The Complete

BEATLES

Mark Lewisohn

STERLING
New York

EMI

The Official story of the Abbey Road years 1962 - 1970

Introductory interview with **Paul McCartney**

Author's acknowledgments

The Complete Beatles Recording Sessions would be an infinitely poorer book were it not for the invaluable assistance of those people directly involved in the story. The following technicians, musicians, production staff and observers of eight magical years of recording sessions generously offered me their time and their memories, and I thank them all warmly.

Malcolm Addey; Kenny Baker; Martin Benge; Pete Best; Anil Bhagwat; Leo Birnbaum; Chris Blair; Peter Blake; Bob Boast; Peter Bown; Jerry Boys; Tony Bramwell; Alan Brown; Jack Brymer; John Burden; Barrie Cameron; Clem Cattini; George Chkiantz; Alan Civil; Tony Clark; Frank Clarke; Peter Coe; Terry Condon; Hunter Davies; Malcolm Davies; Stuart Eltham; Geoff Emerick; Kenneth Essex; Jack Fallon; Eric Ford; Jim Foy; Francisco Gabarro; Brian Gibson; Tony Gilbery; Laurie Gold; Keith Grant; Richard Hale; Dave Harries; Derek Healyey; Alan Holmes; Ted Huntley; Bill Jackman; Jeff Jarratt; Philip Jones OBE; Harry Klein; Bobby Kok; John Kurlander; Richard Langham; Richard Lush; Phil McDonald; George Martin OBE; David Mason; Peter Mew; Mo Miller; Barry Morgan; Rex Morris; Harry Moss; Cris Neal; Alan Parsons; Ron Pender; Bill Povey; Ron Richards; Mike Sammes; Sidney Sax; John Scott; Ken Scott; Mike Sheady; Stephen Shingles; Kenneth Sillito; John Skinner; Keith Slaughter; Norman Smith; Derek Taylor; Chris Thomas; Eddie Thornton; John Timperley; Ken Townsend; Peter Vince; Nick Webb; Andy White.

Very special thanks to Paul McCartney for a splendidly entertaining and illuminating interview.

The supportive role offered to me by *everyone* at Abbey Road Studios throughout the duration of the project has been marvellous. Ken Townsend, the general manager, and a man whose sharp memory spans three decades of sterling service there, offered consistently illuminating recollections, not least about his own inventions which spurred the Beatles on to making more complex recordings and changed all recording practices worldwide. The checking of the technical aspects of this book, undertaken by Townsend, could not have been placed in more appropriate hands. Special thanks also go to Alan Brown and to the good folk in the tape library, for putting up with innumerable "final" requests.

Grateful thanks are due to many people over at EMI in W1, and especially to Terri Anderson, Norman Bates, Mike Heatley, David Hughes, Brian Southall, Bob Street and Tony Wadsworth. A special debt of gratitude is owed to Brian Southall for being the book's editor.

Grateful thanks to Paul Wilkinson for marshalling the design of the book and for his eternal optimism, to Brian Folkard for his timely assistance and to Bryan Dunn, Piers Murray Hill and Isobel Smythe-Wood at Hamlyn.

I am indebted to Linda Mallarkey, Sarah Murgatroyd, Christine Russell and Tracie Smith for transcribing the interview tapes, and to Jenny Caswell at the Musicians' Union for supplying information from its unique archive. And thanks, of course, go to my wife Tarja, for patiently enduring the interminably long hours slaved by her husband over a hot word processor.

Special thanks go to Kathryn Varley at Abbey Road, for without her astute and unremitting belief, vision, persistence and encouragement, this book simply would not exist.

Finally, posthumous salutations to John Barrett, to whom this book is dedicated. I enjoyed the good fortune of meeting John before his sad and appallingly premature death and remember him well, as both a man dedicated to the project and a very fine recording engineer. Thanks, John.

Mark Lewisohn

Abbreviations

Abbreviations in this book are few, and they mostly occur in the initial information part of each date entry. There you may encounter the following:

P Producer
E Balance engineer. (See below.)
2E Second engineer, otherwise known as the Tape Operator/tea boy.
n/a Not applicable - ie, there was no producer on the session.
SI Superimposition, also known as overdub.

Special mention should be made of the role of the technical engineer, distinct from the balance engineer. While the latter would be positioned behind the recording console during a session, adjacent to the producer, the technical engineer would be there or thereabouts, on hand - or on call - to deal with any equipment problems or make suggestions in this area. There was, in the 1960s, and there remains today, a pool of such staff at Abbey Road, and each member would have contributed to Beatles sessions to some degree. But unlike balance engineers, whose names were noted for posterity on recording sheets and tape boxes, history cannot tell us which technical engineers were assigned to which sessions.

Picture credits

Every effort has been made to correctly acknowledge the source and/or copyright holder of each illustration, and EMI Records apologises for any unintentional errors or omissions, which will be corrected in future editions of this book.

Apple Corps: 98 bottom, 102, 129 top left, 177 bottom right, 180 top; Apple/Dezo Hoffman: 19 bottom left, top, centre & bottom right; Apple/Ethan Russell: 165, 169; Beat Publications/Leslie Bryce; 58, 64, 65, 74, 75 left, 93, 94 right, 97, 98 top left & top right, 100, 101, 103, 104, 105 top left & bottom right, 108 top left & bottom right, 122 right, 132 bottom left & top right, 135; Beat Publications/Leslie Bryce/Paul McCartney: 108 centre; Peter Blake (© EMI): 113 top left; Tony Bramwell: 136 top, 138, 140 bottom; Michael Cooper: 106, 112/113 bottom centre, 113 right, 115 top left, top centre & top right, 118 top right; *Daily Mail*: 92 centre; Express Newspapers: 62 bottom right, 63; Robert Freeman: 2, 3, 7, 9, 10, 12, 13, 15, 43 top left & right, 45 bottom left, 46 left & right, 69, 71, 73, 75 right, 76, 79, 80, 81, 82, 87, 88; Richard Hale: 148, 151, 154; The Keystone Collection: 124-125; Richard Langham: 26 bottom centre; Mark Lewisohn: 25 top centre & right, 47 top right, 52 right, 61 bottom, 92 left, 129 bottom right; Linda McCartney: 149, 156 right, 171 left & right, 172 bottom right, 174, 175, 179, 180 bottom left & right, 183, 184, 185, 191; Don McCullin: 136 bottom, 141; Iain Macmillan: 186, 192; *Radio Times*: 94 left, 129 top right, 156 left; Ron Richards: 22 bottom; John Skinner: 45 centre; Times Newspapers/Brodie: 11; Harry Watmough; 17; Andy White: 20.

All other photographs and all studio documentation © EMI Records.

STERLING
New York

An Imprint of Sterling Publishing
387 Park Avenue South
New York, NY 10016

Contents

Preface

Picture yourself as a motorist driving down Abbey Road, a quiet northwest London suburb when suddenly in the pouring rain you are confronted by a strange sight. In front of you standing on a zebra crossing are four tourists, one minus shoes and socks, being photographed by some poor bowler-hatted city gent holding an umbrella looking for all the world as though he has been hijacked especially for the occasion.

This is no rare event. Come rain, hail or shine, never a day goes by when one does not rush to the window following the screech of brakes to witness a similar sight. Why you ask yourself, some twenty years on from the time the Beatles used this same zebra crossing for their album cover, should there still be so much interest? Why also should our mail at Abbey Road Studios contain so many letters asking for information about the Beatles, and why should we have to paint over all the Beatles-related graffiti on our front wall every six months?

It was back in 1931 that the studios officially opened, having been built in the back garden of an old property in St John's Wood. The list of artists, conductors and orchestras who have used the facility reads like a who's who of recording but none has ever captured the imagination of the entire world so much as the Fab Four.

This book really began in the early 1980s when one of our highly talented young balance engineers, John Barrett, became seriously ill. During the time he was undergoing chemotherapy, John asked if there was anything he could do to keep his mind occupied. My suggestion was that he listened through every Beatles tape and logged all relevant details; a job which he did to perfection. He produced a wonderful catalogue with all information colour coded with an attention to detail which was quite incredible.

The story continued in 1982 when Brian Southall, author of the book *Abbey Road*, and myself were asked to give a talk at the annual Beatles' convention in Liverpool. We took John along to sit on the platform and used his new catalogue to respond to any tricky questions. The audience were so enthralled at some of the information given that they asked if a book could be published.

Tragically, in 1984, John Barrett died. But Abbey Road's Kathryn Varley was determined that John's work should be published, and eventually Mark Lewisohn was commissioned to write the book. He has worked tirelessly in his quest for information, interviewing virtually everybody who had any association with the Beatles' recording schedules. Apart from his own extensive research, he has had to filter very carefully all he has been told, for it is amazing how quickly memories get tarnished with age. He has listened to hours and hours of playbacks, and the contents of this book are a tribute to his diligence. Finally it is thanks to Norman Bates, a key figure in EMI Records' Strategic Marketing, that a publishing deal was eventually concluded.

This is not just another Beatles' book. It is the first and only one to tell the story of their recording career. It will, I feel sure, become the definitive reference book for Beatles' fans everywhere. We at Abbey Road sincerely hope you enjoy it.

Ken Townsend
General Manager, Abbey Road Studios

Previously unpublished photographs of the Beatles outside EMI Studios, Abbey Road on 5 March 1963, taken by EMI staff photographer John Dove.

The Paul McCartney Interview

ML: Let me take you back to 6 June 1962. You were just back from your third trip to Hamburg, your first trip to the Star-Club. You still had Pete Best in the group and Brian Epstein had fixed up what was either a test or a session at EMI.

PM: We were told that it was an audition for George Martin. Brian had been going down to London for some time beforehand but we never used to go around with him. I remember endless times of him coming back to Liverpool only to say "Sorry, lads". We used to be at Lime Street station or in the Punch and Judy coffee bar, waiting for hours until his train came in. But it was on one of those occasions that there was some good news, and it was that George Martin had agreed "to think about it, possibly, maybe!". We didn't really get into many of the details although with all of these things we always asked "Did you have to pay any money?". Actually, we had had another audition before then, which was for Decca, with Tony Meehan, the Shadows' ex-drummer.

ML: Did you get to meet Tony at Decca?

PM: No, he was in the control room with Decca's Mike Smith. Brian went in but in those days we didn't go into the control room. It was strictly performance orientated. We were "studio", which was like the stage, and you just didn't go into the "front office". That was where The Big People lived.

ML: What do you remember about having to record 'Love Me Do' with Andy White, the session drummer?

PM: Well, George Martin didn't think that Ringo was a very good drummer. On all these Lita Roza, Alma Cogan records that were in vogue shortly before us, the drummers were pretty good show drummers, so producers were used to hearing a bass drum in the right place, locking in with the bass guitar like it would now. We weren't really bothered with that. Ours was very four in the bar – boom, boom, boom, boom – we used to try and break stages with it. That's what eventually got called the Mersey Beat. So Andy White was the kind of professional drummer that we weren't really used to, and George obviously thought that Ringo was a little bit out of time, a little bit unsteady on tempo. We never really had to be steady on tempo. We liked to be but it didn't matter if we slowed down or went faster, because we all went at the same time. So that was a major disappointment for Ringo.

When we *first* came down in June 1962, with Pete Best, George took us aside and said "I'm not happy about the drummer". And we all went, "Oh God, well I'm not telling him. You tell him … Oh God!" and it was quite a blow. He said "Can you change your drummer?" and we said "Well, we're quite happy with him, he works great in the clubs". And George said "Yes, but for recording he's got to be just a bit

more accurate". Pete had never quite been like the rest of us. We were the wacky trio and Pete was perhaps a little more … sensible; he was slightly different from us, he wasn't quite as artsy as we were. And we just didn't hang out that much together. He'd go home to his Mum's club, the Casbah, and although we'd hang out there with him, we never really went to other places together. So then we changed to Ringo, who'd been with Rory Storm and the Hurricanes, went back to London and found that George didn't even like him! We said, "But you're kidding! This is the best drummer in Liverpool, this guy, he's out of Rory Storm and the Hurricanes! This is class!" And George went, [eyes to the ceiling, stifling a yawn] "Oh yes? Well I still like Andy White!". So then Ringo got to play tambourine instead, which was very humiliating for him. God knows how he must have been brought down – you never can be in someone else's head.

I actually remember a lot of those early sessions. When we first came to the studio to do 'Love Me Do', Dezo Hoffmann, the photographer, was there to take some shots for black-and-white handout photos which we needed. George [Harrison] always hated those because he had a black eye. He'd been bopped in the Cavern by some guy who was jealous over his girlfriend! Anyway, we got on with 'Love Me Do'. We started playing it, [singing] "Love, love me do/you know I love you" and I'm singing harmony then it gets to the "pleeeaase". STOP. John goes "Love me…" and then put his harmonica to his mouth: "Wah, wah, wahhh". George Martin went "Wait a minute, wait a minute, there's a crossover there. Someone else has got to sing 'Love Me Do' because you can't go 'Love Me waahhh'. You're going to have a song called 'Love me waahh'! So, Paul, will you sing 'Love Me Do'!" God, I got the screaming heebeegeebies. I mean he suddenly changed this whole arrangement that we'd been doing forever, and John was to miss out that line: he'd sing "Pleeeeease", put his mouth-organ to his mouth, I'd sing "Love Me Do" and John would come in "Waahhh wahhhh wahhhhhh". We were doing it live, there was no real overdubbing, so I was suddenly given this massive moment, on our first record, no backing, where everything stopped, the spotlight was on me and I went [in shaky singing voice] "Love me doooo". And I can still hear the shake in my voice when I listen to that record! I was terrified. When we went back up to Liverpool I remember talking to Johnny Gustafson of the Big Three and he said "You should have let John sing that line"! John did sing it better than me, he had a lower voice and was a little more bluesy at singing that line.

I also remember those great big white studio sight-screens, like at a cricket match, towering over you. And up this endless stairway was the control room. It was like *heaven*, where the great Gods lived, and we were down below. Oh God, the nerves! Anyway, it worked out well and from then on we

started to get a bit more confidence. So much so that ultimately we started to see what recording was about. George [Martin] was very, very helpful in the early days, he was the mastermind then. But as it went on the workers took over the tools more, and we started to say "We're coming in late, and we might not need you, George. If you can't make it, we'll go in on our own."

ML: In 1960 and 1961 the Beatles were playing every night, two/three times a day sometimes. Did you ever look ahead, long-term, and if you did, did you see yourself as gigging for ever until you stopped, or did you see your goal as being a recording outfit, with records in the shops?

PM: Recording was always the thing. Rather than TV and films. TV and films were a possibility, if we became stars, but records were the main objective. That was what we bought, that was what we dealt in. It was the currency of music: records. That's where we got our repertoire from, the B-sides, the 'Shot Of Rhythm And Blues', the lesser known stuff that we helped bring to the fore, the R&B stuff. Because it was just Cliff before that. I certainly wanted to be like Elvis. We admired very much all the black recording artists and could hear how basic all their recordings were. And Buddy Holly's three chords. We had nice ordinary ambitions really, just to be recording artists.

ML: You were obviously into hearing yourself on disc from the very early days. There were a couple of demo studios in Liverpool, there was one in Manchester, and I know that in 1958 you made recordings of 'That'll Be The Day' and 'In Spite Of All The Danger', which was what, incidentally, a McCartney-Harrison composition?

PM: It says on the label that it was me and George but I think it was actually written by me and George played the guitar solo! We were mates and nobody was into copyrights and publishing, nobody understood – we actually used to think when we came down to London that songs belonged to everyone. I've said this a few times but it's true, we really thought they just were in the air, and that you couldn't actually own one. So you can imagine the publishers saw us coming! "Welcome boys, sit down. That's what you think, is it?" So that's what we used to do in those days – and because George did the solo we figured that he 'wrote' the solo. That wouldn't be the case now: Springsteen writes the record and the guy who plays the solo doesn't 'write' it.

Any time we could get into those demo studios we would have done so. There was one in Hamburg, where we went with members of the Hurricanes to back Lou, who was their ballad singer, to do 'Fever', the Hurricanes' biggest number in the clubs. We all went and I think Rory – who was a bit of an entrepreneur – he probably got the money together. So that was a very early one. And then there was Percy

Phillips' place in Kensington [Liverpool] where we did 'That'll Be The Day' and 'In Spite Of All The Danger'. I remember we all went down on the bus with our instruments – amps and guitars – and the drummer went separately. We waited in the little waiting room outside while somebody else made their demo and then it was our turn. We just went into the room, hardly saw the fella because he was next door in a little control booth. "OK, what are you going to do?" We ran through it very quickly, quarter of an hour, and it was all over. I think we paid £5 for that. It was me, John, George, Colin Hanton on drums and Duff Lowe, five of us. Duff was a friend of mine from school who only played a couple of gigs but he got in because he could play the arpeggio in 'Mean Woman Blues' and only people who are trained to play can do that. Ordinary guys like ourselves can't do that! Anyway, John did 'That'll Be The Day', which was one of our stage numbers, and George played the opening guitar notes and I harmonised with John singing lead. Then on the other side I sang the lead, I think so anyway. It was my song. It's very similar to an Elvis song. It's me doing an Elvis.

ML: Any particular Elvis song?

PM: Yeah, but I'm a bit loathe to say which! "Yeah" is all I'm going to say on that. *I* know which one! It was one that I'd heard at scout camp when I was younger and I'd loved it. And when I came to write the first couple of songs at the age of about 14 that was one of them.

ML: When you signed to EMI and began making records professionally were you deliberately trying to recapture the Sun sound, or the Atlantic sound, or any specific sound?

PM: If the Beatles ever wanted a sound it was R&B. That's what we used to listen to, what we used to like and what we wanted to be like. Black, that was basically it. Arthur Alexander.

ML: That's *heavy* R&B.

PM: Right, heavy R&B. Bo Diddley, you know. When John and Stuart were art students and me and George were at the grammar school next door, we used to go around to John's flat and stay the night on Saturdays – be really wild and stay out all night! Well, we used to think it was very wild, it was very innocent actually. In the mornings I remember waking up with the light coming in and the cathedral out there and you'd been on a mattress on the floor all night, very studenty! Someone had a gramophone and they'd put on 'All By Myself', which was by Johnny Burnette but his brother Dorsey played on it too. Great moments. They were trying to be black. Elvis was trying to be Arthur 'Big Boy' Crudup. So I think we, the Beatles, were initially Elvis-y, Gene Vincent-y, Little Richard-y, Chuck Berry, Fats Domino – on one side. But on the other side it was all the lesser known people

who we secretly hankered after a little bit more: James Ray, 'If You Gotta Make A Fool Of Somebody' – Freddie [and the Dreamers] took that and made it into a comedy record but it was actually a rather serious little waltz song, the first time we'd ever heard waltz done in an R&B song. These were exciting moments for us. Whenever we were asked who our favourite people were we'd say "Black, R&B, Motown".

ML: Can you think of one of your own compositions where you tried to capture that?

PM: 'Love Me Do' was us trying to do the blues. It came out whiter because it always does. We're white and we were just young Liverpool musicians. We didn't have any finesse to be able to actually sound black. But 'Love Me Do' was probably the first bluesy thing we tried to do. 'Please Please Me' was supposed to be a Roy Orbison-type song [sings lyrics in typical Orbison style, adding guitar noises].

> Come on, ching ching
> Come on, ching ching
> Come on, ching ching
> Come on, ching ching
> Please pleeeeeaaase me!

It's very Roy Orbison when you slow it down. George Martin up-tempo'd it, he thought that it was too much of a dirge and probably too like Roy Orbison. So he

cleverly speeded us up and we put in the little scaled riff at the beginning which was very catchy.

ML: You say that George thought it was too much like Roy Orbison. There's no doubt in my mind that George was the right man – probably the only man – for the Beatles, but with his background – comedy, Charlie Drake, Bernard Cribbins…

PM: Guildhall School of Music too, a rather straight background.

ML: …what was it like when you said to him "We want to have a bass sound like in 'A Shot Of Rhythm And Blues' or a particular riff from, say, Little Richard's 'Ooh! My Soul'"?

PM: Very sympathetic. He might not know the song but he was very cool. He was a super-sympathetic guy, George, still is, that is one of his greatest strengths. And it wasn't as if we were young nitwits and yobs, and that he wasn't interested in our opinion. It was exactly the opposite. George was never a cultist about jazz or serious music – although he did once or twice turn me on to bits of classical music, Debussy and other French composers. He was very, very good. George would always listen to oddball ideas, like *Sgt Pepper*: "We'll have a dog noise, a frequency only a dog can hear!". He was amused and we all laughed. It was never serious, but he was very, very sympathetic. For instance, he wanted us to do Mitch Murray's song 'How Do You Do It'. He *knew* it was a number one hit so he gave us it on a demo, a little white acetate. We took it back to Liverpool and said, "What are we gonna do with this? This is what he wants us to do, he's our producer, we'll have to do it, we'll have to learn it." So we did, but we didn't like it and we came back to George and said "Well it may be a number one but we just don't want this kind of song, we don't want to go out with that kind of reputation. It's a different thing we're going for, it's something new." I suppose we were quite forceful really, for people in our position. And he understood. George later took our demo and played it to Gerry [and the Pacemakers] and said "They don't want it, it's a major hit, you do it" and Gerry leapt at the chance. He kept it very similar in tempo to our version which was quite changed from the original demo because it was our arrangement, basically.

ML: Have you heard any of the Beatles' early BBC radio recordings lately? All the stage act material: 'The Hippy Hippy Shake', 'Clarabella', 'A Shot Of Rhythm And Blues' etc?

PM: Yes, some of them are not bad.

ML: Did you think of doing these on record?

PM: I think we probably played them all to George and said "How about this one?" 'Clarabella' was one.

ML: That was an obscure one, the Jodimars.

PM: Yeah, we all had little B-sides and we did the kind of thing that I did many many years later in Jamaica, which was to go in a record shop and look for offbeat suff. You'd have a name like, let's say Johnny Burnette, then we'd know Dorsey Burnette was his brother because he sang on one of the tracks on the album that we liked. So when Dorsey Burnette himself had a single out it might be the B-side we'd be interested in. It was digging round the backs of everything just to find an idea. I've recently recorded 'Cracking Up', the B-side of a Bo Diddley record, just jams and stuff, just rock 'n' roll, but it shows how deeply embedded all this stuff is. All the research we did then is our roots, our musical roots. Black people have gospel choirs. All we had was Sunday School and an absolutely ordinary C of E English upbringing until teenage years, then we went from Cliff Richard to all the very black, exciting and musically interesting stuff. I still know songs that could be hits. I still tell people to try 'Thumbin' A Ride' by the Coasters. A new version of that could be a hit. It's a great number.

ML: It would make a TV commercial hit these days.

PM: Yeah, it would probably be a good Levi's commercial.

ML: You did 'Besame Mucho' at the 6 June 1962 session, which was a staple of your stage act at that time. Now the Coasters did that, and you obviously liked the Coasters, yet your version was nothing like theirs. Where would you have got your arrangement from?

PM: We *were* well into the Coasters but I'm not sure how we came to do that one. It may have been our own arrangement. I looked at the recording scene and realised that a few people were taking offbeat songs, putting them into their acts and modernising them a bit. So I looked at a few songs with that in mind. 'Till There Was You' was one, no one was doing that except Peggy Lee so I thought that'd be nice to play.

ML: Where did you get 'The Honeymoon Song' from? That one always intrigued me.

PM: 'The Honeymoon Song' was Marino Marini, an Italian and his backing group. They used to appear on telly and the greatest thing about them was they had a volume pedal! 'The Honeymoon Song' wasn't a big hit but I liked it, thought it was a nice tune. I was the force behind that, the others thought it was a real soppy idea, which I can see now! I also did 'Falling In Love Again'. We modernised that because, again, it's a lovely song, the Dietrich recording. I used to spend time at home looking at B-sides of this and that and thinking "Oh, we could do a good version of that". And those songs then went down quite well with the club crowds, but when it came to the recording studio there had to be more integrity behind it. This is

another reason why we wouldn't do 'How Do You Do It'. We figured, "Now, wait a minute, we are now starting a reputation, a major reputation, hopefully, so we must be careful as to what we do". We wanted to do 'Love Me Do' first because it was bluesy and we thought we'd keep our integrity with all the lads in Liverpool. They weren't going to say "Oh God, you've gone soppy on us, you've done 'Besame Mucho'!". Mind you, George Martin didn't like 'Besame Mucho'.

ML: What were your early impressions of the EMI Studios in Abbey Road?

PM: I loved it. I loved the variety of artists that went there. These days you go to a recording studio and you tend to see other groups, other musicians, because that's where the industry is now, that's where the money is. But then you'd see Sir Tyrone Guthrie, Barenboim. There'd be a lot of *acting*.

ML: A couple of people have told me how Sir Malcolm Sargent popped in to see you there.

PM: Yeah, in number two. We were working and he came in wearing his navy blue pin-striped suit, carnation, [adopts upper crust voice] "Hello!". George Martin said "Boys, Sir Malcolm Sargent wants to say hello". [Upper crust again] "Hello!", and there was a wave. "Hey, Mal, how you doin' son?" and all that, the irreverent bit. But we were quite pleased, he gave us a big grin and stuff, he seemed like a nice bloke. You'd see classical sessions going on in number one – we were always being asked to turn down because a classical piano was being recorded in number one and they could hear us. And the echo chambers, we used to have a laugh because you could patch in to other people's echo chambers. I remember a Paul Jones session going on and we nearly nicked his echo and put it in one of our 'I Am The Walrus' things. We thought 'We'll have Paul singing on our record!'. One of the great things about Abbey Road was that it almost became our own house, especially by the time *Sgt Pepper* was going on. A lot of people didn't work past ten in the evening and we did. We were pretty free on our time schedule because we weren't touring by then.

ML: Was working late a deliberate thing, so that no one else would be in the building and you'd have the run of the place?

PM: No, we'd just heard that Sinatra recorded late, that's all I can remember. Somebody said "Sinatra never records until ten in the evening" and we thought "That sounds groovy!". It was just a chance observation by someone that made us think "Great, we can have an evening out and then pop along later. Let's try it for a change." So we'd have the whole place, studios one, two and three and we'd move between all those studios. At one point I'd be mixing 'Ob-La-Di' in studio two with Ken Scott. John, I

think, was mixing 'Glass Onion' with Geoff Emerick and George Martin in three, and then I'd play them our mix, which wasn't very good, of 'Ob-La-Di', and their team would then come in and fix my mix up and then we'd go back to 'Glass Onion' and help fix that. We were operating in quite a zany manner. Actually the one thing John didn't like was that I took Ringo during a lull – they were doing something complicated, like a guitar solo or something – and I said to Ringo "Let's go in the other room", and we went into three, I think it was, and recorded 'Why Don't We Do It In The Road', just me and Ringo.

ML: You were also attending other sessions, for other artists, weren't you? Like an Alma Cogan session or Paul Jones or Cilla Black, Billy J Kramer, Cliff Bennett and the Rebel Rousers.

PM: They'd ask me. For example, Cliff Bennett and the Rebel Rousers were friends of ours from Hamburg. Because we were doing so well many people would stick their head around the door and say "Give a listen to this track for us, will you?" And of course if we gave the thumbs-up it was like a blessing, and made them feel better. Cliff Bennett asked me to produce and I loved it. The only reason I don't do all that now is that I'm married with kids. I just don't have the time. But that's something I do like, just to wander in and out of a studio and see who's doing what, "That's good, that guitar solo's no good, you ought to fix that" and just give a few pointers. Yes, I did do quite a bit of that.

ML: What about those songs that you gave away, like 'Bad To Me' and 'It's For You'? Some of those were pretty good songs!

PM: John and I were a songwriting team and what songwriting teams did in those days was wrote for everyone – unless you couldn't come up with something or wanted to keep a song for yourself and it was a bit too good to give away. John and I would get together, "Oh, we gotta write one for Billy J, OK [sings part of 'Bad To Me', simply] 'Birds in the sky will be…'" and we just knocked them out. In our minds there was a very vague formula and we could do it quite easily. I read something just this morning where Geoff Emerick was saying that he and George Martin could sit and not say anything throughout a whole session and people would think they were very weird. It was just that they read each other. It was the same thing with me and John about a Billy J song or a Fourmost song, a Cilla song. Cilla's 'It's For You' was something else, that was something I'd written. You sometimes would pull one out of the drawer and say, "Maybe this would be good for you". 'Misery' was for Helen Shapiro, and she turned it down. [Makes mock pain noise.] It may not have been that successful for her because it's a rather downbeat song, "world's treating me bad, misery". It was quite pessimistic. And in the end Kenny Lynch did it. Kenny used to come out on tour with us and he used to sing it, that was one of his minor hits.

ML: With Bert Weedon on guitar as a session man!

PM: Was he? I know I've never been so surprised in my life as to find a chit in Abbey Road for Ivor Mairants, a session fee chit. I mean, he was a God to us. He had *shops*! You don't do sessions when you've got shops do you?! And I saw the MU form, signed by Ivor. He'd obviously just done a session.

ML: I'd like to throw one or two song titles at you and perhaps you could give me quick two-sentence answers about the writing and recording of them.

PM: You don't get couple-of-sentence answers with me!

ML: 'I Saw Her Standing There'.

PM: I wrote it with John in the front parlour of my house in 20 Forthlin Road, Allerton. We sagged off school and wrote it on guitars and a little bit on the piano that I had there. I remember I had the lyrics "just 17 never been a beauty queen" which John – it was one of the first times he ever went "What? Must change that…" and it became "you know what I mean". That's really the major recollection. To us it was just an opening line that, but – you see I told you you wouldn't get two sentences! – at the time we were 18, 19 whatever, so you're talking to all girls who are 17. We were quite conscious of that. We wrote for our market. We knew that if we wrote a song called 'Thank You Girl' that a lot of the girls who wrote us fan letters would take it as a genuine thank you. So a lot of our songs – 'From Me To You' is another – were directly addressed to the fans. I remember one of my daughters, when she was very little, seeing Donny Osmond sing 'The Twelfth Of Never' and she said "He loves me" because he sang it right at her off the telly. We were aware that that happened when you sang to an audience. So 'From *Me* To *You*', 'Please Please *Me*', '*She* Loves *You*'. Personal pronouns. We always used to do that. '*I* Want To Hold *Your* Hand'. It was always something personal. 'Love *Me* Do', 'Please Please *Me*'…

ML: 'P.S. *I* Love *You*'…

PM: 'Thank *You* Girl.

ML: '*I'll* Get *You*'.

PM: Exactly. We were in a rut, obviously!

ML: Why did you open the song with that "one, two, three, four!"? You didn't open any other songs with a count-in.

PM: There always was a count-in on the front of songs but I think that one was particularly spirited so we thought "We'll keep that one, sounds good".

ML: What about 'Hold Me Tight'? You tried that for the *Please Please Me* LP but it didn't work out.

PM: I can't remember much about that one. Certain songs were just 'work' songs, you haven't got much memory of them. That's one of them.

ML: I suppose that when you've had about 500 compositions published you can't remember them all.

PM: That's what I mean. I remember the name of the tune. Some of them … I wouldn't call them fillers but they were 'work' songs. You just knew that you had a song that would work, a good melody. 'Hold Me Tight' never really had that much of an effect on me. It was a bit Shirelles.

ML: 'All My Loving'. I always consider that as your first major, really major song.

PM: You know, that was on an album and the first person I heard single it out was the disc-jockey David Jacobs, who was pretty hip. Still is actually – he knows pop music. He was always quite an expert, for one of the older generation. I remember him singling it out on his radio show and I think from that moment it did become a big favourite for people. And I heard it differently. Till then I'd heard it as an album track. But when he played it on his radio show, and it went over to however many million people on network BBC, it was like "Woh! That *is* a good one". I always liked it. I think it was the first song where I wrote the words without the tune. I wrote the words on the tour bus during our tour with Roy Orbison. We did a lot of writing then. Then, when we got to the gig, I found a piano and worked out the music. That was the first time that I'd actually written that way.

ML: It's very advanced, quite complex, just one year on from 'Love Me Do'. The Beatles' advancement from year to year, album to album, never ceases to astonish me. It was so tangible.

PM: Yeah, the Beatles were a pretty good group! Not a bad group, I must say! I just heard 'Hello, Goodbye' on the radio this morning and it was very good. We *knew* we were good. People used to say to us, "Do you think John and you are great songwriters?" and I'd say "Yeah, it may sound conceited but it would be

stupid of me to say 'No, I don't' or 'Well, we're not bad' because we are good!". Let's face it, if you were in my position, which was working with *John Lennon*, who was, we know, a great, great man … it's like that film *Little Man, Big Man*, the beginning of it, he says "We wasn't just playing Indians, we was *living* Indians!". And that's what it was. I wasn't just talking about it I was living it. I was actually working with the great John Lennon. And, similarly, he with me. It was very exciting. We wrote 'From Me To You' on the bus too, it was great, that middle eight was a very big departure for us. Say you're in C then go to A minor, fairly ordinary, C, change it to G. And then F, pretty ordinary, but then it goes [sings] "I got arms" and that's a G Minor. Going to G Minor and a C takes you to a whole new world. It was exciting.

ML: And then there was the famous last chord of 'She Loves You', the Glenn Miller one.

PM: That's right. We loved that bit and we rehearsed it a lot. John and I wrote that in a hotel room, on twin beds, during an afternoon off. Your book *The Beatles Live!* really gave me that feeling, that was one of the things I liked about it most: I mean, God bless their little cotton socks, those boys *worked*! They worked their little asses off! Here I am talking about an afternoon off and we're sitting there writing! We just loved it so much. It wasn't work. 'This Boy' was another one done in the bedrooms.

ML: That's a marvellous song, and just a B-side!

PM: Yeah, a monster. Fabulous. And we just loved singing that three-part too. We'd learned that from [singing 'To Know Him Is To Love Him'] "To know know know is to love love love", that was the first three-part we ever did. We learned that in my Dad's house in Liverpool. Anyway, we rehearsed the end bit of 'She Loves You' and took it to George and he just

laughed and said "Well you can't do the end of course, that sixth, it's too like the Andrews Sisters!" and we said "All right we'll try it without" and we tried it without and it just wasn't as good and – this is what I mean about George – then he conceded. "You're right, it's great." But we were both very flexible. We would listen to George's ideas too, because he was a producer and a musician and he obviously knew what he was talking about. There was good to and fro.

One really great thing about work in the early days was that they were better conditions than I enjoy now. If I go into a session now I'm invariably the artist, I'm probably the producer, I'm certainly the bass player and so on and so on. I'm involved with the remix engineer. I'm involved in all the steps. Whereas then the great thing was that you just went in, sang your stuff and then went to the pub. And then *they* mixed it, *they* rang you up if they thought there was a single, you'd just ring them up "Have we got a hit?" – that's all you wanted to know. Great, luxurious conditions if you think about it. Now, as I say, you take everyone's

job and kill yourself into the bargain. I sometimes look back to those days and think "God, which is right? No pay and a lot of time in the pub or a lot of pay and no getting away from the studio?" It's a fine thing to balance.

ML: Listening to the original tapes I was struck by the economy of it all. George Martin or Geoff Emerick or Norman Smith will put the red light on and John Lennon, who must have been very aware of the time, keeps saying "Oh, the red light's on, let's go, let's start".

PM: Oh yeah, whenever the red light was on that was it, we had to go, that was our signal. Now it's very relaxed. I've now got my own studio and we hardly ever put the light on. The other cute thing was that the engineers had to identify each recording. Geoff Emerick was so shy that he didn't want to speak on tape; some people hate to hear their voice on tape. Geoff and the others had to say "RM1", which was remix mono one, or "RS2", later, "remix stereo two", and Geoff would go [fast mumble] "RM1", pressing the button down. He hated doing that. Those are the things you don't get these days.

One thing I'll never forget at EMI was the "pop"/ "classical" switch on the right-hand-side of the console! And the control knobs were great big RAF things, that was the state of the technology then. We used to like them though, and actually they were much better than the fiddly little things these days because then if you put treble on you actually heard treble come on. Now you put treble on and it's nothing. I really do think those valve machines were more fun to work with. A lot of people think that, I know Geoff Emerick does, and I still keep some valve equipment myself because it gives you a record-y type sound. That's why a lot of people won't go to digital. Analogue is warmer, and you can defeat the machine. For example, one trick of our's – 'Ob-la-Di' is one of the songs I did this on – was to over-record an acoustic guitar, so you'd swing the needle into the red and it'd be there, hard, every time you'd played it. The engineer would say "No, no, no, this is not allowed, we have to keep it just before the red or a little into the red!" and we'd be firm and say "No". And the acoustic would come back like an electric, it wouldn't distort too much, it would just mess around with that original sound. It'd make it *hot*. You'd defeated the machine, you'd actually screwed it up a bit. They're harder than ever to defeat now. They've thought of all that. If you're going to work in the red now there's a little computer that comes in and says "Limit!", stops it and brings it back. They're all so clever these days and you can't actually screw up.

Norman Smith was a great engineer, we were all so sad when Norman became a producer because we wanted him as our engineer, he was dynamite. But Geoff was dynamite too, in fact that was the great thing about *all* of the EMI guys. Training. I still think

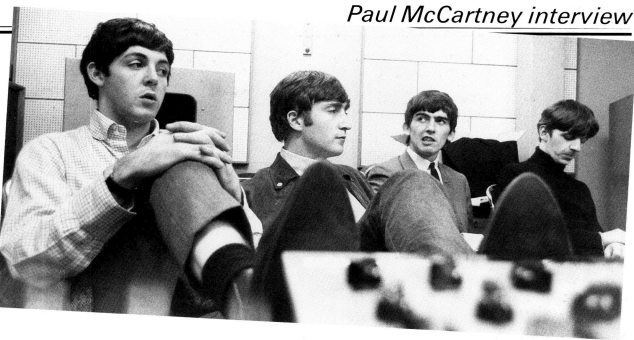

of it in the same breath as the BBC and the government. Anyone you get who's been EMI trained really knows what he's doing. They actually used to have to come to work in ties and suits and white coats which is lovely, like another age! But you listen to the early Beatle recordings, you listen to 'Twist And Shout', it's no less powerful than your current Curiosity Killed The Cat. There's power in John's voice there that certainly hasn't been equalled since, and I know exactly why: it's because he worked his bollocks off that day. We left 'Twist And Shout' until the very last thing because we knew there was one take. The whole album only took a day so it was amazingly cheap, no-messing, just *massive* effort from us. But we were game, we'd been to Hamburg for Christ's sake, we'd stayed up all night, it was no big deal. We started at ten in the morning and finished at ten at night, it sounded like a working day to us! And at the end of the day you had your album. There's many a person now who would love to be able to say that. Me included!

ML: Indeed the *Please Please Me* LP works *because* of the speed in which you did it. It has an urgency, it's a very "instant" album.

PM: That's right. You see I believe in throwaway as a great thing. A great comedian will throw his gags away and I think in music it's very similar. I often find that my demos turn out better than the finished recording. I did a demo for 'Come And Get It' for Badfinger which took about 20 minutes, it was before a Beatles session. Phil McDonald was there and I got in – I always used to get in early because I lived just around the corner – and all the equipment was set up from the day before so I ran in and said "Just do this, Phil, go on, it'll only take 20 minutes" and I threw it away, I mean it's really nice. I did two demos that I was very pleased with. That one and 'Goodbye', for Mary Hopkin, they were nice demos. And I said to Badfinger, "Look, lads, don't vary, this is good, just

copy this down to the letter. It's perhaps a little bit undignified for you, a little bit lacking in integrity to have to copy someone's work that rigidly, but this is the hit sound. Do it like this and we're all right, we've got a hit. No one will know anyway. And if they do say anything say 'Yes, Paul did the arrangement, big deal, it's not unheard of '."

ML: What do you remember of 'Leave My Kitten Alone'? Do you remember that one.?

PM: That was a Johnny Preston song that we'd rehearsed in Liverpool along with all our Cavern stuff and it was just in our repertoire. It wasn't a big one that we used to do, we'd pull it out of the hat occasionally, and we also recorded it.

ML: Do you remember 'Long Tall Sally' as one take? Because to me that's as remarkable as John doing 'Twist And Shout' in one take.

PM: Yeah, it's the same. John and I were very equal. You see, since John's death this thing has emerged – it's quite natural, you can't blame people – he's emerged as the martyr that he didn't want to be. I heard an interview, the day he died, in fact, where he said "I'm not gonna be a bloody martyr, they're all trying to make a martyr of me. I've just got a few things to say, thank you very much, I'll say 'em, goodnight." And obviously this has happened, it was inevitable. When I die the good sides of me will emerge. They'll say, "Oh, did you know he did that in one take? Hey, he wasn't so bad," because I've become known as a soppy balladeer, and John of course did a lot to encourage that myth when we were having rows. He really tried to put that about but he knew otherwise. He was the guy, when I was having trouble with 'Kansas City' – it didn't come off on the first rehearsal – who said "Come on man, you can do it better than this, get up there!".

We were equally raucous and equally balladeering actually. It has become a bit of a myth that I was the balladeer because of 'Yesterday' and John was the shouter because of 'Twist And Shout'. But he wrote songs like 'Good Night', for Ringo, which is the most sentimental little ballad you'll ever hear, and he wrote 'Julia' about his mother, that's a very sentimental piece. Obviously you can't knock his raucous 'Twist And Shout' but there's two sides to everyone.

ML: Tell me about 'I'll Follow The Sun', another very early song I believe.

PM: Yes, I wrote that in my front parlour in Forthlin Road. I was about 16. There's actually a few from then. 'Thinking Of Linking', ever heard of that one?

ML: I know of the title but that's all.

PM: 'Thinking Of Linking' was terrible! I thought it up in the pictures, someone in a film mentioned it [imitates an actor in a film] "we're thinking of linking" and I came out of there thinking "That should be a song. Thinking of linking, people are gonna get married, gotta write that!" But I could never really get past [singing]

> Thinking of linking dah dah
> Thinking of linking dah dah
> Thinking of linking dah dah
> Can only be done by two.

Pretty corny stuff! So 'I'll Follow The Sun' was one of those very early ones. I seem to remember writing it just after I'd had the flu and I had that cigarette – I smoked when I was 16 – the cigarette that's the "cotton-wool" one. You don't smoke while you're ill but after you get better you have a cigarette and it's *terrible*, it tastes like cotton-wool, horrible. I remember standing in the parlour, with my guitar, looking out through the lace curtains of the window, and writing that one.

ML: How come a song like that would take six years to be recorded? It's on your fourth album. Fifty songs had gone under the bridge by that time.

PM: It wouldn't have been considered good enough. I wouldn't have put it up. As I said before, we had this R&B image in Liverpool, a rock and roll/R&B/hardish image with the leather. So I think that songs like 'I'll Follow The Sun', ballads like that, got pushed back to later. We never released 'Yesterday' as a single because we didn't think it fitted our image. In fact it was one of our most successful songs. 'Michelle' we didn't want to release as a single. They might have been perceived as Paul McCartney singles and maybe John wasn't too keen on that.

ML: 'Yesterday' was a single in America in 1965, it was a number one, and the pop papers actually wrote "Paul McCartney is number one without the other Beatles".

PM: Ah, you see, I'd never thought of it like that. In a group, these jealousies don't take much to form.

ML: What about 'If You've Got Trouble', which you and John wrote for Ringo. There's a recording of that. One take and it went no further.

PM: [Laughs and pulls face.]

ML: It was for *Help!* but it didn't happen.

PM: Some of them we just couldn't get behind! I must admit, we didn't really, until later, think of Ringo's songs as seriously as our own. That's not very kind but it's the way it was. Ringo, in fact, had to be persuaded quite heavily to sing. He used to do 'Boys' and 'Matchbox' with us, and with Rory Storm he used to do a set. But generally we never thought of those songs as being that good. To some degree, 'Do You Want To Know A Secret' for George was that way too. I think John and I were really concentrating on "We'll do the real records!" but because the other guys had a lot of fans we wrote for them too. George eventually came out with his own 'Don't Bother Me' but until then he hadn't written one.

ML: What about 'That Means A Lot'? In the end you gave that to PJ Proby but you tried to do it yourself first. There are re-makes and all sorts of things at Abbey Road.

PM: There were a few songs that we were just not as keen on, or we didn't think they were quite finished. This was one of them!

ML: Around 1965/66 you started going to the mix sessions and started being a bit more involved on the production side didn't you?

PM: Yes, we'd started to learn what was involved. We figured that if anyone's going to know how much bass there should be on a record, or how loud the guitar solo should be, or whether 'Hey Jude' should be seven minutes or whether we ought to do the right thing and edit it, it ought to be us. And it was all so fascinating, being allowed to do it, being allowed to actually sit in the studio, because, as I say, on those first sessions you didn't feel you were allowed to join in. During that first audition with Tony Meehan we never even saw him! He was there but we let ourselves in the back door of Decca. But eventually we started to change things. As we got more power they started to let us sit there during a mix. Then you'd say "I don't want to interfere, Geoff, but push my guitar up!". Actually, that was one of the reasons they wouldn't have us there originally, or would prefer that we weren't there, because whoever was present wanted his instrument louder. With two guitarists, with John and George, it was always John saying "put that up a bit" and then George would come in and he'd put his up a bit, then George Martin would be saying "Can you turn the amps down, please?" and John would look at

PM: No, it was nothing to do with that. I was looking for a nice freehold house in London and I was going out with Jane Asher at the time. Her Mum, Margaret Asher, found the house for me. It just happened to be around the corner from the studio so when I moved in there obviously it was very easy for me to get home, and if we wanted to take a break we could go around to my house. *The Girl Can't Help It* was on telly one night and we all bombed over to see it. Chris Thomas hadn't seen the movie and we said "*You haven't seen* The Girl Can't Help It? *It's the best, man, come on over!*" so we all went over to my house to watch it. We'd also use the house as a base. We'd meet at my place and then go around to the studio together. But it was very local, so if someone said "Will you help us produce?" – it wasn't "Oh, I have to come in from Oxford!", it was a pretty simple thing to do.

ML: I remember that the papers made a big deal out of the fact that when you produced the Cliff Bennett record you went around there in your bedroom slippers, you were that local that you just padded around there…

PM: Yes, that was the kind of thing I could do. The *Abbey Road* cover with my famous no shoes on: that was me padding around there in sandals. A nice summer's day, and I went around there with sandals and a suit. It looked fine to me, it seemed great. What the hell's wrong with a pair of sandals!

ML: You were originally going to call the album 'Everest' weren't you?

PM: Yeah, because of Geoff Emerick's cigarettes.

ML: And you were going to fly to the foothills of Everest and have a picture taken?

PM: I don't know. You see, when you're thinking of album titles a lot of loose talk goes around. It's what American film people or advertising people call "Off the top of my head". You have a lot of thoughts that are going to be rejected. We were stuck for an album title and the album didn't appear to have any obvious concept, except that it had been done in the studio and it had been done by us. And Geoff Emerick used to have these packets of Everest cigarettes always sitting by him, and we thought "That's good, it's big and it's expansive".

ML: It says quite a lot.

PM: Yes, it says quite a lot but we didn't really like it in the end. We said "Nah, come on! You can't name an album after a ciggie packet!" But during that time there could have easily been a bit of talk "We'll go to Mount Everest, we'll have that in the background and the picture of us in the foreground". It would have been quite nice, actually! But you'll find this with a lot of the Beatles myths. You know, wanting to put Ghandhi on the cover of *Sgt Pepper* and them having

George and say "How much are you going down? Let's go down to five, alright?" John'd go down to six. "OK, I'm at five!" "You bugger, you're not! You're at six!" There was always this terrible rivalry! You just wanted to be louder. But it's nice to listen to the Beatle records now. There's more guitar than you'll ever hear on a record these days. When you mix now you always mix guitars out, and mix pianos out, it's as if they're only secondary instruments.

ML: There was a really big increase in the bass presence aroung 1966, wasn't there?

PM: That's right. On the original recordings you didn't really hear the bass much, but I started changing style and became more melodic.

ML: It's almost like lead bass on 'Paperback Writer'.

PM: Yeah. Brian Wilson was a big influence, strange really because he's not known as a bass man. If you listen to *Pet Sounds* there's a very interesting bass, it's nearly always a bit offbeat. If you've got a song in C the first bass note will normally be a C. But this would be a G. He'd put the note where it wasn't supposed to be. It still fitted but it gave you a whole new field. I'll never forget putting the bass line in 'Michelle' because it was a kind of Bizet thing. It really turned the song around. You could do that with bass, it was very exciting. The bass on 'Lucy In The Sky With Diamonds' and 'With A Little Help From My Friends' was good too. So yes, the bass became more important, and also we were listening to records that had more bass, in the discos.

ML: Tony Clark cut 'Paperback Writer' and he told me that when he cut it, with all that bass, EMI was

very worried about issuing a single like that, in case the stylus jumped.

PM: That's right. EMI had very firm rules about that, which we always had to break. It wasn't a wilful arrogance, it was just that we felt we knew better. "What do you mean we can't have bass? I was down the disco last night and I heard a record with that kind of bass!" They'd say "Well our rule book says…" and we'd say "They're out of date, come on, let's move!". We were always forcing them into things they didn't want to do. 'Nowhere Man' was one. I remember we wanted very treble-y guitars, which they are, they're among the most treble-y guitars I've ever heard on record. The engineer said "All right, I'll put full treble on it" and we said "That's not enough" and he said "But that's all I've got, I've only got one pot and that's it!" and we replied "Well, put that through another lot of faders and put full treble up on that. And if that's not enough we'll go through another lot of faders and…" so we were always doing that, forcing them. They said "We don't do that" and we would say "*Try it*. Just try it for us. If it sounds crappy, OK, we'll lose it. But it just might sound good." We were always pushing ahead: "*louder, further, longer, more, different*". I always wanted things to be different because we knew that people, generally, always want to move on, and if we hadn't pushed them the guys would have stuck by the rule books and still been wearing ties. Anyway you'd then find "Oh, it worked!" and they were secretly glad because they had been the engineer who'd put three times the allowed value of treble on a song. I think they were quietly proud of all those things.

ML: Did you buy your house in St John's Wood because of its close proximity to EMI Studios?

to tell us to take it off. More often than not these were just ideas that were just a bit left, or a bit right, of centre. We didn't want to do what everyone else wanted to do. Some of them were too expensive but others, like the 'Day In The Life' thing, made a great track. And that song will have earned a whole lot more than that session cost. I met one of the musicians recently, when I went back to Abbey Road – I go back there occasionally, it's a good place to record orchestras, particularly in number one studio – there was a guy who was off the original 'Day In The Life' session, and he said "Oh, I remember that. We came into the studio and down one end was a table with *every* conceivable drink on it." And I said "Oh yeah? I don't really remember that," because I was too involved in the music. I ended up conducting part of it. In fact I did a lot of work on the 'Day In The Life' crescendo because I was getting interested in *avant garde* things and I was generally the bachelor in London with the far-out interests. The others were a little bit more suburbanite, they lived out in Esher and Weybridge and they'd stay out there and not do an awful lot, watch movies or watch telly. And then John would come in and go "Wow! What've you been doing here, putting Beethoven to a home movie?" And I'd be playing him Stockhausen. I never got *known* for being that way because John later superseded me, "Oh, it must have been John who was the Stockhausen freak". In actual fact it wasn't, it was me and my London crowd – Robert Fraser, Miles of *IT* magazine, all those guys, John Dunbar, Peter Asher, the Indica crowd.

With 'A Day In The Life' I said "We'll take 24 bars, we'll count it, we'll just do our song, and we'll leave 24 bare. You could actually hear Mal counting it out, with more and more echo because we thought it was kinda freaky. Then I went around to all the trumpet players and said "Look, all you've got to do is start at the beginning of the 24 bars and go through all the notes on your instrument from the lowest to the highest and the highest has to happen on that 24th bar, that's all. So you can blow 'em all in that first thing and then rest, then play the top one there if you want, or you can steady them out." And it was interesting because I saw the orchestra's characters. The strings were like sheep – they all looked at each other: "Are you going up? I am!" and they'd all go up together, the leader would take them all up. The trumpeters were much wilder.

ML: The frustrated jazz bit coming out perhaps…

PM: The jazz guys, they liked the brief. The musicians with the more conventional instruments would behave more conventionally. But it made for a great noise which was all we wanted, a huge crescendo and we overdubbed it a few times. In studio one they had this facility called ambiophonics and you pick the sound up again. It appears to be a bigger room. As to why anyone would need a bigger room than that I can't imagine!

ML: Tell me about 'The Ballad Of John And Yoko'.

PM: John came to me and said "I've got this song about our wedding and it's called 'The Ballad Of John And Yoko, Christ They're Gonna Crucify Me'" and I said "Jesus Christ, you're kidding aren't you? Someone really is going to get upset about it." He said "Yeah but let's do it". I was a little worried for him because of the lyric but he was going through a lot of terrible things. He came around to my house, wanting to do it really quick, he said "Let's just you and me run over the studio". I said "Oh, all right, I'll play drums, I'll play bass" … I'm not sure if I even played guitar…

ML: No, John played guitar.

PM: …John played guitar. So we did it and stood back to see if the other guys would hate us for it. Which I'm not sure about. They probably never forgave us. John was on heat, so to speak. He needed to record it and so we just ran in and did it.

ML: What about the medley on *Abbey Road*?

PM: I wanted to do something bigger, a kind of operatic moment. There were a few people doing that. 'Teenage Opera' was one. We wanted to dabble and I had a bit of fun making some of the songs fit together, with the key changes. That was nice, it worked out well.

ML: John's 'Polythene Pam' and your 'Bathroom Window' were actually recorded as one, you put them together as one, didn't you?

PM: Yeah, we did that. The nice thing about the way we worked was there were never any rules. Any rules we found ourselves making we would generally try and break. It always seemed an unsafe idea to try and be safe, it never worked. So we did things every which way.

ML: What about Ringo's drum solo?

PM: Ringo would never ever do drum solos. He hated drummers who did lengthy drum solos. We all did. And when he joined the Beatles we said "Ah, what about drum solos then?", thinking he might say "Yeah, I'll have a five-hour one in the middle of your set" and he said "I hate 'em!". We said "Great! We love you!" And so he would never do them. But because of this medley I said "Well, a *token* solo?" and he really dug his heels in and didn't want to do it. But after a little bit of gentle persuasion I said "Yeah, go [taps out the medley drum solo], just do that, it wouldn't be Buddy Rich gone mad", because I think that's what he didn't want do do.

ML: That's the problem. When you do a solo you get compared with people.

PM: Exactly, he didn't like that idea. Anyway, we came to this compromise, it was a kind of a solo. I don't think he's done one since.

ML: Rather difficult to do a five-hour solo in a 30-minute live set, which is what you were doing by the mid-1960s!

PM: [Laughing] Yeah, but some people did those! It was only a 30-minute set but the drummer went on for ever, and lights flashed a lot. Everyone went off and had ciggies and got drunk. By the time the rest of the band came back they were paralytic!

ML: You brought in Glyn Johns for the *Get Back* sessions. What was your thinking behind that? Did you want him as producer?

PM: I don't know really. I just rang him and said "We're going to do some stuff, will you come down?" I think it was just as an engineer. I thought he was one of the best engineers and he was a mate, I knew him from around town. I find it difficult to remember. It might have been that we brought him in as producer, did a lot of work and then felt we ought to get George in. That's the only other thing I can think of, because I think George arrived a bit later.

ML: That period is very sketchy.

PM: To the best I can recall, George was actually the producer but he left us with Glyn to get it together: "All right, you get them all together and when you're ready to record them I'll come in and do it" but in actual fact we probably made a couple of tracks just waiting to record other tracks. It used to be a funny thing, actually, but if the producer went out of the room as, inevitably, they had to do to just take a phone call or something, it was always a very challenging moment. "Try and get it, before he gets back!" Even the engineer would work really fast to try and get the take so that we could say "Hey look, we got it. What took you so long?" when he got back.

ML: Like "Who needs you?"?

PM: It wasn't so much "Who needs you?" It was more like, "Come on, we showed yer!".

ML: Had the Beatles not split, do you think you would have stayed with George Martin or tried others, like Phil Spector? John certainly worked a lot with Spector afterwards, as did George.

PM: Well, I think the reason why we were moving away from George was 'familiarity breeding contempt'. It was just that. And then after that it would have been 'absence makes the heart grow fonder'. Every record we'd ever made had been with George. We'd had immense success, we'd had immense fun, it was great on every single level, but I think you go through ten years and then you stop and

re-assess. Times might have changed. "What am I really trying to do in life?" And John always had a hankering, as did a lot of us, to really produce the greatest, dirtiest rock and roll record ever, and maybe Phil, who'd done some of our favourite songs, the 'River Deep Mountain High' productions that we'd always loved, maybe he was the one. I think we probably wanted to make a 'River Deep Mountain High'. So we did move away occasionally, we often did little things without George. It hurt him when I did the Mike Leander thing on 'She's Leaving Home'. I was just impatient, it was like 'The Ballad Of John And Yoko' and 'Why Don't We Do It In The Road'. You get an idea and you get on fire. And you just think "I could put this fire out and wait but *what the hell! I can't. Come on man!*" Your drive is just too strong. Unfortunately it does steamroller some people's feelings and I always hate that aspect of it because I'm never really aware of it at the time, when you get on a streak and you're writing great. "I won't eat tonight, I just daren't!" If you stop and go back to it it's never quite the same.

ML: In very early 1967, when you were doing 'Penny Lane', you made a 14-minute, very bizarre recording of effects and noises for a 'Carnival of Light' at the Roundhouse. Like 'Revolution 9' but in 1966 rather than in 1968. You seemed to be the leader of that. Do you remember it?

PM: Yes, I was interested in that. I'm now becoming re-interested, in fact. There were millions of threads that we put down in the '60s that I never picked up again. There was a lot of experimental stuff that went on. George's Indian stuff and all of that. It was really just pushing frontiers, that's all we were doing. Everyone else was pushing frontiers too but perhaps we didn't necessarily like what, say, Berio was doing. There was only one Stockhausen song I liked actually! We used to get it in all interviews "Love

Stockhausen!". There was only one, *Gesang der Jünglinge* – 'The Song Of The Young' – that was the only one I ever liked! I thought most of his other stuff was too fruity.

The way I see it, I lived a very urbane life in London. I eventually got my own house there. So I had the metropolis at my fingertips with all this incredible stuff going on, the '60s, and John used to come in from Weybridge in his coloured outfits and we'd meet up. And I'd tell him what I'd been doing: "Last night I saw a Bertolucci film and I went down the Open Space, they're doing a new play there", or "I had dinner with Jagger last night" and it was like "My God! I'm jealous, man." Because I was doing a lot of *avant garde* stuff – it turned out later to be *avant garde*, I thought it was just 'being different'. Making little home movies, showing them to people like Antonioni, it was very exciting, very creative. I do remember John coming in with his big chauffeur and Rolls-Royce, the big, lazy, almost decadent life out in Weybridge and saying "God man, I really envy you". He was starting to feel like he was getting middle-aged and that he was out of it.

ML: You were saying before that you heard 'Hello, Goodbye' on the radio. What do you hear when you hear that, or any Beatles song? Do you hear the recording session? Do you hear the writing of it? Do you hear your singing voice? Your bass guitar?

PM: I hear … [thinks] … all of it. All of those things. A little aspect of each one. The thing that lodges in my memory, in the writing aspect of 'Hello, Goodbye', was the "you say yes, I say no, you say hey, I say hello, you say black, I say white". It almost wrote itself because it was to be 'Hello, Goodbye'. I was thinking of that this morning. From the recording aspect I remember the end bit where there's the pause and it goes [sings] "heba, heba hello'. We had those words and we had this whole thing recorded but it didn't sound quite right, and I remember asking Geoff Emerick if we could *really* whack up the echo on the tom-toms. And we put this echo full up on the tom-toms and it just came *alive*. We Phil Spector'd it. And I noticed that this morning and I said to Linda "Wait! Full echo on the toms, *here we go!* 'Heba, heba hello'" and they came in quite deep, like a precursor to Adam and the Ants.

ML: Do you remember doing the promo films too, at the Saville Theatre? Do you get the whole picture?

PM: Yes, because I directed them. I said "Look, can we get a theatre anywhere? How about Brian's? Is it ever empty for a minute or two? An afternoon? Sure, great." So we went down there, got some girls in Hawaiian skirts, got our *Sgt Pepper* outfits on, and I just ran out there "Get a shot of this! Do this for a bit now! Let's have a shot here! Get a close-up of him! Get the girls on their own! Go back there! Get a wide angle! We'll edit it, we'll make it work." It was very

thrown away. Nice to do stuff like that.

ML: Do you find it irksome that people still ask you Beatles, Beatles, Beatles? I'm here now asking you about B-sides and tracks which haven't even been released yet no one's asking you about 'Zoo Gang' or 'Check My Machine' or 'Lunch Box/Odd Sox'.

PM: That's all right! I don't mind this time!

ML: No, really. Do you not think, "I'm not ashamed of all that, in fact I love it, but, come on, let's live for the present!"?

PM: No no no, I really don't. What I'm finding about all that stuff, all my own contemporary B-sides and strange tracks, is that *it takes time*. People are only just discovering the B-sides of Beatles singles. They're only just discovering things like 'You Know My Name (Look Up The Number)' – probably my favourite Beatles track!

ML: Why on earth…?

PM: Just because it's so insane. All the memories … I mean, what would you do if a guy like John Lennon turned up at the studio and said "I've got a new song". I said "What's the words?" and he replied "You know my name look up the number". I asked "What's the rest of it?" "No, no other words, those are the words. And I wanna do it like a mantra!" We did it over a period of maybe two or three years, we started off and we just did 20 minutes "'You know my name (look up the number)', 'You know my name (look up the number)'" and we tried it *again* and it didn't work. We tried it *again*, and we had these endless, crazy fun sessions. And eventually we pulled it all together and I sang [sings in jazzy style] "You know my name…" and we just did a skit, Mal and his gravel. I can still see Mal digging the gravel. And it was just so hilarious to put that record together. It's not a great melody or anything, it's just unique. Some people haven't even discovered that song yet so I figure that in time they'll get around to more recent stuff, 'Check My Machine', those funny little ones. My big favourite of all of my contemporary work is 'Daytime Nightime Suffering'. I really think that's all right that one. It's very pro-woman.

ML: Yes, it should have been a double-A with 'Goodnight Tonight'. Before we leave 'You Know My Name', was that Brian Jones of the Rolling Stones or was it Brian Jones of the Undertakers playing sax? Because people have never been too sure.

PM: It was Brian Jones of the Stones. He turned up very, very nervous with a sax, and we said "Oh, we thought you'd bring a guitar!" and he'd brought a sax. I invited him to the session. Absolutely definitely Brian of the Stones. Unequivocably, as they say.

ML: Thank you.

The story starts on Tuesday 8 May 1962. The Beatles were in Hamburg, West Germany, four weeks into a seven-week season at the Star-Club, and Brian Epstein – manager of the group – was in London, desperate for someone to give four Liverpool youngsters a break in the record business.

One year before, as manager of a record shop, Epstein had himself been to Hamburg on a retail management course run by Deutsche Grammophon. There he had befriended Bob Boast, a genial man from the prestigious HMV record shop in Oxford Street, London.

So on 8 May, in the sort of position whereby every little contact can help, Epstein walked into the HMV Shop and renewed his acquaintance with Boast. He also played Boast a 7½ ips tape with a few songs from an audition for Decca Records the Beatles had undertaken – and failed – four months earlier. "He said he'd had a very wearing two days, visiting record companies," recalls Boast. "It seems they just weren't prepared to listen. I was, though it was beyond my powers to help him. But at that time we had a small recording studio on the first floor, where budding artists could make 78 rpm demonstration discs. I took Brian there and introduced him to our disc cutter, Jim Foy."

"He wanted me to cut some discs for him," says Foy, "and while I was doing that we started talking. I remarked that the tape sounded very good, to which he replied, rather proudly, that some of the songs were actually written by the group, which was uncommon in those days. I asked whether they had been published, and when he said that they hadn't I told him that the office of Ardmore & Beechwood, one of EMI's music publishing companies, was on the top floor of the shop. Should I fetch the general manager,

Sid Coleman? Epstein said yes. Sid came down, listened to the tape and he too expressed interest. When I'd done the cutting he and Brian went back up to the office."

Coleman's interest was undoubtedly pleasing, but Epstein made his real quest – a recording, not music publishing, contract – clear. Coleman understood, and while Epstein sat opposite him, he made a call to a friend, George Martin, the head of A&R (artists and repertoire) for Parlophone, a small EMI record label.

The phone rang in Martin's office on the fourth floor in EMI's main building in Manchester Square. Judy Lockhart-Smith, George's secretary, answered it. George wasn't there, he was over at the EMI Studios in Abbey Road, St John's Wood, producing Matt Monro's 'When Love Comes Along'. But Epstein took a short walk over to EMI anyway, met Judy and fixed a meeting with George for the next day.

They met at Abbey Road, mid-morning on 9 May. "What I heard wasn't that impressive," says Martin, referring to the new lacquers. "The songs weren't very brilliant, but something there sounded quite interesting. It's no good listening to these, I said, I'll have to see them in person. Bring them down to the studio." A date was fixed: Wednesday 6 June, four days after the Beatles were due back from Hamburg.

When Epstein left he went straight to the Wellington Road post office and dashed off a telegram to the Beatles in Hamburg, telling them the good news, and spicing it with a tiny exaggeration to the effect that the recording contract was already secured. Because of this, as drummer Pete Best recalls, when the group came down on 6 June, they presumed it was a proper recording session, not a test.

It was fortunate for EMI that Martin reacted so positively. Sid Coleman, who wanted the publishing deal, was eager for someone to contract the Beatles as quickly as possible, and was planning to approach Johnny Franz, head of A&R at Philips, if Martin demurred. Furthermore, the other EMI heads of A&R, on the prestigious labels Columbia and HMV, had actually turned the group down before anyone else – even Decca. Confidential letters on file show that on 8 December 1961 Epstein wrote to Ron White, in the EMI sales department, enclosing a copy of 'My Bonnie', a record the Beatles had made in Hamburg in June 1961 backing the singer Tony Sheridan. In mentioning the impending visit to Liverpool of a Decca man, Epstein wrote "I would prefer EMI to have the group". But on 18 December White sent back a respectful apology. The A&R chiefs had heard the disc and were expressing no interest in the Beatles.

The Parlophone Company Ltd has German origins, having been started by a man named Lindstrom. (The label insignia, thought by many to be a £ sign, is in fact a German L.) The company was incorporated in Britain by EMI in 1923, and in 1955 George Martin was put in charge. By 1962 he had an assistant, Ron Richards, and between them they produced records by a number of artists. George concentrated mainly on comedy and variety recordings, his roster including Peter Sellers, Bernard Cribbins, *Beyond the Fringe*, Jim Dale, The Temperance Seven, Matt Monro, Clive Dunn and Scottish musicians like Jimmy Shand. Richards produced Shane Fenton and the Fentones (Fenton later became Alvin Stardust), Paul Raven (later Gary Glitter), Jerry Lordan, Judd Proctor, the Clyde Valley Stompers, and others. It was a busy – if somewhat eclectic – label, which had little chart success and was certainly small time and small budget compared to HMV and Columbia.

Wednesday 6 June

Studio Two/Three?: 6.00-8.00pm. Recording: 'Besame Mucho' (takes unknown); 'Love Me Do' (takes unknown); 'P.S. I Love You' (takes unknown); 'Ask Me Why' (takes unknown).
P: Ron Richards and George Martin.   E: Norman Smith.   2E: Chris Neal.

What, you might wonder, have Darien Angadi, Jill and the Boulevards, Elaine Truss, Thomas Wallis and the Long Riders and the Beatles got in common? The answer is that they were just some of the dozens of young hopefuls who went in 1962 for artists tests/auditions to the lovely old house at 3 Abbey Road, London NW8, built in 1830 and opened as a recording studio in 1931 by The Gramophone Company Ltd, later EMI.

John Skinner, in charge of security, stood in his smart serge uniform on the studio steps during the summer's evening of 6 June. "The Beatles pulled into the car park in an old white van," he says. "They all looked

very thin and weedy, almost under-nourished. Neil Aspinall, their road manager, said that they were the Beatles, here for a session. I thought what a strange name!" The van was unloaded and the group set themselves up in the studio. Precisely which studio is not clear, for memories of the evening are blurred. Skinner and George Martin recall the session taking place in studio three, as do others not present on the day but members of the studio staff at the time, Malcolm Addey, Harry Moss and Keith Slaughter. Conversely, Chris Neal, Ron Richards, Norman Smith and Ken Townsend all swear that it was held in studio two.

Memories are equally blurred about whether the session was actually an artist test (to see if the group were any good), a commercial test (to see if the group could work well inside a recording studio) or even the group's first session proper. The relevant studio documentation has long since been destroyed, although an artist test was the most likely event.

Ron Richards initially took charge of the session. "I used to do most of our rock 'n' roll," he recalls, "so George asked me to have first look at them." Norman Smith was assigned as balance engineer and, because engineers associated with successful artist tests tend to remain with that artist, Smith was installed as the Beatles' engineer thereafter.

"They had such duff equipment," says Smith. "Ugly unpainted wooden amplifiers, extremely noisy, with earth loops and goodness knows what. There was as much noise coming from the amps as there was from the instruments. Paul's bass amp was particularly bad and it was clear that the session wasn't going to get under way until something was done about it." Ken Townsend, on duty in the technical department, recalls what followed. "There was no demand that night for Echo Chamber One, right down in the basement, so Norman and I fetched a very large, very heavy Tannoy speaker from there and I soldered a jack socket onto the input stage of a Leak TL12 amplifier. We were soon back in business."

While all this was going on the Beatles went for a cup of tea, brewed by studio tea-ladies Miss Hawthorne and Miss Hunt. "They asked me where the nearest café was," says Terry Condon, one of the studio's invaluable odd-job men. "But they didn't go. I nipped into the kitchen and made them something to eat."

The equipment wasn't the only thing that made an impression. As they came into the studio Townsend recalls Smith muttering "Good God! What've we got 'ere?" "They dressed quite smartly but they just looked so different to anything we had seen before," says Townsend. Chris Neal, these days re-named Cris Neal to avoid confusion with the record producer of the same name, was the second engineer/tape operator, or 'button pusher' as they were impolitely called. "They were wearing black leather coats which

is why I suddenly thought 'Ah, Beatles'. I remember George Martin taking a quick look at them and going down to the canteen to have a cup of tea!"

So the session got under way, with Ron Richards at the helm. Four songs were recorded, and although documentation no longer exists, each would have been done in about four or five takes. Paul sang 'Besame Mucho', the old Latin crooner, then they layed down three Lennon-McCartney originals, 'Love Me Do', 'P.S. I Love You' and 'Ask Me Why'. It was during 'Love Me Do' that Norman Smith pricked up his ears. "Norman said to me 'Go down and pick up George from the canteen and see what he thinks of this'," recalls Neal. So George Martin came up and took over the rest of the session. When it was over he spoke to the group over the talkback, with them huddled in the far corner of the studio. Then he invited them up to the control room to hear the tapes and discuss technicalities.

"George was giving them a good talking to, explaining about the studio microphones being figure-of-eight, in other words you could stand on either side of them, as opposed to stage mikes which were one-sided," remembers Townsend. "They were really lolling about," says Neal. "Lennon was sitting on a speaker and Harrison, I seem to recall, was lounging on the floor." "We gave them a long lecture about their equipment and what would have to be done about it if they were to become recording artists," says Norman Smith. "They didn't say a word back, not a word, they didn't even nod their heads in agreement. When he finished, George said 'Look, I've laid into you for quite a time, you haven't responded. Is there anything

you don't like?' I remember they all looked at each other for a long while, shuffling their feet, then George Harrison took a long look at George and said 'Yeah, I don't like your tie!' That cracked the ice for us and for the next 15-20 minutes they were pure entertainment. When they left to go home George and I just sat there saying 'Phew! What do you think of that lot then?' I had tears running down my face."

But what of the music? Richards and Martin felt that it was okay, nothing too special. Retrospective judgment is not possible because when it was realised that nothing from that session would be issued, long before anyone could have recognised their historical importance, the tapes – two quarter-inch reels – were destroyed. Remarkably, one of the four songs, 'Besame Mucho', *has* survived, on a private reel discovered in the early 1980s.

George Martin was left to decide whether or not to put the group under contract. This seemed to rest on the question of which Beatle he would make the leader. Most groups then had a leader – Cliff Richard and the Shadows, Johnny Kidd and the Pirates, Shane Fenton and the Fentones. "George and I were walking up Oxford Street one day trying to work out whether it should be Paul – the good looking one – or John, who had the big personality. Neither of us could make up our minds," says Richards. Martin eventually realised that the group was a complete unit and should not be tinkered with. And he decided that he may as well sign them. "I've got nothing to lose," he recalls saying at the time. The standard recording contract was drawn up, it was signed, and the Beatles became an EMI act. The contract was backdated to 4 June, although no one can recall quite why. The likeliest explanation is that this enabled EMI to own the rights to the tapes of the 6 June session, otherwise, legally, they would have belonged to the group. George Martin thinks it may have even been a typing mistake.

Martin may have decided that the group shouldn't be tinkered with, but the group themselves had other ideas. Between 6 June and their next trip to Abbey Road, on 4 September, their drummer, Pete Best, was dismissed from the group in favour of Ringo Starr, ex of Rory Storm and the Hurricanes.

Pete Best's Musicians' Union Session Fees & Expenses payment card, showing his one EMI recording session with the Beatles on 6 June. The handsome drummer, second left, in the June 1962 photograph of the smartly attired group, was dismissed on 16 August, between the Beatles' first and second visits to Abbey Road.

Tuesday 4 September

Studio Two: 7.00-10.00pm. Recording: 'How Do You Do It' (takes unknown); 'Love Me Do' (takes 1-15+). Mono mixing: 'How Do You Do It' (from take 2); 'Love Me Do' (from unknown take number). P: George Martin. E: Norman Smith. 2E: unknown.

Ninety days after the 6 June session, the Beatles returned to Abbey Road to record the two titles for their first single. They flew down from Liverpool Airport in the morning, checked into a small Chelsea hotel and arrived at Abbey Road shortly after lunch.

Recording studio practice in 1962 was strictly regimented. There were three sessions per day: 10.00am-1.00pm, 2.30-5.30pm and 7.00-10.00pm. After that, unless overtime had been agreed and the appropriate Musicians' Union form signed, the day's work would be at an end. (The Beatles' 6 June session was held early, from 6.00-8.00pm, in order to allow the group to drive back north the same evening.) As this book will show, the Beatles successfully challenged this routine and changed – probably forever – the way studios operate.

Stringent timekeeping was not the only curiously staid studio institution back in 1962. Technical engineers still went around in white coats, and in fact continued to do so at Abbey Road until the 1970s. Winston Churchill, before he became 'Sir', visited the studios on one memorable occasion and observing the white-coated staff as he struggled up the steps paused merely to wheeze, "My God. I think I've come to the wrong place. It looks like a hospital."

Between 2.30 and 5.30pm Ron Richards ran the Beatles through a vigorous rehearsal in studio three, with photographer Dezo Hoffmann in attendance. "I remember that we rehearsed 'Please Please Me'," says Richards. "George was playing the opening phrase, later done by John on his harmonica, over and over and over, throughout the song. I said 'For Christ's sake, George, just play it in the gaps!' " In all, the Beatles practised six songs, from which two were selected for recording in the evening session, starting at 7.00pm. One was an automatic choice – 'How Do You Do It' – which George Martin was insisting, in the apparent absence of any stronger original material, would be the group's first single.

" 'How Do You Do It' was brought into my office by the man who wrote it, Mitch Murray, along with Barry Mason, later to write a number of hits himself," recalls Richards. "They offered me first option on the recording and played me Mitch's demonstration acetate. I liked it so much that I immediately called Dick James, the singer turned music publisher, and he signed the song up straightaway. But the acetate stayed in my desk for a long time after that. We didn't know who to give it to. Much later, when George was pondering about the Beatles' first record, I played him Mitch's acetate. He felt that it would be ideal for them and sent a copy to Liverpool right away so that they could learn their parts."

The Beatles themselves felt that the song was absolutely *not* for them, and they told George Martin so during the evening recording session. "We want to perform our own material," they said. George's rejoinder was that when they could write a song as good as this one then he would let them do that instead. Until then…

They recorded the song. "They never shirked on jobs," says Martin. "They didn't really want to do it but in the end they did quite a good job." Listening to it in 1987, it sounds quite pleasant, if innocuous and somewhat lacking in ambition. Clearly the Beatles weren't putting *too* much effort into it. It must have come very close to being released though, because a finished, mastered version of the tape exists in the EMI archive along with other tracks released at the time. Were it intended to remain an outtake it would not have been mastered. But history tells us that the Beatles' first single was 'Love Me Do', and their version of 'How Do You Do It' remains unreleased.

The story had a happy ending. The Beatles' objections led to a lunch appointment between Brian Epstein and Dick James which, in turn, led to James signing up the Beatles' music publishing from January 1963 onwards, an extremely profitable experience. And the song – as recorded during their very first session, on 22 January 1963, by another Epstein-managed Liverpool group, Gerry and the Pacemakers – did go all the way to number one on the charts.

Between the rehearsal and recording sessions, from 5.30 to 7.00pm, George Martin took the Beatles and Neil Aspinall out to dinner, where he regaled them with stories of his recording sessions with Peter Sellers and Spike Milligan. "I took them to a little Italian place, Alpino, in Marylebone High Street. We all had spaghetti and the cost per course was about 3s 9d (19p). It wasn't exactly over-the-top but they thought it was wonderful, real high living!"

After 'How Do You Do It' the Beatles settled down to record 'Love Me Do', first concentrating on the rhythm (backing) track. This took 15 takes to get right. Then the vocals were superimposed, and this too took a long time. The session was far from easy and it ended late into the evening. Says Norman Smith, "I've a feeling that Paul wasn't too happy with Ringo's drumming, and felt that it could be better. He didn't make too good a job of it. I remember too that there was a fair bit of editing to be done." Ken Townsend recalls the studio equipment they used, extremely primitive compared to today's high technology. "Abbey Road designed its own mixing consoles then. In studio two we had the REDD 37,

which had 10 inputs and 2 outputs, with big knobs and levers. Battleship grey was the colour. The tape machines themselves were BTR (British Tape Recorder) models, great hefty jobs. These were originally green but we painted them battleship grey to match the consoles."

Documents show that 'How Do You Do It' and 'Love Me Do' were mixed by Martin and Smith before the day was out, and that an acetate of the two titles was cut for Martin and Epstein to listen to the next morning.

"I looked very hard at 'How Do You Do It'," says George Martin, "but in the end I went with 'Love Me Do'. It was quite a good record."

AN AGREEMENT made the 4ᵗʰ day of JUNE 1962 BETWEEN THE PARLOPHONE COMPANY LIMITED of Hayes in the County of Middlesex (hereinafter called "the Company") of the one part and

B   - 4 -

(11. THE Company shall be entitled to continue this Agreement for 3 (three) successive periods of 1 (one) year each upon giving notice in writing to the Manager. Any notice given under the provisions hereof shall be given before the expiration of this Agreement by registered letter and sent to the address of the Manager last known to the Company. The said notice shall be deemed to have been received by the addressee upon the day on which it would have been received in the course of normal Should this Agreement be extended for a further first period of one year then in respect of records reproducing performances recorded by the Artist during such first extended period the royalty referred to on Cl. 4(a) her shall be increased to 1¼d. (one penny farthing). In the case of any furth extension then in respect of records reproducing performances recorded by the Artists during such further extension the said royalty shall be increa to 1½d (three half pence).

10. THIS Agreement shall be governed by English Law and the High Court of Justice in England shall be the Court of Jurisdiction.

IN WITNESS whereof THOMAS HUMPHREY TILLING on behalf of the Company and BRIAN EPSTEIN have hereunto set their hands the day and year first above mentioned.

SIGNED by the said
THOMAS HUMPHREY TILLING

in the presence of:-

SIGNED by the said
BRIAN EPSTEIN

in the presence of:-

In addition to cabling the Beatles in Hamburg, Brian Epstein also sent a telegram to the fortnightly newspaper *Mersey Beat* (right), boasting that the Beatles had an appointment with EMI on 6 June. Epstein spiced the news somewhat, indicating that the contract was already signed, and the telegram is not without other inaccuracies either, but its place of despatch (Primrose, abbreviation of Primrose Hill, close by Abbey Road) and its date, 9 May, show that Epstein wasted little time in heralding the good news after his meeting with George Martin. As for the contract itself (extracts, left), this was dated 4 June, although no one quite knows why. It was later criticised for showing great thrift in the record company's favour, but this was very much standard fare in the industry at the time. The witness to Epstein's typically flourished signature was R. (Bob) Wooler, announcer/disc-jockey at the Cavern Club and several other Merseyside dance venues at which the Beatles regularly played.

Fifty-year-old Slovak-born photographer Dezo Hoffmann, a London freelancer who worked regularly for *New Record Mirror*, visited the 4 September session to take what was to become an historic set of photographs of the Beatles rehearsing and recording 'Love Me Do'. Dezo attempted to photograph only the right-side of George Harrison's face. The reason why is clear from the one shot in which Dezo failed in his brief: George had a shining black left eye, the result of a skirmish at the Cavern Club!

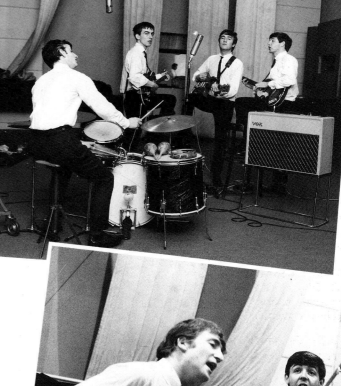

Tuesday 11 September

Studio Two: 10.00am-1.00pm. Recording: 'P.S. I Love You' (takes 1-10); 'Love Me Do' [re-make] (takes 1-18); 'Please Please Me' (takes unknown). Mono mixing: 'P.S. I Love You' (from take 10); 'Love Me Do' (from take 18). P: Ron Richards. E: Norman Smith. 2E: unknown.

The 4 September session really hadn't proved good enough to satisfy George Martin. And because it was the group's first single, it really had to be right.

"We weren't happy with the drum sound on the original 'Love Me Do'," says Ron Richards, who in George Martin's absence was sole producer on 11 September, "so I booked Andy White for the re-make. I used him a lot at the time – he was very good."

Paul McCartney had seen White in action once before, although he didn't know it. White used to drum with Vic Lewis's Orchestra and Paul was there in February 1957 when Lewis played as support act to Bill Haley and the Comets at the Empire Theatre, Liverpool.

White, who was 32 in 1962, much older than the Beatles, takes up the story. "I had already heard of them because I was married to Lyn Cornell of the Vernons Girls, themselves a Liverpool group. They could have been cold towards me but in fact they were very nice, and kidded about. I was impressed because they were doing their own material, whereas most groups at the time were doing covers of American songs or Tin Pan Alley stuff."

And what of Ringo, being deposed on only his second session? "He just sat there quietly in the control box, next to me," says Richards. Then I asked him to play maraca on 'P.S. I Love You'. Ringo is lovely – always easy going. 'What do you want me to do? I'll do it. You don't want me to do anything? Good'. He was never a dedicated 'I've got to get in on the act' type."

'P.S. I Love You' duly featured White on percussion and Ringo on maraca. There was talk of it being the A-side of the single but Richards was quick to scupper that idea. "I was originally a music publishing man, a plugger, so I knew that someone had already done a record with that title. I said to Paul 'You can have it as a B-side, but not an A-side'." So they did it as a B-side, and ten takes later it was in the can.

The re-make of 'Love Me Do' came next, and again Andy White sat in on drums. It took 18 takes before it was perfect. "Ringo didn't play drums at all that evening," recalls Richards. "On 'Love Me Do' he played the tambourine." Today this remains the easiest way of determining which recording of 'Love Me Do' is which. The one without the tambourine is from 4 September, the one with is 11 September.

Towards the end of the session, around 1.00, as the Beatles were attempting to record 'Please Please Me', George Martin came in. "At that stage 'Please Please Me' was a very dreary song," he says. "It was like a

Roy Orbison number, very slow, bluesy vocals. It was obvious to me that it badly needed pepping up." After the session had finished, George told them that the song could be much better if they increased the tempo and worked out some tight harmonies. "I told them to bring it in next time and we'd have another go at it." Ron Richards confirms this. "We were standing in the corridor outside the control room after the session. George was saying 'We haven't quite got 'Please Please Me' right, but it's too good a song to just throw away. We'll leave it for another time…'"

It was not customary in 1962 to keep session tapes once completed songs had been mastered for disc release so the Orbison-like 'Please Please Me' no longer exists. "We didn't keep outtakes then, we had enough problems storing masters," says George Martin today. Fortunately, such a policy ceased in 1963, and from that moment almost every session tape was kept, and still exists today.

Session drummer Andy White, in a photograph taken circa 1962. His Abbey Road payment card for the 1962/63 financial year reveals his fee for the Beatles session on 11 September – a standard £5 15s [£5.75]. White was clearly a regular visitor to Abbey Road at the time.

1897

SESSION FEES & EXPENSES

DRUMS

NAME   A. WHITE

ADDRESS   21, THORKHILL GARDENS, THAMES DITTON, SURREY.

CARD No. 1

PROOF	DATE & REFERENCE		CREDIT	PAYMENTS	MONTHLY BALANCE	YEARLY BALANCE	PROOF
						5. 15. 0	1,902. 15. 0
O	26 APR 62	RET 26. 1,897.		5. 15. 0		13. 5. 0	1,910. 5. 0
O	30 APR 62	RET 32. 1,897.		7. 10. 0		20. 15. 0	1,917. 15. 0
O	1 MAY 62	RET 1. 1,897.		7. 10. 0		26. 10. 0	1,923. 10. 0
O	2 MAY 62	RET 6. 1,897.		5. 15. 0		32. 5. 0	1,929. 5. 0
O	8 MAY 62	RET 16. 1,897.		5. 15. 0		38. 11. 6	1,935. 11. 6
O	14 MAY 62	RET 29. 1,897.		6. 6. 6		46. 13. 0	1,943. 13. 0
O	3 JUL 62	RET 6. 1,897.		8. 1. 6		54. 3. 0	1,951. 3. 0
O	19 JUL 62	RET 26. 1,897.		7. 10. 0		59. 18. 0	1,956. 18. 0
O	23 AUG 62	RET 40. 1,897.		5. 15. 0		65. 13. 0	1,962. 13. 0
O	11 SEP 62	RET 16. 1,897.		5. 15. 0		71. 19. 6	1,968. 19. 6
0. 0 O	5 OCT 62	RET 9. 1,897.		6. 6. 6		77. 14. 6	1,974. 14.
O	11 OCT 62	RET 17. 1,897.		5. 15. 0		83. 9. 6	1,980. 9.
O	12 OCT 62	RET 18. 1,897.		5. 15. 0		89. 4. 6	1,986. 4.
O	19 OCT 62	RET 34. 1,897.		5. 15. 0		96. 2. 6	1,993. 2.
O	9 NOV 62	RET 11. 1,897.		6. 18. 0		103. 0. 6	2,000. 0.
O	14 DEC 62	RET 14. 1,897.		6. 18. 0		108. 15. 6	2,005. 15.
O	25 JAN 63	RET 35. 1,897.		5. 15. 0		116. 17. 0	2,013. 17.
O	30 JAN 63	RET 39. 1,897.		8. 1. 6		117. 8. 6	2,014. 8.
O	25 JAN 63	V 1,897.		11. 6		123. 3. 6	2,020. 3.
O	21 FEB 63	RET 28. 1,897.		5. 15. 0		130. 1. 6	2,027. 1.
O	24 MAR 63	RET 35. 1,897.		6. 18. 0			

741

SESSION FEES & EXPENSES
Bass Guitar

NAME G. Harrison

ADDRESS 25, Upton Green,
Liverpool, 24

CARD No. 1.

PROOF		DATE & REFERENCE			CREDIT	PAYMENTS	MONTHLY BALANCE	YEARLY BALANCE	PROOF
						7.10.0		7.10.0	748.10.0
O	6JUN62	RET	8.	741.		7.10.0		15.0.0	756.0.0
O	4SEP62	RET	4.	741.		5.15.0		20.15.0	761.15.0
O	11SEP62	RET	16.	741.		7.10.0		28.5.0	769.5.0
O	26NOV62	RET	31.	741.		14.10.0		42.15.0	783.15.0
O	31JAN63	RET	13.	741.		7.10.0		50.5.0	791.5.0
O	5MAR63	RET	3.	741.					

1327

SESSION FEES & EXPENSES
E.Guitar

NAME J.P.McCartney

ADDRESS 20, Forthlin Road,
Liverpool, 18

CARD No. 1

PROOF		DATE & REFERENCE			CREDIT	PAYMENTS	MONTHLY BALANCE	YEARLY BALANCE	PROOF
O	6JUN62	RET	8.	1,327.		7.10.0		7.10.0	1,334.10.0
O	4SEP62	RET	4.	1,327.		7.10.0		15.0.0	1,342.0.0
O	11SEP62	RET	16.	1,327.		5.15.0		20.15.0	1,347.15.0
O	26NOV62	RET	31.	1,327.		7.10.0		28.5.0	1,355.5.0
O	31JAN63 11FEB	RET	13.	1,327.		14.10.0		42.15.0	1,369.15.0
O	5MAR63	RET	3.	1,327.		7.10.0		50.5.0	1,377.5.0

1727

SESSION FEES & EXPENSES
Percussion

NAME Richard Starkey

ADDRESS 10, Admiral Grove,
LIVERPOOL.

CARD No. 1

PROOF		DATE & REFERENCE			CREDIT	PAYMENTS	MONTHLY BALANCE	YEARLY BALANCE	PROOF
						7.10.0		7.10.0	1,734.10.0
O	4SEP62	RET	4.	1,727.		5.15.0		13.5.0	1,740.5.0
O	11SEP62	RET	16.	1,727.		7.10.0		20.15.0	1,747.15.0
O	26NOV62	RET	31.	1,727.		14.10.0		35.5.0	1,762.5.0
O	31JAN63 11FEB	RET	13.	1,727.		7.10.0		42.15.0	1,769.15.0
O	5MAR63	RET	3.	1,727.					

1032

SESSION FEES & EXPENSES
E.Guitar

NAME J.W. Lewnow
Lennon

ADDRESS 251, Mew Love Ave.,
Liverpool???

CARD No. 1

PROOF		DATE & REFERENCE			CREDIT	PAYMENTS	MONTHLY BALANCE	YEARLY BALANCE	PROOF
O	6JUN62	RET	8.	1,032.		7.10.0		7.10.0	1,039.10.0
O	4SEP62	RET	4.	1,032.		7.10.0		15.0.0	1,047.0.0
O	11SEP62	RET	16.	1,032.		5.15.0		20.15.0	1,052.15.0
O	26NOV62	RET	31.	1,032.		7.10.0		28.5.0	1,060.5.0
O	31JAN63 11FEB	RET	13.	1,032.		14.10.0		42.15.0	1,074.15.0
O	5MAR63	RET	3.	1,032.		7.10.0		50.5.0	1,082.5.0

Although under a royalties contract, the Beatles still received Musicians' Union payment for each EMI session they performed, until the practice ceased in 1964. At the end of each session they would visit Mr. Mitchell, the studios cashier, who would give them each their money and enter the payments on his card system.

Names and addresses were presumably dictated by each Beatle, explaining why J.W. Lennon of 251 Menlove Avenue, Liverpool became "J.W. Lewnow of 251 Mew Love Ave., Liverpool???" and why the positions of George on electric guitar and Paul on bass guitar were juxtaposed.

Friday 5 October

Single release: 'Love Me Do'/'P.S. I Love You'. Parlophone 45-R 4949.

And so it came out, the fruits of two long recording sessions. Ardent Beatles' fans will be aware that the content of the single changed in 1963. Copies pressed before then featured the 4 September version of 'Love Me Do', Ringo on drums. (Clearly, the 11 September version was not regarded as having been a significant improvement after all.) But later copies, and those available today, feature the Andy White version, from 11 September. The swap took place at the time of the EP release *The Beatles' Hits*, which included the version with Andy. It was decided that future pressings of 'Love Me Do' should all have this take. To ensure this, the master tape of Ringo's version was destroyed.

The single rose to 17 in the charts, a healthy debut. Sales were heavily concentrated in the Liverpool area, leading to speculation, not disproved to this day, that Brian Epstein, as manager of a record shop, surreptitiously 'bought in' copies of the disc, 10,000 it was said. He denied this (he could do little else) but associates have since admitted that it was likely to be true.

The 250 advance copies of 'Love Me Do' made for radio stations and the press carried a mis-spelling, corrected before regular copies were made, showing McArtney instead of McCartney.

The plan of attack for press attention was double-headed. EMI's press relations officer, Syd Gillingham, issued a three-page biography of the group (extract, above right) and Brian Epstein commissioned his own handout from freelance journalist Tony Barrow (extract, above left): Four pages 'with a hard fact driven into every sentence' which even included a selection of six awful jokes and puns on the word Beatles to be used by the press (None were, thankfully.)

Monday 26 November

Studio Two: 7.00-10.00pm. Recording: 'Please Please Me' [re-make] (takes 1-18); 'Ask Me Why' (takes 1-6); 'Tip Of My Tongue' (takes unknown). P: George Martin.   E: Norman Smith.   2E: unknown.

'Please Please Me', restructured to George Martin's specifications, was the perfect choice for the Beatles' second single. And with Ringo Starr back on the drummer's stool there was no more talk of a session man being brought in. In fact, Ringo's drumming on 'Please Please Me' was very competent indeed.

The group arrived at the studio at 6.00pm for a one hour rehearsal. Later, when they started recording, it was decided that 'Please Please Me' should be taped without the distinctive harmonica wailing. This was superimposed later, by doing a tape-to-tape overdub, because it was difficult for John to sing, play harmonica and play guitar simultaneously. Including the harmonica edit pieces the song was recorded in 18 takes, and at the end George Martin spoke to the group over the talkback. "You've just made your first number one." He was not wrong.

After a tea break the group went back to record the B-side, 'Ask Me Why', ensuring that both sides of their second 45, like the first, were Lennon-McCartney compositions. Or rather, McCartney-Lennon. At this time there was a minor dispute between the two aspiring geniuses as to who should have his name credited first. It was not until August 1963 that "John got his way, as usual!" recalls Paul.

'Ask Me Why' was comparatively easy to record, and by take six it was perfect. It wasn't an automatic choice for the B-side however, for the Beatles also taped a third homegrown song, 'Tip Of My Tongue'. But after several attempts they gave up. George Martin was unhappy with the arrangement, and said that it would have to be held over for another time. In fact, they never bothered to revive it, and it was not until July 1963 that it surfaced, recorded by another Epstein artist, Tommy Quickly. They weren't doing Quickly much of a favour: the song was terrible.

The tape library log of daily sessions reveals the four songs played by the Beatles during their 6 June 1962 visit. Adjacent to the term 'artiste manager', quaint 1962 record industry terminology for what would today be 'record producer' is the name Richards, George Martin's assistant Ron Richards. The log sheet for 26 November shows that George Martin also produced another session on that day, and that Cliff Richard was in the studios earlier.

Friday 30 November

Studio Two (control room only): time unknown.
Mono mixing: 'Please Please Me' (from unknown take number); 'Ask Me Why' (from take 6).
P: George Martin.   E: Norman Smith.   2E: unknown.

The Beatles were not present at this remix, and did not begin to attend such sessions until much later.

On 25 February 1963, when George Martin and Norman Smith were remixing for the *Please Please Me* LP, they used this day's mix of 'Please Please Me' for the mono version but did a new mix, from takes 16, 17 and 18, for the stereo. The difference between the mono and stereo is clear: towards the end of the stereo mix John gets one line wrong, as a result of which the following "Come on" is sung with a slight chuckle.

Smith recalls a rather cruel joke played on EMI's great rivals, Decca. "We sent a tape of 'Please Please Me' under plain wrapper to Dick Rowe, the man who turned down the Beatles. We hoped he would think it was from a struggling artist looking for a break, and that maybe he would turn them down a second time! I honestly can't remember what, if anything, he replied."

Friday 11 January

Single release: 'Please Please Me'/'Ask Me Why'. Parlophone 45-R 4983.

Did 'Please Please Me' reach number one? The answer depends on your choice of chart. There was no one accepted record industry 'hit parade' then, as there is now. Rather, each pop music newspaper compiled its own. In *Melody Maker, New Musical Express* and *Disc* 'Please Please Me' did make the top. But it reached only number two in the *Record Retailer* listing, also used by *New Record Mirror*.

Monday 11 February

Studio Two: 10.00am-1.00pm. Recording: 'There's A Place' (takes 1-10); 'Seventeen' (working title of 'I Saw Her Standing There') (takes 1-9). Studio Two: 2.30-6.00pm. Recording: 'A Taste Of Honey' (takes 1-5); 'Do You Want To Know A Secret' (takes 1-8); 'A Taste Of Honey' (takes 6-7); 'There's A Place' (takes 11-13); 'Seventeen' (working title of 'I Saw Her Standing There') (takes 10-12); 'Misery' (takes 1-11). Studio Two: 7.30-10.45pm. Recording: 'Hold Me Tight' (takes 1-13); 'Anna (Go to Him)' (takes 1-3); 'Boys' (take 1); 'Chains' (takes 1-4); 'Baby It's You' (takes 1-3); 'Twist and Shout' (takes 1-2). P: George Martin.   E: Norman Smith.   2E: Richard Langham.

There can scarcely have been 585 more productive minutes in the history of recorded music. For in that small space of time, the Beatles recorded all ten new songs for their first long-player. Together with the four sides of their first two singles, a 14-song album was born.

"It was obvious, commercially, that once 'Please Please Me' – the single – had been a success, we should release an LP as soon as possible," says George Martin. "I asked them what they had which we could record quickly, and the answer was their stage act."

The Beatles' stage act was certainly refined by February 1963. As remarkable as it may seem today, the group had been performing live virtually every night, day in, week out, month in, year out, since mid-1960. Nonetheless, only two recording sessions, 10.00-1.00 and 2.30-5.30, were originally booked for the day, and the third, 7.30-10.45, was only added later. Provided their voices could hold out, George Martin calculated, the group should just about be able to record ten tracks in less than ten hours.

It was a close run thing. The group was not exactly at the peak of physical condition before the day even started, having worked up and down the country through one of the coldest British winters on record. John Lennon had a particularly heavy cold, clearly indicated by his between-takes chatter on the preserved session tapes. So how did they keep going? Norman Smith remembers. "They had a big glass jar of Zubes throat sweets on top of the piano, rather like the ones you see in a sweet shop. Paradoxically, by the side of that, was a big carton of Peter Stuyvesant cigarettes which they smoked incessantly."

Only two songs – both McCartney/Lennon compositions – were attempted in the morning session, 'There's A Place' (John lead vocal) and 'Seventeen' (Paul lead vocal), the latter being the working title of 'I Saw Her Standing There', the pulsating song later selected as the LP opener.

The clock had soon moved around to lunchtime, but the Beatles had other thoughts. "We told them we were having a break," recalls second engineer Richard Langham, "but they said they would like to stay on and rehearse. So while George, Norman and I went round the corner to the Heroes of Alma pub for a pie and pint they stayed, drinking milk. When we came back they'd been playing right through. We couldn't believe it. We had never seen a group work right through their lunch break before."

The afternoon began with Paul singing 'A Taste Of Honey', a song from the 1960 play of the same name. This required him to double-track his vocal (superimpose one recording onto another, slightly out of synchronisation, to produce a fuller sound), take seven onto take five, the only time this was done on the LP. This completed, George took lead vocal on the McCartney/Lennon number 'Do You Want To Know A Secret', the best version – take eight – being a superimposition take of the harmony vocal and two drum sticks being tapped together, onto take six. (The song was later 'given' by the songwriters to another Brian Epstein act, Billy J. Kramer with the Dakotas, who recorded it at Abbey Road during their debut session on 14 March 1963 and took it to number one in the charts.) After more work on 'There's A Place' (overdubbing harmonica onto take ten) and 'Seventeen' (overdubbing handclapping onto take one) the Beatles taped 'Misery', a song John and Paul had written for Helen Shapiro to record (she never did), the two songwriters sharing lead vocal. This was recorded at 30 ips (the studio's normal tape speed was 15 ips) to facilitate easier superimposition of piano at a later date.

Publicity photographs of the Beatles taken 21 January 1963 inside EMI House, Manchester Square.

To augment the release of the 'Please Please Me' single, Brian Epstein again commissioned an independent press release, put together by Tony Barrow and Andrew Oldham through the office of Tony Calder Enterprises. Oldham went on to co-manage the Rolling Stones and, with Calder, found Immediate Records.

Things progressed even more quickly in the evening. Paul sang lead vocal on his composition 'Hold Me Tight', recorded in 13 takes, though only two were complete versions. There were five false starts and one breakdown (an aborted take, owing to an error) and four attempts at recording an edit piece (a short burst to be edited in at a later time). In the end, it was decided that a master version could be edited together from takes nine and 13, but documentation shows that this was never done. When the LP running order was worked out 'Hold Me Tight' was surplus to requirements and the song was left unreleased. It will always remain that way too, for the tape no longer exists. However, the Beatles later taped a re-make of the song which does appear on their second LP.

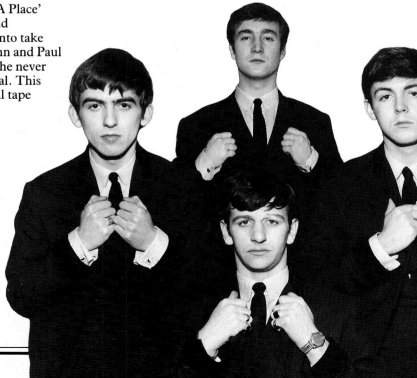

BEATLESBEATLESBEATLESBEATLESBEATLESBEATLESBEATLESBEATLESBEATLESBEATLESBEATLESBEATLESBEAT

here's the first big chart-bustin' bombshell of '63 !!!!

THE BEATLES

have made

THE RECORD OF THE YEAR

RECORDOFTHEYEARRECORDOFTHEYEARRECORDOFTHEYEARRECORDOFTHEYEARRECORDOFTHEYEAR

please, please make sure that you listen to

PLEASE PLEASE ME

coupled with ASK ME WHY

Both titles written, sung and played by

THE BEATLES

Parlophone 45-R 4983

-o-o-o-o-o-o-o-o-o-o-o-o-o-o-o-o-o-o-o-o-o-o-o-o-o-o-o-o-o-o-o-o-o-o-o-o-o-o-o-o-o-o-o-o-o-o

:::: Released Friday 11th January 1963

Four months ago THE BEATLES were already the most popular group in the North West but, so far as the rest of Britain was concerned, their talent and their pop potential was of unknown quantity. In October the group's first Parlophone single, LOVE ME DO, was released and ..... WHAM! ..... THE BEATLES had arrived with a bang which shook the charts before the disc had been in the shops more than 48 hours!

The purpose of this Press Release is to bring you right up to date on the fantastic success story of THE BEATLES and to herald the release of their second Parlophone single, PLEASE PLEASE ME which we predict will put this exceptional vocal/instrumental quartet high up on the NATIONAL TOP TEN CHARTS within the next few weeks.

PICTURES AND BACKGROUND INFORMATION

If your files do not contain the full background story on THE BEATLES (released to the Press on 1st October 1962)

or

If you think we can answer any additional questions which will help you to build a first-rate story for your column

PLEASE DO NOT HESITATE TO CONTACT US

New PHOTOGRAPHS of the group (including individual portraits of the four boys) are freely available for Press use. We are sure you will want to use one when you review PLEASE PLEASE ME

DIRECTION
AND PERSONAL MANAGEMENT

BRIAN EPSTEIN,
Nems Enterprises Limited,
12-14 Whitechapel,
Liverpool.1.

Phone : ROYal 7895

PRESS REPRESENTATIVES.

TONY CALDER ENTERPRISES LTD.,
4th Floor,
Royalty House,
72, Dean Street,
London, W.1.

Phone : REGent 3444 and 0260

Monday 11 February (contd).

After this the Beatles ripped through five cover versions of other artists' material. John sang lead vocal on Arthur Alexander's 'Anna (Go To Him)', recorded in three takes. Ringo took lead vocal for the first time in the recording studio on the Shirelles' 'Boys', recorded in just one take, although because the song required a faded ending this was done at the remix stage, on 25 February. Then John, Paul and George shared the vocals on 'Chains', a minor, contemporary hit for the Cookies, penned by the Brill Building team of Gerry Goffin and Carole King, very inspirational to John Lennon and Paul McCartney in their formative songwriting years. This was captured in four takes although the best was take one and again it was left to be given a faded ending at the remix stage. Following this, in three takes, John sang the Shirelles' 'Baby It's You'.

It was now something like 10.00pm and the studios were due to close down for the evening. But there was one more song to be recorded. Everybody went down to the Abbey Road canteen for coffee, biscuits and a discussion on what the final song might be. Several were considered, and a few friendly arguments broke out. Norman Smith remembers what happened next. "Someone suggested they do 'Twist And Shout', the old Isley Brothers' number, with John taking the lead vocal. But by this time all their throats were tired and sore – it was 12 hours since we had started working. John's, in particular, was almost completely gone so we really had to get it right first time, the Beatles on the studio floor and us in the control room. John sucked a couple more Zubes, had a bit of a gargle with milk and away we went."

What John sang on that first take is what you hear today on record, arguably the most stunning rock and roll vocal and instrumental performance of all time; two-and-a-half minutes of Lennon shredding his vocal cords to bits, audibly ending with a hefty sigh cum groan of relief. It was gone 10.30pm, and the Beatles had completed their first album.

The recording of 'Twist And Shout' had a marked effect on those in the control room, which in studio two is set up high and reached by climbing 20 wooden stairs. Richard Langham recalls "I was ready to jump up and down when I heard them singing that. It was an amazing demonstration." And Cris Neal, who had unofficially popped into the control room to watch the proceedings, has a very definite recollection. "John was stripped to the waist to do this most amazingly raucous vocal. The next morning Norman Smith and I took a tape around all the studio copying rooms saying to everybody 'What the hell do you think of this!' " And George Martin was heard to say "I don't know how they do it. We've been recording all day but the longer we go on the better they get."

Popular myth has the Beatles performing only one take of the song, but infallible studio documentation – written simultaneously to the event – proves that this is not so. They did two, and the second one *was* complete, not a false start or a breakdown. George Martin concurs. "I did try a second take of 'Twist And Shout' but John's voice had gone."

Afterwards, everyone trooped upstairs to hear a playback. "Sessions never normally over-ran past 10.00pm," recalls Richard Langham. "At 10.05 you'd meet half the musicians on the platform of St. John's Wood station, going home. But on this occasion after the first playback they decided they wanted to hear certain songs again. I glanced at Norman and at the clock and said 'Look, I have to be in at nine tomorrow morning, how will I get home?' Brian Epstein said that he would run me home if I played the tape again. So I played the tape and he drove me back to Camden Town in his little Ford Anglia."

Many folk believe that the Beatles also recorded a version of Little Eva's 'Keep Your Hands Off My Baby' during the LP sessions, as reported in the *New Musical Express* edition of 22 February 1963. But the complete set of the day's recording sheets still exist and the song is not mentioned.

Second engineer Richard Langham with the rapidly becoming fab Four. This shot was taken by Norman Smith in September 1963, during the making of *With The Beatles*.

Documentation from an historic day. Ten songs in less than ten hours, and an album still fresh today, more than 25 years on.

RECORDING SHEET

MONO/STEREO TWIN-TRACK.

Sheet: 2 of: Class: Pop! Overall Title L.P.

Date of Session 11-FEB 1963 Job No: 3586 3PMS.

ARTISTIC INFORMATION

ARTISTE(S) AND/OR CAST	The Beatles		CONDUCTOR		
			ORCHESTRA		
			ACCOMPANIMENT		
			ART. DEPT. REP.	G. Martin	

COSTING INFORMATION

MATERIALS USED 5 x 77 ORDER NUMBER
SESSION BOOKED TIME 2.30 - 5.30 COMPANY Parlophone
SESSION ACTUAL 2.30 - 6.00 STUDIO/CONTROL ROOM 2/2
SET-UP/PLAYBACK — ENGINEERS NS RL

TITLES and MATRIX Nos.	AUTHOR/COMPOSER/PUBLISHER	REEL NUMBERS	FALSE STARTS	TAKE No.	FROM	TO	DUR.	M	REMARKS
"Taste of Honey"		E48876		1	complete		2.00		
		TWIN-TRACK		2	B.D		1.00		
				3	B.D		1.00		
				4	complete		2.02		
				5	— .. —		2.00		Best
"Do you want to know a Secret"		— .. —	1,	2	— .. —		1.55		
				3	— .. —		1.55		
			5,	4	— .. —		1.55		
				6	— .. —		2.00		Best.
Superimposition on to two track and Mono		E48877		7	— .. —				
"Do you want to know a Secret"		TWIN-TRACK + Mono		8	— .. —			M	
"A taste of Honey"				6	— .. —				
				7	— .. —			M	
"There's a place"			12,	11	— .. —			M	
				13	— .. —				
"17"			8,	10	— .. —				(ON T9)
			11,	12	— .. —				(ON T1)
"Misery" (No Rhythm)			2,3,4,	1	— .. —				
			5,	6	— .. —		1.42		
			8,9	7	— .. —		1.44		
		E48878	10	11	— .. —		1.44		Best (Recorded at 30 IPS)
		TWIN-TRACK & Mono							

RECORDING SHEET

Date of Session 11-2-63 Job No: 3586 3PMS

COSTING INFORMATION

MATERIALS USED 2 x 77 ORDER NUMBER
SESSION BOOKED TIME 6.30 - 9.30 COMPANY Parlophone
SESSION ACTUAL 7.30 - 10.45 STUDIO/CONTROL ROOM 2/2
SET-UP/PLAYBACK ENGINEERS NS RL

CONDUCTOR									
ORCHESTRA									
ACCOMPANIMENT			George Martin						
ART. DEPT. REP.					TAKE DETAILS				
REEL NUMBERS	FALSE STARTS	TAKE No.	FROM	TO	DUR.	M	REMARKS		
E48878	1,34,	2	complete		1.48				
TWIN-TRACK + Mono.	78,	5	B.D		2.25				
		6	complete		2.26				
		9	— .. —						
	11.	10	EDIT Piece						
		12	— .. —						
		13	— .. —						
	1,2,	3	— .. —						
		—	— .. —						
	2,3,	—	— .. —						
		4	— .. —						
	2,	1	— .. —						
		3	— .. —						
E48879.		1	— .. —						
(TWIN-TRACK		2	— .. —						

RECORDING SHEET

Date of Session 11-FEB. 1963 Job No:

MONO/STEREO TWIN-TRACK. ONLY.

Sheet: 1 of: Class: Pop Overall Title

ARTISTIC INFORMATION

ARTISTE(S) AND/OR CAST	The Beatles		CONDUCTOR		
			ORCHESTRA		
			ACCOMPANIMENT		
			ART. DEPT. REP.	G. Martin	

COSTING INFORMATION

MATERIALS USED 1 x 77 ORDER NUMBER
SESSION BOOKED TIME 10 - 1pm COMPANY Parlophone
SESSION ACTUAL 10 - 1pm STUDIO/CONTROL ROOM 2/2
SET-UP/PLAYBACK 1/2 ENGINEERS NS RL

TITLES and MATRIX Nos.	AUTHOR/COMPOSER/PUBLISHER	REEL NUMBERS	FALSE STARTS	TAKE No.	FROM	TO	DUR.	M	REMARKS
"There's a place"		E48875		1	complete		1.58		
		TWIN-TRACK	3	2	— .. —		1.54		
			5,	4	— .. —		1.50		
			7	6	— .. —		1.51		
				8	— .. —		1.57		
				9	— .. —		1.53		
				10	— .. —		1.50		Best
							2.50		
							2.49		
"17"				1	— .. —		.23		
				2	— .. —		.37		
				3	Edit Piece		.37		
				4	— .. —		2.48		
			6,7,8,	5	complete				
				9					

Wednesday 20 February

Studio One: 10.30am-1.00pm. Recording: 'Misery' (SI takes 12-16); 'Baby It's You' (SI takes 4-6). P: George Martin.   E: Stuart Eltham.   2E: Geoff Emerick.

The Beatles were not present for this overdub session, commonly known then as superimpositions, or SIs. George Martin did all the work, adding piano to 'Misery' and first celeste and then piano to 'Baby It's You'. (The latter piano piece was never used.)

Stuart Eltham was George's regular balance engineer on non-pop group recordings, although he did work on the occasional Beatles session. And a very youthful, fresh-faced Geoff Emerick was the tape operator on this day. Geoff was to play a major role in the Beatles' recordings from 1966 onwards.

Monday 25 February

Studio One (control room only): 10.00am-1.00pm. Editing: 'Seventeen' (working title of 'I Saw Her Standing There') (of takes 9 and 12). Mono mixing: 'Anna (Go To Him)' (from take 3); 'Boys' (from take 1); 'Chains' (from take 1); 'Misery' (from take 16); 'Do You Want To Know A Secret' (from take 8); 'There's A Place' (from take 13); 'Seventeen' (working title of 'I Saw Her Standing There') (from edit of takes 9 and 12); 'Twist And Shout' (from take 1); 'A Taste Of Honey' (from take 7). Stereo mixing: 'Anna (Go To Him)' (from take 3); 'Boys' (from take 1); 'Chains' (from take 1); 'Misery' (from take 16); 'Baby It's You' (from take 5); 'Do You Want To Know A Secret' (from take 8); 'There's A Place' (from take 13); 'Seventeen' (working title of 'I Saw Her Standing There') (from edit of takes 9 and 12); 'Twist And Shout' (from take 1); 'A Taste Of Honey' (from take 7). Studio One (control room only): 2.30-5.45pm. Editing: 'Please Please Me' (of takes 16, 17 and 18). Mono mixing: 'Ask Me Why' (from take 6); 'Misery' (from take 16); 'Baby It's You' (from take 5). Stereo mixing: 'Ask Me Why' (from take 6); 'Please Please Me' (from edit of takes 16, 17 and 18); 'Love Me Do' (from 11 September 1962 mono remix); 'P.S. I Love You' (from 11 September 1962 mono remix); 'Misery' (from take 16). P: George Martin.   E: Norman Smith.   2E: A.B. Lincoln.

Once again the Beatles were not present, as George Martin and his team produced both the mono and stereo masters of the *Please Please Me* album.

Even though the LP was recorded on two-track tape, like all of the Beatles' recordings up to but not including 'I Want To Hold Your Hand', people still wonder why the stereo version of the LP has such peculiar left/right channel separation, with the rhythm (backing) on the left and the vocals on the right. George Martin: "The reason I used the stereo machine in twin-track form was simply to make the mono better, to delay the vital decision of submerging the voices into the background. I certainly didn't separate them for people to hear them separate!"

That said, many students of the group prefer the stereo version because it enables closer scrutiny of individual elements of the recording. For those who simply want a better sound however, the mono version is infinitely superior.

Tuesday 5 March

Studio Two: 2.30-5.30pm. Recording: 'From Me To You' (takes 1-13); 'Thank You Little Girl' [working title of 'Thank You Girl'] (takes 1-13). Studio Two: 7.00-10.00pm. Recording: 'The One After 909' (takes 1-5). P: George Martin. E: Norman Smith. 2E: Richard Langham.

"Brian Epstein and I worked out a plan," says George Martin, "in which we tried – not always successfully – to release a new Beatles single every three months and two albums a year. I was always saying to the Beatles 'I want another hit, come on, give me another hit' and they always responded. 'From Me To You', 'She Loves You', 'I Want To Hold Your Hand'. Right from the earliest days they never failed."

'From Me To You' – to be the Beatles' third single – was a very new song. John and Paul wrote it on 28 February on the artistes' coach travelling down from York to Shrewsbury during a concert tour in which they and others played as support acts to Helen Shapiro. Now, just five days later, they were recording it.

As with all Beatles' recordings of the time, the group performed live in the studio, vocals and instrumentation, treating each take as a separate performance. 'From Me To You' was recorded in seven takes, then six additional edit piece takes were done, featuring harmonica, the guitar solo and the harmonised introduction. The Beatles intended the song to open with a guitar solo, but George Martin suggested that harmonica, augmented with vocals, would be a much better idea. Malcolm Davies, an Abbey Road disc cutter at the time, remembers that

John made a rare visit to him up in the cutting rooms. "Artists never came to the cuts in those days but John popped up to see me because he wanted to borrow my harmonica, thinking it might make a better sound. He brought it back a little later saying that it tasted like a sack of potatoes!"

The B-side, 'Thank You Little Girl' (later, simply, 'Thank You Girl'), was recorded in six takes, with seven additional edit piece takes of the guitar flourish at the end. It was decided that the 'best' was to be an edit of takes six and 13.

Although only two songs were required for the single, the Beatles had two more they wanted to record, both very early Lennon/McCartney compositions, 'The One After 909' and 'What Goes On'. But there was only time for one, so the group spent the evening session concentrating on 'The One After 909'. Four takes of this – plus an edit piece of the middle eight guitar solo through to the end of the song – were put onto tape, though only one was a complete version, the others all breaking down at various points. It was never to progress any further, and the tape remains in the archive, unreleased. The group did revive the song in 1969 however, recording a new version which was released on the *Let It Be* album. The main differences between the two are the rawer instrumentation and

more deliberately monotone vocal of the original, plus the quality of George's guitar solos. On take two of the 1963 version this was so akin to the twanging of a rubber band that John was prompted to comment at the end "What kind of a solo was that!". The solo in the 1969 version was impeccable.

Instrument or Singer	Name	Session Payment	Overtime & Extras	Signature
E. Guitar	J. W. Lennon	7 - 10 - 0		J W Lennon
E. Guitar	G. Harrison	7 - 10 - 0		G. Harrison
Bass Guitar	J. P. McCartney	7 - 10 - 0		J P McCartney
Drums	R. Starkey	7 - 10 - 0		

ENDANCE ...MR. G.H. MARTIN...TRADE MARK...PARLOPHONE... JOB No. 14/233/3RM5

SESSION DETAILS

DATE	TIME	STUDIO
MARCH 5th.	2.30 @ 5.30. 7 - 10 p.m.	No. 2.
TYPE	No. of SIDES	DJ/NP LACQUERS
Stereo/Mono.		

E BEATLES.

TION OF ORCHESTRA/CHORUS

rums.
guitars.

TITLES	Publishers
ios/Artiste(s)	
To be selected.	

Items marked * are non copyright.

	COST DETAILS		CASH
CHEQUE			
Orchestra	4 men @ £7. 0. 0.	28.	0. 0.
Doubling			
Porterage			
Secretarial Fee			
Chorus			
Booking Fee			
Conductor			
Orchestrations	Royalty 1d.		
	Charged to E.M.I. Records Ltd.		
	Type of Contract Period.		

TOTAL COST INCLUDING ADVANCED ROYALTY

33/3Pm5. Date
s or any part thereo
and/or its licencee
including broadcastir
e and I accept the
The Beatles.
Address
en required

More payment sheets, this time for the 5 March session, together with the appropriate 'Red Form' for "4 men".

"I used to sit on my high stool in the studio and the boys would play me what they had brought in to record," says George Martin. "I'd listen to the basic idea of the song, perhaps on an acoustic guitar, then I'd help to decide on the structure of the introduction, where the solo should go, the ending and the final length of the song – never longer than 2'45" otherwise we wouldn't get it on the radio!"

Here, 5 March 1963, having first fortified themselves with Abbey Road tea, George listens as they run through 'From Me To You'.

Out and about on the morning of 5 March 1963, before the afternoon and evening recording session at Abbey Road, working with EMI staff photographer John Dove on LP cover ideas and publicity shots. First stop was EMI House, Manchester Square, where the Beatles changed into suitable clothing, having travelled down by van from St Helens, Lancashire during the night. They then posed for Dove on the iron stairwell outside EMI House before moving on to Montague Place where they grouped themselves around a short-sighted parking meter.

It has often been said that the remarkable arrival of the Beatles onto a jaded British pop scene was inestimably aided by their perfect back-up team. Here, seen chatting while the Beatles change clothes, are the three men vital to the group's success, caught mid-conversation by John Dove's camera lens: record producer George Martin, music publisher Dick James and the Beatles' manager Brian Epstein, as ever, impeccably dressed.

Wednesday 13 March

Studio Two: 10.00am-1.00pm. Recording: 'Thank You Little Girl' (working title of 'Thank You Girl') (SI takes 14-28). Editing: 'Thank You Little Girl' (working title of 'Thank You Girl') (of takes 6, 13, 17, 20, 21 and 23). Mono mixing: 'Thank You Little Girl' (working title of 'Thank You Girl') (from edit of takes 6, 13, 17, 20, 21 and 23). Stereo mixing: 'Thank You Little Girl' (working title of 'Thank You Girl') (from edit of takes 6, 13, 17, 20, 21 and 23). P: George Martin.   E: Norman Smith.   2E: Geoff Emerick.

A harmonica overdubbing session only. Just as well, for John's cold had grown so bad that his voice had disappeared. The previous evening he had been forced to bow out of the Beatles' concert in Bedford, and later on this day, when the group had dashed all the way from London to York, he missed out again.

Thursday 14 March

Studio Two (control room only): 10.00am-1.00pm. Editing: 'From Me To You' (of unknown take numbers). Mono mixing: 'From Me To You' (from edit of unknown take numbers). Stereo mixing: 'From Me To You' (from edit of unknown take numbers). P: George Martin.   E: unknown.   2E: unknown.

Friday 22 March

LP release: *Please Please Me.* Parlophone PMC 1201 (mono). [Stereo LP, Parlophone PCS 3042, issued Friday 26 April 1963.] A: 'I Saw Her Standing There'; 'Misery'; 'Anna (Go To Him)'; 'Chains'; 'Boys'; 'Ask Me Why'; 'Please Please Me'. B: 'Love Me Do'; 'P.S. I Love You'; 'Baby It's You'; 'Do You Want To Know A Secret'; 'A Taste Of Honey'; 'There's A Place'; 'Twist And Shout'.

It wasn't always going to be called *Please Please Me*. George Martin thought of naming it *Off the Beatle Track*, and Paul even doodled a few cover ideas before the idea was dropped. (George clearly retained a liking for it however, for on 10 July 1964 he released an orchestral LP of Beatles tracks with that title.)

The cover of the LP proved to be a problem, as George Martin recalls. "I was a fellow of London Zoo and, rather stupidly, thought that it would be great to have the Beatles photographed outside the insect house. But the zoo people were very stuffy indeed, 'We don't allow these kind of photographs on our premises, quite out of keeping with the good taste of the Zoological Society of London,' so the idea fell down. I bet they regret it now…"

There were other ideas too, as illustrated on these pages. One was to show the Beatles on the spiral stairwell outside EMI's building in Manchester Square. Another was to show them on the steps of Abbey Road studios, kicking their legs in unison. "Those were the sort of dreadful stock ideas every photographer went in for then," says Martin.

Finally George Martin brought in Angus McBean, a distinguished photographer whom he had used for comedy LP covers and who has since worked with the royal family. McBean had the Beatles peer down at him over the entrance stairwell inside the Manchester Square building. It was the first of several fresh, eye-catching Beatles LP covers.

Thursday 11 April

Single release: 'From Me To You'/'Thank You Girl'. Parlophone R 5015.

The Beatles' third single, and a number one smash hit. The group had well and truly 'arrived', and would remain untouchable for the remainder of the decade.

The 45- prefix to catalogue numbers of EMI singles was dropped on March 8 when it was realised that the 45 rpm format was the new industry standard, superseding 78 rpm.

Monday 1 July

Studio Two: 2.30-5.30pm, 7.00-10.00pm. Recording: 'She Loves You' (takes unknown); 'Get You In The End' (working title of 'I'll Get You') (takes unknown). **P: George Martin. E: Norman Smith. 2E: Geoff Emerick.**

Parlophone was dominating British pop music by June 1963, just 12 months after the Beatles had tested for this 'unfashionable' label. The top three places in the mid-month charts were filled by the Beatles, Gerry and the Pacemakers (actually on the Columbia label but produced by George Martin and Ron Richards) and Billy J. Kramer with the Dakotas. Martin took a two-week holiday in mid-June and returned to a full studio diary, for in addition to the label's usual roster of artists, Brian Epstein was supplying several more new acts. The Beatles came in to record on 1 July, Gerry and the Pacemakers 2 July, the Fourmost had their artist test on 3 July, there was a Beatles remix on 4 July, Kramer was in on 16 July, Gerry on 17 July, 18 July was a Beatles remix and a Gerry session, Kramer on 22 July, the Fourmost returned for their first session on 24 July, Cilla Black came for her artist test

on 25 July, there was a Kramer remix on 29 July and the Beatles recorded on the 30th.

'She Loves You' was another very new song, John and Paul having composed it in a Newcastle-upon-Tyne hotel room on 26 June. Paul's initial idea was to have an 'answering' song, him singing "She Loves You" and the others calling back "Yeah Yeah Yeah". John persuaded him to drop the idea.

"I was sitting in my usual place on a high stool in studio two when John and Paul first ran through the song on their acoustic guitars, George joining in on the choruses," recalls George Martin. "I thought it was great but was intrigued by the final chord, an odd sort of major sixth, with George doing the sixth and John and Paul the third and fifths, like a Glenn Miller arrangement. They were saying 'It's a great chord! Nobody's ever heard it before!' Of course I knew that wasn't quite true!"

"I was setting up the microphone when I saw the lyrics on the music stand," says Norman Smith. "I thought I'll just have a quick look. 'She Loves You Yeah Yeah Yeah, She Loves You Yeah Yeah Yeah, She Loves You Yeah Yeah Yeah, Yeah'. I thought Oh my God, what a lyric! This is going to be one that I *do not* like. But when they started to sing it – bang, wow, terrific, I was up at the mixer jogging around."

Precise details of the recording 'takes' no longer exist, but three reels of tape were filled in putting down 'She Loves You' and its B-side 'I'll Get You' (at this stage titled 'Get You In The End'). The record was to become the group's first million seller.

Thursday 4 July

Studio Two (control room only): 10.00am-1.00pm. Editing: 'She Loves You' (of unknown take numbers). **Mono mixing:** 'She Loves You' (from edit of unknown take numbers); 'Get You In The End' (working title of 'I'll Get You') (from unknown take number). **P: George Martin. E: unknown. 2E: unknown.**

MR. WHITE.
MR. R. DOUGHILL.
MR. A. HULLOR.
MR. S. GILLINGHAM.
MR. R. OLDFIELD.
MR. R. McHALE.
MR. A. DEWDNEY.
MR. ... POLLEN.

MR. R. DUNTON.
MR. I. MIDDLETON.
MR. ... GREGORY.
MR. D. WOODWARD.
MR. S. STERN.
MR. G. FRESHWATER.
MR. CANNINGS.
MR. S. WRIGHT.

PARLOPHONE L.P.

'PLEASE PLEASE ME'.

Job No.

3586/3PMS.   April Release: Stereo & Mono.

Cover note:

Tony Barrow.

Cover:

Colour photo of The Beatles.

Artists:

The Beatles.

Side 1.

Recording supervised by George Martin.

I SAW HER STANDING THERE.
(McCartney-Lennon)

MISERY.
(McCartney-Lennon)   Dick James Music.

ANNA.
(Alexander)   Dick James Music.

CHAINS.
(Goffin-King)   Shapiro Bernstein.

BOYS.
(Dixon-Farrell)   Aldon.

ASK ME WHY.
(McCartney-Lennon)   Ardmore & Beechwood.

Side 2.

PLEASE PLEASE ME.
(McCartney-Lennon)   Dick James Music.

LOVE ME DO.
(McCartney-Lennon)   Dick James Music.

P.S. I LOVE YOU.
(McCartney-Lennon)   Ardmore & Beechwood.

BABY IT'S YOU.
(David-Williams-Bacharach)   Ardmore & Beechwood.

DO YOU WANT TO KNOW A SECRET.
(McCartney-Lennon)   Hill and Range.

A TASTE OF HONEY.
(Scott-Marlow)   Dick James Music.

THERE'S A PLACE.
(McCartney-Lennon)   Ambassador.

TWIST AND SHOUT.
(Medley-Russell)   Dick James Music.

Mellin Music.

February 20th. 1963.

G.H. MARTIN.
E.M.I. Records Ltd.

8·3·63

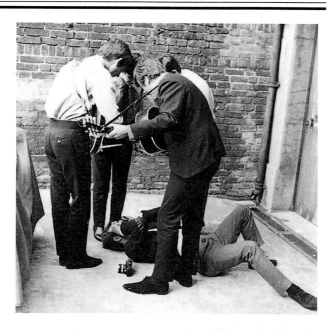

The Beatles at Abbey Road, 1 July 1963, posing for photographs down the left-side of the building (adjacent to the side entrance to studios One and Two) and inside Studio Two with members of staff and a clearly troublesome Beatlemaniac, so near but yet so far to one of her idols. John Lennon and Norman Smith share a joke, seemingly oblivious to the commotion.

PMC
1202

Please Please Me
THE BEATLES

■ **GEORGE HARRISON** (lead guitar)   ■ **JOHN LENNON** (rhythm guitar)
■ **PAUL McCARTNEY** (bass guitar)   ■ **RINGO STARR** (drums)

SIDE ONE

1. I SAW HER STANDING THERE
   (McCartney-Lennon)

2. MISERY
   (McCartney-Lennon)

3. ANNA (GO TO HIM)
   (Alexander)

4. CHAINS
   (Goffin-King)

5. BOYS
   (Dixon-Farrell)

6. ASK ME WHY
   (McCartney-Lennon)

7. PLEASE PLEASE ME
   (McCartney-Lennon)

SIDE TWO

1. LOVE ME DO
   (McCartney-Lennon)

2. P.S. I LOVE YOU
   (McCartney-Lennon)

3. BABY IT'S YOU
   (David-Williams-Bacharach)

4. DO YOU WANT TO KNOW A SECRET
   (McCartney-Lennon)

5. A TASTE OF HONEY
   (Scott-Marlow)

6. THERE'S A PLACE
   (McCartney-Lennon)

7. TWIST AND SHOUT
   (Medley-Russell)

Pop picking is a fast 'n' furious business these days whether you are on the recording studio side listening out, or on the disc-counter side listening in. As a record reviewer I find myself installed halfway in-between with an ear cocked in either direction. So far as Britain's record collecting public is concerned, The Beatles broke into earshot in October, 1962. My natural hometown interest in the group pre-vented me taking a totally unbiased view of their early success. Eighteen months before their first visit to the EMI studios in London, The Beatles had been voted Merseyside's favourite outfit and it was inevitable that their first Parlophone record, LOVE ME DO, would go straight into the top of Liverpool's local hit parade. The group's chances of national chart entry seemed much more remote. No other team had joined the best-sellers via a début disc. But The Beatles were history-makers from the start and LOVE ME DO sold enough copies during its first 48 hours in the shops to send it soaring into the national charts. In all the busy years since pop singles first shrank from ten to seven inches I have never seen a British group leap to the forefront of the scene with such speed and energy. Within the six months which followed the Top Twenty appearance of LOVE ME DO, almost every leading deejay and musical journalist in the country began to shout the praises of The Beatles. Readers of the *New Musical Express* voted the boys into a surprisingly high place via the 1962/63 popularity poll . . . on the strength of just one record release. Pictures of the group spread themselves across the front pages of three national music papers. People inside and outside the record Industry expressed tremendous interest in the new vocal and instrumental sounds which The Beatles had introduced. Brian Matthew (who has since brought The Beatles to many millions of viewers and listeners in his "Thank Your Lucky Stars", "Saturday Club" and "Easy Beat" programmes) describes the quartet as *visually and musically the most exciting and accomplished group to emerge since The Shadows.* Disc reviewing, like disc producing, teaches one to be wary about making long-term predictions. The hit parade isn't always dominated by the most worthy performances of the day so it is no good assuming that versatility counts for everything. It was during the recording of a Radio Luxembourg programme in the *EMI Friday Spectacular* series that I was finally convinced that The Beatles were about to enjoy the type of top-flight national fame which I had always believed that they deserved. The teen-audience didn't know the evening's line-up in advance, and before Muriel Young brought on artists and groups in person, she began to read out their Christian names. She got as far as John . . . Paul . . . and the rest of their Christian names was buried in a mighty barrage of very genuine applause. I cannot think of more than one other group — British or American — which would be so warmly welcomed by the announcement of two Christian

names. To me, this was the ultimate proof that The Beatles (and not just one or two of their hit records) had arrived at the uncommon peak-popularity point reserved for discdom's privileged few. Shortly afterwards The Beatles proved their pop power when they by-passed the lower segments of the hit parade to scuttle straight into the nation's Top Ten with their second single, PLEASE PLEASE ME.

This brisk-selling disc went on to overtake all rivals when it bounced into the coveted Number One slot towards the end of February. Just over four months after the release of their very first record The Beatles had become triumphant chart-toppers!

Producer George Martin has never had any headaches over choice of songs for The Beatles. Their own built-in tunesmith team of John Lennon and Paul McCartney has already tucked away enough self-penned numbers to maintain a steady output of all-original singles from now until 1975! Between them The Beatles adopt a do-it-yourself approach from the very beginning. They write their own lyrics, design and eventually build their own instrumental backdrops and work out their own vocal arrangements. Their music is wild, pungent, hard-hitting, uninhibited . . . and personal. The do-it-yourself angle ensures complete originality at all stages of the pro-cess. Although so many people suggest (without closer definition) that The Beatles have a trans-Atlantic style, their only real influence has been from the unique brand of Rhythm and Blues folk music which abounds on Merseyside and which The Beatles themselves have helped to pioneer since their formation in 1960. This record comprises eight Lennon-McCartney compositions in addition to six other numbers which have become firm live-perform-ance favourites in The Beatles' varied repertoire. The group's admiration for the work of The Shirelles is demonstrated by the inclusion of BABY IT'S YOU (John taking the lead vocal with George and Paul supplying the harmony), and BOYS (a fast rocker which allows drummer Ringo to make his first recorded appearance as a vocalist). ANNA, ASK ME WHY, and TWIST AND SHOUT also feature stand-out solo performances from John, whilst DO YOU WANT TO KNOW A SECRET hands the audio spotlight to George. MISERY may sound as though it is a self-duet created by the multi-recording of two voices belonging to John and Paul. There is only one 'trick duet' and that is on A TASTE OF HONEY featuring a dual-voiced Paul. John and Paul get together on THERE'S A PLACE and I SAW HER STANDING THERE: George joins them for CHAINS, LOVE ME DO and PLEASE PLEASE ME.

TONY BARROW

USE
FMITEX

Thursday 18 July

Studio Two: 7.00-10.45pm. Recording: 'You Really Got A Hold On Me' (takes 1-11); 'Money (That's What I Want)' (takes 1-7); 'Devil In Her Heart' (takes 1-6); 'Till There Was You' (takes 1-3). P: George Martin. E: Norman Smith. 2E: Richard Langham.

The present day notion that pop/rock artists make only one album every two years was certainly not operative in 1963. Quite the reverse, in fact. With *Please Please Me* out just four months, and seemingly parked on a permanent basis at number one on the charts, the Beatles found themselves back at Abbey Road working on the follow-up, at this point untitled but later named *With The Beatles*, in keeping with the Epstein/Martin plan of two LPs and four singles per year.

Sessions for this album quickly revealed the astonishing maturity the Beatles were gaining inside the studio. There were to be cover versions of other artist's songs nestling alongside Beatles originals, just as on *Please Please Me*, yet these all sound far superior on the second album.

'You Really Got A Hold On Me', the first track to be recorded, is a case in point. The Lennon vocal is quite superb, an excellent reading of someone else's material (Smokey Robinson and the Miracles). And the instrumentation, including George Martin on piano, is of an equal calibre. Seven takes of the song – four of them complete, the others false starts – were taped first, followed by four edit pieces, one of which was also a false start. These edits concentrated on just two parts of the song, the word "Baby" and the end riffs. Documentation shows that a basic master could be cut from take seven edited with takes 10 and 11.

The next song to be tackled was 'Money (That's What I Want)', another Tamla Motown number, this time by Barrett Strong. This was done in seven takes, including a piano edit piece. Wrapping up this session of cover versions, the Beatles recorded 'Devil In Her Heart' (originally 'Devil In His Heart' by the Donays, an all-girl group), captured in three takes and three overdubs (including Ringo on maraca), and 'Till There Was You', a Paul McCartney lead vocal on the song from the musical *The Music Man*. Three versions of this were taped, two of which were complete, but they did not prove satisfactory and it was decided that the group would return to the song another time.

Tuesday 30 July

Studio Two: 10.00am-1.30pm. Recording: 'Please Mister Postman' (takes 1-9); 'It Won't Be Long' (takes 1-10). Studio Two: 5.00-11.00pm. Recording: 'Money (That's What I Want)' (piano test, plus takes 8-14); 'Till There Was You' [re-make] (takes 4-8); 'Roll Over Beethoven' (takes 1-8); 'It Won't Be Long' (takes 11-23); 'All My Loving' (takes 1-14). P: George Martin. E: Norman Smith. 2E: Richard Langham.

The interlude between these two album sessions, and the irregular timings (the evening one finished an hour after normal 'lights out'), was due to the fact that the Beatles had a mid-afternoon BBC radio rehearsal and recording session at the Playhouse Theatre, London for the programme *Saturday Club*.

The morning session at Abbey Road saw the Beatles tape a cover version of the Marvelettes' 'Please Mister Postman'. The 'best' was an overdub of take nine onto take seven. Then the group recorded the first new Lennon-McCartney composition for the LP, the superb 'It Won't Be Long'. Eventually selected to open the album, this fast-paced rocker also has plenty of "Yeah"s – like 'She Loves You' – but is technically superior to that song. Despite doing ten takes, two of which were overdubs of the ending, the recording was incomplete when it was time to go off to the BBC.

Resuming in the late-afternoon, the Beatles picked up 'Money' again, George Martin again overdubbing the strident piano chords which distinguish the song. He did a test run first, then recorded edit piece takes 8-14. After this the Beatles did a re-make of 'Till There Was You', starting with take four to take into account the earlier aborted takes. Drums were considered too obtrusive for this quiet ballad so Ringo tapped out the beat on a pair of bongos. Take eight was considered the 'best' version. For one of George Harrison's three vocal contributions to the LP the group next recorded a version of Chuck Berry's rock classic, 'Roll Over Beethoven'. This was recorded in five takes, the 'best' being take five, onto which they added an overdub piece (attempted twice, only one of which was usable) and take eight, an edit piece of the end guitar riff only.

The Beatles then returned to 'It Won't Be Long', recording takes 11-17 and edit pieces 18-23, from which 17 and 21 were chosen as the 'best', to be cut together, and finally, they recorded Paul's magnificent 'All My Loving', by far his best, most complex piece of songwriting yet. It was recorded in just 13 takes (numbered 1-14 but there was no take five), 12-14 being purely overdubs. The master version was an overdub, take 14 onto take 11.

Wednesday 21 August

Studio Three (control room only): 10.00am-1.00pm, 2.00-5.30pm.
Editing: 'Money (That's What I Want)' (of takes 6 and 7); 'You Really Got A Hold On Me' (of takes 7, 10 and 11); 'Roll Over Beethoven' (of takes 7 and 8); 'It Won't Be Long' (of takes 17 and 21).
Mono mixing: 'Devil In Her Heart' (from take 6); 'Money (That's What I Want)' (from edit of takes 6 and 7); 'You Really Got A Hold On Me' (from edit of takes 7, 10 and 11); 'Please Mister Postman' (from take 9); 'Till There Was You' (from take 8); 'Roll Over Beethoven' (from edit of takes 7 and 8); 'All My Loving' (from take 14); 'It Won't Be Long' (from edit of takes 17 and 21).
P: George Martin. E: Norman Smith. 2E: Geoff Emerick.

Mono mixing for the LP.

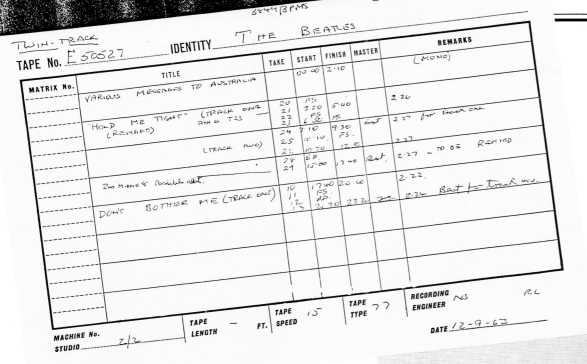

A typical Beatles Emitape box, with the contents detailed on the reverse.

Going up in the world. The Beatles, Brian Epstein and George Martin join top EMI executives (including Sir Joseph Lockwood, chairman, centre, and L.G. Wood, managing director, behind Ringo) for lunch in the Manchester Square boardroom, 18 November 1963.

Friday 23 August

Single release: 'She Loves You'/'I'll Get You'. Parlophone R 5055.

'She Loves You': the record which propelled the Beatles into the national view, its infamous 'Yeah Yeah Yeah' hook line quickly becoming a hackneyed catchphrase. It was the group's first single to sell a million copies in Britain alone, passing the halfway mark on 3 September and the million milestone on 27 November. It also achieved the very rare feat of enjoying two separate spells at number one on the charts, originally occupying the summit for four weeks, spending a further seven in the top three and then returning to the top for another two weeks.

Wednesday 11 September

Studio Two: 2.30-6.00pm. Recording: 'I Wanna Be Your Man' (take 1); 'Little Child' (takes 1-2); 'All I've Got To Do' (takes 1-15). Studio Two: 7.00-10.15pm. Recording: 'Not A Second Time' (takes 1-9); 'Don't Bother Me' (takes 1-7). P: George Martin.   E: Norman Smith.   2E: Richard Langham.

This productive day began with the taping of Ringo's vocal contribution to the LP, 'I Wanna Be Your Man', written by John and Paul. Just the day before, the composers had also offered the song to the Rolling Stones, who recorded it as their second single. The Beatles attempted only one take of the number on this session though, returning to it on 12 September. The same was true of John's 'Little Child', only two takes of which were taped before it was left for another time. The next song however, 'All I've Got To Do', was started and finished in the same session. This superb Lennon number was recorded in 14 takes (eight of which were false starts) and one overdub, take 15.

Recording resumed after dinner with 'Not A Second Time', another classy new Lennon number. Takes one to five concentrated on the basic track while six to nine, the best one, were overdubs onto take five of John's voice, now double-tracked, and George Martin playing the piano. Finally, the group recorded George Harrison's first ever solo composition, 'Don't Bother Me'. Seven takes, three of them overdubs, were recorded but the final result was not satisfactory. The Beatles returned to the song during their next session and tried a 're-make' (ie, they gave it a new structure).

Thursday 12 September

Studio Two: 2.30-6.30pm. Recording: Messages to Australia (takes 1-4); 'Hold Me Tight' [re-make] (takes 20-29). Studio Two: 7.00-11.30pm. Recording: 'Don't Bother Me' [re-make] (takes 10-19); 'Little Child' (takes 3-18); 'I Wanna Be Your Man' (takes 2-7). P: George Martin.   E: Norman Smith.   2E: Richard Langham.

It wasn't only in Britain that the Beatles were enjoying tremendous record sales. On 5 July Brian Epstein verbally agreed to the group undertaking a 1964 concert tour of Australia, and on 2 December the contract was formally signed. Between those dates, in order to satisfy Australian radio, the Beatles recorded four messages for broadcast, three addressed directly to Bob Rogers, disc-jockey at the Sydney station 2SM, and one 'open-message', to be used by any station. These half-scripted, half-spontaneous lines consisted of typically witty Beatles chatter and were the first of a number of speech items the group was to record over the coming years.

The first musical item on the day's agenda was a re-make of 'Hold Me Tight', first attempted on 11 February. To commence with a round number they started this time at take 20, needing to go no further than take 29 before it was right, the final version being an edit of takes 26 and 29.

After a break the group set about another re-make, of George's 'Don't Bother Me', again starting off with a round number, take 10. By take 19 it was finished, the final version being an overdub of take 15 onto take 13, the overdub being a second George Harrison vocal, Paul on claves, John on tambourine and Ringo on an Arabian bongo, all instruments courtesy of the Abbey Road collection! Following this they did 'Little Child', resuming from 11 September. The best basic track was take 7, onto which they overdubbed John's regular harmonica from 13, Paul playing piano from 15 and John's middle eight solo harmonica from 18. Finally, the group returned to 'I Wanna Be Your Man', takes 2-7. But again, it was left unfinished, to be picked up another time.

```
THE BEATLES

CHRISTMAS MESSAGES TO AUSTRALIA - 1963
12th September 1963 - E 50527

TAKE ONE:
Hello Bob Rogers in Australia, this is John Lennon of The
Beatles here. Hope you're okay Bob ...
This is Paul McCartney of The Beatles speaking Bob. I hope
you are still playing our records ...
George Harrison here Bob, just like to say ... hope our record
... our current record does just as well out there as it has
done over here ...
Hello Bob, this is Ringo. Hope they've got the LP over there
and it's selling and hope we can come out and see you sometime
soon.

TAKE TWO:
Hello Bob Rogers in Australia this is John Lennon of The
Beatles here ... We hear you've been playing our records ...

TAKE THREE:
Hello Bob Rogers in Australia this is John Lennon of The Beatles
here in London. We believe you've been playing our records ...
Hi Bob this is Paul here and we'd like to thank you very much
for playing them and keep going pal!
Yeah, this is George Bob ... Just like to say we hope our
current release goes just as well in Australia as it has done
here in England ...
This is Ringo I'd just like to say that we've heard such a
lot of your country that I can't wait to get out there and
see it all.

OPEN MESSAGE TO AUSTRALIA
TAKE ONE:
Hello Australia this is John Lennon of The Beatles here hope
you're all having a great time over there ...
This is Paul speaking, we're hoping to come over soon and
visit Australia.
This is George ... that's if you move it a few thousand miles
nearer.
```

Monday 30 September

Studio Two (control room only): 10.00am-1.15pm. Editing: 'Little Child' (of takes 15 and 18); 'Hold Me Tight' (of takes 26 and 29). Recording: 'Money (That's What I Want)' (three unnumbered takes of SI onto take 7); 'I Wanna Be Your Man' (six takes, numbered 8-13, of SI onto take 7). Mono mixing: 'All I've Got To Do' (from take 15); 'Don't Bother Me' (from take 15); 'Little Child' (from edit of takes 15 and 18); 'Hold Me Tight' (from edit of takes 26 and 29); 'Not A Second Time' (from take 9). P: George Martin.   E: Norman Smith.   2E: Geoff Emerick.

The Beatles were out of the country on well-deserved holidays when this session took place so in addition to the remixing it was George Martin who overdubbed two more piano variations (the second and third takes) on 'Money' and Hammond organ on 'I Wanna Be Your Man' (the 'best' being take 13).

Thursday 3 October

Studio Two: 7.00-10.00pm. Recording: 'I Wanna Be Your Man' (takes 14-15); 'Little Child' (takes 19-21). P: George Martin.   E: Norman Smith.   2E: unknown.
More fine tuning, including the addition of Ringo's maraca to 'I Wanna Be Your Man'.

Thursday 17 October

Studio Two: 2.30-5.30pm, 7.00-10.00pm. Recording: 'The Beatles' Christmas Record' (takes unnumbered); 'You Really Got A Hold On Me' (take 12); 'I Want To Hold Your Hand' (takes 1-17); 'This Boy' (takes 1-17). P: George Martin.   E: Norman Smith.   2E: Geoff Emerick.

This session marked the dawn of a new era for the Beatles at Abbey Road: four-track recording, ushering in entirely new processes. "With four-track one could do a basic rhythm track and then add on vocals and whatever else later. It made the studios into much more of a workshop", says Ken Townsend.

The tapes of 'I Want To Hold Your Hand' reveal that the Beatles had the song perfected before the session, the first take sounding not unlike the last. But one early idea – take two – was to hush the vocal line "And when I touch you". Another – take four – saw Paul introduce the not uncommon 1963 Beatle 'h' into words ("shay that shomthing").

'This Boy', recorded for the B-side of 'I Want To Hold Your Hand' is technically superior to its A-side. While it lacks the immediacy and clever subtleties of 'Hand' it does display a songwriting talent remarkable in its maturity. That the Beatles could afford to virtually throw the track away as a mere B-side speaks volumes for the superb material that was now pouring from them. The song features intricate three-part harmony work, something in which John, Paul and George were naturally adept. "They always experimented with close harmony singing," recalls George Martin, "all I did was change the odd note." The session tapes reveal that the song, although it took 15 takes to perfect (takes 16 and 17 were overdubs), was complete from the start, the only differences being that the middle eight originally featured a guitar solo, and that – like several Beatles recordings of the time – the song originally had a full ending. It was later given a fade-out.

Also on this day the Beatles tried one more take of 'You Really Got A Hold On Me', on four-track, but then gave up, and the group recorded more speech – this time for a flexi-disc to be issued free at Christmas to all members of the rapidly expanding Official Beatles Fan Club. This was the first of seven such discs and it featured the Beatles' cheeky humour (written by press officer Tony Barrow) and offbeat renditions of carols.

Monday 21 October

Studio One (control room only): 10.00am-1.00pm. Mono mixing: 'I Want To Hold Your Hand' (from take 17); 'This Boy' (remixes 1 and 2, from take 15). Editing: 'This Boy' (of mono remixes 1 and 2). Stereo mixing: 'I Want To Hold Your Hand' (remix 1, from take 17). P: George Martin.   E: Norman Smith.   2E: n/a.

Mono mixing for the single, stereo for unforeseen future use.

Wednesday 23 October

Studio Two: 10.00am-1.00pm. Recording: 'I Wanna Be Your Man' (take 16). Mono mixing: 'I Wanna Be Your Man' (from take 16); 'Little Child' (from takes 15 and 18); 'Hold Me Tight' (from takes 26 and 29). P: George Martin.   E: Norman Smith.   2E: unknown.

Still more work on the three difficult tracks.

Tuesday 29 October

Studio Three (control room only): 10.00am-1.00pm. Stereo mixing: 'It Won't Be Long' (from edit of takes 17 and 21); 'All I've Got To Do' (from take 15); 'All My Loving' (from take 14); 'Don't Bother Me' (from take 15); 'Little Child' (from take 21); 'Till There Was You' (from take 8); 'Please Mister Postman' (from take 9); 'Roll Over Beethoven' (from edit of takes 7 and 8); 'Hold Me Tight' (from edit of takes 26 and 29); 'You Really Got A Hold On Me' (from edit of takes 7, 10 and 11); 'I Wanna Be Your Man' (from take 16); 'Devil In Her Heart' (from take 6); 'Not A Second Time' (from take 9); 'Money (That's What I Want)' (from edit of takes 6 and 7). P: George Martin.   E: Norman Smith.   2E: Geoff Emerick and B.T. [Full name unknown.]

Wednesday 30 October

Studio Three (control room only): 2.30-5.30pm. Stereo mixing: 'Money (That's What I Want)' (from take 7). P: George Martin.   E: Norman Smith.   2E: A.B. Lincoln.

Yet another edit of 'Money'. The overdubs on the song were becoming so complicated that to avoid any further two-track to two-track tape copying, two separate two-track mono mixes were used for the stereo album, one for each channel, leading some people to incorrectly interpret the song as a four-track recording. This was the final item of preparation for the LP, and the disc was cut at Abbey Road on November 4.

Friday 22 November

LP release: *With The Beatles*. Parlophone PMC 1206 (mono)/PCS 3045 (stereo). A: 'It Won't Be Long'; 'All I've Got To Do'; 'All My Loving'; 'Don't Bother Me'; 'Little Child'; 'Till There Was You'; 'Please Mister Postman'. B: 'Roll Over Beethoven'; 'Hold Me Tight'; 'You Really Got A Hold On Me'; 'I Wanna Be Your Man'; 'Devil In Her Heart'; 'Not A Second Time'; 'Money (That's What I Want)'.

Eight months to the day from the release of *Please Please Me* came the follow-up LP, *With The Beatles*. With astonishing British advance orders of 300,000, it swiftly passed the half-million and, in 1965, the one million sales marks. It even earned a brief placing in the singles chart, which in the early 1960s was calculated on sales of any record, irrespective of diameter.

Once again, the LP cover set new trends, Robert Freeman's artful photograph of the Beatles in half-shadow having been the subject of much imitation since.

Friday 29 November

Single release: 'I Want To Hold Your Hand'/'This Boy'. Parlophone R 5084.

'I Want To Hold Your Hand' sold one million copies on British advance orders alone and crashed into the charts while 'She Loves You' was enjoying its second spell at number one. Within a week it had replaced its predecessor, and the Beatles were holding numbers one and two, in addition to numbers one and two in the LP charts.

The song was a watershed recording in one other way: it broke the group into the US market, paving the way for a 1964 that would eclipse even 1963 in terms of record sales and all-encompassing Beatlemania.

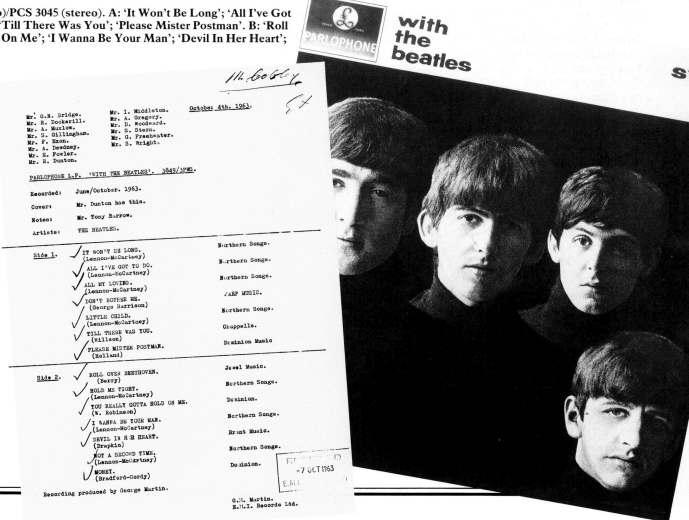

Friday 24 January

Studio One (control room only): 10.00-10.45am. Tape copying: 'I Want To Hold Your Hand' (from take 17). P: n/a. E: Norman Smith. 2E: A.B. Lincoln/Geoff Emerick.

A tape-to-tape copy of the 'I Want To Hold Your Hand' basic rhythm track, take 17 from 17 October 1963; hand-luggage for George Martin and Norman Smith, soon to be leaving for Paris and the Beatles' first EMI recording session outside of Abbey Road.

Wednesday 29 January

EMI Pathé Marconi Studios, 62 Rue de Sevres, Boulogne-sur-Seine, Paris 92, France: Late-morning/afternoon. Recording: 'Komm, Gib Mir Deine Hand' (takes 1-11); 'Sie Liebt Dich' (takes 1-14); 'Can't Buy Me Love' (takes 1-4). Editing: 'Komm, Gib Mir Deine Hand' (of takes 5 and 7). P: George Martin. E: Norman Smith. 2E: Jacques Esmenjaud.

The Beatles, Les Beatles or Die Beatles? On 29 January the four Liverpudlians founds themselves in a French recording studio taping their two most famous songs to date in German. There is a logical explanation for this somewhat bizarre situation. The Beatles were in Paris for a 19-day concert season at the Olympia Theatre. And EMI's West German branch, Odeon, were making overtures to Brian Epstein and George Martin for the group to record in German.

"Odeon was adamant. They couldn't sell large quantities of records unless they were sung in German," recalls George Martin. "I thought that if they were right then we should do it. The Beatles didn't agree, but I persuaded them. Odeon sent over a translator from Cologne to coach the boys although they did know a little German from having played there.

"I fixed the session for late-morning. Norman Smith, myself, and the translator, a chap named Nicolas, all got to the studio on time, but there was no sign of the Beatles. We waited an hour before I telephoned their suite at the George V hotel. Neil Aspinall answered, 'They're in bed, they've decided not to go to the studio'. I went crazy – it was the first time they had refused to do anything for me. 'You tell them they've got to come, otherwise I shall be so angry it isn't true! I'm coming over right now'. So the German and I jumped into a taxi, we got to the hotel and I barged into their suite, to be met by this incredible sight, right out of the Mad Hatter's tea party. Jane Asher – Paul's girlfriend – with her long red hair, was pouring tea from a china pot, and the others were sitting around her like March Hares. They took one look at me and *exploded*, like in a school room when the headmaster enters. Some dived onto the sofa and hid behind cushions, others dashed behind curtains. "You are bastards!" I screamed, to which they responded with impish little grins and roguish apologies. Within minutes we were on our way to the studio. They were right, actually. It wasn't necessary for them to record in German, but they weren't graceless, they did a good job."

First task was to add 'Komm, Gib Mir Deine Hand' vocals to the English rhythm track of 'I Want To Hold Your Hand', mixed down from four-track to two-track. The 'best' versions were takes 5 and 7, with overdubbed handclaps, later edited together. For 'Sie Liebt Dich' ('She Loves You') the Beatles recorded a new rhythm track, the 1 July 1963 two-track tape having been scrapped once the mono master was prepared. This was done in 13 takes, onto which they overdubbed, in one take, the vocals in the rhythm left/vocals right pattern of their earlier two-track tapes. The job was done. "They were extremely pleased to get it over with," recalls Norman Smith. "We all were. I found the studio very odd to work in, the equipment was alien to anything we were used to."

The German songs were clearly completed well within the allotted time for – apart from the fact that a second session, booked for 31 January, could now be cancelled – the Beatles also recorded a new song, English this time, the McCartney gem 'Can't Buy Me Love'. Remarkably, the song was recorded from start to finish in just four takes. Take one shows how Paul originally intended the song, with a very bluesy vocal style similar to his late-1964 offering 'She's A Woman'. John and George add backing vocals in the same vein: "Ooooh satisfied"; "Ooooh just can't buy"; "Ooooh love me too"; "Ooooh give to you" at various junctures, an idea they had discarded by take four. Take two was much the same but take three switches to the style they were eventually to use, except that the song breaks-down. Take four, the final version subject to later remixes, features a vocal overdub by Paul and a lead guitar overdub by George. In what was probably under one hour's work the Beatles had started, altered and completed one of their biggest selling songs. It was to be typical of their industry throughout the year.

A panoramic view of the Beatles in Studio Two on 25 February 1964 (11.40am, according to the trusty studio clock!), recording 'You Can't Do That'. Coats and jackets are slung over chairs, rugs cover the floor to deaden the sound, there is little attempt at prevention of leakage from one microphone to another. A positively sparse picture, compared to the high-tech studios of the 1980s – but the music still sounded great.

Far right: One of two tapes boxes from the 29 January session at the Pathé Marconi studios.

Tuesday 25 February

Studio Two: 10.00am-1.00pm. Recording: 'You Can't Do That' (takes 1-9). Studio Two: 2.30-5.30pm. Recording: 'And I Love Her' (takes 1-2); 'I Should Have Known Better' (takes 1-3). P: George Martin. E: Norman Smith. 2E: Richard Langham.

Early 1964 was the Beatles' busiest ever period. Two days after returning from France they flew to the USA, where 'I Want To Hold Your Hand' had smashed its way to number one within three weeks of release, and all other Beatles records were selling as fast as they could be pressed. It was a sensational visit, three television appearances and three stage shows coinciding with – and promoting – record sales on a scale unmatched by any musical act before or since. Within a few weeks the Beatles held the top *five* positions in the US singles chart simultaneously with the top two places in the LP chart. They had conquered a territory thought impervious to British acts, bar the odd one-off hit, in a manner which would ensure them a place in the modern history books.

Now the Beatles were home again, and on 2 March they were to start shooting their first feature film which, although untitled at this stage, necessitated a crop of new songs to be written and recorded. Some – for the soundtrack – were required before the film

went into production, others – for the tie-in LP – were to be recorded after the film was completed. This day saw the first in a new series of EMI sessions. It was George's 21st birthday too, but work came first.

The most urgent song to be taped was John's inimitable 'You Can't Do That', for the B-side of the 'Can't Buy Me Love' single. It was not a complex recording and by take nine – only the fourth complete take – it was finished. In addition to the Beatles' regular instruments it features Paul on cowbell and Ringo on bongos and what was to become the distinctive 1964 Beatles sound – George Harrison's new 12-string guitar.

Next were two songs for the film, although both were subject to re-makes before they were released. The first two takes of 'And I Love Her', only one of which was a complete version, were much heavier than the final version, with a different guitar intro [similar to that in Scott McKenzie's 1967 'San Francisco (Be

Sure To Wear Flowers In Your Hair)'], Ringo on drums and a lead guitar solo in the middle eight. A great song is a great song in any guise, but the Beatles were wise to re-make this one with a simpler, acoustic sound.

'I Should Have Known Better' was also different at this early stage, John originally opening it with a very Bob Dylan-ish harmonica solo and George ending it with his lead guitar. Only three takes were attempted, and only one of those made it through to the end. Take two was instantly aborted when John broke into hysterics over his harmonica playing. Actually, it is little short of miraculous how the other Beatles were able to record *any* Lennon song without collapsing into laughter, for while Paul or George's 1-2-3-4 count-ins were always appropriately sensible, John's – from the earliest surviving archive tape to the last – were anything but. Only John Lennon could have devised so many demented ways of saying four simple numbers...

Wednesday 26 February

Studio Two (control room only): 10.00am-1.00pm. Mono mixing: 'You Can't Do That' (remixes 1-4, from take 9); 'Can't Buy Me Love' (from take 4). Studio Two: 2.30-5.30pm. Recording: 'I Should Have Known Better' [re-make] (takes 4-22). Studio Two: 7.00-10.00pm. Recording: 'And I Love Her' [re-make] (takes 3-19). P: George Martin. E: Norman Smith. 2E: Richard Langham.

Mono remixes of both sides of the next single provided the morning's work. With Capitol, EMI's US label, now keen to see as much Beatles material as possible, George Martin had a double-edged brief in preparing masters, in some instances making US versions a little different from the UK. 'You Can't Do That' was one such task, George supervising two remixes (numbers two and four) for the USA and keeping remix three for the UK and Europe. Remix one was not used. The remix of 'Can't Buy Me Love' was identical for both territories.

'And I Love Her' and 'I Should Have Known Better', were re-made by the Beatles during the afternoon and evening, the latter song first. The large number of takes should not be taken as an indication that the work was abnormally complicated for very few got beyond the middle eight stage. The final version was take nine, John singing without the harmonica for the first time, with an overdub from take 22 adding a double-track vocal and the harmonica. 'And I Love Her' was quite problematical however. Ringo swapped his drums for bongos and claves midway through the session but the sound was still not quite right. When Norman Smith announced "Take 14" over the talkback, Paul jokingly replied "Ha, take 50!" Again, they ended up leaving it for another time, and yet another re-make.

Thursday 27 February

Studio Two: 10.00am-1.00pm. Recording: 'And I Love Her' [re-re-make] (takes 20-21); 'Tell Me Why' (takes 1-8). Studio Two: 2.30-5.30pm. Recording: 'If I Fell' (takes 1-15). P: George Martin. E: Norman Smith. 2E: Richard Langham.

At last they got 'And I Love Her' right, the second take of this second re-make being considered 'best'. Two more songs for the film were also started and finished on this day, 'Tell Me Why', which by take eight was to everyone's satisfaction, and John's stunning ballad 'If I Fell'.

'If I Fell' could be considered a progression from 'This Boy', with its complex chord structure and intricate harmonies by John and Paul, recorded – at their request – together on one microphone. The song was perfected in 15 takes, although it altered as it evolved. A heavier drum sound was introduced at George Martin's suggestion from take three. John's punchy acoustic guitar opening was introduced at take 11, as was George's plucked lead guitar end piece. "Something like that, you mean?" enquired George after the take was completed – somewhat different to John's utterance at the end of take nine, "I've got an itchy bum". Take 15 of the song was as far as it went.

"More cuff-links. Just what I've always wanted!" George spent virtually all of his 21st birthday in Abbey Road, working, so bearers of gifts – in this instance Dick James – had to travel to St John's Wood.

Paul at the Studio Two piano, 25 February, just three days after the Beatles returned from their triumphant first visit to the USA. British European Airways specially modified its airline bags for the Beatles, adding the letters TLES after the BEA logo.

In the control room, with Dick James and George Martin. Caught on the extreme right is the Beatles' ever faithful assistant Neil Aspinall.

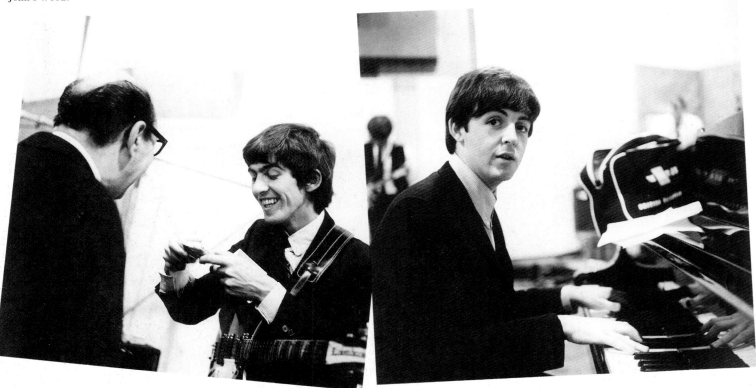

Sunday 1 March

Studio Two: 10.00am-1.30pm. Recording: 'I'm Happy Just To Dance With You' (takes 1-4); 'Long Tall Sally' (take 1); 'I Call Your Name' (takes 1-7). P: George Martin. E: Norman Smith. 2E: Richard Langham.

The Beatles' first Sunday session, three songs in three hours. First was 'I'm Happy Just To Dance With You', penned by John for George to sing. This was recorded in four takes, with all the Beatles on their regular instruments. On takes one and two the group concentrated solely on the rhythm track, take two being the best. Take three was a breakdown and take four introduced vocals for the first time. George double-tracked his to perfection, John and Paul, with slight tape echo, sang the harmony backing vocals while Ringo thumped a distinctive tom-tom sound.

The group spent the rest of the morning taping two songs which would not appear in the film, the first being 'Long Tall Sally'. This is simply a remarkable recording. Just as John had once captured 'Twist And Shout' to perfection in a single take so Paul, doing his greatest ever Little Richard impersonation, put his all

into 'Long Tall Sally'. And again, one take was all that was required. The Beatles' backing – including George Martin on piano – was perfect too, so they didn't even bother with a second take. The first was perfection.

The second song was 'I Call Your Name', a Lennon number originally given to Billy J. Kramer with the Dakotas for the B-side of their August 1963 number one 'Bad To Me', also written by John. Both songs had been recorded at Abbey Road on 27 June 1963 with Paul McCartney in attendance. Now, long after Kramer's recording, Lennon felt that he might try a recording himself.

"Do you think it's a bit much doing Billy J.'s intro and solo? 'Cos it's our song anyroad, innit?" These words, spoken by John over the microphone to

George Martin in the control room, preceded the Beatles' first take. It *was* alright, and it was soon evident too – with all due respect to Kramer – that the writer of the song was capable of giving the only true interpretation. 'I Call Your Name' is a very interesting recording for 1964, its unusual structure being underpinned by a strange middle eight guitar solo, later revealed by Lennon to be an early attempt at ska, the Jamaican beat which was to gain in popularity in the mid-1960s and enjoy a renaissance in the late 1970s. The song was recorded in seven takes, only three of which were complete. The 'best' was take seven, which featured an additional Lennon vocal and a cowbell played by Ringo. But the best middle eight guitar solo was played in take five so this was edited into take seven at the final remix stages.

Tuesday 3 March

Studio One (control room only): 10.00am-1.45pm. Mono mixing: 'I Should Have Known Better' (from take 22); 'If I Fell' (from take 15); 'Tell Me Why' (from take 8); 'And I Love Her' (remix 1, from take 21); 'I'm Happy Just To Dance With You' (from take 4); 'I Call Your Name' (from take 7). P: George Martin. E: Norman Smith. 2E: A.B. Lincoln.

Mono remixes, not only for EMI but also for United Artists, the company making the Beatles' film, the latter urgently requiring copies of the six new songs for the soundtrack, which – together with 'Can't Buy

Me Love' – would form the full complement of seven. One must presume that – at this early stage – 'I Call Your Name' was to have been a part of the film, only to be dropped when the title song 'A Hard Day's

Night' came along. The remix of 'And I Love Her' was later improved upon and was not released on record.

More photographs from 25 February, George working out a guitar phrase, while watching Norman Smith adjust Ringo's drum microphone, and Paul reading what looks like a bunch of fan letters.

Wednesday 4 March

Studio Three (control room only): 10.00-11.00am. Mono mixing: 'I Call Your Name' (from take 7). P: George Martin.   E: unknown.   2E: n/a.

An experimental mix of 'I Call Your Name', never used.

Tuesday 10 March

Studio Two: 10.00am-1.00pm. Stereo mixing: 'Can't Buy Me Love' (from take 4); 'Long Tall Sally' (from take 1); 'I Call Your Name' (from take 7); 'You Can't Do That' (from take 9). Mono mixing: 'Long Tall Sally' (from take 1); 'Komm, Gib Mir Deine Hand' (from edit of takes 5 and 7); 'Sie Liebt Dich' (from take 14). P: George Martin.   E: Norman Smith. 2E: unknown.

The stereo remixes – and the mono remix of 'Long Tall Sally' – were experimental and none was ever released.

Thursday 12 March

Studio Three (control room only): 10.00am-12.00 noon. Stereo mixing: 'Komm, Gib Mir Deine Hand' (from edit of takes 5 and 7); 'Sie Liebt Dich' (from take 14). P: George Martin.   E: Norman Smith.   2E: n/a.

Stereo remixes of the two German-language songs, equalised and compressed with added echo. Copy tapes were despatched to West Germany, and even to the USA, for record release.

Friday 20 March

**Single release: 'Can't Buy Me Love'/'You Can't Do That'.
Parlophone R 5114.**

Truly a worldwide smash hit single, topping the
charts in almost every country of release. In the USA,
where it came out on 16 March, 'Can't Buy Me Love'
sold more than 2,000,000 copies within a week and
earned a gold disc on its day of issue, an
unprecedented achievement. In Britain advance
orders alone passed the 1,000,000 mark.

Thursday 16 April

**Studio Two: 10.00am-1.00pm.
Recording: 'A Hard Day's Night' (takes 1-9).
P: George Martin.   E: Norman Smith.   2E: Geoff Emerick.**

It was Ringo who coined the phrase "a hard day's
night" when, after a long day, he commented to
someone "it's been a hard day" and then, seeing that
it was already night-time, tacked "'s night" on the
end: At this time the Beatles film, nearing completion,
was still untitled, and since Ringo's phrase captured
its mood to perfection it was adopted as the official
title, announced to the press on 13 April. That left
Messrs. Lennon and McCartney with a problem not
previously encountered: writing a song to order, with
the title already set. As ever, they did not disappoint.
Within a few days it was ready for recording, and the
Beatles came to Abbey Road on 16 April to do just
that.

It was not an especially difficult task. Take nine, only
the fifth complete run through, was the 'best'. Using
the four-track equipment to good effect this take has
the basic rhythm on track one, John's first vocal on
track two, his second vocal, with Paul's backing vocal,
bongos, drums and acoustic guitar on track three and
the jangling guitar notes at the end of the song, plus
George Martin's piano contribution, on track four.

Martin recalls why the song opened so distinctively.
"We knew it would open both the film and the
soundtrack LP, so we wanted a particularly strong
and effective beginning. The strident guitar chord was
the perfect launch."

In a picture posed especially for
the camera, the four Beatles
adding vocals and percussion to
the recording of 'You Can't Do
That'.

Monday 20 April

Studio Two (control room only): 2.00-3.15pm. Mono mixing: 'A Hard Day's Night' (from take 9). Stereo mixing: 'A Hard Day's Night' (from take 9). P: George Martin.   E: Norman Smith.   2E: A.B. Lincoln.

Rough mono and stereo remixes of the title track. The tape was taken away by United Artists for the film soundtrack.

Thursday 23 April

Studio Two (control room only): 4.30-5.45pm. Mono mixing: 'A Hard Day's Night' (remix '10', from take 9). P: George Martin.   E: Norman Smith.   2E: David Lloyd.

Another remix of 'A Hard Day's Night', mono only this time, and for disc not film, replacing as 'best' the 20 April mix. To avoid confusion it was named remix ten, although it was still from the original take nine.

Friday 22 May

Studio Two: 10.00-11.00am. Recording: 'You Can't Do That' (SI take 10). P: George Martin.   E: Norman Smith.   2E: A.B. Lincoln/B.T. [Full name unknown]

The Beatles were holidaying abroad when George Martin supervised this overdub session, personally adding a piano track to take nine of 'You Can't Do That', making take ten. But it was never used.

Monday 1 June

Studio Two: 2.30-5.30pm. Recording: 'Matchbox' (takes 1-5); 'I'll Cry Instead (Section A)' (takes 1-6); 'I'll Cry Instead (Section B)' (takes 7-8); 'Slow Down' (takes 1-6). Studio Two: 7.00-10.00pm. Recording: 'I'll Be Back' (takes 1-16). P: George Martin.   E: Norman Smith.   2E: Ken Scott.

The film completed, and holidays taken, the Beatles returned to Abbey Road to record the non-soundtrack side of the *A Hard Day's Night* LP, any songs surplus to requirements being set aside for an EP, *Long Tall Sally*, with that title song and 'I Call Your Name' already in the can.

First song of the day did indeed end up on the EP, Ringo vocalising on a cover version of Carl Perkins' 'Matchbox', an occasional feature of the Beatles' stage act. Perkins was in Britain at the time on a promotional tour and he was at Abbey Road to witness Ringo's recording, although he did not participate. It was captured in five takes, only three of which were complete, with Ringo electing to sing and drum simultaneously.

Next recording was 'I'll Cry Instead', for the LP. This was taped in two parts – 'Section A' and 'Section B' – for editing together at a later date. Six takes of 'A' and two of 'B' saw the song through to satisfactory completion. The Beatles then set about the taping of 'Slow Down', the Larry Williams rocker from 1958. The first three takes concentrated solely on the rhythm track, the best being take three, onto which, from take six, John superimposed his raucous and magnificently delivered vocal. The song was recorded at this stage without piano, which was superimposed onto the four-track tape on 4 June.

After a break the group returned to tape another LP song, 'I'll Be Back', a Lennon vocal in much more gentle mood. They recorded takes 1-16, the first nine comprising the rhythm track and the last seven the vocals, double-tracked, with an acoustic guitar overdub.

Tuesday 2 June

Studio Two: 2.30-5.30pm. Recording: 'Any Time At All' (takes 1-7); 'Things We Said Today' (takes 1-3). Studio Two: 7.00-10.00pm. Recording: 'When I Get Home' (takes 1-11); 'Any Time At All' (takes 8-11). P: George Martin.   E: Norman Smith.   2E: Ken Scott.

Another long and productive day. First song was 'Any Time At All', John belting out the vocal. Seven takes of the basic rhythm track and John's first vocal were attempted but a suitable middle eight had yet to be worked out and the song was left until later to see what might evolve. The next number, 'Things We Said Today', was recorded in three takes. The first was a false start, the second was complete, vocals and rhythm, and the third saw Paul double-track his vocal, Ringo add a tambourine and John add piano. The recording sheets indicate that the piano was to be omitted from the remix, a decision illustrating the luxury of multi-track recording over basic two-track, but because the piano had not been fully separated from the other instruments a little of its sound leaked across into the other microphones, so it can be heard on the finished song after all.

After a break the Beatles taped another new Lennon number, 'When I Get Home', recorded in 11 takes, and they then returned to 'Any Time At All', with a perfected middle eight, piano, guitar and an 'answering' Paul McCartney vocal all being added. Again, take 11 was the 'best' and last take.

Second engineer (tape operator/button pusher) on this session was 17-year-old Ken Scott, destined – like so many others at Abbey Road – for great things in his career, producing David Bowie and Supertramp amongst many others. Ken admits to having been "completely and utterly terrified" at the prospect of working with the Beatles at such a tender age, a situation not improved by an amusing *faux pas* on this day. "At that time four-track tape machines were so large that there was no room for them in the control room. They were sited along the corridor and the only contact you had with the session was via a talkback system. On this particular evening the Beatles were playing back their latest recordings to a few friends who had come in. George Martin was giving me the directions over the talkback and at one point I heard him say "home". So I put the tapes away, switched off the power, put my coat on and left the room. As I was walking along the corridor I saw George standing in the doorway. 'Well,' he said, 'is the tape lined up yet?'. 'I'm sorry?' 'Is the tape of 'When I Get Home' ready yet?' 'Aah, hang on George, I'll just check and see'. I *ran* up that corridor, flicked all the switches and put the tape back on as fast as lightning, acting nonchalantly as if nothing was wrong!"

Cigarette in hand, Norman Smith lifts the four-track faders, watched from a safe distance by tape operator Richard Langham and producer George Martin.

Wednesday 3 June

Studio Two: 3.00-4.00pm. Rehearsing: 'I Want To Hold Your Hand'; 'She Loves You'; 'I Saw Her Standing There'; 'This Boy'; 'Can't Buy Me Love'; 'Long Tall Sally'.

This session, a rehearsal only, was *not* recorded. During a morning photographic assignment on this day Ringo was taken ill with tonsilitis and pharyngitis, just 24 hours before the group was due to leave for a five-country concert tour. It was too late to cancel so Brian Epstein and George Martin came up with a temporary replacement, 24-year-old Jimmy Nicol, a session drummer. Nicol was relaxing in his west London home when Martin's call came through, inviting him to be a temporary Beatle, subject to a hurriedly arranged afternoon rehearsal at Abbey Road.

They rehearsed six songs (the Beatles' standard stage repertoire at this time comprised of just 10!) and Nicol passed the audition. Twenty-seven hours later John, Paul, George and Jimmy were on stage in Copenhagen, giving their first concert.

Press inquisitiveness looked like posing a problem however. A large group of journalists had congregated at the studio and so anxious were they at catching a glimpse of the new Beatle before the rehearsal that they were blocking the side entrance to the studio. "Paul came up to me," recalls studio assistant Terry Condon, "and said 'Sir Terence,' – he often called me that – 'we don't want them all here, getting in the way. Tell them that Jimmy'll enter through the front and then bring him in around the back.' So I beckoned one reporter aside and whispered 'Don't tell the others, but he'll be coming in through the front'. Of course all the others followed him there, Jimmy arrived unnoticed and slipped in the back way. We all had a good laugh about that."

Thursday 4 June

Studio Two: 2.30-7.00pm. Mono mixing: 'Long Tall Sally' (from take 1); 'Matchbox' (from take 5); 'I Call Your Name' (remixes 1 and 2, from takes 5 and 7). Editing: 'I Call Your Name' (of mono remixes 1 and 2). Recording: 'Slow Down' (SI onto take 6). Mono mixing: 'Slow Down' (from take 6); 'When I Get Home' (remix 1, from take 11); 'Any Time At All' (remix 1, from take 11); 'I'll Cry Instead (Section A)' (from take 6); 'I'll Cry Instead (Section B)' (from take 8). Editing: 'I'll Cry Instead' (of mono remixes of takes 6 and 8). P: George Martin. E: Norman Smith. 2E: Richard Langham.

The superimposition on 'Slow Down' was a piano, played by George Martin. These remixes of 'Any Time At All' and 'When I Get Home' were not released.

Tuesday 9 June

Studio Three (control room only): 2.00-5.45pm.
Mono tape copying: 'I Should Have Known Better'; 'If I Fell'; 'Tell Me Why'; 'And I Love Her'; 'I'm Happy Just To Dance With You'; 'I'll Cry Instead'; 'Can't Buy Me Love'; 'A Hard Day's Night'.
Mono mixing: 'A Hard Day's Night' (from take 9); 'Things We Said Today' (from take 3).
P: George Martin. E: Norman Smith. 2E: Ken Scott.

Two identical tapes of the best mono remixes, for Capitol Records and United Artists. The latter – under the film contract – was entitled to release the soundtrack songs on a US album, independently of Capitol, although it too could issue the same songs provided it did not title its collection *A Hard Day's Night*.

Another item for United Artists – for the film track only, not for record release – was a further remix of 'A Hard Day's Night', which by means of an edit was given an extended ending. Finally on this day, 'Things We Said Today' was given a mono remix for record release.

Everything stops for tea… George helps himself to the sugar while Brian Epstein and George Martin discuss matters in hand. The uniformed man in the background is John Skinner, studio security.

Norman Smith operates the four-track recording console. George Martin and his secretary/future wife Judy Lockhart-Smith are in the background. George immerses himself in the latest edition of *Disc*.

Wednesday 10 June

Studio Two (control room only): 10.00-11.00am. Mono mixing: 'I'll Be Back' (remix 1, from take 16). P: George Martin.   E: Norman Smith.   2E: Richard Langham.

Never used.

Friday 19 June

EP release: *Long Tall Sally.* **Parlophone GEP 8913.**
A: 'Long Tall Sally'; 'I Call Your Name'. B: 'Slow Down'; 'Matchbox'.

Not the Beatles' first EP release – their fifth, in fact – but the first to feature otherwise unissued material, hence the first to be detailed here. For the most part, the Beatles and EMI kept singles and LPs as separate entities, good album tracks being saved instead for release on EP records. But on two occasions, here and in December 1967, the Beatles did use the EP format to release new material. None of the four tracks on *Long Tall Sally* had seen prior UK release, although two, the title song and 'I Call Your Name', had already been issued in the USA.

Despite the fact that only one of the four songs was written by Lennon-McCartney, the others having been staple features of the Beatles' pre-fame stage act, *Long Tall Sally* remains arguably the greatest ever EP release by any artist or group.

Monday 22 June

Studio One (control room only): 10.00-11.30am. Mono mixing: 'Any Time At All' (remix 2, for the UK, from take 11); 'Any Time At All' (remix 3, for the USA, from take 11); 'When I Get Home' (remix 2, for the UK, from take 11); 'When I Get Home' (remix 3, for the USA, from take 11); 'I'll Be Back' (remix 2, for the UK, from take 16); 'I'll Be Back' (remix 3, for the USA, from take 16); 'And I Love Her' (remix 2, from take 21). Studio One (control room only):11.30am-1.00pm. Stereo mixing: 'And I Love Her' (from take 21); 'When I Get Home' (from take 11); 'Any Time At All' (from take 11); 'I'll Be Back' (from take 16); 'If I Fell' (from take 15); 'A Hard Day's Night' (from take 9); 'I Should Have Known Better' (from take 22); 'I'm Happy Just To Dance With You' (from take 4); 'I Call Your Name' (remixes 1 and 2, from takes 5 and 7). Editing: 'I Call Your Name' (of stereo remixes 1 and 2). Studio One (control room only): 2.30-5.30pm. Stereo mixing: 'Can't Buy Me Love' (from take 4); 'You Can't Do That' (from take 9); 'Tell Me Why' (from take 8); 'Things We Said Today' (from take 3); 'Matchbox' (from take 5); 'Slow Down' (from take 6); 'Long Tall Sally' (from take 1); 'I'll Cry Instead (Section A)' (from take 6); 'I'll Cry Instead (Section B)' (from take 8). Editing: 'I'll Cry Instead' (of stereo remixes of takes 6 and 8). Studio Two (control room only): 5.45-9.00pm. Tape copying: 'Slow Down' (copy of 4 June mono remix); 'Matchbox' (copy of 4 June mono remix); 'Things We Said Today' (copy of 22 June stereo remix). P: George Martin.   E: Norman Smith.   2E Geoff Emerick.

An exhaustive days remixing, predominantly for the *A Hard Day's Night* LP. The Beatles themselves could not have been further away from the action - they were in Wellington, New Zealand, at the time.

Friday 10 July

Single release: 'A Hard Day's Night'/'Things We Said Today'. Parlophone R 5160. LP release: *A Hard Day's Night*. Parlophone PMC 1230 (mono)/PCS 3058 (stereo). A: 'A Hard Day's Night'; 'I Should Have Known Better'; 'If I Fell'; 'I'm Happy Just To Dance With You'; 'And I Love Her'; 'Tell Me Why'; 'Can't Buy Me Love'. B: 'Any Time At All'; 'I'll Cry Instead'; 'Things We Said Today'; 'When I Get Home'; 'You Can't Do That'; 'I'll Be Back'.

One splendid single and one splendid LP, to tie in with one splendid film. Sales of both formats were vast, on a global scale, and it's worth noting that the LP is comprised entirely of Lennon-McCartney compositions, the only such occurrence in the Beatles' career.

Tuesday 11 August

Studio Two: 7.00-11.00pm. Recording: 'Baby's In Black' (takes 1-14, and 13 [unnumbered] edit pieces). P: George Martin.   E: Norman Smith.   2E: Ron Pender.

A Hard Day's Night had been out just two months when the Beatles began recording another LP, in keeping with the formula of two per year, the second always aimed at the Christmas sales market.

'Baby's In Black', one of the LP's strongest songs, was the first to be recorded. It took 14 takes before the Beatles were satisfied, although only five of those were complete, and five more barely got beyond the first note, a rather distinctive George Harrison guitar twang. After the 14 takes – and John's comment "Can we hear that rubbish back?" – George tried a few variations on this note (none of which was chosen for the finished article), bending it with his tremelo arm, to which George Martin replied "You want the beginning like that, do you?" Clearly, the roles between the Beatles and Martin were beginning to change, with Martin no longer entirely dictating proceedings.

Another industrious session in Studio Two.

IMPORTANT This record is intended for use only on special stereophonic reproducers. If you are doubtful of the suitability of your reproducer for playing this record, we recommend you to consult your record dealer. Most equipment designed for playing stereophonic records may, however, be used with perfect safety for playing normal 33⅓ r.p.m. and 45 r.p.m. microgroove records.

PCS 3058

Songs from the film
A HARD DAY'S NIGHT

THE BEATLES

compositions for the soundtrack while The Beatles were appearing at the Paris 'Olympia' last January. One morning early in March a specially chartered train moved out of Paddington station and the first day's shooting of The Beatles' first feature film got under way.

Reel upon reel of precious film had filled the camera crew's metal cans before a title had been selected for the United Artists picture. Then Ringo casually came up with the name at the end of a particularly strenuous session on the film set. 'It's been a hard day's night that was!' he declared, squatting for a moment on the arm of his canvas chair behind the line of cameras and technicians. The film, which also stars Wilfred Brambell in the role of Paul's (mythical) Irish grandfather, was promptly named 'A HARD DAY'S NIGHT'.

The story depicts something like 48 consecutive hours of activity in the bustling lives of four beat group boys. Named John, Paul, George and Ringo, *A Hard Day's Night* is heard at the very beginning of the film as the boys sing and play over the opening titles. The number features John's double-tracked voice, producing a duet effect. Its brisk, compelling theme crops up in orchestral form elsewhere during the film as part of recording manager George Martin's instrumental soundtrack score.

John's *I Should Have Known Better* makes an early appearance in the film during a railway sequence when the four boys are seen playing cards in the guard's van of the train.

John and Paul share the vocal action on *If I Fell*, the first of four songs featured in extensive theatre/studio sequences which show the group rehearsing and finally performing in a television spectacular. *I'm Happy Just To Dance With You* gives George a chance to handle the lead vocal, *And I Love Her* hands the solo spotlight to Paul who is joined by John for *Tell Me Why*.

The last of the soundtrack's magnificent seven,

Can't Buy Me Love, has already been a worldwide disc hit for The Beatles. In 'A HARD DAY'S NIGHT' it forms the musical backdrop to several different scenes—when the boys are seen chasing across a field after a quick-fire getaway from the television studio and where the incredible race between Beatles, fans and police takes place with the boys tearing along streets and down alleyways in double-quick time!

Creating and perfecting completely new compositions for the soundtrack of 'A HARD DAY'S NIGHT' presented John and Paul with one of the greatest challenges of their pop-penning career. In the past their song-writing had been done at a more leisurely pace. Now they had a shooting schedule deadline to meet and the entire collection of fresh numbers had to be compiled during a season of concerts in Paris and a now legendary visit to America. To assist their work the two boys had a grand-piano moved into their hotel suite at the George V in Paris. By the beginning of March the task was complete and The Beatles had a total of almost a dozen new songs ready for final rehearsal. At every stage of its conception and production care was taken to see that 'A HARD DAY'S NIGHT' would not turn into a continuous parade of Beatle performances. After all The Beatles themselves had agreed that the film

should portray as many different facets of the four boys' individual personalities as possible. Indeed the comedy content was, and is, of paramount importance, and John, Paul, George and Ringo are afforded maximum opportunity to display their on-the-spot sense of humour.

It became apparent that no more than six new songs should be introduced via the soundtrack of the film. To increase this number would have left insufficient screen-time for the action of the plot. On the other hand it seemed most unfair to hold back the remainder of the boys' new songs when each one was of such excellent quality. Eventually the decision was made to record all the material which John and Paul had written and include the extra titles on the second side of this album.

Although the voice of George Harrison is much in evidence throughout this album the solo vocal activity on the second side is shared between the songs' composers, John and Paul. Paul handles the lyrics of *Things We Said Today* and he's heard in duet with John on *I'll Cry Instead*. For the main part John's is the dominant voice featured on *Any Time At All, When I Get Home, You Can't Do That* and *I'll Be Back*. George and Paul back up his efforts strongly on all titles.

When you listen to the second side of this record you will agree that it would have been a pity to cast aside such a fabulous set of songs solely because they couldn't be fitted into the structure of 'A HARD DAY'S NIGHT'. Now, with this album in your library, you have a collection of Beatle recordings which is comprehensive and up to date. At the same time it is interesting to remember that the LP housed within this sleeve is the first-ever album release to be made up entirely of self-composed and self-performed Beatle compositions.

Produced for records by GEORGE MARTIN
Cover Notes by TONY BARROW

SIDE ONE
1. A HARD DAY'S NIGHT
2. I SHOULD HAVE KNOWN BETTER
3. IF I FELL
4. I'M HAPPY JUST TO DANCE WITH YOU
5. AND I LOVE HER
6. TELL ME WHY
7. CAN'T BUY ME LOVE

From the soundtrack of the United Artists film
'A HARD DAY'S NIGHT'

Words and Music:
JOHN LENNON AND PAUL McCARTNEY

SIDE TWO
1. ANY TIME AT ALL
2. I'LL CRY INSTEAD
3. THINGS WE SAID TODAY
4. WHEN I GET HOME
5. YOU CAN'T DO THAT
6. I'LL BE BACK

Words and Music:
JOHN LENNON AND PAUL McCARTNEY

Mr. G. Bridges.
Mr. R. Dockerill.
Mr. A. Maxlow.
Mr. S. Gillingham.
Mr. F. Exon.
Mr. A. Dewdney.
Mr. E. Fowler.
Mr. R. Dunton.

Mr. I. Middleton.
Mr. A. Gregory.
Mr. D. Woodward.
Mr. S. Storm.
Mr. G. Freshwater.
Mr. S. Wright.
Mr. P. Chalmers.

June 18th. 1964.

PARLOPHONE L.P.   'A HARD DAY'S NIGHT'.

Recorded: March, April, May 1964.

Release: July 10th.

Cover:

Note: Mr. Dunton has this.

Artists: THE BEATLES.

Job. No. 3935.aPMS.

Tony Barrow.

Side 1.   Songs from the film 'A Hard Day's Night'.

A HARD DAY'S NIGHT.
I SHOULD HAVE KNOWN BETTER.
IF I FELL.
I'M HAPPY JUST TO DANCE WITH YOU.
AND I LOVE HER.
TELL ME WHY.
CAN'T BUY ME LOVE.

Side 2.

ANY TIME AT ALL.
I'LL CRY INSTEAD.
THINGS WE SAID TODAY.
WHEN I GET HOME.
YOU CAN'T DO THAT.
I'LL BE BACK.

All titles composed by Lennon-McCartney. Published by Northern Songs.

N.B. Side 2 is not to have the heading 'Songs from the film 'A Hard Day's Night'.

Recording produced by George Martin.

C/SS/JLS.
23-6-64

G.H. MARTIN.
E.M.I. Records Ltd.

USE EMITEX

Friday 14 August

Studio Two: 7.00-9.00pm. Recording: 'I'm A Loser' (takes 1-8); 'Mr. Moonlight' (takes 1-4). Studio Two (control room only): 9.00-10.00pm. Mono mixing: 'I'm A Loser' (remix 1, from take 8); 'Baby's In Black' (remix 1, from take 14). Studio Two: 10.00-11.15pm. Recording: 'Leave My Kitten Alone' (takes 1-5). P: George Martin. E: Norman Smith. 2E: Ron Pender.

This new LP, untitled as yet, came too soon after *A Hard Day's Night* for Lennon-McCartney, prodigious composers though they were, to have written a full album's worth of new songs. They had a few, the final total numbering eight, so for the other LP tracks the Beatles had to rely on their old stage favourites.

Of the three songs tackled during this evening session, only one, 'I'm A Loser', was a Lennon-McCartney number, written mostly by John and showing a definite shift in direction away from the 'hand holding' songs to a more autobiographical and introspective slant, influenced by Bob Dylan. It was recorded in eight takes, four of them complete.

The first of the cover versions was 'Mr. Moonlight', John singing lead on this obscure 1962 Dr. Feelgood and the Interns track. Take four was marked down as 'best', although it did not have the Hammond organ and percussion instruments which are so distinctive of the finished record. For the moment 'Mr. Moonlight' featured prominent guitar work by John and George.

At this point two rough mono remixes, of 'I'm A Loser' and 'Baby's In Black', were made, although both songs were later returned to and given improved remixes for record release.

The next track was never returned to, or even remixed, once it was agreed that none of the five takes had captured the song as the Beatles intended. The song was 'Leave My Kitten Alone' and, at the time of writing, it remains unreleased and unheard by the public at large. John took the lead vocal on this R&B track first recorded by Little Willie John in 1959 and covered by Johnny Preston in 1961. Take one was a complete recording, with a subdued Lennon vocal. Take two broke down because, as John said at the end, "I wish I could do it without playing". Take three featured a *searing* Lennon vocal and was complete. Take four was a false start and take five, the 'best', the version which would have been issued had the Beatles wanted it on the LP, featured a different Lennon vocal again, double-tracked, with George on lead guitar, Ringo overdubbing tambourine and Paul the piano. Had it reached remix stage the song would have been given a faded ending, so the original tape cuts off in what seems a rather abrupt – but deliberate – fashion.

Should 'Leave My Kitten Alone' have been left unreleased? The Beatles obviously thought so. But hindsight shows that perhaps it might have made a better LP track than, say, 'Mr. Moonlight', most people's least favourite song on what was to become the *Beatles For Sale* LP.

Ringo steels himself for his debut on timpani, 30 September.

Sunday 23 August

**Live concert at the Hollywood Bowl, 2301 North Highland Avenue, Los Angeles, California, USA.
Recording: 'Introduction' (by announcer); 'Twist And Shout'; 'You Can't Do That'; 'All My Loving'; 'She Loves You'; 'Things We Said Today'; 'Roll Over Beethoven'; 'Can't Buy Me Love'; 'If I Fell'; 'I Want To Hold Your Hand'; 'Boys'; 'A Hard Day's Night'; 'Long Tall Sally'. P: Voyle Gilmore, with George Martin. E: Hugh Davies. 2E: n/a.**

Capitol Records wanted to record the Beatles in concert at Carnegie Hall, New York City on 12 February 1964, but the American Federation of Musicians refused permission. Now – six months later and permission duly received – they taped the group at the famed Hollywood Bowl instead. George Martin was not in favour, but the Beatles didn't mind either way. Capitol was to make an album for issue to the US record market only, since it was felt that UK record buyers – although obsessed with anything by the Beatles – would not be interested in an album of songs already in their collections, even if these were live versions. The show was duly recorded – all 29 minutes of it – the tape was processed, it received the thumbs-down from Capitol and the Beatles on the grounds of poor quality and was confined to the library shelf.

"We recorded it on three-track tape," recalls George Martin, "which was standard US format then. You

would record the band in stereo on two tracks and keep the voice separated on the third, so that you could bring it up or down in the mix. But at the Hollywood Bowl they didn't use three-track in quite the right way. I didn't have too much say in things because I was a foreigner, but they did some very bizarre mixing. In 1977, when I was asked to make an album from the tapes, I found guitars and voices mixed on the same track. And the recording seemed to concentrate more on the wild screaming of 18,700 kids than on the Beatles on stage."

The album, *The Beatles At The Hollywood Bowl*, was in fact a skilful editing job – by Martin and Geoff Emerick – of two concert recordings from the venue, this 1964 one and the Beatles' show a year later, on 30 August 1965, six songs from 1964 and seven from 1965. (Capitol also taped another Beatles show at the Hollywood Bowl, on 29 August 1965, but microphone gremlins prevented any of the songs from being

usable.) This was the best way of coping with what were not only inferior recordings but also erratic stage performances by the Beatles, well into their phase of disliking concerts and touring. "I was against doing the LP at first because I remembered that the boys did not sing too well during the shows," says Martin. "They had no foldback speakers so they couldn't hear themselves sing, and nobody in the audience heard anything either with all that screaming. And it was very difficult to find a three-track machine that worked. Eventually we found an old one which we prevented from overheating by having a vacuum cleaner in reverse, blowing cool air onto it. The first thing Geoff and I did was transfer the original tape onto 24-track and worked from that."

Such is the way a number one album is made, for *The Beatles At The Hollywood Bowl* reached that position on 18 June 1977, 13 years after this first recording was made.

Thursday 27 August

Studio, Capitol Records, 1750 North Vine Street, Hollywood, California, USA. Stereo mixing: 'Introduction' (by announcer); 'Twist And Shout'; 'You Can't Do That'; 'All My Loving'; 'She Loves You'; 'Things We Said Today'; 'Roll Over Beethoven'; 'Can't Buy Me Love'; 'If I Fell'; 'I Want To Hold Your Hand'; 'Boys'; 'A Hard Day's Night'; 'Long Tall Sally'. P: Voyle Gilmore.   E: Hugh Davies.   2E: n/a.

A rough stereo remix of the Hollywood Bowl recording, mixed down to two-track, with added equalisation, reverb and limiting.

Tuesday 29 September

Studio Two: 2.30-6.30pm. Recording: 'Every Little Thing' (takes 1-4); 'I Don't Want To Spoil The Party' (takes 1-7). P: George Martin. E: Norman Smith. 2E: Ken Scott. Studio Two: 7.00-10.45pm. Recording: 'I Don't Want To Spoil The Party' (takes 8-19); 'What You're Doing' (takes 1-7). P: George Martin.   E: Norman Smith.   2E: Ken Scott/Mike Stone.

Back to Abbey Road for the taping of three more LP songs, all Lennon/McCartney compositions. 'Every Little Thing' was first, take four being deemed as 'best', although it was subsequently further improved upon. 'I Don't Want To Spoil The Party' was perfected in 19 takes, just five of those being complete run-throughs. 'What You're Doing' was to prove a somewhat problematical song and was later re-made. On this day the group taped only the rhythm track, take seven being documented as 'best'.

Wednesday 30 September

Studio Two: 2.30-5.30pm. Recording: 'Every Little Thing' (takes 5-9). P: George Martin. E: Norman Smith. 2E: Ken Scott. Studio Two: 6.30-10.30pm. Recording: 'What You're Doing' (takes 8-12); 'No Reply' (takes 1-8). P: George Martin.   E: Norman Smith.   2E: Ken Scott/Mike Stone.

'Every Little Thing', concluded in the afternoon session, was evidently a fun recording. Take six was aborted when Paul burped a vocal instead of singing it, take seven was complete but ended in uproarious laughter. And Ringo was having fun with an instrument new to Beatles recordings – timpani. This appeared for the first time on take nine, along with the guitar intro and piano piece.

After 'Every Little Thing' the Beatles resurrected 'What You're Doing'. Take 11 was documented as being the new 'best' although the entire song was later re-made. At this stage it differed from the final version in that its breaks between choruses were less tight, the middle eight instrumental break was performed an octave above the vocals and it had a 1½ second pause preceding a reprise instrumental coda.

'No Reply' was started and completed in the same session. John's voice was beginning to wilt after the long day in the studios, so Paul was left to do the high register harmonies behind John's lead vocal. George Martin added the piano. Take five was an attempt at making the song longer, 3'17" as opposed to the final version's 2'14". Take eight was that final version, although considerable echo was applied to John's vocal at remix stage.

Tuesday 6 October

Studio Two: 3.00-6.45pm. Recording: 'Eight Days A Week' (takes 1-6). P: George Martin. E: Norman Smith. 2E: Ken Scott. Studio Two: 7.00-10.00pm. Recording: 'Eight Days A Week' (takes 7-13). P: George Martin.   E: Norman Smith.   2E: Ken Scott/Mike Stone.

'Eight Days A Week' was a landmark recording in that it was the first time the Beatles took an unfinished idea into the studio and experimented with different ways of recording it.

Although it was to become the first pop song to feature a faded-up introduction, the session tapes reveal that this was not the original plan. Take one was played straight, no frills, on acoustic guitar. On take two John and Paul introduced a succession of

beautifully harmonised "Ooohs", climbing up the scale, to precede the first guitar strum. On take three they merged the first two ideas, "Ooohs" and acoustic guitar. On take four the "Ooohs" were altered to remain on the same pitch throughout rather than climbing the register. Take five incorporated "Ooohs" at the end as well as the beginning. Take six took the shape of the released version but did not have the faded intro or outro. From then on, until the 'best', take 13, the Beatles concentrated on perfecting

take six, overdubbing a double-tracked Lennon vocal, for instance. The famous faded intro was added at the remix stage and a new outro was taped as an edit piece on 18 October.

The session tape also reveals that another new song, 'I Feel Fine', was being worked out at this time, John strumming its distinctive guitar riff between takes of 'Eight Days A Week'.

Thursday 8 October

Studio Two: 2.30-6.00pm. Recording: 'She's A Woman' (takes 1-7). P: George Martin.   E: Norman Smith.   2E: Ken Scott/Mike Stone.

A superb Paul McCartney composition with blues-style vocal, sung in such a high pitch that he was accused at the time of screeching. Not at all. This fine song was indicative of Paul's fast growing awareness of other forms of popular music, and the ease with which he could slip into those styles.

The recording was quite straightforward, take one sounding not dissimilar from the 'best', take six. They did try a seventh take but six was clearly better. Paul added piano to his vocal and bass playing while Ringo – in addition to his fine drumming – utilised a percussion piece new to Beatles songs, a chocalho, a

cylindrical metal shaker containing lead shot or peas.

The song was not for the in-the-works LP, materialising instead as a single.

Monday 12 October

Studio Two (control room only): 10.00-10.30am. Mono mixing: 'She's A Woman' (remix 1, from take 6). Stereo mixing: 'She's A Woman' (from take 6). **Studio Two (control room only): 2.30-3.00pm.** Mono mixing: 'Eight Days A Week' (remix 1, from take 13). **P: George Martin.   E: Norman Smith.   2E: Ken Scott.**

The mono remix of 'She's A Woman' was for the UK record market only. A remix for the US was done on 21 October.

Friday 16 October

Studio One (control room only): 2.30-5.30pm. Mono mixing: 'No Reply' (remixes 1 and 2, from take 8). **P: George Martin.   E: Norman Smith.   2E: A.B. Lincoln.**

Two mono remixes of the same song, one of which was chosen for the LP, the other relegated to a long shelf-life.

Sunday 18 October

Studio Two: 2.30-11.30pm.
Recording: 'Eight Days A Week' (takes 14-15); 'Kansas City'/'Hey-Hey-Hey-Hey!' (takes 1-2); 'Mr. Moonlight' [re-make] (takes 5-8); 'I Feel Fine' (takes 1-9); 'I'll Follow The Sun' (takes 1-8); 'Everybody's Trying To Be My Baby' (take 1); 'Rock and Roll Music' (take 1); 'Words Of Love' (takes 1-3).
P: George Martin.   E: Norman Smith.   2E: Geoff Emerick.

The Beatles had begun a UK concert tour on 9 October so were having to cram in recording sessions on infrequent days off. This day, a somewhat hectic one, began with the group taping edit pieces for the intro and outro of 'Eight Days A Week' (the intro piece was never used) then swiftly turning their attentions to new recordings. First on the agenda was a cover of Little Richard's 'Kansas City'/'Hey-Hey-Hey-Hey!', recorded at blistering pace in just two takes. But take one was superior by far, so it was labelled 'best' and became another classic one-take Beatles performance. George Martin added a piano contribution though it is barely discernible on record.

Next was a re-make of 'Mr. Moonlight', starting with take five. The Beatles were still undecided about how to perform this number. Although take eight was deemed to be 'best', by take six they had still to think of the addition of Paul playing the Hammond organ. No such problems however beset the next song, 'I Feel Fine'. The song opens with what was described in the press at the time as "an electronic accident". It was no such thing. Right from take one the Beatles had perfected the curious sounding introduction, a Lennon idea of which he was especially proud, with Paul plucking a single bass string and John getting amplifier feedback from his guitar. Takes one to eight concentrated on the rhythm track and the vocals were added on take nine, the final take. After this the Beatles recorded an album track, 'I'll Follow The Sun', the 'best' version being take eight. This take was the first to feature a lead guitar solo in the middle eight, a point in previous takes preserved for an acoustic guitar break.

The Beatles rounded-off the day recording three songs in a total of just five takes. George sang lead vocal on a cover of Carl Perkins' 'Everybody's Trying To Be My Baby', the most notable aspect which was the vast amount of STEED (single tape echo and echo delay) plastered over George's vocal. The echo delay was so great that the record sounds for all the world as if George is singing inside a tin can, and the rhythm backing which leaked onto George's vocal microphone suffers the same fate. After this somewhat unusual recording the Beatles performed a scintillating one-take recording of Chuck Berry's 'Rock and Roll Music', with a slightly echoed Lennon vocal, all the Beatles on their familiar instruments and George Martin again displaying his prowess as a rock 'n' roll pianist. No overdubs, just a magnificent live performance. Finally, John and Paul harmonised on a version of Buddy Holly's 'Words Of Love', the first and only time the Beatles – Holly lovers to the man – performed one of his songs on record, although they had played a number of them on stage before 1963. This was recorded in three takes, only two of which were complete. Take three – with overdubs added onto take two – was the 'best'.

Wednesday 21 October

Abbey Road, Room 65: 2.30-5.45pm.
Mono mixing: 'I Feel Fine' (remixes 1-4 from take 9); 'I'll Follow The Sun' (from take 8); 'She's A Woman' (remix 2, from take 6); 'Everybody's Trying To Be My Baby' (from take 1).
P: George Martin.   E: Norman Smith.   2E: Ron Pender.

Four remixes of 'I Feel Fine'. Remix three was for the British single and remix four for the US. The first two were left unreleased. The second remix of 'She's A Woman' was expressly for the US.

Thursday 22 October

Studio One (control room only): 11.00am-12.00 noon. Mono mixing: 'I Feel Fine' (remix 5, from take 9). P: George Martin. E: Norman Smith. 2E: Ron Pender.

A fifth mono remix of 'I Feel Fine', although this one never saw the light of day.

Monday 26 October

Studio Two (control room only): 10.00am-12.45pm. Mono mixing: 'I Don't Want To Spoil The Party' (from take 19); 'Rock And Roll Music' (from take 1); 'Words Of Love' (from take 3); 'Baby's In Black' (remix 2, from take 14); 'I'm A Loser' (remix 2, from take 8); 'Kansas City'/'Hey-Hey-Hey-Hey!' (from take 1). Studio Two (control room only): 12.45-1.05pm. Stereo mixing: 'Kansas City'/'Hey-Hey-Hey-Hey!' (from take 1). P: George Martin. E: Norman Smith. 2E: Tony Clark. Studio Two: 4.30-6.30pm. Recording: 'Honey Don't' (takes 1-5). Studio Two: 7.30-10.00pm. Recording: 'What You're Doing' [re-make] (takes 13-19); 'Another Beatles Christmas Record' (takes 1-5). Editing: 'Another Beatles Christmas Record' (from takes 1-5). P: George Martin.   E: Norman Smith.   2E: A.B. Lincoln.

Another 'rest day' from the tour, in which the Beatles did anything but rest. Aside from attending all of the mix sessions – perhaps one of the first times they did this – they also recorded the final batch of songs for the LP. First was 'Honey Don't', another Carl Perkins cover version, with Ringo taking the lead vocal. John had previously sung this on stage but Ringo always had at least one vocal per album so he did the recording. It was perfected in five takes, the fifth being 'best', following which the group tried a re-make of 'What You're Doing', takes 13-19. Only three of those seven were complete, and 19 was 'best'.

Finally the Beatles turned their attention towards their Official Fan Club, recording wacky speech and zany versions of Christmas carols for their second annual Christmas flexi disc, sent – as in the previous year – free to all members in mid-December. Once all the "er's", "um's" cusses and rude jokes had been edited out, the master tape was assembled and sent to Lyntone Records for pressing.

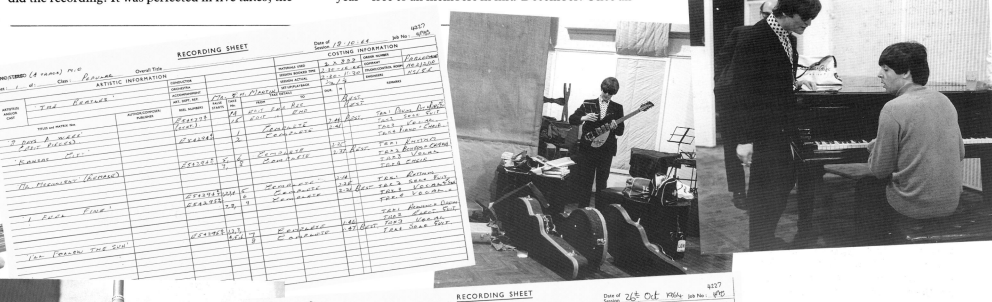

Evidence of more travelling – airline bags and luggage tags – typical of 1964 when the Beatles sandwiched visits to the recording studio between concert tours. Dick James lurks in the background as John talks to Paul at the piano.

Tuesday 27 October

Studio Two (control room only): 10.00am-12.30pm. Mono mixing: 'What You're Doing' (from take 19); 'Honey Don't' (from take 5); 'Mr. Moonlight' (remixes 1 and 2, from takes 4 and 8); 'Every Little Thing' (from take 9); 'Eight Days A Week' (remixes 2 and 3, from takes 13 and 15). Editing: 'Mr. Moonlight' (of mono remixes 1 and 2); 'Eight Days A Week' (of mono remixes 2 and 3). Studio Two (control room only): 12.30-1.00pm. Stereo mixing: 'Eight Days A Week' (remixes 1 and 2, from takes 13 and 15); 'Every Little Thing' (from take 9); 'What You're Doing' (from take 19); 'Honey Don't' (from take 5). Editing: 'Eight Days A Week' (of stereo remixes 1 and 2). P: George Martin.   E: Norman Smith.   2E: Ken Scott.

There can't be many albums released today containing five songs remixed for stereo in half an hour! By comparison with the time spent on the mono mixes it is clear which format was considered the most important in 1964.

Wednesday 4 November

Studio Two (control room only): 10.00am-1.00pm. Stereo mixing: 'I'll Follow The Sun' (from take 8); 'Everybody's Trying To Be My Baby' (from take 1); 'Rock and Roll Music' (from take 1); 'Words Of Love' (from take 3); 'Mr. Moonlight' (remixes 1 and 2, from takes 4 and 8); 'I Don't Want To Spoil The Party' (from take 19); 'I'm A Loser' (from take 8); 'Baby's In Black' (from take 14); 'No Reply' (from take 8); 'I Feel Fine' (from take 9). Editing: 'Mr. Moonlight' (of stereo remixes 1 and 2). P: George Martin.   E: Norman Smith.   2E: Mike Stone.

The remaining stereo mixes for the LP.

Friday 27 November

**Single release: 'I Feel Fine'/'She's A Woman'.
Parlophone R 5200.**

Another massive worldwide success, selling more than a million copies in the USA within a week of issue and more than 800,000 within five days of issue in the UK, passing the million mark on 9 December.

George Martin's original handwritten running-order for the *Beatles For Sale* album, with rough workings and finished item.

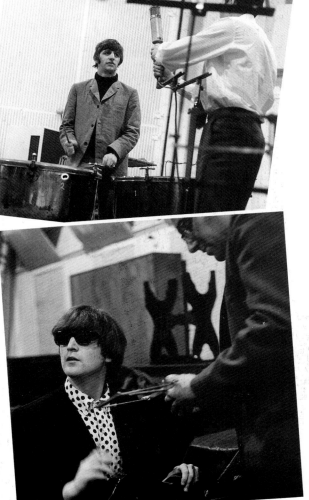

Friday 4 December

LP release: *Beatles For Sale*. **Parlophone PMC 1240 (mono)/PCS 3062 (stereo).**
A: 'No Reply'; 'I'm A Loser'; 'Baby's In Black'; 'Rock And Roll Music'; 'I'll Follow The Sun'; 'Mr. Moonlight'; 'Kansas City'/'Hey-Hey-Hey-Hey!'.
B: 'Eight Days A Week'; 'Words Of Love'; 'Honey Don't'; 'Every Little Thing'; 'I Don't Want To Spoil The Party'; 'What You're Doing'; 'Everybody's Trying To Be My Baby'.

The Beatles' fourth LP in 21 months, and, of course, a top seller worldwide. While no one would classify the album as weak – no Beatles album could be appended with that particular label – it is generally regarded as their *weakest* piece of work, although perhaps this was not entirely their fault. "They were rather war weary during *Beatles For Sale*," says George Martin. "One must remember that they'd been battered like mad throughout 1964, and much of 1963. Success is a wonderful thing but it is very, very tiring. They were always on the go. *Beatles For Sale* doesn't appeal to me very much now, it's not one of their most memorable ones. They perked up again after that…"

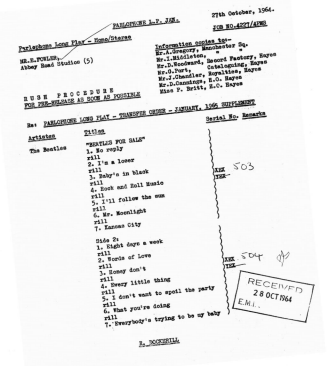

Monday 15 February

Studio Two: 2.30-5.45pm. Recording: 'Ticket To Ride' (takes 1-2). P: George Martin.   E: Norman Smith.   2E: Ken Scott. Studio Two: 7.00-10.30pm. Recording: 'Another Girl' (take 1, and 10 [unnumbered] edit pieces); 'I Need You' (takes 1-5). P: George Martin.   E: Norman Smith.   2E: Ken Scott/Jerry Boys.

Another year, another film, another set of recording sessions; 1965 ushered in a new phase of the Beatles' career, away from concert and other public performances and towards a more serious application in the recording studio. At the same time, the group and George Martin adopted new recording techniques. One was to rehearse songs with a tape machine running, spooling back to record properly over the rehearsed material. Another was to make finished, releasable recordings in just one or two takes; an impressively economical operation which frequently belied the work involved. The secret here was that the rhythm track would usually be taped first and then they would overdub or 'drop in' extra sounds onto the tape at will. In this way, they might superimpose onto an existing take a good many unnumbered overdubs, which in previous years would each have been allotted a new number. So while a

reasonably complex song like, say, 'We Can Work It Out' was perfected in just two takes (and only one of those was complete) it still took four hours and was the result of numerous additions, subtractions and perfections.

These techniques were employed in this first session, in which three songs were taped for the soundtrack of the Beatles' next feature film, still untitled and yet to go into production. The afternoon session was devoted entirely to John's composition 'Ticket To Ride'. Take one of this was an immediate false start and take two was 'best', with drums and bass guitar on track one of the four-track tape, rhythm and lead guitars on track two, John's lead vocal on track three and tambourine, guitars and backing vocals on track four. Paul played both bass guitar and lead guitar on the song, including the characteristic opening

sequence. Ringo's drum pattern – said to have been suggested by Paul – was also outstanding.

Paul's 'Another Girl' was the next song to be taped, and the 'best' version of this was the first and only take, although in ten additional edit pieces George had a go at perfecting a guitar flourish, with tremelo arm in full force, for the very end of the song. The seventh attempt was the best but then the idea was dropped at remix stage. Paul added overdubbed lead guitar on 16 February.

George also took the spotlight for the final song of the day, his composition 'I Need You'. Although completed, with take five being 'best', the song at this stage was predominantly acoustic, its distinctive tone pedal electric guitar, plus double-tracked Harrison vocal, being overdubbed on 16 February.

Tuesday 16 February

Studio Two: 2.30-5.00pm. Recording: 'I Need You' (SI onto take 5); 'Another Girl' (SI onto take 1). P: George Martin.   E: Norman Smith.   2E: Ken Scott. Studio Two: 5.00-7.00pm. Recording: 'Yes It Is' (takes 1-14). Studio Two: 7.00-10.00pm. Recording: 'Yes It Is' (SI onto take 14). P: George Martin.   E: Norman Smith.   2E: Ken Scott/Jerry Boys.

The second day in the week-long period of sessions saw the Beatles overdub double-tracked George Harrison vocals, cowbell percussion and also electric guitar (adorned, for the first time on a Beatles recording, with a foot-controlled tone pedal – later to be known as wah-wah pedal) on 'I Need You', and then overdub another guitar passage, played by Paul, onto take one of 'Another Girl'.

The final song of the day, which took five hours to record, was 'Yes It Is', an exquisite and intricate three-part harmony ballad written by John and sung by John, Paul and George in a style reminiscent of

'This Boy'. 'Yes It Is' was not selected for the film soundtrack in preparation, nor was it included on what was to become the *Help!* album. Instead it appeared merely as the B-side of the Beatles' next single, 'Ticket To Ride', such was the group's embarrassment of songwriting riches. Predominant again was George Harrison and his tone pedal guitar. It took 14 takes to perfect the rhythm track and then three hours for John, Paul and George – all singing live – to get the harmony to everyone's satisfaction. This was recorded as an unnumbered overdub onto take 14. In previous years it would have become take 15.

Wednesday 17 February

Studio Two: 2.00-7.00pm. Recording: 'The Night Before' (takes 1-2). P: George Martin.   E: Norman Smith.   2E: Ken Scott. Studio Two: 7.00-11.00pm. Recording: 'You Like Me Too Much' (takes 1-8). P: George Martin.   E: Norman Smith.   2E: Ken Scott

Two more songs intended for the film soundtrack, although George's 'You Like Me Too Much' was later relegated to the non-soundtrack side of the associated album.

Both songs were typical Beatles 1965, pop music of a superior quality with fine melodies, harmonies and instrumentation. Neither was especially difficult to record, although both featured instruments not previously associated with Beatles songs. John plays electric piano on both numbers and Paul, with George Martin, plays Steinway grand on 'You Like Me Too Much'. Both songs feature the by now almost obligatory double-tracked lead vocals, Paul on 'The

Night Before' and George on 'You Like Me Too Much'.

The Beatles with Brian Epstein and George Martin, receiving awards from EMI chairman Sir Joseph Lockwood, then 60 and a man who commanded respect from everyone – including the Beatles, even if they did call him "Sir Joe"! The presentation, which included numerous awards and national dolls from Japan, was made at EMI Manchester Square on the morning of 16 February 1965.

Thursday 18 February

Studio Two (control room only): 10.00am-1.00pm. Mono mixing: 'Ticket To Ride' (remix 1, from take 2); 'Another Girl' (from take 1); 'I Need You' (from take 5); 'Yes It Is' (from take 14). Studio Two: 3.30-5.15pm. Recording: 'You've Got To Hide Your Love Away' (takes 1-9). Studio Two (control room only): 5.15-6.00pm. Mono mixing: 'The Night Before' (from take 2); 'You Like Me Too Much' (from take 8). Studio Two: 6.00-10.30pm. Recording: 'If You've Got Trouble' (take 1); 'Tell Me What You See' (takes 1-4). P: George Martin. E: Norman Smith. 2E: Ken Scott.

A most interesting and full day's work. John Lennon's lovely 'You've Got To Hide Your Love Away', very much inspired by Bob Dylan, is notable for being the first Beatles recording – excepting the use of Andy White on 'Love Me Do' back on 11 September 1962 – to feature the work of an outside musician, brought in especially for a preconceived purpose. The musician was Johnnie Scott [these days known simply as John Scott] who in addition to being a fine flautist was much in demand at Abbey Road studios at this time as a musical arranger, working with such artistes as Cilla Black.

But it was Scott's talent with the flute which brought him into the Beatles session. He remembers the occasion well. "They told me roughly what they wanted, ¾ time, and the best way of fulfilling their needs was to play both tenor flute and alto flute, the second as an overdub. As I recall, all four of them were there and Ringo was full of marital joys, he'd just come back from his honeymoon." [Ringo married Maureen Cox on 11 February and had returned to

London on the 14th.] In common with all but a scant few of the session musicians the Beatles were to employ in the coming years, Scott went uncredited on any record sleeve note.

'You've Got To Hide Your Love Away', one of the highlights of what was to become the *Help!* LP, has no electrical instruments and was recorded from start to finish in a shortened afternoon session, only two of the nine takes being complete.

Ringo Starr had secured a lead vocal on all Beatles albums so far, with the exception of *A Hard Day's Night*. But since he had yet to provide a self-composition for his outings a suitable 'vehicle' was always provided. For *Please Please Me* it was the Shirelles' song 'Boys'. For *With The Beatles* John and Paul gave him 'I Wanna Be Your Man'. On *Beatles For Sale* he had sung Carl Perkins' 'Honey Don't', and he had sung another Perkins song, 'Matchbox', on the excellent EP *Long Tall Sally*. But what would be his contribution to this new LP? Written especially for the occasion by John and Paul, the answer was a

fast rocker entitled 'If You've Got Trouble'. To this day, in 1987, the song remains unreleased. To be brutally honest, it is not difficult to see why. It was not one of the better Lennon-McCartney numbers by any stretch of the imagination, nor was it brilliantly performed in the one and only take (with at least three overdubs, Ringo's vocal being double-tracked and an extra guitar passage being played by George) which was recorded. There was a fine moment of humour, however. Ringo had a tendency to shout something akin to "Take it, George!" when it came to the middle eight instrumental breaks of his songs. In 'If You've Got Trouble', perhaps sensing that the song needed some very vital boosting, Ringo pleads "Aah, rock on, *anybody*!".

The final song of the day, 'Tell Me What You See', was another offered for the film soundtrack but not selected. Again, there was an interesting array of musical instruments on show. Paul played electric piano and among the instruments described on the tape box as 'Latin American percussion' was a güiro.

Friday 19 February

Studio Two: 3.30-6.20pm. Recording: 'You're Going To Lose That Girl' (takes 2-3). P: George Martin.   E: Norman Smith.   2E: Ken Scott.

Just one song on the menu today, John Lennon's rock ballad 'You're Going To Lose That Girl'. For takes two and three read takes one and two; as a result of an error in the control room, take one of the song was announced as take two.

Take 'three' was the only complete version, take 'two' being a false start. By means of overdubbing, Paul McCartney added a piano to his bass guitar contribution and Ringo added bongos.

Saturday 20 February

Studio Two (control room only): 11.00am-12.00 noon. Mono mixing: 'If You've Got Trouble' (from take 1); 'Tell Me What You See' (from take 4); 'You're Going To Lose That Girl' (from take 3). Studio Two: 12.00 noon-5.15pm. Recording: 'That Means A Lot' (take 1, tape reduction take 1 into take 2, SI onto take 2). Studio Two (control room only): 5.15-6.00pm. Mono mixing: 'That Means A Lot' (from take 1); 'You've Got To Hide Your Love Away' (from take 9). P: George Martin.   E: Norman Smith.   2E: Ken Scott.

With, to date, so few Beatles recordings unreleased in the vault, how bizarre that inside three days the group should tape two songs destined for such a sad fate. For that is exactly what befell the very interesting Lennon/McCartney composition 'That Means A Lot'. The song was written for the new film and the Beatles had two separate attempts at recording it (this day and again on 30 March), neither successful, before they discarded the song and gave it instead to the day's controversial singer P.J. Proby. Said John Lennon at the time, "The song is a ballad which Paul and I wrote for the film but we found we just couldn't sing it. In fact, we made a hash of it, so we thought we'd better give it to someone who could do it well." Proby recorded his version at Abbey Road on 7 April 1965, produced by Ron Richards.

So what was wrong with the Beatles' version? Actually, not a lot. If the Beatles were, as John Lennon indicated, unable to record the song correctly that may have been because it was an over-complex and somewhat unusually structured composition. Two tapes of this day's recording still exist at Abbey Road, the first consisting of four (unnumbered) rehearsal performances and then, having spooled the tape back to the beginning, one take proper, with several overdubs, Paul handling lead vocals and piano, John and George playing their regular guitars and adding backing vocals and maracas, and Ringo playing drums. Then, obviously limited by the four-track tape, George Martin made a tape-to-tape copy, 'bouncing down' the tracks to give more space. Calling this take two the Beatles then overdubbed yet more vocals and guitar work. However, although they may have felt that the recording was not perfect, it was take one which was labelled as 'best', if only until the 30 March re-make.

Five more mono remixes were done on this day too, thereby completing a full set of all 11 songs recorded by the Beatles during the week of 15-20 February. On 22 February the group flew to the Bahamas to begin shooting the film for which the recordings were made, taking with them a copy tape of all 11 remixes for the approval, or otherwise, of the film's producer and director, Walter Shenson and Dick Lester respectively.

Off-beat shots from another publicity photo session, with Neil Aspinall and Mal Evans (in glasses) close at hand.

Tuesday 23 February

Studio Two (control room only): 10.00am-1.00pm. Stereo mixing: 'Yes It Is' (from take 14); 'You've Got To Hide Your Love Away' (from take 9); 'If You've Got Trouble' (from take 1); 'Tell Me What You See' (from take 4); 'I Need You' (from take 5); 'Another Girl' (from take 1); 'Ticket To Ride' (from take 2); 'You Like Me Too Much' (from take 8); 'The Night Before' (remix 1, from take 2); 'You're Going To Lose That Girl' (remix 1, from take 3); 'That Means A Lot' (from take 1); 'You're Going To Lose That Girl' (remix 2, from take 3). P: n/a   E: Norman Smith.   2E: Malcolm Davies.

Stereo remixes of all 11 new songs, made under the supervision of Norman Smith, not George Martin. 'Yes It Is' remains unissued on disc in this form at the time of writing (1987), 'If You've Got Trouble' and 'That Means A Lot' remain unreleased in any form. All of the other songs were released on the stereo *Help!* LP. The second remix of 'You're Going To Lose That Girl' was preferred over the first.

Monday 15 March

Studio Two (control room only): 10.00-11.00am. Mono mixing: 'Ticket To Ride' (remix 2, from take 2). P: n/a.   E: Norman Smith.   2E: unknown.

A new mono remix of 'Ticket To Ride', for use by the film company, United Artists.

Tuesday 30 March

Studio Two: 7.00-10.00pm. Recording: 'That Means A Lot' [re-make] (takes 20-24). P: George Martin.   E: Norman Smith.   2E: Ron Pender/Vic Gann.

"We're calling it take 20," bellowed Norman Smith over the studio talkback system. It was not unknown to begin recording re-makes with a round number, but 20, when the original had only got as far as two, does seem a little drastic.

But whatever the figure, these attempts at 'That Means A Lot', though markedly different from the original, were no more successful than the first. Within eight days the song would be recorded by P.J. Proby for release as a (surprisingly unsuccessful) single.

In fact, Proby's version was not unlike this Beatles re-make, or to be more precise, re-makes. Clearly they still had not decided on the best way to present the song. Take 20 was much faster and brighter than the original versions, more pop-like, with 'answering' electric guitar phrases played by George. Take 21 was different still, the guitar having disappeared. Takes 22-24 all dissolved into anarchy, ideas failing to materialise. They could take the song no further.

Friday 2 April

Studio Two (control room only): 10.00-11.00am. Stereo mixing: 'You're Going To Lose That Girl' (remix 3, from take 3). P: George Martin.   E: Norman Smith.   2E: unknown.

Another attempt at a stereo remix of 'You're Going To Lose That Girl'. But the second remix from 23 February won the day, and this third variation was left to gather dust.

Friday 9 April

Single release: 'Ticket To Ride'/'Yes It Is'. Parlophone R 5265.

The Beatles' first single of 1965, and of course a number one in all countries where pop music was played, bought and sold. Once again, a very classy two-sided performance, far ahead of the field.

Tuesday 13 April

Studio Two: 7.00-11.00pm. Recording: 'Help!' (takes 1-12). P: George Martin.   E: Norman Smith.   2E: Ken Scott.

As purely a working title, the Beatles' second feature film had been called 'Beatles Production 2'. Then a more permanent name was suggested, 'Eight Arms To Hold You'. None of the Beatles cared for that one but since nothing better had materialised they put up with it. Not for long, though, because in the end *Help!* was conceived. And, once again, John Lennon and Paul McCartney had to write a song with that title.

In the end it was almost exclusively written by John, and in later years he would look back on the lyric as being one of his first real 'message' numbers, Lennon pleading for help from somebody, anybody, to help relieve his insecurity.

As far as the recording was concerned, it was not too complicated. Takes one to eight concentrated on the rhythm track, the first vocals being introduced at take nine. Take 10 was complete, take 11 was a false start and the 'best' and final take, numbered 12, saw the introduction of George Harrison's descending, jangly guitar figures which made the song especially distinctive.

Sunday 18 April

Abbey Road, Room 65: 10.00am-12.30pm. Mono mixing: 'Help!' (remixes 1-3, from take 12). Stereo mixing: 'Help!' (remix 1, from take 12); 'The Night Before' (remix 2, from take 2). P: George Martin.   E: Norman Smith.   2E: Phil McDonald.

Three mono remixes of 'Help!', the final one being deemed 'best' for use in the film, plus stereo remixes of both 'Help!' and 'The Night Before', the tapes of which were also taken away by United Artists, but were never used. Neither stereo mix ended up on disc either, 'Help!' being remixed again for that purpose on 18 June, 'The Night Before' having already been done to satisfaction on 23 February.

Monday 10 May

Studio Two: 8.00-11.30pm. Recording: 'Dizzy Miss Lizzy' (takes 1-2); 'Bad Boy' (takes 1-4); 'Dizzy Miss Lizzy' (takes 3-7). Studio Two (control room only): 11.30pm-1.15am. Mono mixing: 'Dizzy Miss Lizzy' (from take 7); 'Bad Boy' (from take 4). Stereo mixing: 'Dizzy Miss Lizzy' (from take 7); 'Bad Boy' (from take 4). P: George Martin.   E: Norman Smith.   2E: Ken Scott.

Larry Williams evening! Recording especially for the North American market, John Lennon steered the group through raucous renditions of two of his favourite songs by the American rocker, 'Dizzy Miss Lizzy' and 'Bad Boy'. Minutes after the final recording, mono and stereo remixes were made of both, to be despatched the next day by air freight to Capitol Records in Los Angeles. Within five weeks they were in the record stores, on the Capitol-compiled LP *Beatles VI*. At best, so the press reported at the time, they might turn up on a British EP later in the year. In fact, 'Dizzy Miss Lizzy' was included on the upcoming *Help!* album but 'Bad Boy' wasn't issued in the UK until the December 1966 compilation *A Collection of Beatles Oldies*.

The Beatles were well versed at performing these songs from their pre-fame stage days so they played them live in the studio, with minimal overdubbing. Take two of 'Dizzy Miss Lizzy' was complete and named 'best' until, obviously feeling that it could be improved upon, the group returned to the song later in the session. Even for what was to become 'best', take seven, they used only three of the four tracks available. 'Bad Boy' was recorded in four takes, the first three being the rhythm track, John singing a guide vocal off microphone. Take four had overdubs of George's guitar, Paul on electric piano, John on organ and Ringo a tambourine, over and above the usual instruments and John's blistering vocal.

Tuesday 8 June

Studio One (control room only): 10.00-10.30am. Stereo mixing: 'I Want To Hold Your Hand' (remix 2, from take 17). P: n/a.   E: Norman Smith.   2E: Ron Pender.

A curious exercise. The motive unknown to this day, Norman Smith here made a new remix of 'I Want To Hold Your Hand', with the vocals placed in the centre of the stereo 'picture'. It was never used.

The Beatles were among the first in Britain to obtain cassette machines. Here, in the control room of Studio Two during the making of the *Help!* LP, they make external (microphone) recordings of their days work.

Monday 14 June

Studio Two: 2.30-5.30pm. Recording: 'I've Just Seen A Face' (takes 1-6); 'I'm Down' (takes 1-7). Studio Two: 7.00-10.00pm. Recording: 'Yesterday' (takes 1-2). P: George Martin. E: Norman Smith. 2E: Phil McDonald.

A remarkable day's work, dominated by Paul McCartney and perfectly illustrating this young man's mastery of three different styles of musical composition and singing. It was on this day that Paul recorded the song which, by public acclaim, will always rank among his best, the beautiful 'Yesterday'.

George Martin remembers the genesis of the song. "I first heard 'Yesterday' when it was known as 'Scrambled Eggs' – Paul's working title – at the George V hotel in Paris in January 1964. Paul said he wanted a one word title and was considering 'Yesterday', except that he thought it was perhaps too corny. I persuaded him that it was all right."

But 'Yesterday' was more than a great song; it was also a trend-setting recording, the use of a string quartet for the first time on a Beatles record paving the way for a new era. The group would continue to utilise strings and orchestras on a regular basis until their final days. "We agreed that it needed something more than an acoustic guitar, but that drums would make it too heavy," says Martin. "The only thing I could think of was strings but Paul was unsure. He hated syrup or anything that was even a suggestion of MOR. So I suggested a classical string quartet. That appealed to him but he insisted 'No vibrato, I don't want any vibrato!'. [Vibrato is oscillation of pitch by, for string players, movement of fingers.] If you're a good violin

player it's very difficult to play without vibrato. Paul told the musicians he wanted it pure. But although they did cut down the vibrato they couldn't do it pure because they would have sounded like schoolboys. I think Paul realised in later years that what he got was right.

"Paul worked with me on the score, putting the cello here and the violin there. There is one particular bit which is very much his – and I wish I'd thought of it! – where the cello groans onto the seventh the second time around. He also liked the idea of holding the very high note on the first [upper] violin in the last section. To be honest, I thought that was a bit boring, but I acceded to his request. The rest of the arrangement was pretty much mine. On the day, I recorded Paul singing and playing guitar simultaneously. Then we overdubbed the strings while Paul had another go at the vocal. But because we didn't use headphones there was leakage from the studio speaker into his microphone, giving the impression of two voices or double-tracking."

Newspapers of the time made a big fuss of the fact that none of the other Beatles played on the recording, and that they were not even in the studio. This myth has persisted for more than 20 years, but while none of the others did play on 'Yesterday', George Harrison, if not John and Ringo, was certainly present, his voice

coming across loud and clear at one point on the original session tape.

The song made a marked impression on those in the studio, not least on the four outside musicians, never credited in writing until now for their contribution. They were not a regular quartet, having been rounded up, only for this one occasion, by the first violinist, Tony Gilbert. Also playing were Sidney Sax (second violin), Francisco Gabarro (cello), and Kenneth Essex (viola). Gabarro, a lovely Spaniard, remembers seeing Paul McCartney in the Abbey Road canteen about a week afterwards. "He came up to me and said 'We have a winner with that 'Yesterday'. I said well good luck! Congratulations!"

What makes Paul's recording of 'Yesterday', the supreme melodic ballad, all the more remarkable is that it directly followed the taping of 'I'm Down', a quasi-soul/rock and roll song delivered by Paul in the most larynx-tearing, cord-shredding style imaginable. This was recorded in seven takes and also features drums, bass, organ (the latter played by John), lead guitar, bongos, rhythm guitar and backing vocals. A powerful combination – and all for a B-side. The other (first) song recorded this day, Paul's folk-rock 'I've Just Seen a Face', was predominantly acoustic, perfected in six takes, with two acoustic guitars and a maraca overdub.

Tuesday 15 June

Studio Two: 2.30-5.30pm. Recording: 'It's Only Love' (takes 1-6). P: George Martin.   E: Norman Smith.   2E: Phil McDonald.

An afternoon session only, recording – and perfecting in six takes – John's mainly acoustic 'It's Only Love'. It was a straightforward taping, George introducing his tone pedal guitar work again for the 'best' take, with John playing his acoustic guitar high up near the neck. Four of the six takes were complete, take three being a false start, take five breaking down when Ringo, very uncharacteristically, made a drumming error. His lone voice apologising to John, was caught by the microphone, "We all make mistakes...!"

Thursday 17 June

Studio Two: 2.30-5.30pm. Recording: 'Act Naturally' (takes 1-13). Studio Two: 7.00-10.00pm. Recording: 'Wait' (takes 1-4). Mono mixing: 'Yesterday' (remixes 1 and 2, from take 2). P: George Martin.   E: Norman Smith.   2E: Phil McDonald.

The rejection of 'If You've Got Trouble', recorded on 18 February, meant that a Ringo Starr vocal had still to be recorded for the now almost completed *Help!* album. Ringo, a fan of country and western music, plumped for a cover version of Buck Owens' 'Act Naturally' and the Beatles recorded it in 13 takes, with George playing acoustic guitar and Paul supplying American style backing vocals. The first 12 concentrated solely on the rhythm track, Ringo adding his vocal only at the last take.

But Ringo very nearly didn't get his quota of one song per LP this time around. Norman Smith takes up the story. "I'd been writing songs since I was a small boy, and in 1965 I wrote one with John Lennon in mind. They were coming towards the end of the *Help!* LP and needed one more song. George Martin and I were in the control room waiting for them to make up their minds and I said 'I know they've heard all this before, but I happen to have a song in my pocket.' George said 'Get on to the talkback and tell them.' But I was too nervous so George called down, 'Paul, can you come up? Norman's got a song for you.' Paul looked shocked. 'Really, Normal?' – that was one of their nicknames for me – 'Yes, really'. So we went across to studio three and I sat at the piano and bashed the song out. He said 'That's really good, I can hear John singing that!' So we got John up, he heard it, and said 'That's great. We'll do it'. Paul asked me to do a demo version, for them all to learn. Dick James, the music publisher, was there while all this was going on and before we went home that night he offered me £15,000 to buy the song outright. I couldn't talk but I looked across at George [Martin] and his eyes were flicking up towards the ceiling, meaning 'ask for more'. So I said 'Look, Dick, I'll talk to you tomorrow about it.'

"I did the demo but the next day the Beatles came in looking a little bit sheepish, long faces. 'Hello, Norm.' I thought, hmm, they're not as excited as me, what's wrong? Sure enough, Paul and John called me down to the studio and they said 'Look, we definitely like your song but we've realised that Ringo hasn't got a vocal on the LP, and he's got to have one. We'll do yours another time, eh?' That was my £15,000 gone in a flash. By the next LP they'd progressed so much that my song was never even considered again." [Not only was Norman's song never again mentioned but 'Act Naturally' was the last cover version the Beatles recorded until the *Get Back* film/album sessions in 1969. In between times only group compositions would feature on Beatles records.]

Curiously, there was one song on that next LP – *Rubber Soul* – which *wasn't* such a great progression. The song was 'Wait', and the reason it didn't sound like late-1965 Beatles is that it was recorded in mid-1965, on this day, as a *Help!* album track. For whatever reason, perhaps it was considered weak or ill-fitting, it was left off *Help!* and was destined to remain unreleased until the Beatles, in need of a song, revived it on 11 November, at the same time overdubbing more sounds. But the original guitars, drums, bass and John and Paul's shared lead vocal were done on this day – take four, the only complete version, being deemed 'best'.

The better of the two mono remixes of 'Yesterday' – also done on this day – was the second one.

Friday 18 June

Studio Two (control room only): 10.00am-12.30pm. Mono mixing: 'I've Just Seen A Face' (from take 6); 'I'm Down' (from take 7); 'It's Only Love' (from take 6); 'Act Naturally' (from take 13); 'Wait' (remix 1, from take 4); 'Help!' (remix 4, from take 12). Studio Two (control room only): 12.30-1.30pm. Stereo mixing: 'I've Just Seen A Face' (from take 6); 'I'm Down' (from take 7); 'Yesterday' (from take 2); 'It's Only Love' (from take 6); 'Act Naturally' (from take 13); 'Help!' (remix 2, from take 12). P: George Martin. E: Norman Smith.   2E: Phil McDonald.

Final mixing for the mono single and LP and the stereo LP. Only 'Wait' remained unreleased – for the time being – although when it did eventually surface more instruments were added and a new remix was necessary.

Friday 23 July

Single release: 'Help!'/'I'm Down'. Parlophone R 5305.

The title song from the film, premiered in London on 29 July. A number one everywhere, of course.

PARLOPHONE E.P. SEPTEMBER — RUSH PROCEEDING FOR PRE-RELEASE AUGUST 7th, 1965
Parlophone Long Play — Mono and Stereo

22nd June, 1965

MR. E. FOWLER
Abbey Road Studios (5)

JOB NO. 15002

M.F.F.

Information copies to:—
Mr. A. Gregory, Manchester Sq.
Mr. I. Middleton,   "
Mr. D. Woodward, Record Factory, Hayes
Mr. G. Port,   Cataloguing, Hayes
Mr. J. Chandler, Royalties, Hayes
Mr. D. Cannings, H.O. Hayes
Miss P. Britt, H.O. Hayes

June 21st. 1965.

PARLOPHONE LONG PLAY — TRANSFER ORDER — SEPTEMBER 1965 SUPPLEMENT

Artist	Title	Serial No.	Remarks
The Beatles	"HELP!"		

1. Help!   13-6-65
rill
2. The Night Before   17-2-65)
rill
3. You've Got To Hide Your Love Away)18-2-65
rill
4. I Need You   15-2-65
rill
5. Another Girl   15-2-65   XEX   549
rill
6. You're Going To Lose That Girl   19-2-65)
rill
7. Ticket To Ride   15-2-65
rill

Side 2.
1. Act Naturally   17-6-65
rill
2. It's Only Love   15-6-65)
rill
3. You Like Me Too Much   17-2-65)
rill
4. Tell Me What You See   18-2-65)
rill
5. I've Just Seen A Face   14-6-65)   XEX 550
rill
6. Yesterday   14-6-65)
rill
7. Dizzy Miss Lizzy   10-5-65)
rill

J.C.H.

R. BOCKERILL

Mr. G.N. Bridge.   Mr. R.N. White.
Mr. R. Oldfield.   Mr. G. Freshwater.
Mr. A. Dewdney.   Mr. I. Middleton.
Mr. R. Dockerill.   Mr. D. Woodward.
Mr. F. Exon.   Mr. F. Chalmers.
Mr. E. Fowler.
Mr. R. Dunton.

PARLOPHONE L.P. 'HELP'!

Artists: THE BEATLES.
Job No. & Release: 15002. August 7th.
Recorded: 1965.
Cover: Design by Robert Freeman — Mr. Dunton has this.

          Photographs and title information with note of lead
          singers on back. No note.

Recording produced by George Martin.

Side 1.   Songs from the film 'HELP!'

          HELP!
          THE NIGHT BEFORE.
          YOU'VE GOT TO HIDE YOUR LOVE AWAY.
          I NEED YOU.
          ANOTHER GIRL.
          YOU'RE GOING TO LOSE THAT GIRL.
          TICKET TO RIDE.
          (All titles Lennon-McCartney – Northern Songs)
          except 'I NEED YOU' (Harrison – Northern Songs.)

          ACT NATURALLY.   Lark Music Ltd.
          (Morrison-Russell)
Side 2.   IT'S ONLY LOVE.   Northern Songs.
          YOU LIKE ME TOO MUCH.   (Harrison)
          TELL ME WHAT YOU SEE.
          I'VE JUST SEEN A FACE.
          YESTERDAY.
          DIZZY MISS LIZZY.   Essex Music.
          (Larry Williams)

          (All titles Lennon-McCartney – Northern Songs except
          where indicated.)

REGISTERED
22 JUN 1965 G.H. Martin.
          E.M.I. Records Ltd.

TRADE MARK
PARLOPHONE
45 R.P.M.
R 5305

NORTHERN
SONGS
NCB

℗ 1965
(7XCE.18280)

SOLD IN U.K. SUBJECT TO
RESALE PRICE CONDITIONS,
SEE PRICE LISTS

HELP!
(from film of same name)
(Lennon—McCartney)
THE BEATLES

MADE IN GT. BRITAIN

Friday 6 August

LP release: *Help!* Parlophone PMC 1255 (mono)/PCS 3071 (stereo). A: 'Help!'; 'The Night Before'; 'You've Got To Hide Your Love Away'; 'I Need You'; 'Another Girl'; 'You're Going To Lose That Girl'; 'Ticket To Ride'. B: 'Act Naturally'; 'It's Only Love'; 'You Like Me Too Much'; 'Tell Me What You See'; 'I've Just Seen A Face'; 'Yesterday'; 'Dizzy Miss Lizzy'.

The soundtrack album of the Beatles' second feature film, alias another fine collection of classic mid-1960s pop music. As with the album *A Hard Day's Night*, the songs on side one appeared in the film, those on side two did not. In the USA, Capitol Records' album of the same name featured just the seven film songs, the other tracks being incidental music recordings by George Martin and his Orchestra. It still sold more than a million there on advance orders alone.

Note. Semaphore experts quickly realised that the message spelt out by the four Beatles on the album cover did not make HELP but NUJV. Not quite such a catchy title…

Sunday 29 August

Live concert at the Hollywood Bowl, 2301 North Highland Avenue, Los Angeles, California, USA. Recording: 'Introduction' (by KRLA disc-jockeys); 'Twist And Shout'; 'She's A Woman'; 'I Feel Fine'; 'Dizzy Miss Lizzy'; 'Ticket To Ride'; 'Everybody's Trying To Be My Baby'; 'Can't Buy Me Love'; 'Baby's In Black'; 'I Wanna Be Your Man'; 'A Hard Day's Night'; 'Help!'; 'I'm Down'. P: Engeman (christian name unknown). E: Hugh Davies. 2E: n/a.

The 23 August 1964 live concert recording from the same venue may well have been lying unreleased in the vault, but that did not prevent Capitol from trying again, taping this and the following night's performances for possible release on record.

But even when the album *The Beatles At The Hollywood Bowl* was released, nothing from this performance was included owing to technical gremlins, not the least of which was a fault on Paul's vocal microphone, which obliterated his singing and introductions on the first four songs.

Monday 30 August

Live concert at the Hollywood Bowl, 2301 North Highland Avenue, Los Angeles, California, USA. Recording: 'Twist And Shout'; 'She's A Woman'; 'I Feel Fine'; 'Dizzy Miss Lizzy'; 'Ticket To Ride'; 'Everybody's Trying To Be My Baby'; 'Can't Buy Me Love'; 'Baby's In Black'; 'I Wanna Be Your Man'; 'A Hard Day's Night'; 'Help!'; 'I'm Down'. P: Voyle Gilmore. E: Pete Abbott. 2E: n/a.

A better recording, though it was dominated by audience screaming of a high decibel level normally associated with an airport runway.

Seven of these 12 songs made it onto *The Beatles At The Hollywood Bowl* in 1977, having been extensively cleaned up and re-processed by George Martin, Geoff Emerick and tape operator Nigel Walker at AIR Studios, London, on 18 January of that year.

Tuesday 12 October

Studio Two: 2.30-7.00pm. Recording: 'Run For Your Life' (takes 1-5). P: George Martin. E: Norman Smith. 2E: Ken Scott/Phil McDonald. Studio Two: 7.00-11.30pm. Recording: 'This Bird Has Flown' (working title of 'Norwegian Wood (This Bird Has Flown)') (take 1). P: George Martin. E: Norman Smith. 2E: Ken Scott.

The Beatles had released two albums of new material in 1963 and 1964, and now in 1965 they had to do the same again. The problem was, they had very little material to work with and time was getting on. John and Paul, really for the first time in their lives, had to force themselves to come up with more than a dozen new songs – which they later admitted was "very impossible"; then, with George and Ringo, they had to zip through a crash series of recording sessions in order to have the LP in the stores by early December. These did not even begin until 12 October.

How very ironic then that the resulting LP, *Rubber Soul*, was acclaimed then and now, and quite rightly so too, as both a high quality product and a major turning point in the group's career, in terms of musical composition and recording technique. *Rubber Soul* has proved a durable and very necessary platform between the impeccable pop music of *Help!* and the experimental ideas of *Revolver*.

John Lennon later admitted that in having to write and record songs so quickly, he would sometimes rely on other records for his initial ideas. Certainly he did this for the first song to be taped in this new set of sessions, 'Run For Your Life', lifting two lines of lyrics from 'Baby Let's Play House', recorded by Elvis Presley. John later admitted this to be one of the reasons he "hated" 'Run For Your Life'. But while his opinion was his prerogative as songwriter, it sounds like a very good song to most other people. It was recorded in five takes, but take five was the only complete version, with added overdubs of acoustic guitar, backing vocals and tambourine.

Even if the first song was "forced", the second to be taped was pure Lennon genius, and one of the most original pop music songs recorded to date. At this stage it was called 'This Bird Has Flown', though it became 'Norwegian Wood (This Bird Has Flown)' when it was re-made nine days after this first attempt. The word re-make can often signify that the first recording had imperfections. Not so for 'This Bird Has Flown', for while it may not have been an exact realisation of what composer Lennon wanted, it was still a *brilliant* recording, quite different but equally as dazzling as the version which ended up on the LP.

'This Bird Has Flown' was recorded in just one take although much rehearsing, head-scratching and overdubbing meant that it took 4½ hours to complete. John's droll vocal, double-tracked in places, of lyrics which gave a new dimension to the usual boy-meets-girl situation (the song was an oblique reference to an extra-marital relationship), being augmented by George Harrison's double-tracked sitar, the Indian instrument being used on a pop record for the first time [though, interestingly, George Martin produced a Peter Sellers session employing both a sitar and a tabla, on 16 October 1959 for the song 'Wouldn't It Be Loverly' on the LP *Songs For Swingin' Sellers*], by superb Paul McCartney vocal harmonies – a naturally acquired and underrated forte – and by Ringo's interesting percussion work, in which he forsook drums in favour of finger cymbals, tambourine and maraca. Add acoustic guitar and bass guitar and you have all the ingredients for...an unreleased Beatles recording, but one which would have graced any album then and indeed now.

The Beatles felt that it wasn't right and gave the song a somewhat heavier approach on the re-make.

For every film soundtrack there must be a film. Leaving behind them EMI Studios and the world of four-track and mono/stereo remixes, this is the Beatles looning in Obertauern Austria, during the shooting of *Help!*, mid-March 1965.

Wednesday 13 October

Studio Two: 7.00pm-12.15am. Recording: 'Drive My Car' (takes 1-4). P: George Martin. E: Norman Smith. 2E: Ken Scott.

The 'best' take of 'Drive My Car', chosen to open the LP, was take four, the only complete run through. But there were numerous overdubs, and by the end of the day the song featured lead vocal by Paul and John plus backing vocal by George, tambourine, lead guitar, rhythm guitar, drums, piano and cowbell.

This session was to prove a landmark in the Beatles' recording career, extending past midnight for the first time. The 10 May 1965 session had also exceeded the bewitching hour but that was for remixing only. There would soon come a time when a session not running into the next day would prove the exception.

October

Saturday 16 October

Studio Two: 2.30-7.00pm. Recording: 'Day Tripper' (takes 1-3). Studio Two: 7.00-12.00pm. Recording: 'Day Tripper' (SI onto take 3); 'If I Needed Someone' (take 1). P: George Martin. E: Norman Smith. 2E: Ken Scott.

Interviewed in 1966, John and Paul admitted that 'Day Tripper' was a "forced" composition, written under the pressure of having to come up with a single. Again, it doesn't show, at least not to an outsider. Other songwriters would have been mighty proud to have come up with a song like that.

The Beatles spent the afternoon rehearsing and recording the rhythm track, with only the final take, the third, making it through to the end. They began the evening session overdubbing the vocals, John and Paul sharing both lead and backing roles.

Finally, with the evening drawing towards midnight the group recorded a basic rhythm track for George Harrison's fine new song 'If I Needed Someone', leaving vocals and additional instruments to be overdubbed in the next session.

Monday 18 October

Studio Two: 2.30-5.45pm. Recording: 'If I Needed Someone' (SI onto take 1); 'In My Life' (takes 1-3). P: George Martin. E: Norman Smith. 2E: Ken Scott.

'If I Needed Someone' was the day's first priority, George's lead vocal being overdubbed onto track three of the four-track tape, John and Paul's backing vocal onto track four. Ringo added a tambourine.

The remainder of the afternoon was spent recording another marvellous new Lennon song, the autobiographical 'In My Life'. After a period of rehearsal, three takes were put down, two of which were complete. The 'best' was take three, with John's lead vocal underscored by Paul, and with lead guitar, tambourine and drums as the rhythm. At this point the middle eight of the song was left open since the Beatles had yet to decide how best to use it. The hole was plugged with an imaginative overdub recorded on 22 October.

Wednesday 20 October

Studio Two: 2.30-6.30pm. Recording: 'We Can Work It Out' (takes 1-2). Studio Two: 7.00-11.45pm. Recording: 'We Can Work It Out' (SI onto take 2). P: George Martin. E: Norman Smith. 2E: Ken Scott.

The second song for the next single. Asked in 1966 whether this one, like its associate 'Day Tripper', was "forced" John and Paul were emphatic in their reply. "No." 'We Can Work It Out' showed complete mastery of the two-minute pop song and is another example of typical Beatles 1965 fare, excellent musicianship being allied with a new lyrical direction, in this instance John's downbeat choruses providing the perfect foil for Paul's positive optimism.

The net result of 525 minutes recording was just two takes, the second, as 'best', with the now obligatory overdubs, not least of which were the vocals which, alone, took the entire evening session to perfect. (Even so, they later decided to add more, these being overdubbed on 29 October.) Instruments used on the recordings included tambourine, drums, acoustic guitar, bass guitar and harmonium (the latter played by John).

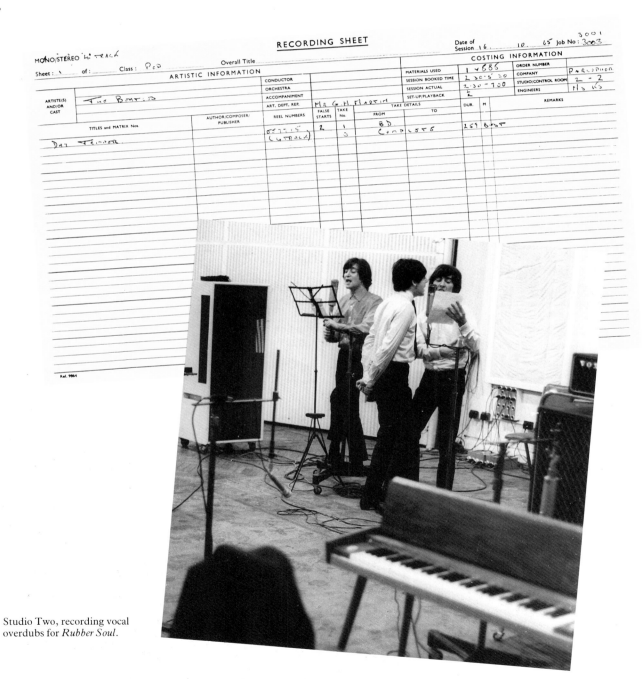

Studio Two, recording vocal overdubs for *Rubber Soul*.

Thursday 21 October

Studio Two: 2.30-7.00pm. Recording: 'Norwegian Wood (This Bird Has Flown)' [re-make] (takes 2-4). Studio Two: 7.00-12.00pm. Recording: 'Nowhere Man' (takes 1-2).
P: George Martin.   E: Norman Smith.   2E: Ken Scott.

The re-make of 'This Bird Has Flown', or rather 'Norwegian Wood'. The title was in the process of changing, hence engineer Norman Smith's talkback announcement "This Bird Has, er…er…Norwegian Wood take three". In the end John compromised and included both elements in the title.

Each of the three takes recorded on this day, numbered two to four (four being 'best'), was different to its predecessor. Take two had a heavy sitar introduction and was recorded without drums or bass. Take three was predominantly acoustic, with two acoustic guitars and Paul's bass, and nothing else bar vocals from John and Paul. This take saw the introduction of the acoustic opening which was to remain for the final version. Take four was that final version, with sitar reinstated.

Norman Smith remembers the difficulty in recording the sitar satisfactorily. "It is very hard to record because it has a lot of nasty peaks and a very complex wave form. My meter would be going right over into the red, into distortion, without us getting audible value for money. I could have used a limiter but that would have meant losing the sonorous quality."

The only other song recorded on this day was John's 'Nowhere Man', and after a period of rehearsal two takes were attempted, one an immediate false start the other only an electric guitar rhythm track recording, save for an elaborate – and later discarded – idea to introduce the song with high register three-part harmony work by John, Paul and George. This was evidently enough for John to realise that the song needed more work, which he must have done quickly for the Beatles taped a re-make the next day.

Friday 22 October

Studio Two: 10.30-11.30am. Recording: 'In My Life' (SI onto take 3). P: George Martin.   E: Stuart Eltham.   2E: Mike Stone.   Studio Two: 2.30-7.00pm. Recording: 'Nowhere Man' [re-make] (takes 3-5). Studio Two: 7.00-11.30pm. Recording 'Nowhere Man' (SI onto take 4). P: George Martin.   E: Norman Smith.   2E: Ken Scott.

First task of the day was to superimpose an instrumental break onto the previously recorded 'In My Life'. But using which instrument? One of the keyboard types certainly, with George Martin playing. The tape box reveals that he originally tried a Hammond organ. Not right. Then he decided on a piano, though there was a problem in playing the type of solo he wanted, baroque style, at the right tempo. The solution was to play at half the speed and then play back the tape at double-speed. It worked, the song was complete, and it went on to become one of the Beatles' most respected pieces of work.

The remainder of the day was spent on the re-make of 'Nowhere Man', the afternoon perfecting the rhythm track, takes three to five, and the evening superimposing vocals onto take four, the 'best' version. A fine piece of work.

Sunday 24 October

Studio Two: 2.30-7.00pm. Recording: 'I'm Looking Through You' (take 1). Studio Two: 7.00-11.30pm. Recording: 'I'm Looking Through You' (SI onto take 1). P: George Martin.   E: Norman Smith.   2E: Ken Scott.

A lot of time to spend on a song later to be re-made entirely differently, not just once but twice. This interesting new Paul McCartney number was stacked with potential but there was obviously some difficulty in recording it to everyone's satisfaction.

That's not to say that anything was wrong with this first recording. In fact, if there was such a thing as an album of the best 'alternate' Beatles recordings this take one of 'I'm Looking Through You' would be an automatic choice along with, so far, 'This Bird Has Flown' and 'And I Love Her'.

Predominant in this version were handclaps and acoustic guitar, maraca, organ, electric guitar and great, great vocals. To this writer it sounds superb, just as good as the re-remake. The Beatles obviously thought differently.

"Now, who does she remind you of?" Paul, George and John during sessions for *Rubber Soul*.

Monday 25 October

Studio Two (control room only): 10.00am-1.00pm. Mono mixing: 'Drive My Car' (from take 4); 'In My Life' (from take 3); 'If I Needed Someone' (from take 1); 'Day Tripper' (remix 1, from take 3); 'Norwegian Wood (This Bird has Flown)' (from take 4); 'Nowhere Man' (from take 4). P: George Martin.   E: Norman Smith.   2E: Ken Scott.

Mono remixes for the LP and single. All made the cut except for 'Day Tripper', a better remix of which was made on 29 October.

Tuesday 26 October

Studio Two (control room only): 10.00am-12.30pm. Stereo mixing: 'Drive My Car' (from take 4); 'Day Tripper' (from take 3); 'In My Life' (from take 3); 'If I Needed Someone' (from take 1); 'Norwegian Wood (This Bird has Flown)' (from take 4); 'Nowhere Man' (from take 4). P: George Martin.   E: Norman Smith.   2E: Ron Pender.

Stereo remixing for the LP. The Beatles were still attending very few of these sessions at this time. Indeed on this occasion they had a prior and perhaps more important engagement – collecting their MBEs from the Queen at Buckingham Palace.

Thursday 28 October

Studio Two (control room only): 5.00-5.30pm. Mono mixing: 'We Can Work It Out' (remix 1, from take 2). P: George Martin.   E: Norman Smith.   2E: Jerry Boys.

A rough remix, not for record but for the Beatles to mime to during the tele-recording of the imminent Granada Television 'spectacular' *The Music Of Lennon And McCartney*, shot at the company's Manchester studios on 1 and 2 November.

It was only when they heard a playback of this remix that the Beatles realised that more vocals needed to be added to the song. These were overdubbed on 29 October, instantly rendering this mix unusable.

Friday 29 October

Studio Two: 2.00-4.00pm. Recording: 'We Can Work It Out' (SI onto take 2). Studio Two (control room only): 4.00-5.00pm. Mono mixing: 'We Can Work It Out' (remixes 2 and 3, from take 2); 'Day Tripper' (remixes 2 and 3 from take 3). P: George Martin.   E: Norman Smith.   2E: Ken Scott.

First job was to superimpose additional vocals onto 'We Can Work It Out'. Then the mono remixing could begin, first two versions of that song – one for record and one for the Granada Television programme – then, improving on the 25 October model, new remixes of 'Day Tripper', again one for record and one for television.

The lunchtime press conference at the Brian Epstein-leased Saville Theatre, London, 26 October 1965, displaying MBE medals acquired that morning.

Wednesday 3 November

Studio Two: 2.30-7.00pm. Recording: 'Michelle' (take 1). Studio Two: 7.00-11.30pm. Recording: 'Michelle' (tape reduction take 1 into take 2, SI onto take 2). P: George Martin. E: Norman Smith. 2E: Ken Scott.

A day spent recording this beautiful new Paul McCartney ballad. In the afternoon the Beatles concentrated on the rhythm track, using up all four tracks of the tape. First task in the evening [although the day was really one continuous session] was to copy this tape onto another, simultaneously mixing down to three tracks. This was called take two. The Beatles then spent the remainder of the day overdubbing the lovely vocal work and guitars onto the newly vacated track.

It was another late finish. Jerry Boys, occasional tape operator on Beatles and other George Martin sessions, remembers popping into the control room late at night, while Paul was still recording his lead vocal. "I stood there quite spellbound. It sounded lovely. George asked me what I thought of the Beatles singing a song with French lyrics and I got the impression that with me being a young chap he was sounding me out, perhaps because they weren't too sure themselves. I said it sounded very pleasant, which it certainly did!"

Thursday 4 November

Studio Two: 11.00pm-3.30am. Recording: 'What Goes On' (take 1); '12-Bar Original' (takes 1-2). P: George Martin. E: Norman Smith. 2E: Ken Scott/Graham Platt.

Deadlines were clearly becoming very tight. It was now less than a month before the desired release date for the new LP and yet only slightly more than half of the songs had been recorded. Several had still to be written.

This prompted two actions. Late-night sessions became not just something the group casually drifted into but a deliberate plan. The session on this day, for example, was booked in advance to end at 3am [it actually finished at 3.30]. Second action, on this day at least, was for the Beatles to revive a couple of previously discarded song ideas. One of them was discarded again and remains unreleased to this day.

It was on 5 March 1963 that the Beatles first attempted to record 'What Goes On', though lack of time meant that the tapes never actually rolled. It was, even then, quite an old Lennon/McCartney song. Now it was revived and handed to Ringo for his statutory one vocal per LP. He also ended up with a joint composing credit too, though what exactly he contributed to warrant this has never been clarified. The song was recorded in one take, with overdubs of Ringo's rockabilly vocal and John and Paul's backing.

The song which was to remain unreleased was actually more of a tune than a song, the Beatles' first attempt at recording a purely instrumental number. "'12-Bar Original', we're calling it" announced Norman Smith over the talkback before the first take, a rather unoriginal – though absolutely accurate – title for what was essentially just a rambling 12-bar blues, typical of the day but certainly untypical of anything the Beatles had ever attempted. Moreover, a listen to the original tape reveals that this was no mere improvised piece of work, take two being identical to what the group was trying in take one before that broke down. Take two was in fact complete – running to an uncommonly long 6'36" – and, furthermore, it was recorded entirely live, without overdubs. Over-riding feature of the number was George's tone pedal lead guitar work and a harmonium persistently played by George Martin. John also played lead guitar, Paul played bass and Ringo the drums.

Saturday 6 November

Studio Two: 7.00pm-1.00am. Recording: 'I'm Looking Through You' [re-make] (takes 2-3). P: George Martin. E: Norman Smith. 2E: Ken Scott.

With this (first) re-make of 'I'm Looking Through You' the Beatles got considerably nearer the sound they were seeking. But obviously not near enough, hence the re-remake recorded on 10 November and completed on the 11th.

This day's attempt was perhaps a little too fast and frenetic. Otherwise it was similar to the final, released version.

Monday 8 November

Studio Two: 9.00pm-3.00am. Recording: 'Beatle Speech' (take 1); 'Won't Be There With You' (working title of 'Think For Yourself') (take 1); 'The Beatles' Third Christmas Record' (takes 1-3). P: George Martin. E: Norman Smith. 2E: Ken Scott.

Time was running out not just for the imminent LP release but also for the group's annual Christmas flexi-disc for its fan club members. Partly for this purpose (ie, in case they said anything particularly witty), and partly for reasons never revealed, George Martin deliberately recorded the Beatles rehearsing George Harrison's 'Think For Yourself' during the early part of this session. They knew they were being recorded, hence they hammed their actions, shouting in mock-Scouse accents, discussing the previous night's television, making jokes about friends and wives, telling George Martin that they'll replace him with Ron Richards and variously calling for either Neil (Aspinall), Mal (Evans) or Norman (Smith). In the end nothing was suitable for the Christmas flexi but, just to ensure the tape was not scrapped, the words "This will eventually be issued" were scrawled on the box. And it was, for in 1967 the tape was lent to the producer of the animated film *Yellow Submarine* and when that film finally appeared, on 17 July 1968, it included a six second snatch of John, Paul and George practising their 'Think For Yourself' vocal harmonising.

Actually, it wasn't quite 'Think For Yourself' yet – that title was cooked up later in the evening. At first it was announced by Norman Smith as 'Won't Be There With You'. Whatever the moniker, it was finally recorded – with overdubs – in one take, with lead, rhythm and bass guitars, plus a fuzz bass, tambourine, maracas and electric piano. The technical people at Abbey Road built fuzz boxes for use with guitars. "It was an electronic device in which you could have controlled distortion," says Ken Townsend, then one of the technical engineers. "You actually made the sound overload."

The Beatles were quite tired towards the end of the evening, when they came to record their Christmas message. They stumbled their way through three takes of unrehearsed banter, a wild, off-key rendition of 'Yesterday' and vaguely witty chat, at one point joking that George Martin had the (obviously unenviable) task of making a releasable record out of it all. As usual, he did just that, editing and remixing the tapes 12 hours later.

Tuesday 9 November

Abbey Road, Room 65: 2.30-5.30pm. Editing: 'The Beatles' Third Christmas Record' (of takes 1-3). Mono mixing: 'Michelle' (remix 1, from take 2); 'What Goes On' (from take 1); 'Run For Your Life' (from take 5); 'Think For Yourself' (from take 1); 'The Beatles' Third Christmas Record' (from edit of takes 1-3). Stereo mixing: 'Think For Yourself' (from take 1); 'Michelle' (from take 2); 'What Goes On' (from take 1). P: George Martin. E: Norman Smith. 2E: Jerry Boys.

More remixing, again in the Beatles' absence. The mono 'Michelle' was re-done on 15 November and this attempt remains unreleased.

Wednesday 10 November

Abbey Road, Room 65: 2.30-5.30pm. Stereo mixing: 'Run For Your Life' (from take 5); 'We Can Work It Out' (from take 2). P: George Martin. E: Norman Smith. 2E: Jerry Boys. Studio Two: 9.00pm-4.00am. Recording:'The Word' (takes 1-3); 'I'm Looking Through You' [re-re-make] (take 4). P: George Martin. E: Norman Smith. 2E: Ken Scott.

Morning stereo remixing, night-time recording. The rhythm track of 'I'm Looking Through You', for the third time of asking, was finally made in a way that pleased everybody. The vocals were superimposed the next day, 11 November. The album sleeve credits Ringo as playing Hammond organ on this song but it cannot be heard on the recording, nor is the instrument detailed on the tape box.

An entirely new song was also recorded during this session, John Lennon's 'The Word', the lyric of which was a prototype 'All You Need Is Love', two years ahead of that world anthem. 'The Word' was perfected in three takes, with Paul on piano as well as bass guitar and George Martin contributing more harmonium work.

Thursday 11 November

Abbey Road, Room 65: 4.00-5.30pm. Mono mixing: 'The Word' (from take 3). Stereo mixing: 'The Word' (remix 1, from take 3). P: George Martin. E: Norman Smith. 2E: Mike Stone. Studio Two: 6.00pm-7.00am. Recording: 'You Won't See Me' (takes 1-2); 'Girl' (takes 1-2); 'Wait' (SI onto take 4); 'I'm Looking Through You' (SI onto take 4). P: George Martin. E: Norman Smith. 2E: Ken Scott.

The deadline had come, the album had to be finished immediately, hence this *marathon* recording session, thirteen hours without any proper break and ending at 7am. Three more songs were needed. Paul came up with one, John another, and for the third they pulled 'Wait', the discarded *Help!* track, out of the tape library, added various bits and pieces and pronounced it fit for inclusion on the new LP. Balance was everything in 1965; a 13-song album was just not done. Fourteen meant seven songs per side and everything hunky-dory.

'You Won't See Me', Paul's song, was recorded in two takes, with various overdubs. According to the record sleeve it featured the Beatles' assistant Mal Evans on Hammond organ, but no such sound is detectable on the tape or disc. There is however a piano, played by Paul.

The other new song, John's 'Girl', was further proof that Lennon wrote some of his best songs under pressure of deadlines. It was a fine song, if perhaps a little naughty. (John later revealed that the scat backing vocal by Paul and George was in fact the word "tit" sung over and over again. And wasn't that heavy breathing that John contributed over and above his sultry vocal?) The song was mainly acoustic, and a fuzz guitar part played by George on the recording was deleted in the remix.

All that was left now was to add tone pedal guitar, tambourine, maraca and more vocals to the five month old 'Wait', and superimpose the vocals onto 'I'm Looking Through You' and the set of recordings was complete. This they did through the early hours of the morning.

Monday 15 November

Studio One (control room only): 2.30-5.30pm. Mono mixing: 'I'm Looking Through You' (from take 4); 'You Won't See Me' (from take 2); 'Girl' (from take 2); 'Wait' (remix 2, from take 4). Stereo mixing: 'Wait' (from take 4); 'I'm Looking Through You' (from take 4); 'You Won't See Me' (from take 2); 'Girl' (from take 2); 'The Word' (remix 2, from take 3). Mono mixing: 'Michelle' (remix 2, from take 2). P: George Martin. E: Norman Smith. 2E: Richard Lush.

Final remixing for the album, including a second stereo mix of 'The Word'. On 16 November George Martin worked out the LP running order and telephoned it over to Abbey Road. On 17 November (and again on the 19th, the EMI pressing plant had problems with the first) disc-cutter Harry Moss made the mono LP, on the 23rd he cut the stereo. Lacquer discs were rushed to the plant, the sleeve was quickly printed and finished copies of the new Beatles LP were in the shops by 3 December.

November 16th. 1965.

Mr. G.N. Bridge.   Mr. I. Middleton.
Mr. R.N. White.   Mr. D. Woodward.
Mr. R. Oldfield.   Mr. F. Chalmers.
Mr. R. Featherstone.   Mr. A. Dawdney.
Mr. J. Florey.   Miss P. Britt.
Mr. R. Dockerill.
Mr. G. Freshwater.   Mr. E. Fowler.
Mr. R. Dunton.

PARLOPHONE L.P. 'RUBBER SOUL'.

Artist: THE BEATLES.
Recorded: October/November, 1965. Job. No. 3003.
Release: December 1965.
Cover: Robert Freeman.
            Recording produced by George Martin.

Side 1.   DRIVE MY CAR.   Paul and John. (with George)
                                 (Paul on piano)

           NORWEGIAN WOOD.   John (with Paul)
           (This Bird has flown) (George on Sitar)

           YOU WON'T SEE ME.   Paul (with John and George)
                                 (Paul on piano:
                                 Mal "organ" Evans on Hammond)

           NOWHERE MAN.   John and Paul and George.
           THINK FOR YOURSELF.   George (with John and Paul) (Paul o...
                                                          fuzz Bass
           THE WORD.   John and Paul and George.
                                 (Paul on piano;
                                 George Martin on harmonium)

           MICHELLE.   Paul (with John and George)

Side 2.   WHAT GOES ON.   Ringo (With Paul and John)
           GIRL.   John (with Paul and George)
           I'M LOOKING THROUGH YOU. Paul (with John)
                                 (Ringo on Hammond Organ)
           IN MY LIFE.   John and Paul.
                                 (George Martin on piano)
           WAIT.   John and Paul.
           IF I NEEDED SOMEONE. George (with John and Paul)
           RUN FOR YOUR LIFE.   John (with Paul and George)

All titles composed Lennon-McCartney except:-
           THINK FOR YOURSELF and IF I NEEDED SOMEONE.
                                 (George Harrison)

All titles published - Northern Songs Ltd.

                                 George Martin.
                                 A.I.R. London.

Far right: The Beatles at work in 1966, a contact sheet from Robert Freeman, favoured Beatles' photographer 1964-66.

Tuesday 30 November

Abbey Road, Room 65: 4.45-5.00pm. Mono mixing: '12-Bar Original' (from take 2). P: n/a. E: Norman Smith. 2E: Ron Pender.

Although it did not figure on the imminent *Rubber Soul* LP, nor any other release, '12-Bar Original' was still remixed in order that – at their request – the Beatles could have acetate discs cut for their private collections.

Friday 3 December

Single release: 'We Can Work It Out'/'Day Tripper'. Parlophone R 5389. LP release: *Rubber Soul*. Parlophone PMC 1267 (mono)/PCS 3075 (stereo). A: 'Drive My Car'; 'Norwegian Wood (This Bird Has Flown)'; 'You Won't See Me'; 'Nowhere Man'; 'Think for Yourself'; 'The Word'; 'Michelle'. B: 'What Goes On'; 'Girl'; 'I'm Looking Through You'; 'In My Life'; 'Wait'; 'If I Needed Someone'; 'Run For Your Life'.

Rubber Soul represented the last time the Beatles would release two albums of wholly new material in one year, breaking the die cast over three successive and sensational years. And it was the last time the group worked with engineer Norman Smith. Smith had joined Abbey Road in 1959 as a tape operator, quickly progressing to be balance engineer. Now it was time to move on and up. In February 1966 he was promoted to the A&R department at EMI, Manchester Square which led to his first role as record producer. In January 1967 he was offered an up and coming group of young Londoners called the Pink Floyd. The rest, as they say, is history. "We all got on so well," says Smith today of his relationship with the Beatles. "They used to call me 'Normal' and, occasionally, '2dBs Smith' because on a few occasions I would ask one of them to turn his guitar amplifier down a couple of decibels. But *Rubber Soul* wasn't really my bag at all so I decided that I'd better get off the Beatles' train. I told George [Martin] and George told Eppy [Brian Epstein] and the next thing I received a lovely gold carriage clock inscribed 'To Norman. Thanks. John, Paul, George and Ringo'."

As a producer, Smith's path did continue to cross with the Beatles' from time to time and when, in 1972, under the name of Hurricane Smith he scored a number one single himself in America [*Cashbox* chart] with 'Oh, Babe, What Would You Say?' John and Yoko Lennon were the first to send a congratulatory telegram.

Another reason for Smith's promotion was that the EMI A&R department had been depleted in August 1965 by the sudden departure of George Martin, Ron Richards and John Burgess, all of whom – together with ex-EMI then Decca staff producer Peter Sullivan – left to form an independent production company, Associated Independent Recordings (London) Limited, better known as AIR. With Martin no longer on the staff, EMI could have allotted another producer to work with the Beatles but this did not happen. The partnership was too successful to break and neither Brian Epstein nor the Beatles would have stood for such an action.

But what of the LP *Rubber Soul?* George Martin neatly sums it up. "It was the first album to present a new, growing Beatles to the world. For the first time we began to think of albums as art on their own, as complete entities." The title was the cause of much speculation at the time, and its origin has never been properly revealed. This author received an unexpected insight into this very subject when listening to the archive tape of the Beatles recording 'I'm Down', 14 June 1965. In between takes, particularly one and two, Paul frequently repeated the words "Plastic soul, man, plastic soul" and then, for the benefit of the other Beatles, and now history, he went on to explain that it was a phrase coined by black musicians to describe Mick Jagger.

Rubber Soul was one of the highlights of John Lennon's career, the sort of peak which Paul McCartney was to achieve a few months later with *Revolver*. And the single 'We Can Work It Out'/'Day Tripper' was one of the highlights of the group's career, a record so strong on both sides that, for the first time, it was officially released as a double A-side. It sold more than a million copies in Britain alone and was yet another number one success around the world.

Wednesday 6 April

Studio Three: 8.00pm-1.15am. Recording: 'Mark I' (working title of 'Tomorrow Never Knows') (takes 1-3). P: George Martin.   E: Geoff Emerick.   2E: Phil McDonald.

The first session for what was to become the significant album *Revolver*. Here was a set of recordings destined to rock the rock world, and change the course of popular music. And its momentous closing song 'Tomorrow Never Knows' was the first to be taped. What a start!

It took just three takes – one of them a breakdown – to record 'Tomorrow Never Knows', although by its very essence the song was also the result of innumerable overdubs, especially of tape loops. (These were superimposed on 7 April.) On this first day the Beatles recorded only the song's rhythm track. (Only?) It was take three which was chosen for the overdubbing of the loops and for the record release, and take two was the breakdown. But take one was a sensational, apocalyptic version, loop less so to speak, which is very close to defying adequate description.

In 1965 the Beatles' recordings had been progressing quite nicely thank you, but here was a *quantum jump* into not merely tomorrow but sometime next week. Take one of 'Mark I', the working title of 'Tomorrow Never Knows' (the latter being a Ringo-ism seized by John as the ideal title for his masterpiece), was a heavy metal recording of enormous proportion, with thundering echo and booming, quivering, ocean-bed vibrations. And peeking out from under the squall was John Lennon's voice, supremely eerie, as if it were being broadcast through the cheapest transistor radio from your local market, and delivering the most bizarre Beatles lyric yet, including one line taken directly from Dr Timothy Leary's version of the Tibetan *Book of the Dead*.

The released version was a somewhat lighter take of the song, although it was still unlikely to rival 'Yesterday' in the ballad stakes. Ringo's drums carried a hypnotic and mournful thud. Paul's bass, high up on the fretboard, matched Ringo note for mesmerising note. There was another eerily live Lennon vocal, a tambourine, one note of an organ playing continuously, two guitar solos, one fuzzed and played backwards the other put through a Leslie organ speaker [see 7 April for explanation], and a jolly honky-tonk piano. All in all, a quite remarkable day's work. Coming less than three years after 'She Loves You', 'Tomorrow Never Knows' reveals an unrivalled musical progression and the Beatles' willingness to first observe the boundaries and then smash right through them.

It would be wrong to assume that the Beatles alone were responsible for this remarkable recording, or for the progressiveness which would be the hallmark of much of their future output. George Martin was, as ever, a vital ingredient in the process, always innovative himself, a tireless seeker of new sounds and willing translator of the Beatles' frequently vague requirements. Now he was joined by engineer Geoff Emerick, promoted to replace Norman Smith.

Emerick's promotion was a shrewd move by the studio management, particularly Bob Beckett, the man in charge of disc-cutters, the job in which Emerick had latterly been employed. "Geoff walked-in green but because he knew no rules he tried different techniques," says tape operator Jerry Boys. "And because the Beatles were very creative and very adventurous, they would say yes to everything. The chemistry of George and Geoff was perfect and they made a formidable team. With another producer and another engineer things would have turned out quite differently." Ron Pender notes "Geoff started off by following Norman Smith's approach because he'd been Norman's assistant for a while. But he rapidly started to change things around, the way to mike drums or bass, for example. He was always experimenting."

One major reason for Emerick's promotion to what was, at this time, probably the most invidious position in the recording world, seems to have been his very inexperience. Here was a young man – a mere 20 – with not only the best-tuned ears in the business and a head full of fresh ideas but, very importantly, no preconceived or irreversible techniques. What he could and would learn from George Martin and the Beatles he could and would repay.

Emerick recalls the circumstances of his promotion. "The studio manager called me to his office and asked whether I'd like to be the Beatles' engineer. That took me a little bit by surprise! In fact it terrified me. I remember playing a game in my head, eeny meeny miney mo, shall I say yes, shall I say no? The responsibility was enormous but I said yes, thinking that I'd accept the blows as they came…"

It wasn't only the personnel which was changing at Abbey Road. The technical boffins were having to respond quickly to the Beatles' needs. "They would relate what sounds they wanted and we then had to go away and come back with a solution," recalls Ken Townsend. "For example, they often liked to double-track their vocals but it's quite a laborious process and they soon got fed up with it. So after one particularly trying night-time session doing just that, I was driving home and I suddenly had an idea…"

Townsend's idea was to affect not just most of the Beatles' future recordings – almost every song on *Revolver* was treated to ADT! – but recording techniques everywhere. Balance engineer Stuart Eltham realised it needed a name, and christened it Artificial Double Tracking, ADT for short. George Harrison told Townsend he should get a medal for inventing it. In layman's terms, ADT is a process whereby a recording signal is taken from the playback head of a tape machine, is recorded onto a separate machine which has a variable oscillator (enabling the speed to be altered) and then fed back into the first machine to be combined with the original signal. In photography, the placement of a negative directly over another does not alter the image. The two become one. But move one slightly and the image widens. ADT does this with tape. One voice laid perfectly on top of another produces one image. But move the second voice by just a few milli-seconds and two separate images emerge.

Phil McDonald remembers that John Lennon was the prime motivation behind Townsend's invention. "After Ken invented ADT John used to say 'Well I've sung it once lads, just track it for me'. He didn't really want to sing something again." Peter Vince, another engineer, concurs. "John was a one or two take man, if you didn't get him then, or if you didn't put the right amount of echo into his cans [headphones] you just wouldn't get the performance from him."

So John, like the others, was very impressed with ADT. But he was no technical genius and made just one attempt to find out how it worked. "I knew he'd never understand it," says George Martin, "so I said 'Now listen, it's very simple. We take the original image and we split it through a double vibrocated sploshing flange with double negative feedback…' He said 'You're pulling my leg. Aren't you?' I replied 'Well, let's flange it again and see'. From that moment on, whenever he wanted ADT he would ask for his voice to be flanged, or call out for 'Ken's flanger.'" The Beatles' influence was so vast that the term 'flanging' is still in use today, more than 20 years on.

Before leaving the events of 6 April it is worth noting that its recording sheets and tape boxes denote the working title of 'Tomorrow Never Knows' as 'Mark I'. Beatles myth – based on insider Neil Aspinall's contemporaneous writings in the group's monthly fan magazine – has it as 'The Void'.

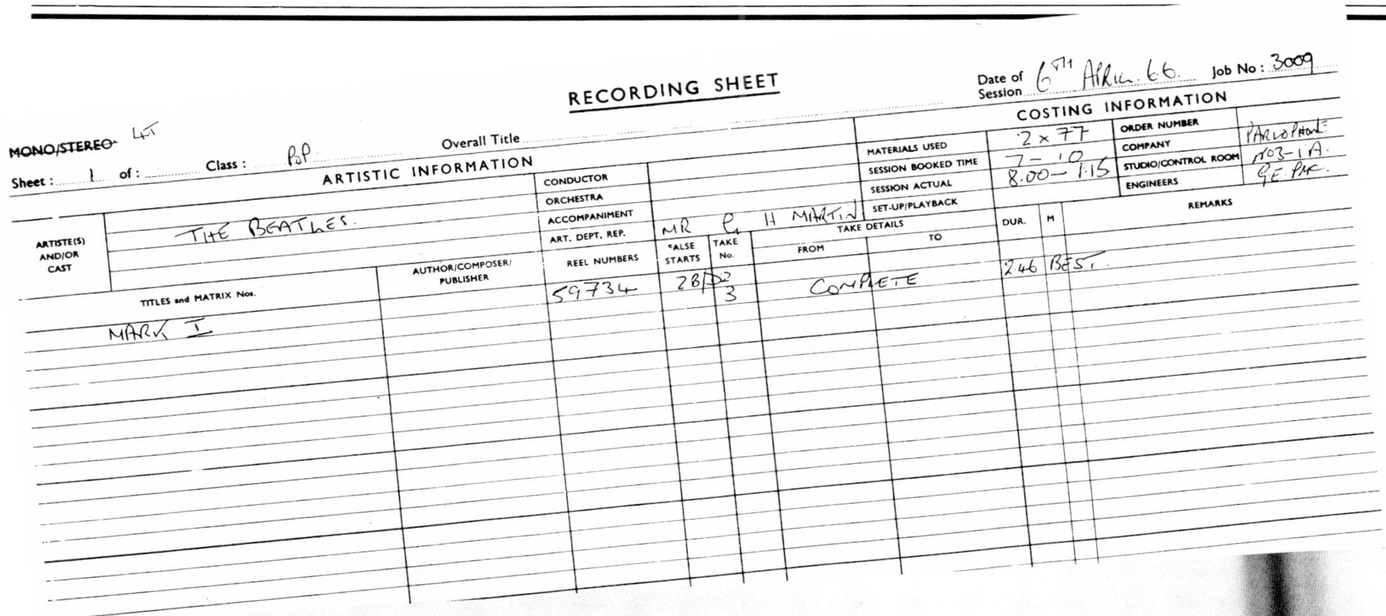

RECORDING SHEET

Date of Session: 6TH APRIL 66. Job No: 3009

MONO/STEREO: 4T

Sheet: 1 of:

Class: POP

Overall Title

ARTISTIC INFORMATION

ARTISTE(S) AND/OR CAST: THE BEATLES.

CONDUCTOR

ORCHESTRA

ACCOMPANIMENT

ART. DEPT. REP.: MR G. H MARTIN

COSTING INFORMATION

MATERIALS USED: 2 x 77

SESSION BOOKED TIME: 7 – 10

SESSION ACTUAL: 8.00 – 1.15

SET-UP/PLAYBACK

ORDER NUMBER

COMPANY: PARLOPHONE

STUDIO/CONTROL ROOM: No3 – 1A.

ENGINEERS: GE PMc

TITLES and MATRIX Nos.	AUTHOR/COMPOSER/ PUBLISHER	REEL NUMBERS	FALSE STARTS	TAKE No.	TAKE DETAILS FROM	TAKE DETAILS TO	DUR.	M	REMARKS
MARK I		59734	2BD	3	COMPLETE		2.46	BEST.	

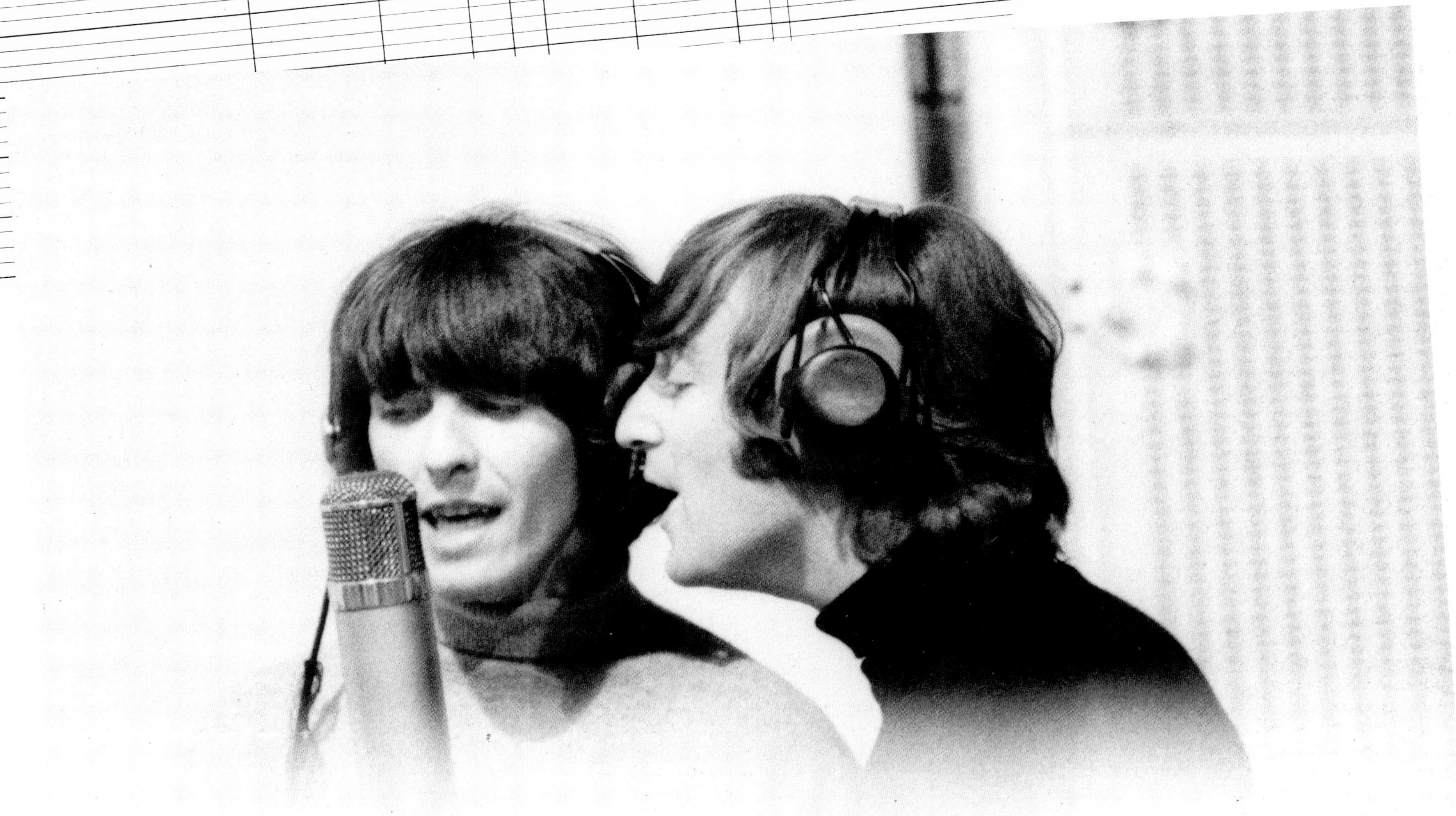

A Robert Freeman shot from the *Revolver* sessions.

Thursday 7 April

Studio Three: 2.30-7.15pm. Recording: 'Mark I' (working title of 'Tomorrow Never Knows') (SI onto take 3). Studio Three: 8.15pm-1.30am. Recording: 'Got To Get You Into My Life' (takes 1-5). P: George Martin.   E: Geoff Emerick.   2E: Phil McDonald.

The entire afternoon was spent overlaying the many and various effects on 'Mark I'. It was, by all accounts, a fun session.

Perhaps the most striking sound on 'Tomorrow Never Knows' is one of tape loops [the sound achieved by tape saturation, by removing the erase head of a machine and then recording over and over on the same piece of tape]. "The tape loop idea started because they all had Brennell machines," recalls Geoff Emerick. "Paul in particular used to make his own loops at home and walk into the studio with bags full of little reels saying 'Listen to this!' The seagull-like noise on 'Tomorrow Never Knows' is really a distorted guitar." (According to studio documentation, other loops used included the sounds of a speeded up guitar and a wine glass.) "We did a live mix of all the loops," says George Martin. "All over the studios we had people spooling them onto machines with pencils while Geoff did the balancing. There were many other hands controlling the panning." "We had five machines running," says Phil McDonald. "Geoff would say 'OK, let's lift that fader, that sounds good'. It was done totally off the cuff. The control room was as full of loops as it was people." "I laid all of the loops onto the multi-track and played the faders like a modern day synthesiser," says Emerick.

'Tomorrow Never Knows' was a groundbreaker in so many ways. No John Lennon vocal had ever sounded like *that* before. *That* was the sound of a voice being fed through a revolving Leslie speaker inside a Hammond organ. Organ notes played through it are given the Hammond swirling effect; voices put through a Leslie emerge in much the same way. "It meant actually breaking into the circuitry," says Emerick. "I remember the surprise on our faces when the voice came out of the speaker. It was just one of sheer amazement. After that they wanted *everything* shoved through the Leslie: pianos, guitars, drums, vocals, you name it!" (Note. The "Leslie'd" Lennon vocal on 'Tomorrow Never Knows' begins 87 seconds into the song. Prior to that it was just treated with ADT.)

This new discovery was again prompted by John Lennon, in conveying his vocal requirement for 'Tomorrow Never Knows'. George Martin remembers "John said to me 'I want to sound as though I'm the Dalai Lama singing from the highest mountain top. And yet I still want to hear the words I'm singing'." Others recall John also requesting that the song have the sound of 4,000 monks chanting in the background.

"John was so impressed by the sound of a Leslie that he hit upon the reverse idea," recalls Emerick. "He suggested we suspend him from a rope in the middle of the studio ceiling, put a mike in the middle of the floor, give him a push and he'd sing as he went around and around. That was one idea that *didn't* come off although they were always said to be 'looking into it'!"

Another distinctive element of 'Tomorrow Never Knows' was Ringo's hypnotic drum sound. "I moved the bass drum microphone much closer to the drum than had been done before," says Emerick. "There's an early picture of the Beatles wearing a woollen jumper with four necks. I stuffed that inside the drum to deaden the sound. Then we put the sound through Fairchild 660 valve limiters and compressors. It became the sound of *Revolver* and *Pepper* really. Drums had never been heard like that before." And Ringo's reaction? "He loved it, there's no question of that. They all loved the sounds. It was exactly what they wanted."

And all this was just one afternoon's work. The remainder of the day saw the group start work on Paul's superb Tamla Motown inspired 'Got To Get You Into My Life', takes one to five. It was to change a great deal before it ended up on disc. Take one of the song, although only a rhythm track, had a one note organ introduction (played by George Martin) supplemented by Ringo's hi-hat, paving the way for a very acoustic number. Before take four the Beatles and George Martin discussed alternative ideas. Take five had the organ and then a full drum intro, heavily limited, and it was also the first to feature vocals. These were not only superb, Paul being backed by John and George, they were different too, Paul singing "Got to get you into my life, somehow, someway" at the instrumental breaks and John and George offering the chant "I need your love" four times over in the refrain. This take was marked 'best' on the tape box, if only temporarily.

Friday 8 April

Studio Two: 2.30-9.00pm. Recording: 'Got To Get You Into My Life' (takes 6-8). P: George Martin.   E: Geoff Emerick.   2E: Phil McDonald.

More work on 'Got To Get You Into My Life', perfecting the rhythm track. Take eight was deemed 'best', later to be overdubbed with vocals, guitar and its distinctive brass passages.

Monday 11 April

Studio Two: 2.30-7.00pm. Recording: 'Got To Get You Into My Life' (SI onto take 8); 'Granny Smith' (working title of 'Love You To') (takes 1-3). Studio Two: 8.00pm-12.45am. Recording: 'Granny Smith' (working title of 'Love You To') (takes 4-6). Studio Two (control room only): 12.45-1.00am. Mono mixing: 'Granny Smith' (working title of 'Love You To') (remix 1, from take 6). P: George Martin.   E: Geoff Emerick.   2E: Phil McDonald.

George's 'Love You To', his first Indian flavoured composition, was untitled at first, then was dubbed 'Granny Smith', after the apple. The song grew more complex with each take. The first, the basic track, had George singing to his own acoustic guitar accompaniment, with Paul supplying backing vocals. The sitar came in at take three and again as an overdub onto take six along with a tabla, bass and fuzz guitar.

George played the sitar but an outside musician, Anil Bhagwat, was recruited to play the tabla. "The session came out of the blue," recalls Anil. "A chap called Angardi called me and asked if I was free that evening to work with George. I didn't know who he meant – he didn't say it was Harrison. It was only when a Rolls-Royce came to pick me up that I realised I'd be playing on a Beatles session. When I arrived at Abbey Road there were girls everywhere with Thermos flasks, cakes, sandwiches, waiting for the Beatles to come out.

"George told me what he wanted and I tuned the tabla with him. He suggested I play something in the Ravi Shankar style, 16-beats, though he agreed that I should improvise. Indian music is all improvisation. I was very lucky, they put my name on the record sleeve. I'm really proud of that, they were the greatest ever and my name is on the sleeve. It was one of the most exciting times of my life."

A rough mono remix of the song was made for George to take away. Also taped on this day was a guitar overdub for 'Got To Get You Into My Life'.

Wednesday 13 April

Studio Three: 2.30-6.30pm. Recording: 'Granny Smith' (working title of 'Love You To') (tape reduction take 6 into take 7, SI onto take 7). Mono mixing: 'Granny Smith' (working title of 'Love You To') (remixes 1-3, from take 7). Editing: 'Granny Smith' (working title of 'Love You To') (of mono remixes 1-3). Studio Three: 8.00pm-2.30am. Recording: 'Paperback Writer' (takes 1-2). P: George Martin.   E: Geoff Emerick.   2E: Richard Lush.

Take seven of 'Granny Smith' was a reduction mix of the four-track take six, creating spare recording tracks. George added another vocal, Ringo contributed tambourine and Paul sang high pitch harmonies on the lines "They'll fill in you in with all the sins you see" though this latter contribution was left out of the mix and, therefore, the record.

The song complete, take seven being 'best', three mono remixes were made – two with ADT, one without – all edited together for record release.

There can't be many number one hit singles on which the French nursery rhyme 'Frère Jacques' is sung. But 'Paperback Writer' is one. It was Paul's idea that John and George should rekindle childhood memories with this unusual backing vocal, recorded on 14 April behind Paul's progressive lead. The song was recorded in just two takes, and one of those was a breakdown. But it was the subject of innumerable overdubs, on this day and again on 14 April.

Eighteen-year-old Richard Lush, another Abbey Road apprentice with a promising future, made his recording session debut as Beatles tape operator on this day. "I was pretty nervous. I'd worked with Cliff and the Shadows and they were very easy going but I knew that Beatles sessions were private. One was rarely allowed to open the door and peek in, and I heard that they took a while to accept new people. It certainly took a while before they knew me as Richard. Until then it was 'Who is that boy sitting in the corner hearing all of our music?' But everything worked out in the end."

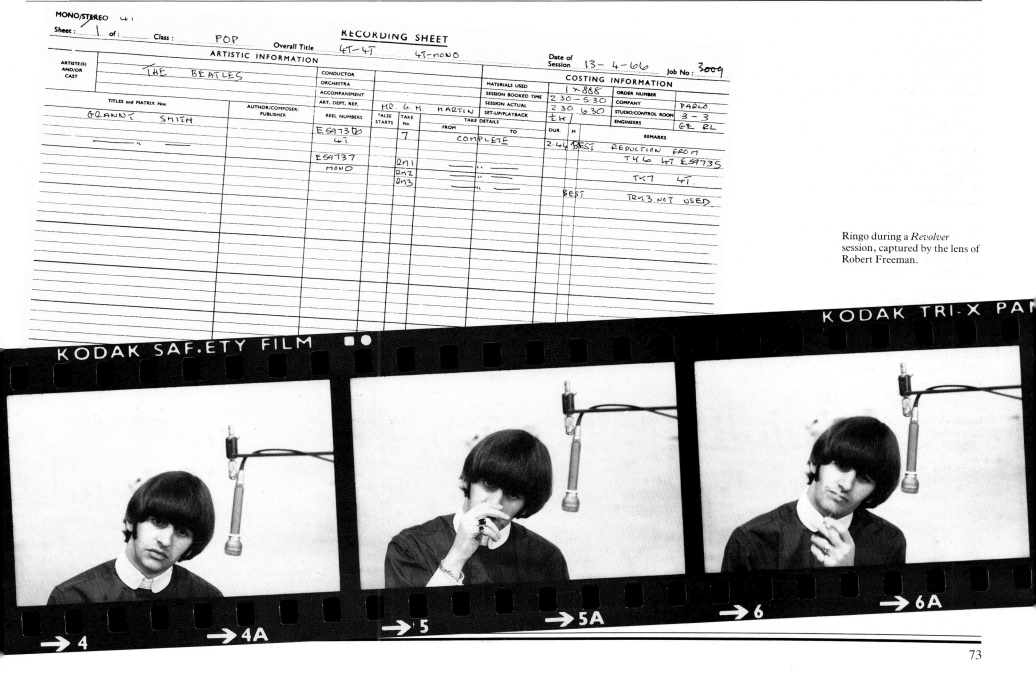

Ringo during a *Revolver* session, captured by the lens of Robert Freeman.

Thursday 14 April

Studio Three: 2.30-7.30pm. Recording: 'Paperback Writer' (SI onto take 2). Studio Three (control room only): 7.30-8.00pm. Mono mixing: 'Paperback Writer' (remixes 1 and 2, from take 2). Studio Three: 8.30pm-1.30am. Recording: 'Rain' (takes 1-5). P: George Martin.   E: Geoff Emerick.   2E: Phil McDonald.

Neither of this day's two songs made it onto *Revolver*, instead making up both sides of a pre-LP single, but both were chock-full of all of the *Revolver* technological advancements: limiters, compressors, jangle boxes, Leslie speakers, ADT.

There had for some time been puzzlement at Abbey Road as to why records cut in America sounded so much better than British cuts. The bass content in particular was greatly diminished on British records. Jerry Boys has a clear recollection of John Lennon demanding to know why the bass on a certain Wilson Pickett record far exceeded any Beatles disc. Certainly one has to listen very intently to hear Paul McCartney's bass playing on Beatles records pre-1966. But on 'Paperback Writer' all that changed. In fact, the bass is the most striking feature of the record.

"'Paperback Writer' was the first time the bass sound had been heard in all its excitement," says Geoff Emerick. "For a start, Paul played a different bass, a Rickenbacker. Then we boosted it further by using a loudspeaker as a microphone. We positioned it directly in front of the bass speaker and the moving diaphragm of the second speaker made the electric current." This was another invention of Ken Townsend's – but he paid the price, being called in to the office of Bill Livy, chief technical engineer, and reprimanded for matching impedances incorrectly!

From his disc-cutting experience, Emerick knew that record companies were loathe to press a million copies of a record if the high bass content was likely to make the stylus jump. Tony Clark, yet another top engineer and producer in later years, cut the master lacquer of 'Paperback Writer'. "It was EMI's first high-level cut and I used a wonderful new machine just invented by the backroom boys, ATOC – Automatic Transient Overload Control. It was a huge box with flashing lights and what looked like the eye of a Cyclops staring out at you. But it did the trick. I did two cuts, one with ATOC and one without, played them to George Martin and he approved of the high-level one."

The other song recorded today was 'Rain'. "One of the things we discovered when playing around with loops on 'Tomorrow Never Knows' was that the texture and depth of certain instruments sounded really good when slowed down," recalls Geoff Emerick. "With 'Rain' the Beatles played the rhythm track really fast so that when the tape was played back at normal speed everything would be so much slower, changing the texture. If we'd recorded it at normal speed and then had to slow the tape down whenever we wanted to hear a playback it would have been much more work."

Playing with backwards tapes on 'Tomorrow Never Knows' had a far reaching effect. "*Revolver* very rapidly became the album where the Beatles would say 'OK, that sounds great, now let's play it backwards or speeded up or slowed down'," says Emerick. "They tried everything backwards, just to see what things sounded like." But apart from satisfying the Beatles' permanent quest for new sounds, backwards tapes have a strong appeal for the listener. "It's because of the enveloping of sound," says Tony Clark. "It draws you in. It's like someone putting their arms around you."

'Rain' features not just instruments slowed down but slowed down vocals too. John's lead on take five of the song, the first to feature vocals, was recorded at 42 cycles per second. Tape machines usually ran at 50. Hence when John's vocal was played back it sounded very fast indeed, halfway to Mickey Mouse. "An offshoot of ADT was that we had a big audio oscillator to alter the frequency of the tape machines," says Emerick. "We would drive it through a power amp and the power amp would drive the capstan wheel and enable you to speed up or slow down the machine at will. John – or George if it was his song – used to sit in the control room on mixes and actually play the oscillator." Again, now that the discovery had been made, few recordings on *Revolver*, or indeed *Sgt Pepper's Lonely Hearts Club Band*, would be spared this new vari-speed technique.

But 'Rain' has one other notable feature – backwards John Lennon vocals in the short reprise at the very end of the song. John always claimed this as his contribution but George Martin remembers it differently. "I was always playing around with tapes and I thought it might be fun to do something extra with John's voice. So I lifted a bit of his main vocal off the four-track, put it onto another spool, turned it around and then slid it back and forth until it fitted. John was out at the time but when he came back he was amazed. Again, it was backwards forever after that."

Phil McDonald's scribbled note detailing the progression and the experiments of the 'Paperback Writer' recording.

Saturday 16 April

Studio Two: 2.30pm-1.30am. Recording: 'Rain' (SI onto take 5, tape reduction take 5 into take 6, takes 7-8). Mono mixing: 'Rain' (remixes 1-4, from take 7). P: George Martin. E: Geoff Emerick. 2E: Phil McDonald.

Eleven hours completing 'Rain', first superimposing tambourine, bass and more vocals, then doing a tape-to-tape reduction to add more overdubs, then producing four mono remixes with plenty of added ADT, the third of which was deemed suitable for disc.

Note. 'Rain' was not remixed for stereo until 2 December 1969.

Sunday 17 April

Studio Two: 2.30-10.30pm. Recording: 'Doctor Robert' (takes 1-7). P: George Martin. E: Geoff Emerick. 2E: Phil McDonald.

A reasonably gimmick-free day, the Beatles recording John's new composition about a certain New York doctor, Charles Roberts, who – it was said – was in the habit of administering hallucinogenic drugs to friends from his 48th Street practice. It was the Beatles' first direct musical reference to drugs.

Only the backing track was recorded on this day: lead guitar, rhythm guitar, bass guitar and drums, plus maracas (played by George), harmonium (by John) and piano (by Paul). The vocals were superimposed on 19 April. At this early stage the song was 2'56" long but in remixing (and there were several of these) it was always edited down to 2'13".

Tuesday 19 April

Studio Two: 2.30-12.00pm. Recording: 'Doctor Robert' (SI onto take 7). Mono mixing: 'Doctor Robert' (remixes 1-3, from take 7). P: George Martin. E: Geoff Emerick. 2E: Phil McDonald.

Vocal overdubs for 'Doctor Robert' and three mono remixes.

Wednesday 20 April

Studio Two: 2.30pm-2.30am. Recording: 'And Your Bird Can Sing' (takes 1-2); 'Taxman' (takes 1-4). Mono mixing: 'And Your Bird Can Sing' (remixes 1-5, from take 2). P: George Martin. E: Geoff Emerick. 2E: Phil McDonald.

A twelve-hour session producing two takes of one song and four of another – nothing of which was ever released in this form.

This day's two takes of 'And Your Bird Can Sing' captured the strident guitar work of the version which was to end up on *Revolver* but that is where the similarity ended. Take one of the song was the rhythm track only, guitars and drums, and it was unrecognisable in this form from the song which finally evolved. Take two, the 'best' for now, had innumerable overdubs, there being at least three Lennon vocals, two McCartney harmony vocals and one from George, plus additional tambourine and bass. The tape also captured hysterical laughter by John and Paul during one of the overdubs, developing into impromptu whistling by the song's end.

Despite making five remixes the song was soon discarded in favour of a re-make on 26 April.

Also recorded on this day were four rhythm track takes of George Harrison's superb new song 'Taxman'. Only two were complete, and at the conclusion of the fourth there was much discussion, caught on tape, about how the song might best be structured. When it was picked up again the next day they started afresh with a new take one.

"Can we please get on with some work?" George Martin waits patiently while Paul and John record the session for posterity.

Thursday 21 April

Studio Two: 2.30pm-12.50am. Recording: 'Taxman' (takes 1-11). P: George Martin.   E: Geoff Emerick.   2E: Phil McDonald.

Takes one through to ten concentrated solely on the rhythm track, the first vocals being introduced at take 11. But although, by this time, the song was close to completion, there were several differences between this and the final version. The "one, two, three, four" spoken count-in had yet to evolve, as had the "Mister Wilson, Mister Heath" refrain sung by John and Paul. In place of the latter was, at this point, a very fast and very high "Anybody gotta bit of money?" sung three times over by John and Paul in a style not dissimilar to that adopted by 1970s group 10CC on some of their hits. The other major difference at this stage was the absence of the rasping lead guitar solo at the end of the song. Here it came to a full ending on three strums of a guitar. (The end solo was in fact a tape copy of the middle eight piece, edited together on 21 June at the final mono and stereo remix stage.)

Friday 22 April

Studio Two: 2.30-11.30pm. Recording: 'Taxman' (tape reduction take 11 into take 12, SI onto take 12); 'Mark I' (working title of 'Tomorrow Never Knows') (SI onto take 3). P: George Martin.   E: Geoff Emerick.   2E: Phil McDonald.

Overdubbing of a cowbell and the "Mister Wilson, Mister Heath" parts onto take 12 of 'Taxman', a reduction mix of take 11. One final superimposition was recorded on 16 May.

Two further overdubs for 'Mark I' ('Tomorrow Never Knows') were taped before this session ended: a whining sitar played by George and an additional Lennon vocal, again put through a Leslie speaker.

Monday 25 April

Abbey Road, Room 65: 10.00-11.00am. Mono mixing: 'Got To Get You Into My Life' (remixes 1 and 2, from take 8). P: n/a.   E: Peter Vince.   2E: n/a.

Rough mono remixes, without echo, for the purpose of cutting acetates. When remixing proper commenced, on 18 May, those were also numbered one and two.

Tuesday 26 April

Studio Two: 2.30pm-2.45am. Recording: 'And Your Bird Can Sing' [re-make] (takes 3-13, SI onto take 10). P: George Martin. E: Geoff Emerick. 2E: Phil McDonald.

"Okay boys, quite brisk, moderato, foxtrot!" Under this somewhat confusing directive from maestro John Lennon the Beatles launched into the re-make of 'And Your Bird Can Sing'. The first attempt, take three, although only a rhythm track, was a *very* heavy recording but the song grew progressively lighter after that, although guitars were always well to the fore. A playback at the end of the 13th take revealed that take 10 had been the best. With Phil McDonald having spooled back the tape the remainder of the session was then spent overdubbing John's lead vocal, with Paul and George backing.

An interesting blend of lead guitar strumming and Paul's bass guitar notes ended the song, and the best version of this section came at the conclusion of take six. Future remixes for the album were edits of the two elements.

Wednesday 27 April

Studio Three (control room only): 6.00pm-11.30pm. Mono mixing: 'Taxman' (remix 1, from take 12); 'And Your Bird Can Sing' (remix 6, from take 10); 'Mark I' (working title of 'Tomorrow Never Knows') (remixes 1-9, from take 3). Studio Three: 11.30pm-3.00am. Recording: 'I'm Only Sleeping' (takes 1-11). P: George Martin. E: Geoff Emerick. 2E: Phil McDonald.

Eleven remixes in one evening – and none was chosen for inclusion on *Revolver*. The Beatles were starting to attend the mix sessions and were making their presence felt. "They found that they could get more control of the sound that they wanted by actually being there for a mix," recalls Phil McDonald. Even so, they still paid little attention to stereo. In fact, to this point, no stereo mixes had been done for any *Revolver* songs.

Just before midnight – an apt time – the Beatles started work on a new song, John's splendidly dreamy 'I'm Only Sleeping'. Again they concentrated on perfecting the rhythm track first, especially as the song was mostly acoustic at this stage, with an extra few bars of strumming starting off the song which were lopped off in the remix.

'I'm Only Sleeping' was eventually to be adorned with elaborate overdubs, done on 29 April and 5 and 6 May.

Thursday 28 April

Studio Two: 5.00-7.50pm. Recording: 'Eleanor Rigby' (takes 1-14, tape reduction take 14 into take 15). P: George Martin. E: Geoff Emerick. 2E: Phil McDonald.

It too was inspired and beautiful. It too – excepting backing vocals – featured just Paul and outside session musicians, no other Beatles. It too was scored by George Martin. But that was where the comparisons ended. 'Eleanor Rigby' was certainly no mere rehash of 'Yesterday'.

Paul McCartney later agreed that, for him, the 1966/67 period was "a pretty hot one". And he is known to favour his work on *Revolver* above most other material. Hardly surprising, really. His contribution to the LP – four of the songs in particular – are outstanding pieces of modern music.

'Eleanor Rigby' is one of those four, the image-conjuring lyric making a perfect marriage with George Martin's great score. Paul attended the session on this day along with John, both sitting up in the studio two control room, conducting their conversations with George Martin via the talkback system, George being down on the studio floor conducting the musicians. This time there were eight – a double string quartet. Tony Gilbert was first violinist, leading Sidney Sax, John Sharpe and Jurgen Hess. The violas were played by Stephen Shingles and John Underwood and the cellists were Derek Simpson and Norman Jones.

Stephen Shingles has a rather caustic memory of the session: "I got about £5 [ie the standard Musicians' Union session fee which was £9] and it made billions of pounds. And like idiots we gave them all our ideas for free." This may be a teensy injustice to George Martin's pre-arranged score which, judging by the tape of the session, the musicians adhered to very closely. Indeed Martin is still very proud of his score. "I was very much inspired by Bernard Herrmann, in particular a score he did for the Truffaut film *Farenheit 451*. That really impressed me, especially the strident string writing. When Paul told me he wanted the strings in 'Eleanor Rigby' to be doing a rhythm it was Herrmann's score which was a particular influence."

Once again the question of vibrato was raised, and it led to an amusing incident. Between takes one and two George Martin asked the players if they could play without vibrato. They tried two quick versions, one with, one without – not classified as takes – and at the end George called up to Paul McCartney "Can you hear the difference?" "Er...not much!" Ironically, the musicians could and they favoured playing without, which must have pleased Paul.

Even with cellos and violins, Paul and Geoff Emerick wanted to get a sound different from any previously wrought from the instruments since gramophone had been invented 68 years previously. The secret was in the microphone technique. "On 'Eleanor Rigby' we miked very very close to the strings, almost touching them," says Emerick. "No one had really done that before; the musicians were in horror."

The eight instruments were recorded across all four tracks of the tape, two per track, so the last job of the day was to mix this down and leave room for Paul's vocal to be overdubbed onto a newly vacated track. The reduction was numbered take 15.

Friday 29 April

Studio Three: 5.00pm-1.00am. Recording: 'Eleanor Rigby' (SI onto take 15). Mono mixing: 'Eleanor Rigby' (remixes 1-3, from take 15). Recording: 'I'm Only Sleeping' (SI onto take 11). P: George Martin. E: Geoff Emerick. 2E: Phil McDonald.

The first task of this session was for Paul to overdub peerless vocals onto 'Eleanor Rigby', double-tracked in places in order to provide harmonies. John and George contributed a few "aah, look at all the lonely people" refrains and the song was complete. Until, that is, another vocal was added on 6 June. Three mono remixes were made today, the third being deemed 'best', but the 6 June overdub made these redundant and a new mix was done on 22 June for inclusion on the LP.

After 'Eleanor Rigby' John overdubbed his lead vocal onto the tape of the previously recorded 'I'm Only Sleeping'. It was the first of three superimposition sessions for the song. On this occasion the tape machine was run at 45 cycles instead of 50, thus speeding up John's voice quite considerably on playback. Just to complicate matters further, the rhythm track onto which John's vocal was superimposed was taped at 56 cycles and played back at 47¾.

Thursday 5 May

Studio Three: 9.30pm-3.00am. Recording: 'I'm Only Sleeping' (SI onto take 11). P: George Martin.   E: Geoff Emerick.   2E: Phil McDonald.

The Beatles had decided to adorn 'I'm Only Sleeping' with the sound of backwards guitars. There are two ways of recording backwards instruments, one easy, one difficult. The easy way is to play the instrument normally and then turn the tape around. The other involves working out the notation forwards, writing it out backwards, then playing it as the notation says, so

that it comes out back to front. This way, although the sound still has the aural attraction of a backwards tape the instrument is actually playing a melodic run of notes.

The Beatles, of course, chose the latter alternative, hence this near six hour session for just the guitar

overdub. In fact, they made it doubly difficult by recording two guitar parts – one ordinary, one a fuzz guitar – which were superimposed on top of one another. Geoff Emerick recalls that this was all George Harrison's idea and that he did the playing.

Friday 6 May

Studio Two 2.30pm-1.00am. Recording: 'I'm Only Sleeping' (SI onto take 11, tape reduction take 11 into takes 12 and 13). Studio Two: (control room only): 1.00-2.15am. Mono mixing: 'I'm Only Sleeping' (remixes 1-4, from take 13) P: George Martin.   E: Geoff Emerick.   2E: Phil McDonald.

Another full day spent on 'I'm Only Sleeping', with added vocal harmonies by John, supported by Paul

and George, reduction mixes to create space for yet more overdubs, and rough remixes.

Monday 9 May

Studio Two: 7.00-11.00pm. Recording: 'For No One' (takes 1-10). P: George Martin.   E: Geoff Emerick.   2E: Phil McDonald.

Ten takes of another superbly crafted Paul McCartney ballad, 'For No One'. The first nine consisted of the rhythm track only, Paul playing piano and Ringo the drums. On the 10th take, the one they felt was best, Paul overdubbed a clavichord (hired, at a cost of five guineas, from George Martin's AIR company) and Ringo additional cymbals and maraca. Paul's lovely

vocal was recorded as an overdub on 16 May and the song's equally lovely French horn solo was overdubbed on 19 May.

There was no role for either John or George in the recording of 'For No One'.

Thursday 12 May

Studio Three (control room only): 1.45-3.30pm. Mono mixing: 'Doctor Robert' (remix 4, from take 7); 'I'm Only Sleeping' (remix 5, from take 13); 'And Your Bird Can Sing' (remixes 7 and 8, from takes 10 and 6). Editing: 'And Your Bird Can Sing' (of mono remixes 7 and 8); 'Doctor Robert' (of remix mono 4). P: George Martin. E: Geoff Emerick. 2E: Jerry Boys.

By making *Help!* a seven-song Beatles album and by reducing *Rubber Soul* to 12 songs (two of those refugees from the British *Help!* LP) Capitol Records had, by 1966, almost enough material to compile a new album of songs unissued in the US to that time. Almost. There were eight available, three more would be ideal. An application was made for three of the new *Revolver* recordings to be sent across for release a few

months earlier than planned. The answer was positive and the mono remixes on this day were made for just such a purpose.

The album, "*Yesterday*". . . *and Today* was issued by Capitol on 20 June 1966 but these three songs were later to be given improved remixes for the British *Revolver* LP so there were some slight differences between the two.

Monday 16 May

Studio Two: 2.30pm-1.30am. Recording: 'Taxman' (SI onto take 12). Tape copying: 'Granny Smith' (working title of 'Love You To') (copies of remix mono 3, numbered mono remixes 4 and 5). Mono mixing: 'Taxman' (remixes 2-5, from take 12). Recording: 'For No One' (SI onto take 10, tape reduction take 10 into takes 13 and 14 [no takes numbered 11 or 12]). Tape copying: 'Taxman' (of remix mono 4); 'Granny Smith' (working title of 'Love You To') (of remix mono 5); 'Mark I' (working title of 'Tomorrow Never Knows') (of remix mono 8). P: George Martin.   E: Geoff Emerick.   2E: Phil McDonald.

A day of overdubs and mixing and, for the purposes of assembling a master reel, of copying some of the best mixes to date. 'Taxman' finally received its "One, two, three, four" intro and Paul overdubbed the lead vocal onto take 10 of 'For No One', recorded at 47½ cycles to make it faster on replay.

None of the four mono mixes of 'Taxman' was ever used.

Wednesday 18 May

Studio Two: 2.30pm-2.30am. Recording: 'Got To Get You Into My Life' (SI onto take 8, tape reduction take 8 into takes 9-11, SI onto take 9). Mono mixing: 'Got To Get You Into My Life' (remixes 1 and 2, from take 9). P: George Martin.   E: Geoff Emerick.   2E: Phil McDonald.

A full day working on Paul's 'Got To Get You Into My Life'.

Eight good takes of the rhythm track had already been recorded (on 8 April) so the task before the group on this day was to overdub the vocals and any extra instruments. There were a number of the latter for Paul had decided that this should be the first Beatles song to feature a strong brass section. Eddie Thornton was one of the five recruits. "I was playing with Georgie Fame and the Blue Flames so I knew the Beatles – John and Paul particularly – from the studios and also from the London night club scene. In fact Paul met Linda Eastman when he was at the Bag O'Nails Club watching us perform. But it was at the Scotch [of St James – the night club] that Paul asked me to do this session with them."

Another of the Blue Flames, tenor sax player Peter Coe, got the job because the group's baritone player, Glenn Hughes, fell sick on the morning of the session. "Georgie [Fame] called me so I rushed up to the EMI Studios. Because I play tenor sax it meant having two tenors instead of a tenor and baritone."

The full line-up of musicians was Thornton (Super-olds trumpet), Coe (tenor sax) and three freelancers, not from the Blue Flames, Ian Hamer and Les Condon (trumpets) and Alan Branscombe (tenor sax). "The Beatles wanted a definite jazz feel," recalls Coe. "Paul and George Martin were in charge. There was nothing written down but Paul sat at the piano and showed us what he wanted and we played with the rhythm track in our headphones. I remember that we tried it a few times to get the feel right and then John Lennon, who was in the control room, suddenly rushed out, stuck his thumb aloft and shouted 'Got it!'. George Harrison got a little bit involved too but Ringo sat playing draughts in the corner."

News of the session leaked out to the press and the names of all five musicians were featured in the pop newspapers in early June. "That led to a lot of extra work for me," says Thornton. "Through working with the Beatles I played wih Jimi Hendrix, Sandie Shaw, the Small Faces and the Rolling Stones."

Geoff Emerick had a clear hand in the recording of the brass. "They were very closely miked for probably the first time – the mikes were right down in the bells of the instruments and then we limited the sound to hell! Prior to this people always miked brass something like six feet away".

The original four-track tape was now full but the vocals previously recorded were no longer thought suitable so they were removed during a tape-to-tape reduction mixdown (actually it was done three times to get the optimum mix, but the first attempt was best). With this done, Paul superimposed a fresh – and sensational – vocal onto the tape, backed by John and George, and then, in another overdub, guitars were superimposed.

The song complete, two mono remixes were made and the 12-hour session was at an end.

Thursday 19 May

Studio Three: 7.00-11.00pm. Recording: 'For No One' (SI onto take 14). P: George Martin.   E: Geoff Emerick.   2E: Phil McDonald.

Alan Civil was the principal horn player in the Philharmonia. "George Martin rang me up and said 'We want a French horn obligato on a Beatles song, can you do it?' I knew George from his very early days at EMI because I'd been doing a lot of freelance work then. So I turned up at Abbey Road and all the bobbysoxers were hanging around outside and trying to look through the windows.

"I thought the song was called 'For Number One' because I saw 'For No One' written down somewhere. Anyway, they played the existing tape to me, which was complete, and I thought it had been recorded in rather bad musical style, in that it was 'in the cracks', neither B-flat nor B-major. This posed a certain difficulty in tuning my instrument. Paul said 'We want something there. Can you play something that fits in?' It was rather difficult to actually understand exactly what they wanted so I made something up which was middle register, a baroque style solo. I played it several times, each take wiping out the previous attempt.

"My friends would ask 'What have you done this week?' and I would say 'Oh, I played wih Otto Klemperer and Rudolf Kempe' – that didn't mean anything to them. But to say that you'd played with the Beatles was amazing. The day would almost go into their diaries as being the day they met someone who'd played with the Beatles. Even now, while only a few people come up to me and say 'I do like your Mozart horn concertos' so many others say 'See that big grey-haired old chap over there? – he played with the Beatles!'. For me it was just another day's work, the third session that day in fact, but it was very interesting."

Note. The Beatles spent most of this day in Abbey Road's huge studio one, shooting promotional film clips for the two sides of their imminent single, 'Paperback Writer' and 'Rain'.

Friday 20 May

Studio One (control room only): 11.00am-12.30pm. Stereo mixing: 'And Your Bird Can Sing' (remixes 1 and 2, from takes 10 and 6); 'Doctor Robert' (remixes 1 and 2, from take 7); 'I'm Only Sleeping' (remixes 1 and 2, from take 13). Editing: 'And Your Bird Can Sing' (of stereo remixes 1 and 2); 'Doctor Robert' (of stereo remixes 1 and 2). P: George Martin.   E: Geoff Emerick.   2E: Phil McDonald.

The first set of stereo mixes for *Revolver* or, rather, for *"Yesterday"*. . . *and Today* and *Revolver*. Since the job involved working from the original four-track tapes George Martin decided that the British remixes may as well be done simultaneously.

But still the mixes were not always identical, Capitol Records receiving remix one of both 'Doctor Robert' and 'I'm Only Sleeping' whereas remixes two of both songs were favoured for the UK. The two mixes of 'And Your Bird Can Sing' were the same.

Thursday 26 May

Studio Three: 7.00pm-1.00am. Recording:'Yellow Submarine' (takes 1-4, tape reduction take 4 into take 5). P: n/a.   E: Geoff Emerick.   2E: Phil McDonald.

There are today two views of 'Yellow Submarine', as there were in 1966. It's either a weak Salvation Army band style singalong or a clever and contagious piece of pop music guaranteed to please the kids, the grannies and plenty others besides.

'Yellow Submarine' was written by John and Paul for Ringo's vocal contribution to *Revolver*. As the group was no longer recording cover versions of other material, and as Ringo had yet to produce any convincing compositions of his own, this was the only way.

Whatever one's opinion of 'Yellow Submarine', one thing is clear: it is a very interesting recording, crammed full of sound effects, party noises, whoops, chants and general silliness. On this day, 26 May, the Beatles recorded the framework of the song – four takes of the rhythm track – and then overdubbed the main vocals. Take five was a tape-to-tape reduction of take four, ready for the later superimposition of the many and varied sound effects.

"I have a clear memory of them doing the rhythm track of 'Yellow Submarine', " says Geoff Emerick, "because George Martin was off with a bad bout of food poisoning and he sent his wife Judy [to be, they married on 24 June 1966] along instead to keep an eye on things, and I suppose to make sure we all behaved ourselves! She sat in George's place at the console making sure that the Beatles got everything they wanted."

Whether it was because of George's absence or not, rehearsals – not recordings – took up most of the session. Just before they launched into take one proper John Lennon, ever the impatient Beatle in the studio, exclaimed "Come on. It's 20 to 10 [ie 9.40] and we still haven't made us a record!" That take one, like all of the rhythm track takes, had a much longer introduction than was eventually released on disc, with acoustic guitar (John), bass guitar (Paul) and tambourine (George) all preceding Ringo's drums and the part of the song where the lyrics would come in.

Take four had the best rhythm track so is it was onto this that all of this day's vocals were superimposed. Ringo's lead – and the backing sung by John, Paul and George – was recorded at 47½ cycles in order that it be speeded up on replay.

The song's other variation at this stage from what would be released on record was a full, rounded ending. On record it was faded out.

The press made them out to be deadly rivals. In truth, the Beatles and the Rolling Stones were good friends. Here Mick Jagger pops in on a Beatles remix for *Revolver*.

Wednesday 1 June

Studio Two: 2.30pm-2.30am. Recording:'Yellow Submarine' (SI onto take 5). P: George Martin.   E: Geoff Emerick.   2E: Phil McDonald.

Sessions don't come much more unusual than this one – the sound effects superimpositions for 'Yellow Submarine'.

Just inside the doorway of studio two at Abbey Road there is a small room cum cupboard called the trap room which houses a many and varied collection of assorted oddments – everything from a cash till to old hosepipes and a football supporter's rattle. Its stock has been sadly depleted over the years but in 1966 it was full to overflowing with such items. The Beatles decided to raid it and almost all of the effects on 'Yellow Submarine' came from there. "The cupboard had everything," remembers Geoff Emerick, "chains, ships bells, hand bells from wartime, tap dancing mats, whistles, hooters, wind machines, thunder-storm machines. . . everything."

Studio staff were brought in to join the fun. John Skinner and Terry Condon were given the task of making whooshing noises. "There was a metal bath in the trap room," says Skinner, "the type people used to bathe in in front of the fire. We filled it with water, got some old chains and swirled them around. It worked really well. I'm sure no one listening to the song realised what was making the noise."

"They had a whole crowd of people in to do the effects," says Emerick. "Brian Jones of the Rolling Stones was there chinking glasses, Marianne Faithfull, Pattie Harrison [George's wife]." These three – and others like George Martin, Neil Aspinall, Mal Evans and the four Beatles – all lent their voices to the song's increasingly raucous choruses. "There was one particular shout that John did," recalls Geoff Emerick. "The door to the echo chamber behind studio two was open so he went and sat there, singing all that 'Full speed ahead Mister Captain' stuff at the top of his voice." After the recording was over Ken Townsend remembers Mal Evans marching around the studio wearing a huge bass drum on his chest, with everyone else in line behind him, conga-style, singing "We all live in a yellow submarine"!

The original tape reveals that overdubs of the effects were plastered throughout the song, although they were only used sporadically on the record. John Lennon blew bubbles in a bucket, and outside session musicians – their names alas lost – were brought in to play traditional brass band instruments.

Ironically, one of the most remarkable overdubs – the one which took the most time to plan and record – never made it onto the finished article. It was a spoken passage by Ringo for the beginning of the song, faded up into the acoustic guitar intro and lasting for as long as 31 seconds. It consisted of at least four separate superimpositions, dominated by Ringo's speaking voice but aided and abetted by George, Paul and John all doing likewise, mixed into one mélange. The theme of the lesson was the walk from Land's End to John O' Groats. [The southernmost tip of England to the northernmost tip of Scotland.] "And we will march to free the day to see them gathered there, from Land O'Groats to John O'Green, from Stepney to Utrecht, to see a yellow submarine. . . ."

Superimposed underneath Ringo's voice while he was saying those words over and over again was the sound of marching feet, not too dissimilar to the sound which John Lennon used to open his 1971 song 'Power To The People'.

It was a most peculiar overdub, although why the Beatles chose to discard it after they had injected such effort is not known. Indeed it is not too clear why they did it in the first place.

"The Land O'Groats to John O'Green bit might have come about because there was a doctor, Barbara Moore I think her name was, who had walked from Land's End to John O'Groats for charity," says Geoff Emerick. "Everyone was talking about her then. As for the sound of marching feet, they did that by putting coal in a cardboard box and sliding it from side to side."

Thursday 2 June

Studio Two: 7.00pm-3.30am. Recording:'Laxton's Superb' (working title of 'I Don't Know', a working title of 'I Want To Tell You') (takes 1-5, SI onto take 3, tape reduction take 3 into take 4). Mono mixing: 'Yellow Submarine' (remix 1, from take 5). P: George Martin.   E: Geoff Emerick.   2E: Phil McDonald.

George Harrison, in securing an unprecedented three compositions on a 14 song Beatles album, was clearly having problems with his song titles. What was in the end to become 'Love You To', itself a title not mentioned in the lyric, had the working title of 'Granny Smith', after the brand of apple. Now, for the song 'I Want To Tell You', the problem evidently arose again, hence this burst of chat on the session tape prior to the recording of take one.

George Martin: "What are you going to call it, George?"
George [who doesn't know]: "I don't know".
John: "Granny Smith Part Friggin' Two! [To George H] You've never had a title for any of your songs!"

In a burst of laconic wit, engineer Geoff Emerick came up with a title, 'Laxton's Superb', another type of British apple. [It was incorrectly spelt on the tape box as 'Laxstone Superbe'] If it was to be 'Granny Smith Part Friggin' Two" then 'Laxton's Superb' fitted the bill perfectly. But midway through the 3 June session the title changed again, this time to the more appropriate 'I Don't Know', humorously based on George's answer to George Martin's original question. By the 6 June remix it had become 'I Want To Tell You'.

As for the recording, five takes of the rhythm track (piano, drums, guitars) were taped before George chose the third as being best and went back to overdub his lead vocal, backed by John and Paul. More instruments – tambourine, maracas and more piano – were also added. A tape-to-tape reduction copy was then made and was numbered (somewhat confusingly) take four. Handclaps were added to this and the song was complete except for a final overdub on 3 June. A quick recording.

"One really got the impression that George was being given a certain amount of time to do his tracks whereas the others could spend as long as they wanted," says Geoff Emerick. "One felt under more pressure when doing one of George's songs."

Friday 3 June

Studio Two: 7.00pm-2.30am. Recording: 'Laxton's Superb' (also 'I Don't Know', both working titles of 'I Want To Tell You') (SI onto take 4). Mono mixing: 'Laxton's Superb' (also 'I Don't Know', both working titles of 'I Want To Tell You') (remixes 1-4, from take 4); 'Yellow Submarine' (remixes 1-5, from take 5). P: George Martin. E: Geoff Emerick. 2E: Phil McDonald.

One final overdub for the song which, during the course of this day, was to become 'I Don't Know'. It was, for the first time on a Beatles recording, a bass guitar superimposition only, something which would become more commonplace during and after 1967. Overdubbing the bass separately, and affording it a vacant track on the four-track tape, allowed greater dexterity with the sound in the remix.

Once Paul's bass overdub was complete the song was given four remixes, though the first attempt was deemed 'best'. 'Yellow Submarine' was also mixed for mono on this day, numbered one to five. [The remix one done the previous night was only a 'rough remix' so it was overlooked when allocating numbers to the new mixes.] One of the first decisions at this stage was to discard Ringo's spoken "Land O'Groats to John O'Green" intro.

Monday 6 June

Studio Three (control room only): 7.00-12.00pm. Tape copying: 'I Want To Tell You' (two copies of remix mono 1, numbered mono remixes 5 and 6). Mono mixing: 'And Your Bird Can Sing' (remixes 9 and 10, from takes 10 and 4); 'For No One' (remixes 1-6, from take 14); 'I'm Only Sleeping' (remixes 5 and 6, from take 13); 'Tomorrow Never Knows' (remixes 10-12, from take 3). Studio Three: 12.00pm-1.30am. Recording: 'Eleanor Rigby' (SI onto take 15). P: George Martin. E: Geoff Emerick. 2E: Phil McDonald.

The fourth anniversary of the Beatles' first visit to EMI's Abbey Road studios, celebrated with an evening of *Revolver* remixing and one final late-night vocal overdub by Paul on 'Eleanor Rigby'.

Remix 11 of 'Tomorrow Never Knows', now no longer 'Mark I', was marked out as the new 'best' and was cut-out for the the master tape of the album. But on the day the LP went into the cutting room, 14 July, George Martin telephoned Geoff Emerick and had him replace it with the original 'best', remix eight.

(Note. Remixes five and six of 'I'm Only Sleeping' should have been numbered six and seven.)

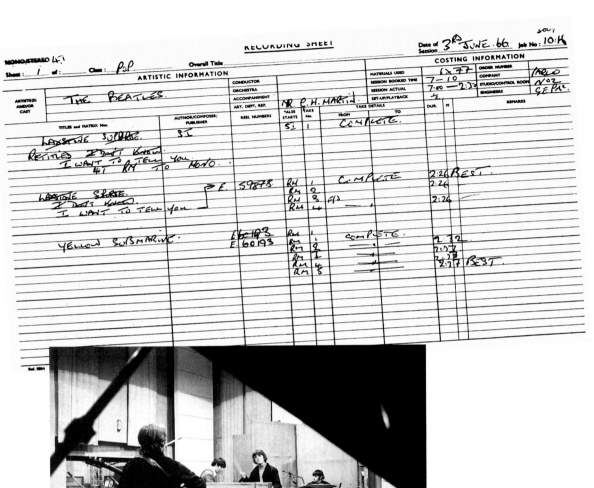

The Beatles recorded much of *Revolver* in Studio Three.

Wednesday 8 June

Studio Two (control room only): 1.00-2.00pm. Editing: 'And Your Bird Can Sing' (of mono remixes 9 and 10). P: n/a. Geoff Emerick. 2E: n/a. Studio Two: 2.30pm-2.30am. Recording: 'A Good Day's Sunshine' (working title of 'Good Day Sunshine') (takes 1-3). P: George Martin. E: Geoff Emerick. 2E: Richard Lush.

One of the quickest recordings on *Revolver:* Paul's 'Good Day Sunshine' (at this point titled 'A Good Day's Sunshine'). The version released on the LP was actually take one, although it had numerous overdubs and could in no way be compared with the truly live take one Beatles recordings of 1963 and 1964.

After a long period of taped rehearsal the group recorded three proper takes of the rhythm track – bass guitar, piano and drums. With take one being 'best' they then spooled back to record an overdub of Paul's lead vocal with John and George backing. More overdubs and drop-ins would also be taped the following day, 9 June.

Thursday 9 June

Studio Two: 2.30-8.00pm. Recording: 'A Good Day's Sunshine' (working title of 'Good Day Sunshine' (SI onto take 1). Mono mixing: 'A Good Day's Sunshine' (working title of 'Good Day Sunshine') (remixes 1-6, from take 1). P: George Martin. E: Geoff Emerick. 2E: Phil McDonald.

A return to more civilised studio hours for the completion of 'Good Day Sunshine' by way of a series of overdubs and drop-ins. Ringo added more drums, particularly the sound of cymbals, and George Martin played a honky-tonk piano solo for the song's middle eight with the tape machine running at 56 cycles per second. All four Beatles then added handclaps and John, Paul and George taped some extra harmonies for the very end of the song. (A close listen to the record reveals the drop-in about nine seconds before the song ends.)

Six remixes were made before home-time, the first of the end vocal overdub only, the other five of the complete song. The sixth was deemed 'best' at this stage but the version which ended up on disc was a new mix done on 22 June, erroneously numbered remix two.

Friday 10 June

Single release: 'Paperback Writer'/'Rain'. Parlophone R 5452.

Twenty-seven weeks had elapsed between the release of the 'Day Tripper'/'We Can Work It Out' single and this, the Beatles' first release of 1966. The original George Martin and Brian Epstein master plan of four singles and two albums per year was now in tatters.

The British sales of 'Paperback Writer' were the lowest for any Beatles single since 'Love Me Do' – but it still sailed to the top of the charts, as it did in all countries. But more important than the figures was the content, the two songs. Both would have fitted snugly onto *Revolver*. Neither would have fitted any previous Beatles' work. The Beatles' music was progressing more rapidly than ever.

Tuesday 14 June

Studio Two: 7.00pm-2.00am. Recording: 'Here, There And Everywhere' (takes 1-4). P: George Martin. E: Geoff Emerick. 2E: Phil McDonald.

Paul McCartney had already shown himself extremely adept at writing beautiful ballads, but they don't come any better than this gorgeous piece of music, 'Here, There And Everywhere'. It has long been Paul's own favourite.

The song was perfected in sessions spread over three days, and on this day four takes were recorded. Just one of those – the fourth – was complete and even then it used only two of the four tracks available. But it was the first to feature any vocal work, the result of a drop-in and at least one overdub. Paul had yet to record his lead but here he was joined by John and George for a take of the charming backing vocals, the highly melodic "oohs" and "aahs". These early takes were faster than the version released on disc, with the vocals speeded up to match.

The great charm of 'Here, There And Everywhere' was undoubtedly its terrific vocal harmonies, shared by Paul, John and George. But although this talent was largely innate it did need promoting, and Geoff Emerick knows where the help came from. "George's [Martin] real expertise was and still is in vocal harmony work, there's no doubt about that. That is his forte, grooming and working out those great harmonies."

George himself is more modest, especially about 'Here, There And Everywhere'. "The harmonies on that are very simple, just basic triads which the boys hummed behind and found very easy to do. There's nothing very clever, no counterpoint, just moving block harmonies. Very simple to do ... but very effective."

Thursday 16 June

Studio Two: 7.00pm-3.30am. Recording: 'Here, There And Everywhere' (takes 5-13, tape reduction take 13 into take 14, SI onto take 14). P: George Martin. E: Geoff Emerick. 2E: Phil McDonald.

The best part of a further nine hours on 'Here, There And Everywhere', with nine more takes and overdubs onto the best rhythm track, take 13.

The sumperimpositions included a second set of lovely backing vocal harmonies by John, Paul and George plus Paul's bass guitar, again occupying a separate track on the tape. When added to the existing acoustic guitar, finger clicks, drums and delicate brushed-cymbals work by Ringo, all four tracks of the tape were full. So this was then reduced to three in a tape-to-tape copy and Paul's lead vocal, slowed down on the tape to sound speeded up on playback, was overdubbed onto the vacant track.

Friday 17 June

Studio Two: 7.00pm-1.30am. Recording: 'Here, There And Everywhere' (SI onto take 14); 'Got To Get You Into My Life' (SI onto take 9). Mono mixing: 'Got To Get You Into My Life' (remixes 3-7, from take 9); 'Here, There And Everywhere' (remix 1, from take 14). P: George Martin. E: Geoff Emerick. 2E: Phil McDonald.

Two final superimpositions. 'Here, There And Everywhere' received an additional Paul McCartney vocal overdub, backing his own lead, and an extra guitar passage was overdubbed onto 'Got To Get You Into My Life'.

This latter SI rendered unusable the previous best mix of the song so five more were produced, the new best being the final one, numbered seven. 'Here, There And Everywhere', meanwhile, received its first remix, later to be improved upon for record release.

Monday 20 June

**Studio One (control room only): 6.00-8.30pm. Mono mixing and recording: 'Got To Get You Into My Life' (tape copy of remix 7 into remix 8 with SI added from take 8).
P: George Martin.   E: Geoff Emerick.   2E: Phil McDonald.**

During the additional mono remixing of 'Got To Get You Into My Life', late at night on 17 June, it was decided that the song's brass section needed beefing up a little. This was done by making a copy of remix seven (calling it remix eight) and then superimposing, fractionally out of sync [synchronisation], the instruments from the original session tape of the 18 May brass overdub.

With this work the song was finally perfect and no further overdubbing or mixing (other than the stereo version) was needed.

Tuesday 21 June

**Studio Three (control room only): 10.00am-1.00pm. Stereo mixing: 'Granny Smith' (working title of 'Love You To') (remixes 1-3, from take 7). Editing: 'Granny Smith' (working title of 'Love You To') (of stereo remixes 1-3). Stereo mixing: 'I Want To Tell You' (remixes 1 and 2, from take 4); 'Here, There And Everywhere' (remixes 1 and 2, from take 14). Mono mixing: 'Here, There And Everywhere' (remixes 2 and 3, from take 14). Studio Three (control room only): 2.30-6.30pm. Mono mixing: 'For No One' (remixes 7 and 8, from take 14); 'Doctor Robert' (remixes 4-6, from take 7); 'Taxman' (remixes 5 and 6, from take 12). Editing: 'Doctor Robert' (of remix mono 6); 'Taxman' (of mono remixes 5 and 6). Stereo mixing: 'For No One' (remix 1, from take 14); 'Taxman' (remixes 1 and 2, from take 12). Editing: 'Taxman' (of stereo remixes 1 and 2). Studio Two: 7.00pm-3.45am. Recording: 'Untitled' (working title of 'She Said She Said') (takes 1-3, tape reduction take 3 into take 4, SI onto take 4). Mono mixing: 'She Said She Said' (remixes 1-3, from take 4). P: George Martin.
E: Geoff Emerick.   2E: Phil McDonald.**

An exceptionally hectic day completing *Revolver*, with the taping of the album's 14th and final track plus mono and stereo mixing galore. (Note. Mono remixes four to six of 'Doctor Robert' should have been numbered five to seven. Mono remixes five and six of 'Taxman' should have been numbered six and seven.)

The new song, John's 'She Said She Said', was untitled at the beginning of the recording session but titled by the end. The lyric recounted the story of an LSD drug trip John had experienced with actor Peter Fonda. With such lines as "...who put all those things in your head/Things that make me feel like I'm mad/And you're making me feel like I've never been born" it is a wonder that the public at large did not realise that substances other than blood were now coursing through the Beatle veins. But it was to remain ignorant for another year, at least.

It took just shy of nine hours to record 'She Said She Said', the group spending most of the time rehearsing through at least 25 takes. Then the recording proper began, with three takes of the rhythm track (in this instance drums, bass and two guitars). Take three was the 'best' so the lead vocal (John) and backing (John and George) were overdubbed onto this. A reduction mix vacated one of the four tracks where an additional guitar and an organ part (played by John) were soon taped. The song now complete, three mono remixes were done, though none made it onto the finished album – that was remix four, from 22 June.

Wednesday 22 June

Studio Three (control room only): 7.00pm-1.30am. Mono mixing: 'Eleanor Rigby' (remixes 4 and 5, from take 15); 'She Said She Said' (remix 4, from take 4); 'Good Day Sunshine' (remix 7, from take 1). Stereo mixing: 'Eleanor Rigby' (remix 1, from take 15); 'She Said She Said' (remix 1, from take 4); 'Good Day Sunshine' (remix 1, from take 1); 'Yellow Submarine' (remixes 1 and 2, from take 5); 'Tomorrow Never Knows' (remixes 1-6, from take 3); 'Got To Get You Into My Life' (remix 1, from take 9). P: George Martin.   E: Geoff Emerick.   2E: Jerry Boys.

Final mono and stereo remixing for the LP.

Friday 5 August

Single release: 'Eleanor Rigby'/'Yellow Submarine'. Parlophone R 5493. LP release: *Revolver*. Parlophone PMC 7009 (mono)/PCS 7009 (stereo). A: 'Taxman'; 'Eleanor Rigby'; 'I'm Only Sleeping'; 'Love You To'; 'Here, There And Everywhere'; 'Yellow Submarine'; 'She Said She Said'. B: 'Good Day Sunshine'; 'And Your Bird Can Sing'; 'For No One'; 'Doctor Robert'; 'I Want To Tell You'; 'Got To Get You Into My Life'; 'Tomorrow Never Knows'.

Revolver is the album which, by common consent, shows the Beatles at the peak of their creativity, welding very strong, economical but lyrically incisive song material with brave studio experimentation. Today, in the late 1980s, it remains one of those rare albums which is able to retain its original freshness and vitality. *Revolver* is a pop masterpiece.

Hindsight also affords us the opportunity to see *Revolver* as the vital plateau between the Beatles' touring activities and what was to become known as their 'studio years'. Although the group had been immensely productive at Abbey Road since 1962, recording the best and most evocative songs of the era, their output had always been worked around other activities, principally inter-continental concert tours, films and marketing strategies like four singles per year and an album at Christmas.

But the Beatles had grown to loathe their concert appearances, sub-30 minute blasts to a distant sea of Beatlemaniacs, forever stifled by screams of adoration through which only rarely could they hear themselves play. In the recording studio the Beatles were striving increasingly for innovation and perfection. On stage they were injecting the basic minimum of care, playing out of time and tune and fluffing lyrics. Worse still, they knew that if their audience *could* hear the screaming and adulation would not diminish one jot because the fans were there merely to pay homage to the group, not hear the music. For four rapidly growing musicians it was an anathema they could no longer bear.

The Beatles' very last concert tour commenced in Chicago on 12 August 1966. As ludicrous as it may seem by today's standards – where most artistes tour only to promote a new album – the Beatles did not perform a solitary song from *Revolver*, released just four days earlier in the USA (and just seven days earlier in the UK). 'Paperback Writer' was included but that was the only concession to 1966, the other songs including 'I Wanna Be Your Man', 'Long Tall Sally' and 'Baby's In Black', all a mere two or three years old but an eternity in the history of Beatles recordings. The problem was that three guitars and a drum kit couldn't possibly reproduce 'Tomorrow Never Knows' on stage.

The punning *Revolver* was just one of a number of potential album titles the Beatles toyed with before they cabled EMI with their final decision from Japan [where they were giving concerts] on 2 July. It could have been 'Abracadabra' but that had already been used by someone else. 'Magic Circles' and 'Beatles on

Safari' were other alternatives.

Both *Revolver* and the single 'Eleanor Rigby'/'Yellow Submarine' were number one hits worldwide. The latter was another double A-sided disc, Ringo thus securing his first lead vocal on a UK Beatles single.

Another eye-catching sleeve: *Revolver*, designed by friend and fellow Brian Epstein-managed musician Klaus Voormann.

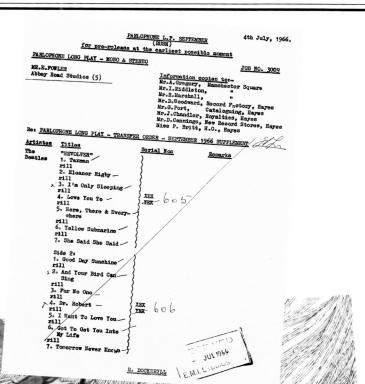

Monday 31 October

Studio One (control room only): 2.30-4.30pm. Stereo mixing: 'Paperback Writer' (remixes 1-3, from take 2). P: George Martin.   E: Geoff Emerick.   2E: Phil McDonald.

When Brian Epstein let it be known to EMI that there would be no new Beatles album available for the Christmas market, and maybe not even a single, EMI took the opportunity to release the first British 'greatest hits' compilation. (It wasn't issued in the US.) The title was *A Collection Of Beatles Oldies*, the reverse of the album sleeve adding the phrase 'But Goldies!'.

The LP was issued in both mono and stereo formats but since some of the songs had never been mixed for stereo – principally Beatles singles, which were released in mono until 1969 – a series of remix sessions were set up. None were attended by as much as a solitary Beatle.

This was the first such session, George Martin planning to remix 'Paperback Writer', 'I Want To Hold Your Hand' and 'She Loves You' in three hours. But 'Paperback Writer' alone took two hours so the others were left for another time.

Monday 7 November

Studio One (control room only): 2.30-5.30pm. Stereo mixing: 'I Want To Hold Your Hand' (remix 1, from take 17). P: George Martin.   E: Geoff Emerick.   2E: Mike Stone.

The third stereo remix of 'I Want To Hold Your Hand', incorrectly numbered as one. Clearly neither of the two previous attempts – 21 October 1963 and 8 June 1965 – had been satisfactory.

Clearly too, the task of remixing old songs was proving more of a handful than was first considered.

George Martin booked the studio on this day to remix three songs, 'She Loves You', 'I Want To Hold Your Hand' and 'From Me To You'. In the end 'She Loves You' was left to the next day and 'From Me To You' was never done. The album's stereo mix of this song is simply the original two-track tape, rhythm on the left channel, vocals on the right. [Keen students of the Beatles' output will be aware that the mono single and stereo LP versions differ, the mono being the only one to have harmonica in the introduction. This was because the single included a harmonica edit piece which was overlooked during the preparation of this album. The 14 March 1963 stereo mix of 'From Me To You' had already been scrapped.]

Tuesday 8 November

Abbey Road, Room 53: 4.00-5.30pm. Stereo mixing: 'She Loves You' (remixes 1 and 2, from single's master tape). P: n/a.   E: Geoff Emerick.   2E: n/a.

For all of his technical skill there was little that Geoff Emerick could do with 'She Loves You'. The original two-track tapes had long been destroyed and all that existed was the mono master tape of the single.

Emerick spent 90 minutes fabricating a 'mock stereo' version of the song – remix two was the 'best' – merely by slashing all of the top frequencies from the left channel to give a bassy sound and slashing all bass from the right channel, giving a trebly, tinny sound. Together they formed the best 'stereo' that could be achieved.

Thursday 10 November

Abbey Road, Room 65: 2.00-4.30pm. Stereo mixing: 'This Boy' (remixes 1 and 2, from takes 15 and 17); 'Day Tripper' (remix 2, from take 3); 'We Can Work It Out' (remix 2, from take 2). Editing: 'This Boy' (of stereo remixes 1 and 2). P: n/a.   E: Peter Bown.   2E: Graham Kirkby.

The final set of stereo mixing. 'Day Tripper' was re-done because the 26 October 1965 remix was not considered good enough. 'We Can Work It Out' was re-done because the original stereo remix, never used, had been scrapped on 9 August 1966.

'This Boy', conversely, from 1963, was treated to its first stereo remix because of a mistake. When the album line-up was dictated by telephone from Manchester Square to Abbey Road someone inadvertently called 'Bad Boy' 'This Boy'. The Abbey Road people, being efficient, had the original four-track tape of 'This Boy' out of the library and remixed before the mistake was spotted.

The error was rectified before the disc cutting stage and the mixes of 'Bad Boy' from 10 May 1965 were used for the mono and stereo LPs.

```
PARLOPHONE L.P.  "A BEATLES COLLECTION OF OLDIES"        9th November, 1966.
Artist:                    THE BEATLES
Release:                        December 1966
Cover & Back:             Mr. Dunton has this in hand
                          Produced by George Martin

SIDE 1.        1)  "SHE LOVES YOU"
               2)  "FROM ME TO YOU"
               3)  "WE CAN WORK IT OUT"
               4)  "HELP!"
               5)  "MICHELLE"
               6)  "YESTERDAY"
               7)  "I FEEL FINE"
               8)  "YELLOW SUBMARINE"

SIDE 2.        1)  "CAN'T BUY ME LOVE"
               2)  "BAD BOY"
               3)  "DAY TRIPPER"
               4)  "A HARD DAY'S NIGHT"
               5)  "TICKET TO RIDE"
               6)  "PAPERBACK WRITER"
               7)  "ELEANOR RIGBY"
               8)  "I WANT TO HOLD YOUR HAND"

               All Songs composed Lennon-McCartney
               and published Northern Songs

                                          GEORGE H. MARTIN
```

Thursday 24 November
Studio Two: 7.00pm-2.30am. Recording: 'Strawberry Fields Forever' (take 1). P: George Martin.   E: Geoff Emerick.   2E: Phil McDonald.

And so the Beatles entered the new phase of their career. No longer the tidy, smiling 'Fab Four', singing boy/girl pop songs on stage. Now they were casually dressed, sometimes mustachioed, smiling-when-they-wanted-to-be-Beatles who would make the greatest ever batch of rock recordings at and for their merest whim, strictly *not* for performing on stage.

The Beatles had scarcely spent a day together since early September, each embarking on solo projects for the first time. Now they had decided to reunite and start the recording of a new album. 'Strawberry Fields Forever' was the first song to be taped although, of course, it was later whipped away for a single and never appeared on a Beatles LP apart from compilations put together outside of the group's direct control.

'Strawberry Fields Forever' captured in one song everything the Beatles had learned in the four years spent inside recording studios, especially 1966, with its backwards tapes, its use of vari-speed and its use of uncommon musical instruments. And it could only have been born of a mind (John Lennon's) under the influence of outlawed chemicals. Strawberry Field is a Salvation Army home in Liverpool, round the corner from where John was brought up. He went there for summer fêtes. 'Strawberry Fields Forever' evokes those childhood memories through a dreamy, hallucinogenic haze. It was, and still is, one of the greatest pop songs of all time.

Of all Beatles recordings, 'Strawberry Fields Forever' is known for being among the most complicated and difficult to record. It is also known that the song changed shape in the studio not once but several times. Both facts are certainly true. Take one, recorded on this night, was not only *magnificent* but as far removed from the final version as possible, the only similarity between it and the record being the song's mellotron introduction. This instrument was the precursor of the string synthesiser and it contained tapes which could be 'programmed' to imitate another instrument, in this instance a flute. "I remember when the Beatles first brought in the mellotron," says Jerry Boys. "It was made mostly for producing sound effects but it also had flutes, brass and string sounds on it. The Beatles used it in a way nobody had ever thought of." "It was a new instrument then," recalls Geoff Emerick. "John had one of the first ones, in a polished wooden cabinet. In the end the Musicians' Union tried to stop manufacture because of the way it reproduced the sounds of other instruments."

During the course of this long and highly inventive evening the Beatles recorded the rhythm track, and a good many overdubs, for take one of the song. By the end of the night it sounded like this: simultaneous with the mellotron, played by Paul, was John's first – and stunning – lead vocal, followed by George's guitar, Ringo's distinctive drums (with dominant use of tomtoms), maracas, a luscious slide guitar piece, John's double-tracked voice and scat harmonies by John, Paul and George. The song came to a full-ending with the mellotron. The entire take was recorded at 53 cycles per second so that it sounded faster on replay but still it lasted only 2'34".

Any lingering doubt about whether or not the Beatles had changed would have crumbled into a thousand pieces had this version of the song been released. But it wasn't. It remains in the vaults today, a reel of magnetic tape which captured a magic night.

'Strawberry Fields Forever', no less, was the song "to be selected".

John during sessions for *Revolver*.

Friday 25 November

Studio, Dick James House, 71/75 New Oxford Street, London WC1: time unknown. Recording: 'Pantomime: Everywhere It's Christmas' (takes unknown). P: George Martin. E: n/a. 2E: unknown.

A temporary departure from the recording of the next LP for a quick visit to the basement studio below the London office of Dick James Music – the Beatles' music publisher – to record the group's fourth annual

Christmas disc for its official fan club.

This recording bears no relation to the Beatles' proper studio work and is included here only for the sake of completeness. Precise details of the session, take

numbers etc, do not exist but the disc – in the form of a pantomime – featured ten separate items including the title song, sung (briefly) by all four Beatles with Paul on piano.

Monday 28 November

Studio Two: 7.00pm-1.30am. Recording: 'Strawberry Fields Forever' (takes 2-4). Mono mixing: 'Strawberry Fields Forever' (remixes 1-3, from take 4). P: George Martin. E: Geoff Emerick. 2E: Phil McDonald.

Back to Abbey Road for more work on 'Strawberry Fields Forever'. For the first time there was no real pressure on the Beatles to deliver a product to a preset deadline. They could, and would, work on a song until they and only they were satisfied with it,

irrespective of time.

One of the three takes of 'Strawberry Fields Forever' recorded today, number three, was a false start. The other two were rhythm track recordings with

overdubs, featuring mellotron, drums, several guitars, bass and maracas. Take four was the temporary 'best' so not only was it given a speeded-up Lennon vocal overdub it was also the subject of three rough remixes for acetate cutting purposes.

Tuesday 29 November

Studio Two: 2.30-8.00pm. Recording: 'Strawberry Fields Forever' (takes 5-6, tape reduction take 6 into take 7, SI onto take 7). Mono mixing: 'Strawberry Fields Forever' (remixes 1-3, from take 7). P: George Martin. E: Geoff Emerick. 2E: Phil McDonald.

Takes five and six of 'Strawberry Fields Forever' were more attempts at recording the rhythm track, growing faster with every session. The first of the two was a false start, the second was complete. John Lennon then overdubbed another experimental vocal and the

entire take was mixed down into take seven, onto which Lennon's vocal was given ADT treatment and more instruments like pianos and bass guitar were superimposed. This take seven was marked 'best', which it was for nine days, but it was hardly the final

version of the song – though that's another story…

Rough remixes, incorrectly numbered again, in this instance one to three, were made of this new 'best', remix three being the one chosen for the cutting of four playback acetate discs.

Friday 2 December

Abbey Road, Room 53: 9.00am-12.00 noon. Mono mixing and editing: 'Pantomime – Everywhere It's Christmas' (from unknown take numbers). P: Tony Barrow. E: Geoff Emerick. 2E: Phil McDonald.

In addition to his post as press officer for Brian Epstein's NEMS Enterprises, Tony Barrow was given the brief of overseeing the production of the annual Christmas flexi-disc for the Beatles' official fan club. In earlier years this meant doing everything from writing the script for the Beatles' "own words" to

liaising with the pressing company, Lyntone Records.

By 1966 the Beatles themselves had assumed the role of script writing but Barrow still continued his other responsibilities. On this day he was logged on the studio recording sheet as producer, meaning that he

advised Geoff Emerick on the placing and order of the various pantomime skits. George Martin, in charge of the special 25 November recording session, was actually 'producer'.

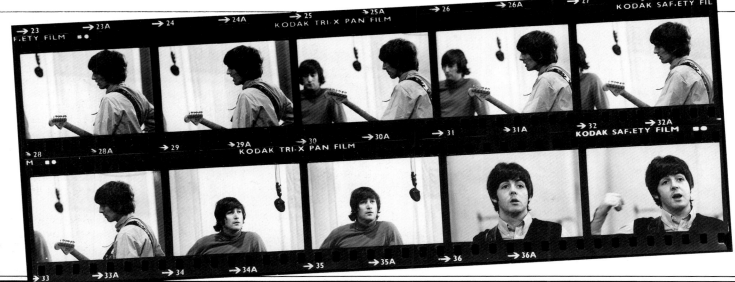

Another Robert Freeman contact sheet, showing the making of *Revolver* in Studio Three, EMI Abbey Road.

Tuesday 6 December

Studio Two: 6.45pm-1.50am. Recording: 'Christmas Messages For Radio London' (takes 1 and 2); 'Christmas Messages For Radio Caroline' (takes 1 and 2); 'When I'm Sixty-Four' (takes 1 and 2). P: George Martin.   E: Geoff Emerick.   2E: Phil McDonald.

The Beatles were fervent supporters and public champions of the so-called 'pirate' radio stations which operated from ships moored off the British coast and had sprung up in the mid-1960s to provide an invaluable alternative to the BBC, still decidedly staid then when it came to the broadcasting of pop music. A disc-jockey from each of the two major pirates, Caroline and London, was even invited to accompany the Beatles during the group's final US tour in August 1966, staying with them as part of the entourage. (For Caroline, Jerry Leighton made the trip, for London it was the zany Liverpudlian and reciprocal Beatles' lover, Kenny Everett.)

To further mark their appreciation of the pirates' efforts, the Beatles taped and had hand-delivered Christmas and New Year goodwill greetings for the staff of the two stations and their listeners. ("Hello, this is John Lennon. All good wishes to everyone everywhere and best of luck for '67!"). These were logged on the tape box and recording sheets as two takes for each station but several dozen short messages were actually recorded.

The greetings were initially spoken unaccompanied but later ones were said above station identification tunes and, later still, some featured the other three Beatles tinkering on studio instruments – any note, any key – behind the Beatle doing the speaking. All of the messages were recorded live although at one point in the proceedings Paul asked George Martin to feed playback tape echo into the studio as they spoke. George replied, with heavy sarcasm, "Do you want to make a production out of it?" George Harrison then chipped in with "Yeah, let's double-track everything!" and John offered his suggestion, "He can double-splange them! That'd be great!"

With the recording of 'Strawberry Fields Forever' finished and complete – or so it was thought – the Beatles now turned their attention to the second song for the next album, Paul's vaudeville-style charmer 'When I'm Sixty-Four'. This was not a new song, the Beatles having performed a variation of it back in their pre-fame Cavern Club days whenever the amplifiers broke down. One plausible reason for the song's revival was that Paul's father, James, had turned 64 years of age in July 1966. The remainder of this session was spent first rehearsing the number and then recording the rhythm track, with Paul playing piano in addition to his normal bass. Two proper takes were taped, both complete, the second being marked 'best'.

Thursday 8 December

Studio One: 2.30-5.30pm. Recording: 'When I'm Sixty-Four' (SI onto take 2). P: George Martin.   E: Geoff Emerick.   2E: Phil McDonald. Studio Two: 7.00pm-3.40am. Recording: 'Strawberry Fields Forever' [re-make] (takes 9-24). Editing: 'Strawberry Fields Forever' (of takes 15 and 24). P: Dave Harries/George Martin.   E: Dave Harries/Geoff Emerick. 2E: Phil McDonald.

"Before the very first recording of 'Strawberry Fields Forever' John stood opposite me in the studio and played me the song on his acoustic guitar. It was absolutely lovely," recalls George Martin. "Then when we actually taped it with the usual instruments it began to get heavy. John didn't say anything but I knew it wasn't what he had originally wanted.

"So I wasn't totally surprised when he came back to me a week or so later and suggested we have another go at recording it, perhaps even bringing in some outside musicians to supplement the Beatles' playing. Together we worked out that I should score the song for trumpets and cellos."

This was that re-made version of 'Strawberry Fields Forever', the cellos and trumpets being added as an overdub on 15 December. But first the Beatles had to tape the new rhythm track. Ironically, both George Martin and Geoff Emerick were absent at the start of the session. "They had tickets for the premiere of Cliff Richard's film *Finders Keepers* and didn't arrive back until about 11 o'clock," says technical engineer Dave Harries, who later became studio manager at George Martin's AIR Studios in London. "Soon after I had lined up the microphones and instruments in the studio that night, ready for the session, the Beatles arrived, hot to record. There was nobody else there but me so I became producer/engineer. We recorded Ringo's cymbals, played them backwards, Paul and George were on timps [timpani] and bongos, Mal Evans played tambourine, we overdubbed the guitars, everything. It sounded great. When George and Geoff came back I scuttled upstairs because I shouldn't really have been recording them."

There was still a very long way to go before 'Strawberry Fields Forever' was ready for record release but Harries' version – or part of it, anyway – was a vital part of that record. "I am very proud of that," says Harries, "it was a very good record. Geoff was moaning because there was a lot of top [treble] on the cymbals. I said it was the only time there'd been top on any Beatles records!"

By the end of the session 15 more takes had been recorded, numbered nine to 24, all of them rhythm only (ie, no vocals). But although nine of those 15 were complete [there was, for some reason, no take numbered 19, nor was there an 8], it was two of the incomplete versions – takes 15 and 24 – which were chosen to take the song into its next stage. Before the end of this long night George Martin and Geoff Emerick edited together the first three-quarters of take 15 with the last quarter of take 24. An attempt to mixdown the two four-track edits into take 25 was started but then aborted for the night, to be continued the next day.

Also done on 8 December, mid-afternoon, was Paul's vocal overdub onto take two of 'When I'm Sixty-Four'. The other Beatles were not present.

December

Friday 9 December

Studio Two: 2.30-10.00pm. Recording: 'Strawberry Fields Forever' (tape reduction from edit of takes 15 and 24 into take 25, SI onto take 25). Mono mixing: 'Strawberry Fields Forever' (remix 4, from take 25). Recording: 'Strawberry Fields Forever' (SI onto take 25). P: George Martin. E: Geoff Emerick. 2E: Phil McDonald.

LP release: *A Collection Of Beatles Oldies*. Parlophone PMC 7016 (mono)/PCS 7016 (stereo). A: 'She Loves You'; 'From Me To You'; 'We Can Work It Out'; 'Help!'; 'Michelle'; 'Yesterday'; 'I Feel Fine'; 'Yellow Submarine'. B: 'Can't Buy Me Love'; 'Bad Boy'; 'Day Tripper'; 'A Hard Day's Night'; 'Ticket To Ride'; 'Paperback Writer'; 'Eleanor Rigby'; 'I Want To Hold Your Hand'.

There was still much overdubbing to be done on 'Strawberry Fields Forever' so to make best use of the limited space on the four-track tape, the previous night's work, the best of which was the edit of takes 15 and 24, was mixed down to just one track and called take 25.

After this it was time to start the series of overdubs for the three vacant tracks. Onto track two Ringo added various bits of percussion, including some decidedly heavy drum sounds, and George added a swordmandel (an Indian instrument, not unlike a table harp). For the purposes of cutting more acetates another quick mono remix was then done before it was back to the overdubbing, this time of yet more backwards cymbals. Rather like the two backward guitar solos in 'I'm Only Sleeping', the taping of the cymbals was no easy task. The pattern was worked out in the normal manner but it was then written down in reverse so that when recorded and the tape was played backwards the sounds would fit the bars precisely.

The 16-song album *A Collection Of Beatles Oldies* was released on this day. The only new track for British Beatles fans was 'Bad Boy', first released in the USA on 14 June 1965. The inclusion of the song on this otherwise hit-packed collection ensured that all Beatles recordings from 1962 to date were available on both sides of the Atlantic.

Thursday 15 December

Studio Two: 2.30-12.00pm. Recording: 'Strawberry Fields Forever' (SI onto take 25, tape reduction take 25 into take 26, SI onto take 26). Mono mixing: 'Strawberry Fields Forever' (remixes 5-9, from take 26). P: George Martin. E: Geoff Emerick. 2E: Phil McDonald.

Four trumpets and three cellos, brilliantly scored by George Martin, provided the distinctive brass and string sound which he and John Lennon had decided was necessary for the re-make of 'Strawberry Fields Forever'. The trumpeters were Tony Fisher, Greg Bowen, Derek Watkins and Stanley Roderick. On cello were John Hall, Derek Simpson and Norman Jones.

The trumpets and cellos were superimposed onto tracks three and four of the four-track tape so once again all four tracks were full and there was another reduction mix, take 25 becoming take 26. Onto this was added two separate recordings of John Lennon's lead vocal, tracks three and four. At the end of the second overdub John Lennon muttered the words "cranberry sauce" twice over. The red acidic berry, famous for complementing roast turkey, had no relevance whatsoever to the song and John's utterance cannot be satisfactorily explained beyond the point that it was just 'typical John Lennon'. One "cranberry sauce" (two on some foreign pressings of the song) even made it onto the finished single, if you listen hard enough. [Further deflating silly Beatles myths, John most certainly did not say "I buried Paul"!]

By the end of the evening the re-make of 'Strawberry Fields Forever' had taken on an intensity of almost frightening proportion. With its frantic strings, blaring trumpets, very heavy drum sound and two manic, exceptionally fast Lennon vocals it was far removed from the original, acoustic take one of the song recorded on 24 November. Would John be satisfied with it now? For the time being, at least, it was labelled 'best' and was thus subjected to more remixing.

Tuesday 20 December

Studio Two: 7.00pm-1.00am. Recording: 'When I'm Sixty-Four' (SI onto take 2, tape reduction take 2 into takes 3 and 4). P: George Martin. E: Geoff Emerick. 2E: Phil McDonald.

Paul McCartney, George Harrison and John Lennon's backing vocal superimposition onto 'When I'm Sixty-Four', with Ringo adding the sound of bells, followed by a reduction mix from take two into takes three and four, the latter being the better.

Wednesday 21 December

Studio Two: 7.00-9.00pm. Recording: 'When I'm Sixty-Four' (SI onto take 4). Studio Two (control room only): 9.00-10.00pm. Mono mixing: 'When I'm Sixty-Four' (remixes 1-3, from take 4). Studio Two: 10.00-11.45pm. Recording: 'Strawberry Fields Forever' (SI onto take 26). P: George Martin. E: Geoff Emerick. 2E: Phil McDonald.

More overdubbing on the two songs which had dominated all sessions since 24 November, 'When I'm Sixty-Four' and 'Strawberry Fields Forever'. The overdub for the former was of three clarinets – two ordinary, one a bass clarinet – played by recruited musicians Robert Burns, Henry MacKenzie and Frank Reidy. For the latter it was yet more vocals by John Lennon and another piano track.

Three mono remixes of 'When I'm Sixty-Four' were made, the 'best' being the third attempt, although it was for demo use only, not the final record.

Thursday 22 December

Studio Two: 7.00-11.30pm. Mono mixing: 'Strawberry Fields Forever' (remix 10, from take 7, and remix 11, from take 26). Editing: 'Strawberry Fields Forever' (of mono remixes 10 and 11, edit numbered remix 12). P: George Martin. E: Geoff Emerick. 2E: Phil McDonald.

"John Lennon told me that he liked both versions of 'Strawberry Fields Forever', the original, lighter song and the intense, scored version," recalls George Martin. "He said 'Why don't you join the beginning of the first one to the end of the second one?' 'There are two things against it,' I replied. 'They are in different keys and different tempos. Apart from that, fine.' 'Well,' he said, 'you can fix it!'"

Here was a prime example of how John's very absence of technical know-how aided his refusal to believe that such feats were not possible. So George Martin and Geoff Emerick came into Abbey Road on 22 December 1966 to see if the Beatle's wish could be complied with.

It could. George and Geoff carefully studied the two versions and realised that if they speeded up the remix of the first version (take seven) and then slowed down the remix of the second (take 26) they might match. They were originally a semitone different. "With the grace of God, and a bit of luck we did it," says Martin. All that was left now was to edit the two pieces together and the song – almost a full month after it was started – was finally finished. "We gradually decreased the pitch of the first version at the join to make them weld together," says Geoff Emerick.

They did it so well that few people, even today, know exactly where the edit is. "That's funny," says George Martin, "I can hear it every time. It sticks out like a sore thumb to me!"

For those who want to know, the edit can be found precisely 60 seconds into the released version of the single, after one of the "let me take you down" lines. But seek it out at your peril: if you hear it once you might never hear the song the same way again.

Thursday 29 December

Studio Three (control room only): 2.30-4.45pm. Mono mixing: 'When I'm Sixty-Four' (remixes 4-7, from take 4). Tape copying: 'Strawberry Fields Forever' (of remix mono 12, numbered remix mono 13). Studio Three (control room only): 4.45-5.40pm. Stereo mixing: 'Strawberry Fields Forever' (remix 1, from take 7, remixes 2 and 4, from take 26). Editing: 'Strawberry Fields Forever' (stereo remixes 1 and 2 edited together as remix 3, stereo remixes 1 and 4 edited together as remix 5). Studio Two: 7.00pm-2.15am. Recording: 'Untitled' (working title of 'Penny Lane') (takes 1-6). Mono mixing: 'Untitled' (working title of 'Penny Lane') (remixes 1 and 2, from take 6). P: George Martin. E: Geoff Emerick. 2E: Phil McDonald.

Interviewed in November 1965 Paul McCartney mentioned that he'd been toying with the idea of writing a song called 'Penny Lane' because he liked the poetry of the name. Penny Lane was, and still is, the name of a road in the suburb immediately to the south of Liverpool city centre, close to where the Beatles grew up.

It took another year for Paul to actually write the song but with its description of the shops and the people and the "blue suburban skies" his 'Penny Lane' was a fine counterpoint to John's 'Strawberry Fields Forever'. Quite why both men – in their typically different ways – should choose to write songs about Liverpool at this point in time, when neither had lived there for more than three years, is not known. But together the two songs would form a dynamite, seemingly thematic, February 1967 single release, although – of course – at this time both were intended for the in-the-works album, not a single.

One of the most distinctive aspects of 'Penny Lane' would be its keyboard sound and this entire evening session saw the recording of these parts. The most important contribution was the main piano piece, so

Paul took great care in perfecting this, recording six takes until he was satisfied, although only the fifth and sixth were seen through to completion. This piano went onto track one of the four-track tape. Happiest with the sixth take he then began to apply the overdubs, working alone in the studio. Onto track two of the tape went another piano, played this time through a Vox guitar amplifier with added reverberation to give an entirely different sound. Onto track three went yet another piano, played at half-speed and then speeded-up on replay to give another different effect. A tambourine was also shaken for this overdub. Superimposed onto track four were two-tone high-pitch whistles from a harmonium, again fed through a Vox guitar amplifier, various strange percussion effects, one of them sounding at times like a machine gun, and extremely fast and sometimes drawn-out cymbal notes.

This was as far as the recording went at this stage. The song was picked up again on 30 December where the next step was to mix these four tracks down to one and then begin the overdubbing process all over again. Two rough mono remixes were made of the recordings done so far.

Earlier in the day, before the new recording, George Martin and Geoff Emerick oversaw more remixing of 'When I'm Sixty-Four' and 'Strawberry Fields Forever'. Four new mono mixes, numbered four to seven, were made of the former, remix six being marked as 'best' for the USA and remix seven being marked 'best' for the UK. (In the end neither was used – see 30 December.) Also made for the North American market was a tape copy of the previous night's final edit mix of 'Strawberry Fields Forever'.

All the mixes of the new songs were mono to this point, so 'Strawberry Fields Forever', being finally complete, was now given its first stereo remix. Remix stereo one was of the first section of the song only, from take seven. Remix two was of the second section only, take 26. Remix three was an edit of remixes one and two. Remix four repeated the work of remix two, the former obviously not quite good enough. Remix five edited together remixes one and four.

Further proof that the Beatles' recordings had become considerably more complicated of late need not be supplied.

Friday 30 December

Studio Two: 7.00pm-3.00am. Mono mixing: 'When I'm Sixty-Four' (remix 8, from take 4). Tape copying: 'Strawberry Fields Forever' (of remix mono 12). Recording: 'Penny Lane' (tape reduction take 6 into take 7, SI onto take 7). Mono mixing: 'Penny Lane' (remixes 1 and 2, from take 7). P: George Martin. E: Geoff Emerick. 2E: Phil McDonald.

The remixes of 'When I'm Sixty-Four' done on 29 December and marked best for the UK and US did not satisfy Paul. He suggested that they scrap all previous mixes and start again, speeding up the new mix to raise it by as much as a semitone, a big difference. Geoff Emerick thinks Paul may have wanted his vocals to take on a more youthful air, as if he were, say, a 16-year-old looking forward to being 64. Certainly when the stereo remix was made, as far away as 17 April 1967, Richard Lush – the tape operator on that session – remembers George Martin being incredulous at how much the mono mix had

been speeded up. "He kept saying 'Surely it can't have been *that* fast'?". It was, and anybody with the luxury of today's vari-speed record turntables or tape machines can hear the song at the right speed if they so wish.

Before continuing with the recording of 'Penny Lane', now no longer 'Untitled', two more mono tape-to-tape copies for the USA were made of 'Strawberry Fields Forever'. Another would be done on 2 January 1967.

On returning to 'Penny Lane' the first task was to

make a reduction mix of the four-track take six, bumping down to just one track on what was called take seven. Onto track four of take seven was overdubbed Paul's lead vocal, backed by John, recorded slow (47½ cycles) so that they sounded speeded up on replay.

It was well into the early hours of the morning by the time these had been taped, so the other overdubs planned for the song had to wait until the next session and another year – 1967. All that was left to do in 1966 was remix 'Penny Lane' as it presently stood for demo purposes. These were again numbered one and two.

Monday 2 January

Studio Two (control room only): 2.30-4.00pm. Tape copying: 'When I'm Sixty-Four' (of remix mono 8); 'Strawberry Fields Forever' (of remix mono 12). P: George Martin. E: Geoff Emerick. 2E: Phil McDonald.

More copies for the USA.

Wednesday 4 January

Studio Two: 7.00pm-2.45am. Recording: 'Penny Lane' (SI onto take 7). P: George Martin. E: Geoff Emerick. 2E: Phil McDonald.

The Beatles returned to the studio with a resumption of the 'Penny Lane' recording; there was still much to add before the song was deemed fit for release. Overdubbed onto track two of take seven was yet another piano part – played by John – and a lead guitar, played by George. Paul added a vocal on track three.

Thursday 5 January

Studio Two: 7.00pm-12.15am. Recording: 'Penny Lane' (SI onto take 7); 'Untitled' (take 1). Mono mixing: 'Untitled' (from take 1). P: George Martin. E: Geoff Emerick. 2E: Phil McDonald.

After overdubbing another McCartney vocal onto 'Penny Lane', replacing the one from the previous evening, the Beatles set to work on the session's main task: preparing a sound effects tape for a 'Carnival of Light', being held at the Roundhouse Theatre, London, later in the month. Paul was the chief instigator behind the commission and he took charge of the creation on tape of the bizarre collection of loops and distortions. Or, as it was described in the press at the time, "a tape of electronic noises".

The Beatles had never made a recording quite like this before, although they were certainly to repeat the exercise again, culminating in 'Revolution 9' on the 1968 double-album *The Beatles*. This day's attempt lasted 13'48", the longest uninterrupted Beatles recording to date, and it was the combination of a basic track and numerous overdubs. Track one of the tape was full of distorted, hypnotic drum and organ sounds; track two had a distorted lead guitar; track three had the sounds of a church organ, various effects (the gargling with water was one) and voices; track four featured various indescribable sound effects with heaps of tape echo and manic tambourine.

But of all the frightening sounds it was the voices on track three which really set the scene, John and Paul screaming dementedly and bawling aloud random phrases like "Are you alright?" and "Barcelona!"

Paul terminated the proceedings after almost 14 minutes with one final shout up to the control room: "Can we hear it back now?" They did just that, a rough mono remix was made and Paul took away the tape to hand over to the 'Carnival of Light' organisers, doubtless pleased that the Beatles had produced for them such an *avant garde* recording.

Geoff Emerick recalls this most unusual session. "When they had finished George Martin said to me 'This is ridiculous, we've got to get our teeth into something a little more constructive'." Twenty years on, George had obviously driven the session entirely from his mind, for when reminded of the sounds on the tape and asked whether he could recall it, he replied "No, and it sounds like I don't want to either!"

Friday 6 January

Studio Two: 7.00pm-1.00am. Recording: 'Penny Lane' (SI onto take 7, tape reduction take 7 into take 8, SI onto take 8, tape reduction take 8 into take 9). P: George Martin. E: Geoff Emerick. 2E: Phil McDonald.

Yet more overdubbing onto the tape of 'Penny Lane': Paul on bass guitar, John on rhythm and Ringo on drums. None of the instruments was taped pure, being heavily limited by engineer Geoff Emerick and recorded at 47½ cycles to speed up on replay. John also overdubbed conga drums, again limited and slowed down.

All four tracks of the tape were full again so a new reduction mix was made, take seven becoming take eight with two vacant tracks. Onto this was overdubbed John and George Martin playing pianos, handclaps and John, Paul and George scat singing at the points where the brass instruments would later be dropped in.

Another reduction mix, take eight becoming take nine, was made before the end of the session, vacating two more tracks of the four-track tape.

The holes in our roads

THERE are 4,000 holes in the road in Blackburn, Lancashire, or one twenty-sixth of a hole per person, according to a council survey.

If Blackburn is typical there are two million holes in Britain's roads and 300,000 in London.

£22 0000

Monday 9 January

Studio Two: 7.00pm-1.45am. Recording: 'Penny Lane' (SI onto take 9). Mono mixing: 'Penny Lane' (remixes 5 and 6, from take 9). P: George Martin. E: Geoff Emerick. 2E: Phil McDonald.

The overdubbing of four flutes and two trumpets and – with three of the six musicians playing extra instruments – two piccolos and a flügelhorn onto 'Penny Lane'. The four flautists were Ray Swinfield, P. Goody, Manny Winters and Dennis Walton and the trumpeters were Leon Calvert and Freddy Clayton.

Two more rough mono remixes were made before the session ended.

Tuesday 10 January

Studio Three: 7.00pm-1.40am. Recording: 'Penny Lane' (SI onto take 9). P: George Martin. E: Geoff Emerick. 2E: Phil McDonald.

Superimpositions of various effects: including scat harmonies and a hand-bell (taken from the trap room and shaken whenever the lyrics mentioned the fireman or his fire-engine).

Thursday 12 January

Studio Three: 2.30-11.00pm. Recording: 'Penny Lane' (SI onto take 9). Mono mixing: 'Penny Lane' (remixes 7 and 8, from take 9). P: George Martin. E: Geoff Emerick. 2E: Phil McDonald.

The second set of classical instrument overdubs onto 'Penny Lane': two trumpets, two oboes, two cor anglais and a double-bass. The trumpeters were Bert Courtley and Duncan Campbell. The oboists, who also doubled with cor anglais, were Dick Morgan and Mike Winfield and the bassist was Frank Clarke.

"They wanted me to play one note over and over, for hours," Clarke recalls.

Tuesday 17 January

Studio Two: 7.00pm-12.30am. Recording: 'Penny Lane' (SI onto take 9). Mono mixing: 'Penny Lane' (remixes 9-11, from take 9). Tape copying: 'Penny Lane' (of remix mono 11). P: George Martin. E: Geoff Emerick. 2E: Phil McDonald.

'Penny Lane' still needed the finishing touch. Paul McCartney realised what it was when he sat watching the second of a five-part, late-night BBC2 television series *Masterworks* at home on the Wednesday evening of 11 January. "He saw me playing Bach's Brandenburg Concerto Number 2 in F Major with the English Chamber Orchestra from Guildford Cathedral," remembers David Mason, recruited for the Beatles session and paid the special Musicians' Union rate of £27 10s for his efforts. "The next morning I got a call and a few days later I went along to the studio. I took nine trumpets along and we tried various things, by a process of elimination settling on the B-flat piccolo trumpet."

True to form, there was no prepared notation for Mason to follow. "We spent three hours working it out," says Mason. "Paul sang the parts he wanted, George Martin wrote them out, I tried them. But the actual recording was done quite quickly. They were jolly high notes, quite taxing, but with the tapes rolling we did two takes as overdubs on top of the existing song. I read in books that the trumpet sound was later speeded up but that isn't true because I can still play those same notes on the instrument along with the record."

Further correcting previous accounts of the story, Mason was never a member of the London Symphony Orchestra. "I was in the New Philharmonia then, now known simply as the Philharmonia, and still am. I've spent a lifetime playing with top orchestras yet I'm most famous for playing on 'Penny Lane'!"

Mason has one other distinctive memory of the session. "Although Paul seemed to be in charge, and I was the only one playing, the other three Beatles were there too. They all had funny clothes on, candy-striped trousers, floppy yellow bow ties etc. I asked Paul if they'd been filming because it really looked like they had just come off a film set. John Lennon interjected 'Oh no mate, we always dress like this!'."

Mason's two trumpet overdubs, his solo in the middle eight and his flourish towards the end of the song, completed the recording of 'Penny Lane', close on three weeks after it had been begun. Three more mono remixes were made before the evening ended, the final edition – remix 11 – being deemed 'best'. A copy of this mix was then made for quick despatch to the USA.

Far left:
John and Paul in Studio Two, the alarm clock vital to the recording of 'A Day In The Life' in the foreground. The *Daily Mail* item which inspired part of the lyric.
The Beatles signed a new nine-year contract with EMI on 27 January 1967, hence it ultimately covered their solo careers up to January 1976.
Left:
Moustaches to the fore! The Beatles with Neil Aspinall and Mal Evans in Studio Two.
Above:
George proudly donning an American anti-Beatles sweatshirt!

Thursday 19 January

Studio Two: 7.30pm-2.30am. Recording: 'In the Life Of . . .' (working title of 'A Day In The Life') (takes 1-4).   P: George Martin.   E: Geoff Emerick.   2E: Phil McDonald.

From little acorns . . . The song which was to become the stunning finale of the Beatles' next album, 'A Day In The Life', started out simply – but no less magnificently – as a stark, bare recording. A clear parallel between take one of 'A Day In The Life' (or 'In The Life Of . . .' as it was on this first day only) and take one of 'Strawberry Fields Forever' can be drawn in that both sowed the seeds of what would become epic recordings, yet at their early stages both were no less beautiful in their simplicity. And both, of course, were John Lennon songs.

Take one of 'A Day In The Life' used just two of the four available tracks: a basic rhythm (bongos, maracas, piano and guitar) on track one and a heavily echoed Lennon vocal on track four. At this stage of the recording the Beatles only knew that *something*

would later be taped for the song's middle eight structure. Precisely what they did not know. But to mark out the place where the unknown item would go they had Mal Evans count out the bars, numbers one to 24. And to enter into the true spirit of the Beatles recordings 1967-style, this laboured counting was plastered with tape echo, increasing with the numbers until by 24 it sounded like he was in a cave. He was also backed by the tinkling of a piano, the notes climbing in tandem with the numbers. To mark the end of the middle eight overdub section an alarm clock was sounded. There was no Paul McCartney vocal yet, merely instruments at the point where his contribution would later be placed, but then John's vocal returned, leading into another Mal Evans one to 24 count and then a single piano – building, building, building, building, stop. Breathtaking stuff indeed.

With take four John began a series of vocal overdubs onto the two vacant tracks, so that by the evening's end the four-track tape included three separate Lennon vocals, all with heavy echo. "There was so much echo on 'A Day In The Life'," recalls Geoff Emerick. "We'd send a feed from John's vocal mike into a mono tape machine and then tape the output – because they had separate record and replay heads – and then feed that back in again. Then we'd turn up the record level until it started to feed back on itself and give a twittery sort of vocal sound. John was hearing that echo in his cans [headphones] as he was singing. It wasn't put on after. He used his own echo as a rhythmic feel for many of the songs he sang, phrasing his voice around the echo in his cans."

Friday 20 January

Studio Two: 7.00pm-1.10am. Recording: 'A Day In The Life' (tape reduction take 4 into takes 5-7, SI onto take 6).   P: George Martin.   E: Geoff Emerick.   2E: Phil McDonald.

Reduction mixes of take four into five, six and seven, each with different console settings. Take six was 'best' and it was overdubbed with another John Lennon vocal, Paul's bass and Ringo's drums.

There was one other new overdub: Paul's vocal contribution, appearing for the first time, and in perfect juxtaposition to John Lennon's. Here was a prime example of how the two songwriters had

evolved: Lennon's song had a beginning and an end but no middle; McCartney's had a middle but no beginning or end. But the two pieces came together like a jigsaw, creating a complete picture and the impression that the two pieces were *intended* as one. The illusion was compounded by the fact that Paul's vocal, the first line of which was "Woke up, fell out of bed", occurred immediately after the alarm clock had been sounded on the original recording to mark the

end of the first 24 bar gap. Making good use of the happy coincidence, the alarm clock was kept on the track permanently.

Actually, Paul re-recorded his vocal on 3 February, instantly wiping out this version. This attempt was just a rough guide, ending on an expletive after he had made an error.

Wednesday 25 January

Studio One (control room only): 6.30-8.30pm. Mono mixing: 'Penny Lane' (remixes 12-14, from take 9). Studio One (control room only): 9.00-10.00pm. Tape copying: 'Penny Lane' (of remix mono 14).   P: George Martin.   E:Geoff Emerick.   2E: Phil McDonald.

The 17 January mono remix of 'Penny Lane', numbered 11, had been considered 'best' and a copy had been sent to Capitol for American pressing. But further thought on the subject resulted in dis-satisfaction with that mix. It had to be improved, so three more mono mixes were made during this evening, the final one – remix 14 – being accepted as

the new 'best' and final master version, the main difference between 14 and 11 being the omission of some David Mason trumpet figures from the very end of the song.

But while it was not too late to substitute new for old in Britain, a few singles using remix 11 had already

been pressed and distributed to US radio stations as advance promotion/broadcast copies, although for the general release the correct mix was used. Those promo copies rank today among the most collectable of all Beatles records.

Monday 30 January

Studio Three (control room only): 7.00-8.30pm. Mono mixing: 'A Day In The Life' (remix 1, from take 6).   P: George Martin.   E: Geoff Emerick.   2E: Richard Lush.

A rough mono remix, for demo purposes only. The Beatles themselves did not attend – they were in Sevenoaks, Kent for the night-time shooting of the 'Strawberry Fields Forever' promotional film. [They would be similarly employed on 31 January, and on 5 and 7 February they made the 'Penny Lane' clip.]

"It's time for tea and *Meet The Wife*". John Lennon's song lyrics could be derived from *any* source.

Wednesday 1 February

Studio Two: 7.00pm-2.30am. Recording: 'Sgt Pepper's Lonely Hearts Club Band' (takes 1-9).   P: George Martin.   E: Geoff Emerick.   2E: Richard Lush.

It wasn't going to be *Sgt Pepper's Lonely Hearts Club Band* until *'Sgt Pepper's Lonely Hearts Club Band'* had come along. That is, the album was not "The Sgt Pepper Project" until the recording of this Paul McCartney song and Paul's realisation soon afterwards that the Beatles could actually pretend they were Sgt Pepper's band, the remaining songs on the LP forming a part of a show given by the fictitious combo.

Nine takes of the rhythm track (drums – with heavy echo – bass and two guitars, one by Paul the other by George) were recorded on this night, and only two of those – one and nine – were seen through to completion. Paul's bass was recorded by direct injection of the sound into the recording console, as opposed to being recorded through an amplifier and a microphone. "I think direct injection was probably used on Beatles sessions for the first time anywhere in the world," says Ken Townsend. "We built our own transformer boxes [called DIT boxes] and plugged the guitars straight into the equipment."

Direct injection, or DI for short, greatly attracted John Lennon, forever keen on short cuts, especially if there was a chance that his vocals might somehow be changed in the process. Stories are legion at Abbey Road of John doing anything to change his voice – a most curious fixation considering that his singing was the envy of all others and is quite properly regarded as being among the best in all rock music. "John came up to the control room one day and asked if we could possibly inject his voice directly into the console," says Geoff Emerick. "George [Martin] replied 'Yes, if you go and have an operation. It means sticking a jackplug into your neck!'"

Thursday 2 February

Studio Two: 7.00pm-1.45am. Recording: 'Sgt Pepper's Lonely Hearts Club Band' (SI onto take 9, tape reduction take 9 into take 10). Mono mixing: 'Sgt Pepper's Lonely Hearts Club Band' (remix 1, from take 10).   P: George Martin.   E: Geoff Emerick.   2E: Richard Lush.

Superimposition of Paul's lead and group backing vocals onto tracks three and four of the 'Sgt Pepper's Lonely Hearts Club Band' tape, followed by a tape-to-tape reduction mix vacating two of the tracks for future overdubs. A demo remix, for acetate purposes, was made of the song as it presently stood.

Friday 3 February

Studio Two: 7.00pm-1.15am. Recording: 'A Day In The Life' (SI onto take 6).   P: George Martin.   E: Geoff Emerick.   2E: Richard Lush.

More overdubs onto take six of 'A Day In The Life' including the re-recorded Paul McCartney vocal. When the Beatles heard the 30 January demo remix of 'A Day In The Life' they must have considered the drum and bass sound unsatisfactory, for they also re-recorded both parts again on this night, wiping out the previous attempt in the process.

Ringo taped his contribution on tomtoms, giving the song a distinctive percussion sound. "That was entirely his own idea," says George Martin. "Ringo has a tremendous feel for a song and he always helped us hit the right tempo first time. He was rock solid and this made the recording of all the Beatles' songs so much easier."

It is true that on only a handful of occasions during all of the several hundred session tapes and thousand of recording hours can Ringo be heard to have made a mistake or wavered in his beat. His work was remarkably consistent – and excellent – from 1962 right through to 1970.

Wednesday 8 February

Studio Two: 7.00pm-2.15am. Recording: 'Good Morning Good Morning' (takes 1-8).   P: George Martin.   E: Geoff Emerick.   2E: Richard Lush.

Eight takes – four of them complete – of the basic rhythm track of John Lennon's new composition 'Good Morning Good Morning', its title inspired by a British television commercial for cornflakes.

By the time the song was readied for release on the LP it had received several overdubs. But at this stage it was a fairly straightforward rhythm recording.

Thursday 9 February

Regent Sound Studio, 164-166 Tottenham Court Road, London W1: time unknown. Recording: 'Fixing A Hole' (takes 1-3).   P: George Martin.   E: Adrian Ibbetson.   2E: unknown.

The first Beatles recording session, expressly for EMI, at a British studio other than Abbey Road. Regent Sound was independently owned, and many a hit record had been taped there including some of the Rolling Stones' earliest hits.

"We couldn't get in to Abbey Road that night," remembers George Martin. "But Regent Sound was a pretty awful little studio, very cramped and boxy." No longer on the EMI staff, Martin was free to travel with the Beatles wherever they were recording. But engineer Geoff Emerick and the usual crew of tape operators were all EMI employees so they couldn't go along, Adrian Ibbetson, chief engineer at Regent Sound, filling the role of Beatles engineer for this 'Fixing A Hole' session. (Procedures have now changed at Abbey Road and staff might be called upon to follow an album project around to any studio.)

After a series of rehearsals (taping at least six unofficial takes), recording of this fine new McCartney composition began in earnest, with three takes of the full song, including vocals – unusual in these days when common Beatles procedure was to tape the rhythm track and overdub vocals later on. The third take was a breakdown but the first two were both very good so onto the tape box was written, rather ambiguously, 'master' for take one and 'final master' for take two. In fact it was only after a little more work had been applied to the song back at Abbey Road on 21 February that the true 'best' emerged, originating from the Regent Sound take two.

The most distinctive instrument on 'Fixing A Hole' was a harpsichord and Neil Aspinall, writing in the magazine *The Beatles Book*, stated that this was played by Paul. But the session tape proves that the harpsichord and bass were played simultaneously so this throws a question mark over Paul's exact role, especially as the bass playing is typical McCartney circa 1967. There is no such query over the identity of the lead guitarist however, George playing his familiar instrument and letting rip on what, for a Beatles song, was an unusually long solo in the middle eight.

Friday 10 February

Studio One: 8.00pm-1.00am. Recording: 'A Day In The Life' (tape reduction take 6 into take 7, SI onto take 7, reduction of take 7 with SI onto take 6, edit piece takes 8-11).   P: George Martin.   E: Geoff Emerick.   2E: Richard Lush.

There can be no doubt that 1967 was a heady year for the Beatles. And 10 February must have ranked as one of the highlights.

It was Paul who decided upon the best way of filling the 24 bar gap in 'A Day In The Life': an orchestral build-up, with perhaps 90 musicians playing from a pre-selected low note to the highest their respective instruments could play. As usual, the task of making this vision a reality fell to George Martin. "At the very beginning I put into the musical score the lowest note each instrument could play, ending with an E-major chord. And at the beginning of each of the 24 bars I put a note showing roughly where they should be at that point. Then I had to instruct them. 'We're going to start very very quietly and end up very very loud. We're to start very low in pitch and end up very high. You've got to make your own way up there, as slide-y as possible so that the clarinets slurp, trombones gliss, violins slide without fingering any notes. And whatever you do, don't listen to the fellow next to you because I don't want you to be doing the same thing.' Of course they all looked at me as though I was mad…" "The orchestra just couldn't understand what George was talking about," says Geoff Emerick, "or why they were being paid to go from one note to another in 24 bars. It didn't make any sense to them because they were all classically trained."

Studio documentation shows that 40 outside musicians were employed [the 39 shown plus one percussionist], their names as follows:
Violin: Erich Gruenberg (leader), Granville Jones, Bill Monro, Jurgen Hess, Hans Geiger, D. Bradley, Lionel Bentley, David McCallum, Donald Weekes, Henry Datyner, Sidney Sax, Ernest Scott.
Viola: John Underwood, Gwynne Edwards, Bernard Davis, John Meek.
Cello: Francisco Gabarro, Dennis Vigay, Alan Dalziel, Alex Nifosi.
Double-bass: Cyril MacArther, Gordon Pearce.
Harp: John Marson.
Oboe: Roger Lord.
Flute: Clifford Seville, David Sandeman.
Trumpet: David Mason, Monty Montgomery, Harold Jackson.
Trombone: Raymond Brown, Raymond Premru, T. Moore.
Tuba: Michael Barnes.
Clarinet: Basil Tschaikov, Jack Brymer.
Bassoon: N. Fawcett, Alfred Waters.
Horn: Alan Civil, Neil Sanders.
Percussion (including timpani): Tristan Fry.

The total cost of the musicians was £367 10s, quite an investment. "It was quite a chaotic session," recalls Alan Civil. "Such a big orchestra, playing with very little music. And the Beatle chaps were wandering around with rather expensive cameras, like new toys,

photographing everything."

Although only 40 musicians were used instead of 90, Paul McCartney got more than he originally requested because the orchestra was recorded four times, on all four-tracks of a tape, and this was then mixed down to one. So he had the equivalent of *160 musicians*. It was clear before the session even began that there might be technical problems and Ken Townsend felt a new invention coming on. "George Martin came up to me that morning and said to me 'Oh Ken, I've got a poser for you. I want to run two four-track tape machines together this evening. I know it's never been done before, can you do it?' So I went away and came up with a method whereby we fed a 50 cycle tone from the track of one machine then raised its voltage to drive the capstan motor of the second, thus running the two in sync. Like all these things, the ideas either work first time or not at all. This one worked first time. At the session we ran the Beatles' rhythm track on one machine, put an orchestral track on the second machine, ran it back did it again, and again, and again until we had four orchestra recordings. The only problem arose sometime later when George and I were doing a mix with two different machines. One of them was sluggish in starting up and we couldn't get the damn things into sync. George got quite annoyed with me actually." George is more forgiving today: "The synchronisation was rather a hit-and-miss affair and the orchestra is slightly out of time in places, but it doesn't matter."

George Martin and Paul McCartney conducted the orchestra, leaving Geoff Emerick to get the sounds down on tape in the correct manner. "It was only by careful fader manipulation that I was able to get the crescendo of the orchestra at the right time. I was gradually bringing it up, my technique being slightly psychological in that I'd bring it up to a point and then slightly fade it back in level without the listener being able to discern this was happening, and then I'd have about 4 dB's in hand at the end. It wouldn't have worked if I'd just shoved the level up to start with."

The recording was made using the unique 'ambiophonics' system of the massive Abbey Road studio one, whereby 100 loudspeakers, fitted symmetrically to all four walls, artificially tailor the acoustics by feeding signals delayed at different intervals, the resulting sound being called 'ambiophony'.

But the technical aspects of the recording tell only half the story. The session was more than anything else an *event*. "The Beatles asked me, and the musicians, to wear full evening dress, which we did," recalls George Martin. "I left the studio at one point and came back to find one of the musicians, David McCallum, wearing a red clown's nose and Erich Gruenberg,

leader of the violins, wearing a gorilla's paw on his bow hand. Everyone was wearing funny hats and carnival novelties. I just fell around laughing!" "I remember that they stuck balloons onto the ends of the two bassoons," says violinist Sidney Sax. "They went up and down as the instruments were played and they filled with air!"

"Only the Beatles could have assembled a studio full of musicians, many from the Royal Philharmonic or the London Symphony orchestras, all wearing funny hats, red noses, balloons on their bows and putting up with headphones clipped around their Stradivari violins acting as microphones," jokes Peter Vince, who – like many of the Abbey Road engineers – attended as a spectator and was highly impressed with what he saw. Tony Clark didn't even bother to go inside the studio; by just standing outside the door he could feel the excitement. "I was speechless, the tempo changes – everything in that song – was just so dramatic and complete. I felt so privileged to be there…I walked out of the Abbey Road that night thinking 'What am I going to do now?' It really did affect me." Malcolm Davies recalls Ron Richards sitting in the corner of the control room with his head in his hands, saying "I just can't believe it…I give up". "He was producing the Hollies," says Davies, "and I think he knew that the Beatles were just uncatchable. It blew him away…"

As Alan Civil noted, the entire session was filmed. In early 1967 the weekly pop music newspapers regularly reported the Beatles' plan to make a television special about the making of *Sgt Pepper's Lonely Hearts Club Band*. It never happened, but the footage shot on this night was to have been the start and it duly captured the craziness of the evening, making for a compelling, if chaotic, little film, with all of the musicians in evening dress, everyone – including John Lennon – wearing silly novelties like upside down spectacles, plastic stick-on nipples, imitation bald heads, red noses, false eyes, fake cigars and knotted handkerchiefs on heads. It also shows George's wife Pattie Harrison and the many friends especially invited along by the Beatles – among them Mick Jagger, Marianne Faithfull, Keith Richard, Mike Nesmith, Donovan and Simon and Marijke of designers the Fool. [Marijke played a tambourine during the orchestral overdub which appeared on the final record.] It shows girl fans being ejected by Neil Aspinall and bubbles floating around the expanse of studio one. Tony Bramwell, an employee of Brian Epstein's NEMS company and in charge of the shooting, remembers the outcome. "It never got shown because the BBC banned the song, thinking it related to drugs. But the party idea was picked up again for the 'All You Need Is Love' broadcast."

It would almost be superfluous to state that the

original tapes of the night's work are immensely absorbing. But they are revealing too, showing how – when the orchestra had packed up and gone home – the Beatles and various friends (at least one female voice is evident) gathered around the studio microphone and attempted to record the song's coda – later a crashing piano chord – which at this stage was going to be a long 'hummmmmm'. "Eight beats, remember" says Paul, leading them into the first take of this edit piece. This and two others (numbered eight to ten) dissolved, understandably, into laughter. But take 11 was good so onto this the ensemble recorded three overdubs, filling the four-track tape. It was undoubtedly a fine idea, and it was to remain the best solution to ending the song until the famous piano chord was recorded on 22 February.

The tapes also reveal how, at the end of the orchestra's tremendous 33½ second build-up near the end of the song, everyone in the studio broke into a spontaneous barrage of applause. This, too, makes for remarkable listening. It must have been a remarkable night in all ways, best summed up by George Martin. "When we'd finished doing the orchestral bit one part of me said 'We're being a bit self-indulgent here'. The other part of me said 'It's bloody *marvellous*!'"

Monday 13 February
Studio Two: 7.00pm-3.30am. Mono mixing: 'A Day In The Life' (remixes 2-5, from take 7). Recording: 'Not Known' (working title of 'Only A Northern Song') (takes 1-9). P: George Martin. E: Geoff Emerick. 2E: Richard Lush.

George Harrison's initial song for *Sgt Pepper's Lonely Hearts Club Band* was 'Only A Northern Song', its title being a wry comment on the fact that it would be published by Northern Songs Ltd, the company 50 per cent owned by Dick James and 50 per cent by John Lennon, Paul McCartney and Brian Epstein's NEMS Enterprises Ltd. George himself was only a contracted songwriter. (Actually, in keeping with George's frequent shortage of songtitles, it was known on this day as 'Not Known'!)

But 'Only A Northern Song' did not end up on *Sgt Pepper*, indeed it didn't show up on record until January 1969 as part of the *Yellow Submarine* film soundtrack album. Once again, Beatles myth has the real story all wrong, one book – basing its "facts" directly from a quote – stating that 'Only A Northern Song' was written very much at the last minute, in the spring of 1968, at 2 o'clock in the morning at Abbey Road "with the London Symphony Orchestra waiting patiently to go home".

There was certainly no London Symphony Orchestra [which the Beatles never contracted anyway] in Abbey Road on this night in February 1967 when the Beatles recorded nine takes of the song's rhythm track – only four complete and the 'best' being take three. Vocals would follow the next day.

Paul holding a playback acetate of one of the latest *Sgt Pepper* mixes.

Tuesday 14 February
Studio Two: 7.00pm-12.30am. Recording: 'Only A Northern Song' (tape reduction take 3 into takes 10-12, SI onto take 12). Mono mixing: 'Only A Northern Song' (remixes 1-3, from take 12). P: George Martin. E: Geoff Emerick. 2E: Richard Lush.

A tape-to-tape reduction of take three to vacate two tracks – done three times to achieve the optimum result, the best being take 12 – and superimposition of two George Harrison lead vocals. Three mono remixes for demo purposes were made, the first being a false start the other two complete.

Thursday 16 February
Studio Three: 7.00pm-1.45am. Recording: 'Good Morning Good Morning' (SI onto take 8, tape reduction take 8 into takes 9 and 10). Mono mixing: 'Good Morning Good Morning' (remix 1, from take 8). P: George Martin. E: Geoff Emerick. 2E: Richard Lush.

Overdubs of vocals and bass guitar onto the basic rhythm recording from 8 February. After a rough remix was made, with ADT applied to John's lead vocal, the four-track tape was subjected to two reduction mixes – the second, numbered 10, being 'best' – ready for more overdubbing, not done for almost a month.

Friday 17 February

Studio Two: 7.00pm-3.00am. Recording: 'Being For The Benefit Of Mr Kite!' (takes 1-7, tape reduction take 7 into takes 8 and 9, SI onto take 9). Mono mixing: 'Being For The Benefit Of Mr Kite!' (remix 1, from take 9).   P: George Martin.   E: Geoff Emerick.   2E: Richard Lush.

Single release: 'Strawberry Fields Forever'/'Penny Lane'. Parlophone R 5570.

John Lennon was very adept at writing songs around contemporary sources or events in his life. A part of the 'A Day In The Life' lyric, first recorded on 19 January, was culled from a 17 January newspaper article. The lyric of 'Being For The Benefit Of Mr Kite!' was derived almost entirely from an original poster advertising a circus near Rochdale, Lancashire in February 1843, bought in an antique shop by Lennon while in Sevenoaks, Kent on 31 January for the filming of the 'Strawberry Fields Forever' promotional clip.

John was also very sure of the title, hence this piece of conversation caught on the original session tape.

Geoff Emerick: "This is 'For The Benefit Of Mr Kite!' take one".
John Lennon: "No. *Being* For The Benefit Of Mr Kite!' "

The first seven takes of the recording were of the rhythm track only: bass, drums and harmonium, but they still managed to convey the right circus atmosphere, especially on the third take, with John dum-dumming the vocal. His first vocal proper was overdubbed onto take seven, the machine running at 49 cycles per second instead of the normal 50. After the take, John – talking to George Martin about future ways of recording the song – could be heard to say "Well, we'll have the Massed Alberts on by then, won't we?" Whether he was being facetious or actually referring to a possible Beatles employment of the Alberts, a somewhat bizarre vocal group produced by George Martin, is not known though certainly the latter event never occurred!

Geoff Emerick has a distinct memory of George Martin playing the harmonium for hours, trying to get the right fairground/circus effect. "You have to pump a harmonium with your feet and he was pumping away for about four hours. He collapsed onto the floor after that, laying there spreadeagled and exhausted!"

Take seven was made into takes eight and nine in a reduction mixdown (the latter was the better), onto which John taped a new lead vocal. The session ended with a rough mono remix of the recording as it presently stood. Studio documents indicate this was taken home by Paul McCartney.

This day, 17 February, saw the UK issue of the single 'Strawberry Fields Forever'/'Penny Lane', the Beatles' third double-A side in four consecutive releases. On the one hand it broke established procedure in Britain, being issued in a limited edition picture sleeve, a most uncommon occurrence in the 1960s. On the other it followed standard 1960s record company practice – the release of the two songs as a single effectively (though it was not always the case) ruling out the opportunity of including the songs on an album. Hence both dropped out of the running for *Sgt Pepper's Lonely Hearts Club Band.*

'Strawberry Fields Forever'/'Penny Lane' is arguably the greatest pop single to be issued by anyone at anytime. Both songs are brilliant and brimful with confidence and high ability. And each is a perfect counterpoint to the other even though they share a similar theme. It was nothing short of high irony that the single should become the Beatles' first in Britain since 'Love Me Do' to fail to reach number one. It sold as many copies as most other Beatles singles but could not overhaul Engelbert Humperdinck's 'Release Me', one of those records which can inexplicably catch on in the pop market, sell millions of copies and stay on the chart for a year.

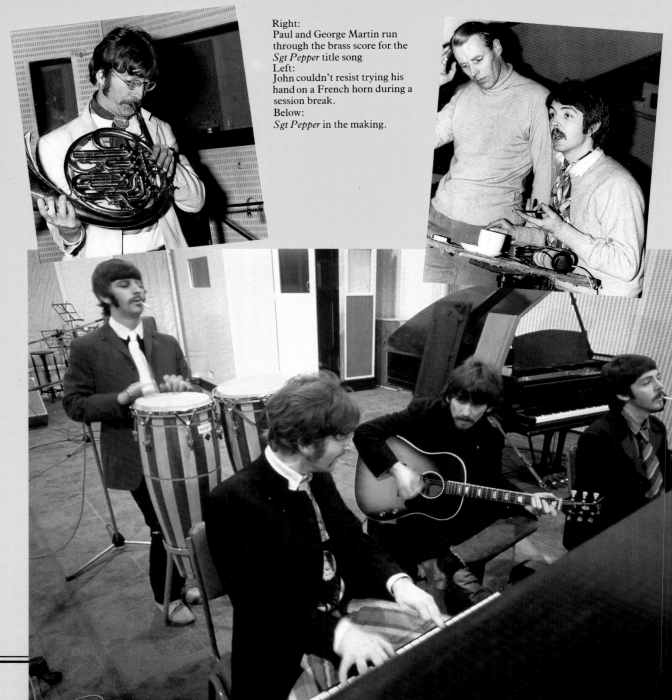

Right:
Paul and George Martin run through the brass score for the *Sgt Pepper* title song
Left:
John couldn't resist trying his hand on a French horn during a session break.
Below:
Sgt Pepper in the making.

Monday 20 February
Studio Three: 7.00pm-2.15am. Recording: 'Being For The Benefit Of Mr Kite!' (unnumbered take). Mono mixing: 'Good Morning Good Morning' (remix 1, from take 10).   P: George Martin.   E: Geoff Emerick.   2E: Richard Lush.

"Beatles songs were quite simple in the early days," says George Martin. "You couldn't play around with them too much. But by 1967 we were building sound pictures and my role had changed – it was now to interpret those pictures and work out how best to get them down on tape. Paul was fine – he could express what he wanted, the sounds he wanted to have. But John was less musically articulate. He'd make whooshing noises and try to describe what only he could hear in his head, saying he wanted a song 'to sound like an orange'. When we first worked on 'Being For The Benefit Of Mr Kite!' John had said that he wanted to 'smell the sawdust on the floor', wanted to taste the atmosphere of the circus. I said to him 'What we need is a calliope'. 'A what?' 'Steam whistles, played by a keyboard.'"

So George Martin looked around for an authentic steam organ, but only automatic models were available, played by punched cards. There were no hand operated models around. The fairground sound would have to be created inside Abbey Road using other equipment.

I knew we needed a backwash, a general mush of sound," says Martin, "like if you go to a fairground, shut your eyes and listen: rifle shots, hurdy-gurdy noises, people shouting and – way in the distance – just a tremendous chaotic sound. So I got hold of old calliope tapes, playing 'Stars and Stripes Forever' and other Sousa marches, chopped the tapes up into small sections and had Geoff Emerick throw them up in the air, re-assembling them at random."

"I threw the bits up in the air but, amazingly, they came back together in almost the same order," says Emerick. "We all expected it to sound different but it was virtually the same as before! So we switched bits around and turned some upside down." "It really worked well," says Martin, proudly. "And of course John was delighted with the end result."

Although the effects tape was done on this day it was not superimposed onto 'Being For The Benefit Of Mr Kite!' until 29 March. Close scrutiny of that overdub (it's the one which appears near the end of the song) reveals that 19 pieces of tape had been edited together by Martin and Emerick.

Also done on 20 February was demo remix one of 'Good Morning Good Morning'. (The 16 February remix had also used that number and, to confuse matters even further, on 6 April, when the song was given two more mono remixes, these were numbered one and two.)

Tuesday 21 February
Studio Two: 7.00pm-12.45am. Recording: 'Fixing A Hole' (take 1, tape reduction take 2 into take 3, SI onto take 3). Mono mixing: 'Fixing A Hole' (remixes 2-6, from take 3). Editing: 'Fixing A Hole' (of mono remixes 3 and 6).   P: George Martin.   E: Geoff Emerick.   2E: Richard Lush.

Should you be attempting to keep track of the take numbers you'll need the following advice. The take one done this day was actually the fourth take because of the three recorded at Regent Sound Studio on 9 February. The intention was that this new recording would be mixed together with the original take three. But the idea was soon dropped and, instead, a reduction mix was made of the Regent Sound take two, the mixdown being called take three. (Not to be confused with the Regent Sound take three.) The Beatles then recorded overdubs for this new take and the song was ready for remixing.

Unfortunately, although these were the song's first ever remixes, there was no remix one. They started with remix two, running through to six. The 'best' was an edit of remix three and remix six.

Wednesday 22 February
Studio Two: 7.00pm-3.45am. Recording: 'A Day In The Life' (edit pieces 1-9). Mono mixing: 'A Day In The Life' (remixes 6-9, from takes 6 and 7). Editing: 'A Day In The Life' (of remix mono 9 and edit piece take 9). Stereo mixing: 'A Day In The Life' (remixes 1-9, from takes 6 and 7). Recording: 'Anything' [aka 'Drum Track (1)'] (take 1).   P: George Martin.   E: Geoff Emerick.   2E: Richard Lush.

There remained the question of how to end 'A Day In The Life'; how to follow the staggering build up of orchestrated sound after the final Lennon lyrics. The 'choir' of voices (as it was so described) taped at the end of the eventful 10 February session was clearly along the right lines, but not powerful enough. Judging by the original tape of this session, Paul was in charge of the special overdub.
Paul: "Have you got your loud pedal down, Mal?"
Mal [Evans]: "Which one's that?"
Paul: "The right hand one, far right. It keeps the echo going."
John: "Keep it down the whole time."
Paul: "Right. On four then. One, two, three…"

What followed was the sound of John, Paul, Ringo and Mal Evans sharing three pianos and simultaneously hitting E major. Bunnggggg.

It took nine takes to perfect because the four players were rarely able to hit the keys at *precisely* the same time. Take seven was a good attempt, lasting longer than any other at 59 seconds. But it was take nine which was considered 'best' so it was overdubbed three more times, with George Martin compounding the sound further on a harmonium, until all four tracks of the tape were full. The resultant wall of sound, which lasted for 53½ seconds (it was faded a little early on the record), was the perfect ending.

Geoff Emerick, up in the control room, once again had to ensure that every last droplet of sound from the studio was captured onto tape. To do this he used heavy compression and all the while was manually lifting the volume faders, which started close to their lowest point and gradually made their way to the maximum setting. "By the end the attenuation was enormous," says George Martin. "You could have heard a pin drop." Pins dropping there are not, but one can hear a rustle of paper and a chair squeaking. Interviewed in 1987, after the compact disc release of *Sgt Pepper's Lonely Hearts Club Band*, Geoff Emerick noted, "Actually the sound could have gone on a bit longer but in those days the speakers weren't able to reproduce it. So we thought there wasn't any more sound but there was – the compact disc proves it."

The Beatles were especially keen to sit in on the remixes of 'A Day In The Life', mono and stereo, and these were done next, utilising the two tape machines in sync, as invented by Ken Townsend on 10 February. But there was still some time left at the end of this session so the Beatles set about recording another of their experimental tapes. Ringo was to the fore in this one, the tape being 22 minutes and 10 seconds of drum beat, augmented by tambourine and congas. Quite what is was meant for is not clear. It was certainly never used, nor was it remixed.

It was customary by 1967 for friends of the Beatles to pop into their sessions at Abbey Road and spend some time chatting. A visitor on this evening was David Crosby of the American group the Byrds.

Thursday 23 February

Studio Two: 7.00pm-3.45am. Stereo mixing: 'A Day In The Life' (remixes 10-12, from takes 6 and 7). Editing: 'A Day In The Life' (of remix stereo 12 and edit piece 9). Recording: 'Lovely Rita' (takes 1-8, tape reduction take 8 into take 9). P: George Martin. E: Geoff Emerick. 2E: Richard Lush.

Once the stereo master of 'A Day In The Life' had been completed it was time to start on an altogether new song, Paul's 'Lovely Rita', all about "meter maids", an Americanism for the British traffic warden, which Paul heard in early 1967.

Takes one through to eight of 'Lovely Rita' filled the four-track tape with the rhythm backing only: George on acoustic guitar on track one, John punching another acoustic on track two, Ringo drumming on track three and Paul playing piano, with tape echo, on track four. Take eight was the best version so far and a reduction mix into take nine saw the piano, drums and guitars share one track. Paul's bass guitar was the only other superimposition done this day; the vocals would follow on 24 February.

Friday 24 February

Studio Two: 7.00pm-1.15am. Recording: 'Lovely Rita' (SI onto take 9, tape reduction take 9 into takes 10 and 11). P: George Martin. E: Geoff Emerick. 2E: Richard Lush.

Paul's lead vocal on 'Lovely Rita' – which appeared for the first time at take nine – was recorded with the tape machine running at 46½ cycles per second – therefore sounding appreciably faster on replay. The previous day's rhythm track recording was also subjected to vari-speed, playing at 46½ cycles. At this stage the song had a longer piano introduction than on the record.

Take nine became takes 10 and 11 in further reduction mixes, ready for more overdubbing on 7 and 21 March.

Tuesday 28 February

Studio Two: 7.00pm-3.00am. Recording: 'Lucy In The Sky With Diamonds' (rehearsal only). P: George Martin. E: Geoff Emerick. 2E: Richard Lush.

It was, by now, customary Beatles procedure to spend unlimited time in the studio rehearsing material before commencing proper recording takes. In the 1980s this seems extravagant in the extreme, studio time being hardly a cheap commodity. But in the 1960s, with EMI recording the Beatles and owning the studios at Abbey Road, the expense of studio time was merely an internal paper transaction and was not deducted from the Beatles' royalty payments. No budget restraints were put on the group, nor onto George Martin, no longer an EMI employee, remember.

"No one ever said to me 'You're spending too much money' or 'You're taking too long over it'. I can only presume that EMI realised it was onto a good thing," Martin says today.

Rehearsals of 'Lucy In The Sky With Diamonds', a marvellous new Lennon song, took so long on this night that no proper recordings were made. These would begin the next day. Peter Vince sums up the feelings of all Abbey Road personnel working on *Sgt Pepper's Lonely Hearts Club Band*. "Although they'd use the studio as a rehearsal room you couldn't just clear off because they might be trying something out –

just piano or bass or drums – and they'd want to come up and listen to the thing before carrying on. So you couldn't just disappear or nod off, you had to be around *all* the time. The night's were so long when you had nothing to do. While they were actually working on the records, wonderful – all those great sounds, wonderful – but what people don't realise is the boredom factor. *Sgt Pepper's Lonely Hearts Club Band* took four months to record and for probably more than half that time all the engineers were doing was sitting around waiting for them to get their ideas together."

Wednesday 1 March

Studio Two: 7.00pm-2.15am. Recording: 'A Day In The Life' (SI onto take 6); 'Lucy In The Sky With Diamonds' (takes 1-7, tape reduction take 7 into take 8). P: George Martin. E: Geoff Emerick. 2E: Richard Lush.

"'Lucy In The Sky With Diamonds' was *not* about LSD," declares George Martin, adamantly. "The title originated when his three-year-old son Julian came home from nursery school with a painting of a girl in his class. John asked him what it was called and Julian replied 'It's Lucy, in the sky, with diamonds'."

Although it was mere coincidence that the initial letters of the song title spelt LSD, there can be little doubt that it was this very substance which provoked such colourful word imagery to flow out of the Lennon head and onto paper. And once again it was important that the sounds captured the *feel* of the song.

The first seven takes concentrated solely on the rhythm track, with piano, acoustic guitar, Hammond organ, drums and maraca all being used. The Hammond, played by Paul, was used for the song's distinctive opening passage, being taped with a special organ-stop to give it a sound not unlike a celeste. There was no lead vocal as yet although John was

singing off microphone to guide the rhythm track. During the early part of the session he was singing the words "Cellophane flowers of yellow and green" in such a way that each was enunciated slowly, separately and precisely. Paul can be heard to suggest he sing them quicker, in one flowing sentence, to which John replied "OK" and did just that.

The final rhythm track, take seven, saw the introduction of a very heavy and very prominent tamboura, an Indian guitar-like instrument which makes a drone sound, and with the tape full the four tracks were then reduced to one all encompassing rhythm track on a new tape, ready for overdubbing on 2 March.

Also taped during this 1 March session was a piano overdub for 'A Day In The Life', take six. It was a strange thing to do considering that the final mono and stereo master remixes had already been made. Whatever the purpose, this additional overdub was never used.

Experiments for the final, crashing chord in 'A Day In The Life'.

Thursday 2 March

Studio Two: 7.00pm-3.30am. Recording: 'Lucy In The Sky With Diamonds' (SI onto take 8). Mono mixing: 'Lucy In The Sky With Diamonds' (remixes 1-11, from take 8). P: George Martin. E: Geoff Emerick. 2E: Richard Lush.

'Lucy In The Sky With Diamonds' was the most varispeeded song on *Sgt Pepper's Lonely Hearts Club Band*. The rhythm track reduction of take seven into take eight had been done at 49 cycles per second. Now, onto track two, was recorded one of two John Lennon lead vocals, backed by Paul (with occasional tape echo), taped at 45 cycles; onto track three was

taped the second Lennon vocal and the second McCartney harmony, recorded this time at 48½ cycles; onto track four went, at normal speed, Paul's bass and George Harrison on fuzzed lead guitar.

'Lucy In The Sky With Diamonds' was one of the quickest *Sgt Pepper* recordings: one night for the

rhythm track, one for overdubs. But the mono remixes done this night, 11 of them, were all wiped from the tape on 3 March when, expressing themselves dissatisfied with any mix – even remix 11 which had been marked 'best' – the Beatles had George Martin start afresh with remixes numbered one to four.

Friday 3 March

Studio Two: 7.00pm-2.15am. Recording: 'Sgt Pepper's Lonely Hearts Club Band' (SI onto take 10). Mono mixing: 'Lucy In The Sky With Diamonds' (remixes 1-4, from take 8). P: George Martin. E: Geoff Emerick. 2E: Richard Lush.

Since it was now clear that Sgt Pepper's Lonely Hearts Club Band was a (pretend) real band, a brass overdub was called for. Four outside musicians were recruited to play French horns – James W. Buck, Neil Sanders, Tony Randall and John Burden. "They didn't really know what they wanted," says Burden, then an ex-London Symphony Orchestra freelancer. "I wrote out phrases for them based on what Paul McCartney was humming to us and George Martin. All four Beatles were there but only Paul took an active interest in our overdub."

John Burden would not have known it but his last observation was not strictly true. John Lennon had tape op Richard Lush record all of the conversation between the four players, Paul McCartney and George Martin. Then, for reasons best known only to himself, he took the tape home for his private collection!

After the musicians had secured Beatles autographs (a common practice) and gone home, George Harrison became the focus of attention with the overdubbing of a stinging – and much distorted – lead guitar solo onto

the same song, now complete except for one final overdub on 6 March.

The session ended with the four new mono mixes of 'Lucy In The Sky With Diamonds', with extensive use of ADT. Remix four was deemed 'best'.

Monday 6 March

Studio Two: 7.00pm-12.30am. Recording: 'Sgt Pepper's Lonely Hearts Club Band' (SI onto take 10). Mono mixing: 'Sgt Pepper's Lonely Hearts Club Band' (remixes 2 and 3, from take 10). Stereo mixing: 'Sgt Pepper's Lonely Hearts Club Band' (remixes 1-8, from take 10). P: George Martin. E: Geoff Emerick. 2E: Richard Lush.

"It was about three or four weeks before the final session when they started thinking about the running order of the songs," says Geoff Emerick. "The concept of it being Sgt Pepper's band was already there when Paul said 'Wouldn't it be good if we get the atmosphere? Get the band warming up, hear the audience settle into their seats, have the songs as different acts on the stage?' "

The sound of the band warming up was easy to find. During the 10 February orchestral overdub for 'A Day In The Life' four tapes had been made of the miscellaneous sound effects, stored away for possible future use. A few seconds was (metaphorically) chopped out of one of the tapes and dropped into track three of the 'Sgt Pepper's Lonely Hearts Club Band' four-track tape.

Most of the song's remaining effects – the sound of an audience settling down, then clapping and laughing – came from an invaluable Abbey Road archive collection of sound effects locked away in a rickety green cabinet in an old storeroom. The curator of the collection was – and still is – balance engineer Stuart Eltham. "The collection began in about 1956," says Eltham, "when Peter Sellers, Spike Milligan, Michael Bentine and others used to make records at Abbey Road. We started to keep bits and pieces. If we did a location recording somewhere we'd keep what outtakes were possible. Then I and people like Ken Townsend used to make recordings in our spare time."

In 'Sgt Pepper's Lonely Hearts Club Band' extracts from "Volume 28: Audience Applause and Atmosphere, Royal Albert Hall and Queen Elizabeth

Hall" were used for the audience murmuring at the start of the song. The applause and laughter was taken, appropriately, from "Volume 6: Applause and Laughter", a tape from the Fortune Theatre, London live recording of the 1961 comedy revue *Beyond The Fringe*, starring Peter Cook, Dudley Moore, Jonathan Miller and Alan Bennett.

When 'Sgt Pepper's Lonely Hearts Club Band' was later segued into the album's following song, 'With A Little Help From My Friends', the edit was masked by one further sound effect: audience screaming from one of the at-this-time unreleased recordings of the Beatles in concert at the Hollywood Bowl!

Master remixes of 'Sgt Pepper's Lonely Hearts Club Band' were made before the session ended, the third mono and the eighth stereo being 'best' respectively.

Tuesday 7 March

Studio Two: 7.00pm-2.30am. Recording: 'Lovely Rita' (SI onto take 11). P: George Martin. E: Geoff Emerick. 2E: Richard Lush.

Harmony vocal and miscellaneous overdubbing onto take 11 of 'Lovely Rita' (a reduction mix of take nine from 24 February). John Lennon led the backing vocals brigade, augmented with very heavy tape echo which, in turn, encouraged a little juvenile microphone messing: moaning, sighing and screaming for the end of the song plus cha-cha-chas and even the

percussive sound of comb and toilet paper! "John always wanted repeat echo in his headphones, it gave him more excitement," says Geoff Emerick. "They'd finished doing the vocal on 'Lovely Rita' and he just started fooling around, using the echo as his inspiration."

Thursday 9 March

Studio Two: 7.00pm-3.30am. Recording: 'Getting Better' (takes 1-7, tape reduction take 7 into takes 8-12).   P: George Martin.   E: Malcolm Addey/Ken Townsend.   2E: Graham Kirkby.

There was a change in the studio personnel for this session, Geoff Emerick and Richard Lush having the night off. Malcolm Addey, another Abbey Road balance engineer with impeccable credentials – he worked on Cliff Richard's 'Move It' as well as most Shadows sessions – was drafted as temporary replacement, aided by Ken Townsend. "Geoff had been doing a lot of late-night work and was getting very tired," says Addey. "I remember the session was booked to begin at 7pm but there was barely a Beatle

in sight much before midnight, and we were sitting around waiting. They eventually straggled in one by one. Ringo came in about 11 and ordered fish and chips. The others arrived later, they all hung around and finally started work at about one in the morning. The ego trip of the big-time artists had started to set in…I know their method of working upset Geoff [Emerick] from time to time."

The song to be worked on this time was a new

McCartney composition, 'Getting Better'. Seven takes of the basic rhythm track were recorded: guitars, bass and drums, with George Martin playing piano, though not via a keyboard but by actually striking the strings.

The four-track tape was then given a reduction mix down to one-track of another tape, done five times to get the optimum mix, the 'best' being take 12. More tapings for 'Getting Better' were done on the next day and again on 21 and 23 March.

Friday 10 March

Studio Two: 7.00pm-4.00am. Recording: 'Getting Better' (SI onto take 12).   P: George Martin.   E: Geoff Emerick.   2E: Richard Lush.

Track one of the tape had the mixed down basic rhythm recording from take seven. Onto track four George Harrison overdubbed a droning tamboura,

Paul McCartney's bass guitar went onto track three and Ringo's drums were superimposed onto track two.

Monday 13 March

Studio Two: 7.00pm-2.30am. Recording: 'Good Morning Good Morning' (SI onto take 10). P: George Martin.   E: Geoff Emerick.   2E: Richard Lush.

Three weeks had elapsed since 'Good Morning Good Morning' had been mixed down to allow for overdubbing, yet the song had not been touched since. John Lennon felt that it needed a few brass instruments, so for this session members of Sounds Inc were recruited to play three saxophones (Barrie Cameron, David Glyde and Alan Holmes), two trombones (John Lee and A.N. Other) and a French horn (Tom someone – no one can recall his surname!). Sounds Inc, previously Sounds Incorporated – the name changed on 14 January 1967 along with the addition of extra players – was a top instrumental group from Kent which had a long history of backing American stars in Europe, Gene Vincent and Little Richard among them. They had first met the Beatles at the Star-Club in April 1962 and in March 1964 they were signed to a management contract by Brian Epstein.

"We were there for about six hours," says Alan Holmes. "The first three hours we had refreshments and the Beatles played us the completed songs for the new LP." Tape operator Richard Lush remembers what happened next. "They spent a long time doing the overdub, about three hours or maybe longer, but John Lennon thought it sounded too straight. So we ended up flanging, limiting and compressing it, anything to make it sound unlike brass playing. It was typical John Lennon – he just wanted it to sound weird."

Follow these instructions to make your very own *Sgt Pepper*: a selection of Geoff Emerick's original notes showing console settings for the remixes.

Wednesday 15 March

Studio Two: 7.00pm-1.30am. Recording: 'Untitled' (working title of 'Within You Without You') (take 1).   P: George Martin.   E: Geoff Emerick.   2E: Richard Lush.

With 'Only A Northern Song' being left off *Sgt Pepper's Lonely Hearts Club Band*, George Harrison came up with another composition as the sole break in an otherwise exclusively Lennon-McCartney album.

'Within You Without You' – typically untitled at this early stage, as were most of George's songs – was perhaps the most Indian flavoured song to appear on a Beatles album, although George was to write and record others for himself later in 1967 for the soundtrack of the film *Wonderwall*.

A beautiful blending of Eastern and Western musical styles, 'Within You Without You' was written early in 1967 at the Hampstead, London home of Klaus Voormann, long time friend of the Beatles, bass player with (at this point) Manfred Mann and designer – Klaus conceived the sleeve for the Beatles' *Revolver* LP.

The recording of 'Within You Without You' was done as one song but was referred to in three parts for easy indentification. The basic track of take one – including parts one, two and three – was taped on this day, lasting 6'25" and featuring an Indian friend (his name regrettably unknown) on tabla and other session men contributing swordmandel, dilruba [a sitar like instrument but played with a bow] and a tamboura. This latter instrument was also played by George and by Beatles assistant Neil Aspinall. The outside musicians were from the Asian Music Circle in Fitzalan Road, Finchley, north London.

" 'Within You Without You' was a great track," says Emerick. "The tabla had never been recorded the way we did it. Everyone was amazed when they first heard a tabla recorded that closely, with the texture and the lovely low resonances."

The song was subjected to overdubs on 22 March and on 3 April but at no time did any of the other three Beatles participate in the recordings.

It was around this time that 'fine artist' Peter Blake was commissioned to provide the design for the *Sgt Pepper's Lonely Hearts Club Band* LP sleeve. Blake visited a few sessions at Abbey Road – one was on this day, another was on 28 March – to meet the Beatles and discuss ideas. Referring to this session Blake recalls "George was there with some Indian musicians and they had a carpet on the floor and there was incense burning. George was very sweet – he's always been very kind and sweet – and he got up and welcomed us in and offered us tea. We just sat and watched for a couple of hours. It was a fascinating, historical time."

Friday 17 March

Studio Two: 7.00pm-12.45am. Recording: 'She's Leaving Home' (takes 1-6).   P: George Martin.   E: Geoff Emerick.   2E: Richard Lush.

The Beatles had never been the sole act produced by George Martin. As head of A&R at Parlophone from 1955 to 1965 he had overseen dozens of artists. Now, even as a freelancer, he still looked after several. If the Beatles thought he was solely at their beck and call they were mistaken. Certainly Paul McCartney made the mistake, expecting George to drop other engagements and meet him to arrange a score for his beautiful new ballad 'She's Leaving Home'. But George refused to break his other commitment so Paul promptly went ahead and had Mike Leander do the score instead. [Leander was also a freelance producer and arranger. Paul had met him when he attended the session at Decca Studios, London for Marianne Faithfull's cover version of 'Yesterday' on 11 October 1965.]

George Martin saw it as a slight and was very hurt, and it was to his great credit that he agreed not only to produce this session but also conduct the ten musicians. Paul McCartney is not in evidence on the original tape so it is unlikely that he attended. "It was just one of those silly things," says Martin. "He was so damned impatient and I was up to my eyes with other work and I just couldn't cope. But Paul realises now, though he was surprised that I was upset."

The score called for four violins, two violas, two cellos, a double-bass and a harp. "I had to change the score a little bit, not very much. Mike Leander did a good job." One change immediately noticeable when comparing the original tape with the released record is that two edits were made of the cello, one after each "bye bye". Paul recorded his vocal before the decision to cut the two pieces was made, and it was done at the mono and stereo remix stages.

The musicians were Erich Gruenberg (leader), Derek Jacobs, Trevor Williams and José Luis Garcia (violins); John Underwood and Stephen Shingles (violas); Dennis Vigay and Alan Dalziel (cellos); Gordon Pearce (double-bass) and Sheila Bromberg (harp), the latter being the first woman especially recruited to play on a Beatles recording.

All six takes of 'She's Leaving Home' recorded on this day were of the strings only. There was little to choose between takes one and six and both were marked 'best' for the time being.

Monday 20 March

Studio Two: 7.00pm-3.30am. Recording: 'Beatle Talk' (take 1); 'She's Leaving Home' (tape reduction take 1 into takes 7-9, tape reduction take 6 into take 10, SI onto take 9). Mono mixing: 'She's Leaving Home' (remixes 1-6, from take 9). Editing: 'She's Leaving Home' (of remix mono 6).   P: George Martin.   E: Geoff Emerick.   2E: Ken Scott.

As the difference between takes one and six of 'She's Leaving Home' was negligible, tape reductions were made of both. But the reduction of take one, numbered take nine, was 'best' so it received the overdub of Paul's lead and John's fine backing vocals, recorded twice over to sound like four voices. This lovely song was now complete because there were no overdubs of any Beatle playing any musical instrument: the only music played on 'She's Leaving Home' was the strings.

The song was then treated to six mono remixes, the sixth being 'best'. As an experiment, ADT was

applied to the song's opening harp passage on remix one, but the idea was dropped after that.

Also taped on this day was 'Beatle Talk', another spoken word recording. Quite what was said is not known for neither the recording sheet nor the tape box are very revealing and the tape itself was taken away by George Martin and never returned.

The hands of Emerick working the four-track for a mono remix, with John, George and Paul in close attendance. Tape operator Richard Lush is in the background.

Tuesday 21 March

Studio Two: 7.00pm-2.45am. Recording: 'Getting Better' (tape reduction take 12 into takes 13 and 14, SI onto take 14); 'Lovely Rita' (SI onto take 11). Mono mixing: 'Lovely Rita' (remixes 1-15, from take 11). Editing: 'Lovely Rita' (of mono remixes 11 and 14). P: George Martin. E: Geoff Emerick. 2E: Richard Lush.

The first task of this session was to overdub lead and backing vocals onto 'Getting Better'. Hunter Davies, of the newspaper *The Sunday Times*, had just been engaged as writer of the Beatles' authorised biography – *The Beatles*, published in September 1968 – and he was at Abbey Road for the first time during this evening. "The Beatles had already done the backing track and now they were doing the vocals," he recalls. "They could hear the backing through their headphones while they were singing but all I could hear was their voices: flat, grainy, hoarse and awfully disembodied [as voices nearly always sound without accompaniment]. I remember thinking 'Why am I such a big fan of theirs, why do I think they're good singers? They're completely out of tune!'"

Only three of the Beatles attended the session. Ringo was not required for vocals on 'Getting Better' so he didn't bother to show. But at one point in the evening, after repeated listening to the 9 and 10 March rhythm track recording of the song, Paul decided that Ringo needed to re-record his drums. He was duly telephoned at home and summoned to the studio. (John picked up the telephone: "Ringo on toast, please", according to Hunter Davies.) But after Paul and Geoff Emerick had played with a few knobs and switches on the console Paul pronounced the original recording fine after all so Ringo was telephoned again and cancelled. "We never heard how he felt," says Davies, "but he must have been pretty choked,

having got himself ready for work and the long drive in from Surrey only to be told he wasn't needed."

Hunter Davies didn't know it, but he was attending rather an infamous Beatles recording session. After running through the vocals of 'Getting Better' a few times John said that he felt ill. George Martin – not knowing the reason why but certainly aware that the studio was, as ever, surrounded by Beatles fans – took John onto the roof of studio two for some fresh spring air, then left him and returned to the studio. After a while Paul called up to the control room "How's John?". "He's on the roof, looking at the stars," replied Martin. Paul joked "You mean Vince Hill?," referring to the singer and then, with George Harrison, bursting into a quick version of 'Edelweiss', Hill's current hit. But what Martin said suddenly struck the two Beatles with force. They knew *why* John was ill – he was in the middle of an LSD trip – and yet he had been left alone on the roof of studio two which has no rails or barriers, just a sheer drop of about 30 feet to the ground below. He was quickly fetched down to the studio before he killed himself.

Geoff Emerick also remembers what happened. "John came up to the control room and was looking up at the ceiling saying 'Cor, look at that George!' God only knows what he was seeing, George certainly couldn't figure it out. So he took him onto the roof and left him. When the others found out they dashed straight

up there to get him down."

Emerick had a big hand in the other item recorded during this session, the piano solo for 'Lovely Rita', played by George Martin with the tape machine running at 41¼ cycles per second, sounding *very* fast on replay. "I used to try out funny things in odd moments and I discovered that by putting sticky tape over the capstan of a tape machine you could wobble the tape on the echo machine, because we used to delay the feed into the echo chamber by tape. So I suggested we did this using a piano sound. The Beatles themselves couldn't think what should go into the song's middle eight and they didn't really like my idea at first, but it turned out fine in the end because of the effect. It gave the piano a sort of honky-tonk feel. In fact, Paul asked me to play the solo when I made the suggestion but I was too embarrassed."

'Lovely Rita' was remixed for mono after this overdub, the tape machine running at 48¾ cycles throughout the song. The same was true of the stereo, done on 17 April.

Norman Smith was working elsewhere in Abbey Road during this evening, producing the first album by Pink Floyd, *The Piper At The Gates Of Dawn*. At around 11pm he brought in his young group to sheepishly meet the Beatles and exchange what Hunter Davies noted as "half-hearted hellos".

Wednesday 22 March

Studio Two: 7.00pm-2.15am. Recording: 'Within You Without You' (SI onto take 1, tape reduction take 1 into take 2). Mono mixing: 'Within You Without You' (remix 1, from take 2). P: George Martin. E: Geoff Emerick. 2E: Richard Lush.

Overdubbing of two more dilrubas – again played by someone recruited especially for the purpose, his name unknown – onto track three of the 'Within You Without You' four-track, taped at 52½ cycles per second to sound slowed down on replay. When this was done the tape was complete and a reduction mix was made, take one becoming take two, followed by a

demo mono remix of the song for acetate cutting.

This session took place in Studio Two at Abbey Road. In the control room of Studio One, between 11.00pm and 12.30am, tape operator Graham Kirkby oversaw a playback of the LP songs completed to date for any Beatle interested in listening.

Thursday 23 March

Studio Two: 7.00pm-3.45am. Recording: 'Getting Better' (SI onto take 14, tape reduction take 14 into take 15, SI onto take 15). Mono mixing: 'Getting Better' (remixes 1-3, from take 15). P and E: Peter Vince. 2E: Ken Scott.

Once again, the usual control room team of Martin, Emerick and Lush was otherwise engaged so Peter Vince assumed the roles of producer and engineer and Ken Scott deputised as tape operator. The vocal overdub for 'Getting Better, taped on 21 March, was re-recorded on this day, hardly surprising considering the events of the original session! This completed, there was another reduction mix, take 14 becoming 15, and onto this Ringo overdubbed bongos. The song was now finished and three mono remixes were made by Vince, the third deemed 'best'.

George shows one of the Indian musicians how he wants 'Within You Without You' to be played.

Left:
Paul instructs the French horn players.
Right:
An original note referring to the overlaying of animal sound effects for 'Good Morning Good Morning'.

Tuesday 28 March

Studio Two: 7.00pm-4.45am. Recording: 'Good Morning Good Morning' (SI onto take 10, tape reduction take 10 into take 11, SI onto take 11, unnumbered take); 'Being For The Benefit Of Mr Kite!' (SI onto take 9). P: George Martin. E: Geoff Emerick. 2E: Richard Lush.

John's lead vocal on 'Good Morning Good Morning' appeared here for the first time, finally filling the original four-track tape. This was then bumped down to two tracks in a reduction mix, onto which a lead guitar solo – played by Paul, not George – and backing vocals, by John and Paul, were overdubbed. The lead vocal was treated to ADT in remixing.

John Lennon – possibly in the absence of any better idea, possibly not – had decided that he would like to end 'Good Morning Good Morning' with a series of animal sound effects. To most people these were applied at random, but to Geoff Emerick there was more to it than that. "John said to me during one of the breaks that he wanted to have the sound of animals escaping and that each successive animal should be capable of frightening or devouring its predecessor! So

those are not just random effects, there was actually a lot of thought put into all that."

Close study of the original tape proves Emerick's memory correct, even though George Martin today describes the story as "fanciful". The song starts off with a cock crowing, then later on there's a cat mewing, dogs barking, horses neighing, sheep bleating, lions roaring, elephants snorting, there's a fox being chased by bloodhounds in a hunt, with the horses galloping, there's a cow lowing and finally a hen clucking.

The effects came once again from the Abbey Road sound effects tape collection, looked after by Stuart Eltham. Two tapes in particular were used: "Volume 35: Animals and Bees" for the lion, elephant, dog,

sheep, cow and the cat, and "Volume 57: Fox-hunt" for the bloodhounds chasing the fox, the tooting and the galloping.

Although the 'Good Morning Good Morning' sound effects were assembled on this day they were not spun into the four-track tape of the song until 29 March.

Before the end of this session 'Being For The Benefit Of Mr Kite!' received some more overdubs. George, Ringo, Mal Evans and Neil Aspinall all played harmonica, John the organ and Paul a guitar solo. There would be more overdubbing for this song on 29 and 31 March before it was considered complete.

Wednesday 29 March

Studio Two: 7.00pm-5.45am. Recording: 'Good Morning Good Morning' (unnumbered take, SI of unnumbered take onto take 11); 'Being For The Benefit Of Mr Kite!' (SI onto take 9); 'Bad Finger Boogie' (working title of 'With A Little Help From My Friends') (takes 1-10, tape reduction take 10 into take 11, SI onto take 11).   P: George Martin.   E: Geoff Emerick.   2E: Richard Lush.

With the addition of a few more animal sound effects to those collated the previous night, and the overdub of these onto take 11 of 'Good Morning Good Morning', this song was complete and ready for mono and stereo remixing (done 6 April).

The elaborate sound effects for 'Being For The Benefit Of Mr Kite!', compiled at such pains on 20 February, were superimposed onto the song today, along with a swirling organ piece, played this time by George Martin.

In all of the recording sessions since 24 November 1966, when *Sgt Pepper's Lonely Hearts Club Band* had been begun, there had been no song with Ringo as lead vocalist. John and Paul put matters to rights with the composition, written especially for him to sing, 'With A Little Help From My Friends', initially – but only very briefly – titled 'Bad Finger Boogie'.

It had already been decided that this song would not merely follow the album's title track but that it would be *joined* to it, 'segued' to use music industry parlance. Hence the song, from the very first take, began with what – on the LP – sounds more like the end of 'Sgt Pepper's Lonely Hearts Club Band', the "Bil-ly Shears" vocal line. Underscoring that line (although the vocals weren't added until later) was a Hammond organ piece played by George Martin. Then, into the song proper, Paul played piano, George lead guitar, Ringo drums and John cowbell.

Ten takes were made using this basic rhythm line-up, the tenth being best. This was then converted into take 11 by a reduction mix which saw all four tracks from the first tape merge into one. Ringo's lead vocal – one of the best he has ever recorded – was then overdubbed onto tracks three and four of the song and more overdubs were taped on 30 March.

Thursday 30 March

Studio Two: 11.00pm-7.30am. Recording: 'With A Little Help From My Friends' (SI onto take 11).
P: George Martin.   E: Geoff Emerick.   2E: Richard Lush.

Before this session – prompting its very late start – the Beatles went to Chelsea Manor [photographic] Studios in Flood Street, Chelsea, London to pose for the splendid Michael Cooper shots which would adorn the Peter Blake designed cover, and the inside-gatefold, of the *Sgt Pepper's Lonely Hearts Club Band* album. A trend-setting session indeed.

On reaching Abbey Road the group settled straight back into the completion of 'With A Little Help From My Friends', adding guitar, tambourine and bass guitar onto track two of the tape and superb backing vocals by John and Paul, with another guitar piece by George, on tracks three and four.

Friday 31 March

Studio Two: 7.00pm-3.00am.
Mono mixing: 'With A Little Help From My Friends' (remixes 1-15, from take 11). Recording: 'Being For The Benefit Of Mr Kite!' (SI onto take 9). Mono mixing: 'Being For The Benefit Of Mr Kite!' (remixes 1-7, from take 9).
P: George Martin.   E: Geoff Emerick.   2E: Richard Lush.

Fifteen mono remixes of 'With A Little Help From My Friends', with extensive use of ADT, were necessary before everyone was satisfied, the 15th being 'best' and it was added to the rapidly filling master spool.

'Being For The Benefit Of Mr Kite!' was also remixed for mono on this day [starting with remix one, although that number had already been used on 17 February]. Seven editions were made but remix four was deemed 'best'. These were only done after the overdub of yet another organ – and a glockenspiel – onto take nine of the original recording.

Saturday 1 April

Studio One: 7.00pm-6.00am. Recording: 'Sgt Pepper's Lonely Hearts Club Band (Reprise)' (takes 1-9). Mono mixing: 'Sgt Pepper's Lonely Hearts Club Band (Reprise)' (remixes 1-9, from take 9). P: George Martin. E: Geoff Emerick. 2E: Richard Lush.

Now more than four months in the making, *Sgt Pepper's Lonely Hearts Club Band* was approaching the end, albeit an enforced end, for Paul had planned to fly out to the USA on 3 April – staying until the 12th – and the master tape had been promised to EMI in between. Except for a special item taped on 21 April – but that's another story! – this had to be Paul's last session. There would be others in his absence though, not least the preparation of all the remaining stereo mixes, but this was Paul's last chance to contribute vocals or instruments to the LP.

With the concept of *Sgt Pepper's Lonely Hearts Club Band* assuming the identity of a show, Paul had hit upon the idea to reprise the title song as the penultimate item, just before the rousing end performance which, it had already been decided

(especially since it was impossible to follow), would be 'A Day In The Life'.

'Sgt Pepper's Lonely Hearts Club Band (Reprise)' was a much tighter version than its parent song, lasting only 1′18″ and being punchier and more rock flavoured, with all four Beatles chanting out the quick-paced vocals. And it was very quickly recorded too: the song was made from start to finish in just this one session – lasting 11 hours, admittedly – and being the only song on the LP *not* to be 'bumped'/reduced on the four-track machine. It was a straightforward rock recording; there was no time for niceties and frills.

"I think the reprise version of the song is more exciting than the first cut of 'Sgt Pepper'," says Geoff

Emerick. "There's a nice quality about it. We recorded the Beatles in the huge Abbey Road number one studio which was quite hard because of the acoustics of the place. It's difficult to capture the tightness of the rhythm section in there."

The Beatles taped nine takes of the rhythm track, with Paul singing along on each one as a guide. With the ninth being 'best' the shared lead vocals were added and by the end the song boasted drums, electric guitar, organ, bass guitar, various percussion instruments, the vocals and more audience sound effects from the Abbey Road collection. Nine mono remixes were made, the ninth being 'best'.

Monday 3 April

Studio One: 7.00pm-3.00am. Recording: 'Within You Without You' (SI onto take 2). Studio Two (control room only): 3.00-6.30am. Mono mixing: 'Within You Without You' (remixes 1-3 from 'Part 1' of take 2, remixes 4 and 5 from 'Parts 2 and 3' of take 2). P: George Martin. E: Geoff Emerick. 2E: Richard Lush.

George's 'Within You Without You' was the last song to be completed for the album. No other Beatles were in the studio for this 11½ hour session, which also saw early mono remixing of the number.

Amid the expanse of Abbey Road studio one, George Martin conducted eight violinists and three cellists through a score he had written based on George Harrison's requirements. Each take of the strings overdub went directly onto track three of the four-track tape, automatically wiping the previous

attempt, and this procedure went on until all were satisfied that it could not be improved any further.

The same technique was applied when, later in the evening, George taped his excellent lead vocal, a sitar part and – just here and there – a dash of acoustic guitar onto track four of the tape.

The eight violinists who played on the session were Erich Gruenberg (leader), Alan Loveday, Julien Gaillard, Paul Scherman, Ralph Elman, David

Wolfsthal, Jack Rothstein and Jack Greene. The three cellists were Reginald Kilbey, Allen Ford and Peter Beavan. All but Gruenberg, who received £11, were paid the Musicians' Union session rate of £9.

Mono mixing of the song was started on this evening [incorrectly numbered from remix one – this had been done before, on 22 March] and it was completed later the same day which by now was 4 April. Again, for remix purposes, the song was divided into three parts.

Tuesday 4 April

Studio Two (control room only): 7.00pm-12.45am. Mono mixing: 'Within You Without You' (remixes 6-11 from 'Part 1' of take 2, remix 12 from 'Parts 2 and 3' of take 2). Editing: 'Within You Without You' (of mono remixes 10 and 12, with SI). Stereo mixing: 'Within You Without You' (remixes 1-3 from 'Part 1' of take 2, remixes 4 and 5, from 'Parts 2 and 3' of take 2). Editing: 'Within You Without You' (of stereo remixes 3 and 5, with SI). P: George Martin. E: Geoff Emerick. 2E: Richard Lush.

Final mono and stereo remixing of 'Within You Without You', with heavy use of ADT. At George Harrison's request a few seconds of laughter was edited onto the end of both mixes, courtesy of the

Abbey Road sound effects collection, "Volume 6: Applause and Laughter".

Thursday 6 April

Studio Two (control room only): 7.00pm-1.00am. Mono mixing: Crossfades for LP; 'Good Morning Good Morning' (remixes 1 and 2, from take 11). Stereo mixing: 'Good Morning Good Morning' (remixes 1-5, from take 11). P: George Martin. E: Geoff Emerick. 2E: Richard Lush.

More mono remixes of 'Good Morning Good Morning' and the first stereo editions. Remix stereo five was deemed 'best' and put on the master reel but the mono mixing would be done again on 19 April.

Malcolm Davies had the task of assembling the *Sgt Pepper's Lonely Hearts Club Band* prototype master tape, utilising George Martin's specification unique for a pop music album – it was to have no 'rills' or gaps between songs. The tape was compiled in such a way

that either the merest split-second of silence separated the songs or they were 'crossfaded', a method of editing two songs together where the first actually merges into the second, done by using three tape machines. There were two crossfades on *Sgt Pepper's Lonely Hearts Club Band*: the title song into 'With A Little Help From My Friends' and the reprised title song into 'A Day In The Life'.

It is interesting to note how – at this stage – the line-up

of songs for the album differed from that finally chosen. While side two of the LP was to remain identical, side one was, at this stage: 'Sgt Pepper's Lonely Hearts Club Band'; 'With A Little Help From My Friends'; 'Being For The Benefit Of Mr Kite!'; 'Fixing A Hole'; 'Lucy In The Sky With Diamonds'; 'Getting Better' and 'She's Leaving Home'.

Friday 7 April

Studio Two (control room only): 7.00pm-1.00am. Stereo mixing: Crossfades for LP; 'With A Little Help From My Friends' (remixes 1-3, from take 11); 'Being For The Benefit Of Mr Kite!' (remixes 1-8, from take 9); 'Fixing A Hole' (remix 1, from take 3); 'Lucy In The Sky With Diamonds' (remixes 1-5, from take 8).   P: George Martin.   E: Geoff Emerick. 2E: Richard Lush.

"The only real version of *Sgt Pepper's Lonely Hearts Club Band* is the mono version," says Richard Lush. "The Beatles were there for all the mono mixes. Then, after the album was finished, George Martin, Geoff [Emerick] and I did the stereo in a few days, just the three of us, without a Beatle in sight. There are all sorts of things on the mono, little effects here and there, which the stereo doesn't have."

Geoff Emerick confirms this view and points out that almost all of the Beatles recording sessions – including those for *Sgt Pepper's Lonely Hearts Club Band* – were monitored in the control room through just one mono speaker anyway, except for when stereo mixing was being done. "We did have two speakers but everything was put through the right hand one. We weren't allowed to monitor on both because they were saved for stereo orchestral recordings!"

Monday 17 April

Studio Two (control room only): 7.00-10.30pm.
Stereo mixing: 'Getting Better' (remix 1, from take 15); 'She's Leaving Home' (remixes 1-6, from take 9); 'When I'm Sixty-Four' (remix 1, from take 4); 'Lovely Rita' (remixes 1 and 2, from take 11).
Editing: 'She's Leaving Home' (of remix stereo 6).
P: George Martin.   E: Geoff Emerick.   2E: Richard Lush.

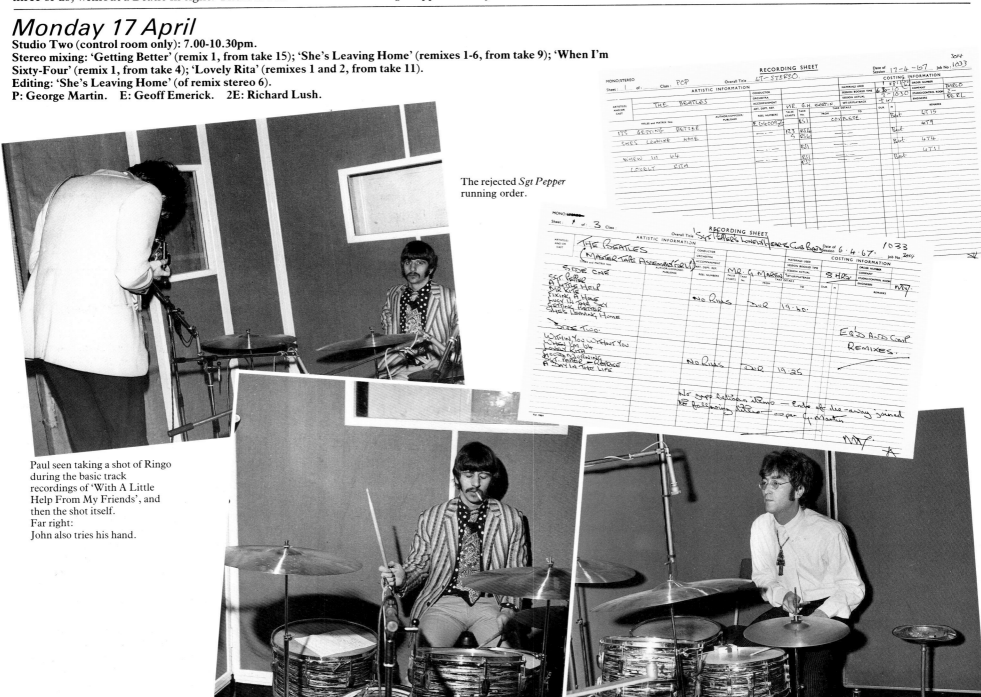

The rejected *Sgt Pepper* running order.

Paul seen taking a shot of Ringo during the basic track recordings of 'With A Little Help From My Friends', and then the shot itself.
Far right:
John also tries his hand.

Wednesday 19 April

Studio Two (control room only): 7.00pm-12.30am. Mono mixing: 'Good Morning Good Morning' (remixes 10-23, from take 11); 'Only A Northern Song' (remix 4, from take 12). P: George Martin.   E: Geoff Emerick.   2E: Richard Lush.

Although the 6 April mono remix two of 'Good Morning Good Morning' had been marked 'best' and placed on the master reel, it did not fit snugly alongside the reprise version of 'Sgt Pepper's Lonely Hearts Club Band'. So the original take 11 of the recording was pulled out of the library again to see how best the two songs could be brought together, either by editing or by means of a crossfade.

It took 14 more remixes before the solution to the problem had been perfected [these started at a round number, 10, although only numbers one and two had been previously used]. It was a brilliant idea based on a complete coincidence: merging the final cluck of the hen at the end of 'Good Morning Good Morning', one of the many animal sound effects, into the similar first guitar note at the beginning of 'Sgt Pepper's Lonely Hearts Club Band (Reprise)'.

"That was one of the cleverest bits of matching a sound effect with an instrument ever done," says Geoff Emerick, proudly, although George Martin is rather more poetic about the edit, claiming that "Sgt Pepper himself was breathing life into the project by this time", intimating that the edit was discovered by chance alone, and that it "just fitted together". Geoff Emerick disagrees that it was an accident. "No no, that was no accident. We fully realised that the cluck matched the guitar. In fact it wasn't a *perfect* match so we shifted the cluck up in time to match correctly. It was a fantastic little thing which will always stick in my mind."

With Paul having returned from the USA the Beatles were due to resume recording sessions on 20 April, picking up 'Only A Northern Song' again for the first time since 14 February. To remind them of the work done so far another demo remix of the song – remix four – was made for the purpose of cutting acetates.

Thursday 20 April

Studio Three (control room only): 5.00-6.15pm. Stereo mixing: 'Sgt Pepper's Lonely Hearts Club Band (Reprise)' (remixes 1-10, from take 9).   P: n/a.   E: Geoff Emerick. 2E: Richard Lush. Studio Two: 7.00pm-2.15am.   Recording: 'Only A Northern Song' (SI onto take 3, SI onto take 11).   P: George Martin.   E: Geoff Emerick.   2E: Richard Lush.

'Sgt Pepper's Lonely Hearts Club Band (Reprise)' was the last song mixed for stereo, remix 10 being 'best'.

Displaying a tremendous appetite for recording, the Beatles were back in the studio working on a non-album song within 45 minutes of those mixes, putting finishing touches to George Harrison's 'Only A Northern Song'. It was a curious session for first they returned to the take three of 13 February, wiping existing material and superimposing in its place bass guitar, a trumpet and a glockenspiel. Then they advanced to take 11 – itself a reduction mix of take three – and added vocals. The two different versions were then mixed together in sync (on 21 April) to give one complete recording.

Friday 21 April

Studio Two: 7.00pm-1.30am. Mono mixing: 'Only A Northern Song' (remixes 1-11, from takes 3 and 11). Recording: 'Edit for LP End' (take 1).   P: George Martin.   E: Geoff Emerick.   2E: Richard Lush.

How does an artist know when – or how – to apply the final brush stroke to a masterpiece? With 'A Day In The Life', *Sgt Pepper's Lonely Hearts Club Band* was already set to end with that tremendous, crashing piano chord lasting more than 40 seconds. But as no silence had been left between each song it would be a pity, the Beatles thought, if there was silence *after* the final chord. Why not put something in the concentric run-out groove? People with automatic players would hear a quick burst of it before their pick-up arm returned to base, people without such luxurious equipment would find the noise in the concentric playing on and on *ad infinitum*, or at least until the arm was manually lifted off.

But what should they do? Geoff Emerick recalls the circumstances. "They were all there discussing how to end the LP but the decision to throw in a bit of nonsense gibberish came together in about 10 minutes. They ran down to the studio floor and we recorded them twice – on each track of a two-track tape. They made funny noises, said random things; just nonsense. We chopped up the tape, put it back together, played it backwards and threw it in." By "threw it in" Emerick means that he edited copies of the "nonsense" into the mono and stereo masters, ready for cutting by Harry Moss. "It took Harry about eight attempts to get it right because the slightest incorrect placing of a stylus at the very beginning of the LP side can put the concentric groove out. We had to enquire if putting musical content in the run-out groove would tear the metal when the records are stamped out at the factory."

It was only after the LP had been released that certain Beatles fans – there will always be a few who play things *backwards* to hear any hidden messages – discovered that this concentric groove gibberish, when played in reverse, revealed a *very* naughty message, totally unintended by the Beatles or anyone in the control room on the night of 21 April 1967. "There was no hidden meaning," insists Emerick.

"I was told by chaps who'd been in the business a long time that cutting things into the run-out grooves was an old idea that they used to do on 78s," says Harry Moss. "Cutting *Sgt Pepper* was not too difficult except that because we couldn't play the masters I had to wait for white label pressings before I could hear whether or not I'd cut the concentric groove successfully. These were the things which, at the time, I used to swear about! It was George Martin who first asked me to do it. I replied 'It's gonna be bloody awkward, George, but I'll give it a go!' "

The Beatles never attended any record cuts, not even this one – done by Moss for mono on 28 April and for stereo on 1 May. "Paul once asked me to cut something for him. I replied 'Are you coming up?' He said 'What for? If I came up you'd only baffle me with science and I wouldn't know what you were doing!' "

The Beatles were not finished with *Sgt Pepper's Lonely Hearts Club Band* yet. Across the spiral of the run-out groove – after the end of the piano chord but before the concentric nonsense – John Lennon suggested that they insert a high-pitch whistle especially for dogs, 15 kilocycles, to make them perk up. This was relatively simple for Harry Moss to do, indeed the tone was not added until the disc cutting stage. "It was done at the same pitch as the police dog whistles, " says Moss. "My dog hears it now when I play the record. The dog will suddenly sit up and look around and I'd think 'Oh yeah, that's the one with the 15 KC on the end!' "

[Subsequent re-pressings of the LP did not include the high frequency tone or the chatter in the concentric groove, but the 1987 compact disc release and the spin-offs from that (in the UK a cassette, in the USA a re-mastered album and cassette) have both.]

Tuesday 25 April

Studio Three: 7.00pm-3.45am. Recording: 'Magical Mystery Tour' (tape loop of coach noise, takes 1-3, tape reduction take 3 into takes 4-8).   P: George Martin.   E: Geoff Emerick.   2E: Richard Lush.

When Paul McCartney was in the USA in early April 1967 he came up with the idea for a Beatles television film about a mystery tour on a coach, and during the flight home on 11 April he jotted down his ideas. He showed them to the other Beatles when they got together a few days later and by the end of that day, between the four of them, a 60-minute 'special' was conceived: *Magical Mystery Tour*.

A working schedule had yet to be drawn up but it was obvious that whenever the film would be made it would require a title song. *Magical Mystery Tour* was very much Paul's concept so it was Paul who wrote it. The first *MMT* recording session took place on this night, 25 April.

Much of the evening was spent in rehearsal, Paul seated at the piano, explaining to the other Beatles his ideas so far. Trumpets were needed, it was decided. (These were overdubbed on 3 May.) After a while recording proper began: a basic rhythm track of two guitars, piano and drums. Three takes were made, the third being 'best' and this was then subjected to five reduction mixes, down to one track of a new tape, the final edition – take eight – being marked 'best basic'.

Although the final content of the song may have been in a state of flux, one thing was clear: coach noises were required, and this meant another raid on the Abbey Road sound effects collection. "Volume 36: Traffic Noise Stereo" satisfied requirements, especially since the sounds of the cars and lorries it contained ranged across a stereo image, passing from left to right or right to left. "I did that leaning over a bridge on the M1 motorway," recalls Stuart Eltham. "It was a quiet day, a Sunday, because that was the only way one could capture the sound of individual vehicles. On any other day all I would have had was a mass of traffic noise."

The coach sound effect was made into a tape loop, to be dropped in to the song at remix stages.

Wednesday 26 April

**Studio Three: 7.00pm-2.00am. Recording: 'Magical Mystery Tour' (SI onto take 8, tape reduction take 8 into take 9).
P: George Martin.   E: Geoff Emerick.   2E: Richard Lush.**

Overdubbing of bass guitar (Paul) onto track two of the new 'Magical Mystery Tour' tape, percussion (maracas, cowbell, tambourines etc by the four Beatles, Neil Aspinall and Mal Evans) onto track three and backing vocal 'shouts' (by John, Paul and George) onto track four, the latter with much added echo.

The four-track tape full once again, another reduction mix was made, take eight becoming nine, ready for more overdubbing on 27 April and 3 May.

Thursday 27 April

Studio Three: 7.00pm-12.45am. Recording: 'Magical Mystery Tour' (SI onto take 9). Mono mixing: 'Magical Mystery Tour' (remixes 1-4, from take 9).   P: George Martin.   E: Geoff Emerick.   2E: Richard Lush.

The addition of vocals onto the two remaining 'Magical Mystery Tour' tracks of tape: Paul's lead and John and George's backing. "All that 'Roll up, roll up for the Magical Mystery Tour' bit was taped very slow so that it played back very fast," says Richard Lush. "They really wanted those voices to sound different."

Four mono demo remixes were made before the session ended, the fourth being 'best', in order that acetate discs could be cut.

Wednesday 3 May

Studio Three: 7.00pm-12.15am. Recording: 'Magical Mystery Tour' (SI onto take 9).   P: George Martin.   E: Malcolm Addey.   2E: Richard Lush.

The brass overdub for 'Magical Mystery Tour', for which four outside musicians were booked. David Mason was one, playing his third Beatles session in as many months, Elgar [Gary] Howarth, Roy Copestake and John Wilbraham were the others.

Geoff Emerick was otherwise employed on this evening and was temporarily replaced as Beatles balance engineer by Malcolm Addey. "Paul McCartney was humming to the musicians the notes that he wanted," recalls Addey, "trying for a long time to get his thoughts across to them. In the end we had to send the trumpet players off for tea while Paul

and George [Martin] worked things out on the studio three piano." Brass musician Philip Jones OBE, though not on the session, is a good friend of those who were and he recalls what they told him about it. "Gary Howarth got so fed up with them not knowing what they wanted that he wrote something out for them himself. It was his idea they used."

The session ran over time, finishing at 12.15am instead of 10.00pm, but everything worked out well in the end and Paul got the sounds that he wanted.

And where *was* Geoff Emerick? He was away on

location, recording – of all things – *Adge Cutler's Family Album with the Wurzels. Recorded LIVE at the Royal Oak, Nailsea, Zummerset!* Ken Townsend also made the trip, and he recalls, "The Beatles only booked the 3 May session a on 27 April, and both Geoff and I immediately said that we wouldn't be available. There's an unwritten rule in the studios which is that if one has been booked for a session one does not switch. The Beatles said 'You can't go to Somerset to record the Wurzels rather than the Beatles!', 'Yes we can!,' said Geoff, 'it's booked and that's that'.

Thursday 4 May

Studio Three (control room only): 7.00-11.15pm. Mono mixing: 'Magical Mystery Tour' (remixes 1-7, from take 9). P: George Martin.   E: Geoff Emerick.   2E: Richard Lush.

Seven mono remixes of 'Magical Mystery Tour' [numbered one to seven irrespective of the one to four made on 27 April]. At this stage the 'best' mix was not

determined, being either five or seven, though neither was used on record owing to an additional overdub being done on 7 November.

Tuesday 9 May

Studio Two: 11.00pm-6.15am. Recording: 'Untitled' (take 1).   P: George Martin.   E: Geoff Emerick.   2E: Richard Lush.

A somewhat unproductive session: more than seven hours of instrumental jamming with little more than 16 minutes being committed to tape. Although the music seemed to lack any direction at least the Beatles knew how to follow each other, though whether this

was pure instinctiveness or whether the "song" was pre-planned is not clear. The instruments used – all well out of tune, incidentally – were an electric guitar, another guitar with a vibrato effect, drums and a harmonium.

Thursday 11 May

Studio One, Olympic Sound Studios, 117 Church Road, Barnes, London SW13: 9.00pm-3.00am. Recording: 'Baby, You're A Rich Man' (takes 1-12, tape reduction take 12 into takes 1 and 2). Mono mixing: 'Baby, You're A Rich Man' (remix 1, from take 2). P: George Martin.   E: Keith Grant.   2E: Eddie Kramer.

Another session outside of Abbey Road, following the 9 February visit to Regent Sound Studio. Olympic was one of the top independent studios in Britain, turning out many hit records. The Rolling Stones had taken to recording there, even though studio manager Keith Grant was equally keen to promote the venue's valuable film soundtrack work.

It was Grant who engineered this session. "I'm a terrible pusher on sessions," he says. "I do a lot of orchestral work and you naturally push people along. The Beatles said that this was the fastest record they'd ever made. They were used to a much more leisurely pace. We started the session at about 9pm and it was finished and mixed by about 3am, vocals and everything. They kept on playing, version after version, then we spooled back to the one they liked and overdubbed the vocals." [It thus became the first Beatles song to be recorded and mixed for record entirely outside of Abbey Road.]

George Chkiantz, tape operator on the session the next

time the Beatles went to Olympic, remembers discussing this session with Keith Grant and Eddie Kramer. "They were both amazed at John Lennon's voice. They'd long been wondering what it would be like to record and they were saying how great it was. They couldn't believe anyone could sing that well."

On 7 June 1967 it was announced to the press that the Beatles had agreed to the making of a full-length animated film to be called *Yellow Submarine* after their song of 1966. They would be providing the soundtrack, it was said, unveiling at least three new songs and allowing use of some others already released. Agreements had actually been signed in early May, however, so the group had *two* projects on the boil – *Magical Mystery Tour* and *Yellow Submarine* – within weeks of the completion of their most ambitious recording project, *Sgt Pepper's Lonely Hearts Club Band* and before it had even been released.

'Baby, You're A Rich Man' was the first song to be

recorded especially for the *Yellow Submarine* film, although it was soon plucked for another destination – the B-side of the next single – and hence never made it onto the soundtrack LP. (It was still used in the film, however.) Numerous instruments can be heard in the song: John played piano, a Clavioline – an electronic keyboard instrument with its own amplifier which plays just one note at a time and can imitate the tonal qualities of various instruments – and sang both lead and backing vocals. Paul played bass, another piano and sang backing vocals, George played lead guitar, sang backing vocals and added handclaps while Ringo played drums and tambourine and also contributed a spot of handclapping. Eddie Kramer, second engineer, reportedly contributed a little vibraphone.

One of the session's two tape boxes offers a tantalising question, adding to the group name The Beatles the words "+ Mick Jagger?" Jagger certainly did attend the session, ostensibly to watch the proceedings, but it is feasible that he sang backing vocals in the free-for-all choruses near the end of the song.

Friday 12 May

Studio Two: 7.00pm-12.30am. Recording: 'All Together Now' (takes 1-9). Mono mixing: 'All Together Now' (remixes 1-6, from take 9).   P: n/a.   E: Geoff Emerick.   2E: Richard Lush.

It must have been the effect of the previous night's work at Olympic which made the Beatles start, finish and mix (for mono) another new song in one evening session – and a short one at that, less than six hours. There was no producer on this occasion however, although Geoff Emerick was in charge of the control room in George Martin's absence.

The song was 'All Together Now', for the *Yellow Submarine* soundtrack, and it was recorded in nine takes – the ninth being 'best' – with innumerable overdubs, and containing two acoustic guitars, a harmonica, bass drum, a triangle, bass guitar, horn, much handclapping and – on top of it all – a Paul McCartney lead vocal and party-style backing vocals

by anyone else who happened to be around. The three words of the title are sung almost 50 times in little over two minutes.

The recording was not unlike 'Yellow Submarine' itself, with much raiding of the studio two trap room for miscellaneous bits of sound effects equipment.

Wednesday 17 May

Studio Two: 7.00pm-2.30am. Recording: 'You Know My Name (Look Up The Number)' (Part 1, takes 1-14). P and E: Geoff Emerick.   2E: Richard Lush.

There can be few more peculiar Beatles recordings than 'You Know My Name (Look Up The Number)', a quirky, anything goes song, conjuring up a seedy night-club atmosphere. And no other Beatles song was to be deliberately held 'in the can' for so long, for it was to remain unissued until March 1970.

The final song was a composite of five different parts, each recorded separately. Part one was tackled on this evening when 14 takes were done – though, with the nature of the recording, little difference could be determined between these and the rehearsals, which were also taped. The best was take 10 – guitars,

drums, bass, handclaps, bongos and a little vocals – and it was marked down for being edited into the master at a later stage.

Thursday 25 May

De Lane Lea Music Recording Studios, 129 Kingsway, London WC2: time unknown. Recording: 'Too Much' (working title of 'It's All Too Much') (takes 1-4).   P: n/a.   E: Dave Siddle.   2E: Mike Weighell.

Another new London location for the Beatles: the basement studio of an office building directly opposite the Holborn London Underground station.

The song recorded on this occasion, the somewhat

chaotic 'Too Much' [later re-titled 'It's All Too Much'], was another *Yellow Submarine* number, composed by George Harrison.

There were scores of rehearsals taped this night in

addition to four takes proper of the rhythm track (organ, lead guitar, bass guitar and drums). The Beatles returned to De Lane Lea on 26 May to continue the work.

Friday 26 May

De Lane Lea Music Recording Studios, 129 Kingsway, London WC2: time unknown. Recording: 'Too Much' (working title of 'It's All Too Much') (tape reduction take 4 into takes 1 and 2, SI onto take 2).   P: n/a.   E: Dave Siddle.   2E: Mike Weighell.

A reduction mixdown from take four of 'It's All Too Much', running at 8'09" at this stage, with additional percussion, George's lead vocal, John and Paul's backing vocals and handclaps. Near to the end of the song George sang a couplet from 'Sorrow', the 1966 hit by the Beatles' friends from years past, the Merseys. John and Paul's backing, meanwhile, started to waver a little, the chanted "too much" eventually becoming "tuba" and then "Cuba". It was that sort of a song.

Peter Blake's original sketch for the LP cover idea, and George Martin's original album label copy. His unusual suggestion that Geoff Emerick receive a sleeve credit as engineer was met with a "???" by an unidentified but clearly high-ranking hand, for the credit never appeared.

PARLOPHONE L.P.   SGT. PEPPER'S LONELY HEARTS CLUB BAND.

Artist: The Beatles.

Recorded: November '66 - April '67.

Cover: Mr. Dunton has this.

Job No.   3014.

Credits: Produced by George Martin.
                  Recording Engineer - Geoffrey Emerick. ???

Side 1.   SGT. PEPPER'S LONELY HEARTS CLUB BAND.
                  WITH A LITTLE HELP FROM MY FRIENDS.
                  LUCY IN THE SKY WITH DIAMONDS.
                  GETTING BETTER.
                  FIXING A HOLE.
                  SHE'S LEAVING HOME.
                  BEING FOR THE BENEFIT OF MR. KITE.

Side 2.   WITHIN YOU WITHOUT YOU.
                  WHEN I'M 64.
                  LOVELY RITA.
                  GOOD MORNING GOOD MORNING.
                  SGT. PEPPER'S LONELY HEARTS CLUB BAND.
                  A DAY IN THE LIFE.

All titles - Lennon-McCartney   Northern Songs   except -
             'Within you without you'
             (George Harrison) Northern Songs.

April 21st.   George Martin.
                  A.I.R. London Ltd.

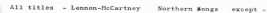

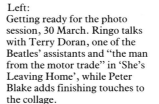

Left:
Getting ready for the photo session, 30 March. Ringo talks with Terry Doran, one of the Beatles' assistants and "the man from the motor trade" in 'She's Leaving Home', while Peter Blake adds finishing touches to the collage.

Above:
Photographer Michael Cooper surveys the cut-outs. Spot the ones not used!

Thursday 1 June

De Lane Lea Music Recording Studios, 129 Kingsway, London WC2: time unknown. Recording: 'Untitled' (no numbered takes). P: George Martin.   E: Dave Siddle.   2E: Mike Weighell.

LP release: *Sgt Pepper's Lonely Hearts Club Band*. Parlophone PMC 7027 (mono)/PCS 7027 (stereo). A: 'Sgt Pepper's Lonely Hearts Club Band'; 'With A Little Help From My Friends'; 'Lucy In The Sky With Diamonds'; 'Getting Better'; 'Fixing A Hole'; 'She's Leaving Home'; 'Being For The Benefit Of Mr Kite!' B: 'Within You Without You'; 'When I'm Sixty-Four'; 'Lovely Rita'; 'Good Morning Good Morning'; 'Sgt Pepper's Lonely Hearts Club Band (Reprise)'; 'A Day In The Life'.

"I was aware that new things were happening," says George Martin, "and I was very excited about it. I loved what the Beatles were doing and I was saying to them 'Let's have another session. Come up with more of these great ideas!' "

Sgt Pepper's Lonely Hearts Club Band was the Beatles' eighth album in a little over four years, released (unusually, on a Thursday) just a few days short of the fifth anniversary of the group's test/audition at Abbey Road studios. It would scarcely be an exaggeration to say that millions of words have been written about the LP, almost every one fulsome in its praise. But what surely stands out most of all is the Beatles' sheer *progression* to this point in time. Here were four musicians, raw and inexperienced in June 1962, changing popular music right about face by June 1967. With their astonishing fame, respect and talent the Beatles made *Sgt Pepper* in a heady atmosphere when, to use the cliché, they could do no wrong, and at a time when they could do virtually *anything* and succeed. Paul McCartney conducting a 40-piece orchestra? No problem!

"There's one thing they always used to say," remembers Phil McDonald. " 'There's no such word as *can't*. What do you mean *can't*?' The word just wasn't in their vocabulary. There was always a way around any problem. If they had an idea – any idea – they thought it must be possible to do it. That's how *Sgt Pepper* was recorded."

Sgt Pepper's Lonely Hearts Club Band typifies the year of 1967 and, as such, must rank as a masterpiece, for surely the prime objective for any piece of music is that it captures the *time* of its recording. Part of the reason for this may be that 1967, in turn, influenced *Sgt Pepper* itself. The clothes worn by the Beatles at the sessions would have made a splendid fashion parade. Drugs – the Beatles were using them more frequently during the recording of *Sgt Pepper* than at any other time – also played a major role, expanding the imagination of four already very creative people. There was even psychedelic lighting inside studio two at Abbey Road, installed at the direct request of the Beatles. Well, sort of psychedelic anyway. . .

"By 1967 the Beatles had become a little bit fed up with studio two at Abbey Road," says Geoff Emerick. "They'd been there for five years, with the plain plaster walls, wooden floor and the huge acoustic sheeting which hangs down there, full of dried seaweed! And the big white lamps in the ceiling were just too much. They asked if the studio could install some psychedelic lighting. Later that same day someone [studio electrician Harry Monk] came along and installed this strange contraption: three five-foot red fluorescent tubes on a microphone stand. I had a lava lamp and a red darkroom lamp at home so I brought them in to brighten up the control room. Then one of the Beatles brought in a stroboscope. I don't suppose they knew that strobes can have a dangerous effect if they're left on too long. Sure enough, after about five minutes of fun they all sat down feeling sick!"

Keith Slaughter has an amusing postscript to this story. "George Harrison came into studio two at Abbey Road quite recently (1986). He came up the stairs and said 'It's just like last time we worked here'. As he was saying this he saw the fluorescent tubes and really burst out laughing, saying 'They're still here!' "

Had the Abbey Road studio personnel been given annual report cards like school children, a number would have been branded 'abuse of equipment', for in their efforts to innovate at the direct request of the Beatles, people often fell foul of the unwritten studio rules. Geoff Emerick vividly recalls one occasion. "John wanted a really unusual vocal sound so I suspended a very thin condenser microphone tied in a plastic bag inside a milk bottle filled with water. Lennon was singing at the top of his voice at this bottle when the studio manager came in. 'What's that noise? How are you getting that?' I was terrified! We both stood around the bottle, shoulders at all angles, trying to hide it.

"The Beatles would say 'We don't want the piano to sound like a piano, we want it to sound like a guitar. But we then want the guitar to sound like a piano.' We used to sit there thinking 'Well why play the wretched thing in the first place?' And we never had the luxury of 1980s gimmick boxes then, just ordinary tape machines."

Jerry Boys, then a tape operator at Abbey Road, now a studio manager in his own right, sums up *Sgt Pepper's Lonely Hearts Club Band* from a technical standpoint. "If you listen to the album now, there are noises which are still impossible to make, even with today's computerised 48-track equipment and all the microchips imaginable. It's a very very clever record. In terms of creative use of recording it has been one of *the* major steps forward."

George Martin, Geoff Emerick and others involved on the production side of *Sgt Pepper* were understandably aggrieved when they later read a John Lennon interview slating the LP. "John later said he thought *Pepper* was a terrible album," says Geoff Emerick. "He said something like 'We don't want to make another album like that rubbish!' which was a ridiculous comment." "John told me he was never satisfied with anything he'd done, Beatles or solo," says George Martin. "In one interview [*Rolling Stone* 1970, published 1971] he was vicious to everybody, including me, for which I hardly ever forgave him. It was completely unwarranted. I met him in Hollywood in 1974 and spent an evening with him. I said 'I don't know if you want to see me, John' and he replied 'Oh, come on George! I was out of my head when I said a lot of those things. Take no notice of what I said.' It was a kind of apology which I was grateful for. But John was a strange person and he did change enormously from the early days."

Quality and value for money were much on the Beatles' minds when *Sgt Pepper* was issued. The record came in what was then a very novel, deluxe colour sleeve, with free cardboard cut-outs and the song lyrics printed in full – a first. The Beatles also posed for a special poster issued by their fan club and even had the publisher of their official monthly magazine use colour for the first time. And the Beatles insisted that the album be issued identically all over the world, even in the USA where Capitol Records fell into corporate line with the UK on a Beatles album for the first time. At one point *Sgt Pepper* was even going to be pressed on coloured vinyl, recalls Tony Bramwell. "It would have been like one of those children's records from Woolworth's, with the splattered colours." Bramwell also remembers the original working title of the LP: " 'One Down, Six To Go', a joky reference to the new contract with EMI."

It is a contentious point that *Sgt Pepper's Lonely Hearts Club Band* represented the Beatles' last real *united* push behind a project, and their last truly creative offering. Certainly after the LP had been completed the Beatles' recordings – throughout the remainder of April, all of May and early June, for example – did display a startling lack of cohesion and enthusiasm, as though they had injected their all into *Sgt Pepper* and now wanted to take things easy. On this day, 1 June 1967, perhaps the most celebrated day in their career, the Beatles went into the studio and recorded nothing but untitled, unplanned, highly tedious and – frankly – downright amateurish instrumental jams, with a bass guitar, an organ, lead guitar with reverb, guitar strings being scraped, drums and tambourine. The single-minded channelling of their great talent so evident on *Sgt Pepper's Lonely Hearts Club Band* did seem, for the moment, to have disappeared.

A rare set of outtakes from the cover photo session.

Friday 2 June

De Lane Lea Music Recording Studios, 129 Kingsway, London WC2: 8.30pm-2.00am. Recording: 'It's All Too Much' (SI onto take 2); 'Untitled' (no numbered takes). P: George Martin.   E: Dave Siddle.   2E: Mike Weighell.

A brass and woodwind overdub onto 'It's All Too Much', with four trumpets and one bass clarinet. The session was booked to start at 8pm and finish at 11pm but it ran over time. David Mason – again – was one of the trumpeters and his diary indicates a finish at 2.00am. "George Harrison was in charge of that session," says Mason. "I don't think he really knew what he wanted." The clarinetist was Paul Harvey.

During the evening the Beatles also found the time to fill two more tapes with the kind of rambling, instrumental and impromptu jamming recorded on the previous night.

Wednesday 7 June

Studio Two: 7.00pm-2.00am. Recording: 'You Know My Name (Look Up The Number)' (SI onto take 9, takes 20-24). P: George Martin.   E: Geoff Emerick.   2E: Richard Lush.

More crazy 'You Know My Name (Look Up The Number)' recordings! After returning to take nine, taped – and at that stage overlooked – on 17 May, and overdubbing various bits and pieces, the remainder of the session was spent working out further ideas. These grew so far apart from the song in hand that the 'You Know My Name (Look Up The Number)' title on the tape box has since been deleted and marked 'Instrumental – Unidentified' instead.

A study of the tape itself reveals almost 20 minutes of rhythm track recording, beginning with take 20 and consisting of an amateurish flute track (played, presumably, by a Beatle), electric guitar, drums, organ and tambourine. At one point Paul McCartney can be heard discussing the chord structure with George Harrison, suggesting the music was pre-planned. But when the playing starts that is the last impression one receives. . .

Thursday 8 June

Studio Two: 7.00pm-1.00am. Recording: 'You Know My Name (Look Up The Number)' (Part 2, takes 1-12; part 3, takes 1-4; part 4, takes 1-6; part 5, take 1). P: George Martin.   E: Geoff Emerick.   2E: Richard Lush.

Another session for 'You Know My Name (Look Up The Number)'. In addition to the Beatles' piano, drums, lead guitar, bass and vibraphone tracks, Brian Jones of the Rolling Stones played alto saxophone on the recording.

The part of 'You Know My Name (Look Up The Number)' numbered five was a most peculiar recording, with sound effects and noises which would not have been out of place in a *Carry On* film soundtrack. Harmonica, bongos, piano, a bird whistle and several other bits and pieces from the studio two trap room were all used.

Friday 9 June

Studio Two (control room only): 7.00-11.00pm. Editing: 'You Know My Name (Look Up The Number)' (take 30, consisting of take 9 of part 1, take 12 of part 2, take 4 of part 3, take 6 of part 4 and take 1 of part 5). Mono mixing: 'You Know My Name (Look Up The Number)' (remix 1, from take 30). P: George Martin.   E: Geoff Emerick.   2E: Richard Lush.

The culmination of the work on 'You Know My Name (Look Up The Number)': a single take (numbered 30) lasting 6'08", rhythm track only.

Vocals would not be added until 30 April 1969. In the meantime a rough mono remix was made for acetate cutting purposes.

Wednesday 14 June

Studio One, Olympic Sound Studios, 117 Church Road, Barnes, London SW13: time unknown. Recording: 'All You Need Is Love' (takes 1-33, tape reduction of take 10). P: George Martin.   E: Eddie Kramer.   2E: George Chkiantz.

It was on 22 May, four days after the contract was signed, that the announcement went out: the Beatles, along with one other item (reported by Magnus Magnusson from the new town of Cumbernauld in Scotland) would represent the BBC – and therefore Britain – in a live television programme to be broadcast worldwide during the evening of Sunday 25 June (UK time). They would be shown working in the recording studio on a new song written especially for the occasion.

Only the Beatles could have been so supremely casual about appearing in the world's first television satellite link-up and being seen by a potential 400 million viewers. "I don't know if they had prepared any ideas but they left it very late to write the song," says Geoff Emerick. "John said 'Oh God, is it that close? I suppose we'd better write something. . .'" 'All You Need Is Love', the song he wrote, was *the* perfect encapsulation and embodiment of the summer of 1967 and its anthemic qualities are as real today as the day it was written. Equally importantly, it fitted the one and only brief given the Beatles by the BBC: keep it simple so that viewers across the globe will understand. Right from the beginning of take one 'La Marseillaise' [the French national anthem] was a vital part of the song, emphasising the international flavour of the occasion.

The first recordings of 'All You Need Is Love', the basic rhythm track and a little vocal work, were made late night on 14 June at Olympic Sound Studios in Barnes, the Beatles playing instruments normally associated with session musicians: John on harpsichord, Paul the double-bass and George dabbling on a violin. Drums were as important as ever so Ringo assumed his familiar role. George Chkiantz was tape operator on the session. "The Beatles were very opportunistic and very positive. At one point we accidentally made a curious sound on the tape and they not only wanted to keep it on the recording they also asked us to deliberately repeat that same sound again. Other groups would have been annoyed but the Beatles capitalised on the mistake.

"They did a four-track to four-track mixdown – with curiously little care we all thought – and George Martin specifically told me to keep any little chatter before the take began."

Monday 19 June

Studio Three: 7.00pm-1.45am. Tape copying: 'All You Need Is Love' (of take 10). Recording: 'All You Need Is Love' (SI onto take 10). P: George Martin.   E: Geoff Emerick. 2E: Richard Lush.

Overdubbing of lead and backing vocals onto tracks three and four of the four-track tape, and drums, piano (played by George Martin) and banjo (John Lennon) onto track two.

Wednesday 21 June

Abbey Road, Room 53: 4.30-5.00pm. Mono mixing: 'All You Need Is Love' (remix 1, from take 10). P: George Martin.   E: Malcolm Addey.   2E: Phil McDonald.   Studio Three (control room only): 7.00-11.30pm. Mono mixing: 'All You Need Is Love' (demo remix, unnumbered). P: George Martin.   E: Geoff Emerick.   2E: Richard Lush.

Two remixes of the Olympic Sound rhythm track for 'All You Need Is Love'. An acetate of the second, unnumbered, was given to Derek Burrell Davis, director of the BBC outside broadcast team for 25 June.

Friday 23 June

Studio One: 8.00-11.00pm. Recording: 'All You Need Is Love' (tape reduction of take 10, takes 34-43 as SI onto take 10). P: George Martin.   E: Geoff Emerick.   2E: Richard Lush.

Enter the orchestra for the first time in the 'All You Need Is Love' story [The full list of musicians can be found under 25 June.]

Saturday 24 June

Studio One: 5.00-8.00pm. Recording: 'All You Need Is Love' (takes 44-47 as SI onto take 10). P: George Martin.   E: Geoff Emerick.   2E: Richard Lush.

Just one day from The Big Event – and to prove the point the Beatles and Abbey Road threw open the usually firmly-closed studio doors to more than 100 journalists and photographers.

The press call took up most of the late-morning period and in the afternoon, from 2.00 to 4.00, there was a rehearsal for the BBC. But afterwards the Beatles and orchestra settled down in studio one to make some additions to the 'All You Need Is Love' rhythm track, made especially important by a late decision – on this day, in fact! – to issue 'All You Need Is Love' as a single after the television broadcast.

Rehearsals for 'All You Need Is Love', 24 June.

Sunday 25 June

Studio One: 2.00pm-1.00am. Recording: 'All You Need Is Love' (takes 48-50; BBC rehearsal takes 1-3; takes 51-53; takes 54-58 [58 being live BBC broadcast]; SI onto take 58).
P: George Martin.   E: Geoff Emerick.   2E: Richard Lush/Martin Benge.

To quote BBC publicity, the *Our World* programme "(was) for the first time ever, linking five continents and bringing man face to face with mankind, in places as far apart as Canberra and Cape Kennedy, Moscow and Montreal, Samarkand and Söderfors, Takamatsu and Tunis". (Actually, the Soviet Union dropped out at the last moment.) As much as these things can be measured, 400 million people across five continents tuned in and saw this Beatles recording session.

It was, as one might well imagine, a hectic, unforgettable day for all concerned. "Horrendous, there's no two ways about it," recalls engineer Geoff Emerick. "To attempt to record what we recorded even *without* the link-up was ridiculous!"

The Beatles spent much of the day perfecting the song and rehearsing for the BBC cameras set up in studio one. These were linked with cables by the score to the outside broadcast van squeezed into the tiny Abbey Road car park. From there the sound and pictures would traverse the world via the Early Bird 'space booster' and Lana Bird and ATS/B satellites.

Take 58 was the all-important broadcast version, although George Martin greatly decreased the chance of an on-air foul-up by having the Beatles play to their own pre-recorded rhythm track of take 10. Only the vocals, bass guitar, the lead guitar solo in the middle eight, drums and the orchestra were actually live.

The pre-taped rhythm made up track one of the four-track tape. Onto track two went the bass, lead guitar solo and drums, track three the orchestra and track four the vocals. An instantaneous remix by Martin and Emerick was fed directly to the BBC van and hence to the world. "It was getting very panicky by transmission time, anything could have gone wrong," says Abbey Road balance engineer Peter Vince, happy to be on the sidelines for once. "I wouldn't have been in Geoff's shoes for all the tea in China." "Of course he wouldn't!," jokes Emerick today. "We actually went on air about 40 seconds early. George and I were having a welcome shot of Scotch whisky when we got the word over the intercom. There was a big panic to hide the bottle and the glasses. We were shoving them under the mixing console!"

The televised sequence of events seem a little corny now and existing studio tapes reveal the considerable rehearsal time which went into this "spontaneous" performance. Broadcaster Steve Race introduced the Beatles playing and singing the basic song, the cameras then cut to the control room where George Martin suggested it was time to bring in the orchestra, the musicians filed in, Mal Evans got into the picture by collecting empty tea cups, then it was back to the studio floor for orchestra and Beatles – all except for Ringo sitting on high stools and surrounded by a large group of friends – to play the song in its entirety. From start to finish the sequence lasted only six minutes but nerves were badly frayed by the end. Tape operator Richard Lush, to whom George Martin addressed the on-air request "Run back the tape please, Richard", recalls ". . . shaking like a leaf even though we rehearsed that bit over and over on the Saturday and Sunday!"

"Lennon was very nervous that day too," says Lush. "He might not have looked it but I was used to working with him and you get to know when someone is nervous."

The broadcast took the form of a party. The orchestral musicians wore formal evening dress while the many friends sitting cross-legged on the studio floor – among them Mick Jagger, Marianne Faithfull, Keith Richard, Keith Moon, Eric Clapton, Pattie Harrison, Jane Asher, Mike McCartney, Graham Nash and his wife, Gary Leeds and Hunter Davies – were dressed in the colourful clothes of the day. (Even though the programme was not broadcast in colour.) There were plenty of streamers, balloons and humorous placards too, and much singing along. At the song's end some of the friends danced the conga around the studio.

Also among the throng – at the special invitation of the Beatles – was Abbey Road studio assistant Terry Condon. "Mal Evans made me wear one of those long, colourful coats – I was no teenager then! – and sit down on the floor for the cameras. It was wonderful fun. When the session was over the girl who had arranged the fantastic flower displays gave me some to take home to the wife and to give to the local hospital. As I walked out of the building I was jumped on by swarms of Beatles fans and was left holding a bunch of stalks!"

With George Martin – looking dapper in a white suit – furiously employed in the studio control room, the task of conducting the 13-man ad hoc orchestra was given to Manfred Mann saxophonist and multi-instrumentalist Mike Vickers. This same ensemble had also been employed on 23 and 24 June for recording and rehearsals. There were four violinists: Sidney Sax (leader), Patrick Halling, Eric Bowie and Jack Holmes; two tenor saxophonists: Rex Morris and Don Honeywill; two trombonists: Evan Watkins and Harry Spain; one accordionist: Jack Emblow; and two trumpeters: Stanley Woods (also doubling on flügelhorn) and David Mason, using the same trumpet as he did for 'Penny Lane'. "We played bits of Bach's Brandenburg concerto in the fade-out," he recalls.

George Martin's score for 'All You Need Is Love' contained extracts from a number of well known pieces of music. In addition to the Brandenburg and the famous introduction from 'La Marseillaise', snatches of 'Greensleeves', Glenn Miller's arrangement of 'In The Mood' and Lennon/McCartney's 'She Loves You' could be clearly distinguished in the fade-out. Except for the burst of 'She Loves You' which was an off-the-cuff Lennonism (during rehearsals he had also been singing 'Yesterday' and 'She'll Be Coming Round The Mountain When She Comes'!), George Martin had woven these pieces of music into the score believing them to be out of copyright. But 'In The Mood' was not, and in late July publishers KPM won a royalty settlement from EMI.

After the excitement was over and the guests had gone home the Beatles still had some work to do. "Later on in the night we overdubbed a snare drum roll by Ringo for the song's intro and John re-did some of his vocal," recalls Geoff Emerick. "Then it was ready for remixing and release a few days later."

Monday 26 June

Studio Two (control room only): 2.00-5.00pm. Mono mixing:

'All You Need Is Love' (remixes 2-10, from take 58). P: George Martin.   E: Geoff Emerick.   2E: Richard Lush.

Mono remixing for the rush release of 'All You Need Is Love' as a worldwide single. Nine mixes were done, five of which were complete, and at the end remix four was adjudged 'best'. "Funnily enough," says George Martin, "although John had added a new vocal, Ringo had added a drum roll and we had done a new mix, few people realised the single was any different to the TV version of the song."

Friday 7 July

Single release: 'All You Need Is Love'/'Baby, You're A Rich Man'. Parlophone R 5620.

Suffice it to say, a worldwide number one single. With the *Our World* promotion it could hardly have failed.

'All You Need Is Love' was the 15th Beatles single in the UK yet was the first time George Martin received a credit as producer on the label of a seven-inch Beatles disc. In the 1980s it seems that even those who make the tea receive credits on record sleeves and labels, and there are also large-type credits for the studio where the record was recorded, mixed and mastered for disc. But in the 1960s very little such information found its way onto records. Not even

Please Please Me, the Beatles' first album, carried a producer's credit for Martin, nor did *Sgt Pepper's Lonely Hearts Club Band* carry an engineer's credit for Geoff Emerick, despite his sterling contribution.

The release of 'All You Need Is Love' occurred just five weeks after the issue of the *Sgt Pepper* LP and yet the single did not appear on the album. Nor were any of the LP tracks issued as singles. Such a quality and quantity of output was the understandable envy of all of the Beatles' contemporaries.

Tuesday 22 August

Chappell Recording Studios, 52 Maddox Street, London W1: time unknown. Recording: 'Your Mother Should Know' (takes 1-8). P: George Martin. E: John Timperley. 2E: John Iles.

The first of two Beatles sessions at Chappell Recording Studios, an independent Central London set-up run by the music store and music publishing company of the same name until its closure in 1979. These two nights interrupted what would otherwise have been a 72-day interlude between Beatles sessions.

"Abbey Road was fully booked on those two nights," says Chappell engineer John Timperley, "but George Martin had been using our studio for quite a few of his other artistes and I had worked with him at Olympic and at IBC in the pre-Beatles days when Abbey Road was booked-up." Another reason for the Beatles choosing Chappell may have been Paul McCartney's attendance at a session there on 20 July, when the Chris Barber Band recorded a version of one of the earliest of all McCartney compositions, the instrumental 'Catcall', (originally 'Catswalk') and Paul contributed background whoops and yelps and a little piano.

'Your Mother Should Know' was very much a McCartney song, in similar vein to 'When I'm Sixty-Four', and although the song was subject to a later re-make at Abbey Road it was the Chappell version, with September overdubs, which made it onto the *Magical Mystery Tour* EP, even though the Chappell system of recording most tapes at 30 ips, half-inch, caused some transfer problems back at Abbey Road.

Wednesday 23 August

Chappell Recording Studios, 52 Maddox Street, London W1: time unknown. Recording: 'Your Mother Should Know' (tape reduction take 8 into take 9, SI onto take 9). P: George Martin. E: John Timperley. 2E: John Iles.

The Beatles' second and last session at Chappell, recording overdubs onto a tape-to-tape reduction and listening to playbacks.

This was the last Beatles session before the death of Brian Epstein who passed away on 27 August, aged just 32, after an accidental, accumulative drug overdose. Although Epstein had been an increasingly infrequent visitor to Beatles sessions he had nonetheless visited Abbey Road on a great number of occasions after that fateful day on 9 May 1962 when he brought along acetates of his unknown Liverpool group and played them to George Martin. Ironically, he also popped into Chappell on this night. "He came in to hear the playbacks looking extremely down and in a bad mood," recalls John Timperley. "He just stood at the back of the room listening, not saying much."

It was nothing less than apt that the 17 October memorial service for Epstein, attended by all four Beatles, should take place 300 metres from the EMI Studios, at the New London Synagogue, 33 Abbey Road.

Tuesday 5 September

Studio One: 7.00pm-1.00am. Recording: 'I Am The Walrus' (takes 1-16). P: George Martin. E: Geoff Emerick. 2E: Ken Scott/Richard Lush.

All four Beatles met up at Paul's St John's Wood house on 1 September, four days after the death of Brian Epstein. They decided many things, one of them being to press on with the *Magical Mystery Tour* project, temporarily postponing a planned visit to India to study Transcendental Meditation. Recording sessions for *MMT* really began in earnest on 5 September; the filming started on the 11th and the two then became intertwined through October. The record, a unique double EP package, was in the shops by early December. The film was premiered by the BBC on Boxing Day.

"*Magical Mystery Tour* was terribly badly organised and it's amazing that anything ever came out of it," says George Martin. "They were into their random period - they said 'If Laurence Olivier walks in this room we'll record it and it'll be great'. All that sort of thing, the John Cage influence. It was chaotic. the [coach] tour itself was dreadful, apparently, but I didn't go on that.

"I tended to lay back on *Magical Mystery Tour* and let them have their head. Some of the sounds weren't very good. Some were brilliant but some were bloody awful. 'I Am The Walrus' was organised – it was organised chaos. I'm proud of that. But there was also disorganised chaos that I'm not very proud of."

Geoff Emerick echoes George Martin's sentiments. "There was something lacking about *Magical Mystery Tour*. It wasn't going to be another album, or another single, it was probably going to be a film. It was a funny period."

Sixteen takes of 'I Am The Walrus', only five of them complete, were recorded on this day, comprising the basic rhythm track of bass guitar, lead guitar, an electric piano and drums, plus an overdub of a mellotron. The first three takes no longer exist because the tape was wound back to its beginning and re-used during the session.

The many other ingredients which were to make 'I Am The Walrus' one of the most peculiar but fascinating and superb Beatles recordings were added in later overdubs.

Wednesday 6 September

Studio Two: 7.00pm-3.00am. Recording: 'I Am The Walrus' (tape reduction take 16 into take 17, SI onto take 17). Mono mixing: 'I Am The Walrus' (remixes 1-4, from take 17). Recording: 'The Fool On The Hill' (take 1); 'Blue Jay Way' (take 1). P: George Martin.   E: Geoff Emerick.   2E: Ken Scott.

A full night's work on *Magical Mystery Tour* songs. First task was to make a reduction copy of 'I Am The Walrus' take 16, mixing down the four-track tape and calling it take 17. Onto this Paul and Ringo then superimposed more bass guitar and drums and John recorded his memorable lead vocal.

With this done four mono remixes of the song were made, the only complete version – the fourth – being marked as 'best'. The reason for this early remixing was to have acetate discs cut, for there was certainly

much work to be done on the recording before it would satisfy either John Lennon or George Martin.

'I Am The Walrus' was John's classic contribution to *Magical Mystery Tour*. Paul's was 'The Fool On The Hill', another superb ballad. Recording proper of this song would not begin until 25 September but on this day he taped a mono two-track demo version for acetate cutting purposes, sitting alone at the piano with no other Beatle on the recording.

Before the session ended the Beatles recorded take one of George Harrison's 'Blue Jay Way', written a month earlier while he was renting a house in the Los Angeles street of that name and was waiting for a fog-delayed friend (Derek Taylor) to arrive. The basic rhythm track was taped on this night, including a Hammond organ part. The vocals, cello and tambourine parts were all overdubbed later.

Thursday 7 September

Studio Two: 7.00pm-3.15am. Recording: 'Blue Jay Way' (tape reduction take 1 into take 2, SI onto take 2, tape reduction take 2 into take 3, SI onto take 3). P: George Martin.   E: Peter Vince.   2E: Ken Scott.

'Blue Jay Way' was to George Harrison what – in recording terms – 'Strawberry Fields Forever' or 'I Am The Walrus' were to John Lennon, in that it seized upon all the studio trickery and technical advancements of 1966 and 1967 and captured them in one song. 'Blue Jay Way' – as it ended up on disc – could not have been the same without Ken Townsend's ADT and its associated "flanging" effect, without the discovery of backwards tapes and without the use of strings scraping away in the background. Just like John's two songs, 'Blue Jay Way' makes fascinating listening for anyone interested in what could be achieved in a 1967 recording studio.

As explained previously, 'Blue Jay Way' was written by George when waiting for a friend to arrive out of the Los Angeles fog. The song manages to capture the *feel* of the fog very well, with its swirling organ parts and extensive use of ADT – at its very widest use – to create a phasing effect of almost two voices. The vocals were taped on this day as were the backing

vocals, sung by George – and occasionally joined by John and Paul – much of which was played backwards on the disc.

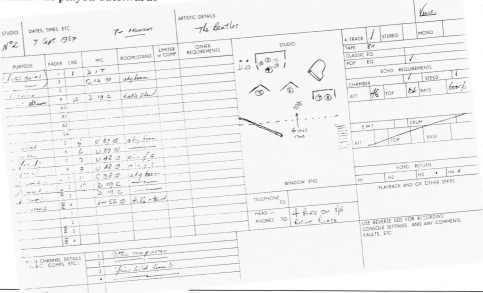

Friday 8 September

Studio Three: 7.00pm-2.45am. Recording: 'Aerial Tour Instrumental' (working title of 'Flying') (takes 1-6, tape reduction take 6 into takes 7 and 8, SI onto take 8). Mono mixing: 'Aerial Tour Instrumental' (working title of 'Flying') (remixes 1-4, from take 8). P: George Martin.   E: Geoff Emerick .   2E: Richard Lush.

'Flying' – or 'Aerial Tour Instrumental' as it was called until well into November (or 'Ariel Tour Instrumental' as it was frequently misspelt) – was more than just the first Beatles instrumental song to be released by EMI [the group recorded another – 'Cry For A Shadow' – in West Germany in 1961 during the sessions in which they backed Tony Sheridan], it was also the first song to be composed jointly by all four members of the group: Harrison/Lennon/McCartney/Starkey as the record label alphabetically – and diplomatically – listed them.

Aside from one-off non-vocal jam or experimental recordings, the Beatles had previously attempted only

one instrumental recording for EMI: '12-Bar Original' from the 1965 *Rubber Soul* sessions, and that had been left unreleased. But *Magical Mystery Tour*, being a film, required a few items of incidental music. 'Flying' was the first to be taped and the only one to make it onto disc.

But the version on record was quite different from the early takes. Those recorded on this first day included, for example, a jazzy, saxophone recording at the end of the song, seemingly copied straight from an unidentifiable modern jazz record!

Take six of the recording saw the debut appearance of

three different organs, recorded and then played backwards on separate tracks. The combination of these with the basic rhythm (drums, guitar and another organ) on track one created a most peculiar sound, a world away from the released version. But this four-track tape was reduced down to two later in the evening and a mellotron (John) and "vocals" by all four Beatles were taped as overdubs. Vocals on an instrumental song? Well, scat chanting then!

The evening was rounded off with four mono remixes of the song as it presently stood, the last version being 'best' and suitable for the cutting of playback acetate discs.

John during the shooting of the 'I Am The Walrus' sequence, probably the film's best. Note his "psychedelic" Rolls-Royce parked nearby.

Paul and the cameraman concoct on-the-spot plans for a beach scene.

Left:
'I Am The Walrus', filmed on location in West Malling, Kent in September 1967.
Above right:
. . . waiting to take him away. Paul in Allsop Place, London NW1 on 11 September 1967, about to board the coach and begin the adventure.

Magical Mystery Tour

Ringo, George, John and Paul
at West Malling.

Saturday 16 September

Studio Three: 7.00pm-3.45am. Recording: 'Your Mother Should Know' [re-make] (takes 20-30). Mono mixing: 'Blue Jay Way' (remix 1, from take 3). Tape copying: 'I Am The Walrus' (of remix mono 4); 'Blue Jay Way' (of remix mono 1). P: George Martin. E: Ken Scott. 2E: Jeff Jarratt.

This tape suggests that Paul McCartney, having already recorded 'Your Mother Should Know' (on 22 and 23 August), wasn't happy with that original attempt but perhaps didn't know how to improve on it. Singing live with the backing, Paul led the Beatles through 11 more, somewhat heavy-sounding takes on this night, the predominant sound of each being a military-style snare drum beat – with additional light cymbals work – by Ringo, plus bongos, a harmonium and jangle piano.

Then the song was left for Paul to ruminate further on what exactly should be done with it.

A demo remix of 'Blue Jay Way' was made on this day and then a 7½ ips reel-to-reel copy of this – and 'I Am The Walrus' – was taken away by a visitor, Gavrik

Losey, assistant to *Magical Mystery Tour* film producer Denis O'Dell, and – point of trivia – producer to George Harrison's executive producer role for the 1974 film *Little Malcolm and His Struggle Against The Eunuchs*.

There was another personnel change in the Abbey Road control room for this session, Ken Scott being promoted to balance engineer on a Beatles session for the first time and Jeff Jarratt (much later to be the man behind the Royal Philharmonic Orchestra's *Hooked On…*series) stepping in as tape operator. "I think Geoff Emerick had burnt himself out doing *Sgt Pepper*," says Scott, "and he had got bored by the whole *Magical Mystery Tour* situation. I'd been cutting for a while and as I was the next one for promotion I was lumbered! By this time the Beatles had taken over

things so much that I was more their right-hand-man than George Martin's. They half knew what they wanted and half didn't know, not until they'd tried everything. The only specific thought they seemed to have in their mind was to be different, but how a song might reach that point was down to their own interpretation and by throwing in as many ideas as possible, some of which would work and some wouldn't."

Monday 25 September

Studio Two: 7.00pm-3.00am. Recording: 'The Fool On The Hill' (takes 1-3, tape reduction take 3 into take 4, SI onto take 4). Mono mixing: 'The Fool On The Hill' (remix 1, from take 4). P: George Martin. E: Ken Scott. 2E: Richard Lush.

The first recording proper of Paul's ballad 'The Fool On The Hill', following the demo made on 6 September. Three takes of the basic rhythm track, including harmonicas played by John and George, were recorded on this day, starting again with take

one. A reduction mixdown then took the song into take four, onto which a recorder (played by Paul), drums and Paul's lead vocal were overdubbed. A mono remix for acetate cutting purposes was made before the session ended.

Tuesday 26 September

Studio Two: 7.00pm-4.15am. Recording: 'The Fool On The Hill' (tape reduction take 4 into take 5, SI onto take 5, tape reduction take 5 into take 6, SI onto take 6). P: n/a. E: Ken Scott. 2E: Richard Lush.

The reduction and numerous overdubs onto 'The Fool On The Hill' made the song barely recognisable from the version begun the previous day, and extended its length from 3'50" to 4'25". (During final remixing for mono and stereo the song was edited down to 2'57".) It was almost a "re-make".

Instruments added on this day, replacing some previously taped, included a piano, an acoustic guitar, drums, another acoustic guitar and a bass guitar. Paul also taped a fresh lead vocal.

In George Martin's absence, Ken Scott took charge of the studio control room for this session – even though it was only his second day as Beatles balance engineer. He was, understandably, a little flustered, as Richard Lush recalls. "He was so nervous that it was just unbelievable. He was saying 'What lights do I use?' and 'What do I do?' I really felt for him that day. The Beatles always put a bit of pressure on their engineers; they expected you to be there doing your job but there wasn't a lot of thanks."

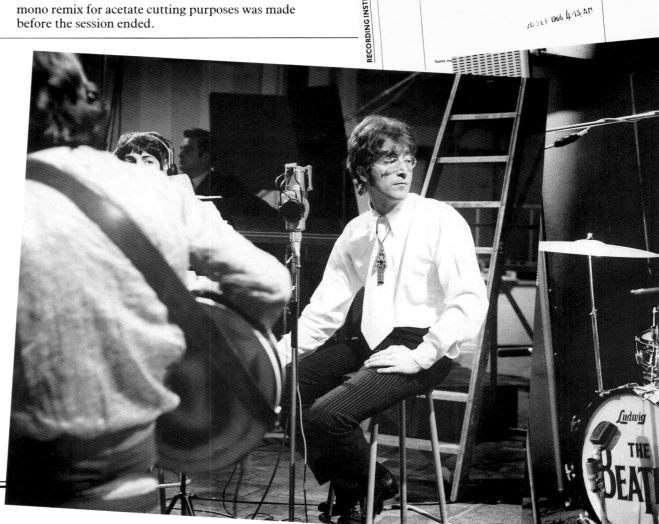

Wednesday 27 September

Studio One: 2.30-5.30pm. Recording: 'I Am The Walrus' (tape reduction take 17 into takes 18-24, with SI onto takes 18-24). Studio Two: 7.00pm-3.30am. Recording: 'I Am The Walrus' (tape reduction take 20 into take 25, SI onto take 25); 'The Fool On The Hill' (SI onto take 6). Mono mixing: 'The Fool On The Hill' (remix 2, from take 6). P: George Martin. E:Ken Scott. 2E: Richard Lush.

'I Am The Walrus' was a Lennon song with everything thrown in but the kitchen sink. In the recordings of 5 and 6 September the rhythm track had been sown together, onto which John had taped his tremendous lead vocal, singing those utterly bizarre lyrics which meant nothing and yet, somehow, formed a picture which either fascinated or disturbed the listener. Or both. On this day, 27 September, two separate overdub sessions saw the taping of 16 more instruments (eight violins, four cellos, a contra bass clarinet and three horns), all producing notes around the bottom end of the scale, plus a choir of 16 voices variously singing "Ho-ho-ho, hee-hee-hee, ha-ha-ha", "Oompah, oompah, stick it up your jumper!", "Got one, got one, everybody's got one" and making a series of shrill whooping noises. Very strange!

"The idea of using voices was a good one," says George Martin. "We got in the Mike Sammes Singers, very commercial people and so alien to John that it wasn't true. But in the score I simply orchestrated the laughs and noises, the whooooooah kind of thing. John was delighted with it."

The 16 instruments were taped in an afternoon session in studio one, George Martin conducting to his own – again superb – score. A reduction mix was made of take 17, vacating one track on the tape, and the musicians made seven attempts at the overdub, the last four of which were edit pieces only. It was then decided that take 20 had been the best version and before the evening session began this was given a further reduction mix, to liberate another track, and re-numbered 25.

The line-up of musicians was as follows. Violins: Sidney Sax (leader), Jack Rothstein, Ralph Elman, Andrew McGee, Jack Greene, Louis Stevens, John Jezzard and Jack Richards. Cellos: Lionel Ross, Eldon Fox, Bram Martin and Terry Weil. Clarinet: Gordon Lewin. Horns: Neil Sanders, Tony Tunstall, Mo [Morris] Miller.

As George Martin has said, eight boys and eight girls from the Mike Sammes Singers, a large group of vocalists who did much session and television work in addition to releasing records themselves, were brought in for the evening session, which had moved across to studio two. [The terms boys and girls are standard in the industry for male and female vocalists. They do not indicate the age of the singers!] The personnel were: Peggie Allen, Wendy Horan, Pat Whitmore, Jill Utting, June Day, Sylvia King, Irene King, G. Mallen, Fred Lucas, Mike Redway, John O'Neill, F. Dachtler, Allan Grant, D. Griffiths, J. Smith and J. Fraser.

It was all in a week's work for the Sammes troupe, as Mike Sammes remembers, with consultation to his diaries. "The next day we did a Kathy Kirby session at Pye Studios, then *The Benny Hill Show* for ATV and we had some men doing recordings for 'The Gang Show' at Chappells!"

Before the session ended the Beatles returned to 'The Fool On The Hill', Paul McCartney adding another vocal. The song was then remixed for mono and labelled 'best' although another overdub on 20 October rendered this unusable.

Thursday 28 September

Studio Two: 4.00-5.30pm. Tape copying: 'Magical Mystery Tour' (of remix mono 7); 'Aerial Tour Instrumental' (working title of 'Flying') (of remix mono 4). Recording: 'I Am The Walrus' (tape reduction of take 25 as SI onto take 17). Studio Two: 7.00pm-3.00am. Mono mixing: 'I Am The Walrus' (remixes 2-5, from take 17). Editing: 'I Am The Walrus' (of remix mono 2). Recording: 'Aerial Tour Instrumental' (working title of 'Flying') (SI onto take 8, takes 1-5 of SI onto take 8). Mono mixing: 'Aerial Tour Instrumental' (working title of 'Flying') (remixes 5 and 6, from take 8). Editing: 'Aerial Tour Instrumental' (working title of 'Flying') (of remix mono 6). P: George Martin. E: Ken Scott. 2E: Richard Lush.

This involved day working on *Magical Mystery Tour* songs began with straightforward 7½ ips tape copying of the title song and 'Flying', in their latest remix incarnations, for the film producer.

Then the work began in earnest, with a reduction mix of take 25 of 'I Am The Walrus' down to just one track and the superimposition of this onto track two of take 17 of the same song. Since take 25 itself was originally a reduction of take 17 the final version of the song contained, in essence, the same rhythm track both with and without the later overdubbing. As part of the evening session – with the Beatles in attendance – this was later remixed for mono and, with remix two deemed 'best', edited down to make the final master. [The numbering was incorrect since remixes one to four had already been used.] But that was not the end of the story because entirely new remixing, with additions, was done on 29 September, rendering even this 'best' mix unusable.

'Flying' (still titled 'Aerial Tour Instrumental' at this stage) was the next song to be looked at, another mellotron (John) a guitar piece (George) and various bits of percussion (Ringo) being overdubbed onto take eight. Then five takes were recorded of an entirely new overdub: tape loops, various effects and backwards tapes, compiled by John and Ringo. The fifth take was deemed 'best' and it found itself on track four of the tape.

Two mono remixes were made of 'Flying' at the end of the session, the second one – remix mono six – being 'best'. But at this stage the song was 9'36" long so it was then edited down to 2'14" for the record. The curious jazz recording which had been evident in the song from take one was deleted.

Friday 29 September

Studio Two: 7.00pm-5.00am. Mono mixing: 'I Am The Walrus' (remixes 6-22, from take 17). Editing: 'I Am The Walrus' (of mono remixes 10 and 22, called remix mono 23). Recording: 'Your Mother Should Know' (tape reduction take 9 into takes 50-52, SI onto take 52). Mono mixing: 'Your Mother Should Know' (remix 20, from take 52). P: George Martin. E: Ken Scott. 2E: Graham Kirkby.

No other Beatles remix session was quite so unusual or inventive. But it wasn't every remix session in which John Lennon took an active role.

Although 17 mono mixes of 'I Am The Walrus' were effected on this night, only two of those were complete. But they were enough, and the final master version was an edit of the two. The first part was from remix 10, up to the lyric "Sitting in an English garden". The other half of the master version – remix 22 – was done with a live feed from a radio, making that unique night-time sound of being flicked through foreign stations. The tuning dial eventually came to rest on the BBC Third Programme [just one day later it was to become Radio 3] while a 190-minute production of Shakespeare's *The Tragedy Of King Lear*

was being broadcast. Parts of Act IV Scene VI can be heard on the record, commencing with the lines, spoken by Gloucester and Edgar respectively, "Now, good sir, what are you?" and "A most poor man, made tame by fortune's blows". The Shakespeare broadcast is particularly evident at the end of the song, from Oswald's "…take my purse" through to Edgar's "Sit you down, father; rest you". Whether the actors concerned – Mark Dignam (Gloucester), Philip Guard (Edgar) and John Bryning (Oswald) – have discovered their appearance on a Beatles record is not known…

Paul McCartney's 'Your Mother Should Know' had now been around for more than two months in an unfinished state, so he and John got together on this

evening to complete it. Ignoring the re-make attempted on 16 September, they delved back to the original 22 and 23 August version taped at Chappell, take nine, gave it three reduction mixes (numbered, in a rather exaggerated fashion, 50-52) and then overdubbed organ (John) and bass guitar (Paul). In this brisk manner the song was finished, and it was treated to a mono remix (numbered 20 although it was the song's first) which was made with the tape machine running at 60½ cycles per second, making it sound laboriously slow on replay. More mixing, devoid of vari-speed, was done on 30 September.

Monday 2 October

Studio Two: 10.00pm-2.30am. Mono mixing: 'Your Mother Should Know' (remixes 21-25, from take 52). Recording: 'Hello Hello' (working title of 'Hello, Goodbye') (takes 1-14, tape reduction take 14 into takes 15 and 16). P: George Martin. E: Ken Scott. 2E: Graham Kirkby.

'Hello, Goodbye' is the archetypal Paul McCartney song: apparently simple but cunningly complex and impossibly infectious.

'Hello, Goodbye' (working title 'Hello Hello') was not a part of the forthcoming *Magical Mystery Tour* package. It was the Beatles' next single which, typically, was released concurrently with a major work while remaining distinctly separate.

There is not one moment on 'Hello, Goodbye' left unfilled by some instrument or voice, the result of sessions on this day and on 19, 20 and 25 October and 2 November. The single was rush-released on 24 November. The first 14 takes concentrated on the basic rhythm track of drums, piano, organ and percussion items like bongos, maracas, conga drums and tambourine. Right from the first take the song featured a reprise ending, nicknamed, somewhat

strangely, the "Maori finale". [When the Beatles made promotional films for the song it was *Hawaiian* girl dancers – actually Londoners with grass skirts on! – who came on to jollify the ending.]

The final mono remixing of 'Your Mother Should Know' was completed before 'Hello, Goodbye' was begun, remix mono 25 being the master. The stereo mix would be done, in a rush as usual, on 6 November.

Friday 6 October

Studio Two: 7.00-12.00pm. Recording: 'Blue Jay Way' (SI onto take 3). P: George Martin. E: Geoff Emerick. 2E: Richard Lush.

Cello and tambourine superimposition onto take three of 'Blue Jay Way'. These were the final additions to the song.

Thursday 12 October

De Lane Lea Music Recording Studios, 129 Kingsway, London WC2: 2.30-8.00pm. Mono mixing: 'It's All Too Much' (remixes 1 and 2, from take 2). P: George Martin. E: Dave Siddle. 2E: Mike Weighell. Abbey Road, Studio Three: 6.30pm-2.00am. Mono mixing: 'Blue Jay Way' (remixes 2-9, from take 3). Editing: 'Blue Jay Way' (of mono remixes 6 and 9). Recording: 'Accordion (Wild)' (working title of 'Shirley's Wild Accordion') (takes 1-8, tape reduction take 8 into takes 9 and 10, SI onto take 10, takes 11-15). Mono mixing: 'Accordion (Wild)' (working title of 'Shirley's Wild Accordion') (remixes 1, 2 and 3, from takes 10, 7 and 14 respectively). P: John Lennon. E: Ken Scott. 2E: Richard Lush.

John Lennon was officially accredited as producer of a Beatles session for the first time on this day. Except that this wasn't really a *Beatles* recording. True, Lennon/McCartney composed the song (and even had it copyrighted), a jaunty ditty titled 'Shirley's Wild Accordion'. True, towards the end of the session Ringo climbed behind his drum kit and tapped out a light beat and Paul McCartney added maraca and a little background yelling. True, its fruits were not even released on record because the song was used solely as incidental music in the *Magical Mystery Tour* film. The star of the song, the main instrumentalist, was the accordion player named in the title, Shirley Evans, accompanied by her musical partner Reg Wale.

Shirley Evans – also brought into the filming of *Magical Mystery Tour*, playing accordion in the coach singalong sequence – was able to play the song by reading music especially arranged and notated – ¾ time – by Mike Leander, recruited by John and Paul to translate their hummed requirements onto paper. It was the second time in seven months that Leander had been employed by the Beatles.

Three mono remixes were made from three different takes of 'Shirley's Wild Accordion'. Of those three, remix two (from take 7) was sub-titled 'Waltz' and remix three (from take 14) 'Freaky Rock'. [Note. The *Magical Mystery Tour* film also included another piece of incidental music, 'Jessie's Dream', copyrighted to

McCartney/Starkey/Harrison/Lennon and played by the Beatles. This was recorded privately, not at EMI.]

Mono remixing of two George Harrison songs was also effected today: 'Blue Jay Way' at Abbey Road (though these mixes were improved upon on 7 November) and 'It's All Too Much' at the De Lane Lea studios where the song had been recorded. This song would also be subjected to later improvements, though in this instance it was *much* later – on 16 October 1968.

IN THE THIRD PROGRAMME
AT 7.30

THE TRAGEDY OF
KING LEAR

by

William Shakespeare

John Gielgud

AS KING LEAR

WITH

Virginia McKenna as *Cordelia*
Barbara Jefford as *Goneril*
Timothy Bateson as *the Fool*
Derek Godfrey as *Edmund*
Michael Goodliffe as *Albany*
Howard Marion-Crawford as *Kent*
Barbara Bolton as *Regan*
Mark Dignam as *Gloucester*
Philip Guard as *Edgar*
Roger Delgado as *Cornwall*

Osw. Let go, slave, or thou diest!
Edg. Good gentleman, go your gait, and let
poor volk pass. And chud ha' been zwaggered
out of my life, 'twould not ha' been zo long as
'tis by a vortnight. Nay, come not near the
old man; keep out, che vor ye, or ise try
whether your costard or my bat be the harder:
chill be plain with you.
Osw. Out, dunghill!
Edg. Chill pick your teeth, zir: come; no
matter vor your foins.
            [*They fight, and* EDGAR *knocks him down.*
Osw. Slave, thou hast slain me:—villain,
        take my purse:
If ever thou wilt thrive, bury my body;   [me
And give the letters which thou find'st about
To Edmund Earl of Gloster; seek him out
Upon the British party:—O, untimely death!
                                        [*Dies.*
Edg. I know thee well: a serviceable villain;
As duteous to the vices of thy mistress
As badness would desire.
    Glo.   What, is he dead?
    Edg. Sit you down, father; rest you.—
Let's see these pockets: the letters that he
speaks of
May be my friends.—He's dead; I am only   [sorry
He had no other death's-man.—Let us see:—
Leave, gentle wax; and, manners, blame us

Filming a promotional clip for 'Hello, Goodbye' at the Saville Theatre, London, 10 November.

Right:
John Lennon at his most creative ... and Mark Dignam, Philip Guard and John Bryning unwittingly make their recording debut with the Beatles.

Thursday 19 October

Studio One: 7.00pm-3.30am. Recording: 'Hello Hello' (working title of 'Hello, Goodbye') (SI onto take 16, tape reduction take 16 into take 17). P: George Martin.   E: Ken Scott.   2E: Richard Lush.

Overdubbing of two different guitar parts, Paul's vocal – echoed in some places, double-tracked in others – and backing vocals by John and George onto 'Hello Hello', still the working title of 'Hello, Goodbye'. Another reduction mix then took the song into take 17.

Friday 20 October

Studio Three: 7.00pm-3.45am. Recording: 'The Fool On The Hill' (SI onto take 6); 'Hello Hello' (working title of 'Hello, Goodbye') (SI onto take 17). P: George Martin. E: Ken Scott.   2E: Phil McDonald.

A session of instrumental overdubs by outside musicians; the Beatles did not play on this evening. Three flautists – brothers Christopher and Richard Taylor plus Jack Ellory – were recruited to add the final touches to 'The Fool On The Hill'. Then, later in the evening, two viola players – Ken Essex and Leo Birnbaum – played on 'Hello, Goodbye'.

As with the flautists, Essex and Birnbaum had been booked to play from 8.00 to 11.00pm but their part of the session overran until 2.30am, resulting in double-time payments to the two musicians. "Paul McCartney was doodling at the piano," recalls Leo Birnbaum, "and George Martin was sitting next to him writing down what Paul was playing." "All of the Beatles were there," says Ken Essex. "One of them was sitting on the floor in what looked like a pyjama suit, drawing with crayons on a piece of paper."

Wednesday 25 October

Studio Two: 7.00pm-3.00am. Mono mixing: 'The Fool On The Hill' (remixes 10-12, from take 6). Editing: 'The Fool On The Hill' (of remix mono 12). Recording: 'Hello Hello' (working title of 'Hello, Goodbye') (tape reduction take 17 into takes 18-21, SI onto take 21). P: George Martin.   E: Ken Scott.   2E: Graham Kirkby.

Superimposition of bass guitar onto 'Hello, Goodbye' and mono mixing [numbered 10-12 although it should have been three to five] of 'The Fool On The Hill', plus editing of the latter to reduce it to 2'57".

Wednesday 1 November

Abbey Road, Room 53: 10.00am-1.00pm. Mono mixing: 'All You Need Is Love' (remix 11, from take 58); 'Lucy In The Sky With Diamonds' (remix 20, from take 8). P: George Martin.   E: Geoff Emerick.   2E: Richard Lush. Studio Three (control room only): 2.30-6.00pm. Recording: 'Untitled Sound Effects' (take 20); 'Hello, Goodbye' (tape reduction take 21 into takes 22-25). Stereo mixing: 'The Fool On The Hill' (remixes 1-5, from take 6). Editing: 'The Fool On The Hill' (of remix stereo 5). P: George Martin.   E: Geoff Emerick.   2E: Graham Kirkby.

New mono remixes of two "old" songs for the soundtrack of the *Yellow Submarine* animated film now in production. This mono mix of 'All You Need Is Love' was, at 3'44", 13 seconds shorter than the original mono single.

Also taped on this day was a short sound effects tape of applause, courtesy of the Abbey Road collection, for inclusion in *Yellow Submarine*. [For some unknown reason this one-off attempt was numbered take 20.] Away from the film, a reduction mixdown of 'Hello, Goodbye' was done – the song's fourth, a

perilous state, owing to the build-up of background noise and hiss which accumulates each time a reduction is made – and 'The Fool On The Hill' became the first *Magical Mystery Tour* song to be treated to stereo mixing. In this instance the fifth remix was 'best'.

Thursday 2 November

Studio Three: 2.30-6.00pm. Recording: 'Hello, Goodbye' (SI onto take 22). Mono mixing: 'Hello, Goodbye' (remixes 1-6, from take 22). P: George Martin.   E: Geoff Emerick.   2E: Jeff Jarratt.

The final overdub for 'Hello, Goodbye': a second bass guitar line played by Paul McCartney. The song was

then given its first remixes, six mono editions, the sixth being deemed 'best'.

Monday 6 November

Studio Three (control room only): 2.30-6.00pm. Stereo mixing: 'Hello, Goodbye' (remixes 1 and 2, from take 22); 'I Am The Walrus' (remixes 1-7, from take 17 and from remix mono 22); 'Your Mother Should Know' (remixes 1 and 2, from take 52); 'Magical Mystery Tour' (remixes 1-4, from take 9). Editing: 'I Am The Walrus' (of stereo remixes 6 and 7). P: George Martin.   E: Geoff Emerick.   2E: Ken Scott.

The stereo mixes of 'Hello, Goodbye' and 'Your Mother Should Know' raised no problems. 'I Am The Walrus' was more difficult because it had to incorporate the live radio feed on the 29 September

mono mix. This is why, from the radio's point of entry to the end of the song, the stereo mix slips into mono. There were no problems with 'Magical Mystery Tour' but acetates cut from its mixes did highlight to the

Beatles the need for more work on the song. This was done quickly – on 7 November – necessitating a new set of mixes, mono and stereo.

Tuesday 7 November

Studio Two (control room only): 2.30-5.45pm. Stereo mixing: 'Blue Jay Way' (remixes 1 and 2, from take 3); 'Flying' (remix 1, from take 8). Editing: 'Blue Jay Way' (of remix stereo 2); 'Flying' (of remix stereo 1). P: George Martin.   E: Ken Scott.   2E: Peter Mew. Studio One: 9.00pm-4.30am. Mono mixing: 'Blue Jay Way' (remixes 20-28, from take 3). Stereo mixing: 'Blue Jay Way' (remixes 10-12, from take 3). Editing: 'Blue Jay Way' (of remix mono 27; of remix stereo 12). Stereo mixing/recording: 'Magical Mystery Tour' (remixes 5 and 6, from remix stereo 4 with new SI). Mono mixing/recording: 'Magical Mystery Tour' (remixes 8-10, from remix mono 7 with new SI). Tape copying: 'I Am The Walrus' (of remix mono 23); 'Your Mother Should Know' (of remix mono 25); 'Flying' (of edit of remix mono 6 and of edit of remix stereo 1); 'Magical Mystery Tour' (of remix mono 10 and of remix stereo 6); 'Blue Jay Way' (of edit of remix mono 27 and of edit of remix stereo 12); 'The Fool On The Hill' (of edit of remix mono 12); 'Strawberry Fields Forever' (of remix stereo 3). P: George Martin.   E: Geoff Emerick.   2E: Graham Kirkby.

The new mixes of 'Magical Mystery Tour' incorporated an additional Paul McCartney vocal line and more sound effects. The new mixing of 'Blue Jay Way' was quite problematical: at one point the stereo

remix was also considered for the mono version, although ultimately this did not happen. The British mono EP was cut for disc on 13 November, the stereo was done on 17 November. The tape copies made at

the end of this session were for Capitol Records, its representative Voyle Gilmore hand-carrying them back to the USA.

Wednesday 15 November

Studio Two (control room only): 10.30-11.00am. Mono mixing: 'Hello, Goodbye' (remix 10, from take 22). Tape copying: 'It's All Too Much' (of remix mono 1); 'All Together Now' (of remix mono 6); 'Only A Northern Song' (of remix mono 6). P: n/a.   E: Geoff Emerick.   2E: Richard Lush.

A new mono remix of 'Hello, Goodbye', eliminating the violas. Under Paul McCartney's direction the Beatles had made three promotional films for this song on 10 November but it was later realised that, in Britain, these might contravene the Musicians' Union ban on miming. Since the viola players were not shown in the films – making the miming transparently obvious – this remix was made and dubbed onto the BBC's copy. It was a wasted task however, for the Beatles' own miming could not be masked and consequently the film was not shown in the UK.

Mono tape copies of 'It's All Too Much', 'All Together Now' and 'Only A Northern Song' were made on this day by Emerick/Lush for the producers of the *Yellow Submarine* film.

Friday 17 November

Abbey Road, Room 53: 10.00am-1.15pm. Stereo mixing: 'I Am The Walrus' (remix 25, from take 17). Editing: 'I Am The Walrus' (of stereo remixes 25 and 7). P: George Martin. E: Geoff Emerick. 2E: Ken Scott

A new remix of the first half of 'I Am The Walrus', for editing into the stereo master.

Friday 24 November

Single release: 'Hello, Goodbye'/'I Am The Walrus'. Parlophone R 5655.

The Beatles' third single of the year, reclaiming for the group the number one UK chart position at Christmas, achieved every year since 1963, bar 1966 when there was no Beatles single released.

Tuesday 28 November

Studio Three: 6.00pm-2.45am. Recording: 'Christmas Time (Is Here Again)' (take 1 [music], takes 1-10 [speech], SI of sound effects onto edit/remix). Mono mixing: 'Christmas Time (Is Here Again)' (of takes 1 [music], 2, 6 and 10 [speech]). P: George Martin. E: Geoff Emerick. 2E: Richard Lush.

The recording session for the Beatles' fifth fan club Christmas record. As in 1966, the Beatles injected considerable time and skill into the disc, preparing a script – essentially a send-up of radio and television programmes – and recording a song written especially for the purpose and copyrighted to Lennon/McCartney/Harrison/Starkey – 'Christmas Time (Is Here Again)', also the name of the overall disc. Short extracts of this song were used on the disc but the Abbey Road tape archive holds the original uncut version, lasting 6′37″ and featuring drums (Ringo), acoustic guitar (George), timpani (John) and piano (Paul) with manually double-tracked vocals by all four Beatles, George Martin and session visitor/actor/friend Victor Spinetti.

The remainder of the recording consisted of skits, messages, jokes, a tap dancing duet courtesy of Ringo and Spinetti, a few words from Mal Evans and George

Martin, a short burst of 'Plenty Of Jam Jars' (by "the Ravellers" – the Beatles on piano/vocals) and a fictitious advertising jingle about the magical properties of "Wonderlust", ideal for your trousers and your hair! The Beatles had great fun doing all of this, spoiling takes with their own laughter and throwing in hilarious cuss words which had to be edited out later.

This was the Beatles' last Christmas fan club disc to be recorded collectively and at Abbey Road. In 1968 and again in 1969 – the last edition – the four Beatles taped their items separately, in their homes or wherever they happened to be. Both discs were edited (there was no "producer", as such) by disc-jockey Kenny Everett, the 1969 edition under his real name, Maurice Cole.

Although the Christmas disc was completed by 2.45, the session did not end until 4.30 because John

Lennon stayed behind to make tapes for the National Theatre production of a play he had written, *Scene Three, Act One*, based on the short piece of the same title in his 1964 book *In His Own Write*. This was John's second solo session at Abbey Road compiling effects tapes, some from special records and tapes, others made especially by him. The first was on 24 November.

John was not the only Beatle presently using Abbey Road for a solo project. George had just begun the recording of his soundtrack for the film *Wonderwall* and had been in to tape sound effects and songs with working titles 'India' and 'Swordfencing' (both later changed) on 22 and 23 November, recruiting classical musicians for the latter session. He was also recording concurrently at De Lane Lea in Kingsway and on 7 January 1968 he flew to India to continue the good work at the EMI studio in Bombay.

Wednesday 29 November

Studio One (control room only): 2.30-5.30pm. Editing: 'Christmas Time (Is Here Again)' (of unnumbered mono remixes). Tape copying: 'Christmas Time (Is Here Again)' (of master version). P: George Martin. E: Geoff Emerick. 2E: Richard Lush.

Editing of the previous night's 1967 Christmas disc mono remixes and tape copying of the master onto a 7½ ips tape for pressing at Lyntone Records.

Friday 8 December

EP release: *Magical Mystery Tour*. Parlophone MMT-1 (mono)/SMMT-1 (stereo). A: 'Magical Mystery Tour'; 'Your Mother Should Know'. B: 'I Am The Walrus'. C: 'The Fool On The Hill'; 'Flying'. D: 'Blue Jay Way'.

Magical Mystery Tour posed a problem for the Beatles and EMI. Six songs was too many for a regular EP, but too few for an LP. One idea, to have an EP playing at LP speed, was considered but discarded because the record would have suffered from loss of volume and fidelity. The problem was solved at the beginning of November: *Magical Mystery Tour* would be packaged as a hitherto untried double-EP set, in a heavy-duty gatefold sleeve with a 28 page booklet, some pages in colour, including all of the song lyrics. The price of this superb package to be 19s 6d [97½p].

That was in the UK. Capitol Records decided that the North American marketplace was too fickle for a

double-EP set, especially since ordinary EPs, commonplace in Britain, had barely taken off there. So Capitol put all the *MMT* songs onto one side of an album and filled the other with the Beatles' five other 1967 song releases outside of *Sgt Pepper's Lonely Hearts Club Band:* 'Hello, Goodbye', 'Strawberry Fields Forever', 'Penny Lane', 'Baby, You're A Rich Man' and 'All You Need Is Love'. [The latter three were issued in "duophonic" form (ie "mock stereo") since true stereo mixes had not yet been made for them. 'All You Need Is Love' was first mixed for stereo on 29 October 1968, 'Penny Lane' did not receive its first stereo remix until 30 September 1971 and 'Baby, You're A Rich Man' until 22 October

1971.] The LP idea was a good one – even if it wasn't what the Beatles themselves wanted – and imports soon found their way into Britain. On 19 November 1976 EMI issued it in the UK [the Capitol version, with three "duophonic" songs] to satisfy public demand.

But whatever the shape and size of the vinyl, *Magical Mystery Tour*, the record, was everything the associated 50-minute television film was not – a runaway success, selling more than a half million copies in the UK and 1½ million in the USA before Christmas 1967 and capping a memorable year for the Beatles.

Friday 12 January

EMI Recording Studio, Universal Insurance Building, Phirozeshah Mehta Road, Fort, Bombay 400001, India: time unknown. Recording: 'Untitled' (working title of 'The Inner Light') (takes 1-5). P: George Harrison.   E: J.P. Sen/S.N. Gupta.   2E: unknown.

In order to continue work on the *Wonderwall* film soundtrack recording, George Harrison flew to India on 7 January 1968 to undertake an intensive, five-day series of sessions at the EMI recording studio in Bombay. [On 5 January, before leaving, George produced another session at Abbey Road and he finished the LP there on 30 January.]

The sessions in Bombay, recorded on quarter-inch two-track mono and stereo tapes, and using local musicians, started on 9 January and ended on the 13th, each day's work beginning around 10.00am and finishing around 7.00pm. They were all personally supervised by Vijay Dubey, who also acted as George's host.

By 12 January *Wonderwall* was all but completed and so, not wishing to waste studio time or under use the pre-booked musicians, George produced a number of ragas for possible use on Beatles records. One of these, to become 'The Inner Light', had a quite exquisite melody and was indeed released by the Beatles (it was the only one thus used) after overdubs had been taped at Abbey Road on 6 and 8 February.

Only the instrumental track of 'The Inner Light' was recorded at this point. The *precise* line-up of musicians is not known although it would have been a selection of the following, all employed by George in Bombay: Ashish Khan (sarod), Mahapurush Misra (tabla and pakavaj), Sharad Jadev and Hanuman Jadev (shanhais), Shambu-Das, Indril Bhattacharya and Shankar Ghosh (sitar), Chandra Shakher (sur-bahar), Shiv Kumar Sharmar (santorr), S.R. Kenkare and Hari Prasad Chaurasia (flute), Vinayak Vohra (taar shehnai) and Rijram Desad (dholak, harmonium and tabla-tarang).

Saturday 3 February

Studio Three: 2.30-6.00pm.
Recording: 'Lady Madonna' (takes 1-3).
Studio Three: 7.00pm-1.30am.
Recording: 'Lady Madonna' (SI onto take 3).
P: George Martin.   E: Ken Scott.   2E: Richard Lush.

The Beatles' oft-postponed visit to India to study Transcendental Meditation under Maharishi Mahesh Yogi was imminent, John and George flying out on 15 February, Paul and Ringo four days later. As they were not scheduled to return until late April the Beatles decided to record a new single for release *in absentia* in mid-March. As it happened, this concentrated series of sessions, ending on 11 February, was more productive than expected and realised *four* new songs, all mixed and ready for issue.

The first of these was 'Lady Madonna', a rocking new Paul McCartney composition with a great boogie feel, accentuated by a double-tracked piano and Paul's strong vocal delivery. 'Lady Madonna' was unlike any previous Beatles song, although – in its intro at least – it was not totally unlike 'Bad Penny Blues', a minor chart hit for the Humphrey Lyttleton Band in 1956, and, ironically, a George Martin production.

In the first 'Lady Madonna' session, this afternoon, three takes of the basic rhythm track were recorded: piano (Paul) and drums (Ringo), the latter using brushes instead of sticks. Then, in the evening, a number of overdubs were made onto take three: Paul's bass, John and George on fuzzed guitars (both instruments played through the same amplifier) and another drum track by Ringo. Paul also added the first of his two lead vocal recordings and John and George contributed scat backing vocals while munching Marmite flavoured crisps. (The crunching was omitted from the remix!)

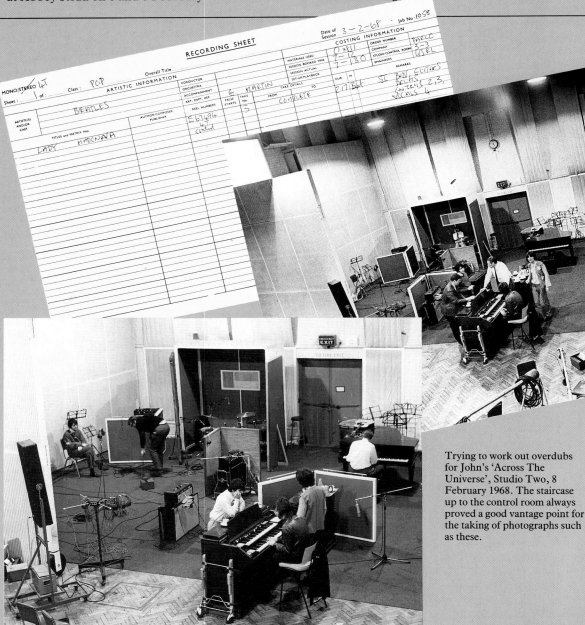

Trying to work out overdubs for John's 'Across The Universe', Studio Two, 8 February 1968. The staircase up to the control room always proved a good vantage point for the taking of photographs such as these.

Sunday 4 February

Studio Three: 2.30-5.30pm. Recording: 'Across The Universe' (takes 1-7). **P:** George Martin. **E:** Ken Scott. **2E:** Richard Lush. Studio Three: 8.00pm-2.00am. Recording: 'Across The Universe' (SI onto take 7, tape reduction take 7 into take 8, SI onto take 8, sound effects takes 1-3). **P:** George Martin. **E:** Martin Benge. **2E:** Phil McDonald.

John's offering for the new single was 'Across The Universe', a beautifully wistful, philosophical number, begun this day and completed on 8 February.

The only problem was, John wasn't entirely sure how to capture on tape the sounds he was hearing in his head. During the first of this day's two sessions – the Beatles had curiously, though temporarily, reverted to the traditional afternoon/evening use of studio time – six takes of 'Across The Universe' were recorded [numbered one to seven but there was no take three]. The first was of the rhythm track only: acoustic guitar (John), tomtoms (Ringo) and tamboura (George), all of the instruments fed through a revolving Leslie organ speaker and subjected to flanging. Take two, a *gorgeous* recording, brought in a sitar introduction by George, also with much flanging, another acoustic guitar and a pure Lennon lead vocal.

The recording chopped and changed during the remainder of the afternoon until take seven, when the rhythm track seemed complete and ready for vocal overdubs, these being the first task of the evening

session. But after John had re-taped his superb vocal contribution, recorded with the machine running slow to play back fast, he and Paul realised that the song was still lacking something: falsetto harmonies, beyond the male vocal range. For any other group in any other studio, finding female vocalists on a Sunday evening without prior arrangement would have been impossible. But all the Beatles had to do was to step outside the front door and invite inside two of the many fans who ritually congregated outside EMI Studios whenever the Beatles were inside, be it daytime or night-time and through sunshine, rain, hail, sleet and snow.

The two girls – Lizzie Bravo, a 16-year-old from Brazil, temporarily living close to Abbey Road, and Gayleen Pease, 17, a Londoner – were understandably thrilled at being the first – and only – Beatles fans ever to be specifically invited inside to contribute to a session. "There was a whole crowd of girls outside and Paul went out to find a couple of suitable ones," recalls Martin Benge, a technical engineer drafted in as replacement balance engineer for Ken Scott who felt unwell during the afternoon. "They were so

excited. They couldn't believe they'd actually been invited by Paul not just inside the building but into the studio itself, to sing with the Beatles."

Once the girls had taped their "nothing's gonna change our world" high harmonies they were thanked and ushered out of the studio so that the Beatles could record the day's final overdub for 'Across The Universe': backwards bass and drums for track four of take eight, newly vacated by a reduction mix of take seven. On 8 February this overdub would be wiped and replaced with more vocals.

Before the session ended the Beatles taped three experimental sound effects for inclusion in 'Across The Universe', though none was. The first of these was subtitled 'Hums Wild', a 15-second take of pure humming, recorded and then overdubbed three more times to fill the four-track tape with a wall of hummed sound virtually identical to the 10 February 1967 experiment for 'A Day In The Life', even in the same key. The other two sound effects were of a guitar and a harp-like sound, the tape box denoting that both were "to be played backwards".

Tuesday 6 February

Studio One: 2.30-8.00pm. Tape copying: 'The Inner Light' (of take 5, numbered take 6). Recording: 'The Inner Light' (SI onto take 6). Mono mixing: 'The Inner Light' (remix 1, from take 6). Studio One: 9.00pm-2.00am. Recording: 'Lady Madonna' (tape reduction take 3 into take 4, SI onto take 4, tape reduction take 4 into take 5, SI onto take 5). Mono mixing: 'Lady Madonna' (remixes 1 and 2, from take 5). **P:** George Martin. **E:** Geoff Emerick. **2E:** Jerry Boys.

A long studio day for the Beatles, all except for Ringo who was busily employed (at the BBC Television Theatre in Shepherd's Bush, London) in afternoon rehearsals and live evening transmission for his guest appearance in Cilla Black's programme *Cilla*. The clear one-hour break between 8.00 and 9.00pm in their Abbey Road sessions on this day intimates that the other three Beatles made sure they watched the show!

'The Inner Light' was all but completed during the afternoon with George adding vocals to a four-track copy tape of the original two-track Bombay stereo. 'The Inner Light' was the last of three Indian-flavoured Beatles songs composed by George and the lyrics were taken almost directly from a poem of the same title from the *Tao Te Ching*, as recommended to George by Juan Mascaró, a Sanskrit teacher at Cambridge University. Strangely, for so beautiful a song, George seemed reluctant to record his vocal, according to tape operator Jerry Boys. "George had this big thing about not wanting to sing it because he didn't feel confident that he could do the song justice. I remember Paul saying 'You must have a go, don't worry about it, it's *good*'."

Certainly the song *was* good, and George's vocal was

perfect. The first of four mono remixes was done at the end of the afternoon session. Three more, including the 'best', would be done on 8 February after a brief additional overdub by John and Paul.

The evening session saw the completion of 'Lady Madonna', with the addition of a second McCartney lead vocal, a second piano piece, handclaps, "See how they run" backing vocals by Paul, John and George and a charming middle eight vocalised brass imitation achieved by the three Beatles cupping their hands around their mouths. "We spent a lot of time getting the right piano sound for 'Lady Madonna'," says Geoff Emerick. "We ended up using a cheaper type of microphone and heavy compression and limiting."

Still the song needed the finishing touch and Paul decided that it must be *real* brass, four saxophones to be exact. Laurie Gold, a session "fixer" for EMI, often used by George Martin and the Beatles, was called into swift action. Harry Klein, a baritone sax player, has a vivid recollection of events. "They were in a real flap to find four musicians and called on Laurie to conjure some up for them. I was in the bath at about 6.30 in the evening when Laurie called and said 'Are you working tonight?' 'No, I'm in the bath!'. 'Well get over to EMI as quick as you can, and how

can I find a tenor player?' I suggested he call Ronnie Scott, the chap who runs the London jazz club, and sure enough when I got to Abbey Road Ronnie was there, along with Bill Jackman (baritone sax) and Bill Povey (tenor sax). Paul didn't recognise Ronnie Scott until we told him who he was.

"There was no written music but we played around with a few riffs until Paul liked what he heard. And then we recorded it – 101 times! I remember there was a big pile of meditation books in the corner of the studio, like the back room of a publisher's office, and I also recall that they asked if we wanted a bite to eat. We were expecting a terrific meal but a few minutes later someone returned with pie and chips!"

Bill Povey recalls, "There was not only no prepared music for us to follow but when Paul called out some chords at us our first reaction was to look at each other and say 'Well, who plays what?'." Bill Jackman remembers, "Paul went through the song on the piano and we were each given a scrap of manuscript paper and a pencil to write out some notes. Had there been music we would have been in and out in about ten minutes. As it was, it took most of the evening, recording it in A-major pitch with the rhythm track playing in our headphones."

Thursday 8 February

Studio Two: 2.30-9.00pm. Recording: 'The Inner Light' (SI onto take 6). Mono mixing: 'The Inner Light' (remixes 2-4, from take 6). Recording: 'Across The Universe' (SI onto take 8). P: George Martin. E: Geoff Emerick/Ken Scott. 2E: Richard Lush. Studio Two (control room only): 10.00pm-12.15am. Mono mixing: 'Across The Universe' (remixes 1 and 2, from take 8). P: George Martin. E: Ken Scott. 2E: Richard Lush.

Aside from the overdubbing of very brief John and Paul backing vocals onto 'The Inner Light', and that song's final mono remixing, this day was spent completing John Lennon's 'Across The Universe'. John was evidently still unsure of what the song needed in the way of instruments. George Martin played an organ and John himself contributed a mellotron piece but both were then wiped off the tape and replaced by a tone pedal guitar part played by John, maracas by George and a piano by Paul. And the backwards bass guitar and drum track recorded at the end of the 4 February session was wiped and replaced by some lovely harmonised backing vocals by John, Paul and George.

" 'Across The Universe' was such a superb performance from John," says Geoff Emerick. "He put so much feeling into the song, and his vocal was just incredible..." It would seem that everyone shared Emerick's view of 'Across The Universe' – except for John Lennon himself, rarely content with his own work even though others were lavishing heaps of praise upon it. When the Beatles sat down to decide which two of the three songs recorded thus far would be used for the imminent single John preferred 'Across The Universe' to remain on the shelf, especially since it was agreed that 'The Inner Light', being such a lovely song, really merited a B-side placing, George Harrison's first for a Beatles single.

So instead of being issued as a single 'Across The Universe' was set aside for use on a charity album for the World Wildlife Fund, conceived by comedian Spike Milligan in December 1967. But the LP – *No One's Gonna Change Our World*, the title based on the lyric of 'Across The Universe' – wasn't released until December 1969, and for that specific purpose the song was adorned with sound effects during a stereo remix session at Abbey Road on 2 October 1969. (See separate entry.) It should be noted that these effects were not *planned* by the Beatles to be a part of the song. 'Across The Universe' (in this February 1968 form, at least – see next paragraph) has yet to be released without the effects, nor has this day's 'best' mono mix (remix two) been issued, since the World Wildlife album was issued only in stereo.

It is popularly believed – but untrue – that the Beatles taped a re-make of this song, the one which appears on the 1970 LP *Let It Be*, a misconception fuelled by the sight of John rehearsing the song during the tie-in film, in a manner all but identical to the version released on the LP. Actually, at no point did the Beatles re-make the song on tape. The version of 'Across The Universe' on the *Let It Be* LP was this same February 1968 recording, with elements of the original four-track tape wiped and replaced by an orchestra and a choir, and with the speed of John's vocal drastically slowed. (Some instruments remained from the original version, including acoustic guitar, maracas and tamboura.) All this work was overseen by Phil Spector in March and April 1970.

Sunday 11 February

Studio Three: 4.00pm-2.00am. Recording: 'Hey Bulldog' (takes 1-10). Mono mixing: 'Hey Bulldog' (remixes 1 and 2, from take 10). P: George Martin. E: Geoff Emerick. 2E: Phil McDonald.

The Beatles were undoubtedly in a productive mood at this point in time. They had completed their planned three songs so quickly, in just four sessions, that a 2.30-midnight session pre-booked for studio two on Saturday 10 February was cancelled. On this day, 11 February, the plan, ostensibly, was for the group to be filmed working in the studio, the clip to be given to television stations worldwide to promote 'Lady Madonna'. But once inside the studio the Beatles decided to record, the result being 'Hey Bulldog', started, finished and mixed for mono in ten hours, and recorded on straight four-track, without any reduction mixes.

There was no question of 'Hey Bulldog' rivalling 'Lady Madonna' for the next A-side. John had composed it specifically for the *Yellow Submarine* film and soundtrack album. [Note. Although it does indeed appear on the latter, only some prints of the film include the 'Hey Bulldog' sequence. It was edited out of most copies.]

While the cameras whirred for the 'Lady Madonna' film John led the Beatles through ten takes of 'Hey Bulldog', following the general instruction he gave to George Martin in the control room at the start of the session, and captured on the original tape: "Just tell us when we get a good one...". All ten takes featured a basic rhythm track of piano, drums, tambourine, lead guitar and bass guitar. Onto take ten was then overdubbed a fuzz bass, deliberately off-beat drums, a rasping middle eight guitar solo, double-tracked Lennon vocals and a single-tracked backing vocal by Paul.

The song, as released on disc, had a curious ending. It was standard practice for the Beatles to ad-lib and mess around after they had reached the point where the song would be faded out on record. In 'Hey Bulldog' they duly began barking, shouting and screaming. But during this day's mono remixing – done, incidentally, at 51 cycles per second – they decided to keep some of the extraneous material in. "That was a really fun song," recalls Geoff Emerick. "We were all into sound texture in those days and during the mixing we put ADT on one of the 'What did he say? Woof woof' bits near the end of the song. It came out really well."

Thursday 15 February

Studio Three (control room only): 4.30-6.00pm. Mono mixing: 'Lady Madonna' (remixes 3-10, from take 5). P: George Martin. E: Geoff Emerick. 2E: Martin Benge.

Final mono remixing of 'Lady Madonna'. A stereo mix would not be done until one was specifically required, at Abbey Road on 2 December 1969 for the Capitol compilation album *Hey Jude*.

Friday 15 March

Single release: 'Lady Madonna'/'The Inner Light'. Parlophone R 5675.

A terrific Beatles single, curiously overlooked today by those analysing the group's output, 'Lady Madonna' was the first of just two 45s released by the Beatles during 1968. It sold more than one million copies in the USA during its first week of release and over a quarter-million in Britain.

Thursday 30 May

Studio Two: 2.30pm-2.40am. Recording: 'Revolution' (working title of 'Revolution 1') (takes 1-18).   P: George Martin.   E: Geoff Emerick.   2E: Phil McDonald.

The lazy, hazy, long hot relaxing days spent by the Beatles in India produced a bumper crop of new songs: at least a dozen ready for recording. During the time it took to tape those many more were written. And by the time these were taped the Beatles no longer had a mere album on their hands, they had the makings, plus more, of a double-album.

Sessions for that double-album – released on 22 November as, simply, *The Beatles* but more commonly known today as the 'White Album' – began on this day at Abbey Road, the group having privately taped, on four-track, a few demos in preceding days at George Harrison's country bungalow in Esher, Surrey. [Studio documentation shows that sessions had been due to begin on 29 May, 2.30-midnight in studio three, but that this was cancelled. And it also shows that on 14 May the group pre-booked studio two at Abbey Road for the 2.30-midnight period of every working week, Monday through to Friday, from 20 May until 26 July. It was only in July that they began to adhere to this.]

The Beatles would be the first Beatles album to appear on their own Apple record label, although – for the group themselves (including almost all of their solo output) – this was a façade since their recordings continued to be owned exclusively by EMI and released by the Parlophone company, with Parlophone catalogue numbers and prefixes.

It was certainly not unknown for the Beatles to record re-makes of certain songs during their sessions at Abbey Road, from 'Please Please Me' to 'Strawberry Fields Forever'. What *was* unusual was for them to release the original *and* re-made versons of the same song. The Beatles did this in 1968 with John Lennon's stunning new composition 'Revolution'. Briefly, the version on *The Beatles* was the first to be taped, and it was titled 'Revolution 1'. On the same album was 'Revolution 9', the second to be recorded. The third version appeared only on the B-side of the group's next single, and this was, simply, 'Revolution'.

The full story of the recordings is a little more complicated. For a start, 'Revolution 1' was itself originally titled 'Revolution' – obviously before it was realised that more than one version would be made. Furthermore, great chunks of 'Revolution 9' were born directly out of the early tapings of 'Revolution 1', being at this stage more than ten minutes long but cut for the LP to a little over four.

On this first day, takes one through to 18 were recorded of the 'Revolution' (ie, 'Revolution 1'), rhythm track – piano, acoustic guitar and drums – each of varying length but averaging about five minutes. There were no takes numbered 11 or 12.

Take 18 was different, substantially different, and it was the basis of the final LP version. It began so soon after the previous take that Geoff Emerick, in punching the talkback button simultaneously with the start of the song, announced "Take 18" over John Lennon's vocal, the first take with vocals, in fact. John deliberately kept Emerick's words as part of the song and thus they appear on the album. Secondly, this take did not stop after five minutes. It kept on and on and on, eventually running out at 10'17" with John's shout to the others and to the control room "OK, I've had enough!". The last six minutes were pure chaos – the sound of a 'Revolution', if you like – with discordant instrumental jamming, plenty of feedback, John Lennon repeatedly screaming "alright" and then, simply, repeatedly screaming, with lots of on-microphone moaning by John and his new girlfriend Yoko Ono, with Yoko talking and saying such off-the-wall phrases as "you become naked" and with the overlay of miscellaneous, home-made sound effects tapes.

There can be no doubt: take 18 of 'Revolution 1' was riveting. But in its present length there was no way it could be released as a single, something the Beatles were actively considering at this point. Before very long the last six minutes would be hived off to form the basis for 'Revolution 9'.

The role of Yoko Ono in the Beatles' recording sessions – at least on John's song material – has been much detailed in other books, while disputes still rage as the whether she had a positive or negative effect on the sessions, and whether or not her presence disturbed the other three Beatles. The 1960s staff at EMI Studios are still divided in their opinions about the positive/negative aspects of Yoko's presence but, clearly, she was there to stay. "John brought her into the control room of number three at the start of the 'White Album' sessions," recalls Geoff Emerick. "He quickly introduced her to everyone and that was it. She was always by his side after that."

Yoko wasn't the only new person to sit in on recording sessions for *The Beatles*. AIR, the production company in which George Martin was a founder director, had recently taken on an assistant, 21-year-old Chris Thomas. He was to stay by George's side for most of the Beatles' remaining 1968 sessions, learning the ropes of being a record producer. Then, in September, George went on holiday and Chris found himself alone in the hot seat. "I wasn't their engineer, that was always Geoff Emerick or Ken Scott. Nor was I their 'producer'. I worked on stuff with them but basically they produced the sessions themselves when George went away. It was John Lennon who insisted that I have a credit on the album's pullout sheet."

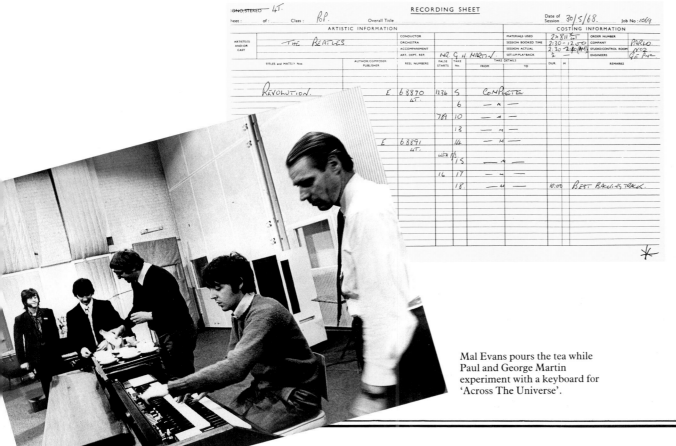

Mal Evans pours the tea while Paul and George Martin experiment with a keyboard for 'Across The Universe'.

Friday 31 May

Studio Three: 2.30-12.00pm. Recording: 'Revolution' (working title of 'Revolution 1') (SI onto take 18, tape reduction take 18 into take 19, SI onto take 19). P: George Martin. E: Geoff Emerick. 2E: Phil McDonald.

The overdubbing of two separate John Lennon vocals and Paul's bass guitar onto take 18 of 'Revolution 1' and tape reduction of this into take 19. Then further overdubbing of Paul and George's backing vocals.

A new technical engineer, Alan Brown, had joined the staff at Abbey Road in November 1967, and he was assigned for stand-by duty at many of the sessions for *The Beatles*, alternating with people like Ken Townsend, Dave Harries, Keith Slaughter, Brian Gibson and Richard Hale. Brown was on duty the night John Lennon added vocals to the recording of 'Revolution 1'. (Gibson was likewise on 4 June when John had another go, but that's another story.) "I was in the control room of studio three and there on the other side of the glass was a figure in semi-darkness going over and over some lines of a song. I knew the voice and sure enough I knew the face. John Lennon was about 30 feet away! He was working on 'Revolution', the slow one, and I remember him going through the song again and again in rehearsal, changing a word or two every time. Each time it would alter very slightly, it would develop and evolve. 'When you talk about destruction ... you can count me out.' 'When you talk about destruction ... you can count me in'."

John Lennon wasn't too sure whether he wanted to be counted 'in' or 'out'. By the time 'Revolution 1' reached vinyl it was both out *and* in. In the faster, single version, 'Revolution', he categorically wanted 'out'.

Tuesday 4 June

Studio Three: 2.30pm-1.00am. Recording: 'Revolution' (working title of 'Revolution 1') (SI onto take 19, creation of tape loops takes 1 and 2, tape reduction take 19 into take 20, SI onto take 20). Mono mixing: 'Revolution' (working title of 'Revolution 1') (unnumbered rough remix, from take 20). P: George Martin. E: Peter Bown. 2E: Phil McDonald.

A day of curious overdubs and experiments for 'Revolution 1'. John re-recorded his lead vocal during this session, opting for the 'in/out' answer to whether he should or shouldn't participate in destruction as a form of revolution. To alter his voice in some way, John recorded the vocal *lying flat on the floor* of studio three. Brian Gibson, technical engineer on the session, remembers it clearly. "John decided he would feel more comfortable on the floor so I had to rig up a microphone which would be suspended on a boom above his mouth. It struck me as somewhat odd, a little eccentric, but they were always looking for a different sound; something new."

(Although not relevant to 'Revolution', Geoff Emerick also recalls one of John's more bizarre studio requests in 1968. "He suggested we mike his voice from behind his back rather than in front and next to his mouth. He was desperate to sound different. 'Why does it have to be there? Why can't it be *there*?' We tried it but you just couldn't get the presence; it sounded the same as ever, only more muffled, so we gave up and returned to putting his vocals through a Fairchild limiter, which we did for almost every Lennon vocal after 1966.")

Geoff Emerick was by no means the only engineer the Beatles were using at this time. Emerick still had duties with other artists so on this day it was Peter Bown, well known in his field for his work on some of the best early British rock records, who sat in with them. "I didn't lay any basic tracks with the Beatles, just overdubs," recalls Bown. Before we had new mains cables laid to St John's Wood, the volts used to go down pretty badly on a cold night and one evening in number three they went down so low that the stabilisers went on the four-track machine and made this awful sound in John Lennon's headphones while he was overdubbing. We fixed up another machine but about ten minutes later it happened again. I remember John coming into the control room saying 'The f***ing machine has broken down *again*? It won't be the same when we get our own studio down at Apple...' I replied 'Won't it?' and left it at that. He went out of the studio and sulked for a while but at the end of the session poked his head around the door and said 'I'm sorry, Pete, I realise it wasn't your fault'."

John's floored vocal wasn't the only unusual vocal overdub recorded on this day. One of the session's tape boxes details "vocal backing mama papa". This was not a guest appearance by the Mamas and the Papas, however, rather a description of a persistent backing vocal (actually "Mama ... Dada ... Mama ... Dada ... Mama ... Dada") sung by Paul McCartney and George Harrison dozens upon dozens of times towards the end of the ten minute recording – but therefore cut out of the truncated version which appeared on the LP.

And also taped on this day was another drum track and various percussive clicks by Ringo, a tone-pedal guitar part by John and an organ part played by Paul. But two tape loops made for dropping in to the recording of 'Revolution 1' never actually made it and remain on the original tape, unused. One was of all four Beatles singing, at length, "Aaaaaaah", very high register. The second was made from a rather manic guitar phrase, played high up the fretboard. A rough mono remix of take 20 was made and was taken away on a plastic spool by John Lennon at the end of the session.

Top:
John, flat out on the floor of Studio Three for his 'Revolution 1' vocal overdub.

Right:
The Beatles line up for the lens of famous photographer Don McCullin during a special photo shoot.

Wednesday 5 June

Studio Three: 2.30pm-1.30am. Recording: 'Ringo's Tune (Untitled)' (working title of 'This Is Some Friendly', a working title of 'Don't Pass Me By') (takes 1-3, tape reduction take 3 into takes 4 and 5, SI onto take 5, tape reduction take 5 into take 6).   P: George Martin.   E: Geoff Emerick.   2E: Phil McDonald.

The second song to be recorded for *The Beatles* was a real first for the Beatles; Ringo's debut solo composition, a country and western flavoured song titled 'Don't Pass Me By'. Strangely, the song took life in the studio as 'Ringo's Tune (Untitled)' and then became, equally temporarily, 'This Is Some Friendly'. Strange because as early as 1963 it was reported in the press, and revealed in a radio interview, that Ringo was halfway through the writing of his own song and even then he was calling it 'Don't Pass Me By'.

The first three takes of 'Don't Pass Me By' concentrated solely on the basic rhythm track of piano (Paul) and drums (Ringo). At the end of the third take Ringo shouted to George Martin in the control room, "I think we've got something there, George!" So onto take three was then overdubbed another piano piece and, oddly, a Christmassy sleigh-bell.

This filled the four-track tape but two reduction mixes, the latter being 'best', took the song through

take four into take five. The first overdub onto take five was Ringo's lead vocal, recorded at 46 cycles per second, but this was immediately wiped and replaced by a bass guitar overdub played by Paul. Paul also recorded a bass part for the other spare track on the tape. Take five then became take six via another reduction mix, ready for more overdubbing, but it was noted on the recording sheet that this reduction was not good, and would be bettered before recording of the song was resumed.

Thursday 6 June

Studio Two: 2.30pm-2.45am. Recording: 'This Is Some Friendly' (working title of 'Don't Pass Me By') (SI onto take 5, tape reduction take 5 into take 7, SI onto take 7). Mono mixing: 'This Is Some Friendly' (working title of 'Don't Pass Me By') (unnumbered rough remix, from take 7). Recording: 'Revolution 9' (sound effects takes 1-12).   P: George Martin.   E: Geoff Emerick.   2E: Phil McDonald.

In returning to take five of 'Don't Pass Me By', both of Paul's bass guitar tracks were wiped and replaced by two Ringo Starr lead vocals, including a part near the end of the song where he audibly counted through from one to eight to mark out the bars! Another reduction took the song into take seven, Paul overdubbing a fresh bass part onto one of the two newly vacated tracks. This still left one track free – and it would remain so until 12 July.

While Ringo's song was approaching completion, 'Revolution 9' began to take shape – credited on the LP to the Beatles, of course, but in reality a John Lennon conception from the outset, assembled (rather than "recorded") almost exclusively by him and Yoko Ono, excepting a little later assistance from George Harrison. John would spend the next few days preparing tapes and loops of sound effects, some of his own making, others culled from his own and the Abbey Road collections. Twelve effects were

compiled on this day, five marked 'Various' and the others titled 'Vicars Poems', 'Queen's Mess', '*Come Dancing* Combo', 'Organ Last Will Test' [sic], 'Neville Club', 'Theatre Outing' and 'Applause/TV Jingle'. It should be noted that not all of these were included in 'Revolution 9'; some were used by Lennon in the imminent stage adaptation at the Old Vic theatre, London of his book *In His Own Write*, directed by friend Victor Spinetti. It opened on 18 June.

Monday 10 June

Studio Three: 2.30-5.45pm. Recording: 'Revolution 9' (sound effects takes 1-3).   P: George Martin.   E: Geoff Emerick.   2E: Phil McDonald.

The Beatles has long been known as the first Beatles album to be a collection of four men's solo recordings rather than a group's united effort. The session documentation and the original tapes do bear this out; aside from the basic tracks of each song, *most* – though even then not all – of which were recorded with all four Beatles present, much of the overdubbing was done by the Beatle who wrote the song.

Never before had one or more of the Beatles left the country while group recording sessions were in progress. But on 7 June 1968 George and Ringo flew to the USA, not returning until 18 June, and sessions continued in their absence; John compiled more sound effects for 'Revolution 9' and on 11 June – completely solo, with John *inside Abbey Road but in another studio* – Paul taped 'Blackbird', even remixing

it for mono until the final and 'best' version was reached.

On this day, 10 June, John compiled more sound effects for 'Revolution 9' in a three-hour session.

Tuesday 11 June

Studio Two: 6.30pm-12.15am. Recording: 'Blackbird' (takes 1-32). Mono mixing: 'Blackbird' (remixes 1-6, from take 32). Studio Three: 7.00-10.15pm. Recording: 'Revolution 9' (unnumbered takes of sound effects).   P: George Martin.   E: Geoff Emerick.   2E: Phil McDonald.

Fortunately, it is only a short walk from the control room of Abbey Road studio two to studio three. Because that's what George Martin, Geoff Emerick and Phil McDonald had to do throughout this evening, in keeping an eye on John Lennon in studio three and Paul McCartney in studio two, both busy on separate ideas for the 'White Album'. In theory, that is, and as detailed on the recording sheets. In reality, the triumvirate production team would have more or less left John to look after his own unique requirements in his own – similarly unique – way, although Chris Thomas remembers going with John

to find sound effects tapes and helping him make up loops.

While John was busy experimenting with sounds, Paul started and finished the recording of 'Blackbird', a lovely new composition which featured his own lead vocal, double-tracked in places via an overdub, accompanied by his acoustic guitar and a metronome gently ticking away in the background. It was a straightforward recording – no reductions necessary – and was perfected by the 32nd run through, just 11 of which were complete.

There was one other addition to the four-track tape: chirruping blackbirds, courtesy of "Volume Seven: Birds of Feather", from the Abbey Road taped sound effects collection, the doors of the trusty green cabinet already being open during this evening for raidings by John Lennon. "I taped that on one of the first portable EMI tape-recorders, in my back garden in Ickenham, about 1965," recalls Stuart Eltham. "There are two recordings, one of the bird singing, the other making an alarm sound when I startled it." Six mono remixes of the song were made before the session in studio two ended, the sixth being 'best'.

Thursday 20 June

Studios One, Two and Three: 7.00pm-3.30am. Recording: 'Revolution 9' (sound effects takes 1 and 2, compilation of master version, with SI).   P: George Martin.   E: Geoff Emerick.   2E: Richard Lush.

Three sessions – 12 to 14 June – had been cancelled in the absence of George and Ringo. But this session went ahead, even though Paul McCartney flew out of London Airport, bound for five days in the USA, one hour before it began.

But Paul's absence did not unduly affect this day's work, which saw the compilation of the 'Revolution 9' master take, now complete but for one final overdub done on 25 June. It was a busy night for all concerned, John Lennon commandeering the use of all three studios at Abbey Road for the spinning in and recording of the myriad tape loops. Just like the 7 April 1966 'Tomorrow Never Knows' session, there were people all over EMI Studios spooling loops onto tape machines with pencils. But instead of Geoff Emerick sitting at the console fading them in and out in a live mix, it was John Lennon, with Yoko closely by his side.

A close study of the four-track tape reveals the loops and effects to include:
· George Martin saying "Geoff … put the red light on," heavily echoed and played repeatedly.
· A choir, supplemented by backwards violins.
· A symphonic piece, chopped up and played backwards.
· A brief extract of the 10 February 1967 'A Day In The Life' orchestral overdub, repeated over and over.
· Backwards mellotron (played by John), miscellaneous symphonies and operas.

The most famous of all the 'Revolution 9' sound effects also made its bow during this evening: the faceless voice uttering "number nine, number nine, number nine". Richard Lush has a detailed memory of the session. "Lennon was trying to do really different things … we had to get a whole load of tapes out of the library and the "number nine" voice came off an examination tape. John thought that was a real hoot! He made a loop of just that bit and had it playing constantly on one machine, fading it in or out when he wanted it, along with the backwards orchestral stuff and everything else."

The identity behind the voice remains unclear to this day. "Abbey Road used to do taped examinations for the Royal Academy of Music," recalls Stuart Eltham. "The tapes aren't around now."

"John was really the producer of 'Revolution 9'," says Richard Lush. "But George Harrison joined him at Abbey Road on that night and they both had vocal mikes and were saying strange things like 'the Watusi', 'the Twist'…"

The original tape does indeed show that John and George went on the studio floor to read out bizarre lines of prose – in voices sometimes equally bizarre – into a couple of microphones, abetted by Yoko Ono humming at a very high pitch. These ran for the duration of 'Revolution 9', being faded in and out of the master at John's whim. Among John's random pieces were "personality complex", "onion soup",

"economically viable", "industrial output", "financial imbalance", "the watusi", "the twist" and "take this brother, may it serve you well". George's contributions included "Eldorado" and, shared with John Lennon and whispered six times over, "There ain't no rule for the company freaks!"

At the end of their long overdub, still whispering, John said to George "We'd better listen to it then, hadn't we?" What they listened to was the sound of a hundred sound effects, tape loops and overdubs and more. Even two decades later one can spend hours trying to pick them out and *still* find new ones.

"In 'Revolution 9' we had the STEED system of tape echo fed via a tape delay system," says Alan Brown. "The track ran for so long that there is one point where the delay runs out and you can hear the tape being re-wound, live. Even that impromptu thing, an accident, contributed to the finished result."

Paul McCartney presumably had little interest in 'Revolution 9', being neither involved in the manufacture of the tape loops nor in the same country when the master was compiled. But it is worth remembering that he had been the first of the Beatles to experiment with sound tapes, his 5 January 1967 'Carnival Of Light' collage being in much similar vein to 'Revolution 9'. "Paul was in America when John did 'Revolution 9'," recalls Richard Lush. "I can't recall exactly what happened later but I know it *didn't* get a fantastic reaction from McCartney when he heard it."

Friday 21 June

Studio Two: 2.30-9.00pm. Recording: 'Revolution' (working title of 'Revolution 1') (SI onto take 20, tape reduction take 20 into takes 21 and 22, SI onto take 22).   P: George Martin.   E: Geoff Emerick.   2E: Richard Lush/Nick Webb. Studio Two: 10.00pm-3.30am. Recording: 'Revolution 9' (SI onto master version). Stereo mixing: 'Revolution 1' (remixes 1-7, from take 22); 'Revolution 9' (remixes 1 and 2, from master version).   P: George Martin.   E: Geoff Emerick.   2E: Richard Lush.

'Revolution 1' – now with that title – was completed on this day with two more overdubs and yet another reduction mixdown, the song's third. The first overdub was of brass: two trumpets and four trombones, John Lennon settling on this arrangement having originally requested two tenor saxophones, a baritone sax, two trumpets and one trombone. The trumpeters were Derek Watkins and Freddy Clayton, the trombonists Don Lang, Rex Morris, J. Power and Bill Povey. Lang had a chart career going back to pre-Beatles days and had also – with his Frantic Five – supplied the opening music every week to a television show watched by the fledgling Beatles and every hip teenager in Britain in 1957/58, 6.5 *Special*!

Paul McCartney was still in the USA so he missed this session. Ringo too, was absent, so it was just John, with Yoko, and George holding the fort. It was George

who supplied the final superimposition for 'Revolution 1', a lead guitar line. Then it was John and George who attended to the final sound effects overdub for 'Revolution 9'.

'Revolution 1' and 'Revolution 9' were remixed for stereo in a 330 minute session which began at 10.00pm, although both were to be improved on 25 June. John Lennon had a marvellous time remixing 'Revolution 9' for stereo, pushing different images through on both channels and panning the words "number nine" across the stereo in fractions of a second.

Entertaining friends: Ringo listens to his Bush gramophone along with Lulu and Davy Jones of the Monkees.

Tuesday 25 June

Studio Two (control room only): 2.00-8.00pm. Stereo mixing: 'Revolution 1' (remixes 8-12, from take 22). Editing: 'Revolution 9' (of remix stereo 2). Tape copying: 'Revolution 1' (of remix stereo 12); 'Revolution 9' (of edit of remix stereo 2). P: George Martin. E: Geoff Emerick. 2E: Richard Lush.

'Revolution 1' and 'Revolution 9' were completed during this session (all that needed to be done to 'Revolution 9' was editing of the stereo master from 9'05" to 8'12"), and tape copies were made of the stereo masters for John Lennon and Apple Corps Ltd. 'Revolution 9' was to have a divided effect on its audience when released on *The Beatles*, most listeners loathing it outright, the dedicated fans *trying* to understand it. It was the first of several John Lennon excursions into the realms of sound collages. He

would later release three albums with Yoko Ono containing little else. It also had an effect on the personnel at Abbey Road, as Brian Gibson remembers. "For weeks afterwards everybody was going around the building muttering 'number nine, number nine, number nine'!"

Paul missed this session too, returning home from the USA while it was in progress. And George Harrison, although inside the studio building, also missed it. He

was employed in studio three, producing and playing guitar on the recording by Apple Records' artist Jackie Lomax of his especially donated composition 'Sour Milk Sea'. [The Harrison-produced Lomax sessions had started on 24 June, but they later switched to Trident Studios, an independent Central London venue. Paul also spent much of his non-Beatles time at Trident during July, producing Mary Hopkin recordings.]

Wednesday 26 June

Studio Two: 7.00pm-3.30am. Recording: 'Untitled' (working title of 'Everybody's Got Something To Hide Except Me And My Monkey') (rehearsal only). P: George Martin. E: Geoff Emerick. 2E: Richard Lush.

The Beatles, chameleon-like from album to album, and with time aplenty on their hands, discovered for themselves a new method of working for *The Beatles*: rehearse and rehearse and rehearse, with everything recorded, but then – in most instances – instead of spooling back to record proper over the rehearsals, treat the rehearsals themselves as the recordings, all takes numbered. Then, in the familiar fashion, go

back to the best basic version and start the process of overdubbing and tape reduction mixdowns. Few songs on *Sgt Pepper's Lonely Hearts Club Band*, the ultimate exercise in economical four-track recording, had gone beyond ten takes. Few songs on *The Beatles* stopped there. One, 'Not Guilty', went as far as *102 takes* – and was still left unissued.

On this night the Beatles set about the basic rhythm track rehearsal/recording of a new John Lennon song, untitled at present but very soon to become no less than 'Everybody's Got Something To Hide Except Me And My Monkey'. On the recording sheet was written 'Various takes; best to be decided'. In fact, the group wiped these and started again on 27 June.

Thursday 27 June

Studio Two: 5.00pm-3.45am. Recording: 'Untitled' (working title of 'Everybody's Got Something To Hide Except Me And My Monkey') (takes 1-6, tape reduction take 6 into takes 7 and 8, SI onto take 8). P: George Martin. E: Geoff Emerick. 2E: Richard Lush.

Six takes of the rhythm track for this still untitled gobbledegook Lennon rocker, the last being 'best'. At this stage the song lasted 3'07" but a reduction mix, to takes seven and eight, was done with the tape machine

running at 43 cycles per second, speeding the song considerably on replay, down to 2'29". [In later remixing it would come down further, to 2'24".] With overdubs onto take eight, the song by the end of the

session included drums, two different lead guitars, a vigorously shaken hand-bell and a chocalho.

Friday 28 June

Studio Two: 7.00pm-4.30am. Recording: 'Untitled' (working title of 'Good Night') (takes 1-5). P: George Martin. E: Geoff Emerick. 2E: Richard Lush.

There were two sides to John Lennon. On the one he was the composer and singer of 'Revolution' and 'Everybody's Got Something To Hide Except Me And My Monkey'. On the other he was the writer of tender ballads like 'Good Night' and 'Julia'.

The recording of 'Good Night' began during this session, although it was clear from the outset that John, though the composer, was handing over the lead

vocal to Ringo, whose doleful, plaintive voice suited the song's mood to perfection. 'Good Night' was a children's lullaby, pure and simple, written for a five-year-young Julian Lennon. Rehearsals and early takes – just John on acoustic guitar, Ringo on vocals – emphasised this, each one opening with an unscripted but positively charming spoken preamble by Ringo, along the lines of "Come on children! It's time to toddle off to bed. We've had a lovely day at the park

and now it's time for sleep." Or, "Put all those toys away. Yes, Daddy will sing a song for you!" Or, "Cover yourself up, Charlie. Pull those covers up and off you go to dreamland!"

[Note. There is no actual Beatles instrumentation on the final version of the song for neither this day's acoustic guitar nor the vocal harmonies recorded on 2 July were used.]

Monday 1 July

Studio Two: 5.00pm-3.00am. Recording: 'Everybody's Got Something To Hide Except Me And My Monkey' (SI onto take 8, tape reduction take 8 into takes 9 and 10, SI onto take 10). P: George Martin. E: Geoff Emerick. 2E: Richard Lush.

Overdubbing of Paul's bass guitar, reduction mixdowns and overdubbing of John's lead vocal.

July

Tuesday 2 July

Studio Two: 6.00pm-12.15am. Recording: 'Good Night' (SI onto take 5, takes 6-15).   P: George Martin.   E: Peter Bown.   2E: Richard Lush.

A new superimposition of Ringo's lead vocal and harmony backing vocals onto 'Good Night'. George Martin took away two copies of take 15 at the end of the session so that he could score the song for an orchestra and choir.

Wednesday 3 July

Studio Two: 8.00pm-3.15am. Recording: 'Ob-La-Di, Ob-La-Da' (takes 1-7, SI onto take 3, SI onto take 7).   P: George Martin.   E: Geoff Emerick.   2E: Richard Lush.

'Ob-La-Di, Ob-La-Da', the song which, in many minds, was the most fun number on *The Beatles* was a very involved recording indeed, spanning the original version and *two* re-makes, and recorded virtually every day from now until mid-July.

Not that the re-makes were drastically different from the song Paul had originally conceived. Just marginally so, indeed the song took shape on this day in much the same manner as it ended, though perhaps a touch more jauntily. Seven takes were recorded of the basic rhythm; Paul on acoustic guitar and Ringo on drums, Paul singing the lead vocal off microphone as a guide.

Take seven was deemed 'best' so a proper lead vocal and another acoustic guitar were then overdubbed. But Paul decided that it was take four which had the better basic rhythm so further improvements to take seven were abandoned and take four received the second acoustic guitar overdub too. Vocals for this take would follow on 4 July.

Thursday 4 July

Studio Two: 7.00pm-2.15am. Recording: 'Ob-La-Di, Ob-La-Da' (SI onto take 4, tape reduction take 4 into take 5, SI onto take 5).   P: George Martin.   E: Geoff Emerick.   2E: Richard Lush.

Overdub of vocals onto take four of 'Ob-La-Di, Ob-La-Da': Paul's lead and high register backing "la-las" by John and George. The four-track tape was then given a reduction into take five (not to be confused with the take five of 3 July) onto which another Paul McCartney lead vocal was superimposed.

Friday 5 July

Studio Two: 5.00pm-1.30am. Recording: 'Ob-La-Di, Ob-La-Da' (SI onto take 5).   P: George Martin.   E: Geoff Emerick.   2E: Richard Lush.

Numerous overdubs onto take five of 'Ob-La-Di, Ob-La-Da'. Between 6.00 and 10.30pm three saxophones and one set of bongos were taped, the saxophonists being James Gray, Rex Morris and Cyril Reuben, with one J. Scott supplying bongos. Rex Morris remembers playing on 'Ob-La-Di, Ob-La-Da' – "the reggae one" – and that "Yoko Ono was there at the session".

An instrument new to Beatles songs was overdubbed between 10.30 and 11.45pm: a piccolo, the flute-like instrument which has the highest range of the orchestra. The identity of its player is not known but Paul must have quickly realised that the instrument was surplus to requirements anyway, for between 11.45pm and 1.00am he wiped the piccolo track with a superimposed guitar overdub after which, barring a short playback, the session was at an end. Chris Thomas recalls that this was no easy guitar overdub, however. "Paul was deliberately overloading the sound through the desk so that it sounded like a bass."

A decidedly unstudio-like activity: Abbey Road receives a visit from a hairdresser, the precious Harrison locks falling onto a makeshift *Daily Mail*.

Opposite:
Another from the Don McCullin promotional series.

Monday 8 July

Studio Two: 5.00pm-3.00am. recording: 'Ob-La-Di, Ob-La-Da' [re-make] (takes 1-12, tape reduction take 12 into take 13, SI onto take 13). Mono mixing: 'Ob-La-Di, Ob-La-Da' (unnumbered rough remix, from take 13). P: George Martin. E: Geoff Emerick. 2E: Richard Lush.

In recording a re-make of 'Ob-La-Di, Ob-La-Da', the Beatles were creating another first: the first time they had especially recruited session musicians and then rejected the recording.

A dozen takes of the new version were taped, the four Beatles playing live (Paul on fuzz bass, Ringo on drums, George on acoustic guitar and John piano), filling the four-track tape. John's part included the released version's distinctive keyboard introduction, though this was born out of frustration as much as inspiration, as Richard Lush recalls. "Looking back now it was great to be involved with the Beatles but there *was* a negative side. They spent so much time doing each song that I can remember sitting in the control room before a session *dying* to hear them start a new one.

"They must have done 'Ob-La-Di, Ob-La-Da' five nights running and it's not exactly the most melodic piece of music. They'd do it one night and you'd think 'that's it'. But then they'd come in the next day and do it again in a different key or with a different feel. Poor Ringo would be playing from about three in the afternoon until one in the morning, with few breaks in between, and then have to do it all over again the next night.

"After about four or five nights doing 'Ob-La-Di, Ob-La-Da' John Lennon came to the session really stoned, totally out of it on something or other, and he said 'Alright, we're gonna do 'Ob-La-Di, Ob-La-Da'. He went straight to the piano and smashed the keys with an almighty amount of volume, twice the speed of how they'd done it before, and said 'This is *it*! Come *on*!' He was really aggravated. That was the version they ended up using."

As regretful as it may seem now, the Beatles' split in 1970 was acrimonious, and many observers attribute the break-up to having started during sessions for *The Beatles*. To a man, the staff working with the group inside Abbey Road confirm this. The sessions were becoming tangibly tense and fraught, and tempers were being lost more easily and more frequently than ever before. It should be stressed that not all sessions were conducted in this atmosphere, but certainly a good many were. And they would continue this way until the end of the group.

This particular session ended at 3.00am after a reduction of take 12 had been made, with lead and backing vocals overdubbed onto tracks three and four and 'Latin American percussion' (maracas and other assorted instruments) superimposed onto the newly vacated track two. A rough mono remix was made of take 13, taken away by Paul McCartney.

Tuesday 9 July

Studio Three: 4.00-9.00pm. Recording: 'Ob-La-Di, Ob-La-Da' [re-re-make] (takes 20 and 21). Studio Three: 10.00pm-3.30am. Recording: 'Ob-La-Di, Ob-La-Da' [re-make] (SI onto take 13, tape reduction take 13 into take 22, SI onto take 22); 'Revolution' (rehearsal only). P: George Martin. E: Geoff Emerick. 2E: Richard Lush.

Evidently, Paul McCartney wasn't very happy with the re-made version of 'Ob-La-Di, Ob-La-Da' either so in a five hour afternoon/evening session he set about taping a re-re-make. But just two takes of this [beginning with a rounded number, 20] were recorded before Paul realised that he wasn't going to improve the song any further. All further work on finishing the song would be applied to the first re-make.

The exact line-up of musicians on that unreleased second re-make of 'Ob-La-Di, Ob-La-Da' is in doubt, for the drumming style was less like Ringo and more like Paul – no mean drummer in his spare moments. This is verified to some extent by a contemporary report in *The Beatles Book* magazine, stating that Ringo arrived at EMI Studios early for the 9 July *evening* session so he popped into a Solomon King session and added a spot of handclapping to one song. This would infer that he was not there in the afternoon. [Abbey Road documentation shows that King did record there on 9 July, taping the single 'A Hundred Years Or More'.]

So in the evening the Beatles, all four of them, returned once again to 'Ob-La-Di, Ob-La-Da', the first re-make version, and turned into the home straight, the chequered flag ahead. The lead and backing vocals taped on 8 July were wiped and replaced by a new set, this time with additional laughing, joking, ho-hos, hee-hees and little asides. (Listen on the record for John shouting "arm" and George shouting "leg" after Paul's first "Desmond lets the children lend a hand", then for George's "foot" after "Molly lets the children lend a hand" in Paul's deliberately twisted final verse.) Handclaps and vocal percussion were also added after another reduction mix, take 13 becoming – to take into account the re-re-make – take 22.

The remainder of the session was devoted to the recording of 'Revolution', strictly speaking a re-make of 'Revolution 1'. Shortly before his death in 1980 John explained the reason for the song's re-make: Paul and George refused to allow the original recording, 'Revolution 1', to be released as the next Beatles single, fearing that it was not upbeat enough. So John decided that the Beatles would record the song fast and loud, but with the same sentiment and – but for one word – the same lyrics.

The resultant recording, 'Revolution', still only made the B-side of the next single, but it was no less a tremendous piece of rock music than Lennon had visioned, ranking with songs like 'This Boy' as the sort of B-side which could have easily been an A-side.

On this night the Beatles played through the song as much in rehearsal as recording, with lead and rhythm guitars, bass, drums and John's lead vocal. But all of the 'Revolution' takes from this session were later wiped, the recording started afresh on 10 July.

Wednesday 10 July

Studio Three: 7.00pm-1.30am. Recording: 'Revolution' (takes 1-10, tape reduction take 10 into takes 11-13, SI onto take 13, tape reduction take 13 into takes 14 and 15). P: George Martin. E: Geoff Emerick. 2E: Richard Lush.

There were few more exciting, hard rocking Beatles recordings than what has become known as the "single version" of 'Revolution'. Perhaps the song's most distinctive sound was of two distorted lead guitars. Phil McDonald, tape operator on the 11 July session, remembers how this was achieved. "John wanted that sound, a really distorted sound. The guitars were put through the recording console, which was technically not the thing to do. It completely overloaded the channel and produced the fuzz sound.

Fortunately the technical people didn't find out. They didn't approve of 'abuse of equipment'."

After ten takes, and an overdub onto the tenth, the basic rhythm of 'Revolution' was blistering, with the two distorted guitars, handclaps and two separate and very heavy drum tracks, compressed and limited and generally squashed to sound hard and uncompromising. A reduction mix took the song into takes 11 to 13, the latter being deemed 'best', and onto this John superimposed a venomous lead and, on another track, a second vocal take, manually double-tracking the odd word here and there (and occasionally going wrong, though the mistakes went uncorrected because of the exciting live feel) to further force his points across. In this second overdub John also gave the song a screaming introduction.

Another reduction mix took the song into takes 14 and 15, ready for more overdubbing in the next session.

Thursday 11 July

Studio Three: 4.00-7.00pm. Recording: 'Revolution' (SI onto take 15). P: George Martin. E: Geoff Emerick. 2E: Richard Lush. Studio Three: 7.00pm-3.45am. Recording: 'Ob-La-Di, Ob-La-Da' (SI onto take 22); 'Revolution' (tape reduction take 15 into take 16, SI onto take 16); 'Ob-La-Di, Ob-La-Da' (tape reduction take 22 into takes 23 and 24, SI onto take 23). Mono mixing: 'Ob-La-Di, Ob-La-Da' (remixes 1 and 2, from take 23). P: George Martin. E: Geoff Emerick. 2E: Phil McDonald.

A day of reductions and overdubs, by the end of which 'Revolution' also included electric piano and bass guitar while 'Ob-La-Di, Ob-La-Da' had three saxophones and bass guitar. The piano was played not by one of the Beatles, however, but by Nicky

Hopkins, brought in especially for the part. Hopkins was to become one of the best known sidemen in rock music in the 1970s, backing the Rolling Stones on tour and contributing piano to many best selling albums, including efforts by John Lennon, George Harrison

and Ringo Starr. (George returned the compliment, playing on four songs on Hopkins' own 1973 album *The Tin Man Was A Dreamer*.)

Friday 12 July

Studio Two: 3.00-11.00pm. Recording: 'Don't Pass Me By' (SI onto take 7). Mono mixing: 'Don't Pass Me By' (remixes 1-4, from take 7); 'Ob-La-Di, Ob-La-Da' (remixes 10 and 11, from take 23). Studio Two: 12.00pm-4.00am. Recording: 'Revolution' (SI onto take 16). Mono mixing: 'Revolution' (remixes 10-13, from take 16). P: George Martin. E: Geoff Emerick. 2E: Richard Lush.

After lying fallow for more than a month, Ringo's 'Don't Pass Me By' was completed today – excepting the song's somewhat quirky introduction, taped as an edit piece on 22 July. The afternoon and most of the evening was devoted to the song; from 3.00 until 6.40 a violin part was recorded by outside musician Jack Fallon, after which Paul added bass guitar and Ringo contributed more piano. Four mono remixes finished it off.

The Beatles were surprised when they saw Jack Fallon, for he was a booking agent as well as a musician and it was he who, when wearing his other hat, had booked the Beatles into their first professionally-organised engagement in the south of England (Stroud) on 31 March 1962, ten weeks before the group's audition/test with EMI. (He later booked them for engagements in Swindon, Lydney, Salisbury and a return to Stroud, too.)

"George Martin had jotted down a 12-bar blues for me. A lot of country fiddle playing is double-stop but Paul and George Martin – they were doing the arranging – suggested I play it single note. So it wasn't really the country sound they originally wanted. But they seemed pleased. Ringo was around too, keeping an eye on his song."

Keen students of the Beatles' recordings will be aware that the mono and stereo versions of 'Don't Pass Me

By' differ considerably at the end of the song, the mono version having several extra seconds of Fallon's fiddle playing. "I thought that they had had enough so I just busked around a bit. When I heard it played back at the end of the session I was hoping they'd scrub that bit out, but they didn't, so there I am on record, scraping away! I was very surprised they kept it in, it was pretty dreadful."

Even allowing for the Beatles' nocturnal recording habits, it was uncommon for the group to *begin* recording at midnight. But that's what happened with

the final overdub session for 'Revolution'. John added another lead guitar to track one of the tape, Paul superimposed another bass guitar part onto track four.

(Note: During the course of recording and remixing *The Beatles*, three tapes of out-takes and studio chatter were compiled at the Beatles' request. Preserved from this session was the sound of Paul, Ringo and George in the studio two control room, announcing "remix ten" for 'Ob-La-Di, Ob-La-Da' with different inflexion and various accents.)

An original, hastily scribbled guide to the lengthy 'Helter Skelter' recordings.

Monday 15 July

Studio Two: 3.30-8.00pm. Mono mixing: 'Revolution' (remixes 20 and 21, from take 16). Recording: 'Ob-La-Di, Ob-La-Da' (SI onto take 23). Mono mixing: 'Ob-La-Di, Ob-La-Da' (remixes 12-21, from take 23). Studio Two: 9.00pm-3.00am. Recording: 'Cry Baby Cry' (approximately 30 unnumbered takes). P: George Martin. E: Geoff Emerick. 2E: Richard Lush.

John Lennon and Paul McCartney had taken home copies of the best (mono) remixes of 'Ob-La-Di, Ob-La-Da' and 'Revolution' after the Friday session. Over the weekend they had clearly dwelt on the songs and decided that both required a little further improving. 'Revolution' only needed slightly different remixing (starting, oddly, with the number 20). But Paul wasn't happy with 'Ob-La-Di, Ob-La-Da' and

he spent considerable time on this day re-recording his lead vocal. When he was done, ten more remixes were made and the song was finished. (Note. 'Revolution', being destined only for a mono single and not the mono/stereo LP, wasn't mixed for stereo until 5 December 1969.)

In the evening the Beatles began the recording of 'Cry

Baby Cry', a new John Lennon composition with *Alice In Wonderland* style lyrics and a distinct nursery rhyme feel. The early recordings were more like rehearsals, and the Beatles filled *four* 30-minute tapes with unnumbered takes. The majority of these were deliberately wiped by the group in recording later 'proper' takes and, on 18 July, a new song, 'Helter Skelter'.

Tuesday 16 July

Studio Two: 4.00-9.00pm. Recording: 'Cry Baby Cry' (takes 1-10, tape reduction take 10 into takes 11 and 12). Studio Two: 10.00pm-2.00am. Recording: 'Cry Baby Cry' (SI onto take 12). P: George Martin. E: Geoff Emerick. 2E: Richard Lush.

A day of concentrated work on 'Cry Baby Cry'. Take ten – a basic track of John's vocal plus bass, organ, drums, and acoustic guitar (later "flanged" in remixing) – was taken into take 12 by a reduction mix onto which, in the evening session, a harmonium (played by George Martin) and piano (John) were added.

Geoff Emerick quit working with the Beatles during this session, no longer able to withstand the rapidly worsening atmosphere and tenseness within the group. He was not to work with them again until 1969, when the Beatles coaxed him away from EMI to be the resident balance engineer at their new Apple studios, and when they coaxed him – and George Martin – to return to Abbey Road as an ex-employee to work on what was to become the *Abbey Road* LP. But, for the time being, he had had enough.

"I lost interest in the 'White Album' because they

were really arguing amongst themselves and swearing at each other. The expletives were really flying. There was one instance just before I left when they were doing 'Ob-La-Di, Ob-La-Da' for the umpteenth time. Paul was re-recording the vocal again [probably 15 July] and George Martin made some remark about how he should be lilting onto the half-beat or whatever and Paul, in no refined way, said something to the effect of 'Well you come down and sing it'. I said to George [Martin] 'Look, I've had enough. I want to leave. I don't want to know any more.' George said 'Well, leave at the end of the week' – I think it was a Monday or Tuesday – but I said 'No, I want to leave *now*, this very minute'. And that was it.

"I went down to the studio to explain it to the group and John said 'Look, we're not moaning and getting uptight about you, we're complaining about EMI. Look at this place, studio two, all we've seen is bricks for the past year. Why can't they decorate it?'

Admittedly the studio did need smartening up a little bit but I knew this was just an outlet for a bigger problem. They were falling apart."

Richard Lush also recalls some anti-EMI feeling on the part of the Beatles. "They always had a bee in their bonnet about EMI being very organised and *establishment*. They thought that *we* were like that too, and of course George Martin was very suit and tie." The situation was aggravated a little by the re-introduction, temporarily as it turned out, of obligatory white coats for the technical engineers.

"They were never really at ease with all that," recalls Martin Benge, one of the white-coat wearers. "I think they felt the place could be much more laid-back and relaxed and much less formal, but that's the way Abbey Road was in those days."

Thursday 18 July

Studio Two: 2.30-9.30pm. Recording: 'Cry Baby Cry' (SI onto take 12). Studio Two: 10.30pm-3.30am. Recording: 'Helter Skelter' (takes 1-3). P: George Martin. E: Ken Scott. 2E: Richard Lush.

There was no session on 17 July; the Beatles attended the world premiere of *Yellow Submarine* at the London Pavilion cinema in Piccadilly Circus and went on from there to a private party. But work resumed on this day with the recording of 'Cry Baby Cry', brought to a conclusion in an extended afternoon/evening session with the overdub of a new Lennon vocal, backing vocals, a new harmonium track, a tambourine and various sound effects.

The remainder of the day/night was spent recording three extended versions of 'Helter Skelter', a new McCartney song invoking the name of a spiral slide at a British fairground.

The version of 'Helter Skelter' which appears on *The Beatles* is entirely different from the versions taped on this day, however. That album recording, a re-make, was begun on 9 September. The 18 July versions

remain unreleased, being – essentially – rehearsals. Take one lasted 10′40″, take two 12′35″ and take three an epic 27′11″, the longest ever Beatles recording. All three versions were similar: drums, bass, lead and rhythm guitars played live – positively no overdubs – with a *very* heavy drum sound, heavy guitars and a magnificent vocal delivery by Paul, with – surprisingly – all but identical lyrics to the re-made version. Each take developed into a tight and concisely played jam with long instrumental passages.

Assigned as technical engineer on the session was Brian Gibson. "They recorded the long versions of 'Helter Skelter' with live tape echo. Echo would normally be added at remix stage otherwise it can't be altered, but this time they wanted it live. One of the versions of 'Helter Skelter' developed into a jam which went into and then back out of a somewhat bizarre version of 'Blue Moon'. The problem was,

although we were recording them at 15 ips – which meant that we'd get roughly half an hour of time on the tape – the machine we were running for the tape echo was going at 30 ips, in other words 15 minutes. We were sitting up there in the control room – Ken Scott, the second engineer and myself – looking at this tape echo about to run out. The Beatles were jamming away, completely oblivious to the world and we didn't know what to do because they all had foldback in their headphones so that they could hear the echo. We knew that if we stopped it they would notice.

"In the end we decided that the best thing to do was stop the tape echo machine and rewind it. So at one point the echo suddenly stopped and you could hear bllllrrrrippppp as it was spooled back. This prompted Paul to put in some kind of clever vocal improvisation based around the chattering sound!"

Friday 19 July

Studio Two: 7.30pm-4.00am. Recording: 'Sexy Sadie' (takes 1-21).   P: George Martin.   E: Ken Scott.   2E: Richard Lush.

'Sexy Sadie' was originally a bitter John Lennon song about Maharishi Mahesh Yogi, written after John had left India in April, somewhat disappointed with the holy man. But John replaced the word "Maharishi" with "Sexy Sadie" to avoid any upset.

'Sexy Sadie' was never officially recorded as 'Maharishi' but at one point during the session John briefly showed Paul how it was originally conceived, and this quick, tongue-in-cheek burst into song was kept for posterity on one of the "interesting bits and pieces" tapes. [See 12 July for explanation.] The expletives were *not* deleted on the tape.

> "You little t*at
> Who the f**k do you think you are?
> Who the f**k do you think you are?
> Oh, you c**t".

At the end of this delightful verse Paul suggested that perhaps it was better that the song was now more sympathetic.

Much of this day's session was spent jamming, and several other items found their way onto 'Beatles Chat'. There were more crude run-throughs of 'Sexy Sadie', with plenty of good humoured Lennon cusses, a new two-verse spur-of-the-moment Lennon song rather uncomplimentary to the memory of Brian Epstein and to his brother Clive, and then a near six minute instrumental jam of George Gershwin's 'Summertime', doubtless inspired by the 1958 rock version – albeit not an instrumental – by Gene Vincent and His Blue Caps.

The real recordings of 'Sexy Sadie', again resembling more of a rehearsal than a serious attempt at taping a releasable version, began with a Lennon shout up to the control room, "See if we're all in tune, George!" Then the group – drums, guitars and organ – went into 21 takes of the song, the lengths varying between 5'36" and 8'00". Some of the versions were bluesy and quite lovely but few came to any thought-out ending. Another 'Beatles Chat' item has Yoko Ono suggesting that the Beatles could do 'Sexy Sadie' better. John, eager to placate the mood, quickly interjected. "Well, maybe *I* can".

By the end of the session John could be heard to enquire, generally, "I don't like the sound very much for a kick-off. Does anybody?" The answer was not captured on the tape but it must have been negative for a re-make was recorded on 24 July.

Monday 22 July

Studio One: 7.00pm-1.40am. Recording: 'Don't Pass Me By' (edit piece takes 1-4); 'Good Night' (takes 23-34, SI onto take 34). P: George Martin.   E: Ken Scott.   2E: Richard Lush.

The Beatles moved into the larger studio one for the completion of the album's two Ringo songs, his own 'Don't Pass Me By' and the Lennon composed 'Good Night'. The larger studio was needed to accommodate the 26 musicians recruited to overdub the lush – John later described it as "possibly over lush" – orchestra for 'Good Night', arranged and conducted by George Martin. The musicians, their names alas now lost, played the following instruments: 12 violins, three violas, three cellos, one harp, three flutes, one clarinet, one horn, one vibraphone and one string bass. A celeste and a piano were also made available for personal use by George Martin.

All previous takes of 'Good Night' were overlooked and the song was recorded anew, from start to finish,

during this evening. The orchestra was taped first, 12 takes beginning, rather oddly, from 23. Then, from 10.30 to 11.50pm, four "boys" and four "girls" from the Mike Sammes Singers – making their second appearance on a Beatles recording – taped the sound of a choir. The singers were Ingrid Thomas, Pat Whitmore, Val Stockwell, Irene King, Ross Gilmour, Mike Redway, Ken Barrie and Fred Lucas. (Mike Redway went on to become a radio personality and Ken Barrie later went into television and sang the theme song of the hugely popular animated children's programme 'Postman Pat' – more than four months on the singles chart in the early 1980s!)

From 11.50pm until 1.40m Ringo recorded his solo lead vocal, this time without any of the charming

preamble evident on 28 June. But this was clearly a lot of fun too, for outtakes kept for posterity on the 'Beatles Chat' tape depict Ringo in fits of laughter between takes and telling jokes aplenty, and it also contains a few seconds of Ringo chatting with George Martin and Ken Scott.

This day's other recording was of a tinkling piano introduction to 'Don't Pass Me By'. Four such edit pieces were recorded, the best being the fourth. But at 45 seconds it was to be substantially edited down (to just eight seconds) on 11 October when it was joined to the remainder of the song and given new mono and stereo remixes.

Tuesday 23 July

Studio Two: 7.00pm-2.30am. Recording: 'Everybody's Got Something To Hide Except Me And My Monkey' (SI onto take 10, tape reduction take 10 into takes 11 and 12, SI onto take 12). Mono mixing: 'Everybody's Got Something To Hide Except Me And My Monkey' (remixes 1-5, from take 12); 'Good Night' (remixes 1-6, from take 34).   P: George Martin.   E: Ken Scott.   2E: Richard Lush.

John's 'Everybody's Got Something To Hide Except Me And My Monkey', was completed during this session, 22 days after take ten had been deemed 'best' and the song presumed finished. The original lead vocal was replaced by a rousing new Lennon version which, after the point where he knew the song would be faded out on disc, developed into frantic, jocular screaming. For tape operator Richard Lush it was a taste of things to come: he would be one of the engineers on *John Lennon/Plastic Ono Band*, John's first studio album of solo music (recorded at Abbey Road between 26 September and 9 October 1970) in which there was plenty of *serious*, primal therapy screaming.

"As usual, John was wanting his voice to sound different," says Lush. "He would say 'I want to sound like somebody from the moon' or *anything* different. 'Make it different!' And at that time there wasn't the range of instant effects available today."

The third reduction mix in the life of 'Everybody's Got Something To Hide Except Me And My Monkey' took the song into take 12. Onto this was overdubbed backing vocals and handclaps and the song was then complete. Five mono remixes of this and six of 'Good Night' brought the session to a close.

The 'Red form' for the 22 July session, showing the instrumental line-up for 'Good Night'.

Wednesday 24 July

Studio Two: 7.00pm-2.30am. Recording: 'Sexy Sadie' [re-make] (takes 25-47); 'Untitled' (one unnumbered take of sound effects).　P: George Martin.　E: Ken Scott.　2E: Richard Lush.

The first of two 'Sexy Sadie' re-makes. Despite the recording of 23 takes (commencing with number 25) on this day, spread over three tapes, and despite the fact that take 47 was labelled 'best', John still wasn't happy with the sound. The re-remake was begun on 13 August.

The Beatles finished this session putting a few sound effects down on tape. It is impossible to say what these consisted of because only one tape was made and this was taken away. But certainly nothing from it was used on record.

Thursday 25 July

Studio Two: 7.00pm-3.15am. Recording: 'While My Guitar Gently Weeps' (take 1).　P: George Martin.　E: Ken Scott.　2E: Richard Lush.

George Harrison had been patient. He too had new songs to record though, to use his own, candid, words – "I always had to do about ten of Paul and John's songs before they'd give me the break". George had suppressed his new material since the LP sessions began on 30 May, but in the end he would tape five songs for *The Beatles*, the first – and the most famous – of these being 'While My Guitar Gently Weeps'.

Like so many Beatles recordings, 'While My Guitar Gently Weeps' was to change considerably from conception to completion. On this first day the Beatles rehearsed several takes, all of which were taken away by George for home listening. But they also taped one proper take, still in the archive at Abbey Road. Or, rather, George Harrison taped it, for take one of 'While My Guitar Gently Weeps' was a solo vocal and acoustic guitar job (joined only near the end by an overdubbed organ) – and a very beautiful job it was too.

"The song changed considerably by the time they had finished with it," says Brian Gibson. "They completed the song on eight-track tape [more of this later] and this gave them the immediate temptation to put more and more stuff on. I personally think it was best left uncluttered."

Certainly a less cluttered recording than this take one could not be imagined. Nor a more exquisite unreleased recording, which – arguably – George has rarely bettered in his entire career. It lasted for all of 3'13", had a final verse not included in the final version and ended with a somewhat ironic "Let's hear that back!" call by Harrison up to the control room.

Monday 29 July

Studio Two: 8.30pm-4.00am. Recording: 'Hey Jude' (takes 1-6).　P: n/a.　E: Ken Scott.　2E: John Smith.

There was no session on Friday 26 July because John and Paul were putting the finishing touches to what was, essentially, a McCartney composition – 'Hey Jude'. The first session for this magnificent tune was therefore held over until the Monday, 29 July. 'Hey Jude' was not meant for the 'White Album'. It was meant for, and released as, a single, one of the Beatles' best known, and certainly their longest.

The Beatles had shown time and again that they would not stand loitering around musical barriers. Barriers were there to be by-passed or even obliterated. One of these was that pop music singles had to last no longer than three minutes. In 1963 it had been more like two. Richard Harris, with 'MacArthur Park', was the first to break that mould; the Beatles soon compounded it with 'Hey Jude', the single release being 7'11" long. Today's ubiquitous "megamixes" are a direct descendant of these songs but twelve-inch singles (thankfully, perhaps) didn't exist in 1968. It is an interesting thought that had they existed – using 1980s practices – 'Hey Jude' probably would have been a regular three minute single, with the full 7'11" version being saved only for the 12-inch.

But although 'Hey Jude' was always going to be a long recording it wasn't always 7'11". On this first day three complete takes were recorded – one, two and six – and they lasted 6'21", 4'30" and 5'25" respectively.

But then again, these were more like rehearsals than attempts at a 'best' recording. Each of the six takes recorded during this session had the live line-up of vocals and piano (Paul), acoustic guitar (John), electric guitar (George) and drums (Ringo). But you cannot keep a great melody down. Each was only a little less superb than the final version.

George Martin had a night off and did not attend the session. Had he done so he would have seen the debut as Beatles' tape operator of John Smith, replacing Richard Lush. Smith, with Ken Scott as balance engineer, would work on all but a few of the remaining sessions for *The Beatles*.

Tuesday 30 July

Studio Two: 7.30pm-3.30am. Recording: 'Hey Jude' (takes 7-23, tape reduction take 23 into takes 24 and 25). Stereo mixing: 'Hey Jude' (remix 1, from take 25).　P: George Martin.　E: Ken Scott.　2E: John Smith.

Rehearsals cum recordings for 'Hey Jude' continued on this night, the song progressing from take seven through to 25, though it was not the Beatles' intention to capture the perfect recording yet. Sessions over the next few days at another studio, Trident, had already been booked for that purpose, and a large orchestra had already been lined up for a session there on 1 August.

But this session was arranged as more than a means of rehearsing 'Hey Jude'. It also took place in order that the Beatles could be filmed for part of a documentary being made by the National Music Council of Great Britain. The resulting colour film, *Music!*, included 2'32" of interesting Beatles footage, compiled from several hours of shooting during this long session (though mostly from take nine of the song), showing the Beatles busking, chatting and rehearsing. The musical takes recorded during this session featured just piano, drums and acoustic guitar – so there was no role for George Harrison. *Music!* showed him in the control room of studio two with George Martin and Ken Scott. "The film crew was supposed to work in such a way that no-one would realise they were there," recalls Scott. "But of course they were getting in everyone's way and everyone was getting uptight about it."

At the end of this session a rough stereo remix was made of 'Hey Jude' take 25, the tape taken away by George Martin, enabling him to arrange the song's orchestral score.

Wednesday 31 July

Trident Studios, Trident House, St Anne's Court, Wardour Street, London W1: 2.00pm-4.00am. Recording: 'Hey Jude' [re-make] (takes 1-4, SI onto take 1).   P: George Martin. E: Barry Sheffield.   2E: unknown.

Trident was a new studio for the Beatles as a group but individually two of the four had been getting to know it quite well of late. The launch of Apple Records was just a month away and George was busy sliding Trident sessions as producer of Jackie Lomax in between Beatles sessions back at Abbey Road. And Paul was doing likewise with Mary Hopkin, and popping in to the occasional James Taylor session too. Trident had two attractions in 1968. It was independent, just like Apple Records. And it had eight-track recording facilities. Abbey Road was still four-track. At least, that's what the Beatles thought.

What the Beatles didn't know – and would remain in the dark about for another few weeks – was that Abbey Road too had eight-track, a new 3M machine.

It just wasn't installed yet. "Whenever we got in a new piece of equipment at Abbey Road it went to Francis Thompson, our resident expert on tape machines, and he would spend about a year working on it," says Ken Townsend. "The joke was always that when he'd finished with it he'd let the studios use it! He was unhappy with the overdub facility, it didn't come directly off the sync head as it did with the Studer four-track, and there was no facility for running the capstan motor vari-speed from frequency control. Francis had to make some major modifications. I remember George Harrison asking why we hadn't got one – 'When are you going to get an eight-track, Ken?' – and we had a wooden replica of the new desk EMI was making to go with it. He said 'When are you going to get a real one, not a wooden one?'."

So the Beatles went to Trident. "Such independent studios were setting up all over London," says Townsend. "They were really trying to attract work and were installing new technology which was leaving the EMIs and the Deccas a bit behind."

Using the eight-track tape facility economically and with care the Beatles set about layering 'Hey Jude', starting afresh with take one, ostensibly a re-make, with a basic rhythm track of piano (Paul), electric guitar (George), acoustic guitar (John) and drums (Ringo). Paul has since revealed that George Harrison wanted to play an answering guitar phrase immediately after each "Hey Jude" vocal, but that he vetoed the suggestion.

Thursday 1 August

Trident Studios, Trident House, St Anne's Court, Wardour Street, London W1: 5.00pm-3.00am. Recording: 'Hey Jude' (SI onto take 1).   P: George Martin. E: Barry Sheffield.   2E: unknown.

'Hey Jude' was completed in a remarkably short time. Between 5.00 and 8.00pm on this day Paul McCartney overdubbed a bass guitar and his lead vocal while the other Beatles contributed backing vocals. (Listen out for an undeleted expletive at 2'59" into the finished record!) Then from 8.00 until 11.00pm the orchestra was recorded for the musical build-up during the song's long refrain. (The bass guitar part was wiped in favour of a separate track for the strings.)

The following 36 instruments were used: ten violins, three violas, three cellos, two flutes, one contra bassoon, one bassoon, two clarinets, one contra bass clarinet, four trumpets, four trombones, two horns, one "percussion" and two string basses. The musicians' names are no longer known, although Bobby Kok was one of the three cellists and Bill Jackman – tenor saxophonist on 'Lady Madonna' – played flute. "We just played the refrain over and over," he recalls, "the repeated riff which plays in the long fade-out." Chris Thomas, George Martin's assistant, was also at the session. "The studio at Trident was long and narrow. When we did the orchestral overdub we had to put the trombones at the very front so that they didn't poke anyone in the back!"

In addition to their playing role, the musicians were asked if they wouldn't mind contributing handclaps and backing vocals ("nah, nah nah nah nah nah nah, nah nah nah nah, Hey Jude") for the powerful build-up in the refrain. Most of the musicians were happy to oblige, especially as it meant a doubled fee, but there was one dissenter who reportedly walked out, saying "I'm not going to clap my hands and sing Paul McCartney's bloody song!".

'Not Guilty' scores a century, proceeding from takes 47 to 101, with 99 the 'best' basic track version.

Friday 2 August

Trident Studios, Trident House, St Anne's Court, Wardour Street, London W1: 2.00pm-1.30am. Stereo mixing: 'Hey Jude' (remixes 1-3, from take 1).   P: George Martin.   E: Barry Sheffield.   2E: unknown.

Three stereo remixes of the completed song, the third being 'best'. (These commenced with remix one despite the 30 July effort with that number.)

Tuesday 6 August

Trident Studios, Trident House, St Anne's Court, Wardour Street, London W1: 5.30-7.30pm. Mono mixing: 'Hey Jude' (remix 1, from remix stereo 3).   P: George Martin.   E: Barry Sheffield.   2E: unknown.

The first mono remix of 'Hey Jude' was made, somewhat unusually, from the best available stereo mix rather than the original eight-track tape. It was re-remixed for mono in the more conventional manner back at Abbey Road on 7 and 8 August.

Wednesday 7 August

Studio Two: 3.00-7.45pm. Tape copying: 'Hey Jude' (of remix mono 1). Studio Two: 8.45pm-5.30am. Recording: 'Not Guilty' (takes 1-46).   P: George Martin.   E: Ken Scott. 2E: John Smith.

Back to Abbey Road. A new song was begun during the marathon evening session, George Harrison's 'Not Guilty'. This was to become something of a marathon in itself – rehearsals/recordings exceeding more than 100 takes for the first time on a Beatles song. And *still* it would be left unreleased!

Having bandied the 100 figure about, it should be explained that by no means were 100 *complete* takes recorded. Only 21 were seen through to conclusion, and the very last take – 102 – was actually a reduction mix of take 99. Takes 1-46 were recorded on this night, all of the live, basic rhythm track only – bass guitar, drums, guitar and electric piano. The first 18 concentrated solely on the song's introduction. Then, from 19 through to 46 just five takes were complete – 26, 30, 32, 36 and 41.

Thursday 8 August

Studio Two: 6.40pm-6.30am. Mono mixing: 'Hey Jude' (remixes 2-4, from take 1). Recording: 'Not Guilty' (takes 47-101). Tape copying: 'Hey Jude' (of remix mono 4, numbered 5); 'Revolution' (of remix mono 21, numbered 5).   P: George Martin.   E: Ken Scott.   2E: John Smith.

"I went to Trident to see the Beatles doing 'Hey Jude' and was completely blown away by it. It sounded incredible," recalls Ken Scott. "A couple of days later, back at Abbey Road, I got in well before the group. Acetates were being cut and I went up to hear one. On different equipment, with different EQ [equalising] levels and different monitor settings, it sounded awful, nothing like it had at Trident.

"Later on, I was sitting in number two control room and George Martin came in. I said 'George, you know that stuff you did at Trident?' 'Yes – how does it sound?' I said 'In all honesty, it sounds terrible!'

'What?' 'There's absolutely no high-end on it, no treble.' Just then Paul McCartney came in and George said to him 'Ken thinks 'Hey Jude' sounds awful'. The look that came from Paul towards me...if looks could kill, it was one of those situations. Anyway, they went down to the studio floor, clearly talking about it, and one by one all the other Beatles came in and joined them. I could see them talking and then look up at me, and then talk again, and then look at me. I thought, 'Oh God, I'm going to get thrown off the session'. Finally, they all came storming up and said 'OK, let's see if it's as bad as you say. Go get the tape and we'll have a listen'. Luckily, they agreed with me,

it did sound bad. We spent the rest of the evening trying to EQ it and get some high-end on it. But for a while there I wanted to crawl under a stone and die."

'Not Guilty' continued on this day with takes 47 to 101 and take 99 deemed 'best'. But this was still a basic rhythm track only, although the instruments had changed to bass guitar, drums, guitar and harpsichord, the latter replacing the electric piano.

Tape copies of the 'Hey Jude' and 'Revolution' mono masters, both numbered five, were made at the end of the session and were taken away by George Martin.

Friday 9 August

Studio Two: 7.30pm-2.00am. Recording: 'Not Guilty' (tape reduction take 99 into take 102, SI onto take 102); 'Mother Nature's Son' (takes 1-25).   P: George Martin.   E: Ken Scott.   2E: John Smith.

Having found the 'best' rhythm track, 'Not Guilty' underwent its first reduction mix, take 99 becoming take 102. Now the overdubbing could begin. Much of this 6½ hour session was thus devoted, with a second drum track, a second lead guitar and a second bass track all being superimposed. The second lead guitar overdub was painstakingly recorded, as Brian Gibson recalls. "George asked us to put his guitar amplifier at one end of one of the echo chambers, with a microphone at the other end to pick up the output. He sat playing the guitar in the studio control room with a line plugged through to the chamber." The final overdub for 'Not Guilty' – also done in the control room – would be recorded on 12 August.

This session was due to finish at 10.00pm and it was around that time that work on 'Not Guilty' was completed for the night. But after the other Beatles had gone home Paul stayed behind to record a fine new acoustic ballad, 'Mother Nature's Son'. Although it was later to receive a brass overdub, the song was to feature no other Beatles, the same as 'Blackbird', already taped, and one other to follow.

'Mother Nature's Son' barely altered from the very first take, and it was just a matter of time, Paul running through the song with live acoustic guitar and vocal, until he hit upon the 'best' take. This was 24, although he did go one beyond – to 25 – just for good

measure. The only difference between the earliest takes and the 'best' was that the guitar intro piece was originally twice the length. The song would be completed on 20 August.

Making his debut on this night as technical engineer on a Beatles session was Richard Hale, and he recalls one of his responsibilities. "I had to look after the headphone amplifier. John Lennon only had one 'can', a single earpiece, which was a specfic request that he had made. He'd use it for vocal overdubs and somebody always had to give him this thing at the start of a session. It had a green Dymo label saying LENNON stuck on it!"

Monday 12 August

Studio Two: 7.00pm-4.15am. Recording: 'Not Guilty' (SI onto take 102). Mono mixing: 'Not Guilty' (remix 1, from take 102). P: George Martin. E: Ken Scott. 2E: John Smith.

The final overdub for 'Not Guilty' was of George Harrison's lead vocal, but as with his second guitar overdub of 9 August, this was no conventional taping. "George had this idea that he wanted to do it in the control room with the speakers blasting, so that he got more of an on-stage feel," recalls Ken Scott. "So we had to monitor through headphones, setting the monitor speakers at a level where he felt comfortable and it wouldn't completely blast out his vocal. I remember that John Lennon came in at one point and I turned to him and said 'Bloody hell, the way you lot

are carrying on you'll be wanting to record everything in the room next door!' The room next door was tiny, where the four-track tape machines were once kept, and it had no proper studio walls or acoustic set-up of any kind. Lennon replied 'That's a great idea, let's try it on the next number!' The next number was 'Yer Blues' [recording commenced 13 August] and we literally had to set it all up – them and the instruments – in this *minute* room. That's how they recorded 'Yer Blues', and it worked out great!"

'Yer Blues' may have worked out great but 'Not Guilty' evidently had not. Although the song was given a rough mono remix at the end of this session, in order that acetates could be cut, the recording never progressed beyond that, and it was never remixed for mono or stereo with a view to inclusion on the double-album *The Beatles*. Happily, George Harrison revived the song on his excellent eponymous album released in 1979, treating it to a much gentler acoustic feel but leaving the lyrics intact from the unreleased 1968 version.

Tuesday 13 August

Studio Two and annexe: 7.00pm-5.30am. Recording: 'Sexy Sadie' [re-remake] (takes 100-107, tape reduction take 107 into takes 108-111); 'Yer Blues' (takes 1-14, tape reduction take 6 into takes 15 and 16, tape reduction extract of take 14 into take 17). Editing: 'Yer Blues' (of takes 16 and 17). P: George Martin. E: Ken Scott. 2E: John Smith.

Perhaps inspired by the 100+ takes of 'Not Guilty', this re-remake of 'Sexy Sadie' began in the customary manner with a rounded number – take 100! The first eight takes, through to 107, were of the new basic track: drums, piano, fuzz guitar and the song's first John Lennon vocal. Take 107 was deemed 'best' and it was given four reduction mixdowns, 108-111, ready for overdubbing to commence on 21 August.

'Yer Blues' – largely recorded, as Ken Scott recounted, in the small annexe to the studio two

control room – was a new John Lennon song, a parody of the British blues scene. The first 14 takes were of the basic track – drums, bass, rhythm and lead guitars. Takes 15 and 16 were reductions of take six and take 17 was a reduction of a part of take 14. Then, for the first time on a Beatles recording, the original four-track tape was itself edited (editing was usually done only at the two-track quarter-inch tape stage), bringing the beginning of take 17 onto the end of take 16. On the finished record the edit is quite clear: it occurs at 3'17" into the song and runs through to the

fade-out. 'Yer Blues' was to be subjected to further recording on 14 August.

Between takes eight and nine of the 'Yer Blues' recording the Beatles (except for Paul, who took a break) lapsed into one of their regular impromptu session jams, in this instance a purely instrumental piece with much electric guitar. It was later cut-out of the original tape and put onto 'Various Adlibs', one of three bits and pieces tapes compiled during sessions for *The Beatles*.

Wednesday 14 August

Studio Two: 7.00pm-4.30am. Recording: 'Yer Blues' (SI onto edit of takes 16 and 17). Mono mixing: 'Yer Blues' (remixes 1-4, from edit of takes 16 and 17). Recording: 'What's The New Mary Jane' (takes 1-4). Mono mixing: 'What's The New Mary Jane' (remix 1, from take 4). Tape copying: 'Yer Blues' (of remix mono 3); 'What's The New Mary Jane' (of remix mono 1). P: George Martin. E: Ken Scott. 2E: John Smith.

'Yer Blues' was seen through to completion – except for a short edit piece taped on 20 August – with the overdub of a second John Lennon vocal. The song was then remixed for mono.

The influence of Yoko Ono on John Lennon's musical ideas was rapidly becoming evident. Together, on John's primitive home equipment, the couple had taped an album's worth of "experimental" recordings, which would be released within a week of *The Beatles* in November 1968 as the controversial *Two Virgins*. For *The Beatles* John – with Yoko's discernible influence – had already compiled the 'Revolution 9' extravaganza. Now, on this day, again with Yoko much in evidence, he set about the recording of a new composition, the downright bizarre 'What's The New Mary Jane'. This too was destined for *The Beatles* but was left off very much at the last minute owing to lack of space and, very probably, peer pressure. It remains unreleased today – even though John later made a second attempt at getting it released. [See 11 September 1969 and 26 November 1969.]

John Lennon and George Harrison were the only

Beatles playing on 'What's The New Mary Jane' and John was the only singer. But Yoko and Mal Evans too – judging by the original session tape – were also joining in the fun. Four takes were recorded, one was a break down, the others lasting 2'35", 3'45" and 6'35". These timings alone illustrate the impromptu nature of the song, although it should be stated that the lyric was identical for each take, so it was clearly scripted in advance rather than being a spur-of-the-moment thought, as would certainly be suggested by the content. The song conveyed a strange message, its title being mentioned not once but with the line "What a shame Mary Jane had a pain at the party" being the underlying theme. For some equally strange reason John always sung "party" with an American drawl *viz*, "pahr-tee".

Throughout all takes John was singing and playing piano, with George on guitar. On take four these instruments were overdubbed a second time and John added a second vocal line. Other oddments: at the end of takes two and four someone vigorously shook a handbell and someone else hammered away at a xylophone. During take four someone deliberately

rustled paper into a microphone. And all the while everyone was cavorting about and laughing hysterically. At the end of take four, the tape caught John saying to the others, "Let's hear it, before we get taken away!"

This day's mono remix of 'What's The New Mary Jane' was faded early, at 3'15", and copies of this and the 'Yer Blues' 'best' mixes were taken away by John.

Thursday 15 August

Studio Two: 7.00pm-3.00am. Recording: 'Rocky Raccoon' (takes 1-9, tape reduction take 9 into take 10, SI onto take 10). Mono mixing: 'Rocky Raccoon' (remix 1, from take 10). Tape copying: 'Yer Blues' (of remix mono 3); 'Rocky Raccoon' (of remix mono 1). P: George Martin. E: Ken Scott. 2E: John Smith.

All four Beatles were in the studio for the recording of a new Paul McCartney song, 'Rocky Raccoon', the basic track of which was acoustic guitar (Paul), drums (Ringo) and bass guitar (John). Another bass and drum track was overdubbed onto take nine and then, this take reduced into take ten, John added harmonica, George Martin added a honky-tonk piano solo and John, Paul and George added backing vocals. Prior to this, George Harrison had been languishing in the control room, as evidenced by his own announcement "take one" at the start of the session, usurping the role of Ken Scott!

For a song recorded and completed so quickly, Paul was surprisingly uncertain of the lyrics, formulating them as he went along and leaving the following rejected ideas in his wake: "roll up his sleeves on the sideboard"; "roll over, Rock…he said ooh, it's OK doc, it's just a scratch and I'll be OK when I get home"; "This hear is the story of a young boy living in Minnesota…**** off!" and "move over doc, let's have none of your cock". As Paul himself later said, between takes, "I don't quite know the words to that verse yet!"

'Rocky Raccoon' was remixed for mono in just one attempt during this evening (the preceding announcement "RM1" being kept for posterity on one of the three ad-lib tapes) and copies of this were made for taking away by John and Paul. Copies of 'Yer Blues' were also made for George and Ringo to take home.

Friday 16 August

Studio Two: 7.00pm-5.00am. Recording: 'While My Guitar Gently Weeps' [re-make] (takes 1-14, tape reduction take 14 into take 15). P: George Martin. E: Ken Scott. 2E: John Smith.

The 25 July acoustic version of 'While My Guitar Gently Weeps' had served its purpose only as a demo for the other Beatles. George Harrison now wanted the song to appear on record in much different form.

Recordings for 'While My Guitar Gently Weeps' would run until 6 September; takes one through to 14 were made on this day, featuring the new basic rhythm track: drums (Ringo), bass (Paul), organ (John) and guitar (George). Take 14 went into 15 via a reduction mix running at approximately 42½ cycles per second, extending the length of the song from 3'53" to 4'53".

There remains a question mark over who produced this session, George Martin's name, as ever, being included on the recording sheet but one of the session's tape boxes clearly stating "The Beatles; Produced by the Beatles". "The 'White Album' was a time when George Martin was starting to relinquish control over the group," recalls Brian Gibson. "There were a number of occasions – holidays, and when he had other recording commitments – when he wasn't available for sessions and they would just get on and produce it themselves. He certainly wasn't around for quite a considerable period of time, although they'd always fall back on him for scoring and arranging things."

Opposite:
Ringo arrives at the EMI Studios for another session on *The Beatles*. This shot, and the two that follow in the next six pages, was secretly taken by Abbey Road technical engineer Richard Hale through a venetian blind at the front of the building. Staff were not generally permitted to take photographs of recording artistes.

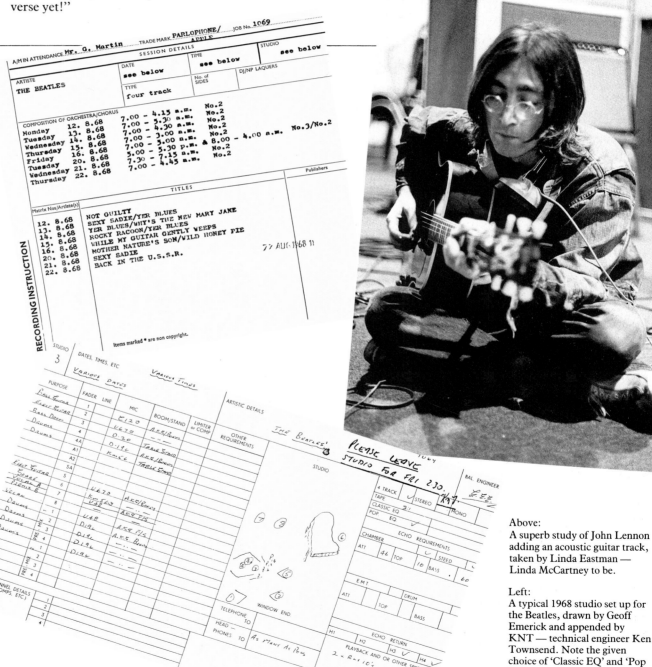

Above:
A superb study of John Lennon adding an acoustic guitar track, taken by Linda Eastman — Linda McCartney to be.

Left:
A typical 1968 studio set up for the Beatles, drawn by Geoff Emerick and appended by KNT — technical engineer Ken Townsend. Note the given choice of 'Classic EQ' and 'Pop EQ'.

Tuesday 20 August

Studio Three: 5.00-5.30pm. Recording: 'Yer Blues' (edit piece take 1). Editing: 'Yer Blues' (of remix mono 3 and edit piece take 1). Mono tape copying: 'Revolution 9' (mono copy 1, from edit of remix stereo 2). P: n/a. E: Ken Scott. 2E: John Smith. Studio Two: 8.00pm-4.00am. Recording: 'Mother Nature's Son' (SI onto take 24; tape reduction take 24 into take 26, SI onto take 26); 'Etcetera' (take 1); 'Wild Honey Pie' (take 1). Mono mixing: 'Mother Nature's Son' (remixes 1-8, from take 26); 'Wild Honey Pie' (remixes 1-6, from take 1). P: George Martin. E: Ken Scott. 2E: John Smith.

Very much at the last minute, George Harrison had decided on a quick trip to Greece, leaving Britain on 17 August and returning on the 21st. So the session scheduled for Monday 19 August was cancelled. But this one went ahead in his absence, with John and Ringo taking the opportunity to complete 'Yer Blues' and oversee the mono mix of 'Revolution 9', with Paul – in another studio – enjoying another solo session.

Taking things chronologically, 'Yer Blues' was completed with the recording of a very short edit piece for the beginning of the song, a "two, three..." count-in shouted by Ringo. This was edited onto the previous 'best' mono remix to make the completed master.

'Revolution 9' was obviously far too complicated to remix for mono from the original four-track tape, as was the customary procedure, so the mono mix was a straightforward dub of the best available stereo mix, the 25 June remix two.

The first task of Paul's evening solo session was to complete 'Mother Nature's Son'. Alan Brown was technical engineer on the session and he has a vivid recollection of its events. "It was quite late at night, the whole building was quiet, and there was Paul playing this enchanting song. I love the phrase "sitting in my field of grass". It has a *completeness* about it. It isn't just any old field, it's a field of grass.

We were all moved by it. Simultaneous to this recording session, Russia was invading Czechoslovakia. Of course we didn't know it at that moment but it did seem such a contrast of events...

"Paul wanted an open effect on his drums [to give a bongos sound] and we ended up leaving the studio itself and putting the drums in the corridor, halfway down, with mikes at the far end. It wasn't carpeted then and it gave an interesting staccato effect." (As a matter of interest, although he cannot recall which song was involved, Ken Scott has a recollection of Paul making a similar request during another session for *The Beatles*. "Right at the back of the building there's a staircase that goes from the basement up to the top floor," he says. "Paul suggested we use that as a natural echo chamber, with a speaker at the bottom and a microphone about half-way up, for the bass drum sound.")

'Mother Nature's Son' also received overdubs of timpani, a second acoustic guitar track and brass instruments during this session. As a stiff reminder that all was not entirely well within the Beatles' ranks, Ken Scott recalls, "Paul was downstairs going through the arrangement with George [Martin] and the brass players. Everything was great, everyone was in great spirits. It felt really good. Suddenly, half way through, John and Ringo walked in and you could cut the atmosphere with a knife. An instant change. It was

like that for ten minutes and then as soon as they left it felt great again. It was *very* bizarre."

John and Ringo were similarly not on hand for two very quick Paul McCartney recordings also done on this eventful evening. The first was a demo recording of a song called 'Etcetera'. "This was a very beautiful song," says Alan Brown. "I recall it was a ballad and had the word "etcetera" several times in the lyric. I only heard it twice: when he recorded it and when we played it back to him. The tape was taken away and I've never heard of it since."

Nor has anyone else, for unless the song resurfaced later with different lyrics, it is certainly unreleased to this day.

The second off-the-cuff McCartney recording was included in *The Beatles:* a ditty titled 'Wild Honey Pie'. In October Paul would record 'Honey Pie' for the same album but the similarity between the two songs ended fairly and squarely with the title. 'Wild Honey Pie' was a 53-second, much overdubbed one-man McCartney performance, with numerous vocals, numerous acoustic guitars and a thumping bass drum in the background. Just one take – with the overdubs, of course – was required to capture the song, spontaneity being the key.

Wednesday 21 August

Studio Two: 7.30pm-7.15am. Recording: 'Sexy Sadie' (tape reduction take 107 into take 112, SI onto take 112, tape reduction take 112 into takes 113-115, SI onto take 115, tape reduction take 115 into takes 116 and 117, SI onto take 117). Mono mixing: 'Sexy Sadie' (remixes 1-5, from take 117). P: George Martin. E: Ken Scott. 2E: John Smith.

An inordinately long session – almost 12 hours – probably caused by George Harrison's return from Greece on this day. It is unlikely that he would have showed up at Abbey Road until part way through proceedings, at the earliest.

The recording of 'Sexy Sadie', begun way back on 19 July, was completed during the session, with three reduction mixes and various overdubs; another Lennon lead vocal, an organ, bass guitar, two sets of backing vocals and a tambourine.

Five mono remixes, the final edition being 'best', concluded the session.

Thursday 22 August

Studio Two: 7.00pm-4.45am. Recording: 'Back In The USSR' (takes 1-5). Tape copying: 'Baby You're A Rich Man' (of remix mono 1).   P: George Martin.   E: Ken Scott.   2E: John Smith.

The tensions within the Beatles came to a head during this session…and Ringo Starr quit the group. Everyone privy to the sad state of affairs was sworn to secrecy and the news didn't reach the press.

"Things were getting very strained on Beatles sessions by this time," recalls Peter Vince. "The engineers would be asked to leave. They'd say 'Go off for a meal' or 'Go off for a drink' and you'd know they were having heavy discussions and didn't want anyone around." Ron Richards, as part of the four-man team at AIR, was still involved with Beatles sessions, albeit on a more administrative level, and he was also still regularly involved as a producer at the EMI Studios. "Ringo was always sitting in the reception area waiting, just sitting there or reading a newspaper. He used to sit there for hours waiting for the others to turn up. One night he couldn't stand it any longer, got fed up and left. George [Martin] told me that he was having trouble with Ringo but I'm not surprised. He left and it was all kept very hush hush. Paul played the drums in his place."

Richard Lush, even though he was not the Beatles' current tape operator, had seen the trouble coming for a while. "Ringo probably had the hardest job in the band, playing for hours and hours, and he probably shared the same view that we occasionally had, 'I played that last night for nine hours. Do I have to do it again?' He had a hard job trying to please them."

Someone who *was* there at this session was Ken Scott. "I remember Ringo being uptight about something, I don't remember what, and the next thing I was told was that he'd quit the band. But work continued. They did 'Back In The USSR' with what I seem to recall was a composite drum track of bits and pieces, possibly with all of the other three playing drums. Within a few days the differences had been sorted out and Ringo came back. Mal Evans completely decorated studio two with flowers, they were all over his drum kit, 'Welcome Back Ringo'."

Scott's recollection is largely confirmed by the original session tapes, for although the early takes reveal Paul as the drummer on the basic track, two more drum tracks were later overdubbed, conceivably while Paul was engaged playing other instruments. And the song was also a composite recording in other ways, with three bass guitar parts, played by John, Paul and George respectively, and both Paul and George playing lead guitar.

But that's jumping the gun. On this first night only the basic rhythm track – first drums (Paul), first lead guitar (George) and first bass (John) – was recorded. The remaining sounds would be recorded as overdubs during the next session.

(Note. A copy of the mono master of 'Baby, You're A Rich Man' was also made on this day, and was taken away by George Martin, the reason unknown.)

Friday 23 August

Studio Two: 7.00pm-3.00am. Recording: 'Back In The USSR' (SI onto take 5, tape reduction take 5 into take 6, SI onto take 6). Mono mixing: 'Back In The USSR' (remix 1, from take 6). Tape copying: 'Back In The USSR' (of remix mono 1); 'Rocky Raccoon' (of remix mono 1); 'Wild Honey Pie' (of remix mono 6); 'Mother Nature's Son' (of remix mono 8); 'Sexy Sadie' (of remix mono 5).   P: George Martin.   E: Ken Scott.   2E: John Smith.

Ironically, Ringo's absence spurred the Beatles into making one of their tightest and best recorded rock songs ever, 'Back In The USSR'. Completed on this day, it was a thumping number and ideal album-opener, a "potboiler" as George Martin was wont to call them. Added to the song during this session were the following: two more drum tracks, two more bass parts, two more lead guitar parts, a piano, lead vocals (Paul), fine Beach Boys style backing vocals (John and

George) and handclaps.

The final and distinctive touch was added in the song's one and only mono remix: the sound of an aeroplane taking off and landing. Eight seconds of this was applied to the beginning of the song, and the sounds then pop up here and there before bringing it to an end. "Someone managed to get that tape for me at London Airport," says Stuart Eltham, curator of

the effects collection from which the sound was borrowed. "There's one of it revving up and taking off and one of it landing. It's a Viscount aeroplane filed in the library as 'Volume 17: Jet and Piston Engine Aeroplane'."

Before the end of this session, four sets of tape copies were made of the latest songs to be completed, duly signed for and taken away by Mal Evans.

Monday 26 August

Studio Two (control room only): 4.00-5.00pm. Mono tape copying: 'Revolution 9' (mono copy 2, from edit of remix stereo 2).   P: n/a.   E: Ken Scott.   2E: John Smith.

The temporary absence of Ringo provided an ideal time for tidying up the work done so far, rather than start any new recordings. In this session another mono

copy was made of the stereo 'Revolution 9', improving on the 20 August model.

Tuesday 27 August

Studio Two (control room only): 4.30-5.00pm. Tape copying: 'Ob-La-Di, Ob-La-Da' (of remix mono 21); 'Blackbird' (of remix mono 6); 'Not Guilty' (of remix mono 1); 'Revolution 9' (of edit of remix stereo 2). P: n/a.   E: Ken Scott.   2E: John Smith.

More copies, taken away by Mal Evans.

Paul arrives at EMI Studios, greeting loyal fans with a wave.

Wednesday 28 August

Trident Studios, Trident House, St Anne's Court, Wardour Street, London W1: 5.00pm-7.00am. Recording: 'Dear Prudence' (take 1).   P: George Martin.   E: Barry Sheffield. 2E: unknown.

Back to Trident for more eight-track recordings. 'Dear Prudence', the subject of this and the next two days' work, was a fine new John Lennon composition, dedicated to Prudence Farrow, sister of the actress Mia Farrow. Prudence and Mia studied Transcendental Meditation with the Beatles in India during the Spring and, so the song goes, Prudence rarely ventured away from her chalet, preferring to meditate in solitude rather than join the others outside and "greet the brand new day".

'Dear Prudence' was a perfectly crafted recording, and the eight-track facility meant that it could be recorded track by track, each one perfected over a number of times while simultaneously wiping previous attempts. This method of working makes the "take one" statistic look distinctly silly for although it was just one 'take' it was innumerable *recordings*.

A basic track was taped first: George's and John's guitars (John supplied the hypnotic picking which opens and the runs throughout the song) and Paul on drums.

Thursday 29 August

Trident Studios, Trident House, St Anne's Court, Wardour Street, London W1: 7.00pm-6.00am. Recording: 'Dear Prudence' (SI onto take 1).   P: George Martin.   E: Barry Sheffield.   2E: unknown.

More contributions to the 'Dear Prudence' eight-track: bass guitar (Paul) and a manually double-tracked lead vocal (John) plus backing vocals, handclaps and tambourine supplied by Paul and George, occasionally joined by Mal Evans with Paul's visiting cousin John and Apple artiste Jackie Lomax.

The original eight-track tape reveals that the end of 'Dear Prudence' was shrouded in deliberate and massed applause from those persons supplying the backing vocals/handclaps, though this was mixed out of the finished master.

Friday 30 August

Trident Studios, Trident House, St Anne's Court, Wardour Street, London W1: 5.00-11.00pm. Recording: 'Dear Prudence' (SI onto take 1).   P: George Martin.   E: Barry Sheffield.   2E: unknown.

Single release: 'Hey Jude'/ 'Revolution'. Apple [Parlophone] R 5722.

A red-letter day in the Beatles' career; the first release bearing the group's own Apple label (even if it was only make believe, the rights and catalogue number staying with the Parlophone series). Issued simultaneously with 'Hey Jude' was Apple Records' first *real* release, Mary Hopkin's 'Those Were The Days' – an enormous worldwide success, produced by Paul McCartney. Seven days later – on 6 September – Apple issued two more singles, Jackie Lomax's 'Sour Milk Sea', written and produced by George Harrison, and 'Thingumybob' by the Black Dyke Mills Band, written and produced by Paul McCartney. A hectic time was guaranteed for all...

'Hey Jude' was more than just the Beatles' longest single, it was also one of their most compelling and commercially successful, selling in excess of eight million copies worldwide and topping the *Billboard* chart in the USA for nine straight weeks, from 28 September to 23 November.

Back at Trident Studios, the recording of 'Dear Prudence' was concluded on this day, with the overdubbing of a piano track and a very short burst of flügelhorn, both played by Paul.

Tuesday 3 September

Studio Two: 7.00pm-3.30am. Tape copying: 'While My Guitar Gently Weeps' (take 15 into take 16). Recording: 'While My Guitar Gently Weeps' (SI onto take 16). Tape copying: 'Revolution' (of take 16, rhythm track only).   P: n/a.   E: Ken Scott.   2E: John Smith.

Recording 'Dear Prudence' at Trident had whetted the Beatles' appetites: they now wanted *all* their recordings to be eight-track. When they got wind of the fact that Abbey Road did have an eight-track machine, the 3M model in Francis Thompson's office, they decided to "liberate" it.

"The studios were never allowed to use any equipment until Francis had said that it was up to standard, which was great, fine, but when you've got four innovative lads from Liverpool who want to make better recordings, and they've got a smell of the machine, matters can take a different course," says technical engineer Dave Harries. "They must have been getting on to Ken Scott about it because Ken called me and suggested we get the machine out of Francis's office and take it along to number two." Understandably, this led to repercussions. "Nearly death!," jokes Harries. "I very nearly got the sack over that."

The availability of multi-track recording is a controversial subject in recording circles. Some say that the more tracks are available the better the recording. [At the time of writing, 1987, there is equipment which can provide up to and even beyond 96 tracks.] Others maintain that rock music can be made much more economically, and point to some of

the greatest of all rock music, made on two- or four-track, *Sgt Pepper's Lonely Hearts Club Band*, for example. The danger of multi-track is a tendency to *over*-record. Brian Gibson recalls one Beatles session where overuse of the eight-track facility resulted in an extraordinary overdub. "There was one song, I can't remember the title, in which they'd added so many instruments that you just couldn't hear the drums any more. So they overdubbed Ringo playing a chair, a red plastic Abbey Road chair, slapping the drum sticks on the cushion and making a thwack to emphasise the snare beat, because they'd buried it."

According to Mike Sheady, soon to be second engineer/tape operator on sessions for *The Beatles*, the eight-track machine was taken from Francis Thompson's office before it was ideally suited for use. "Unless the tape operator remembered to mute the output from the machine when you spooled back and wanted to *hear* the tape travelling past the heads, it would send the spooling noise straight into the Beatles' cans, almost blasting their heads off. They got very uptight about that, understandably, because it can be very disconcerting."

The very first eight-track Beatles recordings at Abbey Road were 'While My Guitar Gently Weeps' overdubs, so the first task was to transfer the existing

tracks onto another tape for use as eight-track. Then the overdubs could begin afresh, with – for this song – six vacant channels now available. The Beatles – or to be more precise George Harrison, for he worked alone on this night – spent the entire session attempting to record a backwards guitar solo for track five of the tape, as Brian Gibson recalls. "George particularly wanted to get the sound of a crying guitar but he didn't want to use a wah-wah [tone] pedal, so he was experimenting with a backwards guitar solo. This meant a lot of time-consuming shuttling back and forth from the studio to the control room. We spent a long night trying to get it to work but in the end the whole thing was scrapped and it was around that time that Eric Clapton started to get involved with the song."

The only other output from this day's session was a copy tape of the 'Revolution' rhythm track from take 16, as completed on 12 July. This was made so that the Beatles could add a new vocal track – and therefore escape the Musicians' Union miming ban – during the shooting of television promotional clips at Twickenham Film Studios on 4 September. For 'Hey Jude' Paul simply sang a new vocal over the existing model. The filming meant that the Beatles missed a day at Abbey Road, returning on 5 September.

Thursday 5 September

Studio Two: 7.00pm-3.45am. Recording: 'While My Guitar Gently Weeps' (SI onto take 16); 'While My Guitar Gently Weeps' [re-remake] (takes 17-44).   P: n/a.   E: Ken Scott.   2E: John Smith.

The grand return to EMI studio two of Ringo Starr, his drum kit smothered in flowers. [Actually, Ringo had rejoined the group the night before, for the filming of the 'Hey Jude' and 'Revolution' promotional clips.]

The first part of this session saw more work on the 'While My Guitar Gently Weeps' eight-track tape, with two separate George Harrison lead vocals plus maracas, more drums and another lead guitar track all being superimposed. Still only six tracks were filled but that was as far as it went. George heard a playback, didn't like what he heard and scrapped everything. The Beatles then started work afresh on a re-remake. The scrapped version was quite different from the released version, with less prominent Harrison vocals and the backwards guitar and organ parts to the fore.

For the re-remake George steered the group through 28 more takes. These were numbered 17 to 44, obviously against George's wishes, for at the beginning of take 17 George himself announced into his vocal microphone "Take one!", as if to emphasise – to himself if no one else – that this new version would be substantially different from its predecessor.

And it was: the re-remade version of 'While My Guitar Gently Weeps' was the one which appeared on *The Beatles*. It had a basic track of drums (Ringo), acoustic guitar and guide vocal (George), lead guitar (John) and, alternately, piano or organ (Paul).

By the end of the session a playback revealed that take 25 was the 'best' version, and the remaining overdubs – filling four more tracks – would be done on 6 September.

(Note. Take 40 developed into an impromptu jam which included briefly busked snatches of 'Lady Madonna' and 'While My Guitar Gently Weeps', both with Paul as vocalist. These were preserved on the 'Beatles Chat' bits and pieces tape.)

Friday 6 September

Studio Two: 7.00pm-2.00am. Recording: 'While My Guitar Gently Weeps' (SI onto take 25). P: n/a. E: Ken Scott. 2E: John Smith.

Perhaps the most famous instance of the Beatles bringing in an outside musician to play on a studio recording was Eric Clapton's marvellous performance on 'While My Guitar Gently Weeps', recorded as an overdub on this day. Not that this was preordained; George only suggested to Eric that he might wish to contribute a few hours earlier, when Eric was giving George a lift from Surrey (where they both lived) into London. Eric was reluctant to help out – "because no one plays on Beatles sessions!" – only for George to retort "So what? It's my song!".

Lead guitarists are known for socialising with others of their ilk; Clapton and Harrison had been friends since 1964, when the Yardbirds, of which Clapton was

an esteemed member, had played support to the Beatles in a series of Christmas shows. Their friendship blossomed especially brightly in the late 1960s and is still strong today.

"Eric behaved just like any session musician," recalls Brian Gibson, "very quiet, just got on and played. That was it…there were no theatrics involved. I remember Eric telling George that Cream's approach to recording would be to rehearse, rehearse, rehearse, spending very little time in the studio itself, whereas the Beatles' approach seemed to be to record, record, record, and then eventually get the right one. The sessions were their rehearsals."

Clapton's superb solo, played on his Les Paul guitar, was just one of a number of overdubs recorded this day, which brought 'While My Guitar Gently Weeps' to a conclusion. Paul played a fuzz bass guitar, George threw in a few very high pitched organ notes, Ringo added percussion, and George – with Paul adding nice backing harmonies – taped his lead vocal.

Aside from making a unique contribution to a great song, Clapton's appearance on a Beatles session had one interesting side effect. As George was later to comment, "It made them all try a bit harder; they were all on their best behaviour".

Monday 9 September

Studio Two: 7.00pm-2.30am. Recording: 'Helter Skelter' [re-make] (takes 4-21). P: Chris Thomas. E: Ken Scott. 2E: John Smith.

"I came back from my holiday," recalls Chris Thomas, "and there was a note from George [Martin] on my desk 'Chris: Hope you had a nice holiday; I'm off on mine now. Make yourself available to the Beatles. Neil and Mal know you're coming down.' It took a while for the Beatles to accept me. Paul was the first one to walk in – I was sitting in the corner wearing a suit and tie! – and he said 'What are you doing here?'. I felt such an idiot, but managed to blurt 'Didn't George tell you?' 'No.' 'Well, George has suggested I come down and help out.' Paul's reply was 'Well, if you wanna produce us you can produce us. If you don't, we might just tell you to **** off!' That was *encouragement*? I couldn't speak after that…"

Despite Thomas's earlier proclamation that he didn't actually *produce* any Beatles sessions [see 30 May] this is how he was described on the relevant recording sheets and tape boxes and, to maintain consistency, the same description will apply in this book, though credence should be given to the fact that, by the autumn of 1968, the Beatles were much in control of their own music, its production and remixes. It is doubtful on this night, for example, that anyone but the group was guiding the session…

The 18 July recording of 'Helter Skelter' had partly fulfilled Paul's wish to create a rock music cacophony. The problem was, with that day's 'best' take running to more than 27 minutes, the song was likely to fill one entire side of an album. So on this day the Beatles

taped a re-make: 18 takes of an equally cacophonous maelstrom, but at the regular length of three to four minutes.

Actually, the length was the only "regular" aspect of the re-make for this was, by all accounts, a *mad* session. "The version on the album was out of control," says Brian Gibson. "They were completely out of their heads that night. But, as usual, a blind eye was turned to what the Beatles did in the studio. Everyone knew what substances they were taking but they were really a law unto themselves in the studio. As long as they didn't do anything *too* outrageous things were tolerated."

All sorts of instruments were being bandied about. The end result – take 21 and additional overdubs recorded the next day, 10 September – was a song in which John played bass guitar and, of all things, a decidedly unskilled saxophone, Mal Evans played an equally amateurish trumpet, there were two lead guitars, heavy drums, a piano, built-in distortion and feedback, backing vocals from John and George, various mutterings and – the icing on the cake – a supremely raucous Paul McCartney lead vocal. If 'Revolution 9' was John's excursion into mayhem on *The Beatles*, 'Helter Skelter' was Paul's. But it was Ringo who added the perfect finishing touch. Having drummed as if his life depended on it, his "I've got blisters on my fingers!" scream was preserved as the song's great climax.

Chris Thomas recalls, "While Paul was doing his vocal, George Harrison had set fire to an ashtray and was running around the studio with it above his head, doing an Arthur Brown! All in all, a pretty undisciplined session, you could say!"

(Note. The remixing of 'Helter Skelter' was a vital ingredient to the song, yet it threw up a major difference between the mono and stereo versions. The mono (done 17 September) ends at 3'36", the stereo (12 October) runs on for almost another minute, to 4'29". The latter has a fade down and up within the song, the former doesn't. The latter has Ringo's blistery shout, the former does not. There are also other, minor differences.)

Tuesday 10 September

Studio Two: 7.00pm-3.00am. Recording: 'Helter Skelter' (SI onto take 21). P: Chris Thomas. E: Ken Scott. 2E: John Smith.

Final overdubbing onto 'Helter Skelter'.

George sprints up the Abbey Road steps en route to another session.

Wednesday 11 September

Studio Two: 7.00pm-3.30am. Recording: 'Glass Onion' (takes 1-34).   P: Chris Thomas.   E: Ken Scott.   2E: John Smith.

John's song for those despised people who dissected his lyrics for hidden – but *almost* always unintended – revelations and conundrums. One of two songs on *The Beatles* to give mention in its lyric to another Beatles song title ('Savoy Truffle' mentioned 'Ob-La-Di, Ob-La-Da'), 'Glass Onion' is peppered with references to the Beatles' recent output: 'Strawberry

Fields Forever', 'I Am The Walrus', 'Lady Madonna', 'The Fool On The Hill' and 'Fixing A Hole'. John also tossed in what may seem a cryptic line, about the "Cast Iron Shore". This is a real place in Liverpool.

'Glass Onion' was not especially difficult to record.

On this day the Beatles ran through 34 takes of the basic rhythm track – drums, bass, lead and acoustic guitars – each version being around 1'50" in length except for take 15 which developed into a six-minute jam. A playback at the end of the session revealed take 33 to have been 'best', and overdubs onto this would begin the next day.

Thursday 12 September

Studio Two: 8.30pm-1.30am. Recording: 'Glass Onion' (SI onto take 33).   P: Chris Thomas.   E: Ken Scott.   2E: John Smith.

Superimposition of John's lead vocal and a tambourine onto 'Glass Onion' take 33.

Friday 13 September

Studio Two: 8.00pm-1.45am. Recording: 'Glass Onion' (SI onto take 33).   P: Chris Thomas.   E: Ken Scott.   2E: John Smith.

Superimposition of an additional drum track and a piano onto 'Glass Onion' take 33.

Monday 16 September

Studio Two: 7.00pm-3.00am. Recording: 'I Will' (takes 1-67). Tape copying: 'I Will' (take 65 into take 68). Recording: 'Glass Onion' (SI onto take 33).   P: Chris Thomas.   E: Ken Scott.   2E: Mike Sheady.

A very interesting session, almost exclusively for Paul's plaintive new ballad 'I Will'. It featured three Beatles only, with George not involved.

Using a four-track tape machine, Paul, John and Ringo recorded 67 straight takes of the new song, Paul singing and playing acoustic guitar, Ringo playing maraca and tapping cymbals and John tapping out a beat with wood on metal. Not all takes were complete, of course, and Paul wasn't entirely settled on the final lyric until late in the day. (Or, more precisely, night.)

Given the opportunity, and an acoustic guitar, Paul is wont to slip into a few ad-lib songs. He did, several times, during this session, and one of the off-the-cuff numbers made it onto the *The Beatles*. Take 19 of 'I Will' (again, with the Paul/John/Ringo line-up) was in

fact an untitled – and uncopyrighted – ditty along the lines of "Can you take me back where I came from, can you take me back?" It lasted 2'21" in all and was cut-out and copied for keeping on two of the 'odds and ends' tapes. From one of those a 28-second section, from 1'51" to 2'19", was itself cut-out for inclusion in the finished album, slotted between 'Cry Baby Cry' and 'Revolution 9'.

Other ad-lib pieces from 'I Will' were take 35, a very brief and impromptu version of 'Step Inside Love' (the song written by Paul especially for Cilla Black, recorded by her at Abbey Road on 28 February 1968 and rush-released on 8 March); 'Los Paranoius', a 3'48" make-it-up-as-you-go-along piece, painfully rhyming "paranoius" with "come on and join us", and including mouth-trumpet noises; and 'The Way

You Look Tonight', a short number, the lyric of which was derived almost entirely from 'I Will'.

But what of 'I Will' itself? A playback shortly before the end of the long session revealed that take 65 had been the 'best' version. To allow for more overdubbing without resorting to a reduction mixdown, the four-track tape was then copied across to another for use as an eight-track.

Before the session ended there was one small addition to make to the 'Glass Onion' tape. Either John or Paul hit upon the idea of including a few notes from a recorder at the point where the song's lyric mentioned 'The Fool On The Hill'. The recorder made a nice, if brief, parody and was probably played by Paul. It was double-tracked, recorded as two overdubs, for tracks six and eight.

Tuesday 17 September

Studio Two: 7.00pm-5.00am. Mono mixing: 'Helter Skelter' (remix 1, from take 21). Recording: 'I Will' (SI onto take 68). Tape copying: 'Cry Baby Cry' (take 12 into take 13).   P: Chris Thomas.   E: Ken Scott.   2E: Mike Sheady.

'I Will' was completed during this session with the overdubbing, all by Paul, of a backing vocal, a clever baritone dum-dum-dum impersonation of a bass guitar and a second acoustic guitar track. The lead vocal would be treated to ADT at the remix stages. 'Helter Skelter' was remixed for mono on this day in the aforementioned manner of ending the song at 3'36" rather than the full length 4'29".

Finally, the completed four-track tape of 'Cry Baby Cry', last used on 18 July, was copied across for future eight-track overdubbing. But nothing more would ever be added.

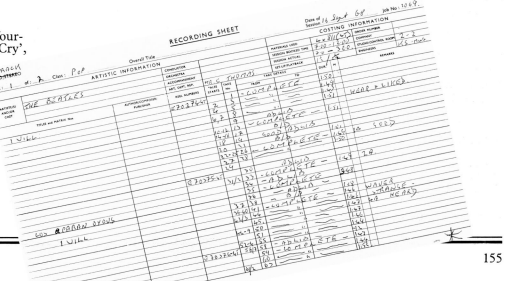

Wednesday 18 September

Studio Two: 5.00pm-4.30am. Recording: 'Birthday' (takes 1-20). Tape copying: 'Birthday' (take 20 into takes 21 and 22). Recording: 'Birthday' (SI onto take 22). Mono mixing: 'Birthday' (remix 1, from take 22). P: Chris Thomas. E: Ken Scott. 2E: Mike Sheady.

"I had mentioned to Paul a couple of days earlier about *The Girl Can't Help It* being on television during this evening," says Chris Thomas. [This was the first British TV transmission of the classic 1956 rock and roll film, shown on BBC2 between 9.05 and 10.40pm in the series *The Hollywood Musical*.] "The idea was to start the session earlier than usual, about five o'clock in the afternoon, and then all nip around the corner to Paul's house in Cavendish Avenue, watch the film and go back to work.

"So on the day Paul was the first one in, and he was playing the 'Birthday' riff. Eventually the others arrived, by which time Paul had literally written the song, right there in the studio. We had the backing track down by about 8.30, popped around to watch the film as arranged and then came back and actually finished the whole song. It was all done in a day!"

'Birthday' is a remarkable recording, displaying Paul McCartney's great versatility. Just the day before he had been working on 'I Will', a ballad in anyone's book; now he was writing – right there in the studio – one of the Beatles' most compelling rock and roll songs, and lending it the McCartney power vocal in a style reminiscent of 'Long Tall Sally'.

'Birthday' was also the sort of song into which any idea would fit. When the other Beatles arrived they all tossed in little contributions here and there, just as, when the recordings started, session visitors Pattie Harrison and Yoko Ono were recruited to add backing vocals. The recordings began on four-track but were transferred across to eight-track to accommodate all the overdubs and instruments which, for the record, were: drums, lead guitar, bass guitar, tambourine, piano, handclaps (helped out by Mal Evans), the backing vocals and the lead vocal, predominantly Paul but joined on occasions by John.

Between 4.30 and 5.00 in the morning the completed 'Birthday' recording was remixed for mono. The stereo would be done on 14 October.

Thursday 19 September

Studios One and Two: 7.15pm-5.30am. Recording: 'Piggies' (takes 1-11). P: Chris Thomas. E: Ken Scott. 2E: Mike Sheady.

Basic track recordings for a splendidly acerbic social comment George Harrison song, easily as biting (and equally lacking in subtlety!) as his 'Taxman'.

"All four Beatles were there for the session and we were working in number two," recalls Chris Thomas. "I wandered into number one and found a harpsichord, not knowing that it had been set up overnight for a classical recording. So we discussed wheeling the thing into number two but Ken Scott said 'No, we can't, it's there for another session!'. So we moved our session into number one instead.

"George Harrison agreed that my harpsichord idea was a good one and suggested that I play it. [Thomas had studied part-time at the Royal Academy of Music as a child.] This I did, but while George and I were tinkling away on this harpsichord he started playing another new song to me, which later turned out to be 'Something'. I said 'That's great! Why don't we do that one instead?' and he replied 'Do you like it, do you really think it's good?'. When I said yes he said 'Oh, maybe I'll give it to Jackie Lomax then, he can do it as a single!'." [George never did give Lomax 'Something' – his best known and most recorded composition – but he did give it to Joe Cocker, and played guitar on Cocker's version, some months before the Beatles issued the song in September 1969. But although taped first, Cocker's version was released second, in November 1969.]

Eleven takes were made of the 'Piggies' basic rhythm track on this night: harpsichord (Thomas), acoustic guitar (George), tambourine (Ringo) and a good bass line by Paul, his individual string plucking managing to evoke the sound of a pig grunting. That was as far as 'Piggies' went for the moment but overdubbing would begin and end on 20 September.

Interestingly, 'Something' was not the only future Beatles song (indeed, future Beatles *single*) which first saw the light of day during this session. "There were a couple of other songs around at this time," recalls Chris Thomas. "Paul was running through 'Let It Be' between takes." And technical engineer Alan Brown has a 1968 'White Album' recollection – the precise date unknown – of assisting Paul McCartney to quickly tape a demo version of 'The Long And Winding Road' at the grand piano in studio one, and then handing over the spool of tape to Paul.

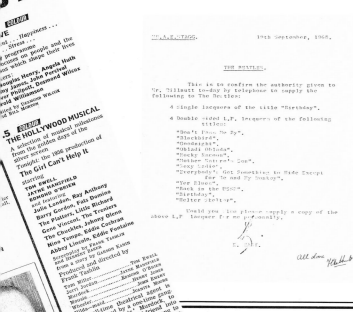

Left:
Even by late 1968, with many millions of records sold worldwide, the Beatles still had to await formal clearance from EMI before receiving advance pressings of their latest recordings. In 1969 and 1970 they finally by-passed the system by having acetate discs cut at Apple.

Friday 20 September

Studio Two: 7.00-11.00pm. Tape copying: 'Piggies' (take 11 into take 12). Recording: 'Piggies' (SI onto take 12). P: Chris Thomas. E: Ken Scott. 2E: Mike Sheady.

The completion of 'Piggies', with space made for overdubs by a four-track to eight-track tape copy of take 11 – called take 12. The first superimposition was of George's lead vocal, with ADT later added to the phrases "play around in" and "damn good whacking". In one verse George wanted to capture a nasal sound, as if he was pinching his nose while singing. Ken Townsend was technical engineer on the session. "We fed the microphone signal through a very sharp echo chamber filter, an RS106, so that it chopped off everything above and below the 3.5 kilohertz level, creating a very narrow band of sound."

While this was going on, John Lennon was up in the control room creating a tape loop of pigs snorting and grunting, using a tape from the Abbey Road sound effects collection. "There's a tape called 'Animals and Bees' [volume 35] which includes pigs," says Stuart Eltham. "It's from an old EMI 78rpm record and the Beatles may have used a combination of that and their own voices. That always works well – the new voices hide the 78rpm scratchiness, the original record hides the fact that some of the sounds are man-made."

Monday 23 September

Studio Two: 7.00pm-3.00am. Recording: 'Happiness Is A Warm Gun In Your Hand' (working title of 'Happiness Is A Warm Gun') (takes 1-45). P: Chris Thomas. E: Ken Scott. 2E: Mike Sheady.

It was, so John said, three different songs, unfinished and sharing not a single theme, woven together to form one complete number. A listen to 'Happiness Is A Warm Gun' (originally titled 'Happiness Is A Warm Gun In Your Hand') confirms this. But the decision to weld them into one was clearly made before John brought the song into the studio, for right from the first take it was complete as we now know it. As for the odd title, that came – as did several Lennon song ideas – from a magazine advert.

"'Happiness Is A Warm Gun' went to a great many takes," says Chris Thomas. "We used to make jokes out of it. 'Take 83!'" Eighty-three takes it did not reach, but it did make 70 rhythm track recordings rather effortlessly, mostly because of the complicated tempo changes between 3/4 and 4/4 time. The first 45 were taped during this session – bass, drums, John's lead guitar, his guide vocal and George's fuzzed lead guitar – and there was then much discussion between the Beatles, captured on tape, about how to play the song and how some sections were easier/more difficult than others.

Tuesday 24 September

Studio Two: 7.00pm-2.00am. Recording: 'Happiness Is A Warm Gun In Your Hand' (working title of 'Happiness Is A Warm Gun') (takes 46-70). P: Chris Thomas. E: Ken Scott. 2E: Mike Sheady.

Twenty-five more takes of the 'Happiness Is A Warm Gun' rhythm track, the instrumental line-up being the same as for the previous session.

A playback at the end of the session revealed that take 53 had been the best version for the first half of the song, but that take 65 had been the best for the second half. It was therefore decided that the two should be edited, and that the overdubbing be done onto the edited 'best' take. This was done on 25 September.

Wednesday 25 September

Studio Two: 7.30pm-5.00am. Editing: 'Happiness Is A Warm Gun In Your Hand' (working title of 'Happiness Is A Warm Gun') (of takes 53 and 65, called take 65). Recording: 'Happiness Is A Warm Gun In Your Hand' (working title of 'Happiness Is A Warm Gun') (SI onto take 65). Studio Two (control room only): 5.00-6.15am. Mono mixing: 'Happiness Is A Warm Gun In Your Hand' (working title of 'Happiness Is A Warm Gun') (remixes 1 and 2, from take 65). P: Chris Thomas. E: Ken Scott. 2E: Mike Sheady.

With the 'best' take of 'Happiness Is A Warm Gun' edited together from takes 53 and 65, but still called take 65, overdubbing could begin. This was completed by 5 o'clock in the morning, with the following additions to the eight-track tape: John's lead vocal, splendid "bang bang, shoot shoot" backing vocals by John, Paul and George, an organ, a piano, a tuba (virtually deleted in the remixes), a snare drum beat, a tambourine and a bass guitar.

This completed version did differ from the released model, however, for while applying ADT to the lines beginning "I need a fix" it was decided to mix out John's vocal the first time he sang the line, leaving that brief passage purely instrumental. (On the record, one can just make out the word "down" where the vocal was re-introduced for the next part a split second too early.)

Opposite: Another Linda McCartney action shot of John Lennon.

Thursday 26 September

Studio Two (control room only): 7.00pm-1.30am. Mono mixing: 'Happiness Is A Warm Gun' (remixes 3-12, from take 65); 'What's The New Mary Jane' (remixes 1 and 2, from take 4); 'Glass Onion' (remixes 1 and 2, from take 33); 'I Will' (remixes 1 and 2, from take 68). Recording 'Glass Onion' (one unnumbered take of sound effects). P: Chris Thomas. E: Ken Scott. 2E: Mike Sheady.

More mono remixes for 'Happiness Is A Warm Gun' and 'What's The New Mary Jane' (the latter commencing with remix one, although there had also been a remix one on 14 August), plus first-time mono mixes of 'Glass Onion' and 'I Will'.

John Lennon must have found the mono mixes of 'Glass Onion' lacking in something, and he decided that sound effects were needed. The remainder of the session was spent compiling a bizarre four-track tape – never used – lasting 2'35" but identical from beginning to end. Track one had a telephone ringing, track two had one note of an organ, track three had the BBC television soccer commentator, Kenneth Wolstenholme, shouting "It's a goal!", with the crowd roaring in the background, and track four had the sound of a window being smashed. A strange concoction!

On his return from holiday, George Martin was presented with a set of five acetate discs of the songs worked on in his absence. ('Birthday' was omitted and, presumably because there had been no mixes yet, so was 'Piggies'). In response to John's searching for the finishing touch to 'Glass Onion' George suggested strings. These were scored by Martin and recorded as an overdub on 10 October, rendering this day's mixes – and the sound effects – unusable.

Tuesday 1 October

Trident Studios, Trident House, St Anne's Court, Wardour Street, London W1: time unknown. Recording: 'Honey Pie' (take 1). Mono mixing: 'Honey Pie' (unnumbered rough remix, from take 1). P: George Martin. E: Barry Sheffield. 2E: unknown.

"I like this kind of hot kind of music!" Paul McCartney showing his versatility again – 'Honey Pie' is a hot 1920s-style jazzy number, with a lovely melody and blissful saxophones and clarinets, as scored by George Martin.

The Beatles returned to Trident Studios for no other reason than a week's change of scenery (which in this instance ran Tuesday to Saturday rather than the Monday to Friday schedule so consistent throughout *The Beatles*). Certainly Trident could not offer the Beatles any more than Abbey Road now that the latter also had eight-track facilities.

Once again, the final version of a Beatles recording at Trident was a "take one" though it should be stressed that there would certainly have been rehearsal takes too, though these were wiped before all the overdubbing began.

The basic track of 'Honey Pie' was recorded during this night-time session (the precise start/finish time is not known): piano (Paul), bass (George), drums (Ringo) and electric guitar (John). A rough mono remix was made for, and taken away by, George Martin in order that he could write the brass and woodwind arrangement.

Wednesday 2 October

Trident Studios, Trident House, St Anne's Court, Wardour Street, London W1: 4.00pm-3.30am. Recording: 'Honey Pie' (SI onto take 1). P: George Martin. E: Barry Sheffield. 2E: unknown.

Overdubs for 'Honey Pie': lead vocal and lead guitar, both the work of Paul McCartney.

Thursday 3 October

Trident Studios, Trident House, St Anne's Court, Wardour Street, London W1: time unknown. Recording: 'Savoy Truffle' (take 1). P: George Martin. E: Barry Sheffield. 2E unknown.

The Beatles, John Lennon especially, had more than once taken inspiration for song compositions from the printed word. But never before had a Beatles song been derived from a chocolate box. George Harrison's 'Savoy Truffle' was. Much of its lyric – indeed its title – came out of Mackintosh's Good News chocolates. George has since revealed that it was Eric Clapton's virtual chocolate addiction which led him to reach out for the Good News with one hand and the guitar with the other!

The recording of 'Savoy Truffle' was to span two studios, Trident and Abbey Road. During this day a basic track of drums, bass and lead guitars was recorded. The eight-track tape does not reveal any role for John Lennon on 'Savoy Truffle' at any stage in its recording.

Friday 4 October

Trident Studios, Trident House, St Anne's Court, Wardour Street, London W1: 4.00pm-4.30am. Recording: 'Martha My Dear' (take 1); 'Honey Pie' (SI onto take 1); 'Martha My Dear' (SI onto take 1). P: George Martin. E: Barry Sheffield. 2E: unknown.

It is difficult to say for sure, even by referring to the master eight-track recording, but 'Martha My Dear' – excepting the strings and horns overdub – may well have been another one-man Paul McCartney recording. Parts were recorded both before and after a six-hour brass, woodwind and string overdub for this and for 'Honey Pie', with a vocal line, piano and drums being recorded first as the basic track for the recruited musicians to follow.

What is certain is that 'Martha My Dear' was a one-man composition, a typical McCartney ballad, melodious and sentimental. Contrary to popular opinion, it was *not* about Paul's sheepdog of the same name. He may have got the title from his canine friend but that was where the association ended.

Between 6.00 and 9.00pm seven musicians recorded their parts for 'Honey Pie'; between 9.00pm and midnight 14 musicians did likewise for 'Martha My Dear'. The seven for 'Honey Pie' were: Dennis Walton, Ronald Chamberlain, Jim Chester, Rex Morris and Harry Klein (saxophones), Raymond Newman and David Smith (clarinets). The 14 for 'Martha My Dear' were: Bernard Miller, Dennis McConnell, Lou Sofier and Les Maddox (violins), Leo Birnbaum and Henry Myerscough (violas), Reginald Kilbey and Frederick Alexander (cellos), Leon Calvert, Stanley Reynolds and Ronnie Hughes (trumpets), Tony Tunstall (French horn), Ted Barker (trombone) and Alf Reece (tuba). Leon Calvert also contributed a flügelhorn part.

The period between midnight and the 4.30 end of session saw Paul wipe the existing 'Martha My Dear' vocal track with a new one (later applied with ADT), adding handclaps at the same time. He then turned his attention to 'Honey Pie', recording a quaint touch: the vocal line "now she's hit the big time!" which was heavily limited, chopping off the signals at both ends of the frequency range, and superimposed with the sound of a scratchy old phonograph, to make the end product like a vocal from a very early and worn 78 rpm record.

(Note. Since George Martin had a score prepared – and musicians booked – for this first recording session of 'Martha My Dear', one must deduce that he had been given a home-recorded McCartney demo tape of the song in advance with which to devise his arrangement.)

Saturday 5 October

Trident Studios, Trident House, St Anne's Court, Wardour Street, London W1: 6.00pm-1.00am. Recording: 'Savoy Truffle' (SI onto take 1); 'Martha My Dear' (SI onto take 1). Mono mixing: 'Honey Pie' (remix 1, from take 1); 'Martha My Dear' (remix 1, from take 1); 'Dear Prudence' (remix 1, from take 1). Stereo mixing: 'Honey Pie' (remix 1, from take 1); 'Martha My Dear' (remix 1, from take 1). P: George Martin. E: Barry Sheffield. 2E: unknown.

Overdubbing of an ADT'd George Harrison lead vocal onto 'Savoy Truffle' and bass and electric guitars – both played by Paul – onto 'Martha My Dear'.

The latter song, along with 'Honey Pie' and 'Dear Prudence' – an earlier Trident recording – was then remixed for mono. ('Dear Prudence' would be done again at Abbey Road, on 13 October when the stereo mix was being made.) Then 'Honey Pie' and 'Martha My Dear' were remixed for stereo, though again these too would be changed back at Abbey Road and copied from the NAB equalisation system of recording preferred at Trident to the CCIR method favoured at EMI.

Monday 7 October

Studio Two: 2.30pm-7.00am. Tape copying: 'Honey Pie' (of remix mono 1 and of remix stereo 1); 'Martha My Dear' (of remix mono 1 and of remix stereo 1). Stereo mixing: 'While My Guitar Gently Weeps' (remix 1, from take 25). Mono mixing: 'While My Guitar Gently Weeps' (remixes 1 and 2, from take 25). Recording: 'It's Been A Long Long Long Time' (working title of 'Long Long Long') (takes 1-67). P: George Martin. E: Ken Scott. 2E: Mike Sheady.

A 16½ hour session in which a new song was started: George's 'Long Long Long', at this point called 'It's Been A Long Long Long Time' but later abbreviated by the writer because he felt the title itself too long. The session tapes reveal that George was in a happy mood throughout, laughing, joking and bursting into busked versions of other songs, including 'Dear Prudence'. At one point he enquired of Paul and Ringo (again, John was not present for the session, nor for the song's overdubs), "Where did Mal get those joss-sticks? They're like Rishikesh joss-sticks!" Richard Lush attended many a Beatles session where joss-sticks were burned. "The people at Abbey Road didn't particularly like them," he recalls, "especially when the carpet and the whole studio was stinking of them, be it strawberry or whatever was the flavour of the month."

Whisper it quietly, but Alan Brown still has an authentic and unused Beatles joss-stick, in its original wrapper, picked up off the floor after a session had ended. "They used to burn several at once, sticking them into the slots of the acoustic screens. I'd go home at night my clothes reeking of them! I've never smelt joss-sticks of quite the same quality that they used. They had them specially brought in from India." Brown proves this by producing the 20-year-old packet and pointing to the details: "Special Durbar Agar Bathi, Sri Satyanarayana Parimala Factory. Proprietors: MV Narayana Rao Sons, Mysore, India."

It took 67 run-throughs of the basic rhythm track – acoustic guitar and vocal (George), organ (Paul) and drums (Ringo) – before the 'best' version of 'Long Long Long' was found and onto which the overdubs would be made. But there was one additional sound taped on this day. Chris Thomas, attending as George Martin's assistant, recalls, "There's a sound near the end of the song [best heard on the right stereo channel] which is a bottle of Blue Nun wine rattling away on the top of a Leslie speaker cabinet. It just happened. Paul hit a certain organ note and the bottle started vibrating. We thought it was so good that we set the mikes up and did it again. The Beatles always took advantage of accidents."

Just to compound the sound, Ringo recorded an extra spurt of fast drumming for the same passage.

Tuesday 8 October

Studio Two: 4.00pm-8.00am. Recording: 'It's Been A Long Long Long Time' (working title of 'Long Long Long') (SI onto take 67); 'I'm So Tired' (takes 1-14); 'The Continuing Story Of Bungalow Bill' (takes 1-3). P: George Martin. E: Ken Scott. 2E: Mike Sheady.

By 1968-standards this was fast going. Two new songs started and finished – with no overdubs to follow – in one session … albeit a 16-hour one. It was as well that the Beatles kept toothbrushes at the Abbey Road studios for pre-breakfast use.

It must be no coincidence that both were John Lennon songs. It had latterly become clear that the particular composer of each Beatles song was setting the pace for his particular number in the recording studio, and although there were times when John too might spend days or weeks on just one song, he was still prone to making his songs *instant*. Session tapes at Abbey Road largely reveal Lennon as a man in a hurry, "Quick, quick, the red light's on, let's go, let's make a *record!*"

'I'm So Tired' was the first of the two, a lethargic rocker with interesting changes in tempo to match a lyric which shared more with John's *Revolver* song 'I'm Only Sleeping' than a similarly bleary-eyed title. But unlike 'I'm Only Sleeping', 'I'm So Tired', was not an especially complex recording, with the eight-track tape looking like this by the song's completion; 1) bass 2) drums 3) guitars 4) John lead vocal 5) vocal fills by John, with Paul 6) drums, guitar, electric piano 7) drums 8) organ, distant guitar. The ending of 'I'm So Tired' – and also the ending of this session's second new song – featured an obscure Lennon muttering, in this instance "Monsieur, monsieur, how about another one?".

That second song, 'The Continuing Story Of Bungalow Bill', was a different kettle of fish altogether; a fun song written, like 'Dear Prudence', about one of the other Transcendental Meditation

students who was with the Beatles in India earlier in the year. The basic track of 'The Continuing Story Of Bungalow Bill' was recorded in a mere three takes and although it was then crowded with overdubs, the song showed the Beatles far removed from the days of *Sgt Pepper*, with a slap-happy, slapdash recording, preserving imperfections in an effort to capture the right atmosphere. In fact, the recording of 'Bungalow Bill' was something of a free-for-all, with everyone in the studio shouting out the choruses, applauding, whistling and backing John's lead vocal. Yoko Ono sang one line solo – "not when he looked so fierce" – the first female lead vocal line on a Beatles recording. And Maureen Starkey, Ringo's wife, was also one of the assembled chorale. Adding mellotron to the song was Chris Thomas. "That night was really fast going," he recalls. "Everyone who was in the vicinity of the studio joined in on 'The Continuing Story Of

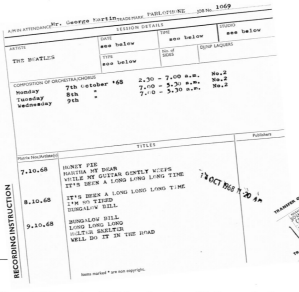

Bungalow Bill'. Yoko sang her line and I played a mandolin-type mellotron bit in the verses and the trombone-type bit in the choruses."

On record, the song began with a short Spanish acoustic guitar solo, but this was recorded separately and then edited on to the beginning of take three. The end of the song, meanwhile, was a north of England accented Lennon "Eh up!" which, when the album master tape was compiled, provided a perfect cue for the beginning of the next song, George's 'While My Guitar Gently Weeps'.

It was work on another Harrisong, 'Long Long Long', which had started this productive session, George contributing a second acoustic guitar track and a second, manually double-tracked lead vocal, and Paul adding a bass track.

The combined label copy and disc cutting instruction sheets for *The Beatles*. These newly designed forms replaced the typed memos used in previous years.

Wednesday 9 October

Studio Two: 7.00pm-5.30am. Stereo mixing: 'The Continuing Story Of Bungalow Bill' (remixes 1 and 2, from take 3). Mono mixing: 'The Continuing Story Of Bungalow Bill' (remix 1, from take 3). Recording: 'Long Long Long' (SI onto take 67). Tape copying: 'Helter Skelter' (of take 3). P: George Martin. E: Ken Scott. 2E: John Smith. Studio One: time unknown. Recording: 'Why Don't We Do It In The Road' (takes 1-5). P: n/a. E and 2E: Ken Townsend.

Overdubbing of a sporadic Paul McCartney backing vocal, and a piano played by Chris Thomas, onto the now re-titled 'Long Long Long'. These completed the song subject to remixing.

Another new number was recorded during this session, Paul McCartney inviting Ken Townsend to join him in studio one, where the technical engineer did a spot of balance engineering and tape operating while Paul quickly taped the basic track of his short and risqué 'Why Don't We Do It In The Road'. Excepting a drum track played by Ringo as an overdub on 10 October, this was to be yet another McCartney solo recording for *The Beatles*, taped on a four-track machine. Five takes of lead vocal and

acoustic guitar were recorded first, and a piano track was then overdubbed onto take five. The first four takes proved that Paul was still structuring the song in the studio – not that it was ever a particularly complicated matter. "I want to do one quiet verse, one loud verse, that's it really," was his instruction to Ken Townsend. Each take then began with Paul thumping the sounding board of his acoustic guitar before, as he predicted, going into a high-pitch vocal, switching to the rocking McCartney voice midway through the song. It was only at take five that Paul's vocal took on the more raucous tone throughout.

(Note. During this session, Paul withdrew from the tape library the original 18 July recordings of 'Helter Skelter' and made a copy of the longest take – the 27'11" version – for his own private collection.)

Thursday 10 October

Studio Two: 7.00pm-7.15am. Recording: 'Piggies' (SI onto take 12); 'Glass Onion' (SI onto take 33). Stereo mixing: 'Glass Onion' (remixes 1 and 2, from take 33); 'Rocky Raccoon' (remix 1, from take 10); 'Long Long Long' (remixes 1-4, from take 67). Mono mixing: 'Glass Onion' (remixes 10 and 11, from take 33). P: George Martin. E: Ken Scott. 2E: John Smith. Studio Three: time unknown. Recording: 'Why Don't We Do It In The Road' (SI onto take 5, tape reduction take 5 into take 6, SI onto take 6). P: n/a. E and 2E: Ken Townsend.

The double-album approaching completion, three songs were finished during this marathon session: George's 'Piggies', John's 'Glass Onion' and Paul's 'Why Don't We Do It In The Road'. The first two titles were completed by means of strings, played by the same eight musicians: Henry Datyner, Eric Bowie, Norman Lederman and Ronald Thomas (violins); Eldon Fox and Reginald Kilbey (cellos); John Underwood and Keith Cummings (violas).

While these activities were under way in studio two, Paul McCartney, again with Ken Townsend at the helm, went into studio three and added the finishing touches to his 1'40" rocker 'Why Don't We Do It In The Road'. More vocals, handclaps, a bass track and drums (Ringo's sole role) were added to take five and, since this was a four-track tape, this was then treated to a reduction mixdown, tracks one and four being mixed together to form track one of the new take six.

The one track vacated by the reduction was then filled with a McCartney electric guitar overdub.

(Note. The mono mixes of 'Glass Onion' were numbered 10 and 11 to make them distinct from the two previous editions, one and two from 26 September, done before the strings were overdubbed.)

Friday 11 October

Studio Two: 3.00-6.00pm. Recording: 'Savoy Truffle' (SI onto take 1). Studio Two (control room only): 6.00-12.00pm. Mono mixing: 'Piggies' (remixes 1-4, from take 12); 'Don't Pass Me By' (remix 1, from take 7 and edit of edit piece 4); 'Good Night' (remixes 1 and 2, from take 34). Stereo mixing: 'Piggies' (remixes 1-3, from take 12); 'Don't Pass Me By' (remix 1, from take 7 and edit of edit piece 4); 'Good Night' (remix 1, from take 34). P: George Martin. E: Ken Scott. 2E: John Smith.

'Savoy Truffle', recorded at Trident, still needed some finishing touches. One was a brass overdub, recorded in a three-hour afternoon session on this day. "George Martin suggested that I score 'Savoy Truffle' for saxophones," says Chris Thomas. "I must say that I found it a real chore." Six saxophonists were called in to perform the overdub, two baritone players (Ronald Ross and Bernard George) and four tenor players (Art Ellefson, Danny Moss, Harry Klein and Derek Collins).

Brian Gibson recalls, "The session men were playing really well – there's nothing like a good brass section letting rip – and it sounded fantastic. But having got

this really nice sound George turned to Ken Scott and said 'Right, I want to distort it'. So I had to plug-up two high-gain amplifiers which overloaded and deliberately introduced a lot of distortion, completely tearing the sound to pieces and making it dirty. The musicians came up to the control room to listen to a playback and George said to them 'Before you listen I've got to apologise for what I've done to your beautiful sound. Please forgive me – but it's the way I want it!' I don't think they particularly enjoyed hearing their magnificent sound screwed up quite so much but they realised that this was what George wanted, and that it was their job to provide it."

After the 'Savoy Truffle' overdub the remainder of the session was devoted to remixing. (These included some numerical errors, 'Don't Pass Me By' having already had a remix mono one, and 'Good Night' having already had mono remixes one and two.) Ringo was evidently in the control room for these new versions, for his own announcement "'Good Night', remix two" was preserved on one of the odds and ends tapes.

Saturday 12 October

Studio Two (control room only): 7.00pm-5.45am. Stereo mixing: 'Everybody's Got Something To Hide Except Me And My Monkey' (remix 1, from take 12); 'Helter Skelter' (remixes 1-5, from take 21); 'Mother Nature's Son' (remixes 1 and 2, from take 26); 'Ob-La-Di, Ob-La-Da' (remixes 1-4, from take 23). Mono mixing: 'Everybody's Got Something To Hide Except Me And My Monkey' (remix 1, from take 12); 'Mother Nature's Son' (remixes 1 and 2, from take 26); 'Ob-La-Di, Ob-La-Da' (remix 10, from take 23); 'Long Long Long' (remix 1, from take 67). P: George Martin. E: Ken Scott. 2E: John Smith.

"The Beatles would go to extremes with the 'White Album'," recalls Ken Scott. "Like when it came to mixing they would say 'Right, let's add full top [treble] and full bass to everything'. Some of the time it would sound good, sometimes it wouldn't. When it

did they would say 'OK, let's do it like that'. Most people just used top and bass where necessary, trying to keep the sound as natural as possible. The Beatles weren't necessarily after a natural sound."

(Note, for those keeping notes. The following songs were allotted incorrect mono remix numbers: 'Everybody's Got Something To Hide Except Me And My Monkey', 'Mother Nature's Son' and 'Ob-La-Di, Ob-La-Da'.)

Sunday 13 October

Studio Two: 7.00pm – 6.00am. Recording: 'Julia' (takes 1-3). Stereo mixing: 'Julia' (remix 1, from take 3); 'Dear Prudence' (remix 1, from take 1); 'Wild Honey Pie' (remixes 1 and 2, from take 1); 'Back In The USSR' (remix 1, from take 6); 'Blackbird' (remix 1, from take 32). Mono mixing: 'Julia' (remix 1, from take 3); 'Dear Prudence' (remixes 1-5 from take 1); 'Blackbird' (remix 10, from take 32). P: George Martin. E: Ken Scott. 2E: John Smith.

The 32nd and final song intended for *The Beatles* was a gentle and touching new John Lennon composition, 'Julia', named after his late mother but also including a reference to Yoko in its lyric. 'Julia' was a solo Lennon recording – the only such occurrence during the Beatles' career – and it was recorded simply, on a four-track machine: acoustic guitar and vocal taped twice over, the two vocal recordings allowing for an effective word overlap on the word "Julia" itself. The

song was finished in very little time, and it was immediately mixed for both mono and stereo.

(Note. The mono remix numbering of 'Dear Prudence' was incorrect, remix one having already been made.)

Monday 14 October

Studio Two: 7.00pm-7.30am. Stereo mixing: 'I Will' (remix 1, from take 68); **'Birthday'** (remix 1, from take 22). **Recording: 'Savoy Truffle'** (SI onto take 1). **Mono mixing: 'Savoy Truffle'** (remixes 1-6, from take 1); **'While My Guitar Gently Weeps'** (remixes 10 and 11, from take 25); **'Long Long Long'** (remixes 2 and 3, from take 67). **Stereo mixing: 'Savoy Truffle'** (remixes 1 and 2, from take 1); **'While My Guitar Gently Weeps'** (remixes 10-12, from take 25); **'Yer Blues'** (remixes 1-5, from takes 16 and 17 and edit piece take 1); **'Sexy Sadie'** (remixes 1-3, from take 117); **'What's The New Mary Jane'** (remixes 1 and 2, from take 4). **P: George Martin. E: Ken Scott. 2E: John Smith.**

And then there were three. On the morning of 14 October Ringo flew out with his family to Sardinia for a two-week holiday, leaving the final remixing and judgement on the double-album's running order to the remaining three Beatles and the production team.

The final recording for *The Beatles* took place during this session, with overdubs for 'Savoy Truffle': a second electric guitar, an organ, tambourine and bongos. These recorded, the song joined the remixing queue, with several songs still requiring stereo mixes. Stereo, though soon to replace mono, was still of secondary importance in 1968.

Perhaps the most interesting set of remixes was for 'While My Guitar Gently Weeps'. "I was given the grand job of waggling the oscillator on the 'Gently Weeps' mixes," says Chris Thomas. "Apparently Eric Clapton insisted to George [Harrison] that he didn't want the guitar solo so typically Clapton. He said the sound wasn't enough of 'a Beatles sound'. So we did this flanging thing, really wobbling the oscillator in the mix. I did that for hours. What a boring job!"

Tuesday 15 October

Studio Two: 6.00-8.00pm. Stereo mixing: 'Happiness Is A Warm Gun' (remixes 1-4, from take 65); **'I'm So Tired'** (remixes 1-5, from take 14); **'Cry Baby Cry'** (remixes 1-3, from take 12). **Mono mixing: 'I'm So Tired'** (remixes 1-3, from take 14); **'Cry Baby Cry'** (remix 1, from take 12). **P: George Martin. E: Ken Scott. 2E: John Smith.**

More mono and stereo remixing.

Wednesday/Thursday 16/17 October

Abbey Road, Rooms 41 and 42 and Studios One, Two and Three: 5.00pm (Wednesday)–5.00pm (Thursday). Mono mixing: Crossfades and edits for LP; 'Why Don't We Do It In The Road' (remix 1, from take 6). **Stereo mixing: Crossfades and edits for LP; 'Why Don't We Do It In The Road'** (remix 1, from take 6). **P: George Martin. E: Ken Scott. 2E: John Smith. Studio Two (control room only): time unknown. Tape copying: 'It's All Too Much'** (of take 2, called take 196). **Mono mixing: 'It's All Too Much'** (remix 1, from take 196). **Stereo mixing: 'It's All Too Much'** (remix 1, from take 196). **P: n/a. E: Ken Scott. 2E: Dave Harries.**

"I remember arriving at the studios on Thursday 17 October 1968, 9.00am, to find the Beatles still there," says Alan Brown. "They had been there all night, finalising the master tapes for what we now call the 'White Album' and banding it up [putting the songs in order and editing the master]. They were all over the place, room 41, the front listening room – anywhere – almost every room they could get. It was a frantic last minute job."

This was the Beatles' first and only 24-hour-session, and in addition to being frantic, it took place without George Harrison, who flew out to Los Angeles during the daytime hours of 16 October, leaving John, Paul and George Martin, with Ken Scott and John Smith, the problematic task of working out the LP running order from the 31 songs available. (As 'Not Guilty' was not remixed for stereo one can assume that it wasn't a final contender for a place on the double-album.)

Even working to the tried and trusted George Martin formula of opening each side of vinyl with a strong song, and ending it with one difficult to follow, the 31 songs were just too varied and wide-ranging in styles to slip easily into categories. In the end, after dropping 'What's The New Mary Jane' altogether, there was an *approximated* structure, the heavier rock songs ('Birthday', 'Yer Blues', 'Everybody's Got Something To Hide Except Me And My Monkey', 'Helter Skelter') mostly ended up on side C, George Harrison's four songs were spread out one per side, no composer had more than two songs in succession and

each side lasted between 20 and 25 minutes. And, as a joke, most of the songs with an animal in the title ('Blackbird', 'Piggies', 'Rocky Raccoon') were placed together, in succession, on side B.

Another decision was to link each successive song, either with a crossfade, a straight edit or simply by matching the dying moment of one with the opening note of the next. *The Beatles*, like *Sgt Pepper's Lonely Hearts Club Band*, had none of the customary three-second gaps between songs. 'Back In The USSR' faded straight into 'Dear Prudence'. 'The Continuing Story Of Bungalow Bill' cut straight into 'While My Guitar Gently Weeps'. A part of Paul's uncopyrighted and untitled ad-lib along the lines of "Can you take me back where I came from" was plucked from one of the three odds and ends tapes and used to usher in 'Revolution 9' along with a bizarre piece of studio control room chatter, from the same source, which had Alistair Taylor, office manager at the Beatles' Apple Corps, apologising to George Martin – and beseeching forgiveness – for not bringing him a bottle of claret. (The recording date of this little item was never documented.)

At some point during the 24-hour-session the 1967 recording 'It's All Too Much' was dusted off the shelf, copied and remixed for mono and stereo for release on the impending soundtrack album of songs from the *Yellow Submarine* film. (The mono mix was numbered one, although there had been a remix mono one on 12 October 1967.) For reasons known only to themselves, Ken Scott and Dave Harries falsely numbered the copy of the original take two *take 196 –* the highest Beatles take count ever!

Finally, it is worth noting that after recording 32 songs in five months, the supply of new material was not exhausted. In its November 1968 issue, *The Beatles Book* magazine reported that two new songs, 'Polythene Pam' and 'Maxwell's Silver Hammer' had been written just too late for *The Beatles*. Both would be recorded in 1969 – along with two more album's worth of material!

Friday 18 October

Studio One (control room only): 12.00 noon-1.00pm. Tape copying: 'Yer Blues' (of edit of remix mono 3 and edit piece take 1); 'Don't Pass Me By' (of remix mono 1). P: n/a. E: n/a.   2E: John Smith.

Ironing out master tape imperfections: copies of two existing mono mixes. The four sides of *The Beatles*, mono version, were cut for disc by Harry Moss at Abbey Road on 18 and 19 October. The stereo discs were cut on 21 October.

Tuesday 29 October

Studio Three (control room only): 10.00am-1.00pm. Stereo mixing: 'Hey Bulldog' (remixes 1-3, from take 10); 'All Together Now' (remix 1, from take 9); 'All You Need Is Love' (remixes 1-6, from take 58); 'Only A Northern Song' (remix 1, from remix mono 6).   P: n/a.   E: Geoff Emerick.   2E: Graham Kirkby.

The remaining stereo remixes for the *Yellow Submarine* soundtrack album. 'Only A Northern Song' was a "mock stereo" mix, worked from the master mono remix rather than the original four-track tape, presumably because the mono mixes had been problematical in themselves, being derived from two tapes played in sync. To date [1987] there is no true stereo mix available for 'Only A Northern Song'.

Friday 22 November

LP release: *The Beatles*. Apple [Parlophone] PMC 7067-7068 (mono)/PCS 7067-7068 (stereo). A: 'Back In The USSR'; 'Dear Prudence'; 'Glass Onion'; 'Ob-La-Di, Ob-La Da'; 'Wild Honey Pie'; 'The Continuing Story Of Bungalow Bill'; 'While My Guitar Gently Weeps'; 'Happiness Is A Warm Gun'. B: 'Martha My Dear'; 'I'm So Tired'; 'Blackbird'; 'Piggies'; 'Rocky Raccoon'; 'Don't Pass Me By'; 'Why Don't We Do It In The Road'; 'I Will'; 'Julia'. C: 'Birthday'; 'Yer Blues'; 'Mother Nature's Son'; 'Everybody's Got Something To Hide Except Me And My Monkey'; 'Sexy Sadie'; 'Helter Skelter'; 'Long Long Long'. D: 'Revolution 1'; 'Honey Pie'; 'Savoy Truffle'; 'Cry Baby Cry'; 'Revolution 9'; 'Good Night'.

A massive out-pouring of Beatles recordings: 30 in one double set. This was what the Beatles wanted – and they were in charge. But George Martin probably wished that he still held the upper hand. "With the 'White Album' they'd come back from India with 32 songs and they wanted to record every one of them. I listened to them all and there were some which I didn't think were that great. But a split had already taken place and they were wanting to do their own things, so the whole of the album, because there was so much to do, became fragmented, with two – sometimes three – studios in use at any one time. I almost became Executive Producer, running from one studio to another and handling one particular thing while the Beatles and Chris Thomas got on with other things.

"I really didn't think that a lot of the songs were worthy of release, and I told them so. I said 'I don't want a double-album. I think you ought to cut out some of these, concentrate on the really good ones and have yourself a really super album. Let's whittle them down to 14 or 16 titles and concentrate on those.'"

The Beatles, obviously, chose to ignore this advice. One frequently aired explanation for the great quantity of the songs on *The Beatles* and for the way that they were recorded, several being entirely solo efforts, is best summed up in George Harrison's own words "[by 1968] the rot had already set in". Another is that with John and Paul as prodigious as ever, and with George – and even Ringo – writing more than ever, there was certainly much material to be pooled, yet none of the four seemed prepared to sacrifice his own interests. George Martin even thinks that in releasing 30 songs in one batch, the Beatles may have been attempting to partly fulfil, in as quick a manner as possible, a pre-set song quota in the group's nine-year recording contract, signed with EMI in January 1967.

But whether *The Beatles* is viewed as the Beatles' ninth album of new material, or as merely a collection of solo material, it must be the music by which the set is finally judged. And in that department it was a winner, a very enjoyable product and an *enormous* seller all around the world. The annual collection of facts and feats, *The Guinness Book Of Records*, still quotes *The Beatles* as having sold "nearly two million" copies in its first week of US release.

After the amazing sleeve for *Sgt Pepper's Lonely Hearts Club Band*, it seemed in 1968 that some people were awaiting the cover of *The Beatles* as anxiously as the records inside. It did not disappoint, being a stark white sleeve, conceived by influential "fine artist" Richard Hamilton, as the perfect minimalist antidote to the scores of increasingly garish *Sgt Pepper* imitations flooding the market by late 1968. The only markings on the sleeve of *The Beatles* were the embossed title and an individual serial number. But inside the record wallets were the free goodies: a poster with a fascinating Richard Hamilton collage of personal Beatles photographs and ephemera, and four individual colour shots of the Beatles taken in late 1968 by John Kelly. (It is interesting to note that this was not always the concept. In June, shortly after beginning sessions for the double-album, the Beatles commissioned various designers and printers to come up with sleeve ideas, one being a transparent cover which would reveal a colour photograph as the record was pulled out of the wallet. And *The Beatles* was not always going to be the title. At one point the double-album was going to be *A Doll's House*, after Henrik Ibsen's 19th century masterpiece.)

John, Paul, George and Ringo in the autumn of 1968: the four giveaway photographs enclosed within *The Beatles*.

Friday 17 January

LP release: *Yellow Submarine*. Apple [Parlophone] PMC 7070 (mono)/PCS 7070 (stereo). A: 'Yellow Submarine'; 'Only A Northern Song'; 'All Together Now'; 'Hey Bulldog'; 'It's All Too Much'; 'All You Need Is Love'. B: 'Pepperland'; 'Sea Of Time'/'Sea Of Holes'; 'Sea Of Monsters'; 'March Of The Meanies'; 'Pepperland Laid Waste'; 'Yellow Submarine In Pepperland'.

A new album by the Beatles? Not quite. Half by the Beatles, half "original film score, composed and orchestrated by George Martin, produced by George Martin". Side A was the Beatles, side B the score.

Perhaps the most puzzling aspect of the LP was the time it had taken to see the light of day. *Yellow Submarine*, albeit a highly successful film in both critical and box-office terms, had been on release for all of seven months before this (supposedly) accompanying soundtrack album was issued. The songs themselves were even older.

One reason for the delay was the November 1968 release of *The Beatles*, which the group felt was of greater import and must take precedence. Another was that George Martin wanted to re-record his side of the album. (He had originally taped the film score at Olympic Sound Studios, with Keith Grant and George

Chkiantz assisting.) On 22 and 23 October 1968, personally conducting the 41-piece George Martin Orchestra and sharing production duties with John Burgess and Ron Richards, he re-taped everything in two three-hour sessions in studio one, Abbey Road. The engineer was Geoff Emerick, tape operator Nick Webb. Stereo remixing and editing was done on 24 and 25 October, Martin producing, Emerick and Mike Sheady assisting. The stereo album was cut at Abbey Road by Harry Moss on 22 November, the mono (simply a monaural cut of the stereo) was done on 25 November.

The Beatles were mildly criticised at the time of this LP release for giving less than their usually excellent value-for-money. Lovely though George Martin's score was, fans of the group were having to buy a full-price album for just four "new" songs by the group (even the most recent was 11 months old), two

of the six titles – 'Yellow Submarine' itself and 'All You Need Is Love' – having long been released. The group evidently took the criticism to heart, for there remains in the EMI library a master tape for a seven-inch mono EP, to run at LP speed, 33⅓ rpm, compiled and banded on 13 March 1969 by Abbey Road employee Edward Gadsby-Toni, with the following line-up: Side A: 'Only A Northern Song'; 'Hey Bulldog'; 'Across The Universe'. Side B: 'All Together Now'; 'It's All Too Much'. (Note the bonus inclusion of 'Across The Universe', long finished and mixed but, as of March 1969, still awaiting issue on the World Wildlife Fund charity album.)

The EP was never issued. Perhaps the Beatles, never too enamoured with any part of the *Yellow Submarine* project, felt that they were better off washing their hands of the whole affair.

Wednesday 22 January

Apple Studios, 3 Savile Row, London W1: time unknown. Recording: 'Going Up The Country'; 'All I Want Is You' (working title of 'Dig A Pony'); 'I've Got A Feeling'; 'Don't Let Me Down'; 'Rocker'; 'Save The Last Dance For Me'; 'Don't Let Me Down'; 'All I Want Is You' (working title of 'Dig A Pony'); 'I've Got A Feeling'; 'Bathroom Window' (working title of 'She Came In Through The Bathroom Window'). P: George Martin? E: Glyn Johns. 2E: n/a.

The start of the infamous *Get Back* – or *Let It Be* – sessions, and of the most confusing and frustrating period in the Beatles' entire career. So much about the *Get Back* project needs lengthy clarification...

Recording sessions for *The Beatles* had proved to the group, in no small way, that they had entered a tense and difficult period. Paul McCartney, with Brian Epstein dead, now the driving force for unity and action within the group, could think of only one solution: to have the group "get back" to what had united them best: four musicians in live performance, be they on film or on stage with an audience. But definitely live. None of the other three was very enthusiastic. John suggested that the Beatles simply call it a day and break up. George Harrison, vehemently against going back on the road as the Beatles, refused, but agreed to the making of a film. Ringo's view was not known.

So on 2 January 1969 the Beatles met at Twickenham Film Studios to begin rehearsing new songs for a live television show, transmission worldwide. And they arranged for the rehearsals to be filmed too, for transmission at some unforeseen time.

But the disharmony could not be suppressed. On 10 January, complaining of being pestered and criticised by Paul, and disenchanted with the television show idea, George Harrison walked out and quit the group, just as Ringo had done five months earlier at Abbey

Road. He returned after a few days but he had made his point. Plans for the television show went the same way as plans for concerts – even unannounced and impromptu ones – in the bin.

So what could the Beatles do now? The answer was to continue with the sessions for the benefit of the film cameras, which would capture the group recording an album instead of rehearsing for television. The last rehearsal session at Twickenham was on Thursday 16 January. The following Monday, 20 January, the Beatles and the cameras moved into Central London, to the Beatles' new recording studio in the basement of their Apple headquarters at 3 Savile Row, near Piccadilly Circus.

The *Get Back* recording sessions, to use the Beatles' own words in a later advertisement for the 'Get Back' single, saw the group "as nature intended . . . as live as can be in this electronic age . . . [with] no electronic 'watchamacallit'". In other words, having pioneered perfectionist multi-track rock recordings, the Beatles were returning to basics, "warts and all", "the Beatles with their socks off", forsaking technical trickery, ADT, tape loops, overdubbing and all. The Beatles wanted every song on this new album to be strictly live – even with live mistakes.

Although filming switched to Apple on 20 January the first session was not held until the 22nd. The delay lay in the fact that Apple Corps had an offshoot company

called Apple Electronics, run by a Greek closely befriended by the Beatles, Alexis Mardas. Alexis was so clever in his field that he was dubbed 'Magic Alex' by the group and, installed in their Savile Row office in July 1968, they asked him to install a basement recording studio. Mardas promised miracles. Abbey Road had eight-track facilities. Apple would have 72. And away with those awkward studio "baffles" around Ringo and his drum kit! (Placed there to prevent leakage of the drum sound onto the other studio microphones.) Magic Alex would install an invisible sonic beam, like a force field, which would do the work unobtrusively.

Hardly surprisingly, it all worked out very differently – and the Beatles lost two day's work.

"The mixing console was made of bits of wood and an old oscilloscope," recalls Dave Harries. "It looked like the control panel of a B-52 bomber. They actually tried a session on this desk, they did a take, but when they played back the tape it was all hum and hiss. Terrible. The Beatles walked out, that was the end of it." Keith Slaughter, Harries' colleague, remembers, "George Martin made a frantic call back to Abbey Road. 'For God's sake get some decent equipment down here!'"

Alan Parsons, later a top engineer and producer and, later still, the man behind the highly successful Alan Parsons Project, was in January 1969 a teenage tape operator newly employed at Abbey Road, and he went down to Apple along with the borrowed equipment. He too clearly remembers Mardas's invention. "The metal was an eighth of an inch out around the knobs and switches. It had obviously been done with a hammer and chisel instead of being properly designed and machined. It did pass signals but Glyn Johns [more of whom later] said 'I can't do anything with this. I can't make a record with this board'." Abbey Road duly lent Apple two four-track consoles to go with its own 3M eight-track tape machine.

And what happened to Magic Alex's rejected masterpiece? "The mixing console was sold as scrap to a secondhand electronics shop in the Edgware Road for £5," says Geoff Emerick. "It wasn't worth any more."

Glyn Johns had been approached by Paul McCartney in December 1968 to be the balance engineer – bordering on "Producer" – for the *Get Back* sessions. Johns was the first ever freelance balance engineer in Britain and by 1963, aged just 21, he was working with acts like the Rolling Stones and Georgie Fame. By 1969 he had also worked with the Who, the Kinks, the Small Faces, Traffic, Chris Farlowe and the Steve Miller Band, to name but a few. (Actually, Glyn had worked with the Beatles too – on 19 April 1964, when the group had a one-off session at IBC Studios, 35 Portland Place, London, pre-recording the soundtrack for a television show called *Around The Beatles*. Johns was second engineer on that occasion.)

Johns began work right from the start of *Get Back*: on 2 January at Twickenham Film Studios, overseeing any sound problems and ensuring that the film's soundtrack recording went smoothly. Johns was in the film-makers union, unlike Geoff Emerick who was unable to attend for this very reason, and unlike Dave Harries and Keith Slaughter, who both went to Twickenham and were caught out, nearly causing an industrial stoppage when they touched a cable which was the sole responsibility of one of the film crew.

None of the Twickenham sessions was properly taped, that is, they were not recorded in the customary recording studio manner. These were strictly rehearsals, not proper sessions, and only one very brief spoken ad-lib was issued on disc from the two weeks at Twickenham. It is the film's magnetic-track recordings of the 90-plus hours of unused footage which has served as the source of the countless illegal ("bootleg") albums of so-called "*Get Back* outtakes".

George Martin's precise involvement in *Get Back* was unclear. He was there for some sessions but not for others. Unfortunately, the documentation is sketchy, but his voice is evident on only some of the tapes; for the others – with the Beatles addressing their chat, enquiries, requests and musical instructions directly to Johns – one must assume that Martin was absent.

Similarly, for the remixing, a question mark remains over George's precise role, although Glyn Johns was in attendance at *every* session. Indeed, the Beatles' work stopped in February when Johns had to fly to the USA to produce pre-booked sessions with the Steve Miller Band. Matters had become so confusing by April that the 'Get Back' single was issued without any producer's credit. (Note. Where George Martin's voice is absent on the *Get Back* session tapes, and where his name is not detailed on the tape boxes, entries will show a producer's credit of "George Martin?")

Glyn Johns – nicknamed Glynis by John Lennon – was not the only new face on these sessions. A fine American organist named Billy Preston happened to be in the Apple reception area on 22 January, and he was literally grabbed by George Harrison and cajoled into joining the Beatles sessions to alleviate the tense atmosphere and – since overdubbing was out – add a vital fifth instrument to the live sound. The Beatles had known Preston since 1962, when he was a teenage member of Little Richard's backing group, sharing a two-week bill with the Beatles at the Star-Club, Hamburg. Preston sat-in on almost all of the *Get Back* sessions, even though he returned to the USA in early February for a brief concert tour of Texas. By this time Preston was an Apple recording artiste, having signed a contract with the company on 31 January. His first album, the recording of which began on 5 May at Olympic Sound Studios, was largely produced by George Harrison and wholly mixed by Glyn Johns.

When studying details of the songs taped during the *Get Back* recordings, it is vital to consider the fact that these sessions – later described by George Harrison as "the low of all-time" and as "hell . . . the most miserable sessions on earth" by John Lennon – were, by their very nature, largely unplanned and impromptu. The Beatles would drift in and out of songs and jam almost incessantly, leaving little in the way of finished items in their wake. They would chat, tell jokes and have arguments while the tapes were running. It was then, and remains so today, quite impossible to catalogue the recorded "takes". In some instances, take numbers announced for the film crew were also used on the Apple tape boxes, thus the first take of a song might be announced as "take 32". Some sessions were difficult to catalogue at all, even briefly, and many tape boxes were left blank – until Paul McCartney found time to plough through them, writing short notes on the box labels.

This book will list the *Get Back* songs in the order of recording, hence the same title may occur two or three times in a single session, indicating that the Beatles left and then returned to a song later. Most importantly, any songs or ad-libs which found their way onto either the aborted *Get Back* or the released *Let It Be* LPs will be detailed for the day of recording.

From this day's work, for example, Glyn Johns selected several items for the ill-fated *Get Back* LP: 'Don't Let Me Down', with John Lennon – composer and lead singer – exhorting Ringo to give him a good crash on the cymbals to "give me the courage to come screaming in"; a Lennon spoken message "We'll do 'Dig A Pony' straight into 'I've Got A Fever'" [meaning 'I've Got A Feeling'] a quick instrumental, titled 'Rocker' by Paul McCartney on the tape box; a jam of the Drifters' 1960 hit 'Save The Last Dance For Me'; and more sundry chat. Left unused was a very brief Paul McCartney run-through of Canned Heat's 'Going Up The Country' which served only to illustrate something he was saying about that group.

Billy Preston was first evident on the second of two tapes recorded this day, making his debut on electric piano when the Beatles were working out the chord structure for Paul McCartney's 'Bathroom Window', later recorded for the *Abbey Road* LP as 'She Came In Through The Bathroom Window'.

Glum faces and bad times: George, Ringo, Yoko, John and Paul listen to a playback of a clearly uninspiring *Get Back* session tape in the basement studio at Savile Row, January 1969.

Thursday 23 January

Apple Studios, 3 Savile Row, London W1: time unknown. Recording: 'Get Back'; 'Blues'; 'Get Back'. P: George Martin.   E: Glyn Johns.   2E: Alan Parsons.

'Get Back', the title song for the current crop of recordings, was a new Paul McCartney number originally conceived with a political bias and controversial lyrics like "don't dig no Pakistanis taking all the people's jobs, get back to where you once belonged". This is how the group rehearsed the song at Twickenham, but by the time sessions reached Apple the lyric had changed and the title . . . well, Paul had his own ideas in that direction. George Martin, over the talkback: "What are you calling this, Paul?" Paul: "'Shit'. 'Shit', take one."

Approximately ten takes of 'Get Back' were recorded on this day, the tenth being marked 'best', although it was never released. Also taped was another untitled jam, most suitably named 'Blues' on the tape box. This was a one-minute instrumental blast, led by Billy Preston on electric piano.

Alan Parsons made his debut as Beatles tape operator on this day, the control room on 22 January having been occupied by Glyn Johns alone, as engineer and tape operator.

Although insufficient documentation is available to detail the precise start/finish times of the Savile Row sessions, it is known that the Beatles had not only returned to pre-1965 recording methods with *Get Back* but to pre-1965 time routines too, possibly because of the film crew's requirements. Most sessions began late-morning, between 10.00 and 11.00am, and ended in the late afternoon, around 5.00pm. One or two ran through until 10.00pm.

Friday 24 January

Apple Studios, 3 Savile Row, London W1: time unknown. Recording: 'On Our Way Home' (working title of 'Two Of Us'); 'Teddy Boy'; 'Maggie Mae'; 'On Our Way Home' (working title of 'Two Of Us'); 'Dig It' (version one); 'Dig A Pony'; 'I've Got A Feeling'. P: George Martin?   E: Glyn Johns.   2E: Neil Richmond.

'On Our Way Home', later re-titled 'Two Of Us', was a new Paul McCartney song, which – in addition to being recorded by the Beatles – Paul later "gave" to a trio of New Yorkers collectively called Mortimer for their debut Apple single release at the end of June, although their version failed to materialise and Mortimer never did have any product released by Apple. One of the Beatles' takes of the song from this day was included on the unissued *Get Back* LP, with a little chat from Paul concluding, "And so we leave the little town of London, England".

Between takes of 'On Our Way Home', the Beatles burst into a 38-second, hammed-up version of 'Maggie Mae', the traditional Liverpool song about an infamous local lady of the night. This was included, in its entirety, on both the *Get Back* and *Let It Be* albums, with the composer credit reading "Trad. arr. Lennon/McCartney/Harrison/Starkey".

'Teddy Boy' was a new McCartney song presented to the Beatles for the first time on this day. The group recorded three versions – two breakdowns and a complete 5'42" take in which Paul showed the others how to play the song, adding, at the end, "[there's] that one for further consideration". Glyn Johns included an extract of this on the *Get Back* album, even though it included bad guitar feedback and John Lennon, clearly growing bored, breaking off into a country hoe-down dance "take your partners, dosi-do...". The Beatles' 'Teddy Boy' remains unreleased, but Paul re-recorded the song for his first solo album, *McCartney*, released on 17 April 1970.

The Beatles recorded two versions of an impromptu John Lennon number called 'Dig It'. The first, on this day, was never issued, and it featured a simple lyric (variations on "Can you dig it, yeah?") and heavy electric instrumentation, including a slide guitar. But

John's childlike spoken message at the end of the song – "That was 'Can You Dig It' by Georgie Wood, now we'd like to do 'Hark The Angels Come'" – *was* released, tacked onto the end of the other version of 'Dig It' on both the *Get Back* and *Let It Be* albums.

The day's recordings of both 'Dig A Pony' and 'I've Got A Feeling' were included on the *Get Back* LP, with a little chat before, in-between and after.

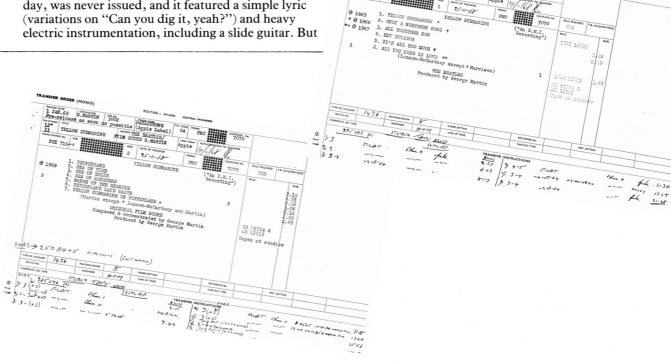

Saturday 25 January

Apple Studios, 3 Savile Row, London W1: time unknown. Recording: 'Untitled Jamming'; 'On Our Way Home' (working title of 'Two Of Us'); 'Bye Bye Love'; 'George's Blues (Because You're Sweet And Lovely)' (working title of 'For You Blue'); 'Let It Be'. P: George Martin?   E: Glyn Johns.   2E: Alan Parsons.

'Untitled Jamming' was just that: a very brief and entirely instrumental piece. 'Bye Bye Love' was a quick, jammed recording of the 1957 Everly Brothers classic, John and Paul sharing the lead vocals during a break from the taping of 'Two Of Us'. George Harrison recorded a version of this song for his 1974 solo album *Dark Horse*.

Two new recordings were begun on this day. 'George's Blues', which was eventually re-titled 'For You Blue', and Paul's 'Let It Be'. But whereas the latter would be subjected to later improvements, 'For You Blue' was completed on this first day. The sixth take was included on the *Get Back* album, and – with further editing and remixing – on *Let It Be*.

Sunday 26 January

Apple Studios, 3 Savile Row, London W1: time unknown. Recording: 'Dig It' (version two); 'Shake Rattle And Roll'; 'Kansas City'; 'Miss Ann'; 'Lawdy Miss Clawdy'; 'Blue Suede Shoes'; 'You Really Got A Hold On Me'; 'Tracks Of My Tears'; 'Let It Be'; 'George's Demo' (working title of 'Isn't It A Pity'); 'Let It Be'; 'The Long And Winding Road'. P: George Martin.   E: Glyn Johns.   2E: Neil Richmond.

This second version of 'Dig It' was the one which, substantially abbreviated, appeared on the *Get Back* and *Let It Be* albums. This recording was 12′25″ in duration, the *Get Back* version faded-in 8′27″ into the song, the *Let It Be* version used only the part from 8′52″ to 9′41″. Although the *Let It Be* album had the composer credit as Lennon/McCartney/Starkey/Harrison, 'Dig It' was essentially a Lennon song, and one in which anything went: early lyrics borrowed from 'Twist And Shout', later lyrics gave mention to the FBI, CIA, BBC, B.B. King (the singer), Doris Day (the actress) and Matt Busby (then manager of Manchester United soccer club). Heather Eastman, six-years-old and six weeks away from becoming Paul's step-daughter, contributed amusing backing vocals during the early part of the song and George Martin shook a percussive shaker.

A long rock and roll medley followed, beginning with 'Shake Rattle And Roll' (the original 1954 Joe Turner version), 'Kansas City' (the 1959 Wilbur Harrison version, very different from the Little Richard copy which the Beatles had covered on *Beatles For Sale* in 1964), 'Miss Ann' (Little Richard 1956, released 1957), 'Lawdy Miss Clawdy' (Lloyd Price, 1952), 'Blue Suede Shoes' (the original Carl Perkins version, 1956) and 'You Really Got A Hold On Me' (the Miracles – with Smokey Robinson – from 1962, as covered on *With The Beatles*). George Harrison was presently re-discovering his affection for Robinson and the Miracles, buying up as many of their albums as he could find. After the medley had ended, George led the Beatles into a mostly instrumental version of 'Tracks Of My Tears' (1965, but not a hit until 1969). (In the 1970s George recorded two tribute songs to Robinson: 'Ooh Baby (You Know That I Love You)'

and 'Pure Smokey', the latter also being the title of one of Robinson's own LPs.)

Two other songs were taped on this day, Paul McCartney's ballad 'The Long And Winding Road', which would be returned to, and a George Harrison demo, untitled, recorded solo with vocal and lightly strummed lead guitar, which would not. When titled this song became 'Isn't It A Pity' but it was never recorded by the Beatles as a group, and it didn't surface publicly until 30 November 1970, when it was one of the outstanding songs on George's triple-album *All Things Must Pass*. (The recording of this particular song – which ended up 7′07″ in duration – began at Abbey Road on 2 June 1970.) On this day the song was just 3′03″ long, with George delightfully la-la-ing where a massive orchestral track, scored by John Barham, would be overdubbed in the 1970 version.

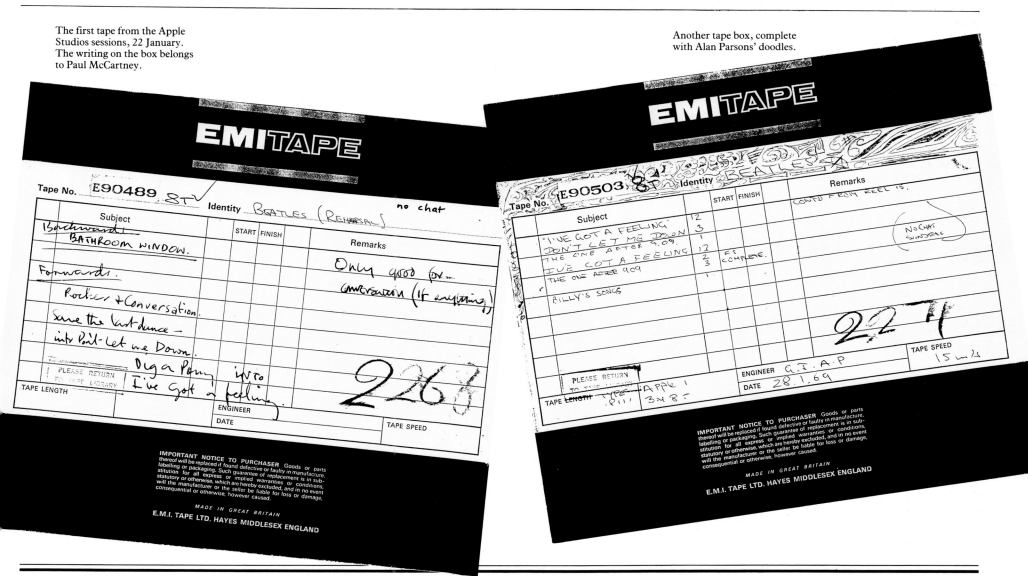

The first tape from the Apple Studios sessions, 22 January. The writing on the box belongs to Paul McCartney.

Another tape box, complete with Alan Parsons' doodles.

Monday 27 January

Apple Studios, 3 Savile Row, London W1: time unknown. Recording: 'Untitled Jamming'; 'Get Back'; 'Oh! Darling'; 'Get Back'; 'I've Got A Feeling'; 'The Walk'; 'I've Got A Feeling'. P: George Martin.   E: Glyn Johns.   2E: Alan Parsons.

'Untitled Jamming' was precisely that: 10'54" in duration, heavy, unstructured . . . and barely listenable to.

The Beatles had at least 14 different attempts at perfecting 'Get Back' during this session. After what was loosely called take nine (though it was more like the 18th) John and Paul could be heard to agree on its definite progress: "nearly" (meaning "nearly there"). When, after a short diversion, the Beatles returned to the song they did indeed record a releasable recording:

the one which closes the *Let It Be* album. (This differed from the version – not yet recorded – chosen for the single.) The recording was preceded by a little jokey chat, also included on *Let It Be*: a few sentences beginning with John's inimitable parody line "Sweet Loretta Fart she thought she was a cleaner but she was a frying pan". The 'Get Back' recordings then continued with at least six more takes.

Among the other songs taped on this day was a rehearsal run-through of a new McCartney rocker,

'Oh! Darling', later to appear on the *Abbey Road* LP, and a jammed cover version of 'The Walk', a major US hit for Jimmy McCracklin in March 1958.

The *audio vérité* nature of the *Get Back* tapings was never better illustrated than during this session. Immediately after the recording of 'Oh! Darling' John Lennon gave vent to a whoop of delight, exclaiming "I've just heard that Yoko's divorce has just gone through. Free at last!" And with that, he burst into song, "I'm free at last . . ."

Tuesday 28 January

Apple Studios, 3 Savile Row, London W1: time unknown. Recording: 'Dig A Pony'; 'Get Back'; 'Love Me Do'; 'Get Back'; 'Don't Let Me Down'; 'I've Got A Feeling'; 'Don't Let Me Down'; 'The One After 909'; 'I've Got A Feeling'; 'The One After 909'; 'Billy's Song (1)'; 'Billy's Song (2)'; 'Teddy Boy'. P: George Martin.   E: Glyn Johns.   2E: Alan Parsons.

An interesting and productive day. Productive because both sides of the Beatles' next single – 'Get Back' and 'Don't Let Me Down' – were recorded. Interesting because the Beatles resurrected two of their earliest songs, 'Love Me Do' and 'The One After 909'.

'Dig A Pony' was the subject of the pre-lunchtime session, with several takes recorded, and with much in the way of discussion between each about how best to play the song.

A 1969 Beatles re-recording of 'Love Me Do' – the song which started it all – sounds tempting. Unfortunately, the sound itself was quite the reverse. As with most *Get Back* recordings, it was more of an impromptu jam – slow and somewhat bluesy – than a serious attempt at a re-make. Paul handled the vocal, with John supporting, and although complete, at

2'20", and although the *Get Back* project was supposed to be capturing the Beatles' rough edges, this recording was just too rough to be considered for release.

The next two recordings, done successively, were released however, the Beatles and Billy Preston suddenly becoming a cohesive unit for the taping of 'Get Back' and 'Don't Let Me Down'. Both were excellent recordings, worthy of the single release. 'Get Back' was faded-out for disc as it continued for some considerable time, ending with forced "ho-ho-hos" from Paul McCartney. (This end section was included as the final item on the unreleased *Get Back* LP, faded up and out for 37", and it was also used over the end titles of the *Let It Be* film.)

Several jammed versions of 'The One After 909', first recorded – and left unissued – on 5 March 1963, were

taped during this session, though again none was released. And two untitled Billy Preston demos were taped, Preston making good use of the four musicians around him. As far as can be ascertained, neither song, both of which were 'southern' style blues, was ever issued in finished form. Finally, Paul McCartney led the Beatles through another rehearsal take of 'Teddy Boy'.

At the end of the session the tape caught a good deal of conversation between the four Beatles about whether they should be rehearsing or recording. Or maybe they shouldn't be bothering at all? And filming. When would it end, and what songs would they do? All four contributed opinions and ideas, although it was patently obvious by the questions, answers and attitudes that the project was not going at all well.

Wednesday 29 January

Apple Studios, 3 Savile Row, London W1: time unknown. Recording: 'I Want You' (later known as 'I Want You (She's So Heavy)'); 'The One After 909'; 'Not Fade Away'; 'Mailman Bring Me No More Blues'; 'Teddy Boy'; 'Besame Mucho'. P: George Martin.   E: Glyn Johns.   2E: Alan Parsons.

Another song first aired in the *Get Back* sessions and destined for later re-recording (in this instance, not too much later) was 'I Want You', released on *Abbey Road* as 'I Want You (She's So Heavy)'.

Among the oldies jammed by the Beatles on this day were two Buddy Holly numbers, 'Not Fade Away' (a major hit for the Rolling Stones in 1964) and the more obscure 'Mailman Bring Me No More Blues'. Both had been Holly B-sides, in 1957 and 1961 respectively, the latter posthumously. A third dip back through the years brought a burst of 'Besame Mucho', the song performed by the Beatles back at the group's EMI audition/test on 6 June 1962, although this time it was delivered in a decidedly more up-tempo manner, with a terrific vocal by Paul.

Nothing from this day was released on disc, although

the performance of 'Besame Mucho' was included in the *Let It Be* film.

Thursday 30 January

Apple Studios (Roof), 3 Savile Row, London W1: time unknown. Recording: 'Get Back' (two versions); 'Don't Let Me Down'; 'I've Got A Feeling'; 'The One After 909'; 'Dig A Pony'; 'God Save The Queen'; 'I've Got A Feeling'; 'Don't Let Me Down'; 'Get Back'. P: George Martin. E: Glyn Johns. 2E: Alan Parsons.

There was only one way that the Beatles could fulfil the original *Get Back* plan – performing live the songs they had been rehearsing and recording – and yet still appease those opposed to going back on the road. And that was for the group to give an unannounced live performance in public in which, although very audible, they were quite invisible to the crowds which quickly gathered. They played up on the high roof of the Apple building.

The rooftop gig, an idea conceived on 26 January, was the first of two consecutive *performances* which concluded the *Get Back* recordings. On 31 January the Beatles ran through numbers *inside* Apple. But this day's work has passed into history as the last "live" performance the Beatles ever gave, even if it couldn't be classified as a "concert".

The 42-minute rooftop show (about half of which comprises the sensational close to the *Let It Be* film), a lunchtime blast into the cold wind – imagine a high London rooftop in January; little wonder Ringo borrowed wife Maureen's red mac, and John borrowed Yoko's fur wrap – is preserved in its entirety on two eight-track audio tapes at EMI, engineered down below in the basement by Glyn Johns, sadly unable to be an eye-witness to the events, with Alan Parsons, a highly impressed Beatles fan, as tape operator. [The eight-track tapes were recorded as follows: 1) Paul vocal; 2) John (and George) vocal; 3) Organ (Billy Preston); 4) Bass (Paul); 5) sync track for film crew; 6) Drums (Ringo); 7) Guitar (John); 8) Guitar (George).]

For the film crew and the Apple/EMI sound engineers it was a long day. Alan Parsons recalls, "It was after about a week at Apple that Paul said 'Wait a minute, it's all very well doing this live stuff in the studio but why don't we just play the songs in front of a few people? Set the gear up on the roof and see how it turns out.' Instant panic stations, everybody saying 'My God, they're on the roof tomorrow!' But nobody ever questioned the Beatles. 'They want to do it on the roof? Fine, it will be done'. The next day was very windy and early in the morning Glyn sent me out to buy ladies stockings to put over the mikes, to prevent the wind from getting into them. I felt a right prat going into Marks and Spencer's and asking for a pair of stockings. 'What size sir?' 'Oh, it doesn't matter.' The look they gave me was very, very weird!"

Dave Harries and Keith Slaughter, technical engineers, ran into similar problems with authority. "Early that morning," recalls Harries, "at about five o'clock, we were driving towards London in an EMI car, full of ropes and blocks and tackle, bits of wood, amplifiers, speakers, God knows what, and we got pulled by the law in Kings Langley. We had these big

coats and hats on and looked for all the world like a couple of burglars. The copper asked where we were going and we said 'If we told you, you wouldn't believe us . . ' so he let us go!"

Much was commercially used from the 42 minutes on the roof, on both the *Get Back* and *Let It Be* albums and in the *Let It Be* film. What follows is a detailed description of the full rooftop repertoire, as preserved on the eight-track tapes, with a guide to how it was made available.
1) Setting-up. Film director shouts "All cameras, take one!" The first song is a rehearsal of 'Get Back', the end of which is greeted with fairly light applause which clearly reminds Paul of a cricket match, so he steps back to the microphone and mutters something about Ted Dexter [Sussex and England player of the time]. John Lennon says "We've had a request from Martin Luther . . .".
2) Another version of 'Get Back' [The *Let It Be* film has a well-matched edit of these first two 'Get Back' versions.] At the end of the song John Lennon says "Had a request for Daisy, Morris and Tommy".
3) 'Don't Let Me Down' [*Let It Be* film], straight into . . .
4) 'I've Got A Feeling' [*Let It Be* film and LP], with John saying at the end, "Oh, my soul . . . [applause] . . . so hard". (George sings a little on 'I've Got A Feeling'; he is otherwise vocally silent during the rooftop performance.)
5) 'The One After 909', ending with John sarcastically reciting a line of Conway Twitty's 1959 US hit 'Danny Boy'. [*Let It Be* film and LP, and *Get Back* LP.]
6) 'Dig A Pony', with a false start ("one, two, three . . . HOLD IT . . . [Ringo blows nose] . . . one, two, three"). Ends with John saying "Thank you brothers . . . hands too cold to play the chords". [*Let It Be* film and LP, though for the latter Phil Spector edited out the song's opening and closing "All I want is . . ." vocal lines.] The eight-track tape also has a brief rehearsal of the song before it began, and John asking for the words. In the film an assistant can be seen kneeling before John with the lyrics attached to a clipboard.

7) Alan Parsons has changed tapes, the first one being full. While waiting for him the Beatles and Billy Preston have strummed through a quick version of the national anthem, 'God Save The Queen'. The new tape catches a few seconds of this, but it is not released on record or seen in the film.
8) 'I've Got A Feeling', second rooftop version. [Not released on record or seen in the film.]
9) 'Don't Let Me Down', second rooftop version. [Not released on record or seen in the film], straight into . . .
10) 'Get Back', the third rooftop version, somewhat distracted owing to police presence, seeking to bring the show to a close. The song almost breaks down but lurches to a finish, with Paul ad-libbing "You've been playing on the roofs again . . . and you know your Momma doesn't like it . . . she's gonna have you arrested!" At the end of the song, Paul acknowledges the fervent applause and cheering from Ringo's wife Maureen with "Thanks, Mo!" and then John, having stepped away from the microphone, returns to add, somewhat hammily, "I'd like to say 'thank you' on behalf of the group and ourselves and I hope we passed the audition!". [Paul's and John's comments, but not this 'Get Back' song, were included on the unreleased *Get Back* LP. The *Let It Be* LP employs a skilful crossfade from the 27 January studio version of 'Get Back' to the closing ad-lib comments from the rooftop, implying that the song was from the rooftop performance. The *Let It Be* film is the only publicly available true version, with the lurching version of 'Get Back' and the closing ad-libs.]

"That was one of the greatest and most exciting days of my life," says Alan Parsons. "To see the Beatles playing together and getting an instant feedback from the people around them, five cameras on the roof, cameras across the road, in the road, it was just unbelievable . . . a magic, magic day." Dave Harries recalls, "There were people hanging off balconies and out of every office window all around. The police were knocking on the door – George Martin went white! We really *wanted* to stop the traffic, we *wanted* to blast out the entire West End . . ."

Out of sight. The Beatles on the roof of their Apple building in Savile Row, London, making light of their problems and giving a splendid last live performance, 30 January 1969.

Friday 31 January

Apple Studios, 3 Savile Row, London W1: time unknown. Recording: 'The Long And Winding Road'; 'Lady Madonna'; 'The Long And Winding Road'; 'Let It Be'; 'On Our Way Home' (working title of 'Two Of Us'). P: George Martin. E: Glyn Johns. 2E: Alan Parsons.

The "Apple Studio Performance" – as described on the tape boxes – in other words, the final recording of those numbers unsuitable for the rooftop show: two piano songs and one acoustic number. The Beatles also ventured into a jam of 'Lady Madonna' which, although later mixed by Glyn Johns as a potential LP track, was barely releasable by any stretch of the imagination. For these recordings the Beatles and Billy Preston arranged themselves into stage formation on and around a platform. Paul was the focus of attention throughout, as can be seen in the *Let It Be* film.

Using take numbers from the film clapperboard, the group recorded three takes (10-12) of 'Two Of Us', seven takes (13-19) of 'The Long And Winding Road'

and nine of 'Let It Be' (20-27, 27 consisting of two audio takes). The unreleased *Get Back* LP included take 19 of 'The Long And Winding Road' and take 27 of 'Let It Be'. It also included a few lines of chat (John: "Are we supposed to giggle in the solo?", Paul: "Yeah.") which was said before the recording of 'Let It Be' take 23 but appears on the LP after the take 27 version. Instead, before the song, the LP included Paul saying, as he did on the original tape, "Sync the second clap, please", mimicking the film director's instruction to his crew.

The *Let It Be* LP itself used all three songs, the above two plus take 12 of 'Two Of Us', although by that time two of the songs had been substantially overdubbed: 'Let It Be' on 30 April 1969 and

4 January 1970 and 'The Long And Winding Road' on 1 April 1970. (The 'Let It Be' single used this same version too, although it sounded different to both LP versions owing to differences in the remix. See 4 January 1970.)

Overdubbing, of course, somewhat defeated the *Get Back* principle, but – it seemed – the Beatles were already on the verge of abandoning their ideas. After an excellent take of 'Let It Be' (take 25), John announced "OK, let's track it," then sharply drew in his breath and added, in a sarcastic, slap-my-wrist fashion, "You bounder, you cheat!"

Wednesday 5 February

Apple Studios, 3 Savile Row, London W1: time unknown. Stereo mixing: 'I've Got A Feeling' (two versions); 'Don't Let Me Down'; 'Get Back' (two versions); 'The One After 909'; 'Dig A Pony'. P: George Martin? E: Glyn Johns. 2E: Alan Parsons.

Stereo mixes, ending with a tape compilation, of the 30 January rooftop recordings.

Saturday 22 February

Trident Studios, Trident House, St Anne's Court, Wardour Street, London W1: time unknown. Recording: 'I Want You' (later known as 'I Want You (She's So Heavy)') (takes 1-35). P: Glyn Johns. E: Barry Sheffield. 2E: unknown.

There was, at best, a fine dividing line between the end of *Get Back* and the beginning of sessions for what was to become *Abbey Road*. Although work on the latter did not begin in earnest until July, a number of that album's songs were well under way by that time.

One was 'I Want You', a fine John Lennon song begun now with 35 takes of the basic track and John's guide vocal (one experimental take was sung by Paul McCartney), almost completed in April and finally

finished in August. (The 29 January recording at Savile Row was merely a rehearsal run-through.) But why Trident, and why the three-week delay between the final Savile Row session and this day? Trident because – with filming now complete – Apple Studios was undergoing a re-build and technological re-think, the Alexis Mardas plans – as well as his mixing desk – scrapped and the borrowed consoles returned to Abbey Road. Presumably, the Beatles were keen to see out the project in an independent studio.

Alternatively, Abbey Road may have been fully booked by other artistes.

The delay was caused by the temporary absence of Glyn Johns and Billy Preston, both in the USA in early February but both back in London to contribute to this session, and by the London hospitalisation of George Harrison between 7 and 15 February for the removal of tonsils.

Sunday 23 February

Trident Studios, Trident House, St Anne's Court, Wardour Street, London W1: time unknown. Editing: 'I Want You' (later known as 'I Want You (She's So Heavy)') (unnumbered master, from takes 9, 20 and 32). P: Glyn Johns. E: Barry Sheffield. 2E: unknown.

Take nine of 'I Want You' had the best Lennon vocal for the early part of the song, take 20 had the best middle eight, take 32 was best for the rest. In this

session the three were edited into one all-encompassing master take.

Monday 24 February

Trident Studios, Trident House, St Anne's Court, Wardour Street, London W1: time unknown. Tape copying: 'I Want You' (later known as 'I Want You (She's So Heavy)') (of unnumbered Trident master). P: n/a. E: Barry Sheffield. 2E: unknown.

A safety copy of the edited master.

Tuesday 25 February

Abbey Road, studio unknown: time unknown. Recording: 'Old Brown Shoe' (takes 1 and 2); 'All Things Must Pass' (takes 1 and 2); 'Something' (take 1). P: n/a.   E and 2E: Ken Scott.

Perhaps as a 26th birthday present to himself, George Harrison went to Abbey Road alone on this day and, with just Ken Scott in the control room, recorded elaborate eight-track demos of three of his latest compositions, presumably for the other Beatles to learn their parts for future, proper recording.

The three each had a different fate. 'Old Brown Shoe' was a Beatles B-side, 'Something' an *Abbey Road* album track and the A-side of a single, 'All Things Must Pass', never to be recorded by the Beatles, was an outstanding song on – and title track of – George's 1970 triple-album.

Like the preceding George Harrison demos for 'While My Guitar Gently Weeps' and 'Isn't It A Pity', these three songs were quite lovely in their simplicity, George recording several vocal parts, guitar and piano. (There were no drums on any of the three songs.) 'All Things Must Pass' and 'Something' were especially beautiful, and 'Something' had the additional bonus of an extra four-line verse not included on the finished recording. [See George's book *I Me Mine*, page 153, for the lyrics.]

Monday 10 March

Olympic Sound Studios, 117 Church Road, Barnes, London SW13: time unknown. Stereo mixing: 'Get Back'; 'Teddy Boy'; 'On Our Way Home' (working title of 'Two Of Us'); 'Dig A Pony'; 'I've Got A Feeling'; 'The Long And Winding Road'; 'Let It Be'; 'Rocker'; 'Save The Last Dance For Me'; 'Don't Let Me Down'; 'Because You're Sweet And Lovely' (working title of 'For You Blue'); 'Get Back'; 'The Walk'. P: George Martin?   E: Glyn Johns.   2E: unknown.

It was now six weeks since the end of the *Get Back* recordings, six weeks in which, it seems, the Beatles had all but washed their hands of the entire project. One day in early March, John Lennon and Paul McCartney called Glyn Johns into Abbey Road and pointed to a big pile of eight-track tapes: the result of those ten January days at Savile Row. "Remember that idea you had about putting together an album?," they asked. "There are the tapes, go and do it."

As one might well imagine, this was a stiff undertaking for Johns: he was being given a free hand to compile the new Beatles album. Armed with the Apple tapes, Glyn booked time at his favourite studio, Olympic Sound, and began assembling the *Get Back* album. At least one aspect was easy: it was to be stereo only, mirroring the pro-stereo movement which escalated at the end of the 1960s, leading to the swift, virtual extinction of mono recordings.

Tuesday 11 March

Olympic Sound Studios, 117 Church Road, Barnes, London SW13: time unknown. Stereo mixing: 'On Our Way Home' (working title of 'Two Of Us'); 'The Long And Winding Road'; 'Lady Madonna'. P: George Martin?   E: Glyn Johns.   2E: unknown.

More *Get Back* remixing.

Wednesday 12 March

Olympic Sound Studios, 117 Church Road, Barnes, London SW13: time unknown. Stereo mixing: 'The Long And Winding Road'; 'Let It Be'. P: George Martin?   E: Glyn Johns.   2E: unknown.

Mixing of different 31 January takes of 'The Long And Winding Road' and 'Let It Be', unreleased.

Left:
George, Paul and Ringo during sessions for *Abbey Road*, July 1969, photographed by Linda McCartney.

Above:
George caught by the lens of Linda McCartney.

Thursday 13 March

Olympic Sound Studios, 117 Church Road, Barnes, London SW13: time unknown. Stereo mixing: 'I've Got A Feeling'; 'Dig It' (version one); 'Dig It' (version two); 'Maggie Mae'; 'Shake Rattle And Roll'; 'Kansas City'; 'Miss Ann'; 'Lawdy Miss Clawdy'; 'Blue Suede Shoes'; 'You Really Got A Hold On Me'. P: George Martin? E: Glyn Johns. 2E: unknown.

The last work on the *Get Back* LP until 7 May. The six rock and roll oldies mixed on this day were left unreleased, even though at one stage an album full of just such material was considered.

Wednesday 26 March

Abbey Road, studio unknown: time unknown. Mono mixing: 'Get Back' (remixes 1-4). P: George Martin? E: Jeff Jarratt. 2E: n/a.

Seeking to rush-release a single, the Beatles asked EMI Studios to remix 'Get Back' for mono. This was done by Jeff Jarratt, it was met with approval and acetates were cut. It was not, however, the *final* mix.

Monday 7 April

Olympic Sound Studios, 117 Church Road, Barnes, London SW13: time unknown. Mono mixing: 'Get Back' (remix 5); 'Don't Let Me Down' (remix 1). Stereo mixing: 'Get Back' (remix 1); 'Don't Let Me Down' (remix 1). P: George Martin? E: Glyn Johns. 2E: Jerry Boys.

On Sunday 6 April British radio disc-jockeys John Peel and Alan Freeman broadcast acetate copies of 'Get Back', announcing its rush-release as a single on 11 April. But Paul McCartney still wasn't entirely happy with the mixing, so he quickly booked studio time with Glyn Johns at Olympic for the Monday – Easter Monday – to try again. Jerry Boys, ex-EMI Studios tape operator, volunteered to help out.

"Only Paul came along," Boys remembers. "They'd already done a mono mix of 'Get Back' and had acetates cut and didn't like it. We tried it again but it wasn't really happening any better and when we went to compare the two we hit a problem because Paul didn't have a tape of that first mix with him, just an acetate. He and Glyn were very concerned with what the new mix was going to sound like on a cheap record player. Purely by chance, I happened to have a cheap record player in the back of my car, which I'd brought along to Olympic to have someone repair. We had an acetate cut from the new mix and then, using my record player, we were able to decide which of the two mixes was better. So the very first playing of the 'Get Back' single, which sold millions, was on my little player!"

Also completed on this day were stereo remixes of 'Get Back' and 'Don't Let Me Down', for issue, initially, in the USA.

Friday 11 April

Single release: 'Get Back'/'Don't Let Me Down'. Apple [Parlophone] R 5777.

The first commercial output from the *Get Back* sessions: 'Get Back' itself and 'Don't Let Me Down', both recorded at Savile Row on 28 January and remixed on 7 April. Owing to the late remixing, copies of the single did not reach the stores until several days after this rather optimistic release date. But it nonetheless sailed straight to the top of the charts all over the world.

Neither the A- nor B-side carried a producer's credit, hardly surprising considering the confused roles of George Martin and Glyn Johns. But the record label for both sides did bear one new name, the two songs being officially accredited to "The Beatles with Billy Preston". "A great honour," said Preston.

George Martin at the keyboard, photographed by Linda McCartney.

Tape operator John Kurlander's detailed recording sheet for 'The Ballad Of John And Yoko', a swift and effective eight-track, eight-hour session by John and Paul.

Monday 14 April

Studio Three: 2.30-9.00pm. Recording: 'The Ballad Of John And Yoko (They're Gonna Crucify Me)' (working title of 'The Ballad Of John And Yoko') (takes 1-11). Studio Three (control room only): 9.00-11.00pm. Stereo mixing: 'The Ballad Of John And Yoko (They're Gonna Crucify Me)' (working title of 'The Ballad Of John And Yoko') (remixes 1-5, from take 10). P: George Martin.   E: Geoff Emerick.   2E: John Kurlander.

On 23 and 24 April 1960 John Lennon and Paul McCartney performed as a duo in a public house in Caversham, Berkshire, calling themselves the Nerk Twins. Nine years on, the act was resurrected: this 14 April 1969 recording session – the fruit of which was released as a fine Beatles single – featured just John and Paul. Ringo was elsewhere, filming his role in a new Peter Sellers movie, *The Magic Christian*. George, it was said, was out of the country.

As a song, 'The Ballad Of John And Yoko' was unlike any other Beatles single, its lyric recounting the recent days in the life of the newly married Lennons. Later in the year, John recorded these sort of songs with his new group, the Plastic Ono Band, and had the band existed at this time 'The Ballad Of John And Yoko' would probably have been theirs. For the present, John's sole musical vehicle was the Beatles.

As a recording, 'The Ballad Of John And Yoko' represented highly efficient use of the studio and the eight-track facility. Indeed, the session finished one hour ahead of the booked time. Concentrating first on perfecting the basic rhythm track, John and Paul recorded eleven takes of simultaneous drums (Paul) and acoustic guitar/lead vocal (John). A study of the original session tape provides an amusing insight into the session and clearly reveals that despite the wranglings, arguments and bitter business squabbles so widely reported of them in 1969, John Lennon and Paul McCartney's great talent, humour, musical understanding and togetherness shone through from start to finish. Five of those 11 takes broke down in precisely the same spot, Paul erroneously adding an extra snare drum fill before the vocal line "Made a lightning trip to Vienna". Take two broke down because, as John explained, "Un string avec caput, Mal!" And there was one lovely moment, before take four, where John said to the drumming Paul "Go a bit faster, Ringo!" and Paul replied to the guitar-wielding John "OK, George!"

Take ten was the 'best' basic track, although John and Paul did make one more attempt, in a higher pitch (G Major). Returning then to take ten, they overdubbed: bass guitar (Paul), lead guitar (John), second lead guitar (John), piano (Paul), backing vocal (Paul), maracas (Paul) and, finally, percussive thumps on the back of an acoustic guitar (John). The song was mixed for stereo in the last two hours of the session, becoming the Beatles' first stereo single in Britain and, consequently, their first release not to be mixed for mono.

"'The Ballad Of John And Yoko' was a very fast session," recalls Geoff Emerick, working on a new Beatles recording for the first time in nine months. "It was a really good record too, helped by Paul's great drumming and the speed in which they did it all."

It was also a fast release, its 30 May issue occurring while 'Get Back' was still number one in the charts.

Wednesday 16 April

Studio Three: 2.30-5.00pm. Recording: 'Old Brown Shoe' (take 1). P: George Martin.   E: Phil McDonald.   2E: Richard Lush. Studio Three: 7.00pm-2.45am. Recording: 'Old Brown Shoe' (takes 1-4); 'Something' (takes 1-13). Stereo mixing: 'Old Brown Shoe' (remixes 1-3, from take 4). P: George Martin.   E: Jeff Jarratt.   2E: Richard Lush.

There were three take ones of George Harrison's 'Old Brown Shoe': the solo demo version on 25 February, a second demo version taped during this afternoon and a proper take one, recorded a couple of hours later, simultaneously wiping the afternoon demo.

Much the same can be said for George's 'Something', too, with a 25 February demo, takes one through to 13 taped on this day, and then, takes one to 14 of a re-make done on 2 May.

'Old Brown Shoe', started first, was a terrific up-tempo Harrison number recorded, quite strictly, in just four takes. The first complete run-through, take two, showed just how well the song had been worked out in advance, and how each of the Beatles seemed to know his part. The live instruments were drums (Ringo), lead guitar and vocals (George), jangle piano (Paul) and rhythm guitar (John). Onto take four was overdubbed bass and lead guitars and fine backing vocals by John and Paul. George also re-taped his lead vocal, huddled into a small corner of the studio to lend a tight but natural echo. The song's highly distinctive and impressive bass sound was actually a fine combination of matching lead and bass guitar notes played by George and Paul.

'Old Brown Shoe' was mixed for stereo at the end of the session – remix three being 'best' – presumably because the Beatles considered the song to be finished. But additional overdubs taped on 18 April rendered these mixes unusable.

Work on 'Something' was restricted to basic track recordings: bass (Paul), drums (Ringo), guitar (George) and piano (George Martin). John Lennon was present but did not contribute and there were no vocals at this stage.

Friday 18 April

Studio Three: 2.30-10.30pm. Recording: 'Old Brown Shoe' (SI onto take 4). Studio Three (control room only): 10.30pm-1.00am. Stereo mixing: 'Old Brown Shoe' (remixes 5-23, from take 4). Studio Two: 1.00-4.30am. Recording: 'I Want You' (later known as 'I Want You (She's So Heavy)') (SI onto unnumbered Trident master; reduction of unnumbered Trident master, called take 1; SI onto take 1). Stereo mixing: 'I Want You' (later known as 'I Want You (She's So Heavy)') (unnumbered rough remix, from take 1). P: Chris Thomas.   E: Jeff Jarratt.   2E: John Kurlander.

'Old Brown Shoe' was completed during this Chris Thomas-supervised session, with a Hammond organ overdub (wiping, in the process, John's rhythm guitar track) and an additional lead guitar track, put through a Leslie speaker. Both overdubs were played by George Harrison. The song was then remixed for stereo, following the three mixes done on 16 April, but beginning this day with remix five.

George Harrison, John Lennon, Chris Thomas, Jeff Jarratt and John Kurlander then went into studio two to work on 'I Want You': overdubbing multi-tracked Lennon/Harrison guitars for the song's momentous finale onto the 23 February Trident master; then creating a reduction mixdown (called take one) of that master and then overdubbing yet more guitar parts onto that take one; finishing off with a rough stereo remix of the song's latest incarnation. "John and George went into the far left-hand corner of number two to overdub those guitars," recalls Jeff Jarratt. "They wanted a *massive* sound so they kept tracking and tracking, over and over."

Sunday 20 April

Studio Three: 7.00pm-12.45am. Recording: 'I Want You' (later known as 'I Want You (She's So Heavy)') (SI onto take 1); 'Oh! Darling (I'll Never Do You No Harm)' (working title of 'Oh! Darling') (takes 1-26). Stereo mixing: 'Oh Darling (I'll Never Do You No Harm)' (working title of 'Oh! Darling') (remix 1, from take 26). P: Chris Thomas.   E: Jeff Jarratt. 2E: John Kurlander.

'Oh! Darling' had first been aired in the recording studio in rehearsal form at Apple on 27 January. Now recording proper commenced, with 26 live takes of the basic track: bass and guide vocal (Paul), drums (Ringo), piano (John) and guitar via a Leslie (George). A Hammond organ part was overdubbed onto take 26 and a stereo remix was made at the end of the session. The song would undergo many more overdubs before completion (during which, for example, the Hammond organ part was wiped) and at this stage recordings were more like a well-planned rehearsal, lapsing into the occasional brief but wild musical jam, like take seven, which melted into a Lennon-led blast of Joe South's contemporary hit 'Games People Play'. Also taped this day were overdubs for the 18 April reduction of 'I Want You': Hammond organ and a set of conga drums brought in especially for the session by Mal Evans.

Friday 25 April

Abbey Road, Room 4: 11.30am-12.30pm. Mono mixing: 'On Our Way Home' (working title of 'Two Of Us') (remix 1). P: n/a.   E: Peter Mew.   2E: Chris Blair.

A rough mono remix, for acetate cutting purposes, of the 31 January Beatles recording of 'Two Of Us', in order that Paul could present the song to the New York trio Mortimer. [See 24 January.]

Saturday 26 April

Studio Two: 4.30pm-4.15am. Recording: 'Oh! Darling' (SI onto take 26); 'Octopus's Garden' (takes 1-32). P: Chris Thomas/the Beatles.   E: Jeff Jarratt.   2E: Richard Langham.

Apart from the overdub of Paul's lead vocal onto 'Oh! Darling' – the first of several such recordings – this session was spent perfecting the basic track for a new composition by Ringo, 'Octopus's Garden'. Ringo did not have a lead vocal on the as yet unissued *Get Back* album, the first time this had occurred in the Beatles' recording career. [Ringo did compose 'Octopus's Garden' during the *Get Back* period, as can be seen in the 26 January sequence of the *Let It Be* film, however it was not recorded or even rehearsed on tape at this point.]

This was a fun and creative session, judging by the original tape, with the Beatles running through 32 takes before hitting upon the 'best'. These consisted of bass (Paul), drums and simultaneous guide vocal (Ringo), guitars (George and John). George handled the main guitar intro, putting the sound through a Leslie speaker. The song was already much like the finished article at this early stage – excepting the later overdubs, of course – with the same lyrics and basic instrumental ideas. Ringo sniggered and laughed quite frequently during the session, and made a fine, self-mocking jibe after take eight (not quite as good as the others) "Well, that was *superb*!"

The recording sheet for this session quotes "Beatles" as the producer, although Chris Thomas has a distinct memory of being around in the control room while it was in progress and Jeff Jarratt was also at the helm, as he recalls. "I was really thrown in at the deep end. George Martin informed me that he wouldn't be available. I can't remember word for word what he said to me, but it was something like 'There will be one Beatle there, fine. Two Beatles, great. Three Beatles, fantastic. But the minute the four of them are there that is when the inexplicable charismatic thing happens, the special magic no one has been able to explain. It will be very friendly between you and them but you'll be aware of this inexplicable *presence*.' Sure enough, that's exactly the way it happened. I've never felt it in any other circumstances, it was the special chemistry of the four of them which nobody since has ever had."

Returning to the Beatles' control room on this day was Richard Langham, veteran of the 1963/64 Beatles sessions. Langham had spent several years in Europe in the mid-1960s, recently re-joining the staff at Abbey Road. Actually, the first Beatles-related task for Langham on his return occurred earlier this day, 26 April, between 2.30 and 4.15pm: making the second stereo remix of a remarkable 22-minute recording, 'John And Yoko' taped by that duo in studio two at Abbey Road between 11.00pm and 4.30am on 22 April, with Jeff Jarratt as balance engineer and John Kurlander as tape op. (Its first stereo remix was also done in that session.) "The nice thing about working with John and Yoko," recalls Jarratt, "was seeing just how much in love they were. They had a fantastic relationship, even though they took a lot of 'stick' for it. The 'John And Yoko' recording was fantastic, though quite unpleasant. John managed to get hold of a highly sensitive microphone from a local hospital and we recorded their heart beats. The mike was so good that you heard all the gurgly noises and everything going on inside the stomach!" [The recording was issued on 7 November 1969, comprising one side of John and Yoko's *The Wedding Album*.]

Tuesday 29 April

Studio Three: 7.30pm-1.00am. Recording: 'Octopus's Garden' (SI onto take 32). Stereo mixing: 'Octopus's Garden' (remixes 1-4, from take 32). P: Chris Thomas.   E: Jeff Jarratt.   2E: Nick Webb.

The re-recording, as an overdub, of Ringo's lead vocal for 'Octopus's Garden', and four stereo remixes of that song, the fourth deemed 'best'. Presumed completed, the tape stayed on the shelf for some time, until mid-July, when it was revived for more overdubbing and mixing.

Before this session began, there was a four-hour playback of recently recorded titles in the control room of studio three, 2.30-6.30pm.

Top:
John Lennon, by Linda McCartney.

Wednesday 30 April

Studio Three: 7.15pm-2.00am. Recording: 'Let It Be' (SI onto take 27); 'You Know My Name (Look Up The Number)' (SI onto take 30). Mono mixing: 'You Know My Name (Look Up The Number)' (remixes 1-3, from take 30). P: Chris Thomas. E: Jeff Jarratt. 2E: Nick Webb.

A most interesting session, which began with a lead guitar overdub onto the 'best' 31 January recording of 'Let It Be' (called take 27 as that was the film slate take number). Glyn Johns used this overdubbed version for his *Get Back* album, the only deviation from the original live premise that Johns made. (It was this solo which featured on the single release, too.)

The remainder of the session was handled solely by John and Paul, and it saw the revival of a 22-month-old rhythm track recording, for overdubbing of vocals and sound effects: 'You Know My Name (Look Up The Number)', recorded through May and June 1967

but left unfinished after a master edit had been compiled of its constituent parts on 9 June 1967. "John and Paul weren't always getting on that well at this time," recalls Nick Webb, "but for that song they went onto the studio floor and sang together around one microphone. Even at that time I was thinking 'What are they doing with this old four-track tape, recording these funny bits onto this quaint song?' But it was a fun track to do."

All of the song's bizarre vocals were added on this day, along with simple sound effects: Mal Evans running a spade through a heap of gravel, John and Paul

handclapping, coughing, spluttering and slipping in the odd vocal reminiscent of Bluebottle in *The Goon Show*. But much of this was later edited out, for when the song was finally released, in March 1970, it was 4'19" in duration. These recordings were still 6'08". [See 26 November 1969 for more details.] For the moment, three new mono remixes were made, the third being 'best'.

Before this session began, there was another playback of recently recorded titles in the control room of studio three, 2.30-6.15pm.

Thursday 1 May

Studio Three (control room only): 2.30-7.00pm. Stereo mixing: 'Oh! Darling' (remixes 2-4, from take 26). P: Chris Thomas. E: Jeff Jarratt. 2E: Nick Webb.

(Note. After this session, from 7.00-10.45pm, John Lennon, as producer, presided over three more stereo remixes of 'John And Yoko', from the 22 April recording and an inferior re-make done at Abbey Road on 27 April.)

Friday 2 May

Studio Three: 7.00pm-3.40am. Recording: 'Something' [re-make] (takes 1-36). P: Chris Thomas. E: Jeff Jarratt. 2E: Nick Webb.

A re-make of George's 'Something', incorporating the song's third take one in as many months. This re-make spanned three months too, finally being completed with an orchestral overdub on 15 August and stereo mixing four days later. In between times it underwent numerous perfections and two reduction mixdowns.

The basic track was recorded at this first stage: bass (Paul), drums (Ringo), guitar (John), piano (Billy Preston) and guitar via a Leslie speaker (George). There would be no vocal recording for some time. The main difference between these early versions of 'Something' and the finished master was that these were much longer in duration. Take 36, the 'best' basic track, was 7'48", compared to the final timing of 3'00". The difference was due entirely to a long, repetitious and somewhat rambling, piano-led four-note instrumental fade-out.

There was a two-hour break in the middle of this session, from 11.00pm until 1.00am.

Linda McCartney's picture of husband Paul, deep in thought during a session for *Abbey Road*.

Extract from the unwritten EMI Studios rule book: All tapes being taken away from the premises must be signed for . . . even if you're John Lennon.

Monday 5 May

Studio One, Olympic Sound Studios, 117 Church Road, Barnes, London SW13: 7.30pm-4.00am. Recording: 'Something' (SI onto take 36). P: George Martin.   E: Glyn Johns.
2E: Steve Vaughan.

The first of a four-day booking by the Beatles at Olympic Sound Studios, with Glyn Johns returning to the helm. In this session the group recorded overdubs for 'Something', with Paul improving on his bass track and George doing likewise with his "Leslie'd" guitar track.

Tuesday 6 May

Studio One, Olympic Sound Studios, 117 Church Road, Barnes, London SW13: 3.00pm-4.00am. Recording: 'You Never Give Me Your Money' (takes 1-36). Stereo mixing: 'You Never Give Me Your Money' (remix 1, from take 30). P: George Martin.   E: Glyn Johns.   2E: Steve Vaughan.

So far, any post-January songs recorded for the "shelf" and destined, eventually, for the *Abbey Road* LP, found themselves on side one of that album. There was a reason for this: much of side two was to form a medley.

It is difficult to pin a precise date on the conception of any idea, although the *Abbey Road* medley must have been born right around this time in 1969, for this day's session at Olympic saw its first recording: a superb, upbeat ballad 'You Never Give Me Your Money' (the title and lyric directly inspired by the fast developing business problems at Apple). Although the song, as it appeared on the LP, did have a full ending, the first recorded takes did not. They ended abruptly, as if to juxtapose with another, just before the point where the finished song went into the vocal line "one, two, three, four, five, six, seven, all good children go to heaven".

After this session the song lay dormant until reaching completion in July, but the basic track was recorded on this day: piano and guide vocal (Paul), drums (Ringo), distorted electric guitar (John) and chiming electric guitar, put through a Leslie (George). A rough stereo remix of the 'best', take 30, ended the session.

Wednesday 7 May

Studio One, Olympic Sound Studios, 117 Church Road, Barnes, London SW13: 8.00pm-7.30am. Stereo mixing: Inserts for the *Get Back* LP. P: George Martin.   E: Glyn Johns.
2E: Steve Vaughan.

Whether they cared for the project or not, it made sense for the Beatles to release *Get Back* now that the LP was close to completion. In line with their intention of showing themselves "warts and all", and emphasising the "live" feel of the LP, *Get Back* included several snatches of chatter and jokes from the original sessions, the sort of thing which will always occur during any session by any artiste, but which is usually kept well clear of the master tape. With *Get Back* the little scraps were not only left in, but in some instances they were *put* in. This session was dedicated to just such a task.

Friday 9 May

Studio One, Olympic Sound Studios, 117 Church Road, Barnes, London SW13: 3.00-11.00pm. Stereo mixing: Inserts for the *Get Back* LP. P: George Martin.   E: Glyn Johns.
2E: Steve Vaughan.

More of the same, plus a playback of the completed and mixed titles.

Wednesday 28 May

Studio One, Olympic Sound Studios, 117 Church Road, Barnes, London SW13: time unknown. Stereo mixing: 'Let It Be' (of take 27). Master tape banding and compilation: *Get Back*
LP. P: George Martin.   E: Glyn Johns.   2E: Steve Vaughan.

At last *Get Back* was finished, even though George was the only Beatle in the country to see and approve it. The other three were either holidaying or working abroad. John and Yoko were two days into their second bed-in for peace, in Montreal.

Get Back was a remarkable project from beginning to end, ill-conceived and certainly ill-fated to such an extent that the original LP was never released, having been rejected by the Beatles. A variation was issued, re-worked, re-jigged and regurgitated – *Let It Be* – but, some say, whatever charm the original *Get Back* had, *Let It Be* managed to lose. Conversely, there are those who opine that *Let It Be* was at least a presentable album, compared with *Get Back* which, despite a sterling effort by Glyn Johns to capture the "live" feel, fails to come across as anything more than a tired rock group going through the motions. That it could follow within two years of *Sgt Pepper's Lonely Hearts Club Band* speaks volumes for the apathy within the Beatles at this time.

The line-up of this unreleased LP, with recording dates in parentheses, was as follows. Side A: 'The One After 909' [30 January]; 'Rocker' [22 January]; 'Save The Last Dance For Me' [22 January]; 'Don't Let Me Down' [22 January]; 'Dig A Pony' [24 January]; 'I've Got A Feeling' [24 January]; 'Get Back' [28 January, the single release version]. Side B: 'For You Blue' [25 January]; 'Teddy Boy' [24 January]; 'Two Of Us' [24 January]; 'Maggie Mae' [24 January]; 'Dig It' [26 January]; 'Let It Be' [31 January and 30 April overdub]; 'The Long And Winding Road' [31 January]; 'Get Back (reprise)' [28 January].

The Beatles had tried to come full circle with *Get Back*, returning not merely to early recording techniques but even arranging to shoot a re-creation of their first LP cover, *Please Please Me*, using the same photographer, Angus McBean. The Beatles, John especially, were very keen to strike precisely the same pose that they had done in 1963; and they were equally keen to word the *Get Back* cover in a fashion identical to *Please Please Me*, adding the legend "with Let It Be and 11 other songs" under the title.

Although *Get Back* was not released, the cover photograph session wasn't wasted. A subtly different but otherwise identical shot, placed side by side with one of its 1963 counterparts, was used by EMI Records for its 1973 Beatles compilations *1962-1966* and *1967-1970*, giving a marvellous visual example of just how much the Beatles had changed from one end of the 1960s to the other.

Friday 30 May

Single release: 'The Ballad Of John And Yoko'/'Old Brown Shoe'. Apple [Parlophone] R 5786.

Released hot on the trail of 'Get Back', 'The Ballad Of John And Yoko' was a memorable single, the perfect embodiment of a snappy, bright three-minute pop single and the diary-like songwriting of John Lennon which was to re-surface later, though without the clarity of this recording. Another number one!

Tuesday 1 July

Studio Two: 3.00-7.30pm. Recording: 'You Never Give Me Your Money' (SI onto take 30). P: George Martin.   E: Phil McDonald.   2E: Chris Blair.

June 1969 was omitted from the Beatles' recording calendar because of holidays, but 22 of the 31 days of July saw Beatles studio action of one sort or another and the group block-booked the 2.30-10.00pm slot in studio two every day from 1 July until 29 August.

Paul was the only Beatle in the studio on this day, overdubbing a lead vocal onto the 6 May basic track recording of 'You Never Give Me Your Money'. John Lennon could not have attended even had he wanted to: along with Yoko, his son Julian and her daughter Kyoko, he was involved in a motor accident while on holiday in Scotland and was hospitalised there until 6 July.

The day marked the start of a new, if short-lived, recording era for the Beatles, as George Martin recalls. "*Let It Be* was a miserable experience and I never thought that we would get back together again. So I was very surprised when Paul rang me up and said 'We want to make another record. Will you produce it for us, *really* produce it?' I said 'Yes, if I am *really* allowed to produce it. If I have to go back and accept a lot of instructions which I don't like I won't do it.' It *was* really good, even though the boys tended to do their own items, sometimes in different studios at the same time and I had to be dashing from one place to another."

Ringo listening to the latest *Abbey Road* recording.

Wednesday 2 July

Studio Two: 3.00-9.30pm. Recording: 'Her Majesty' (takes 1-3); 'Golden Slumbers' (working title of 'Golden Slumbers'/'Carry That Weight') (takes 1-15). P: George Martin. E: Phil McDonald. 2E: Chris Blair.

One major advantage for Paul McCartney in living so close to EMI Studios was that he invariably arrived first for a session, strolling the short distance in no more than five minutes. This meant that he was often the first to start work. On this day, before the arrival of George and Ringo (John was still in hospital), Paul used the solo studio time to record another of his very quick, spontaneous link-tracks: the 23-second 'Her Majesty'. A simpler recording could not be imagined: it took just three takes, only two of which were complete, before Paul had it right, singing live to his own acoustic guitar accompaniment, and using just two of the tape's eight available tracks. At the end of take three, balance engineer Phil McDonald called over "Do you wanna hear it?" Paul replied "Yeah", went upstairs, heard a playback, liked what he heard and 'Her Majesty' joined the list of songs for medley consideration.

Chris Blair, temporarily appointed as tape operator on Beatles sessions, had a harder time of it than Paul. "They hadn't got a tape op," he recalls, "and Allan Stagge, then studio manager, called me to his office to ask if I might like to help out. He said that he wouldn't pressurise me into doing it. [This was a reference to the fact that several EMI engineers and tape operators no longer wanted to work with the Beatles, disliking the sometimes tense atmosphere between the group and the control room staff, "the 'us' and 'them' situation", as one engineer has called it.] I was extremely nervous on the session and my mind went completely blank. Paul sat down and did 'Her Majesty' and I couldn't for the life of me think how to spell Majesty on the tape box. I rang upstairs, all around the building, asking people how to spell Majesty!"

After George and Ringo arrived at the studio the three Beatles began the recording of another new McCartney number, 'Golden Slumbers'. In truth, the song was not new at all, at least some of the lyrics were not. They – and the title – originated in a late 16th-century prose by the British playwright Thomas Dekker. Paul had seen the prose set to music in a book of children's nursery rhymes but not knowing how to read the chord sequence he had invented his own melody. Fifteen takes of the 'Golden Slumbers' basic rhythm track – piano and guide vocal (Paul), drums (Ringo) and bass (George) were recorded before this session was concluded.

These 'Golden Slumbers' recordings, including the 'best' take, were more than three minutes in duration because they actually consisted of what the *Abbey Road* LP sleeve detailed as two songs: 'Golden Slumbers' and 'Carry That Weight'. These two were not segued; they were *recorded* as one. On the finished LP, the end of 'Golden Slumbers'/'Carry That Weight' occurs immediately before the beginning of 'The End' (which consisted of a guitar passage and the McCartney vocal "Oh yeah, alright, are you gonna be in my dreams tonight?").

Thursday 3 July

Studio Two: 3.00-8.30pm. Editing: 'Golden Slumbers' (working title of 'Golden Slumbers'/'Carry That Weight') (of takes 13 and 15, called take 13). Recording: 'Golden Slumbers' (working title of 'Golden Slumbers'/'Carry That Weight') (SI onto take 13, tape reduction take 13 into takes 16 and 17). P: George Martin. E: Phil McDonald. 2E: Chris Blair.

Takes 13 and 15, together, comprised the best basic track of 'Golden Slumbers'/'Carry That Weight' so they were duly edited, and the edit – still called take 13 – was then overdubbed with a rhythm guitar (Paul), lead guitar (George), two lead vocals by Paul and then, in unison, Paul, George and Ringo chanting the 'Carry That Weight' vocals. With the eight-track tape complete, a reduction mixdown (done twice, 17 being 'best') was made.

Friday 4 July

Studio Two: 2.45-5.30pm. Recording: 'Golden Slumbers' (working title of 'Golden Slumbers'/'Carry That Weight') (SI onto take 17). P: George Martin. E: Phil McDonald. 2E: Chris Blair.

The first overdub onto the newly-reduced 'Golden Slumbers'/'Carry That Weight' tape. Also committed to the Beatles' tape on this day was a goodly portion of the live BBC Radio 2 broadcast of Britain's Ann Jones winning the Wimbledon Ladies' tennis championship, beating Billie-Jean King in a 71-minute three-setter. "We were sitting there listening to the final before the Beatles came in," recalls Dave Harries, technical engineer. "We had it coming through the mixing console. Then they came in and we thought, 'Oh blimey, that's it', especially when they pulled faces and went 'Uggghhh'. But they said we could carry on listening for a while and then, a few minutes later, one of them asked how Ann Jones was getting on, so we put it through on the studio speakers so that they could listen too!"

Monday 7 July

Studio Two: 2.30-11.45pm. Recording: 'Here Comes The Sun' (takes 1-13). P: George Martin. E: Phil McDonald. 2E: John Kurlander.

A fine session for a very fine song. 'Here Comes The Sun', has been acclaimed, quite justifiably, as one of the best songs on *Abbey Road*, giving its composer, George Harrison, another great triumph to match 'Something'.

The inspiration for 'Here Comes The Sun' came, once again, from Eric Clapton – although in a more obtuse way than usual. Apple business dealings were steadily growing more tiresome and one fine spring day George played truant, resting in the sunny back garden of Clapton's home, with Clapton's guitar. His sense of liberation immediately inspired 'Here Comes The Sun' and the recording captures that feeling to perfection, right from the opening acoustic guitar chords which ring out, joyously.

Once again, only three Beatles took part in the session, with John still absent through injury. The original tapes reveal a light-hearted atmosphere. When take one broke down, George exclaimed, sadly, "One of me best beginnings, that!" And at the end of take four, Ringo – celebrating his 29th birthday this day – called up to the control room "Turn me down a little bit, if you *don't* mind" – meaning, reduce the level of the drum sound in his headphones.

Take 13 was the 'best' basic track – bass (Paul), drums (Ringo) and acoustic guitar/guide vocal (George) – and the last hour of the session, 10.45 until 11.45pm, was spent re-recording and perfecting the acoustic guitar as an overdub onto take 13.

Tuesday 8 July

Studio Two: 2.30-10.45pm. Recording: 'Here Comes The Sun' (SI onto take 13, tape reduction take 13 into takes 14 and 15). Studio Two (control room only): 10.45-11.15pm. Mono mixing: 'Here Comes The Sun' (unnumbered rough remix, from take 15). P: George Martin.   E: Phil McDonald.   2E: John Kurlander.

The overdubbing of George's lead vocal, wiping the previous guide track, and of superb harmonised backing vocals by George and Paul, manually double-tracked. These were sufficient to complete the eight-track tape, so take 13 was given a reduction mixdown (done twice to achieve the optimum version) and then a rough mono remix of take 15 was made for George to take away.

Wednesday 9 July

Studio Two: 2.30-10.15pm. Recording: 'Maxwell's Silver Hammer' (takes 1-21). P: George Martin.   E: Phil McDonald.   2E: John Kurlander.

'Maxwell's Silver Hammer' was not an entirely new song. It was almost recorded in October 1968 as a last-minute addition to *The Beatles*. Then it was rehearsed (*not* recorded) in January 1969 at Twickenham Film Studios, as seen in the *Let It Be* film. Now, six months later, the song was recorded for real at Abbey Road and for *Abbey Road*.

'Maxwell's Silver Hammer' is one of those songs which inspires partisan feelings among listeners; you either love it or you hate it. John Lennon, so he later said, fell into the latter category, and did not enjoy the sessions. "It's a question of having patience," says Geoff Emerick. "Paul had it and John didn't. John was always a bit fidgety and restless, wanting to get on, 'yeah, that's good enough, a couple of takes, yeah, that's fine' but Paul could hear certain refinements in his head which John couldn't."

This, in fact, was John's first session after his car crash recuperation. Phil McDonald, balance engineer, recalls, "We were all waiting for him and Yoko to arrive. Paul, George, Ringo downstairs and us upstairs. They didn't know what state he would be in. There was a definite 'vibe'; they were almost afraid of Lennon before he arrived, because they didn't know what he would be like. I got the feeling that the three of them were a little bit scared of him. When he did come in it was a relief and they got together fairly well. John was a powerful figure, especially with Yoko – a double strength."

As a couple, John and Yoko certainly were inseparable. Yoko was injured more seriously than John in the crash and, because she was pregnant, she was ordered to have complete bed rest. To remain by John's side, her bed was brought into the recording studio during Beatles sessions. Stories are legion at Abbey Road of "The Bed", and here are two. Martin Benge: "We were setting up the microphones for the session and this huge double-bed arrived. An ambulance brought Yoko in and she was lowered down onto the bed, we set-up a microphone over her in case she wanted to participate and then we all carried on as before! We were saying 'Now we've seen it all, folks!'"

Ron Richards: "I popped into one of the later sessions in number three [the bed was wheeled around between studios two and three, depending on where John was working] and there was Yoko in this blooming double-bed. I couldn't believe it! John was sitting at an organ, playing, and I went up to him and said 'What the bloody hell is all this?' and he was *very* touchy about it, so I kept quiet and walked out."

The basic track of 'Maxwell's Silver Hammer' was recorded, takes one through to 21, during this session, although there were no takes numbered six to ten. The last two-and-a-quarter hours were spent overdubbing guitars.

Thursday 10 July

Studio Two: 2.30-11.30pm. Recording: 'Maxwell's Silver Hammer' (SI onto take 21). Stereo mixing: 'Maxwell's Silver Hammer' (remixes 1-13, from take 21). P: George Martin.   E: Phil McDonald. 2E: John Kurlander.

Various overdubs onto 'Maxwell's Silver Hammer': piano (Paul), Hammond organ (George Martin), anvil (Ringo), guitar via a Leslie (George) and vocals (Paul lead, plus Paul, George and Ringo backing). Thirteen stereo remixes were made at the end of the session, suggesting perhaps that the song was considered finished. Not so …

"There was a proper blacksmith's anvil brought to the studio for Ringo to hit," recalls Geoff Emerick, who was just beginning to become involved with sessions for *Abbey Road*. "They had it rented from a theatrical agency."

Two Georges at Abbey Road, pictured by Linda McCartney.

July

Friday 11 July

Studio Two: 2.30-12.00pm. Recording: 'Maxwell's Silver Hammer' (SI onto take 21); 'Something' (SI onto take 36). Stereo mixing: 'Something' (remixes 1-4, from take 36). Recording: 'Something' (tape reduction take 36 into take 37); 'You Never Give Me Your Money' (SI onto take 30). P: George Martin. E: Phil McDonald. 2E: John Kurlander.

Apart from the overdubbing of a further guitar and another vocal onto 'Maxwell's Silver Hammer', this session was devoted to overdubbing two of the earlier *Abbey Road* recordings. 'Something' received a new George Harrison lead vocal, rough stereo remixes and then a reduction mixdown for further superimpositions (at this point the song was cut from 7'48" to 5'32": 3'00" of the main song and 2'32" of the instrumental coda). And 'You Never Give Me Your Money' received a bass guitar track from its composer, Paul McCartney.

Tuesday 15 July

Studio Three: 2.30-6.00pm. Recording: 'You Never Give Me Your Money' (SI onto take 30). Studio Two (control room only): 6.00-11.00pm. Stereo mixing: 'You Never Give Me Your Money' (remixes 1-6, from take 30). P: George Martin. E: Phil McDonald. 2E: Alan Parsons.

More recordings for 'You Never Give Me Your Money': vocals and chimes, the latter for use near the end of the song. Six rough stereo remixes followed.

Wednesday 16 July

Studio Three: 2.30-7.00pm. Recording: 'Here Comes The Sun' (SI onto take 15). Studio Two: 7.00pm-12.30am. Recording: 'Something' (SI onto take 36, tape reduction take 36 into takes 38 and 39). P: George Martin. E: Phil McDonald. 2E: Alan Parsons.

A day of George Harrison overdubs, with handclaps and a harmonium being added to 'Here Comes The Sun' and lead vocal (George), backing vocals (Paul) and handclapping (George, Paul and Ringo) being added to take 36 of 'Something', even though a reduction of this take had previously been made.

Now, with the new overdubs, the reduction was done again, into takes 38 and 39, the latter being 'best'. George Harrison was evidently in the studio two control room for the mixdowns, for he was able to remind Phil McDonald that the latter model should be numbered 39.

Thursday 17 July

Studio Three: 2.30-6.30pm. Recording: 'Oh! Darling' (SI onto take 16). Studio Two: 6.30-11.15pm. Recording: 'Octopus's Garden' (SI onto take 32). P: George Martin. E: Phil McDonald. 2E: Alan Parsons.

"Perhaps my main memory of the *Abbey Road* sessions is of Paul coming into studio three at two o'clock or 2.30 each afternoon, on his own, to do the vocal on 'Oh! Darling'," says Alan Parsons. "That was a feature of the *Abbey Road* sessions: you very rarely saw all four Beatles together. It was either John or Paul or George working on their various things, perhaps only getting together to hear something back. But Paul came in several days running to do the lead vocal on 'Oh! Darling'. He'd come in, sing it and say 'No, that's not it, I'll try it again tomorrow'. He only tried it once per day, I suppose he wanted to capture a certain rawness which could only be done once before the voice changed. I remember him saying 'five years ago I could have done this in a flash', referring, I suppose, to the days of 'Long Tall Sally' and 'Kansas City'."

John Kurlander also witnessed these overdubs. "I think Paul wanted this 'first thing in the morning' quality, or maybe it was 'last thing at night'. Whatever it was, he came in early each day, an hour before anybody else, to do his piece, always replacing the previous one until he got the one he liked."

(Note. On this day, Paul overdubbed the vocal onto take 16 of the recording but all future work was added to take 26.)

The recording of 'Oh! Darling' had begun in April, and it was another April number which took up the evening session: backing vocals (Paul and George), a piano (Paul) and sound effects being added to the basic track of Ringo's 'Octopus's Garden'. This song was not altogether dissimilar to 'Yellow Submarine' and, like that number, 'Octopus's Garden' had some interesting sound effects incorporated into the recording. Paul and George were responsible for creating most of these, singing in very high pitch and having Phil McDonald use limiters and compressors to produce a gargling vocal sound, matching the song's lyric about being "under the sea". Not wishing to be outdone, Ringo thought back to 'Yellow Submarine' and came up with the idea of blowing bubbles into a glass of water. "That was miked very closely to capture all the little bubbles and sounds," recalls Alan Brown, technical engineer on the session.

Friday 18 July

Studio Three: 2.30-8.00pm. Recording: 'Oh! Darling' (SI onto take 26); 'Octopus's Garden' (SI onto take 32). Studio Two (control room only): 8.00-10.30pm. Mono mixing: 'Octopus's Garden' (remixes 1-7, from take 32). Stereo mixing: 'Octopus's Garden' (remixes 10-14, from take 32). P: George Martin.   E: Phil McDonald.   2E: Alan Parsons.

Another attempt by Paul to capture the right vocal for 'Oh! Darling', plus an attempt by Ringo to do likewise with 'Octopus's Garden', onto which sundry percussion was also added. Rough mono and stereo remixes of this latter title brought the session to a close.

Monday 21 July

Studio Three: 2.30-9.30pm. Recording: 'Come Together' (takes 1-8). Studio Two (control room only): 9.30-10.00pm. Tape copying: 'Come Together' (of take 6, called take 9). P: George Martin.   E: Geoff Emerick/Phil McDonald.   2E: John Kurlander.

John Lennon had kept a low profile during recent Beatles recording sessions and he hadn't offered a new song composition to the group since 'The Ballad Of John And Yoko' on 14 April. (He and Yoko had released 'Give Peace A Chance' however, as the Plastic Ono Band.) In fact, new compositions were generally a little thin on the ground at this time, with recordings for the last new song, 'Maxwell's Silver Hammer', having begun on 9 July.

But John returned with a vengeance in this session, scorching through some terrific takes of his 'Come Together', recording the basic track on a four-track machine, then later copying the 'best' take (six) across to eight-track. Take one was a magnificent version, marked by a supreme Lennon vocal free of the massive tape echo which was applied later. Freed too from the restrictions of a guitar, John was able to sing while simultaneously clapping his hands (again, later applied with tape echo) immediately after each time he sang the line "Shoot me!". There was only one guitar on the tape at this stage and that was George's, Paul played bass and Ringo played drums. John tapped a tambourine part-way through, too. It was a memorable recording.

"On the finished record you can really only hear the word 'shoot'," says Geoff Emerick, "the bass guitar note falls where the 'me' is." This was Emerick's first full day back as the Beatles' balance engineer. "I started working with them again at Paul McCartney's request, just a week after I had left EMI to run Apple Studios. I went back to Abbey Road as the first freelance engineer that had walked in the building."

[It is interesting to note how, due to the Beatles, EMI – and particularly EMI Studios – suffered two exoduses of staff. In 1965, with the mirrored success and fame of George Martin, he, Ron Richards and John Burgess left to form AIR, taking with them others like Emerick, Dave Harries, Keith Slaughter and various secretarial staff in later years. (And Norman Smith left Abbey Road for Manchester Square to shore up the A&R department.) With Apple, the Beatles tempted away Emerick, Ron Pender, Malcolm Davies (the first to go, he cut the masters for 'Hey Jude' and Mary Hopkin's 'Those Were The Days' at Apple in August 1968), Phil McDonald, John Smith, John Barrett, Eddie Klein and several others. They also offered jobs to Terry Condon and John Skinner but both turned the offers down.]

Tuesday 22 July

Studio Three: 2.30-9.30pm. Recording: 'Oh! Darling' (SI onto take 26); 'Come Together' (SI onto take 9). P: George Martin.   E: Geoff Emerick/Phil McDonald.   2E: John Kurlander.

Another McCartney attempt at the 'Oh! Darling' lead vocal, plus overdubbing of a new lead vocal, electric piano, rhythm guitar and maraca onto 'Come Together'.

Wednesday 23 July

Studio Three: 2.30-11.30pm. Recording: 'Oh! Darling' (SI onto take 26); 'Come Together' (SI onto take 9); 'Ending' (working title of 'The End') (takes 1-7). P: George Martin. E: Geoff Emerick/Phil McDonald.   2E: John Kurlander.

Three weeks since the commencement of 'Golden Slumbers'/'Carry That Weight', with its open-ending to facilitate the following song in the medley, that number was begun, its start dovetailing perfectly into its LP predecessor. At this point the piece had no title other than 'Ending' but it would become 'The End'. Never was a title so apt; aside from the 23-second 'Her Majesty', tacked right on the very end of the LP, almost into the run-out groove, 'The End' was the last song on the last-recorded Beatles album.

A good deal of rehearsal time must have preceded the rolling of tapes during this session, for – after John Lennon counted the group in – right from take one this was a tight recording, picking up with some lead guitar notes and paving the way for Ringo's one and only drum solo on a Beatles song. The group had seven attempts at the song and, interestingly, the style of the drum solo changed with each. The final edition, take seven, was a highly effective one, the solo lasting almost 16 seconds. It was spread over two of the available eight recording tracks, a major breakthrough. On Beatles recordings the drums only usually occupied one.

Interestingly, the final eight-track tape reveals that when this song's many overdubs had been recorded, other instruments featured alongside Ringo's drum piece: two lead guitars and a tambourine. But these were omitted in the final remix to leave the solo just that – solo.

(Note. The 'best' take, seven, was only 1'20" in duration at this stage. Later additions like a lengthy lead guitar solo, more drums, an orchestra, vocals and a piano track doubled that duration to 2'41", although tight editing of the best mix brought it back down to 2'05".)

After the recording finished, at 11.30pm, the Beatles, George Martin, Phil McDonald and John Kurlander trooped across to the control room of studio two for a one-hour playback, ending at 12.30am. One other recording they would have heard was another Paul McCartney attempt at a lead vocal for 'Oh! Darling', taped before the 'Ending' session began. This was actually the final attempt; the released version.

Thursday 24 July

Studio Two: 2.30-3.30pm. Recording: 'Come And Get It' (take 1). Stereo mixing: 'Come And Get It' (remix 1, from take 1). Tape copying: 'Come And Get It' (of remix stereo 1). P: n/a. E: Phil McDonald. 2E: John Kurlander. Studio Two: 3.30-10.30pm. Recording: 'Here Comes The Sun-King' (working title of 'Sun King'/'Mean Mr Mustard') (takes 1-35). P: George Martin. E: Geoff Emerick/Phil McDonald. 2E: John Kurlander.

The rate at which the Beatles were giving away new compositions to other artistes (as opposed to other artistes recording cover versions) had slowed to a trickle compared to the days of 1963 and 1964. But they hadn't stopped altogether, indeed the launch of Apple Records had provided a minor resurgence, with George giving Jackie Lomax 'Sour Milk Sea' and Paul donating 'Goodbye' to Mary Hopkin and 'Come And Get It' to Badfinger. To best illustrate lyrics and arrangement it was customary for the songwriter(s) to provide the artiste with a demo version, roughly recorded, usually with an acoustic guitar or piano.

In the case of the Beatles, demos were usually recorded privately, with acetate discs cut likewise, usually by music publisher Dick James. But Paul recorded 'Come And Get It', solo though with overdubs, at Abbey Road before this day's Beatles session. John Lennon was there in the control room – his voice can be heard on the session tape – but it was Paul, and Paul alone, who did the recording, first singing and playing piano, live, then – after a call up to Phil McDonald "OK, give us it on headphones and

I'll track it" – overdubbing a double-tracked vocal with maracas, then drums, then bass guitar. It was mixed for stereo, a copy of that mix was made for Paul to give to Badfinger, and the job was done. All in one hour! And that wasn't all. Paul also produced the Badfinger recording, done at Abbey Road in one day on 2 August, which was virtually a note-for-note copy of his version, with only a slight increase in the tempo being responsible for the timing differences: Paul's version being 2'32", Badfinger's hit (number four in the charts) 2'21".

John Lennon may have later declared his dislike for the medley side of *Abbey Road* but he contributed a large part of it. Recorded on this day was 'Sun King' and 'Mean Mr Mustard' – the two were not segued, they were taped as one straight recording – although for a while they masqueraded under the eventually discarded and certainly confusing first-line title 'Here Comes The Sun-King', nothing whatever to do with George's 'Here Comes The Sun'. The title had changed by 29 July.

'Sun King' and 'Mean Mr Mustard' were both Lennon compositions, totalling 3'37" in duration (2'31" and 1'06" respectively), both with somewhat odd lyrics. The former drifted into nonsense Spanish and Italian verse, the latter was all about a most peculiar chap who, among other unsavoury habits, kept "a ten-bob note up his nose". The basic track of this double-recording was taped during this 24 July session: bass, drums, electric and rhythm guitars and a John Lennon guide vocal, and once again this original tape displays the cohesion of the Beatles as a musical unit, with a thorough understanding between the four. All the basic ideas were there right from Ringo's delicately brushed cymbal which signalled the start. Even when the session suddenly slipped into a jam session – John singing a complete version of 'Ain't She Sweet' and then, clearly in Gene Vincent mood, following with 'Who Slapped John?' and 'Be-Bop-A-Lula' – the sound, though busked and impromptu, was also good and precise. These would undoubtedly have made strong contenders for the *Get Back* album had they been recorded in January and not July 1969.

Friday 25 July

Studio Two: 2.30pm-2.30am. Recording: 'Here Comes The Sun-King' (working title of 'Sun King'/'Mean Mr Mustard') (SI onto take 35); 'Come Together' (SI onto take 9); 'Polythene Pam'/'She Came In Through The Bathroom Window' (takes 1-39). P: George Martin. E: Geoff Emerick/Phil McDonald. 2E: John Kurlander.

Just as 'Sun King' and 'Mean Mr Mustard' were recorded as one continuous piece, so were 'Polythene Pam' and 'She Came In Through The Bathroom Window' (the latter having first been rehearsed at Apple on 22 January). But whereas the two former titles were both John Lennon songs, 'Polythene Pam' and 'She Came In Through The Bathroom Window' were not: the first was entirely John, the second entirely Paul. With the exception of 'A Day In The Life' – a Lennon song for which McCartney contributed a small section – this was the first time that a song from John and a song from Paul had been recorded *as one*.

Encompassing both songs in this manner, the recordings began with some sharp Lennon jabs of a 12-string acoustic guitar (the start of 'Polythene Pam') and ended with Paul's vocal line "...on the phone to me, oh yeah" (the close of 'She Came In Through The Bathroom Window'). In between, on this first day, was a basic track of bass (Paul), drums (Ringo), lead guitar (George) and that acoustic guitar (John), plus off-mike guide vocals from John and Paul where applicable. There was an amusing moment when John commented that Ringo's drumming style for the recording "sounds like Dave Clark!" (It wasn't meant as a compliment.) Perhaps this explains why the drum

track – along with the lead vocal and bass guitar tracks – was taped again later in the session – between 10.30pm and 2.30am – as an overdub onto take 39. The songs' remaining overdubs, and they were many, were made on 28 and 30 July.

Also recorded during this session were overdubs for 'Sun King'/'Mean Mr Mustard' (vocals, piano and organ) and for 'Come Together' (vocal harmonies).

Monday 28 July

Studio Three: 2.30-8.00pm. Recording: 'Polythene Pam'/'She Came In Through The Bathroom Window' (SI onto take 39). Studio Two (control room only): 8.00-8.30pm. Recording: 'Polythene Pam'/'She Came In Through The Bathroom Window' (tape reduction take 39 into take 40). P: George Martin. E: Geoff Emerick/Phil McDonald. 2E: John Kurlander.

Numerous overdubs for 'Polythene Pam' and 'She Came In Through The Bathroom Window': another lead vocal, acoustic and electric guitars, tambourine

and other bits of percussion, electric piano and an ordinary piano. The last half-hour of the session was

spent making a reduction mixdown to facilitate future, additional taping.

Tuesday 29 July

Studio Three: 2.30-10.45pm. Recording: 'Come Together' (SI onto take 9); 'Sun King'/'Mean Mr Mustard' (SI onto take 35). P: George Martin. E: Geoff Emerick/Phil McDonald. 2E: John Kurlander.

A guitar overdub for the middle part of 'Come Together' and vocal, piano, organ and percussion

overdubs onto 'Sun King'/'Mean Mr Mustard'.

A Linda McCartney photograph showing an increasingly typical late-1960s Beatles control room scene: artiste at the console, producer observing. Such a situation would have been laughingly dismissed — were it not downright impossible — earlier in the decade.

The recording sheet for the first trial edit of the *Abbey Road* medley. Note the positioning of 'Her Majesty'.

Wednesday 30 July

Studio Two (control room only): 2.00-3.30pm. Recording: 'You Never Give Me Your Money' (tape reduction take 30 into takes 37-42). Studio Three: 3.30-10.30pm. Recording: 'Come Together' (SI onto take 9); 'Polythene Pam'/'She Came In Through The Bathroom Window' (SI onto take 40); 'You Never Give Me Your Money' (SI onto take 40); 'Golden Slumbers'/'Carry That Weight' (SI onto take 17). Studio Two (control room only): 10.30pm-2.30am. Stereo mixing: 'You Never Give Me Your Money' (remix 1, from take 40); 'Sun King'/'Mean Mr Mustard' (remix 1, from take 35); 'Her Majesty' (remix 1, from take 3); 'Polythene Pam'/'She Came In Through the Bathroom Window' (remix 1, from take 40); 'Golden Slumbers'/'Carry That Weight' (remix 1, from take 17); 'Ending' (working title of 'The End') (remix 1, from take 7). Editing, crossfading and tape compilation: 'You Never Give Me Your Money'; 'Sun King'/'Mean Mr Mustard'; 'Her Majesty'; 'Polythene Pam'/'She Came In Through The Bathroom Window'; 'Golden Slumbers'/'Carry That Weight'; 'Ending' (working title of 'The End'). P: George Martin.   E: Geoff Emerick/Phil McDonald.   2E: John Kurlander.

A session involving overdubbing of: guitars onto 'Come Together'; vocals, percussion and guitar onto 'Polythene Pam'/'She Came In Through The Bathroom Window'; vocals onto a new reduction mix of 'You Never Give Me Your Money'; and vocals onto 'Golden Slumbers'/'Carry That Weight'. These activities occupied the 2.00-10.30pm time slot, but there was no going home yet.

The time had come to piece together the constituent parts of the album medley, to see how the songs moulded together and which required additional work and perfecting. Few of the songs were yet in a finished state, 'The End', for example, did not have any vocals, but this trial edit was designed to highlight any major faults in the *theory* of the medley, or 'The Long One'/'Huge Melody', as it was presently called by the Beatles and the production staff.

Once every song had been treated to a rough stereo remix the editing and crossfading began, in this order: 'You Never Give Me Your Money', 'Sun King'/'Mean Mr Mustard', 'Her Majesty', 'Polythene Pam'/'She Came In Through The Bathroom Window', 'Golden Slumbers'/'Carry That Weight' and 'The End'. The total duration was 15′30″. Fine. A few stitches to be

picked up here and there, but otherwise fine, it all fitted well. Except for one song.

"We did all the remixes and crossfades to overlap the songs, Paul was there, and we heard it together for the first time," recalls John Kurlander. "He said 'I don't like 'Her Majesty', throw it away,' so I cut it out – but I accidentally left in the last note. He said 'It's only a rough mix, it doesn't matter', in other words, don't bother about making a clean edit because it's only a rough mix. I said to Paul 'What shall I do with it?'. 'Throw it away,' he replied.

"I'd been told never to throw anything away, so after he left I picked it up off the floor put about 20 seconds of red leader tape before it and stuck it onto the end of the edit tape. The next day, down at Apple, Malcolm Davies cut a playback lacquer of the whole sequence [Mal Evans took the tape to Apple on 31 July, returning it to EMI on the same day] and, even though I'd written on the box that 'Her Majesty' was unwanted, he too thought, 'Well, mustn't throw anything away, I'll put it on at the end'. I'm only assuming this, but when Paul got that lacquer he must have *liked* hearing 'Her Majesty' tacked on the end. The Beatles always picked up on accidental things. It

came as a nice little surprise there at the end, and he didn't mind. We never remixed 'Her Majesty' again, that was the mix which ended up on the finished LP."

Thus is solved a long-standing Beatles mystery: why, on the *Abbey Road* LP, the final acoustic guitar chord is missing from 'Her Majesty'. The answer is that it was left buried in this unreleased rough edit of the medley, at the beginning of 'Polythene Pam'. And this also explains the appearance of a crashing electric guitar chord at the *beginning* of the acoustic 'Her Majesty' – it is actually the last note of the 'Mean Mr Mustard' rough remix. Dave Harries was involved in the session too: "They cut it all again for the final mix but they did it in much the same way because I believe that you can take 'Her Majesty', edit it back in and it will almost fit."

The most problematic crossfade in the medley was of 'You Never Give Me Your Money' into 'Sun King' and this was tried several times during the session, the best idea, so far, being to merge the songs on an organ note. Paul would come up with the perfect solution on 5 August.

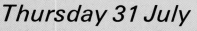

George Harrison trying an experiment with Paul's Fender 'Jazz Bass' guitar.

Thursday 31 July

Studio Two: 2.30pm-1.15am. Recording: 'You Never Give Me Your Money' (SI onto take 30); 'Golden Slumbers'/'Carry That Weight' (SI onto take 17). P: George Martin.   E: Geoff Emerick/Phil McDonald.   2E: John Kurlander.

The experimental edit of the medley proved to Paul that the 30 July reduction mix of 'You Never Give Me Your Money', which took the song from take 30 into take 40, was unnecessary. Ignoring the additional vocal overdub onto the latter, he returned to take 30

and completed the recording on this day, taping bass and piano tracks.

The only other overdubs taped this day were drums, timpani and a vocal for 'Golden Slumbers'/'Carry

That Weight'. Ringo and Paul both had attempts at achieving the right timpani sound, but the tape does not reveal who recorded the final superimposition.

Friday 1 August

Studio Two: 2.30-10.30pm. Recording: 'Because' (takes 1-23, SI onto take 16). P: George Martin.   E: Geoff Emerick/Phil McDonald.   2E: John Kurlander.

It has been said before, but there was more to John Lennon than rock, rock, rock, and it would indeed be a foolish person who thought John capable of only raunchy material. 'Because' was one of the most beautiful of all Beatles recordings, an exquisite three-part harmony venture, and it was pure Lennon, excepting, that is, a little influence from Ludwig Van Beethoven. It was Beethoven's piano sonata in C Sharp minor, opus 27 number two ('The Moonlight Sonata') which inspired 'Because'. Yoko was playing it on the piano one day and John, in clearly

inspirational mood, reversed the chords, added some simple but eloquent lyrics and the song was written. As simple as that.

A total of 23 takes of the basic track were recorded on this day, take 16 being 'best'. This consisted of George Martin playing a Baldwin spinet electric harpsichord, John playing a repeated electric guitar riff and Paul adding bass. Ringo was there too, gently tapping out a beat on the hi-hat, but this was for the musicians' headphones only – it was not recorded on the tape.

"Ringo was our drum machine," says George Martin today. "Having done the backing track," he continues, "John, Paul and George sang the song in harmony. Then we overlaid it twice more, making nine-part harmony altogether, three voices recorded three times. I was literally telling them what notes to sing."

(George has described here the song after a 4 August overdub. On this first day just one of those three-part vocal recordings was made, between 7.30 and the 10.30pm end of the session.)

Monday 4 August

Studio Two: 2.30-9.00pm. Recording: 'Because' (SI onto take 16). P: George Martin.   E: Geoff Emerick/Phil McDonald.   2E: John Kurlander. Studio Three (control room only): 7.15-8.45pm. Stereo mixing: 'Something' (unnumbered rough remix, from take 39); 'Here Comes The Sun' (unnumbered rough remix, from take 15). P: George Harrison. E: Phil McDonald.   2E: Alan Parsons.

The taping of the magnificent 'Because' three-part harmony vocals was concluded on this day with the filling of two more tracks on the eight-track tape. The sum total of nine parts coalesced joyfully on the finished recording, marking a nostalgic throwback

from this last Beatles album to some of the group's earliest recordings, like 'This Boy' and 'Yes It Is'.

When his vocal duties had been discharged, George Harrison nipped into the control room of studio three,

with Phil McDonald and Alan Parsons, to produce rough stereo remixes of 'Something' and 'Here Comes The Sun'. These revealed to him that both required additional overdubbing; an acetate of the 'Something' mix was given to George Martin so that he could arrange an orchestral score.

Tuesday 5 August

Studio Three (control room only): 2.30-6.30pm. Recording: 'You Never Give Me Your Money' (sound effects takes 1-5). Abbey Road, Room 43 and Studio Two: 6.30-10.45pm. Recording: 'Because' (SI onto take 16); 'Ending' (working title of 'The End') (SI onto take 7). P: George Martin. E: Geoff Emerick/Phil McDonald. 2E: John Kurlander.

Home experimentation with Brennell tape machines had not ended with *Revolver*. Paul McCartney, in particular, would still spend spare time in the sound equipment room of his St John's Wood house, making tape loops. On this day, 5 August 1969, Paul took a plastic bag containing a dozen loose strands of mono tape into Abbey Road, where – together with the production staff – he spent the afternoon in the studio three control room transferring the best of these onto professional four-track tape. The effects – sounding like bells, birds, bubbles and crickets chirping – allowed for a perfect crossfade in the medley, made on 14 August, from 'Sun King' into 'You Never Give Me Your Money', solving the problem first brought to light in the experimental edit on 30 July. (Note. Inside the plastic bag was another tape loop which Paul intended for George's 'Here Comes The Sun'. It was never used.)

It seems somehow apt that the Beatles should have been among the first to make use of a new musical instrument which, after their demise, would shape the future of rock music almost as profoundly as they had done: the synthesizer, as invented by one Dr Robert Moog. Compared to today's microchip micro-everything, the early "Moog's" were veritable monstrosities, with a huge bank of wires and a large two-tiered keyboard. George Harrison, in particular, expressed great interest in the invention and bought one early in 1969, recording an album at his home, *Electronic Sounds*, full of its strange noises, which was released in May by Apple's short-lived "experimental" offshoot, Zapple. Now, in early August, George had his Moog transported into EMI for the *Abbey Road* sessions, and with Mike Vickers – the Manfred Mann instrumentalist who also conducted the 'All You Need Is Love' orchestra – recruited as expert consultant/programmer, the Beatles began to make constructive use of the instrument in the closing weeks of the *Abbey Road* sessions.

"The Moog was set up in Room 43," recalls John Kurlander, "and the sound was fed from there by a mono cable to whichever control room we were in. All four Beatles – but particularly George – expressed great interest in it, trying out different things."

"Everybody was fascinated by it," says Alan Parsons. "We were all crowding around to have a look. Paul used the Moog for the solo in 'Maxwell's Silver Hammer' but the notes were not from the keyboard. He did that with a continuous ribbon-slide thing, just moving his finger up and down on an endless ribbon.

It's very difficult to find the right notes, rather like a violin, but Paul picked it up straight away. He can pick up anything musical in a couple of days."

"I think the Beatles used the Moog with great subtlety," says Nick Webb. "Others in a similar situation would probably have gone completely over the top with it. It's there, on the record, but not obtrusively. Perhaps they weren't sure it was going to catch on!"

'Because' was the recipient of the first Moog overdubs, played by George and recorded twice, for the last two available tape tracks, in a studio two session commencing at 6.30pm. With this, the song was complete.

The final overdub on this day was of vocals for 'The End', the song's first.

(Note. Concurrent with these activities, between 8.00 and 9.30pm, balance engineer Tony Clark and tape operator Alan Parsons were in the control room of studio three making a stereo reel-to-reel tape copy from an ordinary cassette of some of John and Yoko's latest privately recorded sounds. The tape was taken away by the Lennons' assistant, Anthony Fawcett.)

Wednesday 6 August

Studio Three: 2.30-11.00pm. Recording: 'Here Comes The Sun' (SI onto take 15). P: George Martin. E: Phil McDonald. 2E: Alan Parsons. Abbey Road, Room 43 and Studio Two (control room only): 2.30-11.00pm. Recording: 'Maxwell's Silver Hammer' (tape reduction take 21 into takes 22-27, with simultaneous SI). P: George Martin. E: Tony Clark. 2E: John Kurlander. Studio Two (control room only): 11.00pm-1.00am. Stereo mixing: 'Maxwell's Silver Hammer' (remixes 14-26, from take 27). P: George Martin. E: Tony Clark/Phil McDonald. 2E: John Kurlander.

Two simultaneous sessions. In studio three George Harrison overdubbed guitar onto 'Here Comes The Sun'; in Room 43, fed into studio two, Paul recorded his Moog synthesizer overdub onto simultaneous reduction mixdowns of 'Maxwell's Silver Hammer', with ten stereo remixes concluding the session (numbered 14-26 but there were no remixes 19-21).

"I got involved in the last three weeks of *Abbey Road*," says Tony Clark. "They kept two studios running and I would be asked to sit in studio two or three – usually three – just to be there, at the Beatles' beck and call, whenever someone wanted to come in and do an overdub. At this stage of the album I don't think I saw the four of them together."

Thursday 7 August

Studio Two (control room only): 2.30-6.00pm. Stereo mixing: 'Come Together' (remixes 1-10, from take 9). Studio Three: 6.00-12.00pm. Recording: 'Ending' (working title of 'The End') (SI onto take 7). P: George Martin. E: Geoff Emerick/Phil McDonald. 2E: John Kurlander.

Stereo remixing of 'Come Together' in studio two (ten versions, the first being 'best') and vocals/electric guitar overdubs for 'The End' in studio three.

An afternoon (2.30-5.30pm) booking for the Beatles in studio three was not required and the studio remained empty.

Friday 8 August

Studio Two: 2.30-9.00pm. Recording: 'Ending' (working title of 'The End') (SI onto take 7); 'I Want You' (later known as 'I Want You (She's So Heavy)') (SI onto unnumbered Trident master). P: George Martin. E: Geoff Emerick/Phil McDonald. 2E: John Kurlander. Studio Three: 5.30-9.45pm. Recording: 'Oh! Darling' (SI onto take 26). P: George Martin. E: Tony Clark. 2E: Alan Parsons.

The recording session may not have started until 2.30 in the afternoon but at 10.00 in the morning the four Beatles gathered together at EMI Studios for a quite different purpose. With photographer Iain Macmillan balanced up a step-ladder in the middle of Abbey Road, John, Ringo, Paul and George strode across the zebra [pedestrian] crossing just outside the studio gates while Macmillan snapped away. The Beatles crossed the road several times while Macmillan took six quick shots, a friendly policeman obligingly holding up traffic. A while later, Paul studied the six transparencies with a magnifying glass, and picked the best of the six for the sleeve of *Abbey Road*.

With the probable exception of their own *Sgt Pepper's Lonely Hearts Club Band*, the Beatles' cover for *Abbey Road* is the most imitated and famous of all rock music sleeves. To this day, and doubtless for a long time to come, not a single day passes without tourists visiting the zebra crossing to pose for their own cameras, many removing their shoes and socks to walk barefoot *à là* Paul McCartney on 8 August 1969, a fine summer's day. (In two of the shots he had shoes on, in the other four he did not.)

A certain section of Beatles fans interpreted Paul's barefootedness as an indication – especially when allied with other "clues" – of his death and replacement by a McCartney clone, a fact kept strictly hush-hush by the other Beatles. Why else would there be a Volkswagen Beetle in the *Abbey Road* cover picture, especially one with the number plate ending 281F? (This was taken to read 28 IF by the same obsessives, implying that Paul would have been 28 IF he were still living – in fact he would have been 27.) As the then Abbey Road tape operator Chris Blair jokes, "Every morning – except for that one – I parked my car by the studio. The guy with the VW, he lived in the block of flats next door, always parked there too. Because of the LP sleeve he had his number plates taken time and time again. I just wonder what my old Morris Minor would be worth now had I parked it there that morning…" (More than £2,300, Chris. That's the price which the actual LMW 281F Volkswagen sold for at a Sotheby's auction in 1986!)

The cover shoot took about ten minutes in all but it was too early to start the recording session, booked for 2.30. To kill time, Paul took John back to his Cavendish Avenue house, George went with Mal Evans to London Zoo in nearby Regent's Park and Ringo went shopping. They re-grouped back at EMI in time for the afternoon session.

After the overdub of drums and bass onto 'The End', two sessions ran concurrently for the remainder of the evening. Paul went alone into studio three to overdub lead guitar and tambourine onto 'Oh! Darling' while, in studio two, John added Moog synthesizer sounds and effects, and Ringo added drums, to the original 23 February Trident master recording of 'I Want You', *not*, note, the 18 April reduction mixdown of same. (The released version was an edit of the two.)

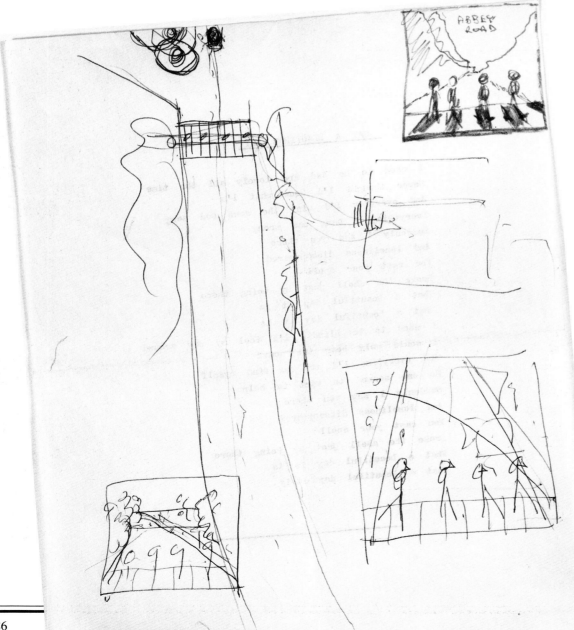

Paul McCartney's sketched ideas for the *Abbey Road* album cover, upon which (in the top right corner) photographer Iain Macmillan made a more detailed plan, executed almost exactly on 8 August.

Monday 11 August

Studio Three (control room only): 1.00-2.00pm. Mono tape copying: 'Dig It' (of 13 March stereo mix); 'Maxwell's Silver Hammer' (of remix stereo 18). P: n/a.   E and 2E: Phil McDonald. Studio Two: 2.30-11.30pm. Recording: 'I Want You (She's So Heavy)' (SI onto take 1); 'Oh! Darling' (SI onto take 26); 'Here Comes The Sun' (SI onto take 15). Tape copying: 'I Want You (She's So Heavy)' (of take 1). Editing: 'I Want You (She's So Heavy)' (from take 1 into unnumbered Trident master). P: George Martin.   E: Geoff Emerick/Phil McDonald.   2E: John Kurlander.

'I Want You' only became titled 'I Want You (She's So Heavy)' during and after this session, which saw the re-recording of tremendous harmony vocals by John, Paul and George, constantly repeating the one line "she's so heavy" onto tracks four and seven of the 18 April take one reduction mixdown. With this, the song was complete, although John Lennon was clearly undecided about which version to release – the

original Trident master, with overdubs, or the 18 April reduction of same, with different overdubs. At this point he had the new "she's so heavy" inserts cut into *both* versions to delay the final decision, not made until 20 August.

The next overdub was of vocal harmonies for 'Oh! Darling', also bringing the song to completion, and

then George ended the session by adding more guitars to 'Here Comes The Sun'.

Earlier in the day, Phil McDonald supervised mono tape copies of two stereo mixes – 'Dig It' (from *Get Back*) and 'Maxwell's Silver Hammer'. These were taken Mal Evans to Malcolm Davies at Apple for the cutting of acetate discs.

Tuesday 12 August

Studio Two (control room only): 7.00pm-2.00am. Stereo mixing: 'Oh! Darling' (remixes 5-9, from take 26); 'Because' (remixes 1 and 2, from take 16); 'Maxwell's Silver Hammer' (remixes 27-36, from take 27). P: George Martin.   E: Geoff Emerick/Phil McDonald.   2E: John Kurlander.

More stereo mixing.

Wednesday 13 August

Studio Two (control room only): 2.30-9.15pm. Stereo mixing: 'You Never Give Me Your Money' (remixes 20-27, from take 30). P: George Martin.   E: Geoff Emerick/Phil McDonald.   2E: Alan Parsons.

A fresh batch of stereo mixes for 'You Never Give Me Your Money', starting with number 20 and ending with 27, but with 23 'best'.

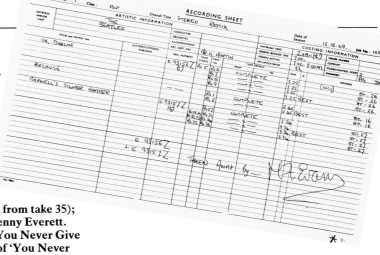

Thursday 14 August

Studio Two (control room only): 2.30pm-2.30am. Stereo mixing: 'Sun King'/'Mean Mr Mustard' (remixes 20-24, from take 35); 'Maxwell's Silver Hammer' (edit piece remix 37, from take 27). Mono recording: John Lennon interviewed by Kenny Everett. Stereo mixing: 'Polythene Pam'/'She Came In Through The Bathroom Window' (remixes 20-32, from take 40); 'You Never Give Me Your Money' into 'Sun King'/'Mean Mr Mustard' (stereo crossfade remixes 1-11, from sound effects take 5 of 'You Never Give Me Your Money'). Editing: 'Maxwell's Silver Hammer' (of stereo remixes 34 and 37); 'Sun King'/'Mean Mr Mustard' (remix stereo 22) joined to 'Polythene Pam'/'She Came In Through The Bathroom Window' (remix stereo 32). P: George Martin.   E: Geoff Emerick/Phil McDonald.   2E: Alan Parsons.

Remixing, crossfading and editing of finished songs for the medley. During this 12-hour session, stereo remixes of 'Sun King'/'Mean Mr Mustard' and 'Polythene Pam'/'She Came In Through The Bathroom Window' were joined together by means of a hard edit, without the merest hint of a gap between the two. And eleven attempts at crossfading 'You Never Give Me Your Money' into 'Sun King'/'Mean Mr Mustard', via Paul's 5 August tape loop sound effects, resulted in what was presumed for the moment to be the master, although it would be re-made again on 21 August.

Also on this day, 'Maxwell's Silver Hammer' was completed with a stereo remix of an edit piece, which was then cut into the previous 'best', remix 34.

The only break from the *Abbey Road* activity occurred when disc-jockey Kenny Everett visited the control

room of studio two to interview John Lennon. This was not the first time Everett had been to EMI Studios to interview one or more of the Beatles, but it was the first time such a visit was documented on a daily recording sheet because, on this occasion, Everett utilised studio equipment and a studio tape, the only copy of which he took away with him.

The EP Collection

Twist and Shout · The Beatles
Twist and Shout
THE BEATLES
mono

FROM ME TO YOU · THANK YOU GIRL
PLEASE PLEASE ME · LOVE ME DO
THE BEATLES' HITS
mono
THE BEATLES
Photo: Angus McBean

I SAW HER STANDING THERE
MISERY · ANNA · CHAINS
PARLOPHONE
THE BEATLES
No. 1

PARLOPHONE
BEATLES FOR SALE No. 2
EMI
mono
Photo: Robert Freeman

PARLOPHONE · EMI
ANY TIME AT ALL · I'LL CRY INSTEAD
THINGS WE SAID TODAY · WHEN I GET HOME
mono
Extracts from the Album
A HARD DAY'S NIGHT
THE BEATLES

ROCK AND ROLL MUSIC · NO REPLY
EIGHT DAYS A WEEK · I'M A LOSER
mono
BEATLES FOR SALE
Photo: Robert W

Friday 15 August

Studio One into Studio Two (control room): 2.30-5.30pm. Recording: 'Golden Slumbers'/'Carry That Weight' (SI onto take 17); 'Ending' (working title of 'The End') (SI onto take 7).
Studio One into Studio Two: 7.00pm-1.15am. Recording: 'Something' (SI onto take 39); 'Here Comes The Sun' (SI onto take 15). P: George Martin. E: Geoff Emerick/Phil McDonald. 2E: Alan Parsons.

It made sound economic sense – in time as well as money – to save all the *Abbey Road* orchestral overdubs until the closing days of the LP and do them in one go. During this long session orchestral tracks were taped for 'Golden Slumbers'/'Carry That Weight', 'The End', 'Something' and 'Here Comes The Sun'.

For the first time on a Beatles session, close-circuit television was employed to link two studios. (Previously, as Phil McDonald humorously recounts, the linking was subject to the vagaries of voice: "All right, Bert? Are you ready?") While George Martin was conducting the recruited musicians through his own immaculate scores in the huge studio one, the remainder of the production team – Geoff Emerick, Phil McDonald and Alan Parsons – were monitoring the proceedings, sound and vision, in the control room of studio two. For 'Something', George Harrison shuttled back and forth between studio one, where he shared the conductor's podium with George Martin for a time, and studio two, where he oversaw the sound recording, virtually as "producer", and where – on the floor of the studio – he taped a new and memorable lead guitar solo for the song's middle eight (actually, barely different from the song's previous best guitar track).

The names of the musicians are, alas, no longer on file, but a listing of the instruments is, and these were as follows:–
For 'Golden Slumbers'/'Carry That Weight' and 'The End': 12 violins, four violas, four cellos, one string bass, four horns, three trumpets, one trombone and one bass trombone.
For 'Something': 12 violins, four violas, four cellos and one string bass.
For 'Here Comes The Sun': four violas, four cellos, one string bass, two clarinets, two alto flutes, two flutes, two piccolos.

"It was a mammoth session," recalls Alan Brown. "We had a large number of lines linking the studios and we were all walking around the building with walkie-talkies trying to communicate with each other. The orchestral overdub for 'The End' was the most elaborate I have ever heard: a 30-piece playing for not too many seconds – and mixed about 40 dBs down. It cost a lot of money: all the musicians have to be paid, fed and watered; I screw every pound note out of it whenever I play the record!"

Monday 18 August

Studio Two: 2.30-10.30pm. Stereo mixing: 'Golden Slumbers'/'Carry That Weight' (remixes 1 and 2, from take 17). Recording: 'Ending' (working title of 'The End') (SI onto take 7).
Stereo mixing: 'Ending' (working title of 'The End') (remixes 1-6, from take 7). P: George Martin. E: Geoff Emerick/Phil McDonald. 2E: Alan Parsons.

Stereo mixing, with one new overdub: Paul's very brief (four seconds) piano track for 'The End', preceding his wonderfully philosophical line "And, in the end/the love you take/is equal to the love you make".

Tuesday 19 August

Studio Two: 2.00pm-4.00am. Stereo mixing: 'Ending' (working title of 'The End') (remixes 1-3, from take 7); 'Golden Slumbers'/'Carry That Weight' and 'Ending' (working title of 'The End') (crossfade/edit for master); 'Something' (remixes 1-10, from take 39). Recording: 'Here Comes The Sun' (SI onto take 15). Stereo mixing: 'Here Comes The Sun' (remix 1, from take 15). P: George Martin. E: Geoff Emerick/Phil McDonald. 2E: Alan Parsons.

George's two songs were completed this day, 'Here Comes The Sun' receiving a Moog synthesizer overdub onto take 15, played by the composer, and then both this song and 'Something' being mixed for stereo.

For 'Here Comes The Sun' this was the one and only mix, done with the original tape running at approximately 51 cycles per second, bringing the duration of the remixed song down to 3'05"; for 'Something' this was the second set of stereo remixes, numbers one to four having been made on 11 July. (One other numbering confusion this day was for 'The End', with stereo remixes one to three being made, despite the one to six numbering of the previous day's attempts.) These new mixes of 'Something' finally discarded any remnant of the instrumental jam which was tacked onto the end of the original recording, but which had been gradually whittled away during interim reduction mixdowns.

Some of Geoff Emerick's console settings for the final *Abbey Road* remixes.

Wednesday 20 August

Studio Three (control room only): 2.30-6.00pm. Stereo mixing: 'I Want You (She's So Heavy)' (remixes 1-8, from take 1, remixes 9 and 10, from unnumbered Trident master). Editing: 'I Want You (She's So Heavy)' (of stereo remixes 8 and 10). Studio Two (control room only): 6.00pm-1.15am. Master tape banding and tape copying: *Abbey Road* LP. P: George Martin.   E: Geoff Emerick/Phil McDonald.   2E: Alan Parsons.

John Lennon's 'I Want You (She's So Heavy)', the first *Abbey Road* recording, begun in February, was not finished and mixed until today. In the intervening six months it had slowly become one of the most complex of all Beatles recordings.

The story so far: the Beatles, with Billy Preston, and with Glyn Johns as producer, recorded 35 takes at Trident in February, the 'best' being an edit of nine, 20 and 32. On 18 April, at Abbey Road, without Preston, and with Chris Thomas, John and George overdubbed guitars onto that Trident 'best', authorised a reduction mixdown of same (called take one) and then added overdubs onto that. More followed on 20 April, but on 8 August – with George Martin – John and Ringo added an overdub back onto the original Trident tape and on 11 August a copy of that day's take one overdub was also edited into the Trident tape. So by 20 August there were two tapes, largely – but not totally – identical, from which to make a final master.

How they did this was to remix both and then edit the two mixes togther. The finished article has 'take one' for the first 4'37" and the original Trident tape for the remaining 3'07", the break occurring after the vocal line "she's so…". The song, in total, was 7'44" in duration but the end was a sudden, full volume slash in the tape: it did not fade out or reach a natural conclusion, the inference being that it could have gone on forever. Actually, the tape would have run out at 8'04" but the suddenness of the ending was powerful. "We were putting the final touches to that side of the LP," recalls Alan Parsons, "and we were listening to the mix. John said 'There! Cut the tape there'. Geoff [Emerick] cut the tape and that was it. End of side one!"

John Lennon was especially keen to incorporate both the original Trident tape and its own reduction mixdown because the former had a vital and unique overdub: the synthesizer taped on 8 August. John had used the Moog in conjuction with a white noise generator to produce a swirling, gale-force wind effect for the last three minutes of the song (on the record the white noise comes in at around 5'10"). Extraneous tape noise is the bane of a recording producer or engineer's life, to be kept at a low level, or out, at all times. And here was John Lennon *deliberately* introducing white noise onto a Beatles recording. It was to cause EMI engineers great concern in 1987 when they were digitally re-mastering *Abbey Road* for release on compact disc. On record the noise was tolerable but with the increased dynamic range of CD it posed a real problem.

There remains to this day a myth about 'I Want You (She's So Heavy)': that one can hear a muffled shout of disapproval from the control room after John Lennon, all but tearing his larynx to pieces, shouts "Yeeaahhh!" during the recording (on the finished master this occurs at 4'32"), the inference being that someone was instructing John to keep his voice down. Never, *never* would anyone have issued such an instruction about a vocal in such a fashion! Close scrutiny of the original Trident tapes reveals the indecipherable shout to belong to a fellow Beatle, off-microphone, taped on 22 February, and that it was certainly not one of disapproval. There *was* one occasion during the recording of 'I Want You (She's So Heavy)', on 18 April, that Jeff Jarratt asked George Harrison to turn his guitar volume down a little. "I was getting a bit of pick-up so I asked George to turn it down a little. He looked at me and said, drily, 'You don't talk to a Beatle like that'."

After the complexities of 'I Want You (She's So Heavy)', the remainder of this long session was dedicated to compiling and banding the final master tape for the entire *Abbey Road* album. At this point it had two variations from the final, released format: the two sides of the album were reversed, i.e. side B was side A and vice versa, so that the medley was on side A and the album finished with the slashed guitar chord of 'I Want You (She's So Heavy)'. And the placing of 'Octopus's Garden' and 'Oh! Darling' was transposed, with 'Octopus's Garden' first.

All four Beatles attended this decisive *Abbey Road* mix and running-order session. It was the last time that they were together inside the recording studio from where they had changed the face of popular music.

Paul adding a vocals and keyboards overdub, photographed by wife Linda.

Thursday 21 August

Abbey Road, Room 4: 1.00-2.00pm. Tape copying/editing/reinserting: 'Ending' (working title of 'The End') (take 7). P: n/a.   E: Phil McDonald.   2E: n/a. Studio Two (control room only): 2.30-12.00pm. Stereo mixing: 'You Never Give Me Your Money' into 'Sun King'/'Mean Mr Mustard' (stereo crossfade remix 12, from sound effects take 5 of 'You Never Give Me Your Money'); 'Ending' (working title of 'The End') (remix 4, from take 7). P: George Martin. E: Geoff Emerick/Phil McDonald.   2E: Alan Parsons.

The final, and best, attempt at crossfading 'You Never Give Me Your Money' into 'Sun King'/'Mean Mr Mustard', and a new remix of 'The End', the result of Phil McDonald having edited the song's orchestral overdub earlier this day. Both items were inserted into the finished master.

Monday 25 August

Studio Two (control room only): 2.30-8.00pm. Editing: 'Maxwell's Silver Hammer' (of master); 'Ending' (working title of 'The End') (of master). Recording: 'Maxwell's Silver Hammer' (unnumbered sound effects takes). Tape copying: *Abbey Road* LP masters. P: George Martin.   E: Geoff Emerick/Phil McDonald.   2E: Alan Parsons.

Editing of the master tape itself: 'Maxwell's Silver Hammer' down by seven seconds to 3'26", and 'The End', down by 36 seconds to 2'05". Various sound effects for the start of 'Maxwell's Silver Hammer' were made during this session but were not used.

Concluding this final session for *Abbey Road*, a safety copy of the master was made, and then both this and the original were taken away by Geoff Emerick for cutting by Malcolm Davies at Apple, the first British Beatles album to be cut anywhere other than at EMI, and by anyone other than Harry Moss.

Thursday 11 September

Studio Three (control room only): 2.30-5.30pm. Stereo mixing: 'What's The New Mary Jane' (remixes 1-3, from take 4). Tape copying: 'What's The New Mary Jane' (of stereo remixes 1-3). P: Malcolm Davies. E: Tony Clark. 2E: Chris Blair.

The Beatles may have overlooked 'What's The New Mary Jane' – recorded on 14 August 1968 for *The Beatles* though left unreleased – but John Lennon hadn't. He was considering issuing the song as a Plastic Ono Band single, and to this end he added new overdubs in a 26 November session at EMI. But first, to refresh his memory, Lennon despatched Malcolm Davies to EMI from Apple to oversee new stereo remixes of the original.

Three new mixes were made, with John's lead vocal placed at different points in the stereo and each one including, at the end, John's comment "Let's hear it, before we get taken away!" Copies of the three were then put onto a 7½ ips spool and were taken back to Apple by Davies for John Lennon's listening pleasure.

(Note. John was the next Beatle to return to Abbey Road, recording and self-producing the harrowing Plastic Ono Band single 'Cold Turkey' on 25 September, assisted by Tony Clark and Neil Richmond. That same day he also remixed tapes of the Plastic Ono Band's debut concert performance, in Toronto, Canada on 13 September, for release on 12 December 1969 as the album *Live Peace In Toronto 1969*.)

Friday 26 September

LP release: *Abbey Road*. Apple [Parlophone] PCS 7088 (stereo only). A: 'Come Together'; 'Something'; 'Maxwell's Silver Hammer'; 'Oh! Darling'; 'Octopus's Garden'; 'I Want You (She's So Heavy)'. B: 'Here Comes The Sun'; 'Because'; 'You Never Give Me Your Money'; 'Sun King'/'Mean Mr Mustard'; 'Polythene Pam'/'She Came In Through The Bathroom Window'; 'Golden Slumbers'/'Carry That Weight'; 'The End'; 'Her Majesty'.

Considering *Abbey Road* as it should be considered – the last Beatles album, even though it was the penultimate release – it is an astonishing piece of work, quite possibly the best album the group made. Astonishing because the animosity within the group was largely submerged during the sessions and was not allowed to interfere with what, in the end, the Beatles were all about: music. All four Beatles shone on *Abbey Road*: John's compositions and vocal work, Paul's supreme musical craft in the long medley, George's skilful musicianship and two marvellous songs, and Ringo's truly excellent drumming throughout. Even if, as the studio engineers have testified, the four Beatles really only came together for the recording of the basic tracks, with overdubs being applied in a mostly solo fashion, somehow the sum of those four parts did make a whole unit, which was the vital ingredient missing from *The Beatles*, recorded in much the same way.

"*Abbey Road* was a kind of *Sgt Pepper* mark two," says George Martin, who has publicly stated his preference for the former. "It was innovatory but in a controlled way, unlike *The Beatles* and *Let It Be* which were a little beyond control. One side of *Abbey Road* was very much John – let's rock a little, let it all hang out. The other side was Paul – perhaps even symphonic. The segues were my idea, to have a continuous piece of music. Wherever possible we would design a song that way."

But how did the Beatles themselves measure the album? Alan Parsons recalls, "When the album was finished we were listening to a playback and Tony Hicks of the Hollies came in and joined us, hearing the LP from start to finish. He said to Paul 'I think

Right:
Iain Macmillan's original shot for the other side of the *Abbey Road* album cover, here minus the sleeve lettering.

Going the other way this time . . . and with shoes too!

this album is every bit as good as *Pepper*' but Paul disagreed with him. 'No, I don't think it's as good as *Pepper*, but I do like George's song, I think that's the best. 'Something' is the best song George has ever written.'" Perhaps as expected, John Lennon later dismissed the entire album, and was especially condemnatory about the long medley. "Even before they began the album I remember John saying that he wanted all of his songs on one side and all of Paul's on the other," recalls Phil McDonald.

Although the bad feelings were largely submerged during the sessions, there were some heavy moments. "You didn't want to get involved," says Phil McDonald, "but people would be walking out, banging instruments down, not turning up on time and keeping the others waiting three or four hours, then blaming each other for not having rehearsed or not having played their bit right. It was very distressing." One member of the studio personnel closely involved with the LP, who prefers to remain anonymous, recalls a very bitter row between John Lennon and George Harrison during the time that Yoko was attending sessions in her double-bed. "She

got up and took a digestive biscuit off the top of George's Leslie speaker cabinet. George saw this from the control room window and got into a big argument with John. The biscuit thing was soon forgotten; it seemed to me that they just wanted an excuse to argue, to air their pent-up resentments."

In naming their album *Abbey Road*, the Beatles bestowed instant world fame upon the studio in which they had recorded almost all of their output, and since the day of the LP release the studio building has taken on an almost tangible aura of magic, and – like the zebra crossing outside – it is visited *daily*, still, by tourists from all over the world. Ken Townsend, now general manager of the complex which actually calls itself Abbey Road Studios these days (having changed – because of the Beatles' LP connection – from plain old EMI Studios in the 1970s) was recently travelling on a train in deepest Japan. "Some 16- or 17-year-old girls came up to us and tried to practise their English language. They asked us for our business cards. When I handed mine over they instantly said 'Ah, Abbey Road, Beatles!'. Thanks to the Beatles, Abbey Road is a worldwide, household name."

But it was nearly so different. "At one point the album was going to be titled 'Everest', after the brand of cigarettes I used to smoke," recalls Geoff Emerick. "Paul often glanced at the packet of cigarettes because it had a silhouette picture of Mount Everest. He liked the idea." John Kurlander recalls, "It was around July, when it was very hot outside, that someone mentioned the possibility of the four of them taking a private plane over to the foothills of Mount Everest to shoot the cover photograph. But as they became more enthusiastic to finish the LP someone – I don't remember whom – suggested 'Look, I can't be bothered to *schlep* all the way over to the Himalayas for a cover, why don't we just go outside, take the photo there, call the LP *Abbey Road* and have done with it?' That's my memory of why it became *Abbey Road*: because they couldn't be bothered to go to Tibet and get cold!"

Thursday 2 October

Abbey Road, Room 4: 9.30-11.00am. Stereo mixing: 'Across The Universe' (remixes 1 and 2, from take 8). P: George Martin.   E: Jeff Jarratt.   2E: Alan Parsons.

The World Wildlife Fund charity album was, at last, about to reach fruition, and – as planned – it was to include the Beatles' 4/8 February 1968 recording of 'Across The Universe', so nearly a March 1968 single and so nearly a bonus addition to a *Yellow Submarine* EP.

The Beatles' 'Across The Universe' was the most important catch for the charity album in terms of making a sellable commodity, so a slight variation on its lyric served as a most appropriate LP title: *No One's Gonna Change Our World*. The album was compiled and banded by George Martin at Abbey Road on 3 October, with John Kurlander assisting.

As the opening track of a wildlife charity album, it was felt that 'Across The Universe' should start and finish with added wildlife sound effects. Once again the old doors of the green EMI sound effects tape cabinet were opened, with suitable tapes – of birds twittering, birds flying and, oddly, children in a playground – being selected for use. Twenty seconds of effects opened the song and a short burst came in, overlapping the music, near to the close.

Apart from the addition of effects, the most radical difference between the new remix and the original Beatles session tape was the marked speeding up of the entire song. Timings tell the whole story. Without

the effects, and played at normal speed, the song was 3'37" in duration. With 20 seconds of effects added, but the entire song speeded up, it was 3'47". And, of course, it just *sounds* fast. Perhaps even too fast. When Phil Spector got hold of the original February 1968 tape for the *Let It Be* album he slowed down the 3'37" recording to 3'46" *without* the effects.

Friday 31 October

Single release: 'Something'/'Come Together'. Apple [Parlophone] R 5814.

The first release in Britain of a Beatles single from an album already issued. *Please Please Me*, *A Hard Day's Night*, *Help!*, *Revolver* and *Yellow Submarine* – plus of course *A Collection Of Beatles Oldies* – all contained either previously issued or simultaneously issued singles; *With The Beatles*, *Beatles For Sale*, *Rubber Soul*, *Sgt Pepper's Lonely Hearts Club Band* and *The Beatles* contained no singles at all.

It was Allen Klein, the new business manager at Apple, who instigated the release of 'Something', to spur George's career in giving him his first A-side, to bring in extra money and – Klein being an American – simply to do things the American way. Issuing singles

off albums was standard practice in the USA; in Britain it wasn't so until the mid 1970s.

'Something' was not a number one hit in Britain (it made number three) but it reached the top in the USA and sold well over two million copies worldwide. But, more than anything else, it was a magnificent song and a magnificent, worthy single.

Wednesday 26 November

Studio Two: 7.00pm-3.00am. Tape copying: 'You Know My Name (Look Up The Number)' (of remix mono 3, called remix mono 4). Editing: 'You Know My Name (Look Up The Number)' (of remix mono 4). Stereo mixing: 'What's The New Mary Jane' (remix 4, from take 4). Stereo mixing with simultaneous overdub: 'What's The New Mary Jane' (remix 5, from take 4). Editing: 'What's The New Mary Jane' (of remix stereo 5, called remix stereo 6). Tape copying with simultaneous editing: 'What's The New Mary Jane' (of stereo remixes 4 into 5). Tape copying: 'What's The New Mary Jane' (of stereo remixes 4 and 5). P: Geoff Emerick/John Lennon. E: Mike Sheady. 2E: Nick Webb.

Strictly speaking, this session belongs in a book about the recordings of the Plastic Ono Band. It was booked for the Plastic Ono Band and its fruits were meant for a Plastic Ono Band single, even though it didn't come out.

John Lennon was determined to have 'What's The New Mary Jane' released. It was his song, even if it was registered as a Lennon/McCartney copyright and was, ostensibly, a Beatles recording. And the same for 'You Know My Name (Look Up The Number)' too. Clearly, there was no place for this on a Beatles album. He wanted it out, which is precisely why he had got together with Paul McCartney on 30 April 1969 to overdub vocals onto the 22-month-old rhythm track tape. If the Beatles wouldn't release the songs he would issue them under the name of Plastic Ono Band.

The intention of this 26 November session was two-fold: to edit 'You Know My Name (Look Up The Number)' down from the unwieldy 6'08" duration to a more releasable length for an A-side, and to record additional overdubs for 'What's The New Mary Jane' and then make several different remixes and edits of

different durations, one of which would be issued as the B-side of the single. The former task was easy enough. A copy was made of the previous 'best' mono remix – remix mono three from 30 April – and that copy, named remix mono four, was duly edited down to 4'19".

For 'What's The New Mary Jane' it was a little more complicated. Remix stereo five was more than just a mix of the 14 August 1968 take four; it had additional (and suitably bizarre) vocals and sound effects simultaneously overdubbed by John and Yoko onto the two-track tape – not quite customary studio procedure but this is what John wanted. Remix stereo six was an edited version of this new recording. Other variations followed, with various mixes edited together and copied, but at the end of the day, and after five hours of editing, the two sides of a Plastic Ono Band single were ready for pressing.

Copies were duly pressed and Apple announced a rush-release date of 5 December 1969, catalogue number APPLES 1002. Rather cryptically, Apple also announced, in a press release, that the recording featured John and Yoko singing "[with instrumental

support from a group] of many of the greatest show business names of today" – taken by the press, quite rightly, as a thinly veiled reference to the Beatles. For reasons unknown (though there are two main possibilities: the other Beatles may have objected; EMI may have objected to Apple issuing what was really a Beatles/EMI recording) the record never appeared. By Monday 1 December it was "on hold" and it never came off that hold.

'What's The New Mary Jane' remains unissued to this day. But this 26 November 1969 edit of 'You Know My Name (Look Up The Number)' *was* released – by the Beatles, as the B-side of 'Let It Be' on 6 March 1970. As irrefutable proof that it was the same version, the APPLES 1002-A matrix detail, though crossed through, is visible in the run-out groove of original pressings of this Beatles single. (Recent pressings have changed.)

Hence the inclusion of this session in this book.

Tuesday 2 December

Studio Two (control room only): 2.30-5.30pm. Stereo mixing: 'Lady Madonna' (remix 1, from take 5); 'Rain' (remix 1, from take 7); 'Octopus's Garden' (remixes 1 and 2, from take 32). P: George Martin. E: Geoff Emerick/Phil McDonald. 2E: Richard Lush.

In September 1969 Allen Klein, acting for the Beatles, engineered a new royalties deal with EMI/Capitol, one aspect of which was that it gave the latter party the right to re-package, and make compilation albums of the Beatles' recordings. Capitol was not slow off the mark, and on 26 February 1970 it issued in the USA *Hey Jude*, a ten-song collection spanning the years 1964-1969. The album was only issued in stereo but since some of the ten songs had never been mixed for stereo those mixes had to be newly made. Capitol was not prepared to issue "mock stereo" as it had for its original *Magical Mystery Tour* album.

As ever, the remixing task fell to EMI Studios back at Abbey Road, since it was the sole holder of the multi-track tapes. 'Lady Madonna' and 'Rain' were thus remixed for stereo on this day.

'Octopus's Garden', newly remixed for stereo on this day without the bass, piano and lead guitar tracks, was done for a quite different purpose, however. Along with Lulu, the Hollies, Spike Milligan, Dudley Moore, Blue Mink and Pan's People, Ringo Starr appeared in a musical sequence in a George Martin television "spectacular", *With A Little Help From My*

Friends, produced by Yorkshire Television for transmission between 6.00 and 7.00pm over the entire IBA network on Christmas Eve, 24 December 1969. Ringo sang 'Octopus's Garden', but to ensure that he did not fall foul of the Musicians' Union ban on miming to records he re-recorded the vocal – along with three outside musicians contributing bass, piano and lead guitar – at Abbey Road on 8 December. The Beatles' other instrumentation remained.

Friday 5 December

Abbey Road, Room 4: 2.30-5.15pm. Stereo mixing: 'Hey Jude' (remixes 20 and 21, from take 1); 'Revolution' (remix 1, from take 16). P: George Martin. E: Geoff Emerick/Phil McDonald. 2E: Neil Richmond.

Stereo mixes for the Capitol *Hey Jude* album. 'Hey Jude' itself had been mixed for stereo before, three times on 2 August 1968, but those were obviously unsatisfactory. 'Revolution' – the B-side single version – had never been mixed for stereo.

The two final sessions by "Micky, Tich and I".

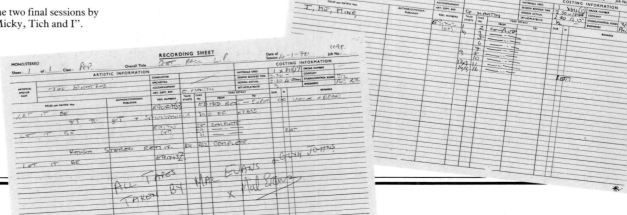

Monday 8 December

Studio Two: 10.00am-12.15pm. Tape copying with simultaneous recording: 'Octopus's Garden' (takes 1-10). P: George Martin.   E: Martin Benge.   2E: Richard Lush.

Ringo's vocal recording – with other musicians supplying bass, lead guitar and piano – for George Martin's *With A Little Help From My Friends*. Ten takes were recorded onto one track of a new two-track tape, with the 2 December remix two running simultaneously on the other. The tenth was 'best' and

was used for the television transmission.

(Note. Ringo, with George Martin producing, had begun the taping of his first album, *Sentimental Journey*, at Abbey Road on 27 October 1969 – becoming the first Beatle to record a solo album,

excepting the "experimental" Apple and Zapple albums by John Lennon and George Harrison and the live Toronto album by Lennon. Sessions for Ringo's LP would continue sporadically, at EMI and elsewhere, until 13 March 1970.)

Friday 12 December

LP release: *No One's Gonna Change Our World*. Regal [Zonophone] Starline SRS 5013 (stereo only).

The debut disc appearance of 'Across The Universe': the first song on side A of an 11-song charity album,

alongside Bruce Forsyth, Harry Secombe, Spike Milligan, Rolf Harris and others.

Saturday 3 January

Studio Two: 2.30pm-12.15am. Recording: 'I Me Mine' (takes 1-16). P: George Martin.   E: Phil McDonald.   2E: Richard Langham.

The last time that the four Beatles were together inside EMI Studios was 20 August 1969. But that was not the last Beatles recording session. On this day – and again on 4 January – Paul, George and Ringo got together at Abbey Road to help complete the still unreleased *Get Back* album. John Lennon was in Denmark, enjoying a four-week vacation, and his absence prompted a telling moment during the session, preserved on the eight-track session tape. Before launching into take 15 of 'I Me Mine', George invented and mock-read a formal press statement to the handful of people in the studio: "You all will have read that Dave Dee is no longer with us. But Micky and Tich and I would just like to carry on the good work that's always gone down in number two."

The Beatles had not previously recorded 'I Me Mine'.

It is assumed that they had, for in a part of the *Let It Be* film shot at Twickenham in the first half of January 1969, there is a charming sequence in which George plays the song to Ringo on an acoustic guitar, having composed it in five minutes flat just the night before. But it is perhaps worth stressing once again that nothing from Twickenham was truly recorded: taping did not begin until 22 January at Savile Row and, there, 'I Me Mine' never re-surfaced.

One year on, in January 1970, with neither the *Get Back* film nor its associated album released, rough cuts of the former showed that George's acoustic strumming of 'I Me Mine' was to be included in the finished print, prompting this EMI recording session. It was to be in the film, so it had to be on the LP too.

Sixteen basic track takes of 'I Me Mine' were recorded first, with George playing acoustic guitar and singing a guide vocal, Paul playing bass and Ringo drums. Between takes six and seven an instrumental jam developed, and before take 12 George led the trio into a delightful version of Buddy Holly's 'Peggy Sue Got Married', proving that, given the chance to jam, the Beatles would always return to their musical roots.

Take 16 was the 'best' version and overdubs of electric piano, electric guitar, new lead and backing vocals, an organ and a second acoustic guitar completed the song. It is important to note that throughout this session – including the 'best' take – 'I Me Mine' was only 1'34" in duration. After Phil Spector had overseen overdubs, re-produced and re-edited it for *Let It Be*, it was 51-seconds longer, at 2'25".

Sunday 4 January

Studio Two: 2.30pm-4.00am. Recording: 'Let It Be' (SI onto take 27, tape reduction edit of take 27 into takes 28-30 with simultaneous SI, SI onto take 30). Stereo mixing: 'Let It Be' (remixes 1 and 2, from take 30). P: George Martin.   E: Phil McDonald.   2E: Richard Langham.

'Let It Be' was the one song from the *Get Back* sessions which already had an overdub: a lead guitar solo for the middle eight, taped at EMI on 30 April 1969. Several more were taped on this day.

The first of these was a fine Harrison/McCartney harmonised backing vocal onto the 31 January 1969 recording. This was then given three tape reductions (take 27 becoming 28-30), all with a simultaneous overdub of brass, scored by George Martin: two trumpets, two trombones and a tenor saxophone.

Take 30 was the best reduction and brass overdub, so onto this was added another – more stinging – lead guitar solo by George, drums by Ringo, maracas by Paul, and – right at the end of the song – some cellos, again scored by George Martin.

Again, it was Glyn Johns who was given the task of compiling the updated *Get Back* album: he attended this session and took away all of the tapes – plus the 'I Me Mine' tape from the previous day. But while the revised *Get Back* – see 5 January 1970 – did include 'I Me Mine', Glyn refused to consider this revamped version of 'Let It Be', remaining as faithful as possible to the no overdub concept of *Get Back*.

It is widely believed that there are two different takes of 'Let It Be' publicly available – the single released (in the UK) on 6 March and the *Let It Be* LP version (ditto) 8 May 1970. Certainly the lead guitar solos in the middle eight differ considerably, and the LP version has a longer duration. But, in truth, these are one and the same version. That is, they derive from the same tape. By the conclusion of this 4 January

1970 session the eight-track master tape had two lead guitar solos, playing side by side: the 30 April 1969 overdub and this new overdub. In remix stereo two, used for the single, the newer overdub was mixed out, leaving the 30 April 1969 version on its own. The opposite was then done for the album: the 30 April 1969 solo was mixed out, leaving the 4 January 1970 solo on its own. Not mixed out of the single version, but certainly mixed very low, were the brass and cello overdubs. The LP gives them prominence. To date, no commercially released version of 'Let It Be' features the true and complete eight-track recording, with both solos playing simultaneously.

When *Get Back* became *Let It Be*, an additional recording session took place on 1 April, with Ringo Starr contributing. But this 4 January session was the last recording date by the Beatles – a band.

Monday 5 January

Studio One, Olympic Sound Studios, 117 Church Road, Barnes, London SW13: time unknown. Stereo mixing: 'I Me Mine' (remix 1, from take 16); 'Across The Universe' (remix 3, from take 8). Master tape banding and compilation: *Get Back* LP. P, E and 2E: Glyn Johns.

And still *Get Back* dragged on. In June 1969 the delay was blamed on the late production of a lavish book being prepared about the sessions. An August release date was then announced but quickly shelved. In late July it was announced that another album (*Abbey Road*) would precede *Get Back* and that the latter would be issued in November, coinciding with the film. By August this had become December. By November it had become "the New Year". In the meantime, acetate copies of Glyn Johns' original *Get Back* LP had reached radio stations in North America, as a consequence of which "bootleg" albums had surfaced.

Film and book problems had undoubtedly caused a delay. But so had the Beatles' procrastinative contempt for the whole project. If they did want it out at all they could not decide in which form. Added to which, they could not unanimously agree to liking Glyn Johns' first *Get Back* album. Now, in January 1970, Johns was commissioned to go away and yet again come up with a new Beatles album. There was but one new instruction; he must make it tie-in with the as-yet unissued film.

By the end of this day at Olympic, Johns had compiled a new 44-minute *Get Back* master tape. It lacked 'Teddy Boy' – because it would not be seen in the film and, presumably, because Paul had told Glyn Johns on 4 January that he was about to re-record the song for his first solo album. But it added the newly taped 'I Me Mine' and, for the same reason – that it would be seen in the film – it also added 'Across The Universe'.

'Across The Universe', almost two years old, was now on public release via the World Wildlife Fund album. Glyn Johns – in preserving the intimate, live nature of *Get Back* – somehow had to create an impromptu version which *seemed* different from the Wildlife release, and *seemed* like a *Get Back* recording, even if it was derived from the same original 1968 four-track tape, loaned by Abbey Road. Johns mixed out the Gayleen Pease and Lizzie Bravo backing vocals, mixed out the Beatles' own backing vocals, faded the song early at 3'24" for a slight crossfade into the reprise version of 'Get Back' and rightly ignored the wildlife sound effects. And he preceded the song with six seconds of spoken preamble, just like all the other *Get Back* songs: John saying "Are you alright, Richard [Starkey]?".

Glyn Johns' mix of 'I Me Mine' kept the song at its true length of 1'34" and, again, deliberately included some chat at the start. George: "Are you ready, Ringo?" Ringo: "Ready, George!" Johns did not tamper further with 'Let It Be', although he did move the song from side B to the end of side A.

The line-up of the revised *Get Back* album, the culmination of 12 months' work, was as follows, with recording dates – 1969 unless otherwise stated – in parentheses. Side A: 'The One After 909' [30 January]; 'Rocker' [22 January]; 'Save The Last Dance For Me' [22 January]; 'Don't Let Me Down' [22 January]; 'Dig A Pony' [24 January]; 'I've Got A Feeling' [24 January]; 'Get Back' [28 January, the single release version]; 'Let It Be' [31 January and 30 April overdub]. Side B: 'For You Blue' [25 January]; 'Two Of Us' [24 January]; 'Maggie Mae' [24 January]; 'Dig It' [26 January]; 'The Long And Winding Road' [31 January]; 'I Me Mine' [3 January 1970]; 'Across The Universe' [4/8 February 1968]; 'Get Back (reprise)' [28 January].

This *Get Back*, like its predecessor, remains unreleased. The Beatles still couldn't agree whether or not they liked it, and – additionally – John Lennon couldn't see why Glyn Johns wanted to be credited as producer, even in an unpaid capacity. In March, Phil Spector was brought into see what he could do.

Tuesday 27 January

Studio Two (control room only): 10.00-11.30am. Stereo mixing: 'The Inner Light' (remix 1, from take 6). P: Geoff Emerick.   E: Peter Bown/Jeff Jarratt.   2E: John Barrett.

The first stereo remix of 'The Inner Light' from 1968, for some indefinable future use. (Well into the future; 7 December 1981, as part of *The Beatles*, a bonus EP issued with *The Beatles EP Collection* boxed set.)

Later in the day on 27 January, at 7.00pm, John Lennon began the recording in studio three of the Plastic Ono Band's third and terrific single 'Instant Karma!'. At the suggestion of George Harrison – who played lead guitar on the recording – Phil Spector was recruited as producer. And, impressed with Spector's work on the song – not to mention his other, remarkable production credentials – Lennon and Harrison soon orchestrated the employment of Spector on the *Get Back* tapes.

Saturday 28 February

Abbey Road, Room 4: time unknown. Stereo mixing: 'For You Blue' (remixes 1-8). P: Malcolm Davies.   E: Peter Bown.   2E: Richard Langham.

Between Glyn Johns and Phil Spector there was ex-EMI then Apple man Malcolm Davies. These remixes of 'For You Blue' were a Davies production, included on neither the *Get Back* nor *Let It Be* LPs, and unreleased still. Remix stereo two was 'best'.

Friday 6 March

Single release: 'Let It Be'/'You Know My Name (Look Up The Number)'. Apple [Parlophone] R 5833.

The Beatles, to all intents and purposes, had now split. Irrevocably. Paul had almost completed his debut album, John had an album and three singles by the Plastic Ono Band already on release, Ringo's debut album was one week away from completion and George was thinking seriously of his first solo LP, the recording of which began at EMI on 26 May. On 10 April 1970, one week before his own album release, Paul announced to the world that the Beatles were finished.

But this single kept the pretence going a little longer, the impression being that these were two new recordings. Not so. The basic track of 'Let It Be' was 14 months old, and the B-side, the rejected Plastic Ono Band edit of 'You Know My Name (Look Up The Number)', had been begun 34 months previously, and was still monophonic!

'Let It Be' was issued in a picture sleeve in the UK, still a rare occurrence, the same sleeve that would be used for the *Let It Be* album. This told the real story: the four Beatles were pictured individually, with heavy black lines separating each face. Even the title seemed apt.

A number one in the USA, a number two in Britain.

Monday 23 March

Abbey Road, Room 4: time unknown. Stereo mixing: 'I've Got A Feeling' (remixes 1 and 2); 'Dig A Pony' (remixes 1 and 2); 'I've Got A Feeling' (remixes 3-6); 'The One After 909' (remixes 1-3); 'I Me Mine' (remixes 1-3, from take 16); 'Across The Universe' (remixes 1-8, from take 8). Editing: 'I've Got A Feeling' (of stereo remixes 1 and 2, called remix stereo 3; of stereo remixes 4, 5 and 6, called remix stereo 4); 'I Me Mine' (of stereo remixes 1, 2 and 3, called remix stereo 2). P: Phil Spector.   E: Peter Bown.   2E: Roger Ferris.

Enter Phil Spector and *Let It Be*, exit George Martin, Glyn Johns and *Get Back*. Phil Spector was – in 1970 – and remains – in 1987 – possibly the most revered and famous rock record producer of all time, the man behind some of the classic songs of the rock era, like Ike and Tina Turner's 'River Deep Mountain High', the Righteous Brothers' 'You've Lost That Lovin' Feelin'', the Crystals' 'Da Doo Ron Ron', the Ronettes' 'Be My Baby' and scores of others.

But Phil Spector was – and, again, is – also a highly intense and enigmatic personality, bringing the volatile temperament of an "artist" into the studio control room. Spector had actually been a recording artist himself – 'To Know Him Is To Love Him', his 1958 composition, recorded with two others as the trio the Teddy Bears, was a Beatles stage favourite in the group's pre-fame years, and the Beatles were also great fans of The Spector Productions, the songs and sounds which bore the man's highly distinctive "wall of sound". Almost all of Spector's output carried the stamp of a dominating and forceful producer: they were perhaps more *his* records than the actual artiste's. Only John Lennon and George Harrison, both to work with Spector individually in the early 1970s, proved capable of wresting complete control from the American producer many called "a genius".

One of the two EMI Studios balance engineers assigned to work with Spector at Abbey Road in these Easter 1970 sessions was Peter Bown, and he has a vivid recollection of events. "We did all the *Let It Be* remixes in room four, working from the original

Apple Studios' eight-track tapes, the ones which had caused such consternation. The tapes had seven tracks of music and one sync pulse track for the film camera. I got on quite well with Spector except that he wanted tape echo on *everything*, seemed to take a different pill every half an hour and had his bodyguard with him. I explained to him that this was a British recording studio and that he was safe, but the bodyguard used to come along and sit outside the door … he wasn't there by the end though, I think Spector felt safe in the end. According to some of the stories I've heard about American recording studios, some quite nasty things can happen there.

"We also had the accountant guy [Allen Klein] sitting in on the remix sessions, goodness knows why, and George Harrison was here most of the time, watching. George and I got on like a house on fire. We got the remixes done to the satisfaction of those concerned and the album came out. It had my name on it, the only one that did … the only problem was that it was the worst of the lot."

Spector's stamp on *Let It Be* was to become more pronounced as the days passed, and in this first session he worked on some of the less complex song material. He remixed two versions of 'I've Got A Feeling', one studio (28 January 1969) and one rooftop (30 January), eventually selecting the latter for the LP. He remixed 'Dig A Pony' from the rooftop recording, literally editing out the "All I want is…" backing vocals which both opened and closed the recording. He then did a straight mix of the rooftop

'The One After 909'.

Spector also made his aforementioned extended remix of George's 'I Me Mine' and had his first crack at remixing – again – the February 1968 recording of 'Across The Universe'. He would return to, and remix, both songs again, but these mixes served an invaluable purpose, being the guide recordings which played in the headphones of the orchestra and choir during a lavish overdubbing session on 1 April.

The start and finish times of this Spector session are no longer on file, but it is interesting to note that Paul McCartney, with Tony Clark, was in the control room of Abbey Road studio three, probably simultaneously, between 3.00 and 7.00pm, overseeing the making of copy master tapes of his first solo album, *McCartney*, recorded in secret at EMI and elsewhere in the early months of 1970 under the studio pseudonym of Billy Martin.

But perhaps he wasn't even aware of what was going on in the building, as George Martin comments. "It wasn't until after *Abbey Road* had been out for some time that I heard John was working on *Let It Be* again, although we'd previously mastered it. I was surprised because it was John who originally wanted it honest, with no extra musicians, no voices overdubbed, just like a performance. Paul was also surprised because he didn't know either. And I know he was particularly upset with 'Let It Be' and 'The Long And Winding Road', with all of the strings and choirs."

Wednesday 25 March

Abbey Road, Room 4: time unknown. Stereo mixing: 'For You Blue' (remix 1, remixes 2-8 of edit piece only); 'Teddy Boy' (remixes 1 and 2); 'Two Of Us' (remixes 1 and 2). Editing: 'For You Blue' (of stereo remixes 1 and 5, called remix stereo 1); 'Teddy Boy' (of remix stereo 2). P: Phil Spector.   E: Peter Bown.   2E: Roger Ferris.

The Spector touch was both light and clear on his remix of 'Two Of Us', lending the song, and in particular the acoustic guitar work, a crispness and brightness previously lacking. 'Two Of Us' was probably Spector's best achievement on *Let It Be*.

It is particularly interesting to note that Spector remixed 'Teddy Boy' for possible inclusion on *Let It Be*, even if, ultimately, it failed to make the cut. Its inclusion would have made the film and LP differ, when his main task was to ensure otherwise, and it would have been issued almost simultaneously with Paul's new, solo version of the song. Spector did two mixes of 'Teddy Boy', one faithful to the 25 January 1969 recording, the other a considerable edit, bringing the duration down to 3'10".

Mixing 'For You Blue' presented no special problems. The 'best' was an edit of remix one, the body of the song, and remix five, the intro only.

Another *Get Back* album, compiled by Glyn Johns on 5 January 1970 and including, for the first time, 'I Me Mine' (from 3 January) and 'Across The Universe' (from February 1968). It remains unreleased.

197

Thursday 26 March

Abbey Road, Room 4: time unknown. Stereo mixing: 'The Long And Winding Road' (remix 1); 'Let It Be' (remixes 1-4, from take 30); 'Get Back' (remixes 1-5); 'Maggie Mae' (remixes 1 and 2). Editing: 'Let It Be' (of stereo remixes 1-4, called remix stereo 1); 'Get Back' (of stereo remixes 3 and 5, called remix stereo 3). P: Phil Spector.   E: Peter Bown.   2E: Roger Ferris.

'The Long And Winding Road' was remixed on this day as a prelude to the 1 April overdub, in the same way that 'I Me Mine' and 'Across The Universe' had been mixed on 23 March.

Phil Spector's sharpening of the Beatles' percussion sound came to a head with his remixes of 'Let It Be',

adding such a degree of tape echo to Ringo's hi-hat that this instrument becomes virtually the sole focus of attention. Spector also edited a repeat verse into the end of the song, thereby extending the duration, and plumped for the 4 January 1970 overdubbed lead guitar solo in the middle eight, omitting the 30 April 1969 recording and falsely intimating that his mix was

from a different take to the single released in March.

'Maggie Mae' was a simple remix, identical to Glyn Johns' version, and 'Get Back' was remixed from the 27 January 1969 recording, with John Lennon's joky introduction "Sweet Loretta Fart...".

Friday 27 March

Abbey Road, Room 4: time unknown. Stereo mixing: 'Dig It' (remix 1); dialogue and miscellaneous pieces (remixes 1-8). P: Phil Spector.   E: Mike Sheady.   2E: Roger Ferris.

Apart from the stereo mix of 'Dig It', faded up at the start, faded down at the end and including only 49 seconds of the original 12'25" version two recording, this Good Friday session was devoted to mixing and selecting short items of music and dialogue from the Apple Studios tapes for possible LP inclusion. One of these was John's "That was 'Can You Dig It' by Georgie Wood, now we'd like to 'Hark the Angels Come'", which Spector crossfaded onto the end of his 'Dig It' remix and which, rather cleverly, introduced the next LP song, the hymn-like 'Let It Be'.

Other snippets included the film director's "Quiet please!" order which Glyn Johns had used to precede his mix of 'For You Blue', John and Paul sending up American comedians Rowan and Martin with a quick skit comprising "Say goodnight, John; Goodnight John. Goodnight Paul", the Beatles discussing the nature of the Apple recording sessions and the burst of 'God Save The Queen' from the rooftop performance.

Only two other snippets from this collection were ultimately selected for *Let It Be*: the McCartney and

Lennon comments at the end of the rooftop show: "Thanks Mo..."/"...hope we passed the audition" (Spector crossfaded these onto the end of his studio version of 'Get Back', implying that the song was a rooftop recording though, at the same time, placing the comments, logically, at the close of the album); and John's risqué "'I Dig A Pygmy' by Charles Hawtrey and the Deaf Aids. Phase one, in which Doris gets her oats" (which Spector added to the beginning of side A).

Monday 30 March

Abbey Road, Room 4: time unknown. Stereo mixing: 'For You Blue' (unnumbered stereo remixes). P: Phil Spector.   E: Mike Sheady/Eddie Klein.   2E: Roger Ferris.

A most interesting Phil Spector idea, rejected and not released, in which he made a 16-second tape loop of the instrumental break in 'I Me Mine' and overlaid extracts from the film soundtrack, to which he had unlimited early access.

Several mixes were made in this fashion, utilising such *cinéma vérité* moments from the rooftop performance

element of the film as the old woman's "I just can't see that it makes sense!", the young girl's "Yeah, I think it's great ... livens up the office hours, anyway", the bowler-hatted vicar's "Nice to have something for free in this country at the moment, isn't it?", the taxi driver's "Is it their new record? Oh, great, I'm all in favour of it!" and the pompous businessman's "This type of music is all right in its place, it's quite

enjoyable. But I think it's a bit of an imposition to absolutely disrupt all the business in this area..."

But only one tiny scrap of extra dialogue from the film soundtrack – indeed from the entire Twickenham sessions – made it onto the final *Let It Be* LP, and it was none of these. It was John's "Queen says no to pot-smoking FBI movement".

Wednesday 1 April

Studio One and control room Studio Three: 7.00pm-? Recording: 'Across The Universe' (tape reduction take 8 into take 9, SI onto take 9); 'The Long And Winding Road' (tape reduction of 31 January 1969 recording into takes 17-19, SI onto take 18); 'I Me Mine' (tape reduction extended edit of take 16 into takes 17 and 18, SI onto take 18). P: Phil Spector. E: Peter Bown.   2E: Richard Lush.

The climax of Phil Spector's work on *Let It Be*: the overdub of lavish orchestral and choral tracks onto 'Across The Universe', 'The Long And Winding Road' and 'I Me Mine'. It was the very last recording session for a Beatles album, and it featured the work of a real-life Beatle: Ringo, who played drums on all three songs to augment the orchestra.

Brian Gibson was the technical engineer assigned to the session and it is one which he will never forget. "Phil Spector is one of the weirdest persons I have ever met in the recording industry. He's totally paranoid. A most odd character, extremely insecure. He has that famous 'Phil Spector Sound' that consists of lots of echo and everything. But whereas all the record producers that I've encountered have in the

back of their mind the way a song will sound when finally mixed, at the recording stage they tend to leave tracks completely dry, perhaps with just a bit of monitor echo, but certainly without any of the effects added later.

"On *Let It Be*, though, Spector worked in the completely opposite way. He wanted to hear it, while it was being recorded, *exactly* the way it would sound when finished: with all the tape echo, plate echo, chamber echo, all the effects. This was horrendously difficult in studio one which is, technically, quite primitive. Spector was on the point of throwing a big wobbly – '*I wanna hear this!*', '*I wanna hear that!*', '*I must have this!*', '*I must have that!*' – when Ringo took him quietly aside and said 'Look, they can't do that,

they're doing the best they can. Just cool it.' Ringo didn't need to do that but I think he could see that Spector was getting towards the end of his tether and was giving everybody a hard time. He wanted everyone to know who he was, he liked to assert himself."

It seems that little would stand in Spector's way during this session, as Gibson further recalls. "On 'The Long And Winding Road' he wanted to overdub orchestra and choir but there weren't the available tracks on the tape, so he wiped one of Paul's two vocal tracks in order to put the orchestra on."

According to Peter Bown it wasn't only the EMI staff who were upset with Spector's production methods.

"My God, do I remember that session! Spector had three sets of [musical] parts for the musicians but he'd only booked them in for two. Out of the blue he distributed these extra parts, without intimating that there would be any extra payment. I warned Phil that he'd never get away with it, and of course the orchestra got up and walked out. I worked with these musicians often and knew them well, so I went into the control room, put a wedge under the door and tried to keep out of it. I got home very very late, well after midnight, and took the phone off the hook because I knew Spector would try and call. The moment I put it back Spector was on the line, asking me to return to the studio and continue, which I did.

The musicians got their extra payment. This session was on the first of April 1970 – but it was one April Fool's joke which did *not* come off."

Spector did not arrange and conduct the orchestral scores himself. Richard Hewson, a top musical arranger (he arranged Mary Hopkin's 'Those Were The Days', produced by Paul McCartney, and was later to orchestrate Paul's *Thrillington* album), was brought in for that purpose. But the size and scope of the ensemble was pure Spector. Here was the "wall of sound" on a Beatles record: 18 violins, four violas, four cellos, a harp, three trumpets, three trombones, one set of drums (Ringo), two guitarists and 14

vocalists: a total of 50 musicians and a total bill to EMI of a then massive £1,126 5s.

As a study of Phil Spector's "wall of sound" production methods it is interesting to note from the eight-track tapes how he recorded these 50 musicians. 'Across The Universe' had general strings on track four; violins on five; brass, drums and more strings on six; the choir on seven; brass, drums and choir on eight. 'The Long And Winding Road' had strings on six; brass and drums on seven; the choir on eight. 'I Me Mine' had brass and drums on track four; strings on six; no choir.

Thursday 2 April

Abbey Road, Room 4: time unknown. Stereo mixing: 'The Long And Winding Road' (remixes 10-13, from take 18); 'I Me Mine' (remixes 10-12, from take 18); 'Across The Universe' (remixes 10-13, from take 9). Editing: 'The Long And Winding Road' (of stereo remixes 10 and 13); 'I Me Mine' (of stereo remixes 11 and 12). P: Phil Spector.   E: Peter Bown. 2E: Roger Ferris.

The remixing of the songs overdubbed the previous day; the final work on *Let It Be*.

By dividing the released version of 'I Me Mine' into eight verses (the third and sixth being the "I me me mine" choruses), one can observe how Phil Spector managed to extend the song from 1'34″ to 2'25″ so

convincingly well. When he reached the fifth verse, after the line "flowing more freely than wine", he stopped the tape and spooled back to verse two, picking up again with "all through the day". He then let the song follow its natural course, repeating some of verses two and five and all of verses three and four, and adding an extra 51 seconds.

With each verse sporting different lyrics, Spector gambled that no one would guess he had more than halved again the length of the original recording.

And, sure enough, no one did.

Friday 8 May

LP release: *Let It Be*. Apple [Parlophone] PCS 7096 (stereo only). A: 'Two Of Us'; 'Dig A Pony'; 'Across The Universe'; 'I Me Mine'; 'Dig It'; 'Let It Be'; 'Maggie Mae'. B: 'I've Got A Feeling'; 'The One After 909'; 'The Long And Winding Road'; 'For You Blue'; 'Get Back'.

Everyone has a view about *Let It Be*. Most critics and fans feel the album to be a shoddy work, patchy in quality and well, *well* over-produced by Phil Spector. George Martin was reportedly shocked and stunned when he heard what Spector had done to the *Get Back* tapes. Glyn Johns has poured nothing but scorn and vitriol on Spector's production. Most importantly of all, Paul McCartney was highly aggrieved with *Let It Be*, and not just with Spector's production techniques. He disliked the whole package, which included a lavish book [no longer sold] which added 33% to the retail price, and what he viewed as the "blatant hype" on the back cover of the LP, the like of which he felt had never before been employed to sell a Beatles record.

But Paul McCartney's main grouse was with 'The Long And Winding Road' – indeed he even quoted this song in his High Court action to dissolve the Beatles' legal partnership, using it as an example of how the other Beatles were trying to ruin his personal reputation. Spector's extensive layering of a heavenly choir, strings and brass had taken a simple piano ballad into the world of Mantovani. While Paul was by

no means averse to employing orchestras he always used them "dry" and with subtlety. Paul claims, still, that he was not given the opportunity to approve or disapprove of Spector's work, and that the first time he heard the album was after its release. John Lennon and Phil Spector both denied this, and Spector claimed to hold a telegram from Paul approving of the mixes.

In fairness to Spector, he did precisely what John Lennon and George Harrison had commissioned him to do: make a package suitable for public release and to accompany the film [world premiere in New York, 13 May 1970]. The best producer in the world or not, he couldn't re-write or re-record the songs, which were mostly of second-class Beatles standard, recorded at a time of boredom, arguments and intense bad feeling within the group, recorded live on borrowed sound equipment, deliberately devoid of the superior studio polish so characteristic of the Beatles' post-1965 output. True, everyone felt that *Let It Be* was shoddy, but had either of the two Glyn Johns albums been issued public reaction may have been even more hostile. John Lennon thought that Spector

did the best possible job, that he "worked wonders" with 'Across The Universe', generally tightened up the LP and made it listenable to. "He was given the shittiest load of badly recorded shit with a lousy feeling to it ever, and he made something out of it." [*Rolling Stone* 1970, published 1971.]

Those who accuse Spector of destroying the original *Get Back* premise – a simple, straightforward album, no overdubs, no edits, no orchestras – should also consider that it was the Beatles themselves who first betrayed the concept, recording overdubs on 30 April 1969 and 3-4 January 1970, and that the second Glyn Johns album in particular, compiled at the Beatles' request on 5 January 1970, included overdubs too.

It was just this very type of non-creative bickering which brought the Beatles era to a sad and bitter close.

But the Beatles' recordings of the years 1962-1970, the greatest, most memorable and most remarkable song catalogue in the history of popular music, will live on forever.

Discography

These discographies detail all Beatles records issued in the UK and the USA between 1962 and 1970, showing original release dates and original catalogue numbers. They also show current catalogue numbers where they differ from the original, and numbers for the more recent mediums of cassette and compact disc.

Neither discography includes pre-/post-1970 reissues nor post-1970 issues or compilations, nor does the US edition list the numerous interview, 'group versus group', commentary and narrated records issued there in the heat of Beatlemania, between 1964 and 1966.

UK SINGLES

'Love Me Do'/'P.S. I Love You', first issued 5 October 1962. Parlophone 45-R 4949.
'Please Please Me'/'Ask Me Why', first issued 11 January 1963. Parlophone 45-R 4983.
'From Me To You'/'Thank You Girl', first issued 11 April 1963. Parlophone R 5015.
'She Loves You'/'I'll Get You', first issued 23 August 1963. Parlophone R 5055.
'I Want To Hold Your Hand'/'This Boy', first issued 29 November 1963. Parlophone R 5084.
'Can't Buy Me Love'/'You Can't Do That', first issued 20 March 1964. Parlophone R 5114.
'A Hard Day's Night'/'Things We Said Today', first issued 10 July 1964. Parlophone R 5160.
'I Feel Fine'/'She's A Woman', first issued 27 November 1964. Parlophone R 5200.
'Ticket To Ride'/'Yes It Is', first issued 9 April 1965. Parlophone R 5265.
'Help!'/'I'm Down', first issued 23 July 1965. Parlophone R 5305.
'We Can Work It Out'/'Day Tripper', first issued 3 December 1965. Parlophone R 5389.
'Paperback Writer'/'Rain', first issued 10 June 1966. Parlophone R 5452.
'Eleanor Rigby'/'Yellow Submarine', first issued 5 August 1966. Parlophone R 5493.
'Strawberry Fields Forever'/'Penny Lane', first issued 17 February 1967. Parlophone R 5570.
'All You Need Is Love'/'Baby, You're A Rich Man', first issued 7 July 1967. Parlophone R 5620.
'Hello, Goodbye'/'I Am The Walrus', first issued 24 November 1967. Parlophone R 5655.
'Lady Madonna'/'The Inner Light', first issued 15 March 1968. Parlophone R 5675.
'Hey Jude'/'Revolution', first issued 30 August 1968. Apple [Parlophone] R 5722.
'Get Back'/'Don't Let Me Down', first issued 11 April 1969. Apple [Parlophone] R 5777.
'The Ballad Of John And Yoko'/'Old Brown Shoe', first issued 30 May 1969. Apple [Parlophone] R 5786.
'Something'/'Come Together', first issued 31 October 1969. Apple [Parlophone] R 5814.
'Let It Be'/'You Know My Name (Look Up The Number)', first issued 6 March 1970. Apple [Parlophone] R 5833.

Note: All UK singles still available at January 1988.

UK EPs

Twist And Shout, first issued 12 July 1963. Parlophone GEP 8882 (mono).
A: 'Twist And Shout'; 'A Taste Of Honey'.
B: 'Do You Want To Know A Secret'; 'There's A Place'.

The Beatles' Hits, first issued 6 September 1963. Parlophone GEP 8880 (mono)
A: 'From Me To You'; 'Thank You Girl'.
B: 'Please Please Me'; 'Love Me Do'.

The Beatles (No 1), first issued 1 November 1963. Parlophone GEP 8883 (mono).
A: 'I Saw Her Standing There'; 'Misery'.
B: 'Anna (Go To Him)'; 'Chains'.

All My Loving, first issued 7 February 1964. Parlophone GEP 8891 (mono).
A: 'All My Loving'; 'Ask Me Why'.
B: 'Money (That's What I Want)'; 'P.S. I Love You'.

Long Tall Sally, first issued 19 June 1964. Parlophone GEP 8913 (mono).
A: 'Long Tall Sally'; 'I Call Your Name'.
B: 'Slow Down'; 'Matchbox'.

Extracts From The Film A Hard Day's Night, first issued 6 November 1964. Parlophone GEP 8920 (mono).
A: 'I Should Have Known Better'; 'If I Fell'.
B: 'Tell Me Why'; 'And I Love Her'.

Extracts From The Album A Hard Day's Night, first issued 6 November 1964. Parlophone GEP 8924 (mono).
A: 'Any Time At All'; 'I'll Cry Instead'.
B: 'Things We Said Today'; 'When I Get Home'.

Beatles For Sale, first issued 6 April 1965. Parlophone GEP 8931 (mono).
A: 'No Reply'; 'I'm A Loser'.
B: 'Rock And Roll Music'; 'Eight Days A Week'.

Beatles For Sale (No 2), first issued 4 June 1965. Parlophone GEP 8938 (mono).
A: 'I'll Follow The Sun'; 'Baby's In Black'.
B: 'Words Of Love'; 'I Don't Want To Spoil The Party'.

The Beatles' Million Sellers, first issued 6 December 1965. Parlophone GEP 8946 (mono).
A: 'She Loves You'; 'I Want To Hold Your Hand'.
B: 'Can't Buy Me Love'; 'I Feel Fine'.

Yesterday, first issued 4 March 1966. Parlophone GEP 8948 (mono).
A: 'Yesterday'; 'Act Naturally'.
B: 'You Like Me Too Much'; 'It's Only Love'.

Nowhere Man, first issued 8 July 1966. Parlophone GEP 8952 (mono).
A: 'Nowhere Man'; 'Drive My Car'.
B: 'Michelle'; 'You Won't See Me'.

Magical Mystery Tour, first issued 8 December 1967. Parlophone MMT-1 (mono §)/SMMT-1 (stereo).
A: 'Magical Mystery Tour'; 'Your Mother Should Know'.
B: 'I Am The Walrus'.
C: 'The Fool On The Hill'; 'Flying'.
D: 'Blue Jay Way'.

Note: Unless marked §, all UK EPs still available at January 1988. With five additional songs (see US discography for details), *Magical Mystery Tour* is now also available as a UK album [Parlophone PCTC 255 (stereo LP)/TC-PCS 3077 (stereo cassette)/CDP 7 48062 2 (stereo compact disc)].

UK ALBUMS

Please Please Me, first issued 22 March 1963. Parlophone PMC 1202 (mono LP §)/PCS 3042 (stereo LP)/TC-PMC 1202 (mono cassette)/CDP 7 46435 2 (mono compact disc).
A: 'I Saw Her Standing There'; 'Misery'; 'Anna (Go To Him)'; 'Chains'; 'Boys'; 'Ask Me Why'; 'Please Please Me'.
B: 'Love Me Do'; 'P.S. I Love You'; 'Baby It's You'; 'Do You Want To Know A Secret'; 'A Taste Of Honey'; 'There's A Place'; 'Twist And Shout'.

With The Beatles, first issued 22 November 1963. Parlophone PMC 1206 (mono LP §)/PCS 3045 (stereo LP)/TC-PMC 1206 (mono cassette)/CDP 7 46436 2 (mono compact disc).
A: 'It Won't Be Long'; 'All I've Got To Do'; 'All My Loving'; 'Don't Bother Me'; 'Little Child'; 'Till There Was You'; 'Please Mister Postman'.
B: 'Roll Over Beethoven'; 'Hold Me Tight'; 'You Really Got A Hold On Me'; 'I Wanna Be Your Man'; 'Devil In Her Heart'; 'Not A Second Time'; 'Money (That's What I Want)'.

A Hard Day's Night, first issued 10 July 1964. Parlophone PMC 1230 (mono LP §)/PCS 3058 (stereo LP)/TC-PMC 1230 (mono cassette)/CDP 7 46437 2 (mono compact disc).
A: 'A Hard Day's Night'; 'I Should Have Known Better'; 'If I Fell'; 'I'm Happy Just To Dance With You'; 'And I Love Her'; 'Tell Me Why'; 'Can't Buy Me Love'.
B: 'Any Time At All'; 'I'll Cry Instead'; 'Things We Said Today'; 'When I Get Home'; 'You Can't Do That'; 'I'll Be Back'.

Beatles For Sale, first issued 4 December 1964. Parlophone PMC 1240 (mono LP §)/PCS 3062 (stereo LP)/TC-PMC 1240 (mono cassette)/CDP 7 46438 2 (mono compact disc).
A: 'No Reply'; 'I'm A Loser'; 'Baby's In Black'; 'Rock And Roll Music'; 'I'll Follow The Sun'; 'Mr Moonlight'; 'Kansas City'/'Hey-Hey-Hey-Hey!'.
B: 'Eight Days A Week'; 'Words Of Love'; 'Honey Don't'; 'Every Little Thing'; 'I Don't Want To Spoil The Party'; 'What You're Doing'; 'Everybody's Trying To Be My Baby'.

Help!, first issued 6 August 1965. Parlophone PMC 1255 (mono LP §)/PCS 3071 (stereo LP)/TC-PCS 3071 (stereo cassette)/CDP 7 46439 2 (stereo compact disc).
A: 'Help!'; 'The Night Before'; 'You've Got To Hide Your Love Away'; 'I Need You'; 'Another Girl'; 'You're Going

To Lose That Girl'; 'Ticket To Ride'.
B: 'Act Naturally'; 'It's Only Love'; 'You Like Me Too Much'; 'Tell Me What You See'; 'I've Just Seen A Face'; 'Yesterday'; 'Dizzy Miss Lizzy'.

Rubber Soul, first issued 3 December 1965. Parlophone PMC 1267 (mono LP §)/PCS 3075 (stereo LP)/TC-PCS 3075 (stereo cassette)/CDP 7 46440 2 (stereo compact disc).
A: 'Drive My Car'; 'Norwegian Wood (This Bird Has Flown)'; 'You Won't See Me'; 'Nowhere Man'; 'Think For Yourself'; 'The Word'; 'Michelle'.
B: 'What Goes On'; 'Girl'; 'I'm Looking Through You'; 'In My Life'; 'Wait'; 'If I Needed Someone'; 'Run For Your Life'.

Revolver, first issued 5 August 1966. Parlophone PMC 7009 (mono LP §)/PCS 7009 (stereo LP)/TC-PCS 7009 (stereo cassette) CDP 7 46441 2 (stereo compact disc).
A: 'Taxman'; 'Eleanor Rigby'; 'I'm Only Sleeping'; 'Love You To'; 'Here, There And Everywhere'; 'Yellow Submarine'; 'She Said She Said'.
B: 'Good Day Sunshine'; 'And Your Bird Can Sing'; 'For No One'; 'Doctor Robert'; 'I Want To Tell You'; 'Got To Get You Into My Life'; 'Tomorrow Never Knows'.

A Collection Of Beatles Oldies, first issued 9 December 1966. Parlophone PMC 7016 (mono LP §)/PCS 7016 [now FA 41 3081 1] (stereo LP)/TC-FA 41 3081 4 (stereo cassette).
A: 'She Loves You'; 'From Me To You'; 'We Can Work It Out'; 'Help!'; 'Michelle'; 'Yesterday'; 'I Feel Fine'; 'Yellow Submarine'.
B: 'Can't Buy Me Love'; 'Bad Boy'; 'Day Tripper'; 'A Hard Day's Night'; 'Ticket To Ride'; 'Paperback Writer'; 'Eleanor Rigby'; 'I Want To Hold Your Hand'.

Sgt Pepper's Lonely Hearts Club Band, first issued 1 June 1967. Parlophone PMC 7027 (mono LP §)/PCS 7027 (stereo LP)/TC-PCS 7027 (stereo cassette)/CDP 7 46442 2 (stereo compact disc).
A: 'Sgt Pepper's Lonely Hearts Club Band'; 'With A Little Help From My Friends'; 'Lucy In The Sky With Diamonds'; 'Getting Better'; 'Fixing A Hole'; 'She's Leaving Home'; 'Being For The Benefit Of Mr Kite!'.
B: 'Within You Without You'; 'When I'm Sixty-Four'; 'Lovely Rita'; 'Good Morning Good Morning'; 'Sgt Pepper's Lonely Hearts Club Band (Reprise)'; 'A Day In The Life'.

The Beatles, first issued 22 November 1968. Apple [Parlophone] PMC 7067-7068 (mono LPs §)/PCS 7067-7068 (stereo LPs)/TC-PCS 4501 (stereo cassettes)/CDP 7 46443 2 (stereo compact discs).
A: 'Back In The USSR'; 'Dear Prudence'; 'Glass Onion'; 'Ob-La-Di, Ob-La-Da'; 'Wild Honey Pie'; 'The Continuing Story Of Bungalow Bill'; 'While My Guitar Gently Weeps'; 'Happiness Is A Warm Gun'.
B: 'Martha My Dear'; 'I'm So Tired'; 'Blackbird'; 'Piggies'; 'Rocky Raccoon'; 'Don't Pass Me By'; 'Why Don't We Do It In The Road'; 'I Will'; 'Julia'.
C: 'Birthday'; 'Yer Blues'; 'Mother Nature's Son'; 'Everybody's Got Something To Hide Except Me And My Monkey'; 'Sexy Sadie'; 'Helter Skelter'; 'Long Long Long'.
D: 'Revolution 1'; 'Honey Pie'; 'Savoy Truffle'; 'Cry Baby Cry'; 'Revolution 9'; 'Good Night'.

Yellow Submarine, first issued 17 January 1969. Apple [Parlophone] PMC 7070 (mono LP §)/PCS 7070 (stereo LP)/TC-PCS 7070 (stereo cassette)/CDP 7 46445 2 (stereo compact disc).
A: 'Yellow Submarine'; 'Only A Northern Song'; 'All Together Now'; 'Hey Bulldog'; 'It's All Too Much'; 'All You Need Is Love'.
B: [Seven soundtrack instrumental cuts by the George Martin Orchestra.]

Abbey Road, first issued 26 September 1969. Apple [Parlophone] PCS 7088 (stereo LP)/TC-PCS 7088 (stereo cassette)/CDP 7 46446 2 (stereo compact disc).
A: 'Come Together'; 'Something'; 'Maxwell's Silver Hammer'; 'Oh! Darling'; 'Octopus's Garden'; 'I Want You (She's So Heavy)'.
B: 'Here Comes The Sun'; 'Because'; 'You Never Give Me Your Money'; 'Sun King'/'Mean Mr Mustard'; 'Polythene Pam'/'She Came In Through The Bathroom Window'; 'Golden Slumbers'/'Carry That Weight'; 'The End'; 'Her Majesty'.

Let It Be, first issued 8 May 1970. Apple [Parlophone] PCS 7096 (stereo LP)/TC-PCS 7096 (stereo cassette)/CDP 7 46447 2 (stereo compact disc).
A: 'Two Of Us'; 'Dig A Pony'; 'Across The Universe'; 'I Me

Mine'; 'Dig It'; 'Let It Be'; 'Maggie Mae'.
B: 'I've Got A Feeling'; 'The One After 909'; 'The Long And Winding Road'; 'For You Blue'; 'Get Back'.

Note: Unless marked §, all UK albums in all formats still available at January 1988.

US SINGLES

§ 'Please Please Me'/'Ask Me Why', first issued 25 February 1963. Vee Jay VJ 498.
§ 'From Me To You'/'Thank You Girl', first issued 27 May 1963. Vee Jay VJ 522.
§ 'She Loves You'/'I'll Get You', first issued 16 September 1963. Swan 4152.
'I Want To Hold Your Hand'/'I Saw Her Standing There', first issued 26 December 1963. Capitol 5112 [now A-6278].
§ 'Please Please Me'/'From Me To You', first issued 30 January 1964. Vee Jay VJ 581.
§ 'Twist And Shout'/'There's A Place', first issued 2 March 1964. Tollie 9001.
'Can't Buy Me Love'/'You Can't Do That', first issued 16 March 1964. Capitol 5150 [now A-6279].
§ 'Do You Want To Know A Secret'/'Thank You Girl', first issued 23 March 1964. Vee Jay VJ 587.
§ 'Love Me Do'/'P.S. I Love You', first issued 27 April 1964. Tollie 9008.
§ 'Sie Liebt Dich'/'I'll Get You', first issued 21 May 1964. Swan 4182.
'A Hard Day's Night'/'I Should Have Known Better', first issued 13 July 1964. Capitol 5222 [now A-6281].
'I'll Cry Instead'/'I'm Happy Just To Dance With You', first issued 20 July 1964. Capitol 5234 [now A-6282].
'And I Love Her'/'If I Fell', first issued 20 July 1964. Capitol 5235 [now A-6283].
'Matchbox'/'Slow Down', first issued 24 August 1964. Capitol 5255 [now A-6284].
'I Feel Fine'/'She's A Woman', first issued 23 November 1964. Capitol 5327 [now A-6286].
'Eight Days A Week'/'I Don't Want To Spoil The Party', first issued 15 February 1965. Capitol 5371 [now A 6287].
'Ticket To Ride'/'Yes It Is', first issued 19 April 1965. Capitol 5407 [now A-6288].
'Help!'/'I'm Down', first issued 19 July 1965. Capitol 5476 [now A-6290].
'Yesterday'/'Act Naturally', first issued 13 September 1965. Capitol 5498 [now A-6291].
'We Can Work It Out'/'Day Tripper', first issued 6 December 1965. Capitol 5555 [now A-6293].
'Nowhere Man'/'What Goes On', first issued 21 February 1966. Capitol 5587 [now A-6294].
'Paperback Writer'/'Rain', first issued 30 May 1966. Capitol 5651 [now A-6296].
'Eleanor Rigby'/'Yellow Submarine', first issued 8 August 1966. Capitol 5715 [now A-6297].
'Strawberry Fields Forever'/'Penny Lane', first issued 13 February 1967. Capitol 5810 [now A-6299].
'All You Need Is Love'/'Baby, You're A Rich Man', first issued 17 July 1967. Capitol 5964 [now A-6300].
'Hello, Goodbye'/'I Am The Walrus', first issued 27 November 1967. Capitol 2056.
'Lady Madonna'/'The Inner Light', first issued 18 March 1968. Capitol 2138.
'Hey Jude'/'Revolution', first issued 26 August 1968. Apple [Capitol] 2276.
'Get Back'/'Don't Let Me Down', first issued 5 May 1969. Apple [Capitol] 2490.
'The Ballad Of John And Yoko'/'Old Brown Shoe', first issued 4 June 1969. Apple [Capitol] 2531.
'Something'/'Come Together', first issued 6 October 1969. Apple [Capitol] 2654.
'Let It Be'/'You Know My Name (Look Up The Number)', first issued 11 March 1970. Apple [Capitol] 2764.
'The Long And Winding Road'/'For You Blue', first issued 11 May 1970. Apple [Capitol] 2832.

Note: Unless marked §, all US singles still available at January 1988.

US EPs

The Beatles, first issued 23 March 1964. Vee Jay VJEP 1-903 (mono).
A: 'Misery'; 'A Taste Of Honey'.
B: 'Ask Me Why'; 'Anna (Go To Him)'.

Four By The Beatles, first issued 11 May 1964. Capitol EAP 1-2121 (mono).
A: 'Roll Over Beethoven'; 'All My Loving'.
B: 'This Boy'; 'Please Mister Postman'.

4 By The Beatles, first issued 1 February 1965. Capitol R-5365 (mono).
A: 'Honey Don't'; 'I'm A Loser'.
B: 'Mr Moonlight'; 'Everybody's Trying To Be My Baby'.

Note: None of these US EPs available at January 1988.

US ALBUMS

§ *Introducing The Beatles*, first issued 22 July 1963. Vee Jay VJLP 1062.
A: 'I Saw Her Standing There'; 'Misery'; 'Anna (Go To Him)'; 'Chains'; 'Boys'; 'Love Me Do'.
B: 'P.S. I Love You', 'Baby It's You', 'Do You Want To Know A Secret'; 'A Taste Of Honey'; 'There's A Place'; 'Twist And Shout'.

Meet The Beatles!, first issued 20 January 1964. Capitol T-2047 (mono LP §)/ST-2047 (stereo LP)/4XT-2047 (stereo cassette).
A: 'I Want To Hold Your Hand'; 'I Saw Her Standing There'; 'This Boy'; 'It Won't Be Long'; 'All I've Got To Do'; 'All My Loving'.
B: 'Don't Bother Me'; 'Little Child'; 'Till There Was You'; 'Hold Me Tight'; 'I Wanna Be Your Man'; 'Not A Second Time'.

The Beatles' Second Album, first issued 10 April 1964. Capitol T-2080 (mono LP §)/ST-2080 (stereo LP)/4XT-2080 (stereo cassette).
A: 'Roll Over Beethoven'; 'Thank You Girl'; 'You Really Got A Hold On Me'; 'Devil In Her Heart'; 'Money (That's What I Want)'; 'You Can't Do That'.
B: 'Long Tall Sally'; 'I Call Your Name'; 'Please Mister Postman'; 'I'll Get You'; 'She Loves You'.

A Hard Day's Night, first issued 26 June 1964. United Artists UA 6366 (mono LP §)/UAS 6366 [now Capitol SW-11921] (stereo LP)/Capitol 4XW-11921 (stereo cassette).
A: 'A Hard Day's Night'; 'Tell Me Why'; 'I'll Cry Instead'; 'I'm Happy Just To Dance With You'. [Plus two soundtrack instrumental cuts by George Martin & Orchestra.]
B: 'I Should Have Known Better'; 'If I Fell'; 'And I Love Her'; 'Can't Buy Me Love'. [Plus two soundtrack instrumental cuts by George Martin & Orchestra.]

Something New, first issued 20 July 1964. Capitol T-2108 (mono LP §)/ST-2108 (stereo LP)/4XT-2108 (stereo cassette).
A: 'I'll Cry Instead'; 'Things We Said Today'; 'Any Time At All'; 'When I Get Home'; 'Slow Down'; 'Matchbox'.
B: 'Tell Me Why'; 'And I Love Her'; 'I'm Happy Just To Dance With You'; 'If I Fell'; 'Komm, Gib Mir Deine Hand'.

Beatles '65, first issued 15 December 1964. Capitol T-2228 (mono LP §)/ST-2228 (stereo LP)/4XT-2228 (stereo cassette).
A: 'No Reply'; 'I'm A Loser'; 'Baby's In Black'; 'Rock And Roll Music'; 'I'll Follow The Sun'; 'Mr Moonlight'.
B: 'Honey Don't'; 'I'll Be Back'; 'She's A Woman'; 'I Feel Fine'; 'Everybody's Trying To Be My Baby'.

The Early Beatles, first issued 22 March 1965. Capitol T-2309 (mono LP §)/ST-2309 (stereo LP)/4XT-2309 (stereo cassette).
A: 'Love Me Do'; 'Twist And Shout'; 'Anna (Go To Him)'; 'Chains'; 'Boys'; 'Ask Me Why'.
B: 'Please Please Me'; 'P.S. I Love You'; 'Baby It's You'; 'A Taste Of Honey'; 'Do You Want To Know A Secret'.

Beatles VI, first issued 14 June 1965. Capitol T-2358 (mono LP §)/ST-2358 (stereo LP)/4XT-2358 (stereo cassette).
A: 'Kansas City'/'Hey-Hey-Hey-Hey!'; 'Eight Days A Week'; 'You Like Me Too Much'; 'Bad Boy'; 'I Don't Want To Spoil The Party'; 'Words Of Love'.
B: 'What You're Doing'; 'Yes It Is'; 'Dizzy Miss Lizzy'; 'Tell Me What You See'; 'Every Little Thing'.

Help!, first issued 13 August 1965. Capitol MAS-2386 (mono LP §)/SMAS-2386 (stereo LP)/4XAS-2386 (stereo cassette).
A: 'Help!'; 'The Night Before'; 'You've Got To Hide Your Love Away'; 'I Need You'. [Plus three soundtrack instrumental cuts by George Martin & Orchestra.]
B: 'Another Girl'; 'Ticket To Ride'; 'You're Going To Lose That Girl'. [Plus three soundtrack instrumental cuts by George Martin & Orchestra.]

Rubber Soul, first issued 6 December 1965. Capitol T-2442 (mono LP §)/ST-2442 [now SW-2442] (stereo LP)/

4XW-2442 (stereo cassette).
A: 'I've Just Seen A Face'; 'Norwegian Wood (This Bird Has Flown)'; 'You Won't See Me'; 'Think For Yourself'; 'The Word'; 'Michelle'.
B: 'It's Only Love'; 'Girl'; 'I'm Looking Through You'; 'In My Life'; 'Wait'; 'Run For Your Life'.

"Yesterday". . . and Today, first issued 20 June 1966. Capitol T-2553 (mono LP §)/ST-2553 (stereo LP)/4XT-2553 (stereo cassette).
A: 'Drive My Car'; 'I'm Only Sleeping'; 'Nowhere Man'; 'Doctor Robert'; 'Yesterday'; 'Act Naturally'.
B: 'And Your Bird Can Sing'; 'If I Needed Someone'; 'We Can Work It Out'; 'What Goes On'; 'Day Tripper'.

Revolver, first issued 8 August 1966. Capitol T-2576 (mono LP §)/ST-2576 [now SW-2576] (stereo LP)/4XW-2576 (stereo cassette).
A: 'Taxman'; 'Eleanor Rigby'; 'Love You To'; 'Here, There And Everywhere'; 'Yellow Submarine'; 'She Said She Said'.
B: 'Good Day Sunshine'; 'For No One'; 'I Want To Tell You'; 'Got To Get You Into My Life'; 'Tomorrow Never Knows'.

Sgt Pepper's Lonely Hearts Club Band, first issued 2 June 1967. Capitol MAS-2653 (mono LP §)/SMAS-2653 (stereo LP)/4XAS-2653 (stereo cassette)/CDP 7 46442 2 (stereo compact disc).
A: 'Sgt Pepper's Lonely Hearts Club Band'; 'With A Little Help From My Friends'; 'Lucy In The Sky With Diamonds'; 'Getting Better'; 'Fixing A Hole'; 'She's Leaving Home'; 'Being For The Benefit Of Mr Kite!'.
B: 'Within You Without You'; 'When I'm Sixty-Four'; 'Lovely Rita'; 'Good Morning Good Morning'; 'Sgt Pepper's Lonely Hearts Club Band (Reprise)'; 'A Day In The Life'.

Magical Mystery Tour, first issued 27 November 1967. Capitol MAL-2835 (mono LP §)/SMAL-2835 (stereo LP)/4XAL-2835 (stereo cassette)/CDP 7 48062 2 (stereo compact disc).
A: 'Magical Mystery Tour'; 'The Fool On The Hill'; 'Flying'; 'Blue Jay Way'; 'Your Mother Should Know'; 'I Am The Walrus'.
B: 'Hello, Goodbye'; 'Strawberry Fields Forever'; 'Penny Lane'; 'Baby, You're A Rich Man'; 'All You Need Is Love'.

The Beatles, first issued 25 November 1968. Apple [Capitol] SWBO-101 (stereo LPs)/4XWB-101 (stereo cassettes)/CDP 7 46443 2 (stereo compact discs).
A: 'Back In The USSR'; 'Dear Prudence'; 'Glass Onion'; 'Ob-La-Di, Ob-La-Da'; 'Wild Honey Pie'; 'The Continuing Story Of Bungalow Bill'; 'While My Guitar Gently Weeps'; 'Happiness Is A Warm Gun'.
B: 'Martha My Dear'; 'I'm So Tired'; 'Blackbird'; 'Piggies'; 'Rocky Raccoon'; 'Don't Pass Me By'; 'Why Don't We Do It In The Road'; 'I Will'; 'Julia'.
C: 'Birthday'; 'Yer Blues'; 'Mother Nature's Son'; 'Everybody's Got Something To Hide Except Me And My Monkey'; 'Sexy Sadie'; 'Helter Skelter'; 'Long Long Long'.
D: 'Revolution 1'; 'Honey Pie'; 'Savoy Truffle'; 'Cry Baby Cry'; 'Revolution 9'; 'Good Night'.

Yellow Submarine, first issued 13 January 1969. Apple [Capitol] SW-153 (stereo LP)/4XW-153 (stereo cassette)/CDP 7 46445 2 (stereo compact disc).
A: 'Yellow Submarine'; 'Only A Northern Song'; 'All Together Now'; 'Hey Bulldog'; 'It's All Too Much'; 'All You Need Is Love'.
B: [Seven soundtrack instrumental cuts by the George Martin Orchestra.]

Abbey Road, first issued 1 October 1969. Apple [Capitol] SO-383 [now SJ-383] (stereo LP)/4XJ-383 (stereo cassette)/CDP 7 46446 2 (stereo compact disc).
A: 'Come Together'; 'Something'; 'Maxwell's Silver Hammer'; 'Oh! Darling'; 'Octopus's Garden'; 'I Want You (She's So Heavy)'.
B: 'Here Comes The Sun'; 'Because'; 'You Never Give Me Your Money'; 'Sun King'/'Mean Mr Mustard'; 'Polythene Pam'/'She Came In Through The Bathroom Window'; 'Golden Slumbers'/'Carry That Weight'; 'The End'; 'Her Majesty'.

Hey Jude, first issued 26 February 1970. Apple [Capitol] SW-385 [now SJ-385] (stereo LP)/4XJ-385 (stereo cassette).
A: 'Can't Buy Me Love'; 'I Should Have Known Better'; 'Paperback Writer'; 'Rain'; 'Lady Madonna'; 'Revolution'.
B: 'Hey Jude'; 'Old Brown Shoe'; 'Don't Let Me Down'; 'The Ballad Of John And Yoko'.

Let It Be, first issued 18 May 1970. Apple [Capitol] AR-34001 [now SW-11922] (stereo LP)/4XW-11922 (stereo cassette)/CDP 7 46447 2 (stereo compact disc).
A: 'Two Of Us'; 'Dig A Pony'; 'Across The Universe'; 'I Me Mine'; 'Dig It'; 'Let It Be'; 'Maggie Mae'.
B: 'I've Got A Feeling'; 'The One After 909'; 'The Long And Winding Road'; 'For You Blue'; 'Get Back'.

Note: Unless marked §, all US albums in all formats still available at January 1988. US compact disc releases of the Beatles' albums recorded up to and including 1966 follow the British issue pattern.

The following British-format Beatles albums were issued in the USA in 1987:
Please Please Me, Capitol CLJ-46435 (mono LP), C4J-46435 (mono cassette).
With The Beatles, Capitol CLJ-46436 (mono LP), C4J-46436 (mono cassette).
A Hard Day's Night, Capitol CLJ-46437 (mono LP), C4J-46437 (mono cassette).
Beatles For Sale, Capitol CLJ-46438 (mono LP), C4J-46438 (mono cassette).
Help!, Capitol CLJ-46439 (stereo LP), C4J-46439 (stereo cassette).
Rubber Soul, Capitol CLJ-46440 (stereo LP), C4J-46440 (stereo cassette).
Revolver, Capitol CLJ-46441 (stereo LP), C4J-46441 (stereo cassette).

ALL YOU NEED . . . ARE THESE CDs

If you do not possess any Beatles recordings and wish to obtain the whole set, perhaps on compact disc, or if you wish to upgrade your existing collection to a pristine audio quality set of every commercially available recording made by the group, these are the compact discs you need to purchase.
Please Please Me, With The Beatles, A Hard Day's Night, Beatles For Sale, Help!, Rubber Soul, Revolver, Sgt Pepper's Lonely Hearts Club Band, Magical Mystery Tour, The Beatles, Yellow Submarine, Abbey Road, Let It Be and two new CD collections issued in 1988:

Past Masters: Volume One, first issued 7 March 1988. CDP 7 90043 2.
'Love Me Do'; 'From Me To You'; 'Thank You Girl'; 'She Loves You'; 'I'll Get You'; 'I Want To Hold Your Hand'; 'This Boy'; 'Komm, Gib Mir Deine Hand'; 'Sie Liebt Dich'; 'Long Tall Sally'; 'I Call Your Name'; 'Slow Down'; 'Matchbox'; 'I Feel Fine'; 'She's A Woman'; 'Bad Boy'; 'Yes It Is'; 'I'm Down'.

Past Masters: Volume Two, first issued 7 March 1988. CDP 7 90044 2.
'Day Tripper'; 'We Can Work It Out'; 'Paperback Writer'; 'Rain'; 'Lady Madonna'; 'The Inner Light'; 'Hey Jude'; 'Revolution'; 'Get Back'; 'Don't Let Me Down'; 'The Ballad Of John And Yoko'; 'Old Brown Shoe'; 'Across The Universe'; 'Let It Be'; 'You Know My Name (Look Up The Number)'.

Index

Glossary

The world of recording has its own vocabulary. This book contains some phrases unique to the industry, and others which are common words with different interpretations, including the following:

Acetate A reference disc, cut for evaluation purposes and not used for processing.

ADT Artificial Double Tracking. An Abbey Road invention using electronic methods to simulate the natural double tracking of an instrument, particularly vocals.

Ambience The reverberation characteristic of a room.

A&R Artist and Repertoire. Record companies call the department from which artists are handled 'A&R'.

ATOC Automatic Transient Overload Control. An EMI piece of equipment formerly used in disc cutting to flatten peak overload of signals.

Backing track A pre-recorded track to be used for superimposing or overdubbing further instruments or vocals.

Banding Assembling a series of songs into a particular running order.

Board See **Mixing console**.

Bouncing Used in multi-track tape recording to mix and bounce some tracks onto another unused track.

Breakdown An uncompleted take.

Bumping The process of bouncing between two tracks.

Cardioid The polar pattern of a microphone, shaped like a heart, with the highest sensitivity at the front and minimum at the back.

CCIR A European standard for equalisation of tape machines.

Compressor A piece of equipment which deliberately squeezes the dynamic range.

Console See **Mixing console**.

Crossfade Replaying simultaneously from two tape machines and recording onto a third.

Cue See **Foldback**.

Cut The process of making a lacquer or copper from the master tape.

Cut out A piece of tape removed with scissors or razor blade.

Cutting lathe An electrical/mechanical piece of equipment used for cutting a disc, before being sent to the record factory for processing.

Decibel (dB) The common unit of sound measurement, being one tenth of a bel.

Demo Short for demonstration. Usually a tape or disc used for artistic assessment.

Desk See **Mixing console**.

Direct Injection (DI) A method whereby the sound produced by a musical instrument is fed straight into the mixing console, often by means of a DI box. Avoids the use of microphones, thus improving separation.

Double tracking The act of recording the same thing again on a separate track thus re-inforcing the sound when the two are added together. Relies on the fact that two performances are slightly different.

Drop in To insert a new section while a tape is running by switching to record at the appropriate time and switching out and back to replay on completion.

Drop out Loss of recorded signal on a tape usually caused by blemish on the surface or by poor contact with the tape machine heads, frequently due to dirt or oxide build-up.

Dry Sound which has little or no reverberation.

Echo chamber A highly reverberant room with reflective surfaces and, at Abbey Road, large drainpipes! Original sound is sent to a loudspeaker and microphones pick up the new sound with added echo.

Echo plate A large metal vibrating plate which produces artificial reverberation. EMT from Germany manufactured those used on Beatles sessions.

Edit Splicing of tape to improve the overall performance.

Eight-track A tape machine or tape having eight totally independent tracks.

Equalisation Changing of the frequency response, normally on the mixing console, to change the sound.

Fade out The reduction of a signal to an inaudible level, often used on songs with no logical ending.

Fader The volume control on a mixing console, normally a slider, but occasionally a rotary pot.

Fairchild limiter An American piece of equipment used for limiting signal peaks.

False start A take which is immediately aborted.

Feedback Usually undesirable, the return of some of the original sound to its source such as a microphone, thus creating acoustic feedback.

Filter An electronic device for filtering sound.

Flanging A variation of ADT by constantly changing tape speed to give a similar effect to phasing.

Foldback Circuitry in a mixing console enabling engineer/producer to talk to artists on speakers or headphones.

Foldback speakers Speakers used for communication from control room.

Four-track A tape machine or tape having four totally independent tracks.

Fuzz box A device which deliberately overloads or distorts the signal, used particularly with guitars.

High-gain amplifier An amplifier which significantly increases the level of the signal.

IPS Inches per second, related to the speed the tape travels over heads.

Jangle A particular type of piano.

Lacquers An aluminium blank coated with nitro-cellulose, used for disc cutting.

Leslie speaker A particular type of loudspeaker used in organs, normally rotating.

Limiter A device which flattens the peaks of signals, without altering the lower levels.

Loop A piece of magnetic tape of finite length in the form of a continuous loop.

Master tape The final tape from which the record may be cut.

Mastered version The particular tape used for mastering.

Middle eight A linking passage in a song, originally eight bars in the middle.

Mixdown The process of reducing a multi-track tape to the master stage.

Mixed out Removed during the mixing stage.

Mixing console The prime piece of equipment in a control room, enabling the engineer to adjust levels, tones and other criteria.

Monitor setting The nominal position at which the level of a loudspeaker is normally set.

Mono remix Remix from several tracks down to only one.

NAB equalisation system American-type equalisation on tape machines.

Outtake A piece of recorded tape, not to be used as a master.

Overdub The process of adding new sound to previously recorded sounds.

Panning The physical positioning between left and right of a sound source in a stereo picture.

Re-make To do it again.

Reduction mix A means of vacating recording tracks by mixing together existing ones and transferring them to a lesser number of tracks on a different tape.

Remix To reduce from many tracks to a master tape.

Reverb Reverberation – the degree of ambience in a room.

Rhythm track Normally a track containing bass, drums and guitars.

Riff A musical phrase which gives a song its particular identity, usually repeated.

Rill A gap inserted between two songs, normally of silence, used as a marker.

Session tapes The original tapes as recorded on the session.

STEED An Abbey Road invention to add both a delayed signal and tape loop to create an effect.

Stereo remix Reduction from multi-track to a stereo master.

Superimposition (SI) See **Overdub**.

Sync head The recording head when used in replay mode.

Sync pulse track The track of a tape machine onto which a timing pulse is recorded.

Tape delay system The use of magnetic tape to create a time delay.

Tape-to-tape The transfer of a signal from one tape machine to another.

Three-track tape A tape with three independent tracks.

Two-track tape A tape containing two independent tracks.

Vari-speed To vary the capstan speed of a tape machine.

White label pressing A test pressing for evaluation purposes.

White noise generator A generator which produces noise containing a mixture of all frequencies.

The Recording Technology

It is now more than 25 years since the Beatles made their first recordings in Abbey Road Studios. They were perhaps fortunate in that during their early career changes in recording technology were taking place around them, the combination of which enabled them to be instrumental in pioneering new techniques, and in so doing change the face of recording for ever.

It had only been some 12 years earlier that the most significant development in modern recording technology, the tape machine using magnetic tape, had been introduced into Abbey Road. This quickly replaced the previous method of recording directly onto wax, and by 1950 EMI's own BTR machines were providing a degree of flexibility which revolutionised the recording process. Tape could be cut and spliced using non-magnetic scissors, and for the first time this enabled a series of takes to be joined or edited together to produce a flawless performance. Simultaneously the record itself was changing with the old 78s soon to be superseded by the 45rpm single and the 33rpm long playing record. This created a requirement for post-production rooms, the most essential of which was the disc cutting room, and a new range of cutting equipment utilising lacquer blanks coated with a layer of nitro-cellulose raised the quality enormously.

EMI's Alan Blumlein had been working on experimental stereo in the early 1930s, but it was not until 1954 that Abbey Road began to record stereo in earnest. Mixing consoles were moving from fixed record racks to desk tops, valves became smaller and soon the transistor was to play its part. Microphones, particularly condenser types from Neumann in Germany, and AKG in Austria, improved the frequency response picked up from the studio, and then by 1960 the first four-track tape machines were introduced, initially from Telefunken and then from Studer were introduced. A new range of mixing consoles together with comprehensive tone controls and filters from EMI's own research labs, as well as other electronic devices such as echo chambers, echo plates, limiters and compressors began to provide new creative tools for the recording engineers. And of course the electric guitar had begun to make its mark.

It was with many of these developments in their early stages that the Beatles first came to Abbey Road. Classical recording was often the first to use new systems and four-track machines were used primarily for opera, so that orchestra could be laid onto two tracks and soloists and chorus on the other two. Recording sessions were of fixed three-hour periods, in which four songs were normally recorded, for which each musician received a fee fixed by the Musicians' Union.

In the early days the Beatles too had to abide by the rules. But after they exploded on to the world stage they were soon to change the role of the recording studio forever. They demanded that the studio be used as a workshop to contrive new sounds, they created open-ended studio hours, and they brought the best out of the engineers around them. The Beatles became too successful for anyone to doubt their wisdom. Others followed their work style and soon a flood of independent studios were being built to satisfy the demand; equipment manufacturers sprung up supplying new equipment; and new tape machines were being developed with a virtually unlimited number of tracks – all sparked off by the Beatles' extraordinary recording work described in this book.

Ken Townsend
General Manager, Abbey Road Studios